A **MUTTS** TREASURY

CAT CRAZY

PATRICK McDONNELL

**Andrews McMeel
Publishing, LLC**

Kansas City • Sydney • London

Other Books by Patrick McDonnell

Mutts
Cats and Dogs: Mutts II
More Shtuff: Mutts III
Yesh!: Mutts IV
Our Mutts: Five
A Little Look-See: Mutts VI
What Now: Mutts VII
I Want to Be the Kitty: Mutts VIII
Dog-Eared: Mutts IX
Who Let the Cat Out: Mutts X
Everyday Mutts
Animal Friendly
Call of the Wild
Stop and Smell the Roses
Earl & Mooch
Our Little Kat King
Bonk!
A Shtinky Little Christmas

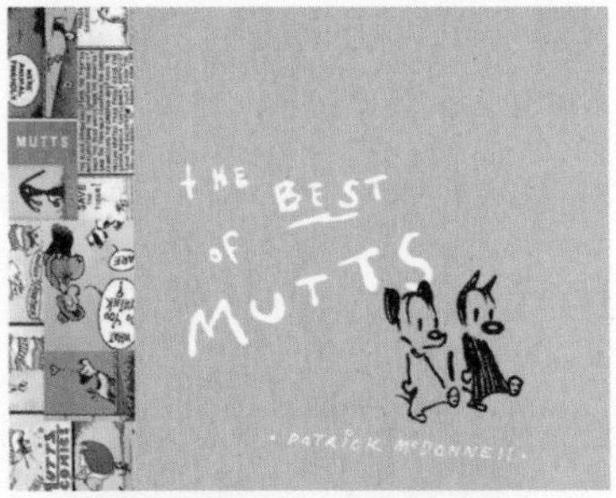
THE BEST OF MUTTS
PATRICK McDONNELL
The Best of Mutts

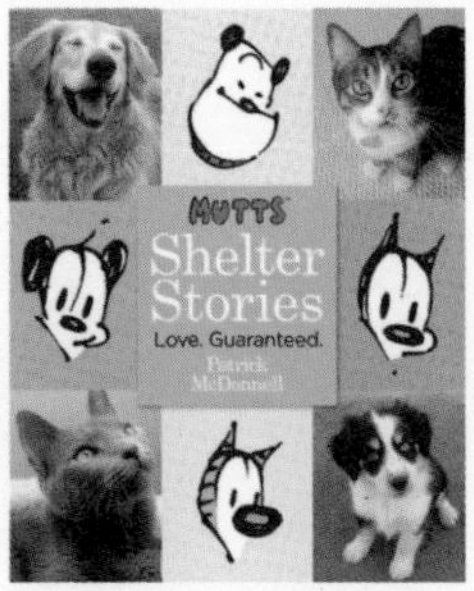
MUTTS
Shelter Stories
Love. Guaranteed.
Patrick McDonnell
Shelter Stories

Mutts Sundays
Sunday Mornings
Sunday Afternoons
Sunday Evenings

Mutts is distributed internationally by King Features Syndicate, Inc. For information, write to King Features Syndicate, Inc., 300 West Fifty-Seventh Street, New York, New York 10019, or visit www.KingFeatures.com.

Andrews McMeel Publishing, LLC, an Andrews McMeel Universal company, 1130 Walnut Street, Kansas City, Missouri 64106.

13 14 15 16 17 POA 10 9 8 7 6 5 4 3 2 1

ISBN: 978-1-4494-3725-1

Library of Congress Control Number: 2013903239

Printed on recycled paper.

Mutts can be found on the Internet at
www.muttscomics.com

Cover design by Jeff Schulz

ATTENTION: SCHOOLS AND BUSINESSES
Andrews McMeel books are available at quantity discounts with bulk purchase for educational, business, or sales promotional use. For information, please e-mail the Andrews McMeel Publishing Special Sales Department: specialsales@amuniversal.com

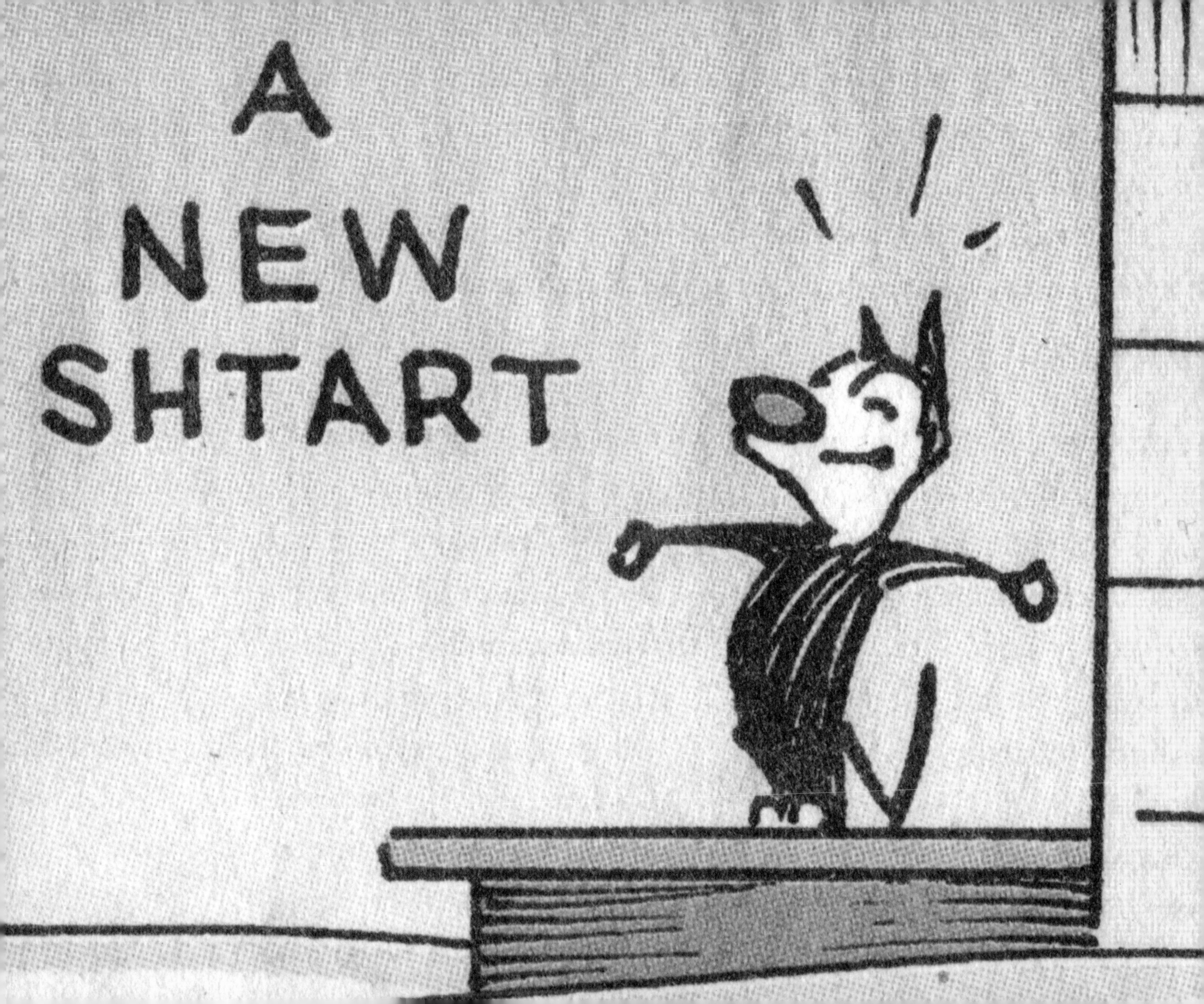
A NEW SHTART

TO A NEW DAY

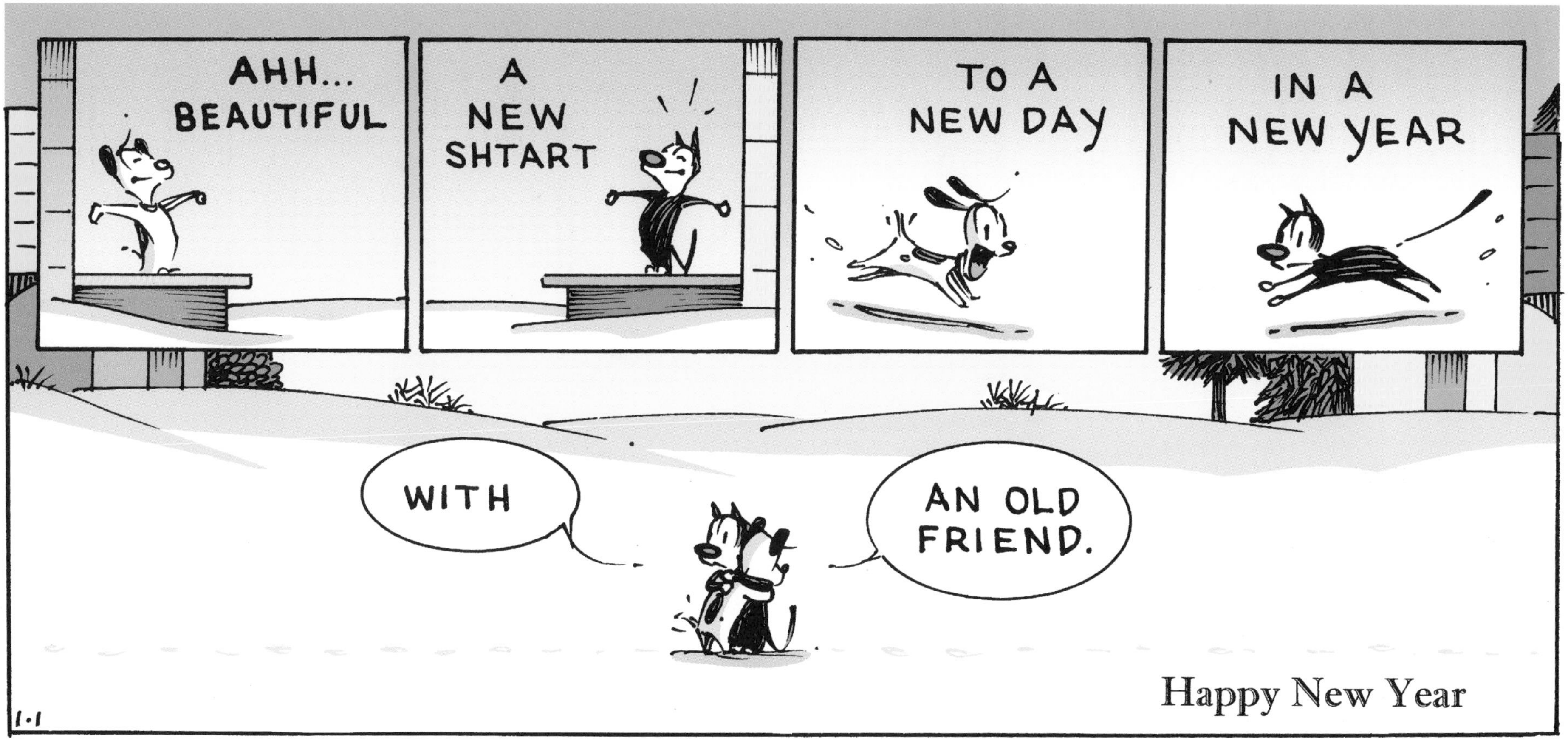
AHH... BEAUTIFUL
A NEW SHTART
TO A NEW DAY
IN A NEW YEAR
WITH
AN OLD FRIEND.
Happy New Year
1.1

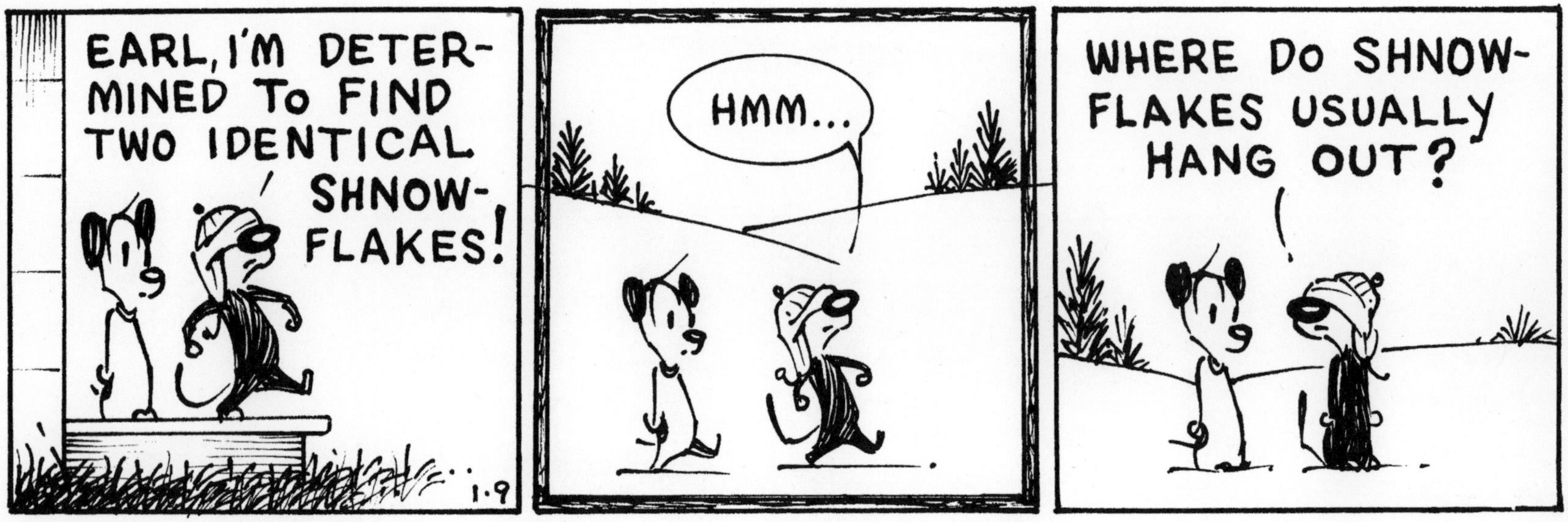
EARL, I'M DETERMINED TO FIND TWO IDENTICAL SHNOWFLAKES!
1·9
HMM...
WHERE DO SHNOWFLAKES USUALLY HANG OUT?

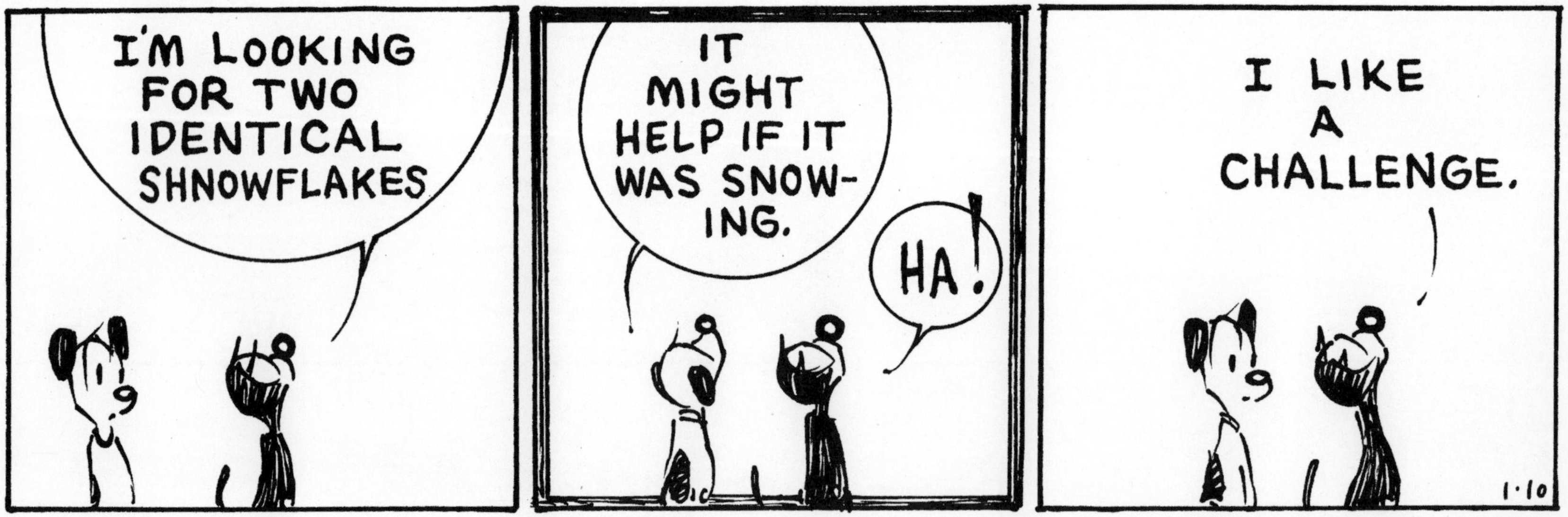
I'M LOOKING FOR TWO IDENTICAL SHNOWFLAKES
IT MIGHT HELP IF IT WAS SNOWING.
HA!
I LIKE A CHALLENGE.
1·10

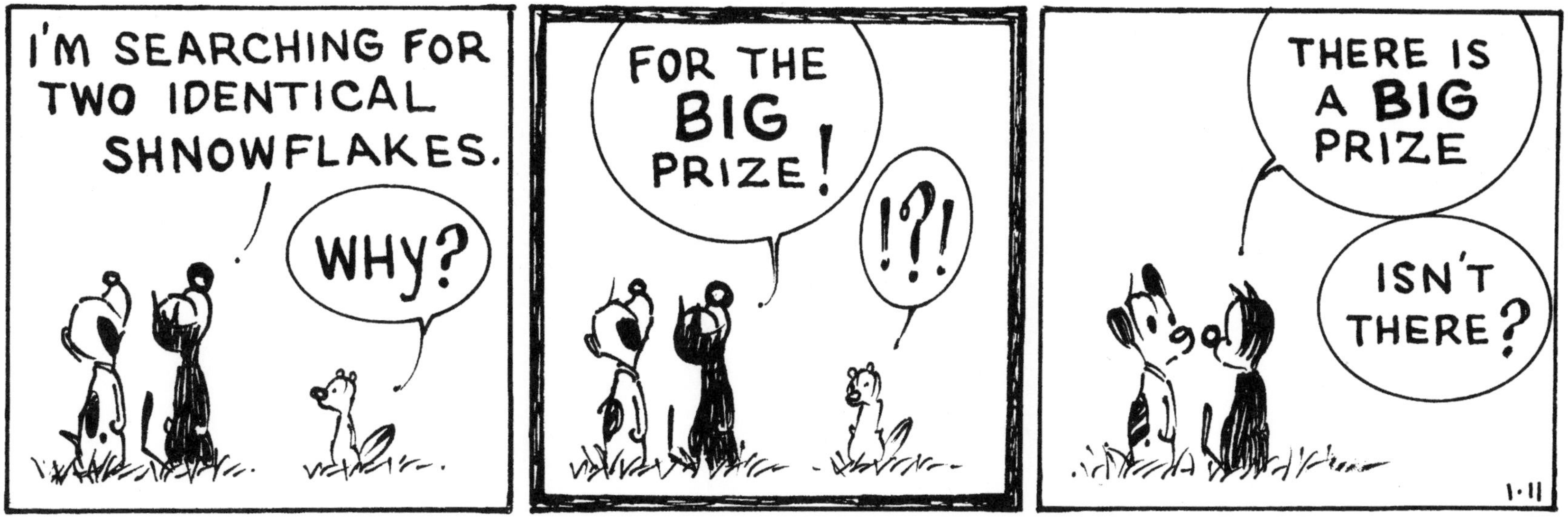
I'M SEARCHING FOR TWO IDENTICAL SHNOWFLAKES.
WHY?
FOR THE BIG PRIZE!
!?!
THERE IS A BIG PRIZE
ISN'T THERE?
1·11

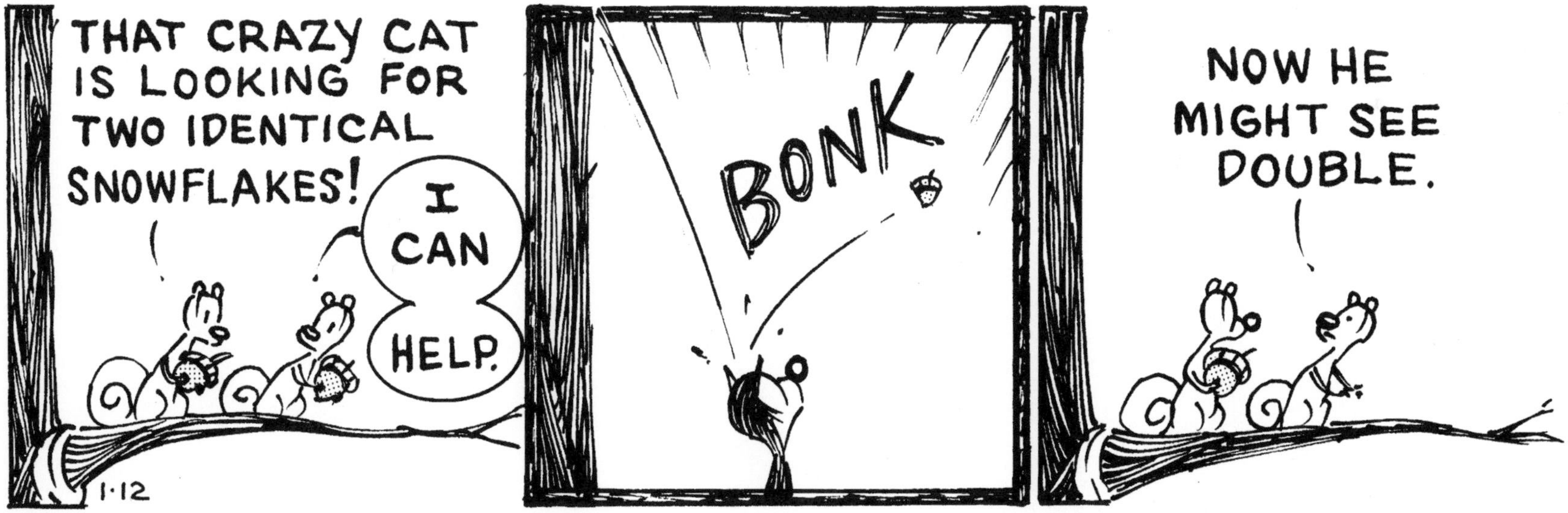
THAT CRAZY CAT IS LOOKING FOR TWO IDENTICAL SNOWFLAKES!
I CAN HELP.
BONK
NOW HE MIGHT SEE DOUBLE.
1·12

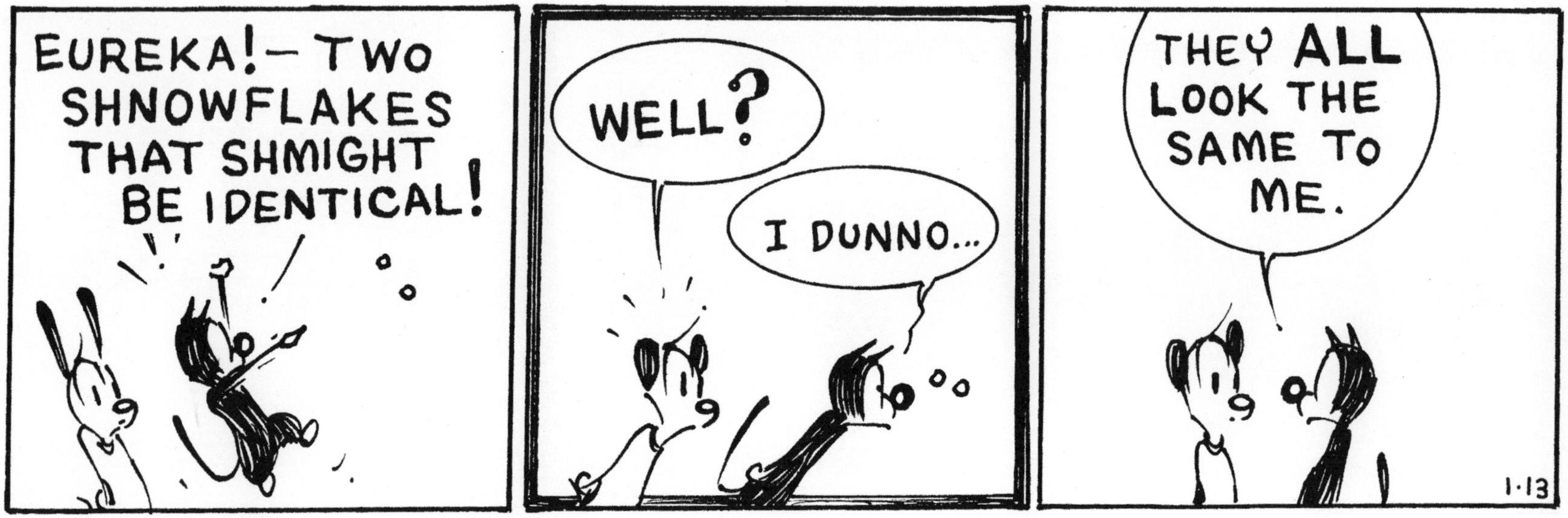
EUREKA! – TWO SHNOWFLAKES THAT SHMIGHT BE IDENTICAL!
WELL?
I DUNNO...
THEY ALL LOOK THE SAME TO ME.
1·13

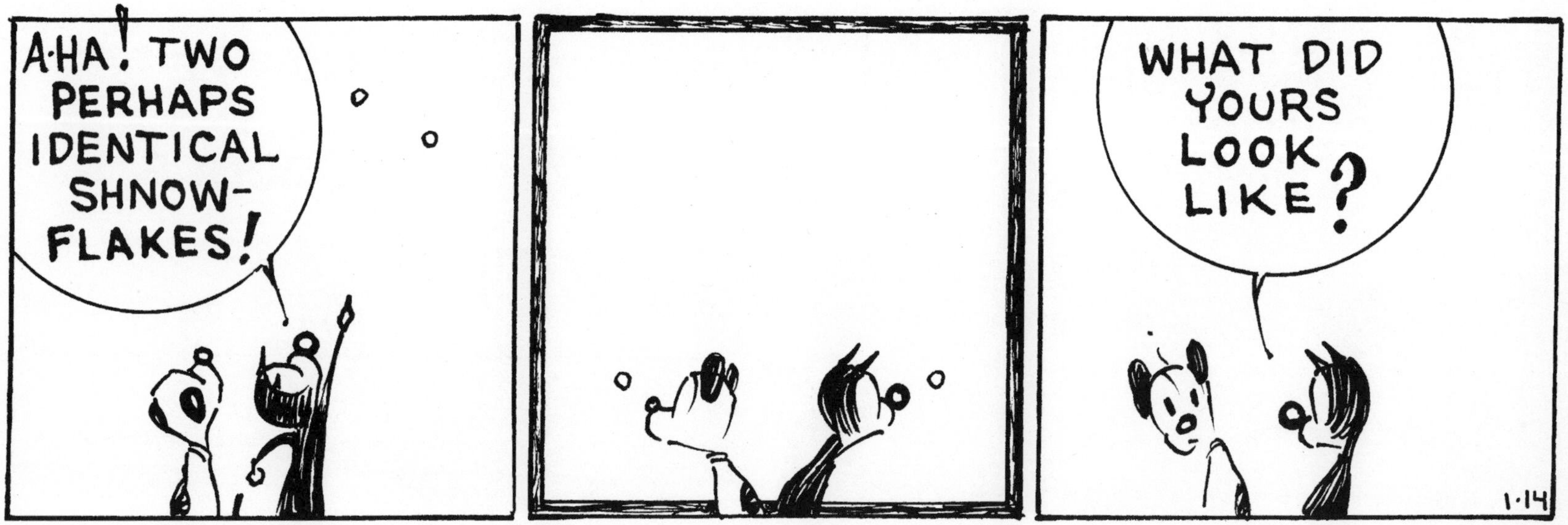
A·HA! TWO PERHAPS IDENTICAL SHNOW-FLAKES!
WHAT DID YOURS LOOK LIKE?
1·14

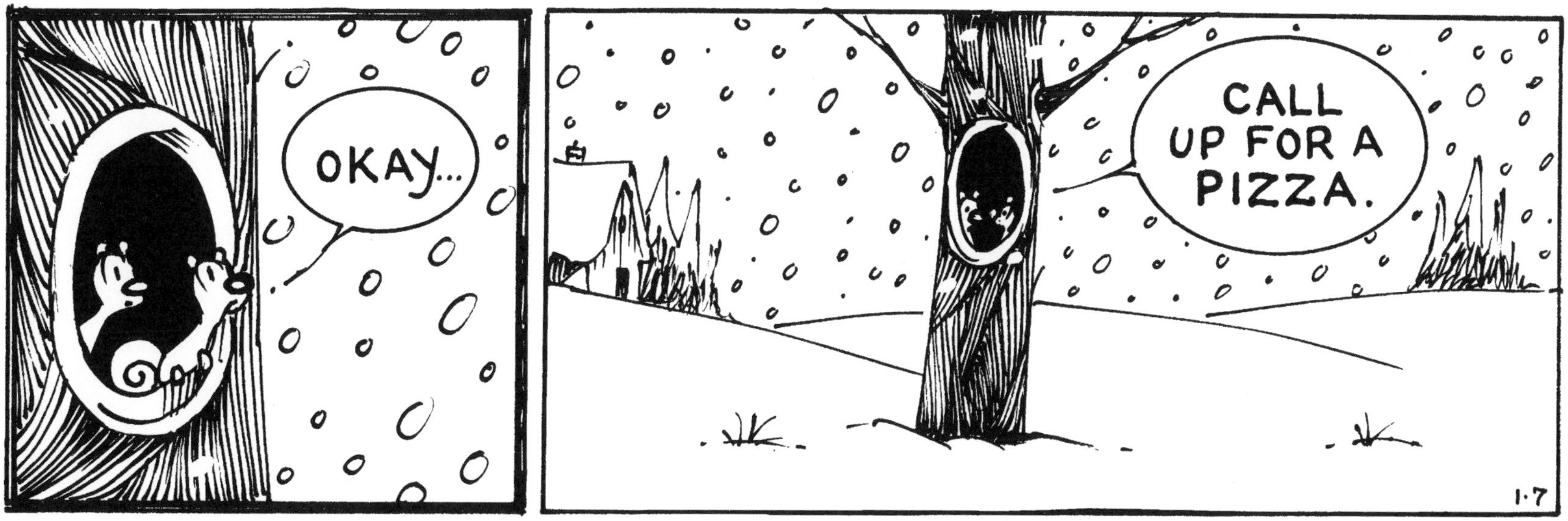
OKAY...
CALL UP FOR A PIZZA.
1·7

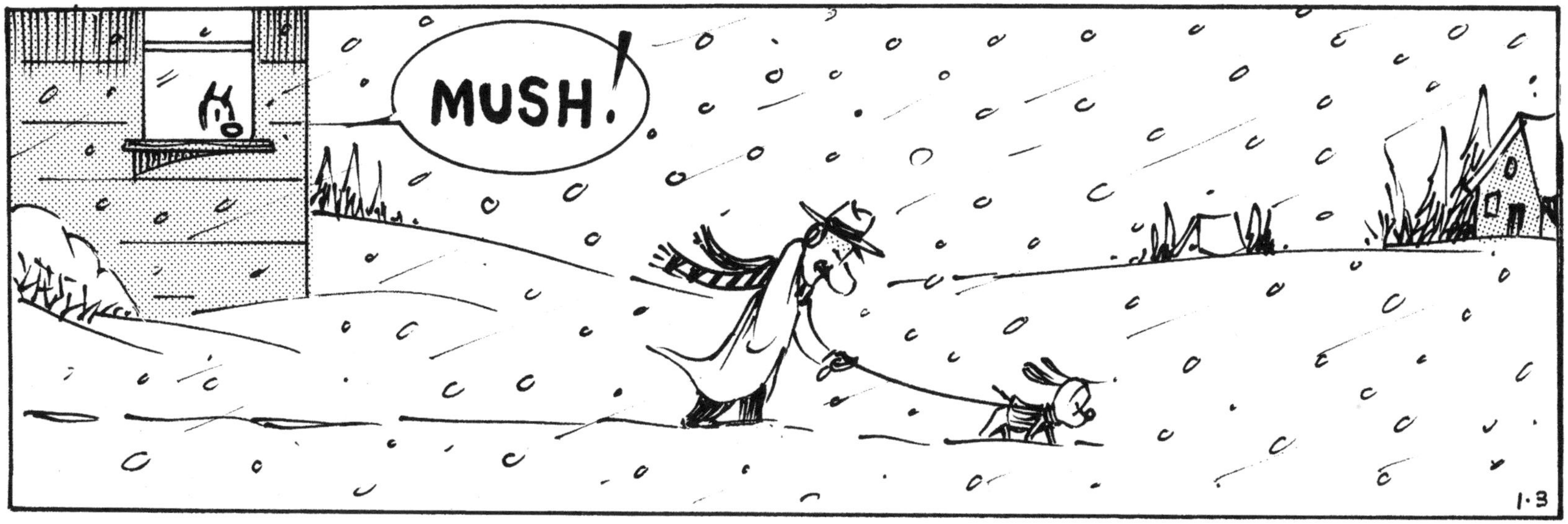
MUSH!
1·3

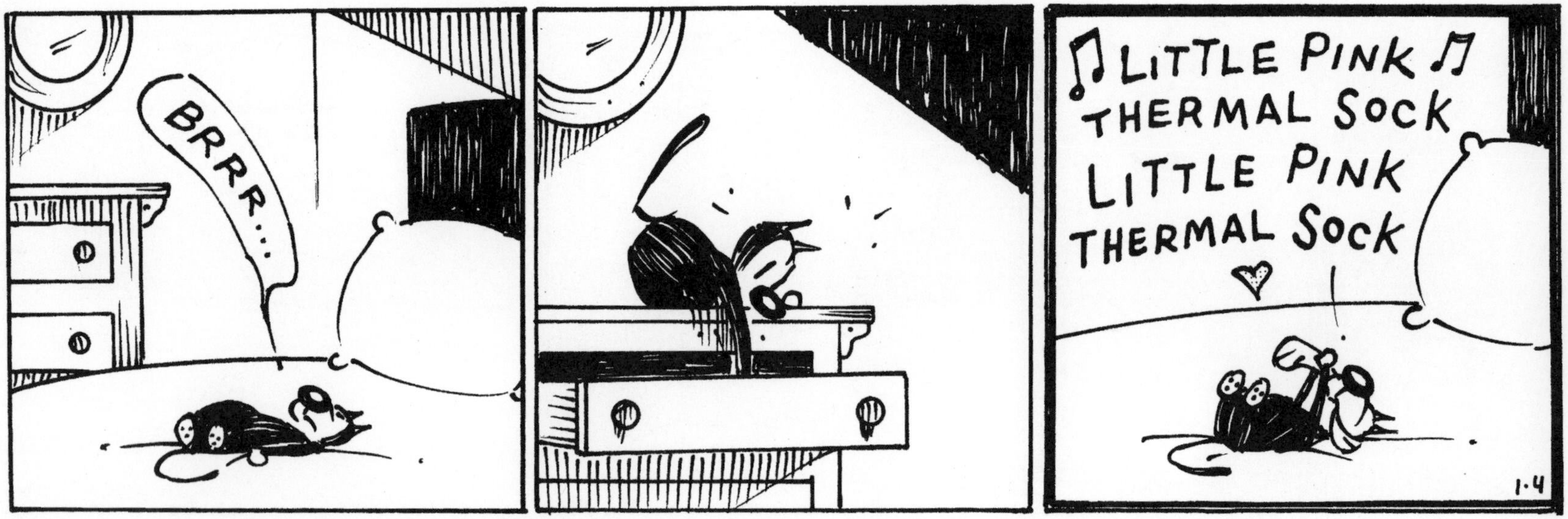
BRRRR...
♫ LITTLE PINK ♫
THERMAL SOCK
LITTLE PINK
THERMAL SOCK
1·4

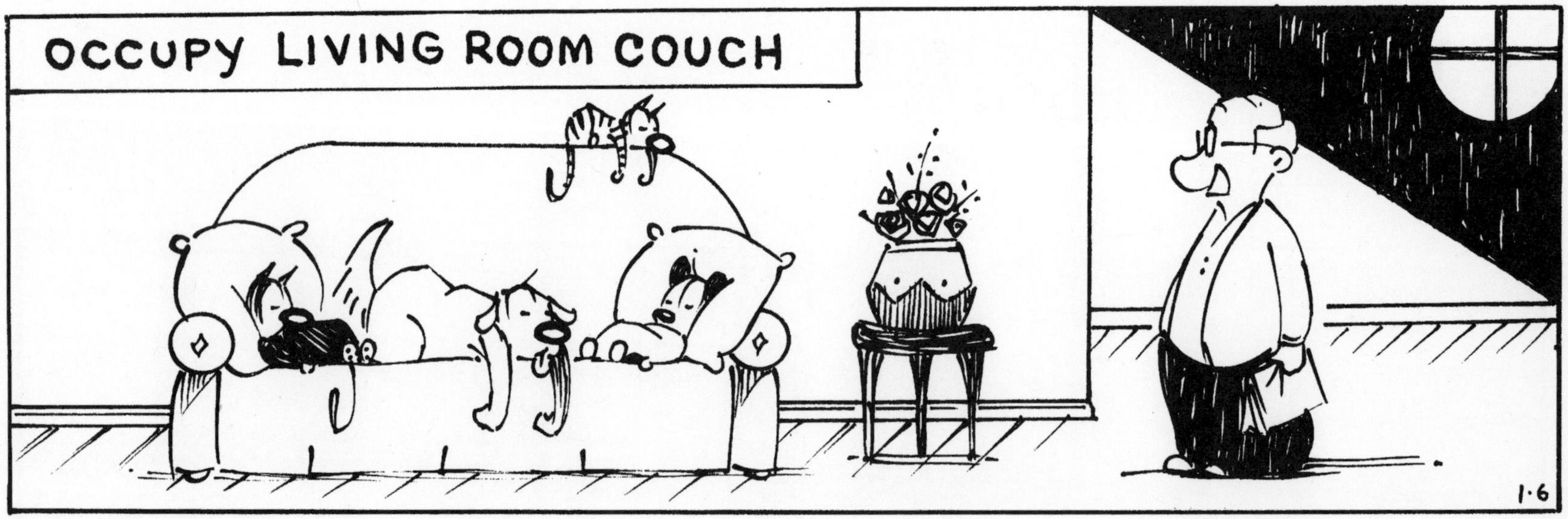
OCCUPY LIVING ROOM COUCH
1·6

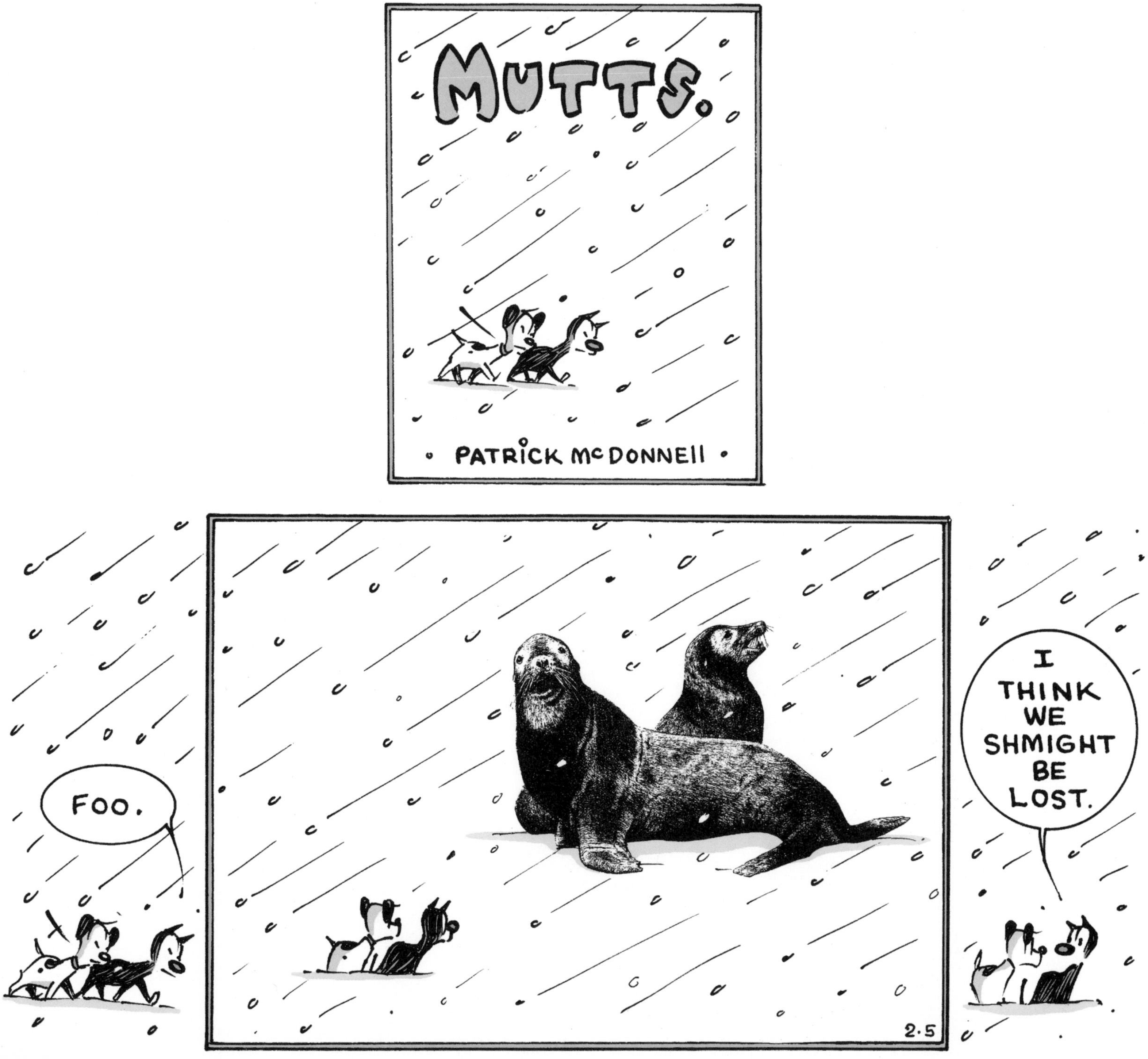
MUTTS.
PATRICK McDONNELL
FOO.
I THINK WE SHMIGHT BE LOST.
2.5

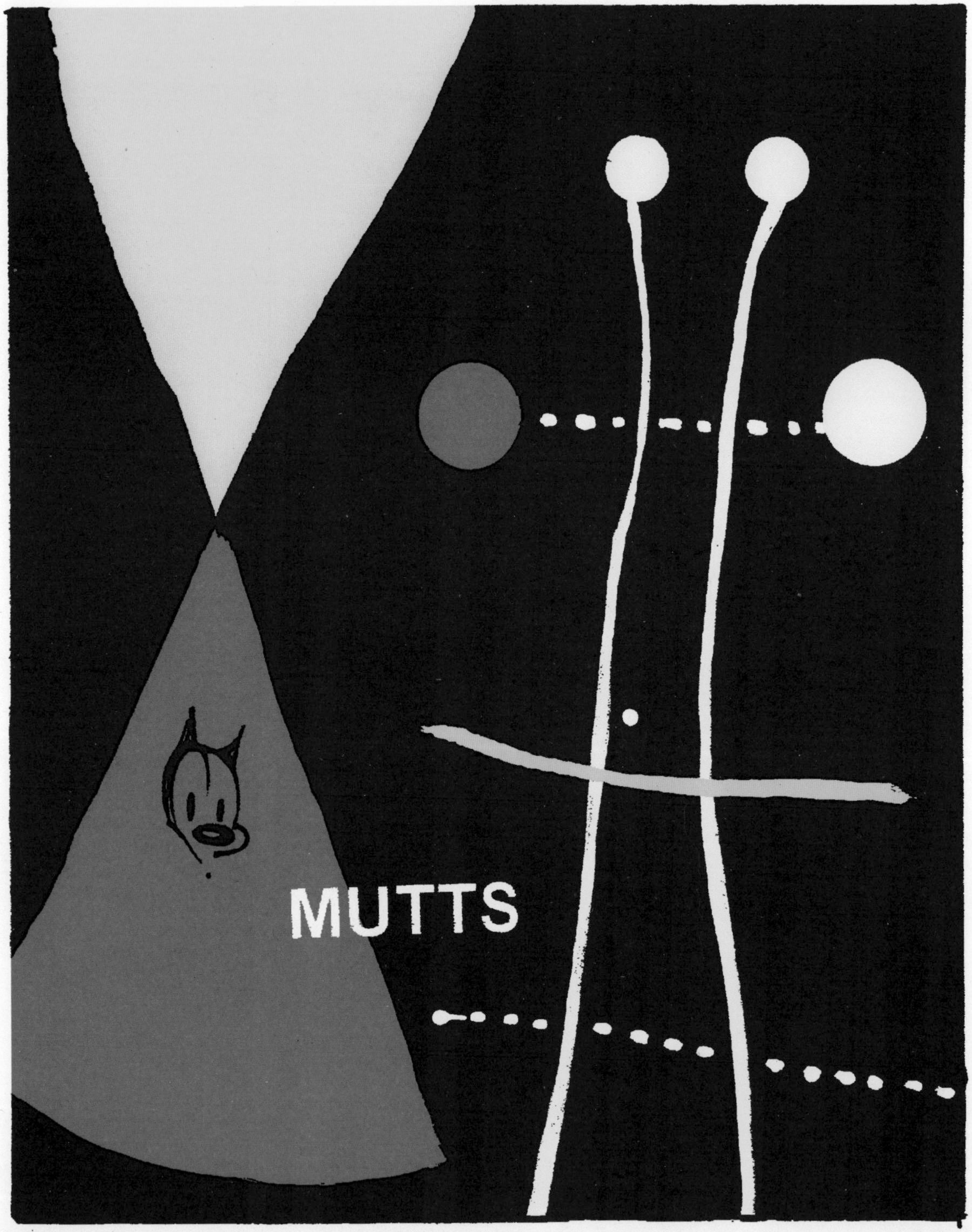
MUTTS

FOO
THESE CAT TREE CONDOS ARE GETTING OUT OF HAND.
1·8

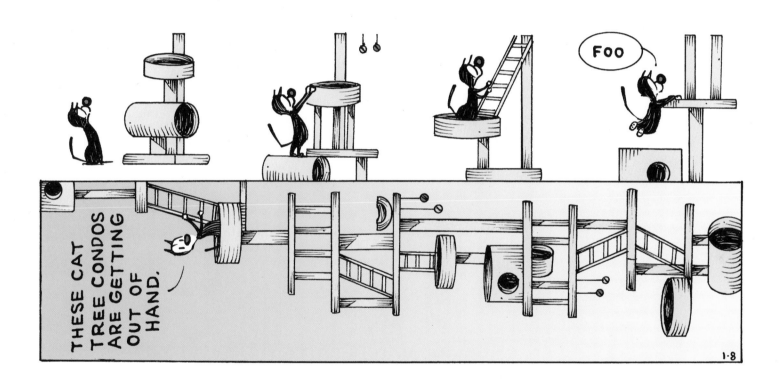

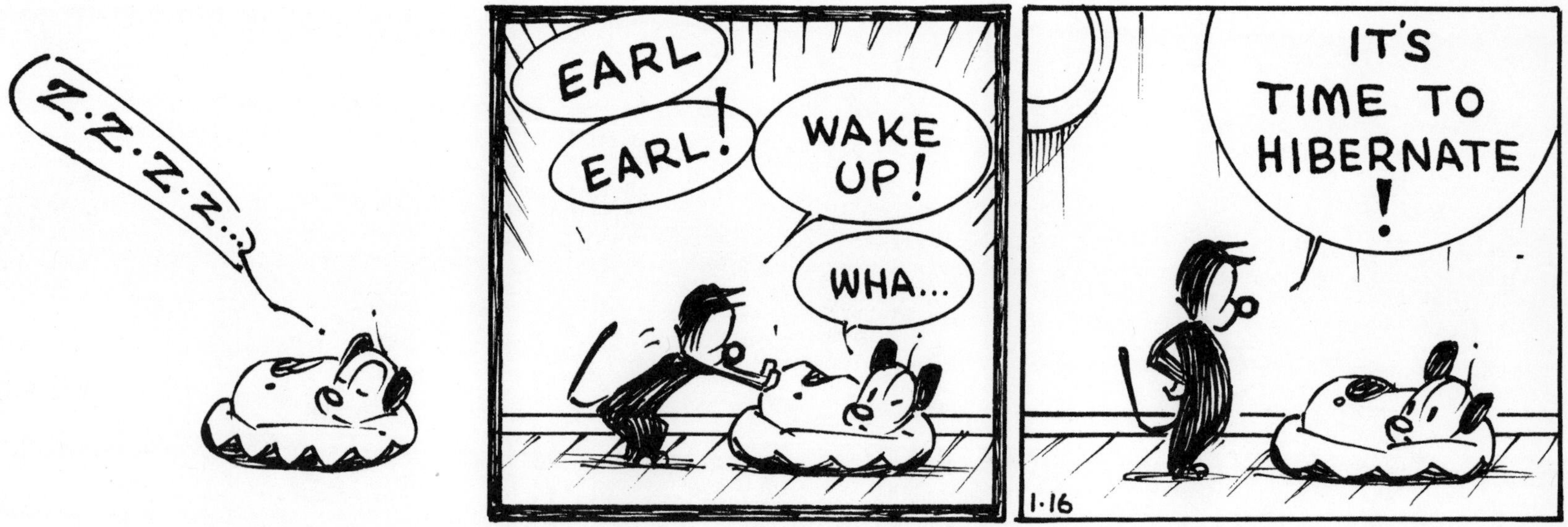
Z·Z·Z·Z...
EARL
EARL!
WAKE UP!
WHA...
IT'S TIME TO HIBERNATE!
1·16

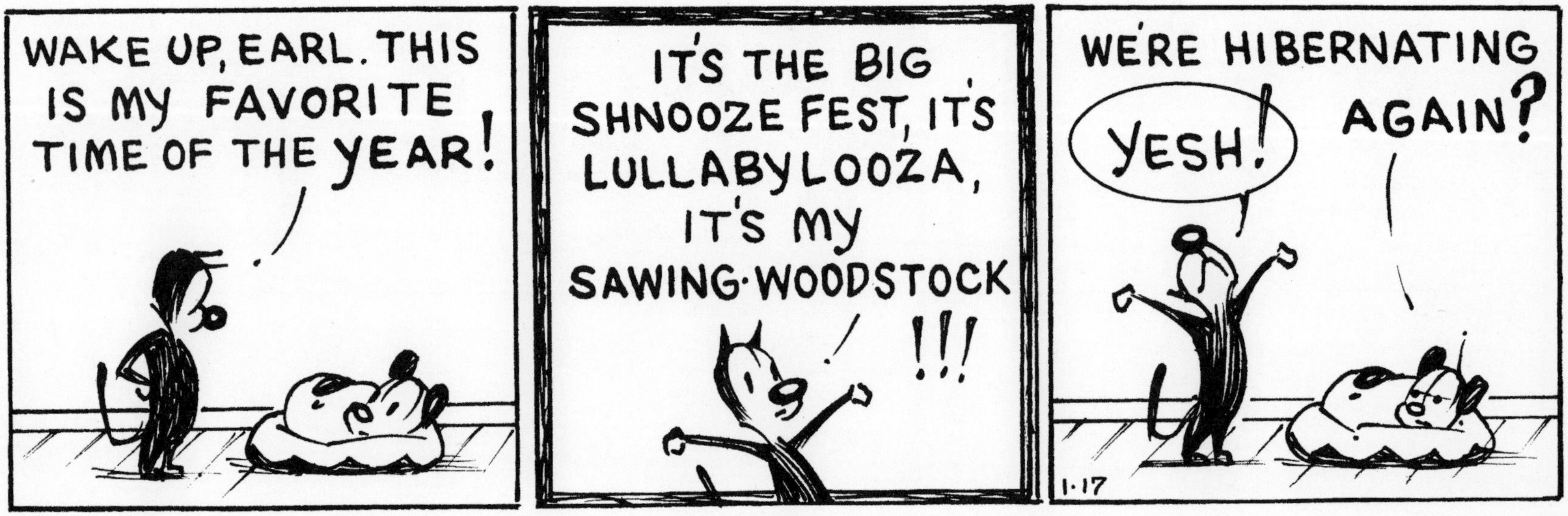
WAKE UP, EARL. THIS IS MY FAVORITE TIME OF THE YEAR!
IT'S THE BIG SHNOOZE FEST, IT'S LULLABYLOOZA, IT'S MY SAWING·WOODSTOCK!!!
WE'RE HIBERNATING AGAIN?
YESH!
1·17

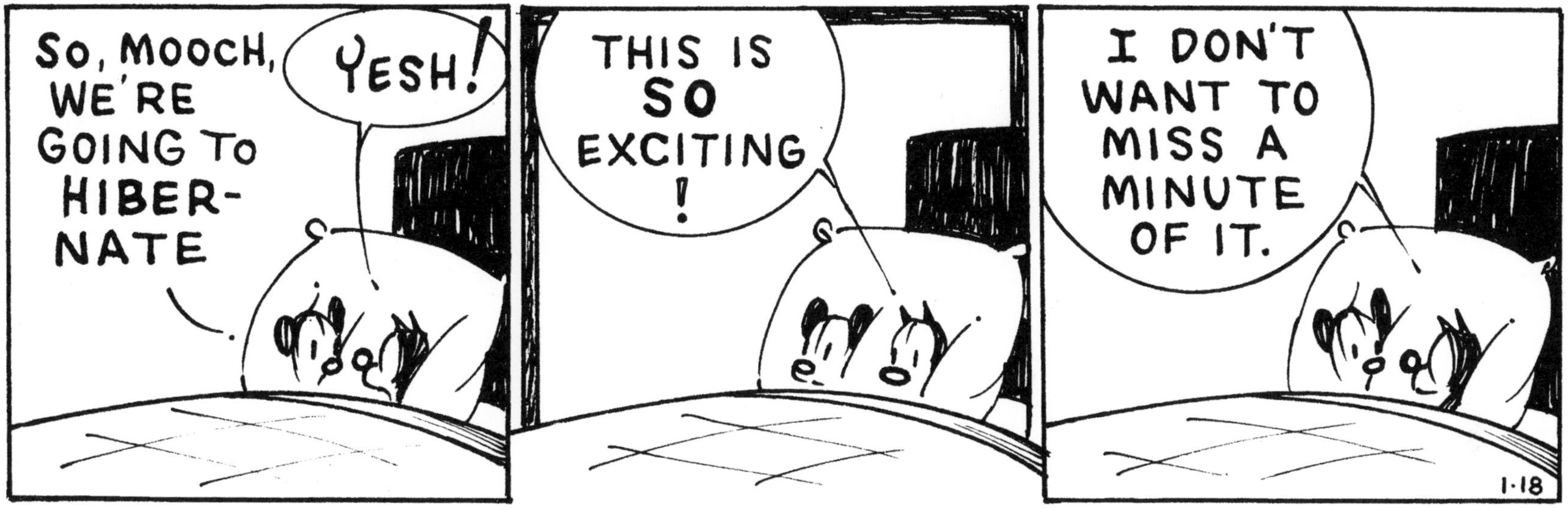
SO, MOOCH, WE'RE GOING TO HIBER-NATE
YESH!
THIS IS SO EXCITING !
I DON'T WANT TO MISS A MINUTE OF IT.
1·18

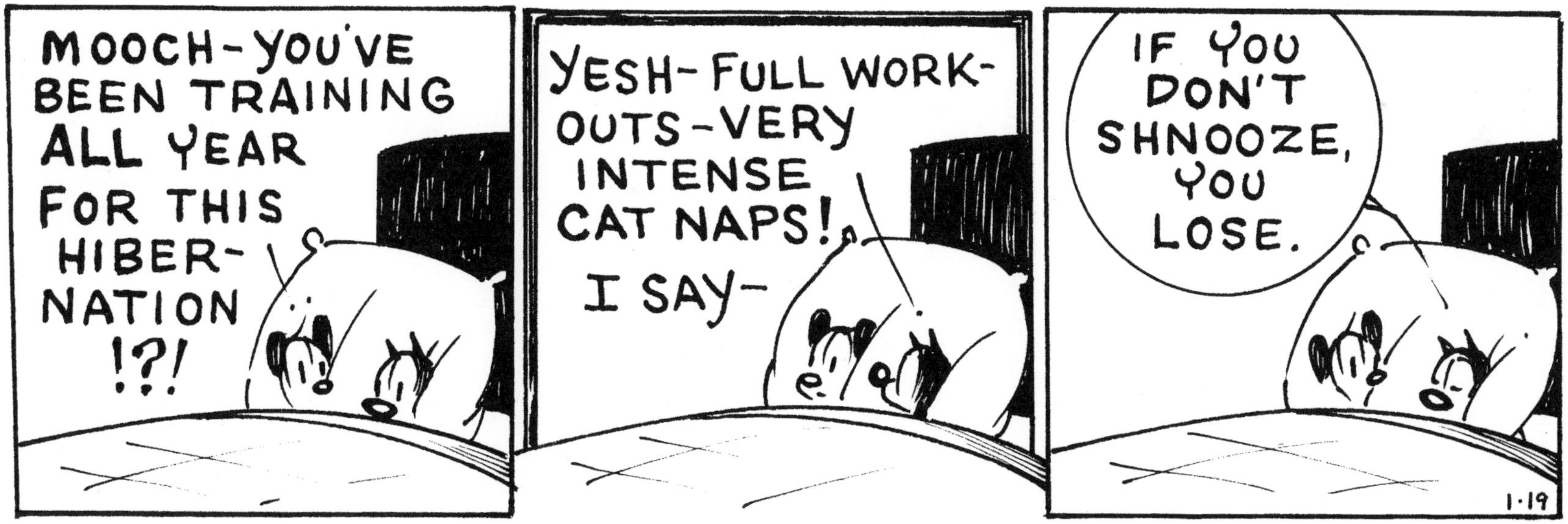
MOOCH - YOU'VE BEEN TRAINING ALL YEAR FOR THIS HIBER-NATION !?!
YESH - FULL WORK-OUTS - VERY INTENSE CAT NAPS! I SAY-
IF YOU DON'T SHNOOZE, YOU LOSE.
1·19

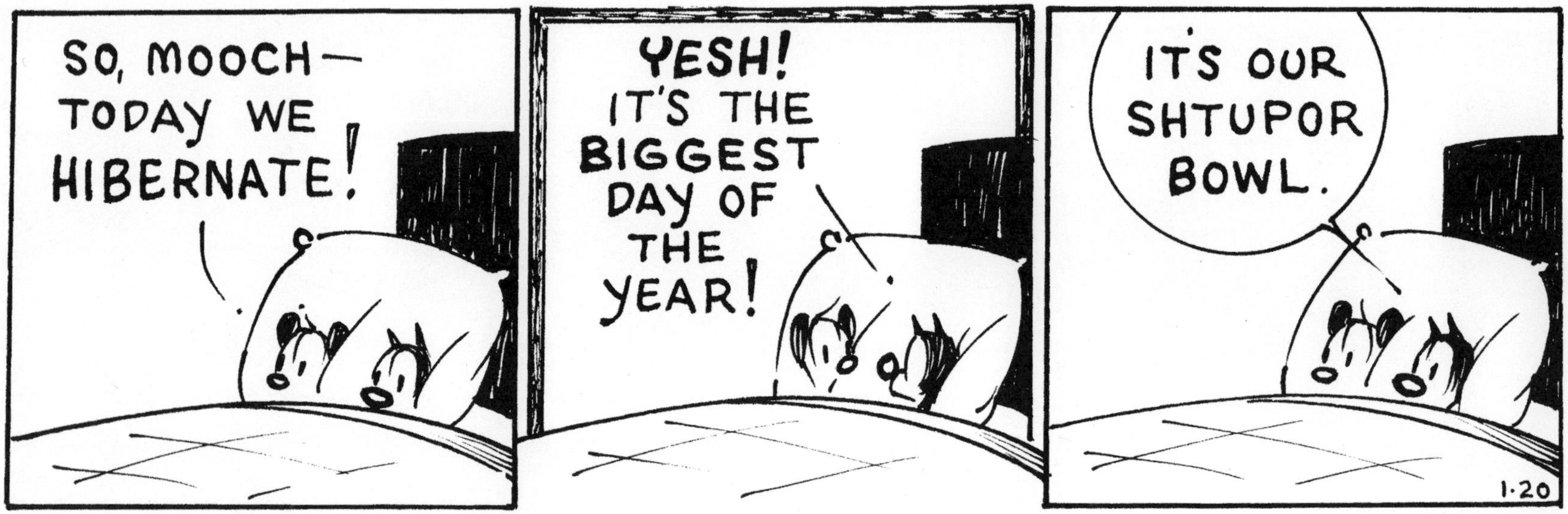
SO, MOOCH— TODAY WE HIBERNATE!
YESH! IT'S THE BIGGEST DAY OF THE YEAR!
IT'S OUR SHTUPOR BOWL.
1·20

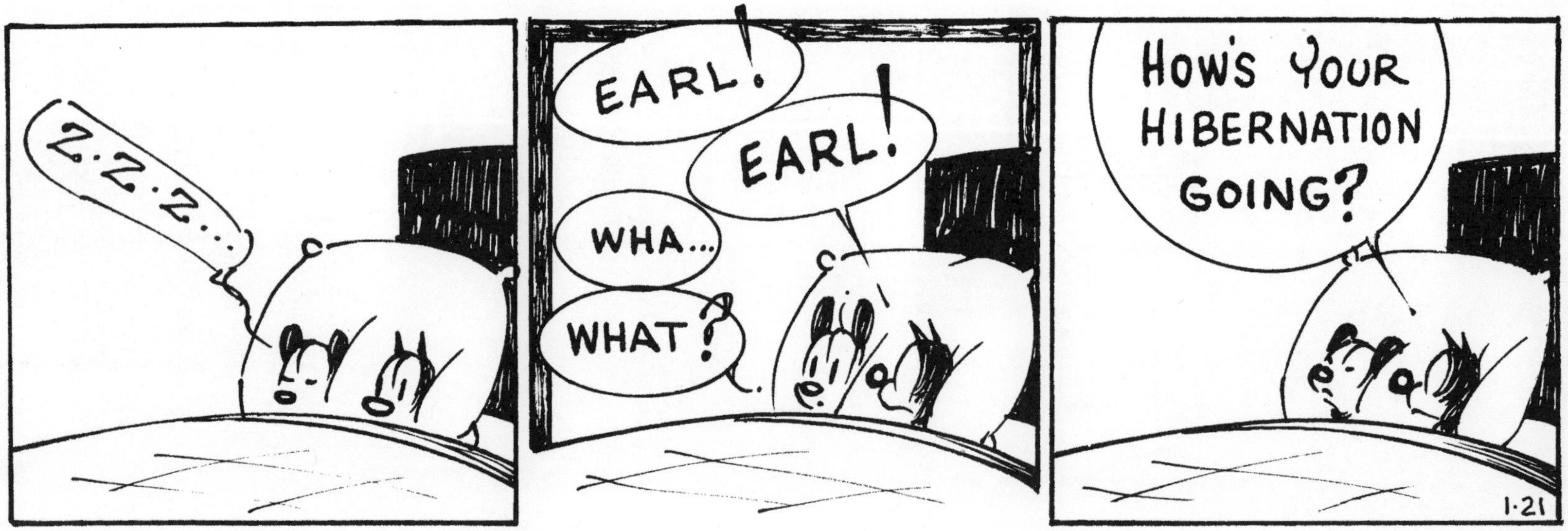
Z·Z·Z...
EARL!
EARL!
WHA...
WHAT?
HOW'S YOUR HIBERNATION GOING?
1·21

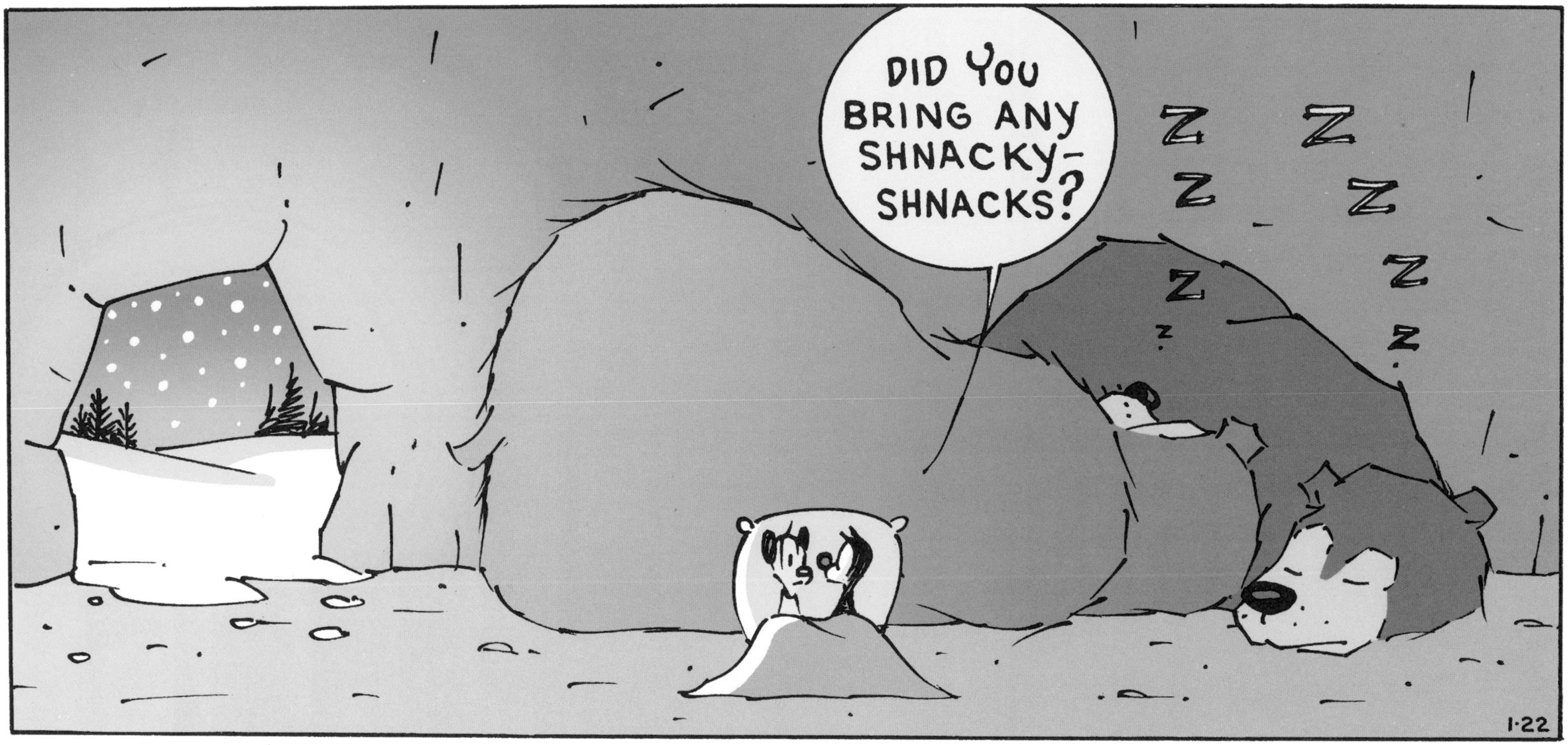
DID YOU BRING ANY SHNACKY-SHNACKS?
Z Z Z Z Z Z Z Z
1·22

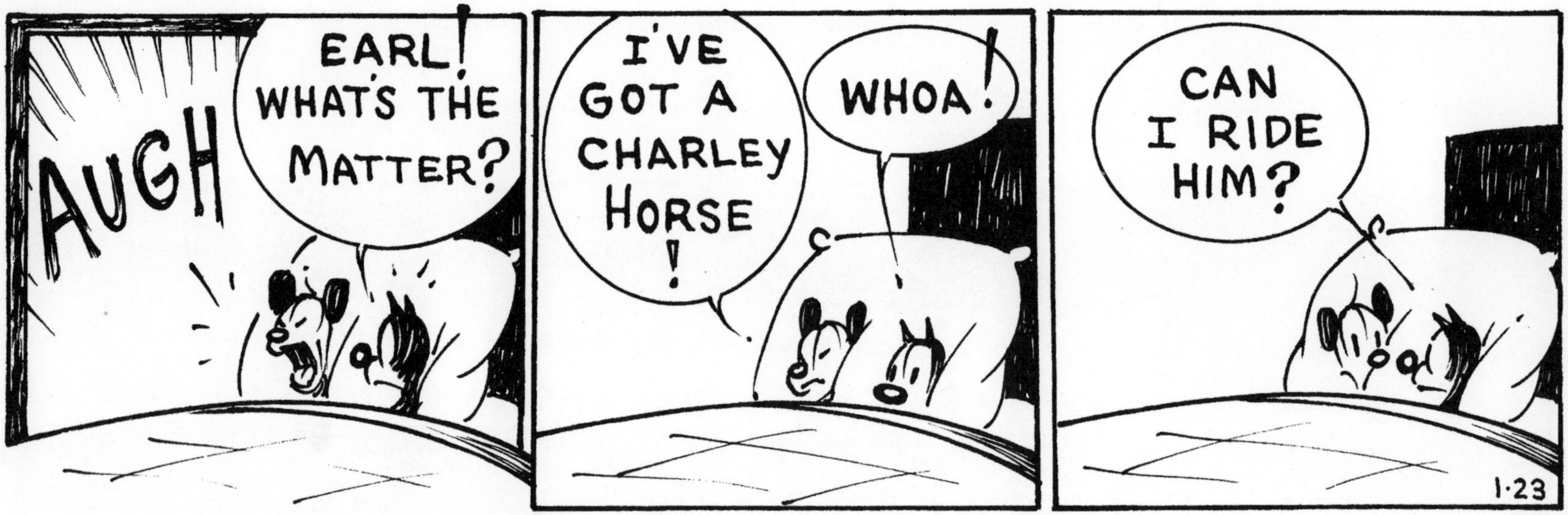
AUGH
EARL! WHAT'S THE MATTER?
I'VE GOT A CHARLEY HORSE!
WHOA!
CAN I RIDE HIM?
1·23

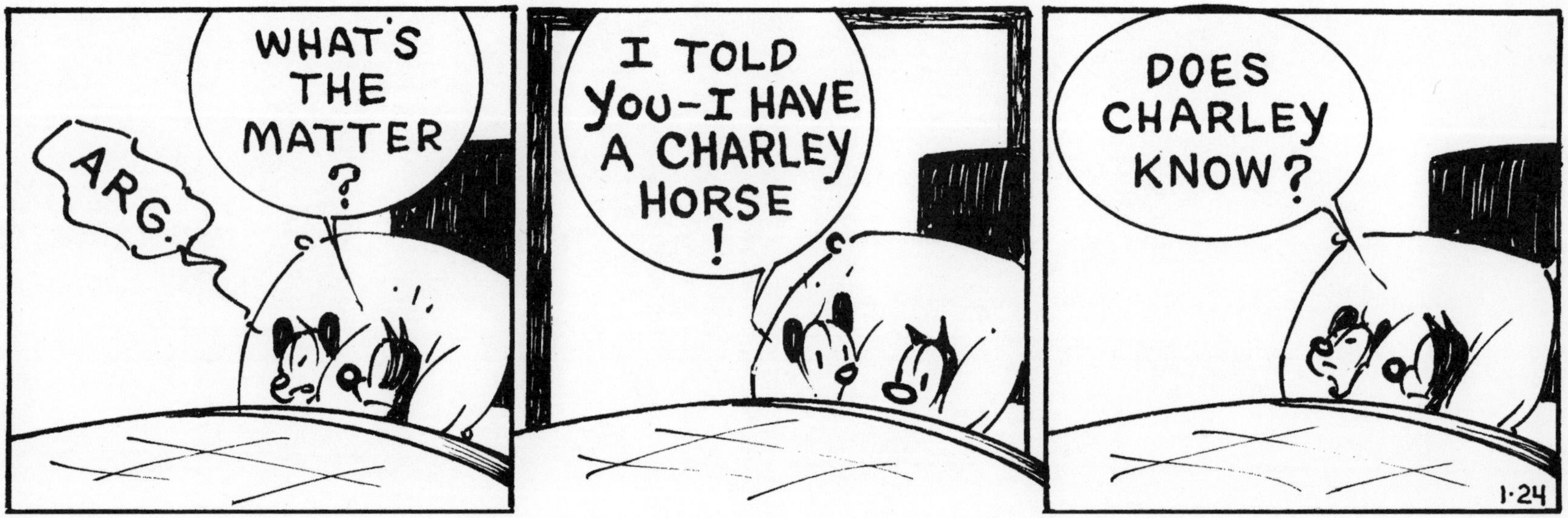
WHAT'S THE MATTER?
ARG.
I TOLD YOU-I HAVE A CHARLEY HORSE!
DOES CHARLEY KNOW?
1·24

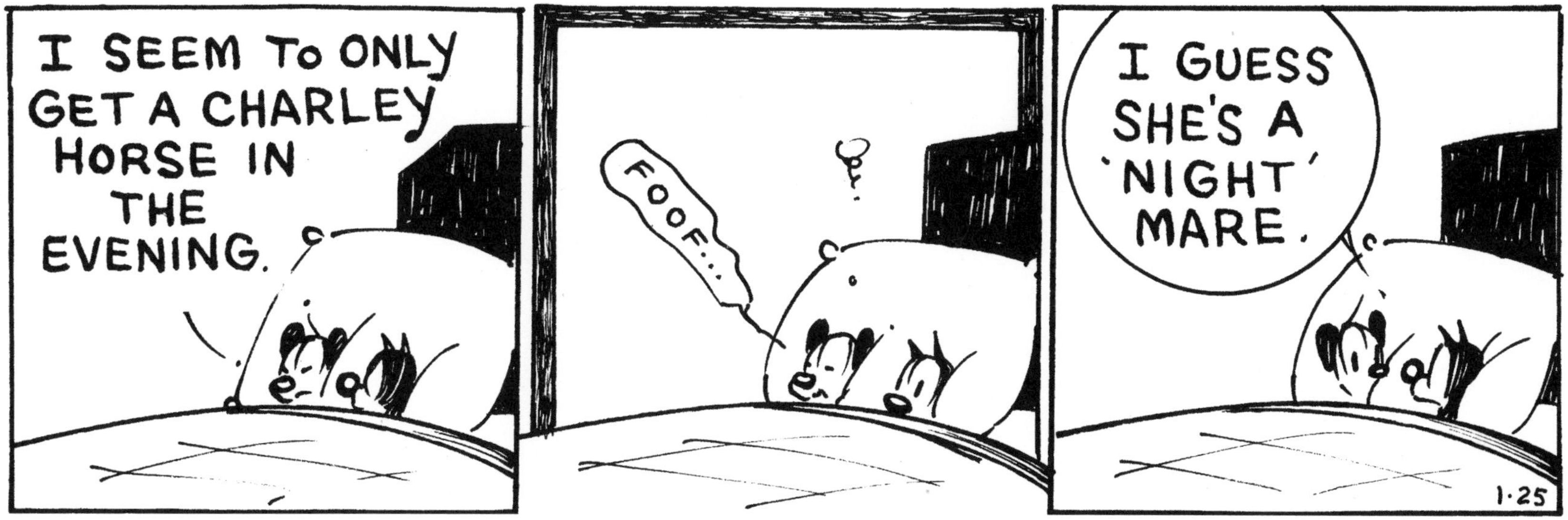
I SEEM TO ONLY GET A CHARLEY HORSE IN THE EVENING.
FOOF...
I GUESS SHE'S A 'NIGHT' MARE.
1·25

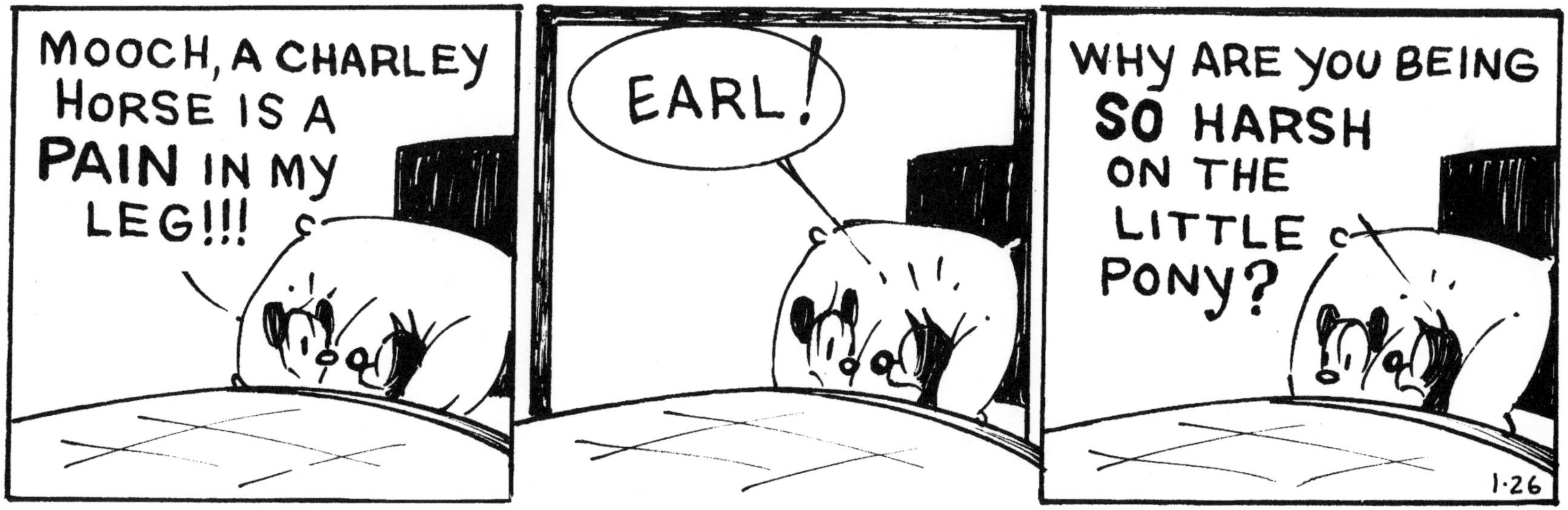
MOOCH, A CHARLEY HORSE IS A PAIN IN MY LEG!!!
EARL!
WHY ARE YOU BEING SO HARSH ON THE LITTLE PONY?
1·26

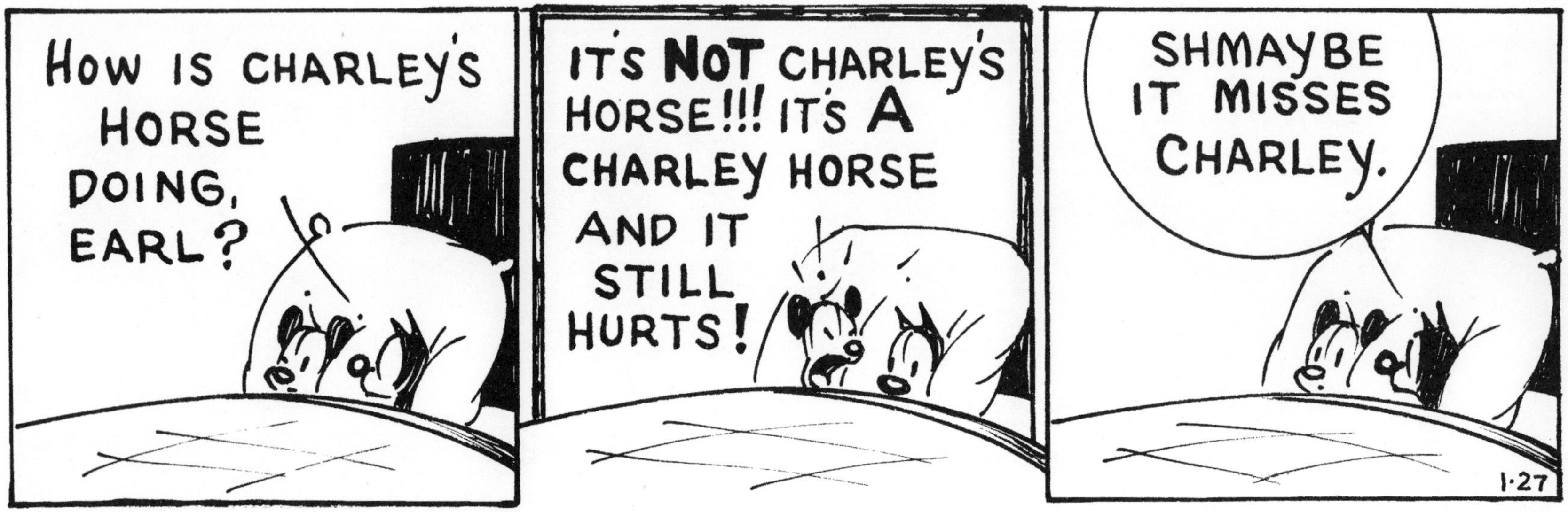
HOW IS CHARLEY'S HORSE DOING, EARL?
IT'S **NOT** CHARLEY'S HORSE!!! IT'S **A** CHARLEY HORSE AND IT STILL HURTS!
SHMAYBE IT MISSES CHARLEY.
1·27

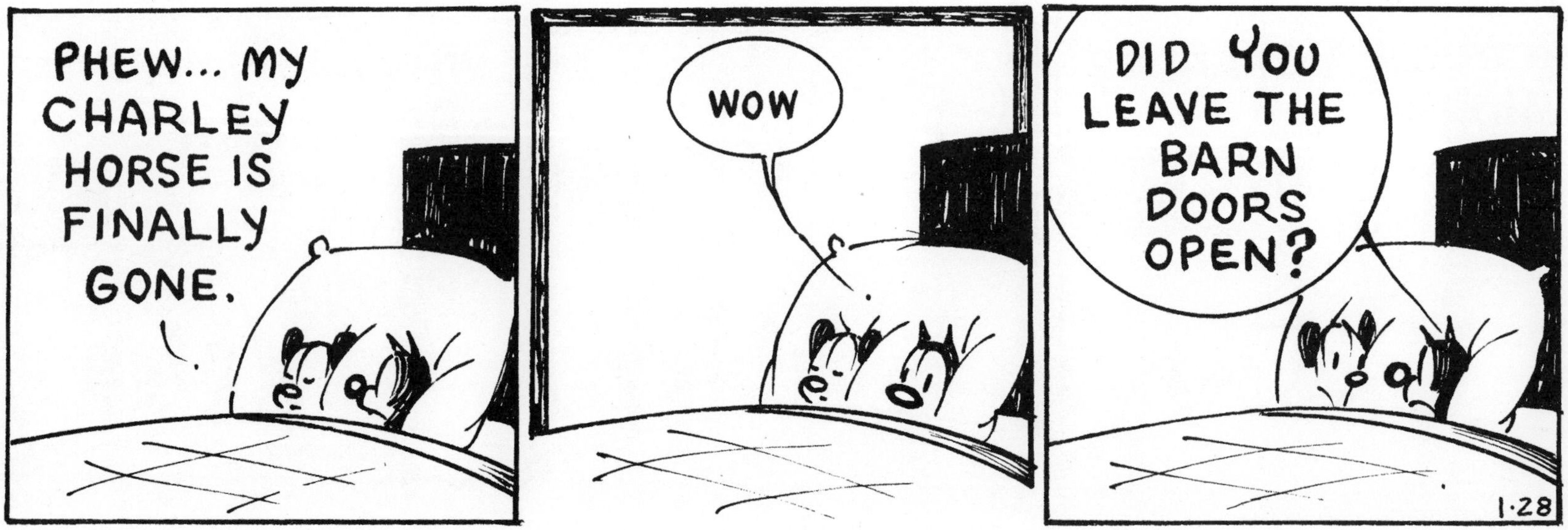
PHEW... MY CHARLEY HORSE IS FINALLY GONE.
WOW
DID YOU LEAVE THE BARN DOORS OPEN?
1·28

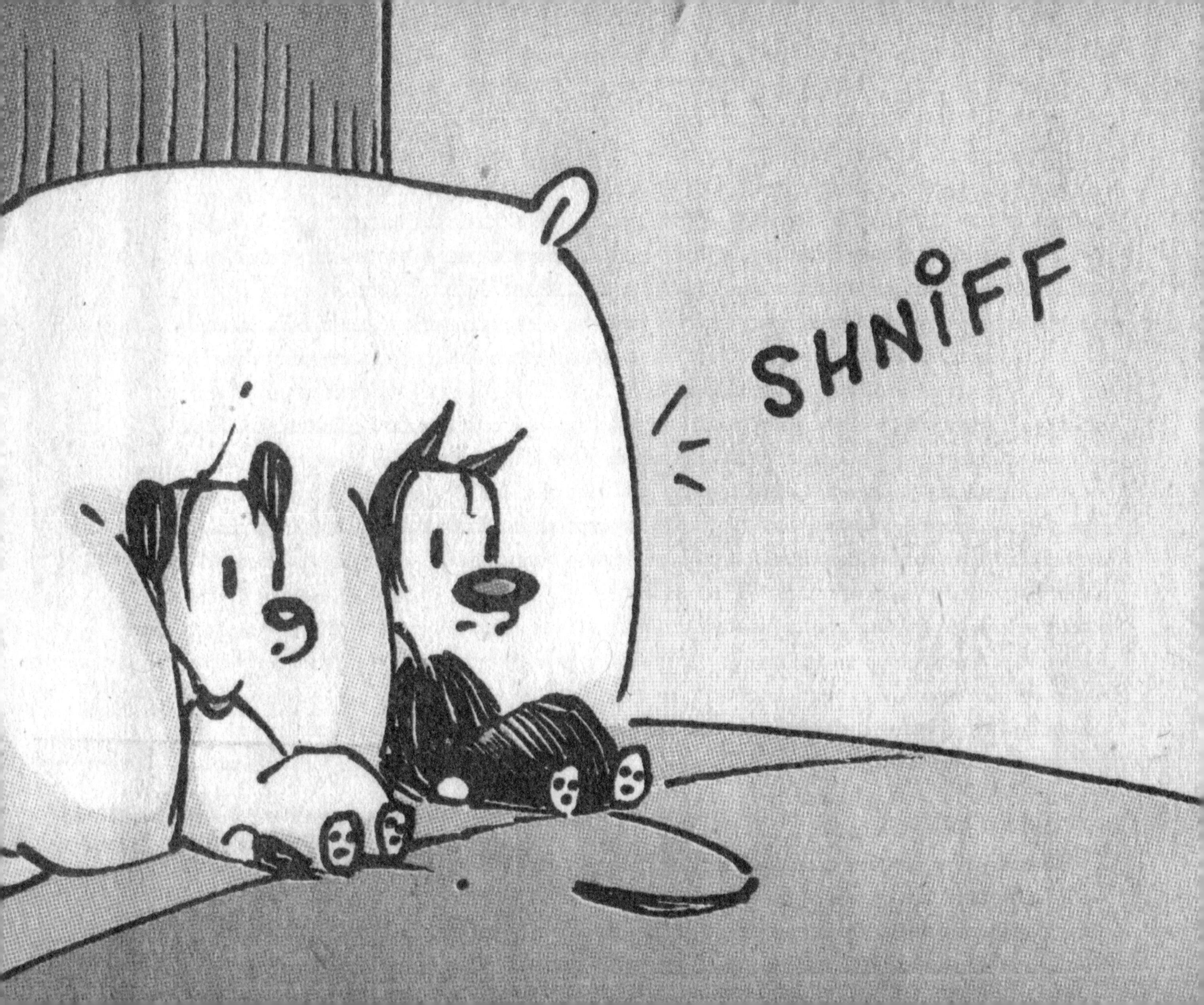
SHNIFF

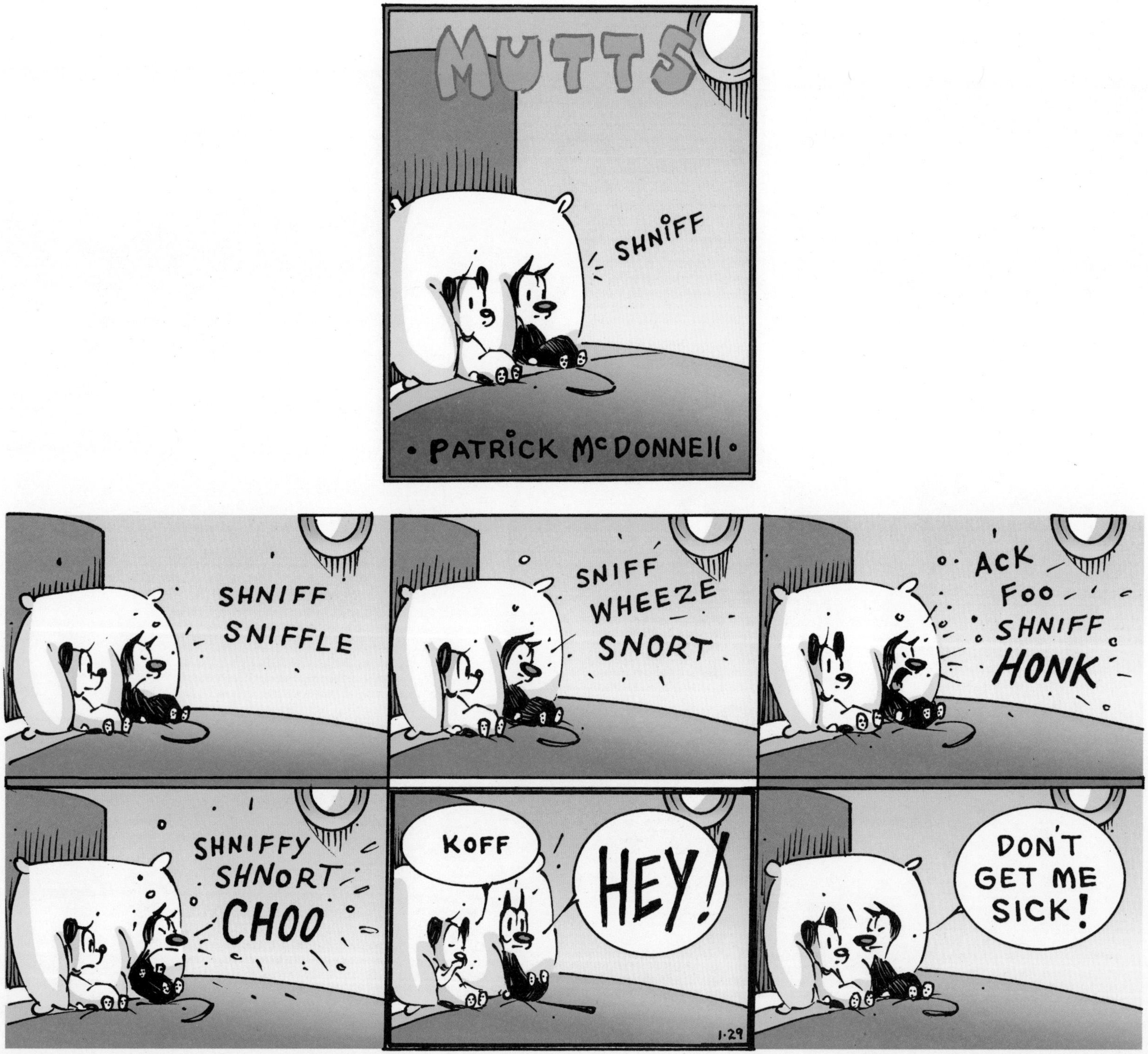
MUTTS
SHNIFF
• PATRICK McDONNELL •
SHNIFF SNIFFLE
SNIFF WHEEZE SNORT
ACK FOO SHNIFF HONK
SHNIFFY SHNORT CHOO
KOFF
HEY!
1·29
DON'T GET ME SICK!

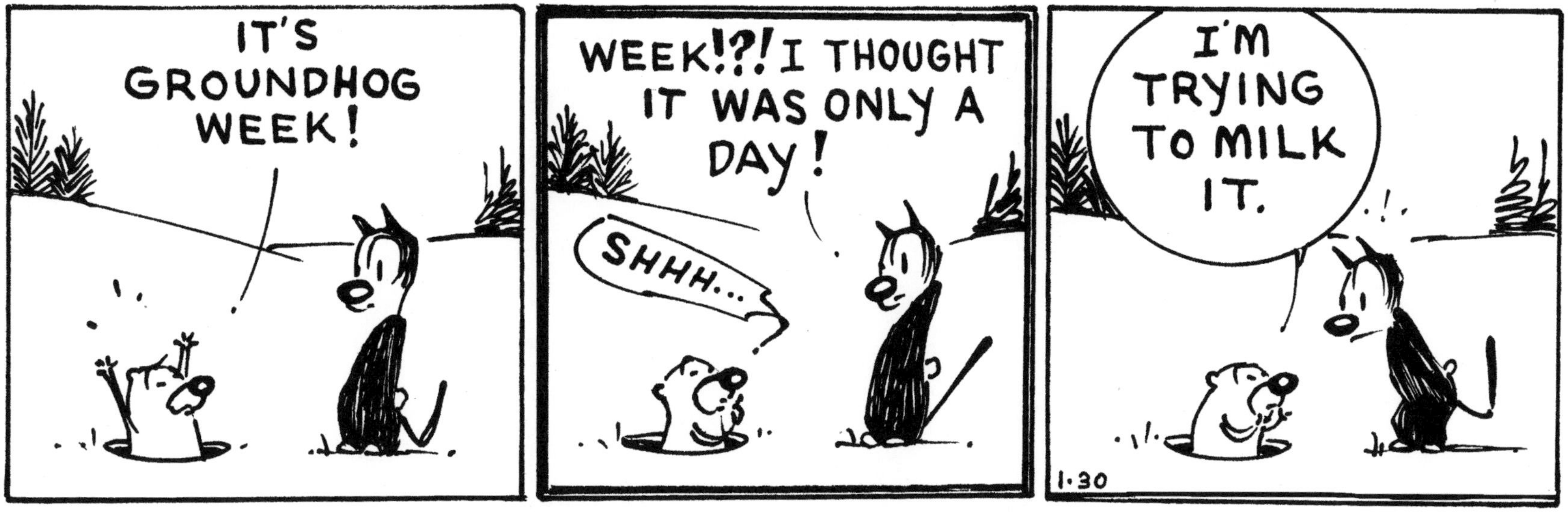
IT'S GROUNDHOG WEEK!
WEEK!?! I THOUGHT IT WAS ONLY A DAY!
SHHH...
I'M TRYING TO MILK IT.
1·30

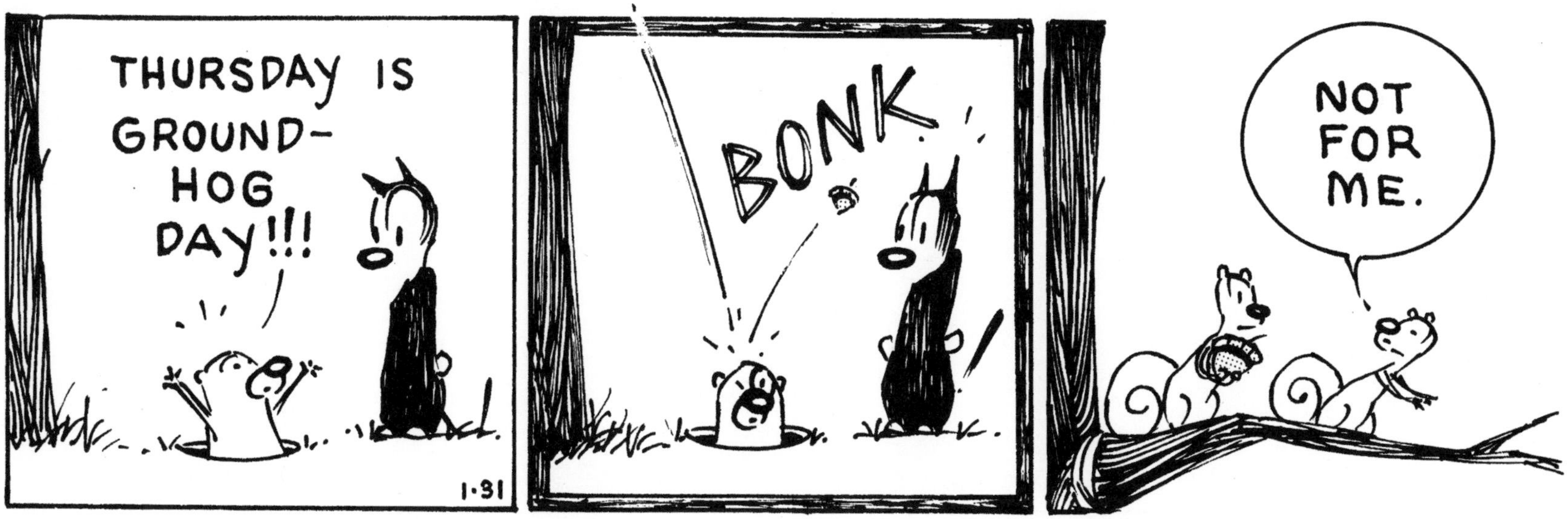
THURSDAY IS GROUND-HOG DAY!!!
BONK
NOT FOR ME.
1·31

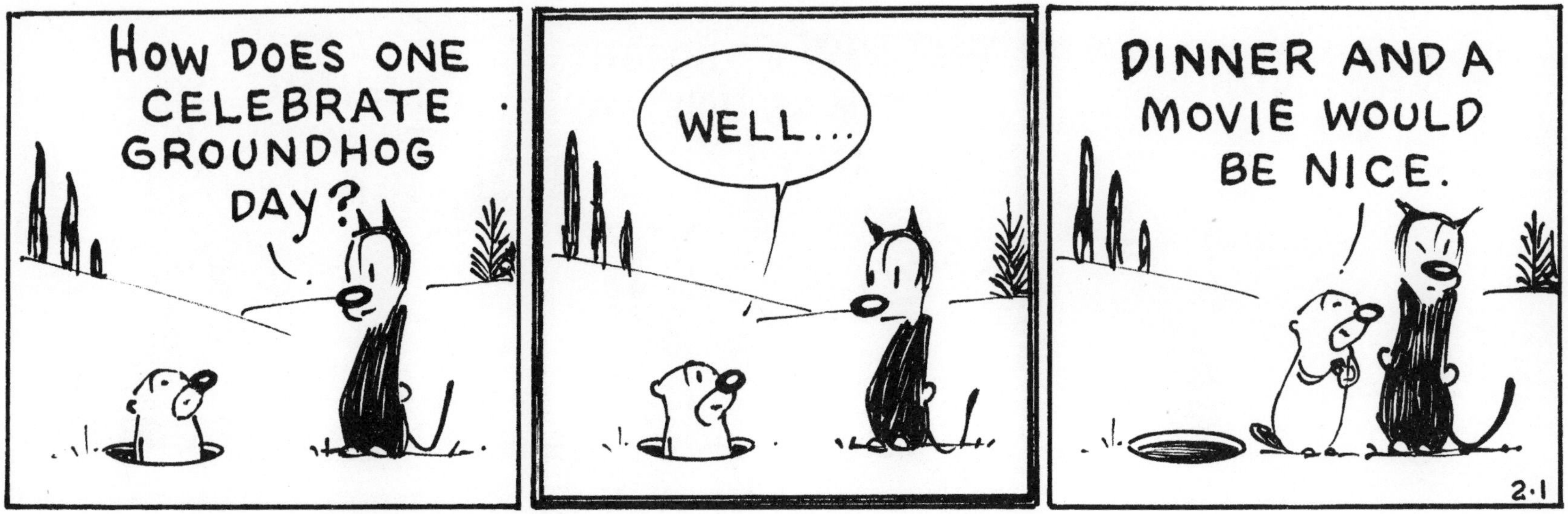
HOW DOES ONE CELEBRATE GROUNDHOG DAY?
WELL...
DINNER AND A MOVIE WOULD BE NICE.
2·1

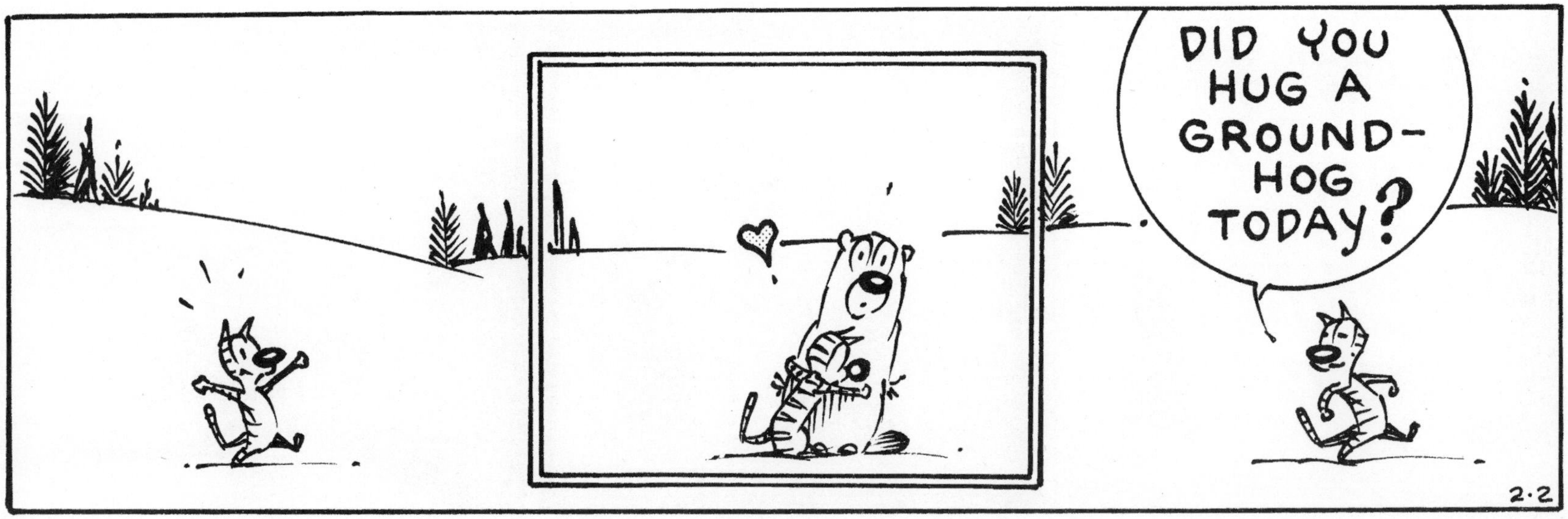
DID YOU HUG A GROUND-HOG TODAY?
2·2

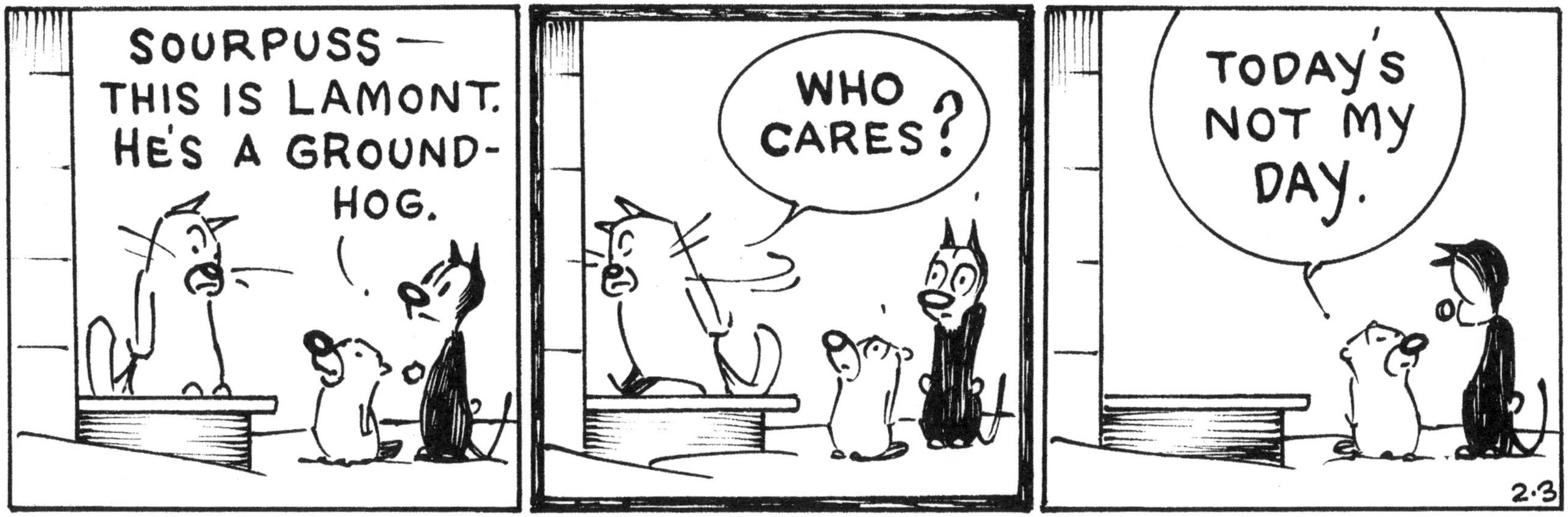
SOURPUSS — THIS IS LAMONT. HE'S A GROUND-HOG.
WHO CARES?
TODAY'S NOT MY DAY.
2·3

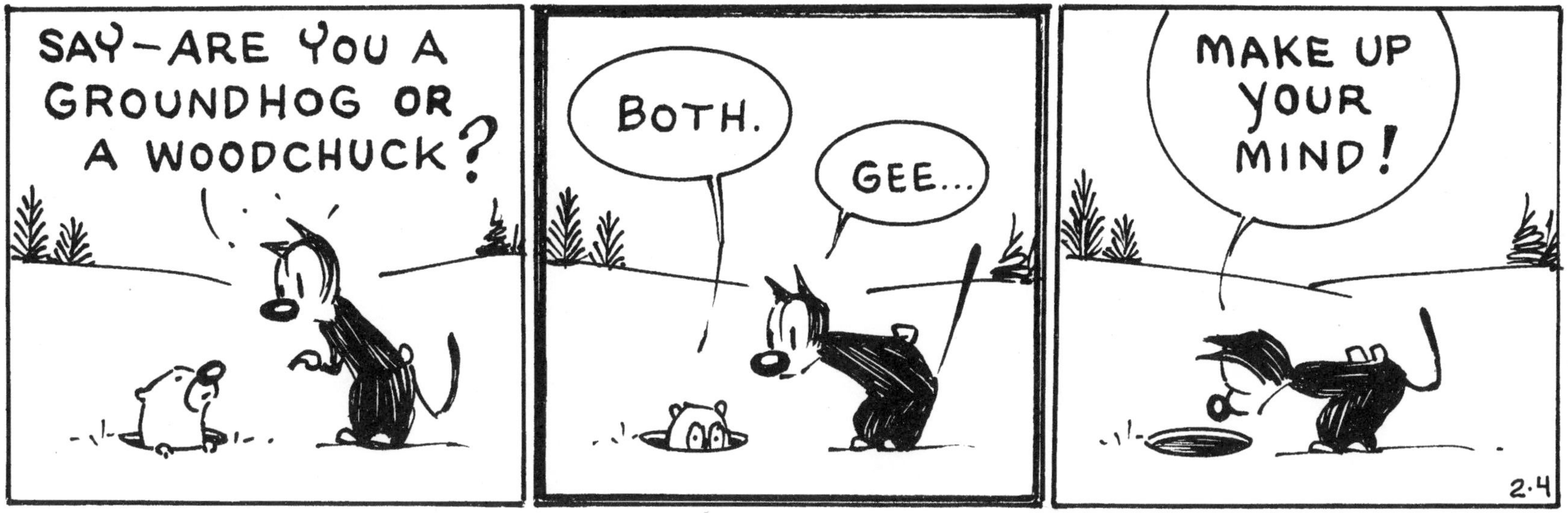
SAY—ARE YOU A GROUNDHOG OR A WOODCHUCK?
BOTH.
GEE...
MAKE UP YOUR MIND!
2·4

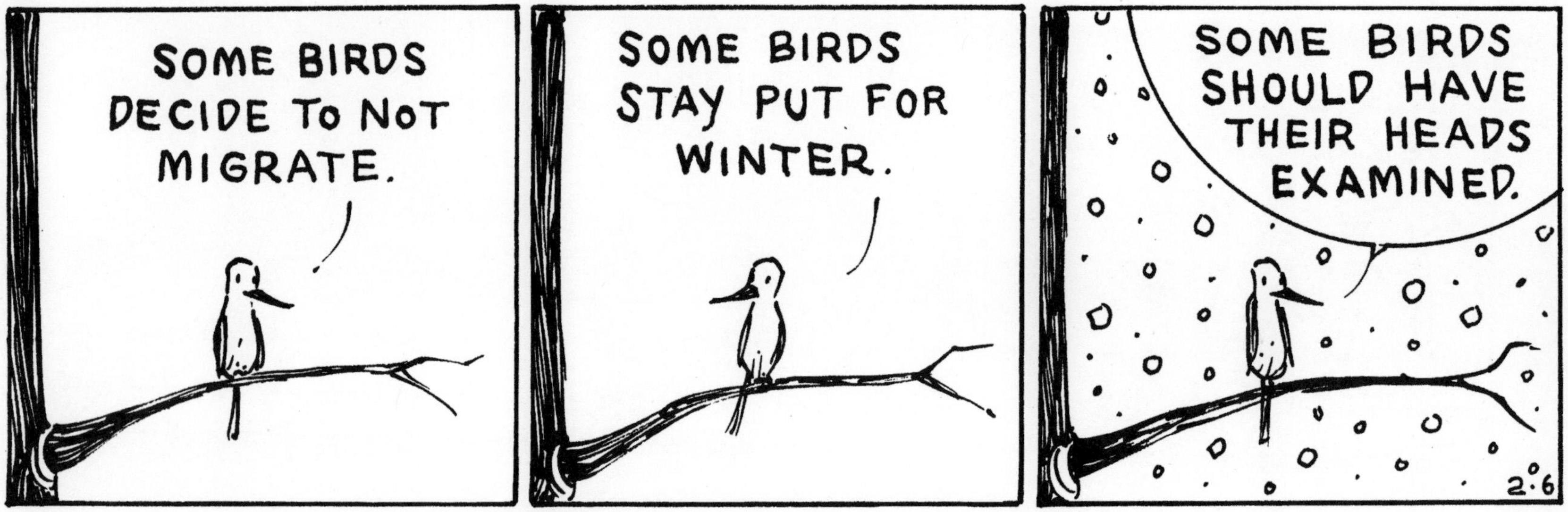
SOME BIRDS DECIDE TO NOT MIGRATE.
SOME BIRDS STAY PUT FOR WINTER.
SOME BIRDS SHOULD HAVE THEIR HEADS EXAMINED.
2·6

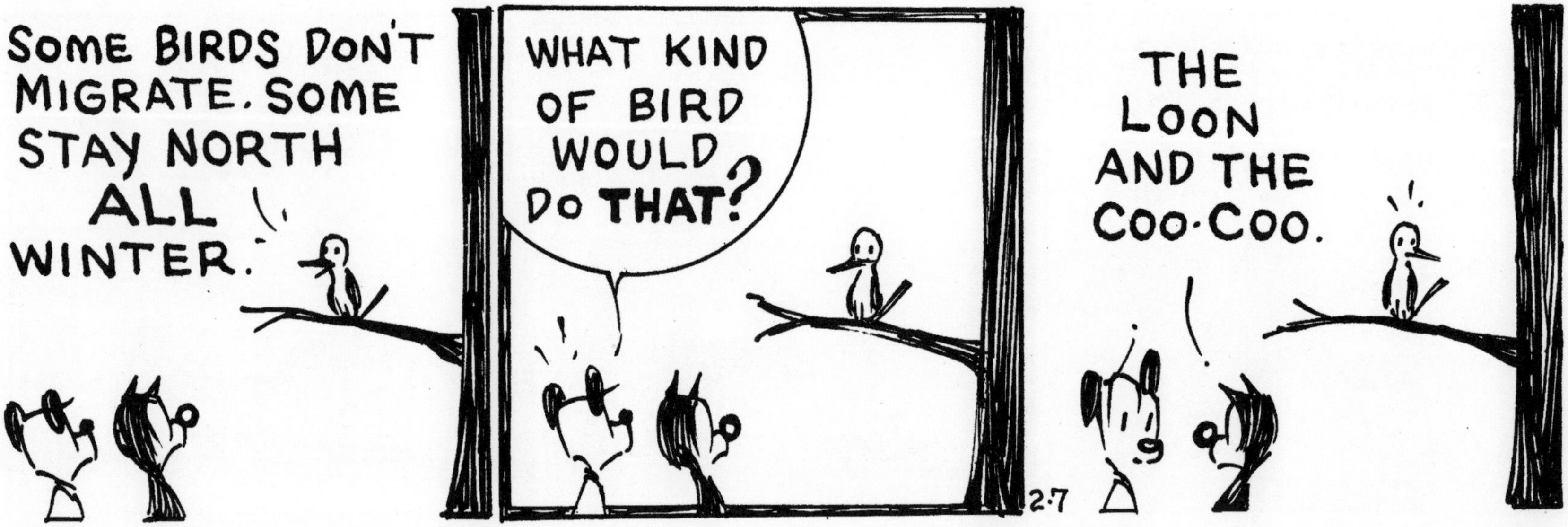
SOME BIRDS DON'T MIGRATE. SOME STAY NORTH ALL WINTER.
WHAT KIND OF BIRD WOULD DO THAT?
2·7
THE LOON AND THE COO·COO.

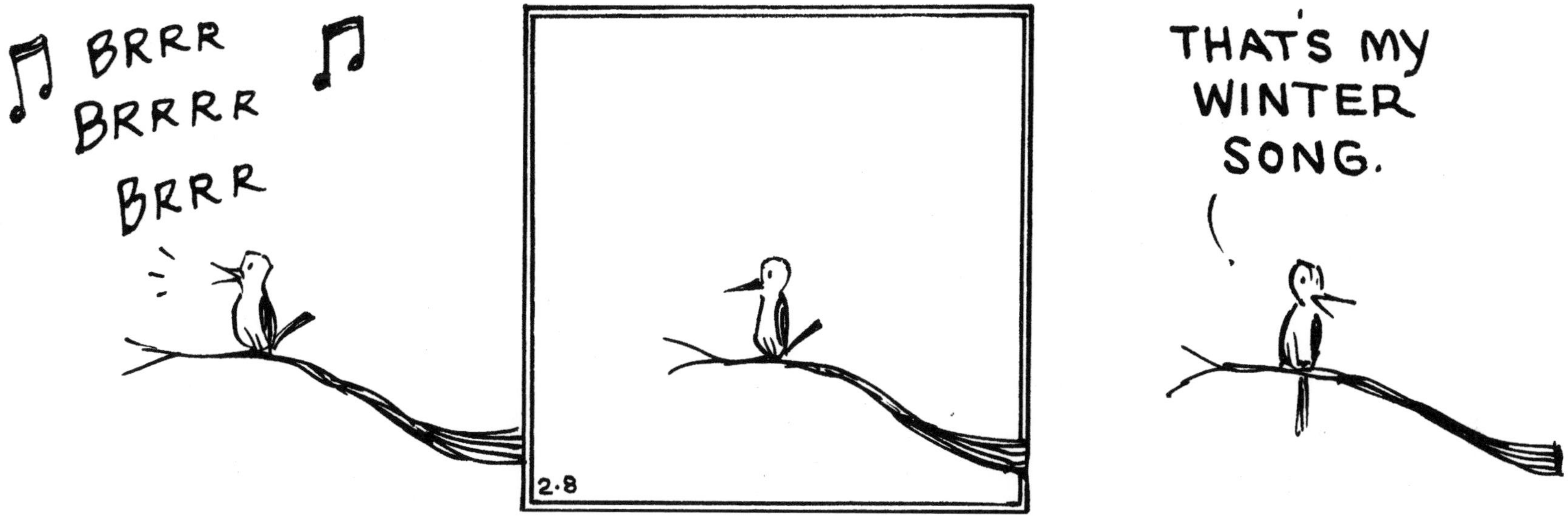
BRRR
BRRRR
BRRR
THAT'S MY WINTER SONG.
2·8

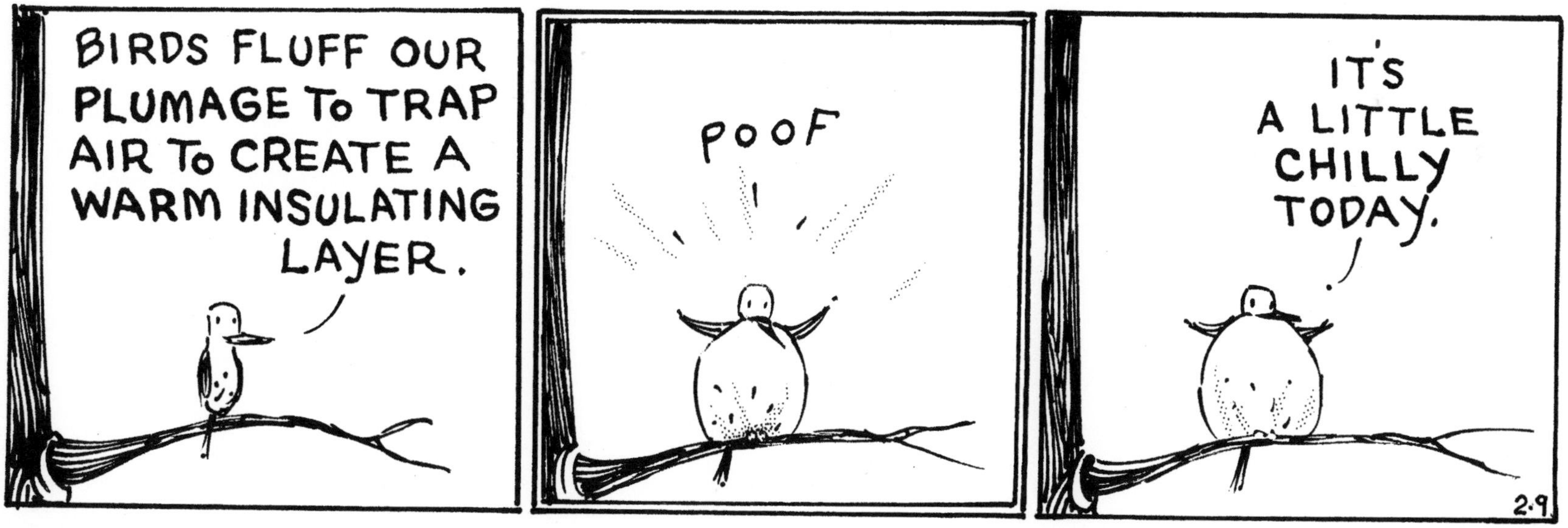
BIRDS FLUFF OUR PLUMAGE TO TRAP AIR TO CREATE A WARM INSULATING LAYER.
POOF
IT'S A LITTLE CHILLY TODAY.
2·9

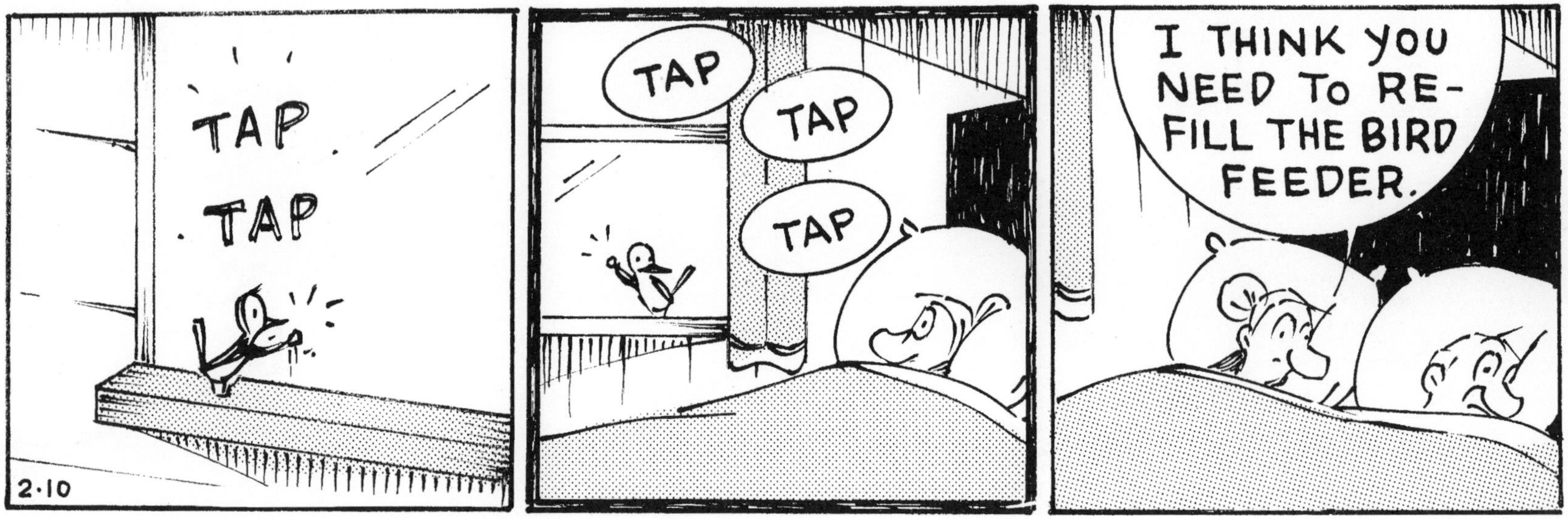
TAP
TAP
TAP
TAP
TAP
I THINK YOU NEED TO RE-FILL THE BIRD FEEDER.
2·10

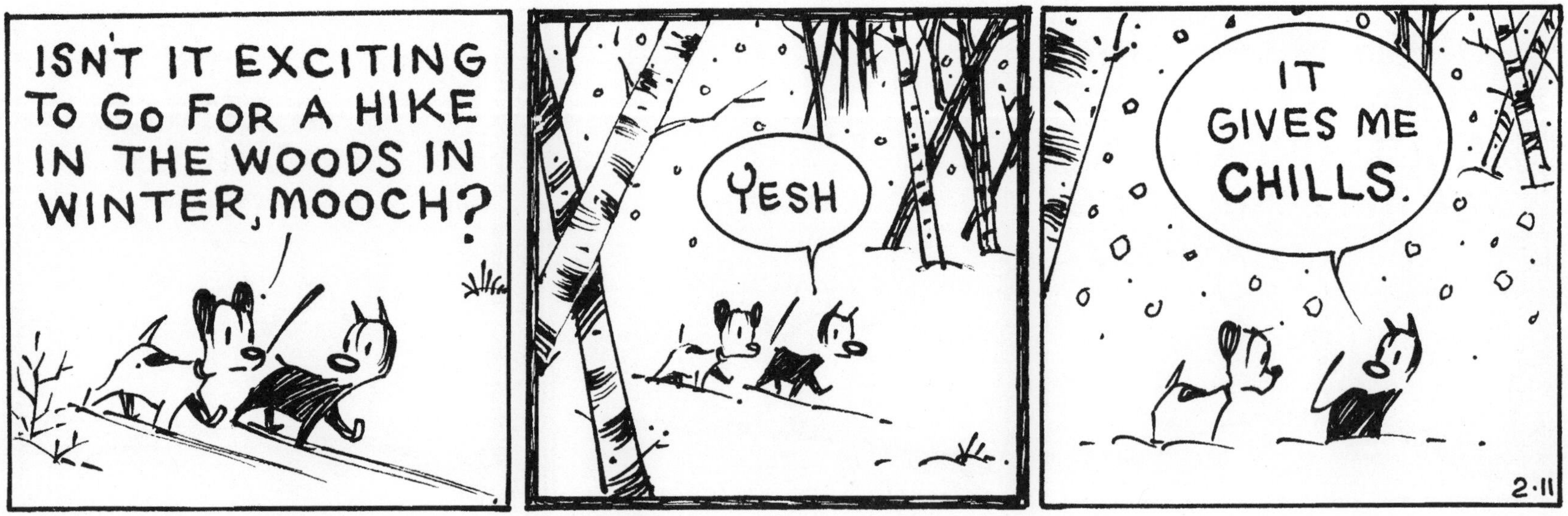
ISN'T IT EXCITING TO GO FOR A HIKE IN THE WOODS IN WINTER, MOOCH?
YESH
IT GIVES ME CHILLS.
2·11

My heart is ever at your service.

~ William Shakespeare

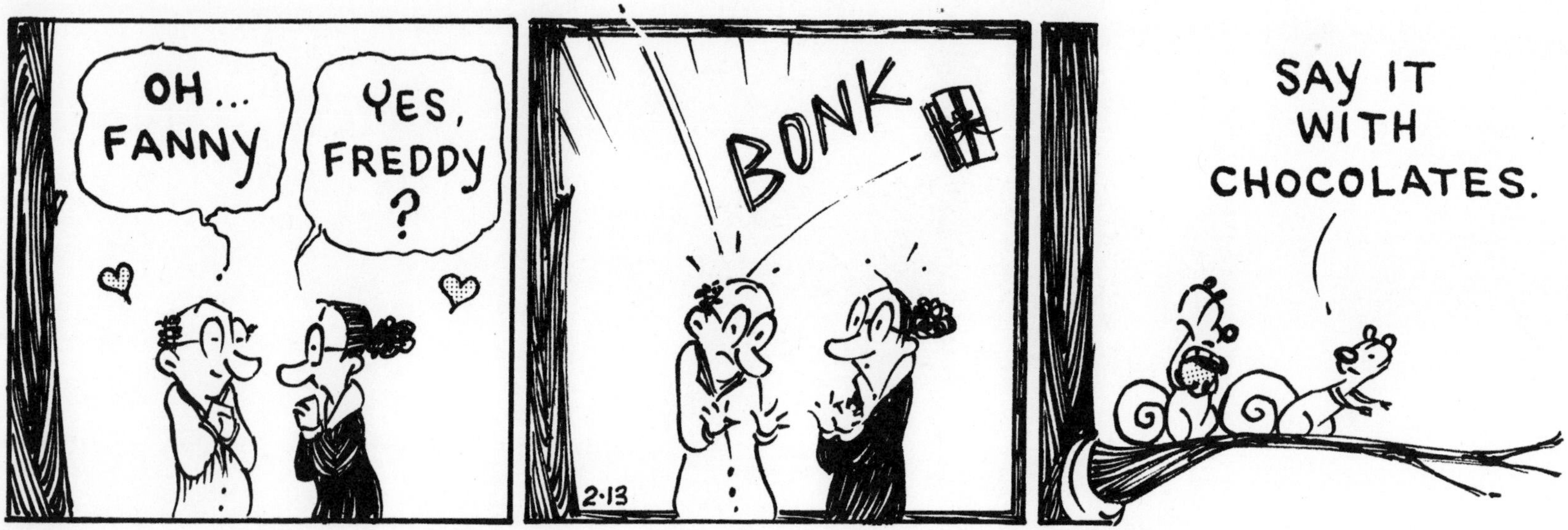
OH... FANNY
YES, FREDDY?
BONK
2·13
SAY IT WITH CHOCOLATES.

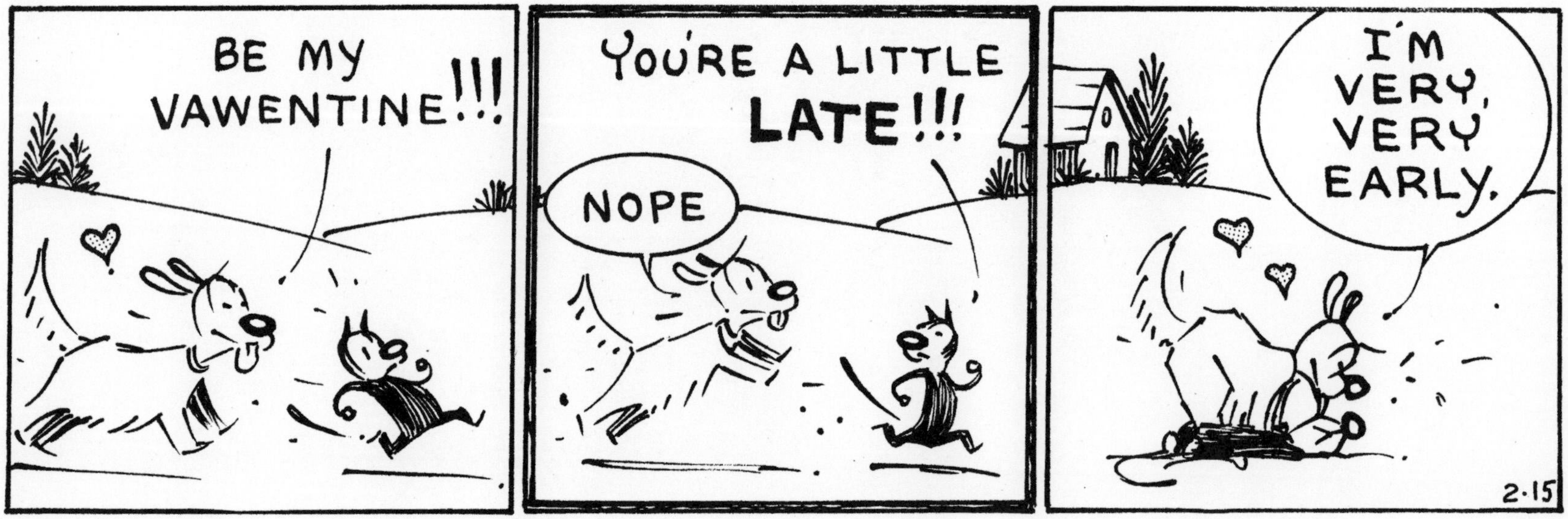
BE MY VAWENTINE!!!
YOU'RE A LITTLE LATE!!!
NOPE
I'M VERY, VERY EARLY.
2·15

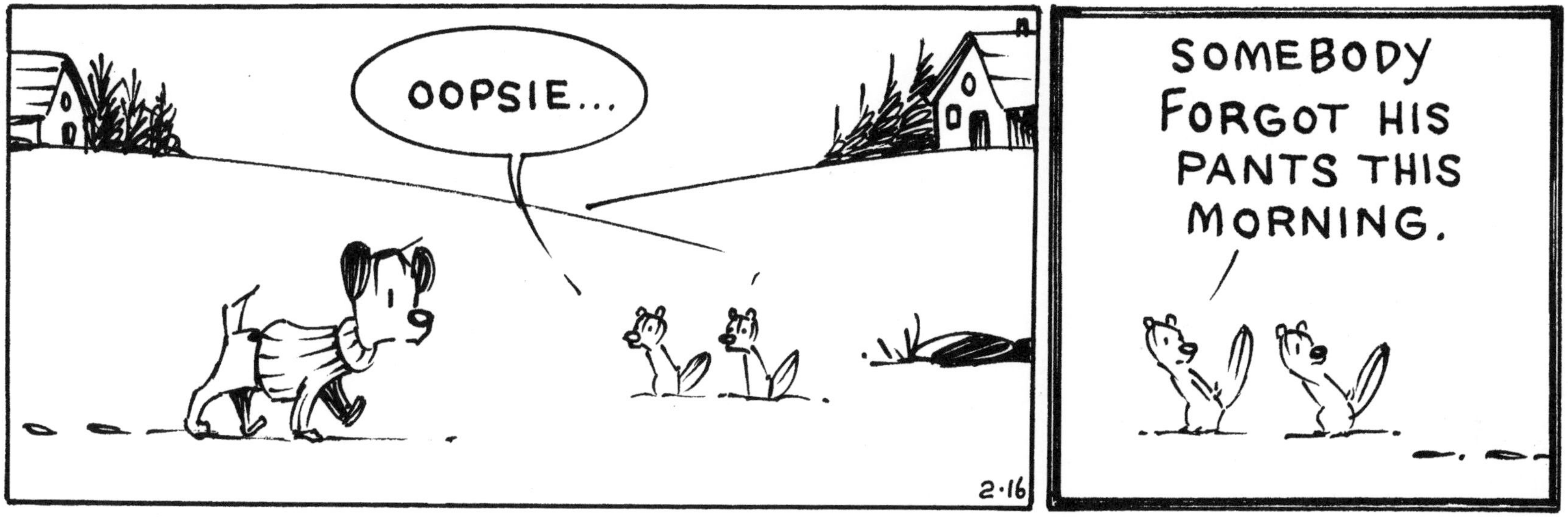
OOPSIE...
2·16
SOMEBODY FORGOT HIS PANTS THIS MORNING.

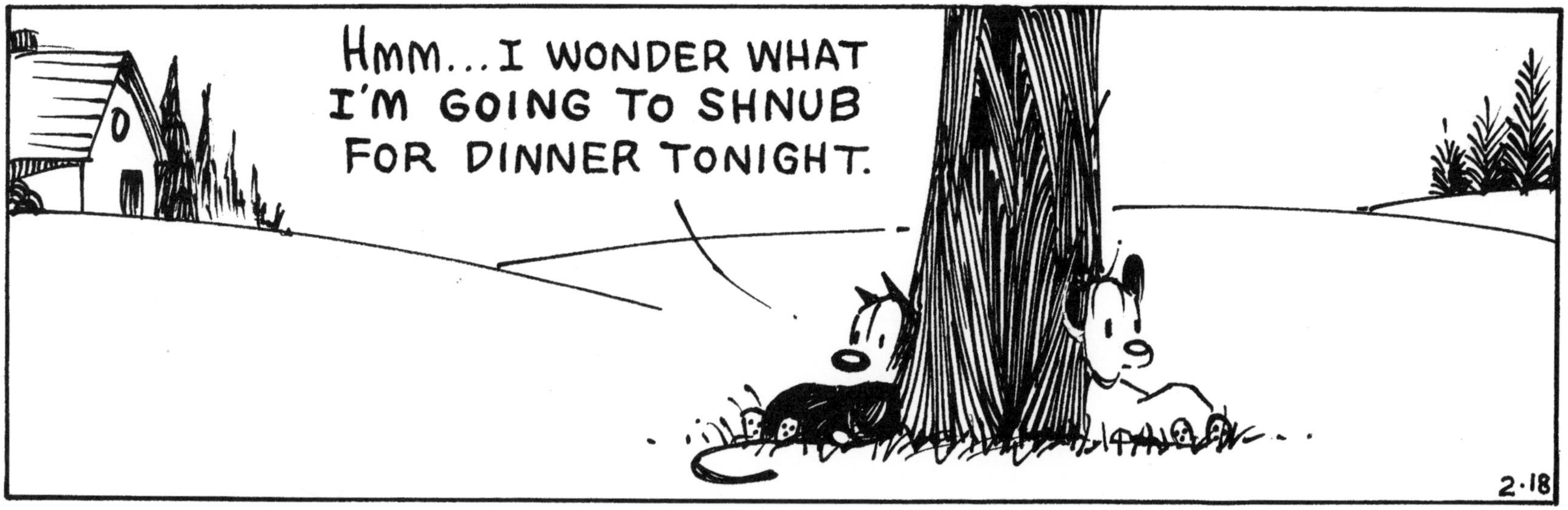
HMM...I WONDER WHAT I'M GOING TO SHNUB FOR DINNER TONIGHT.
2·18

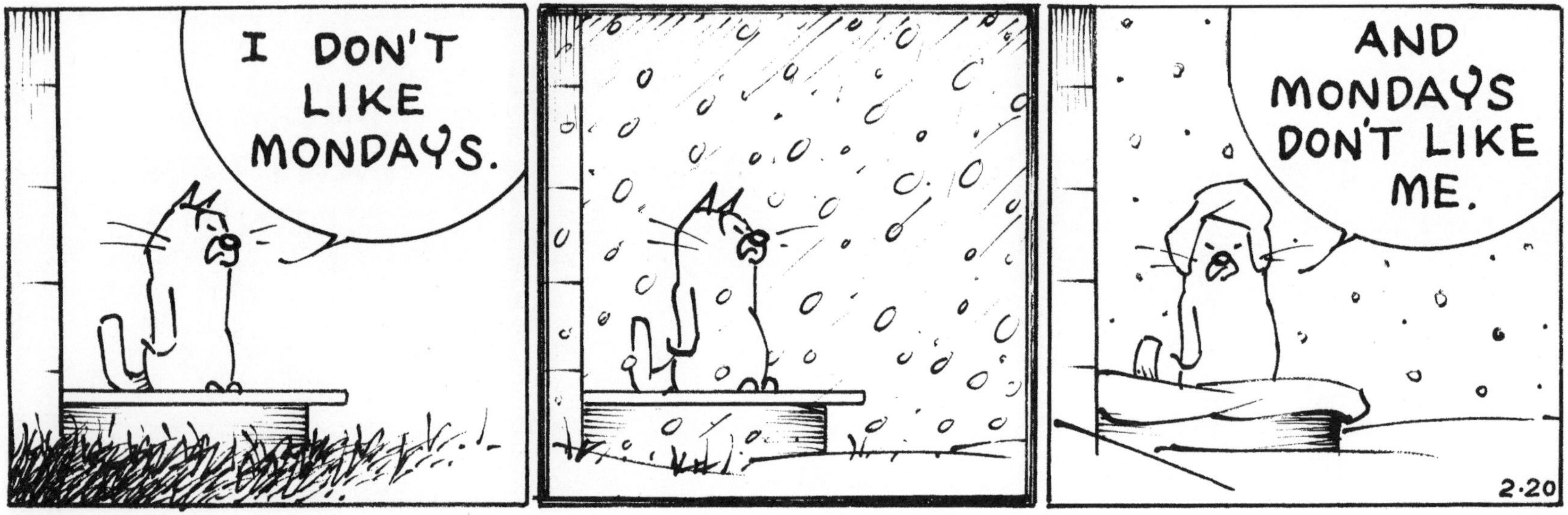
I DON'T LIKE MONDAYS.
AND MONDAYS DON'T LIKE ME.
2·20

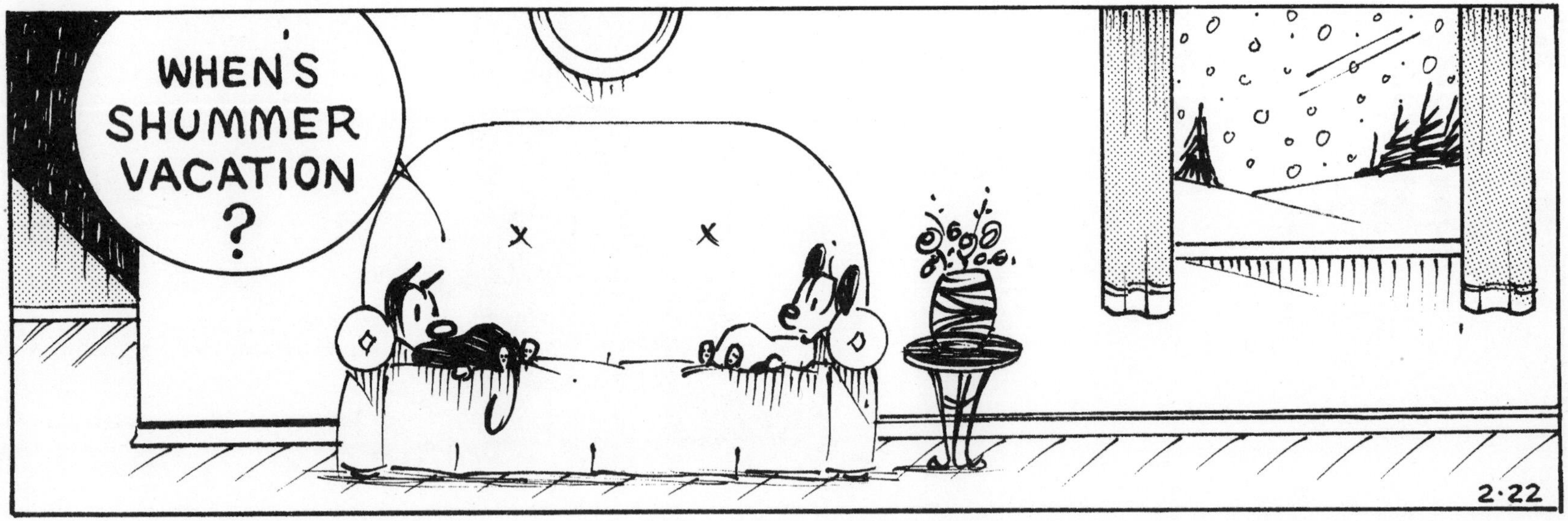
WHEN'S SHUMMER VACATION ?
2·22

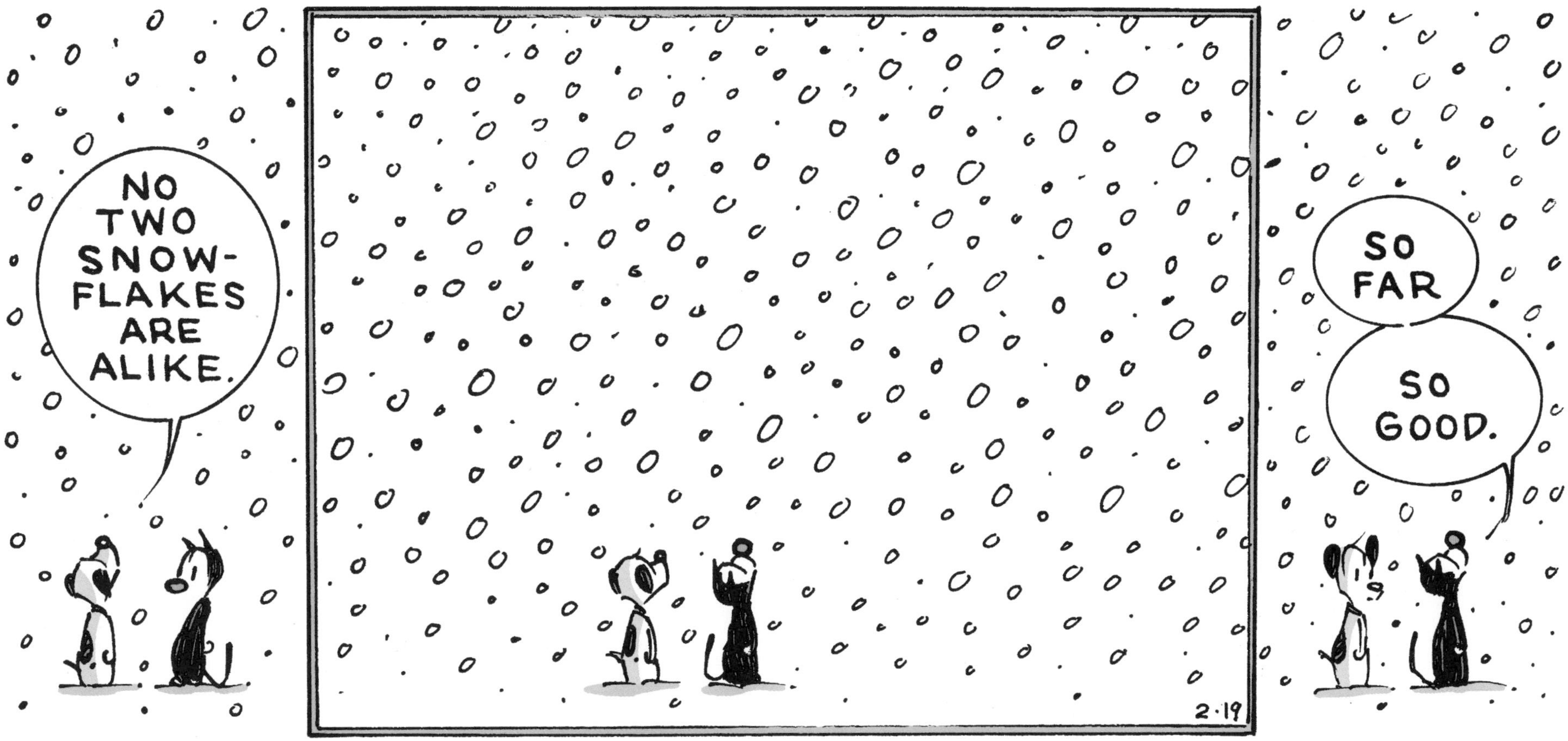
NO TWO SNOW-FLAKES ARE ALIKE.
SO FAR
SO GOOD.
2·19

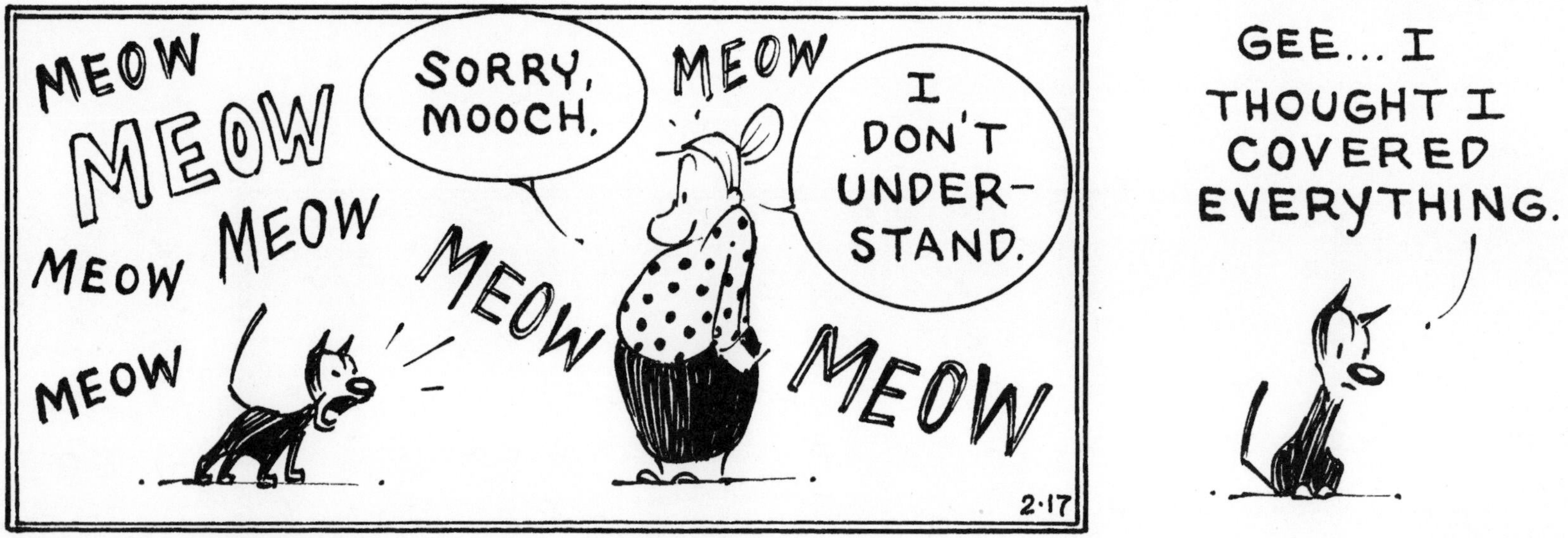
MEOW
MEOW
MEOW
MEOW
MEOW
SORRY, MOOCH.
MEOW
MEOW
I DON'T UNDER-STAND.
MEOW
2·17
GEE... I THOUGHT I COVERED EVERYTHING.

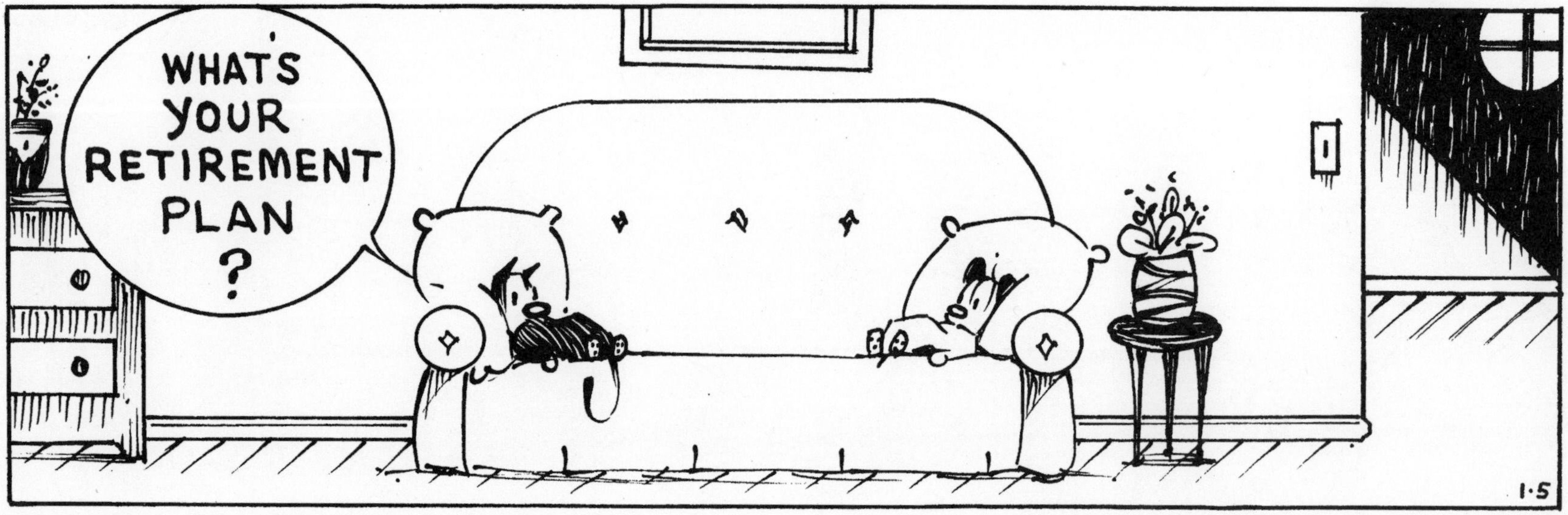
WHAT'S YOUR RETIREMENT PLAN ?
1·5

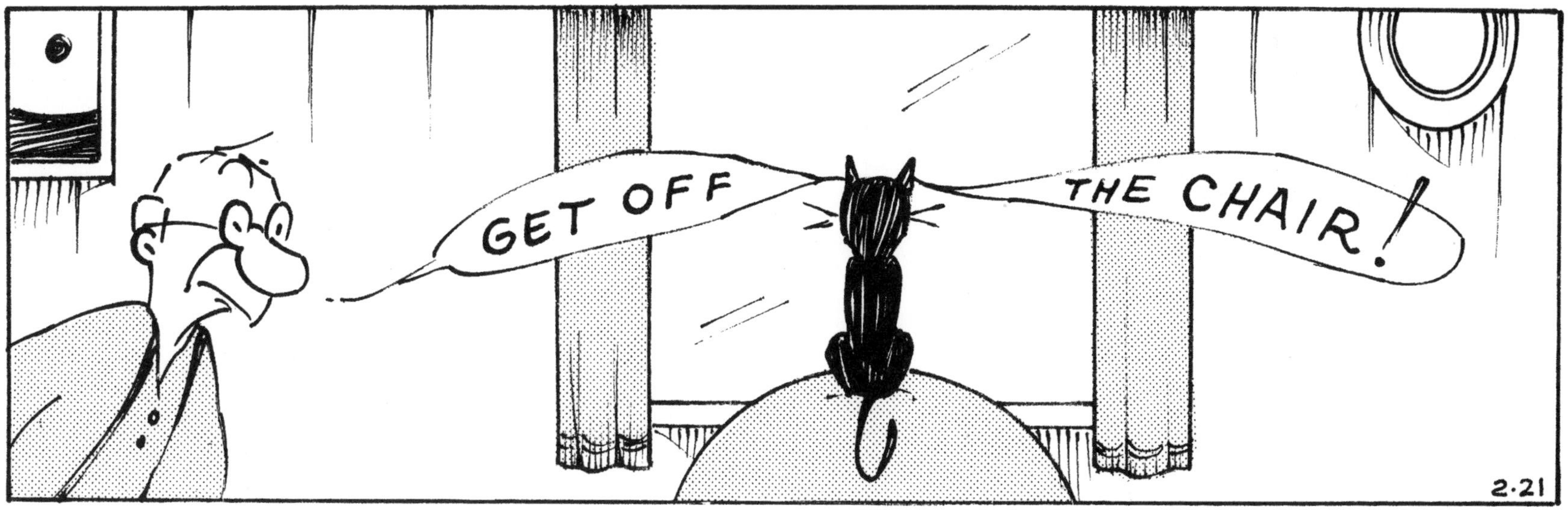
GET OFF THE CHAIR!
2·21

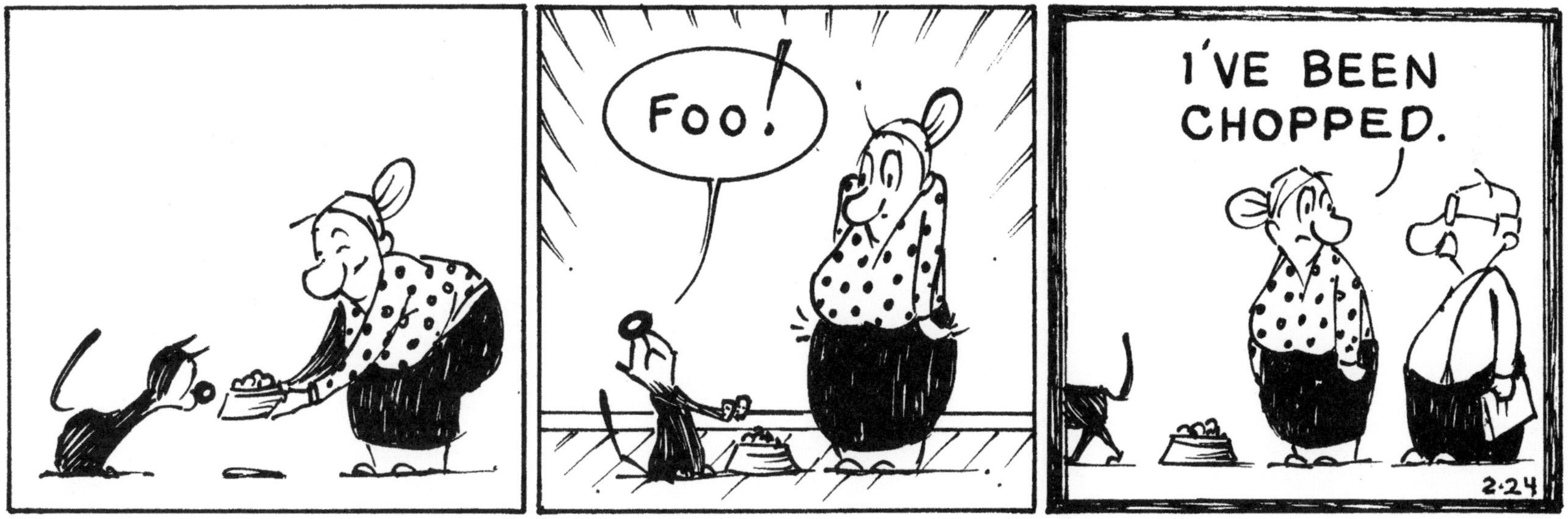
FOO!
I'VE BEEN CHOPPED.
2·24

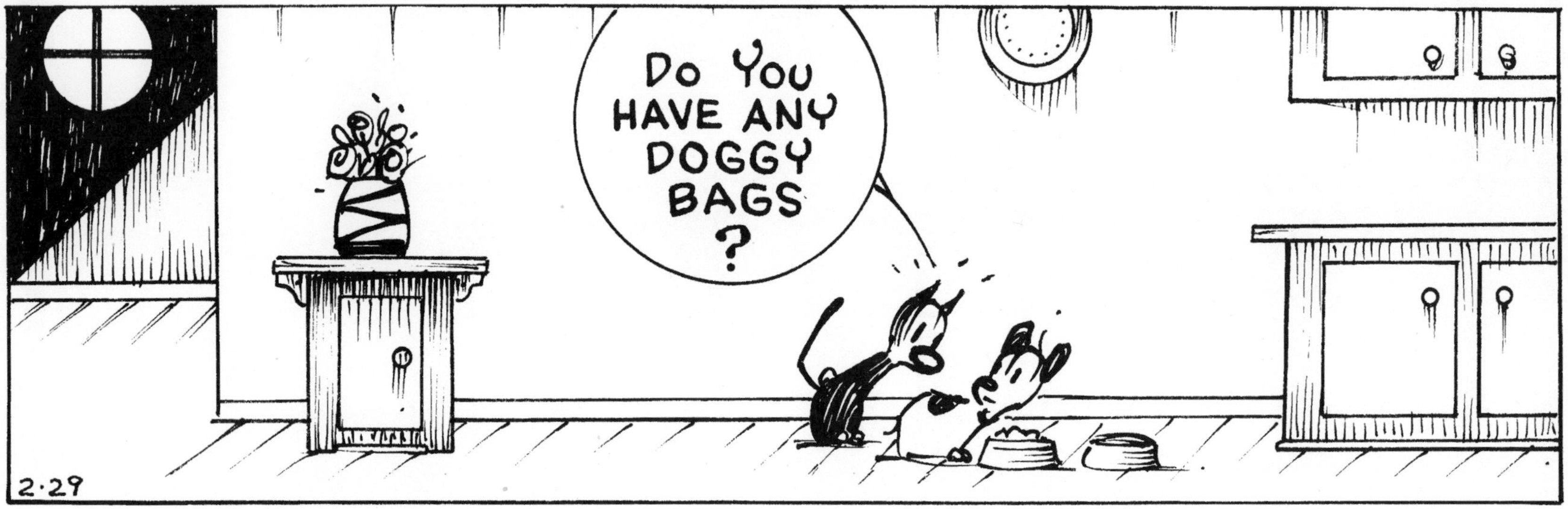
DO YOU HAVE ANY DOGGY BAGS ?
2·29

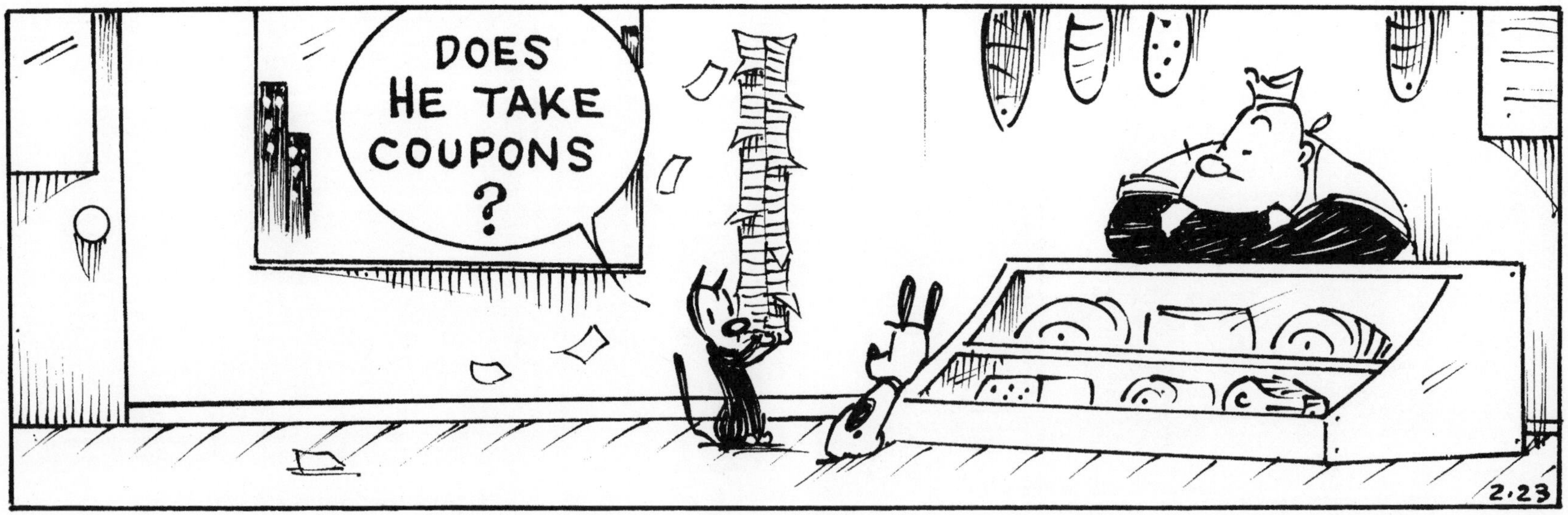
DOES HE TAKE COUPONS ?
2·23

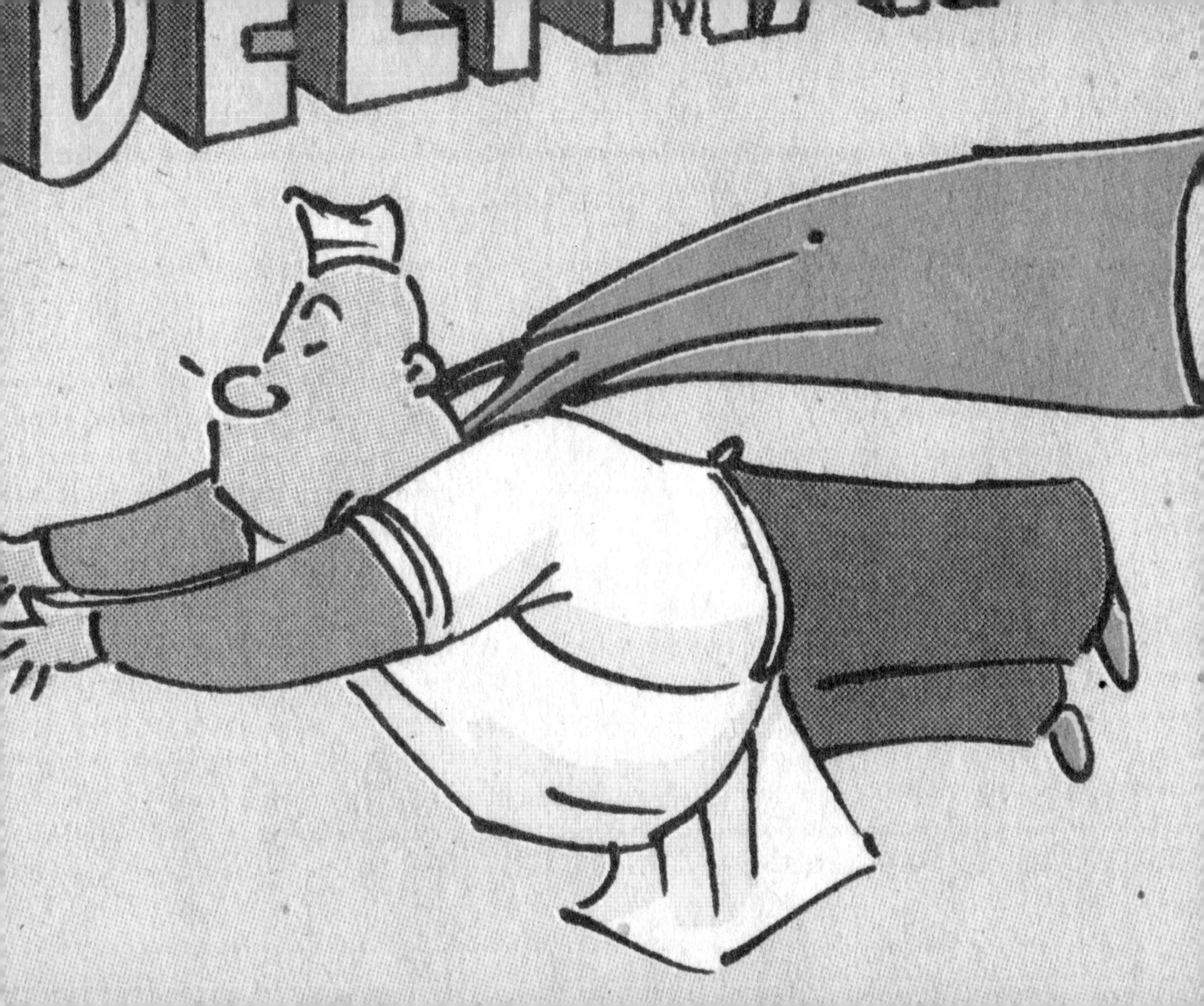

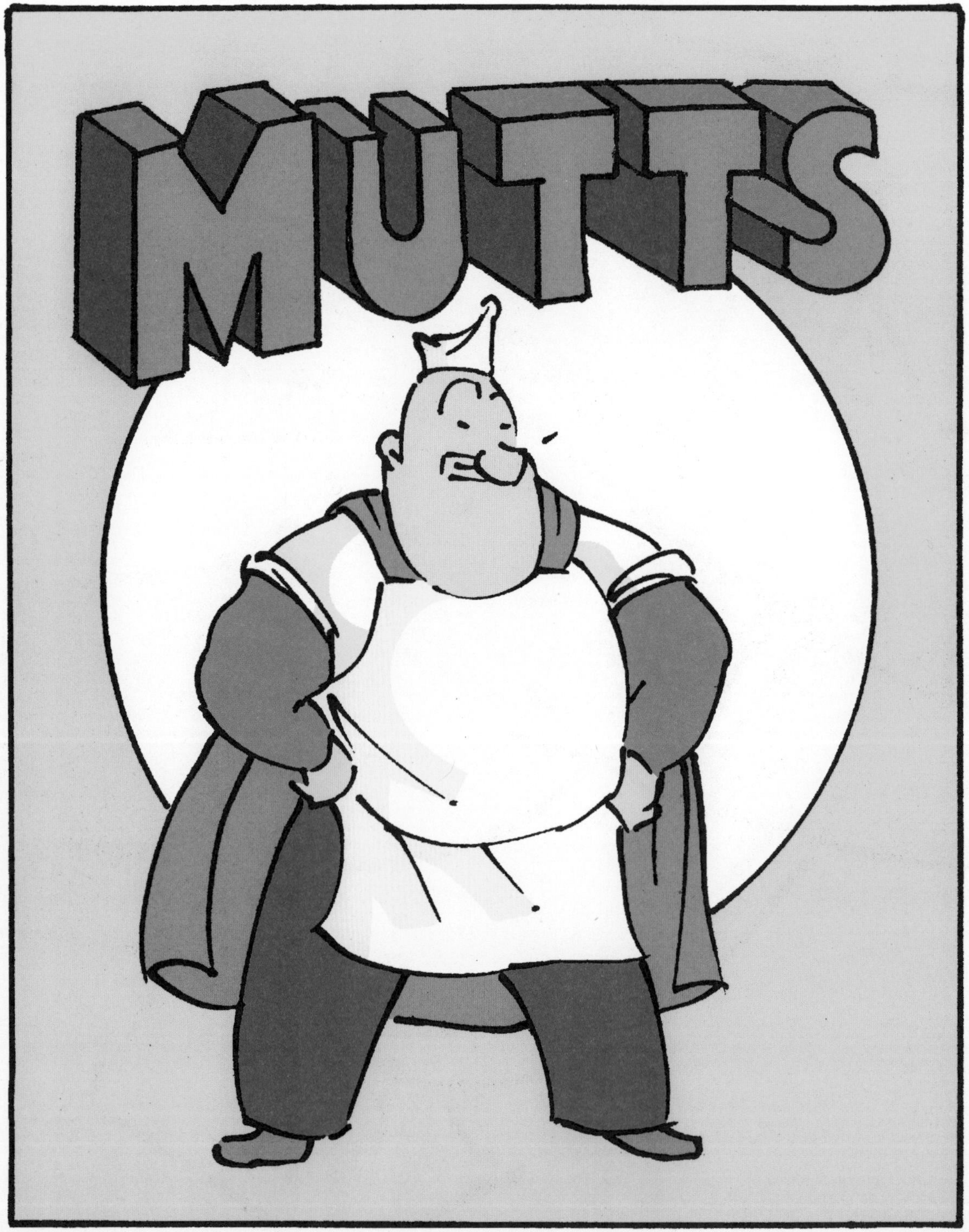
MUTTS

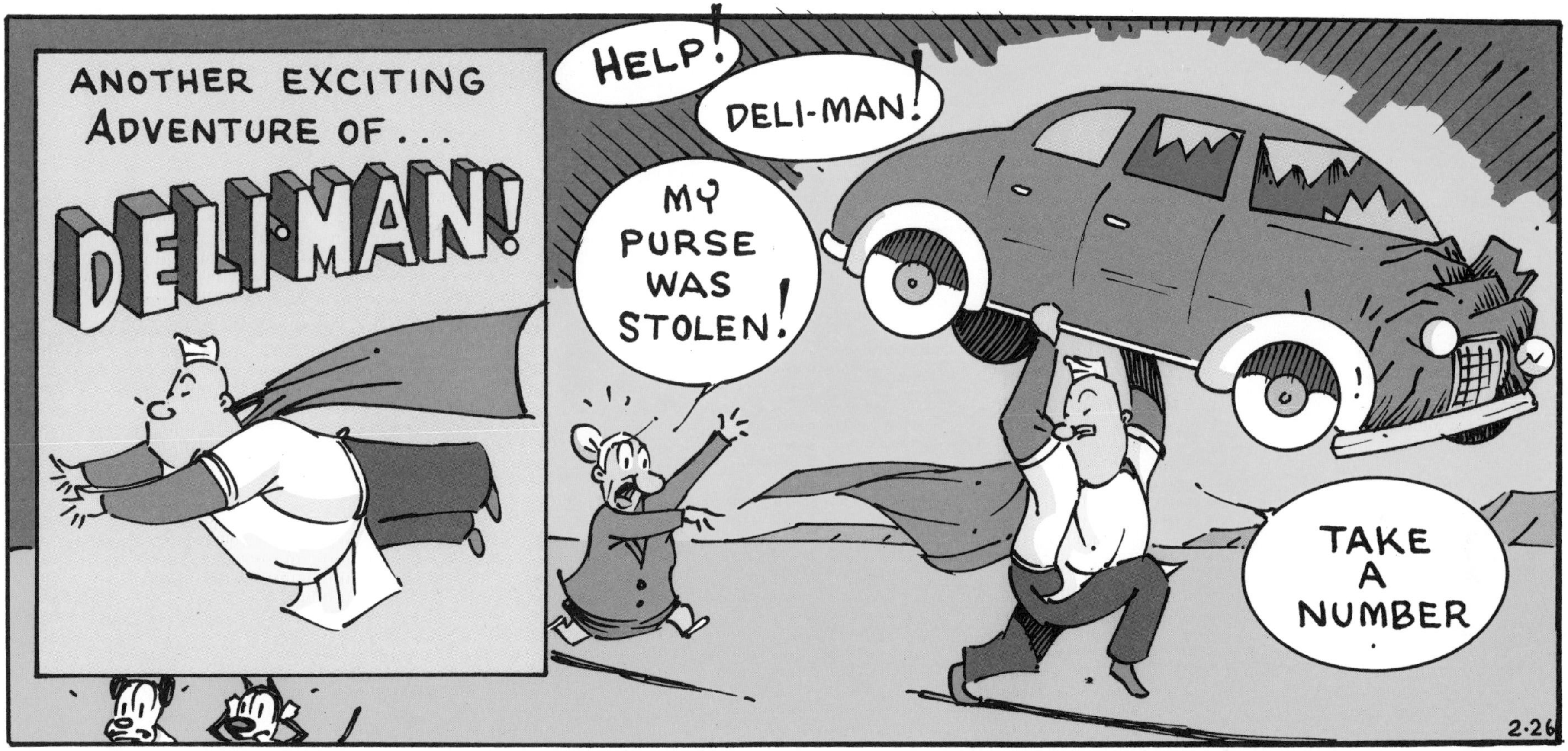
ANOTHER EXCITING ADVENTURE OF . . .
DELI-MAN!
HELP!
DELI-MAN!
MY PURSE WAS STOLEN!
TAKE A NUMBER.
2·26

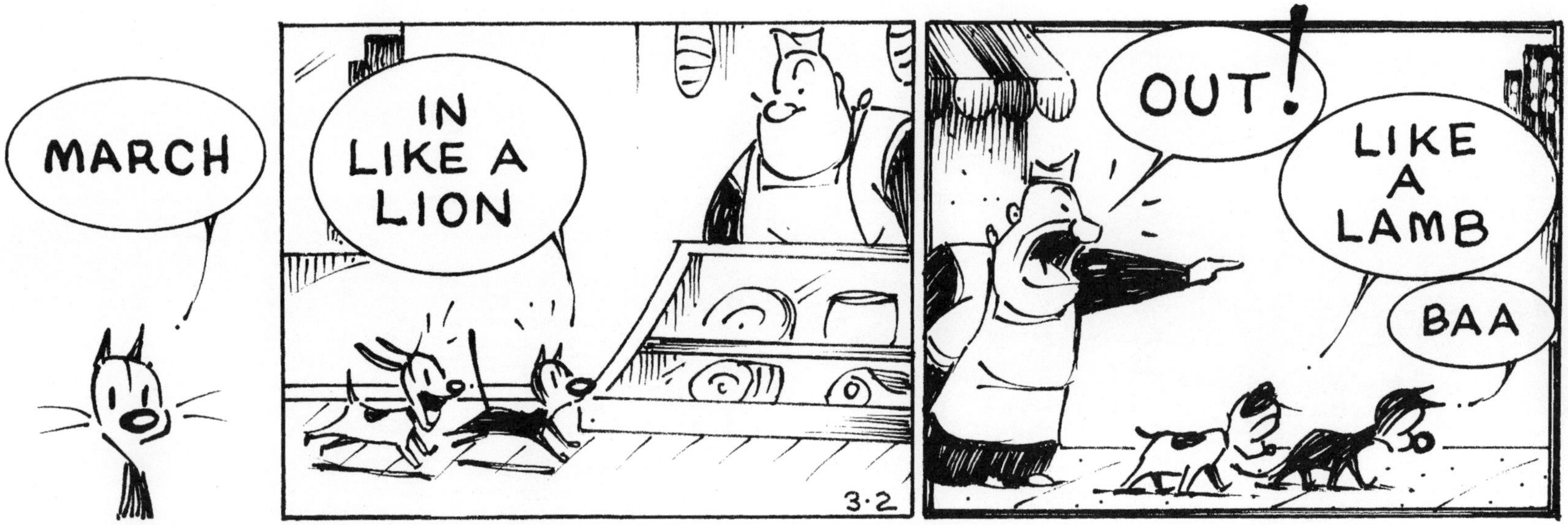
MARCH
IN LIKE A LION
3·2
OUT!
LIKE A LAMB
BAA

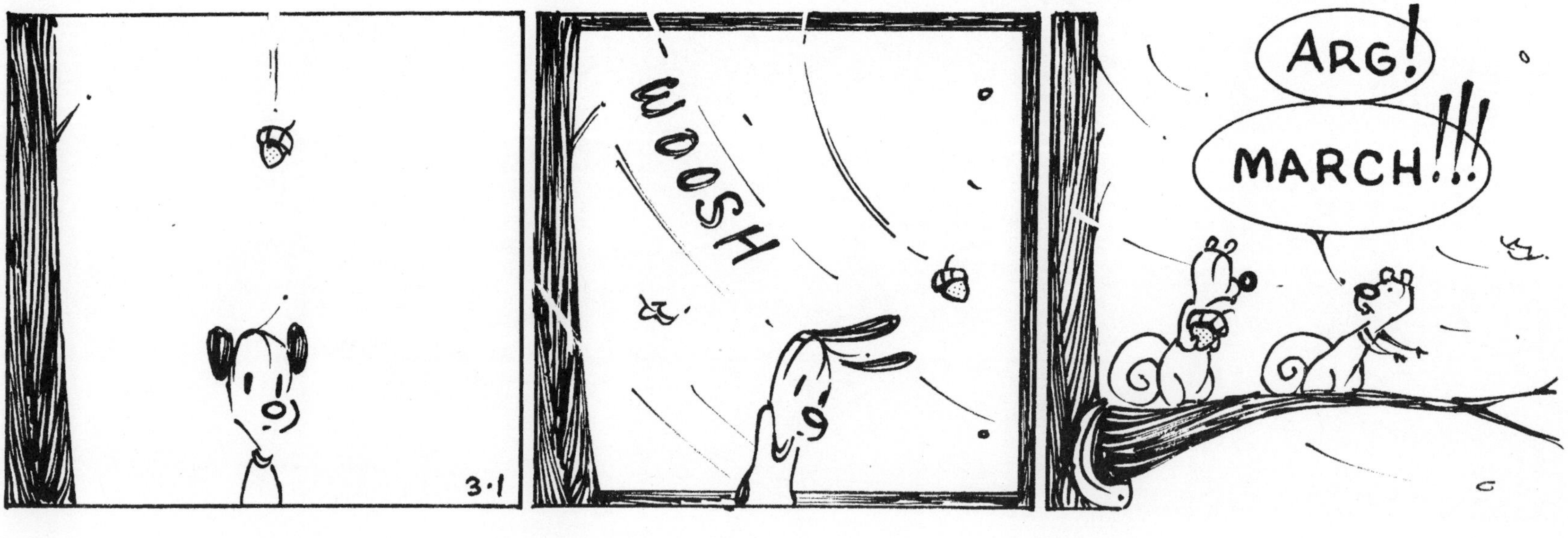
3·1
WOOSH
ARG!
MARCH!!!

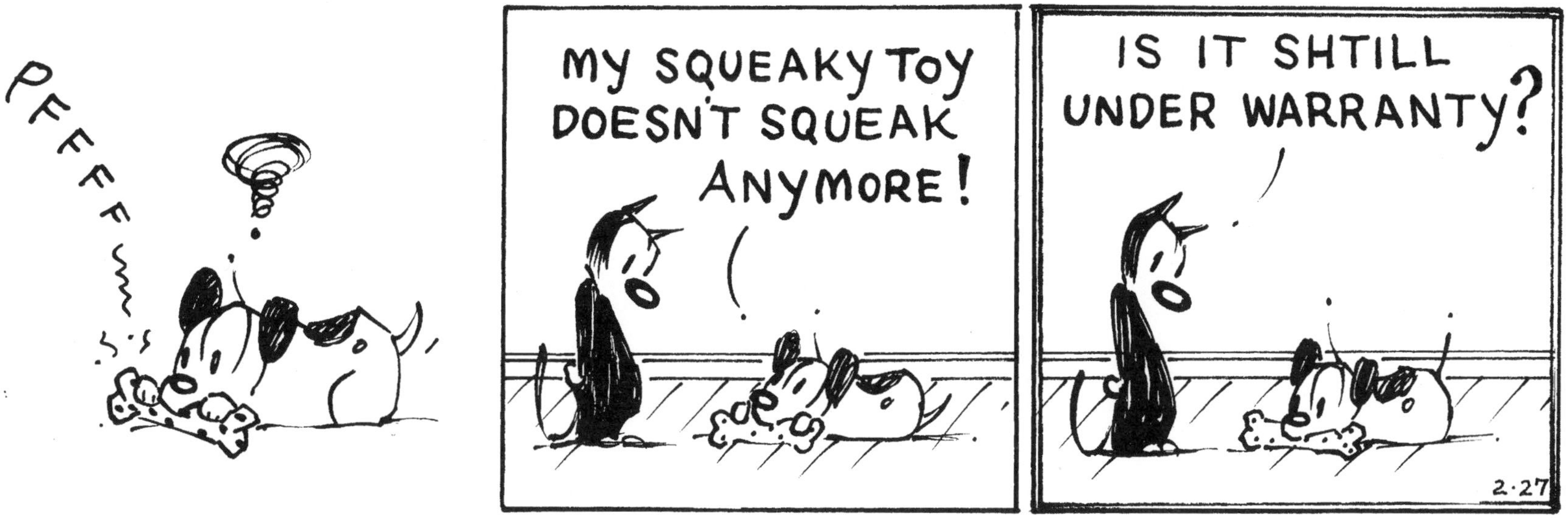
PFFFF
MY SQUEAKY TOY DOESN'T SQUEAK ANYMORE!
IS IT SHTILL UNDER WARRANTY?
2·27

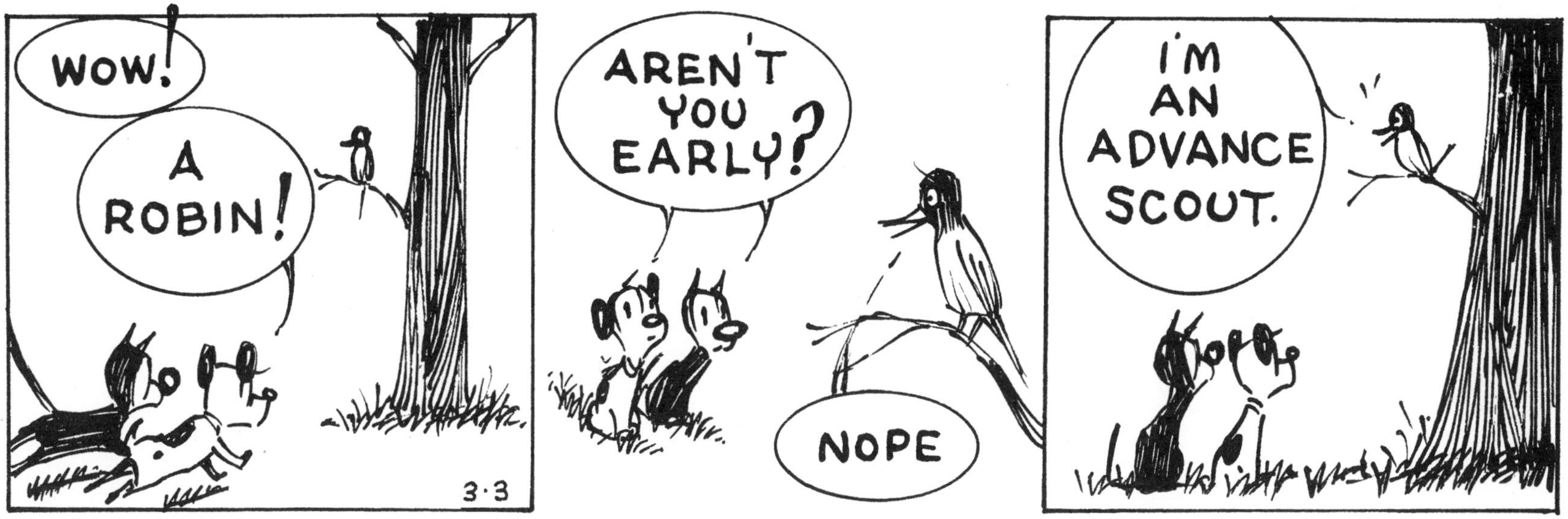
WOW!
A ROBIN!
3·3
AREN'T YOU EARLY?
NOPE
I'M AN ADVANCE SCOUT.

Mutts

THERE GOES OLD MAN WINTER.
GOOD.
HE COULD USE A LONG VACATION.
3·11

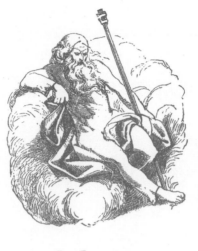

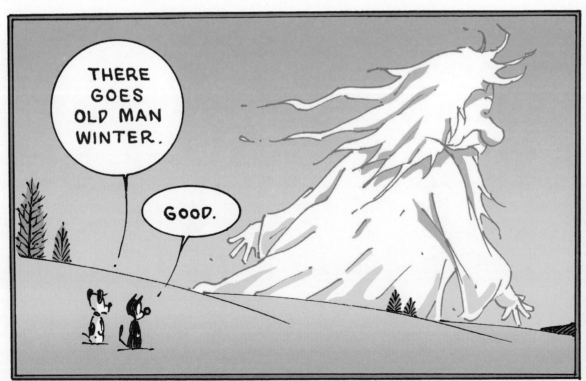

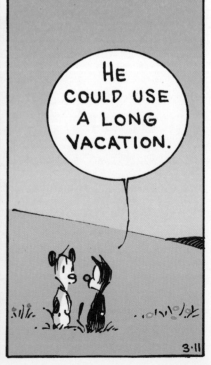

MUTTS

PATRICK McDONNELL

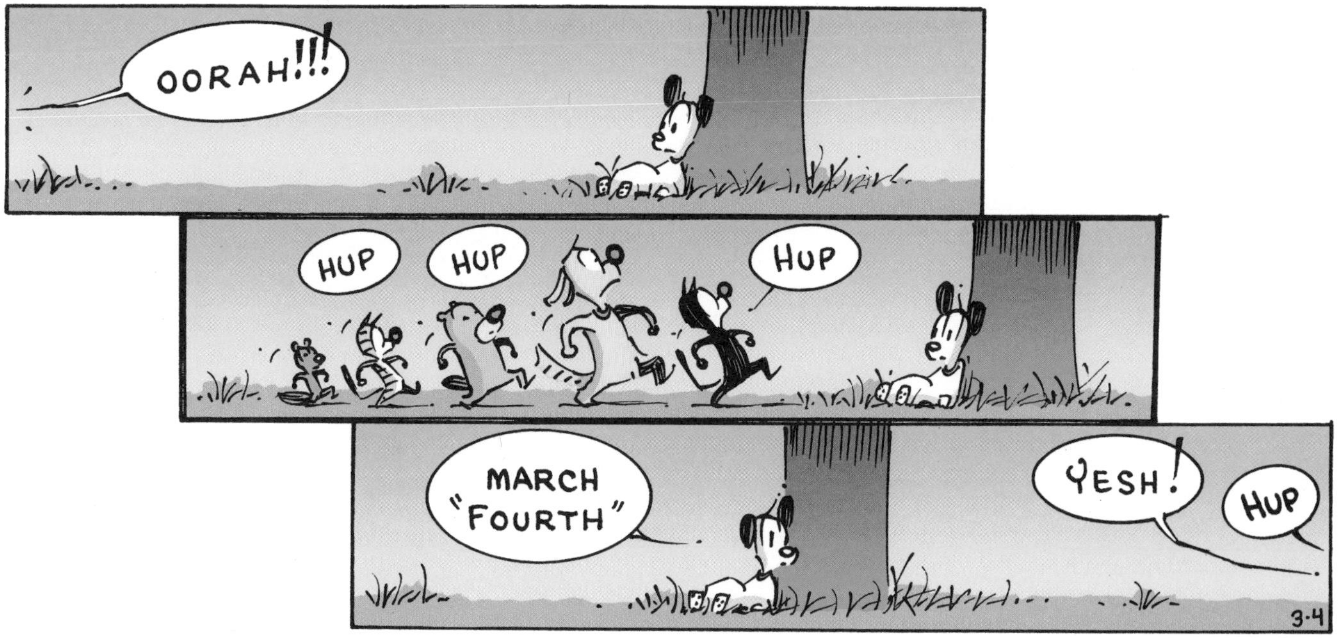
OORAH!!!
HUP
HUP
HUP
MARCH "FOURTH"
YESH!
HUP
3·4

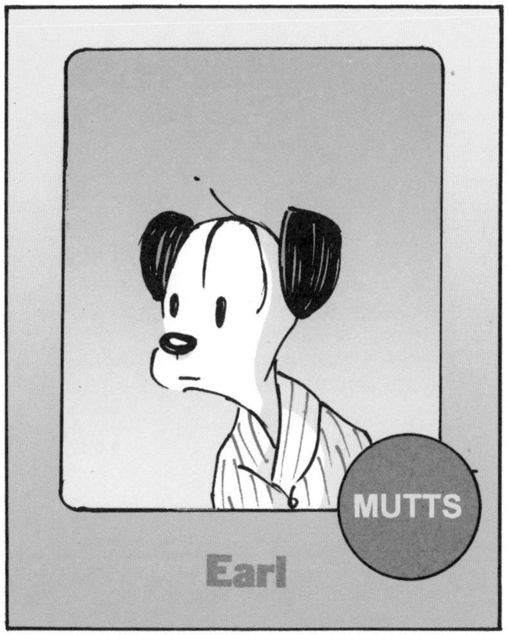
MUTTS
Earl

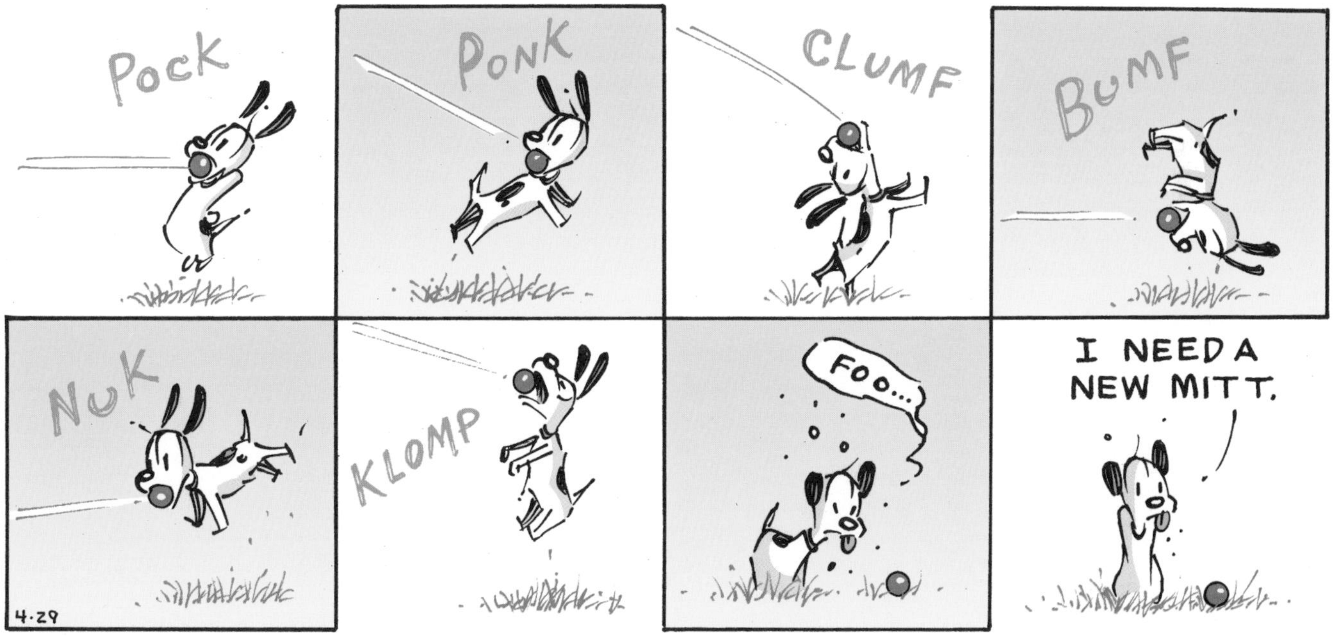
POCK
PONK
CLUMF
BUMF
NUK
KLOMP
FOO...
I NEED A NEW MITT.
4·29

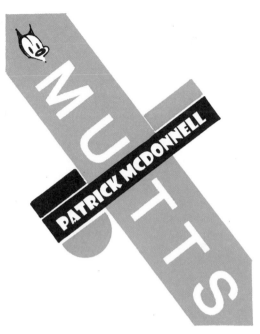

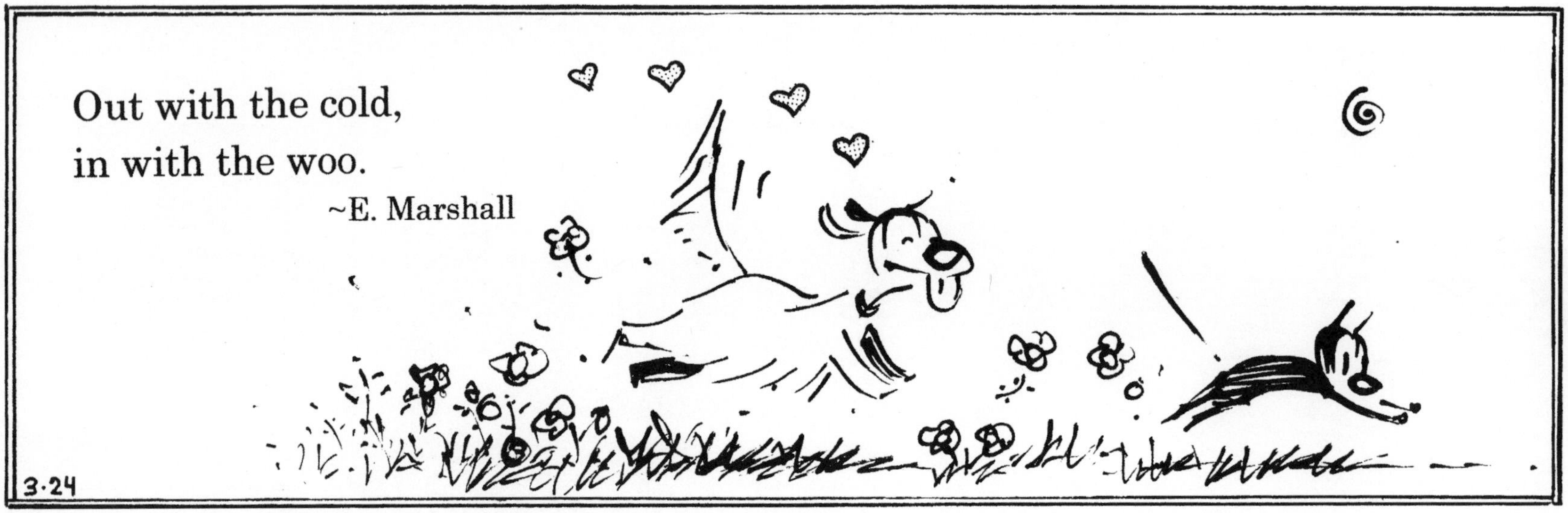
Out with the cold,
in with the woo.
~E. Marshall
3·24

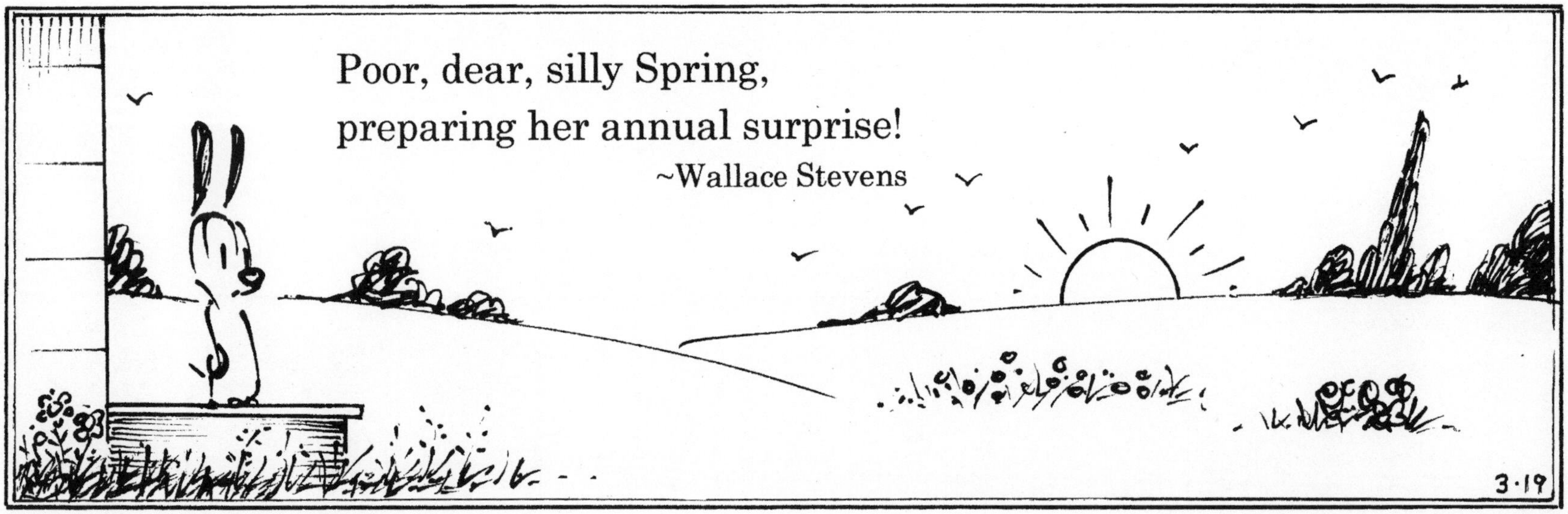
Poor, dear, silly Spring,
preparing her annual surprise!
~Wallace Stevens
3·19

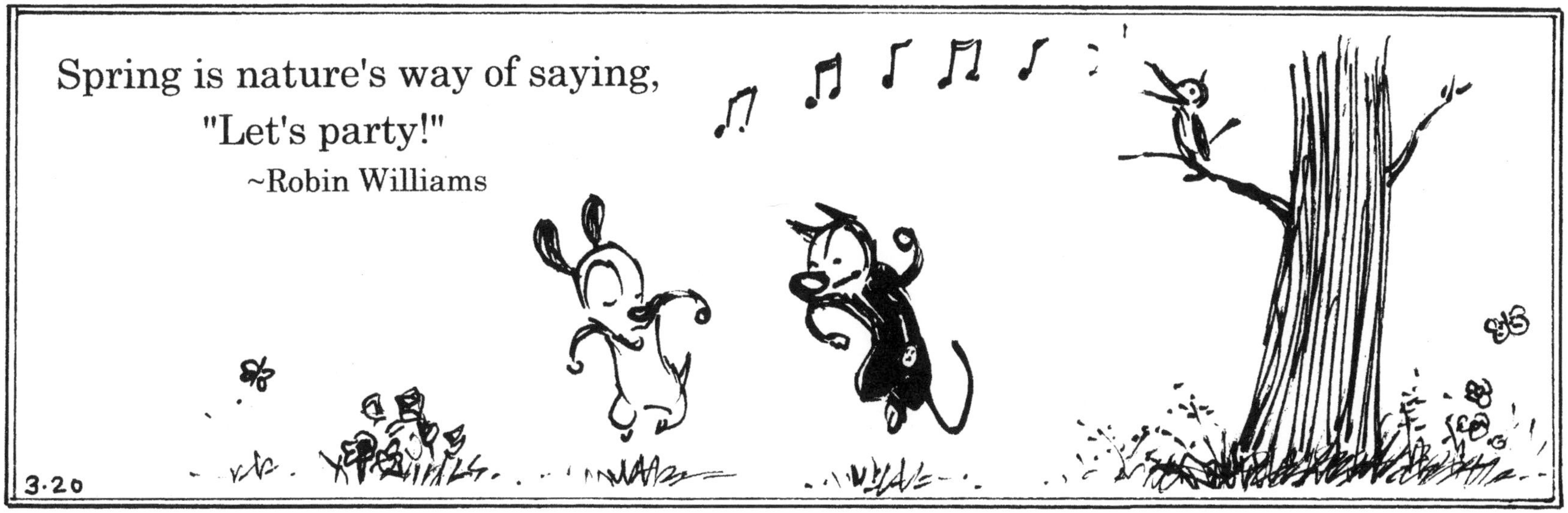
Spring is nature's way of saying,
"Let's party!"
~Robin Williams
3·20

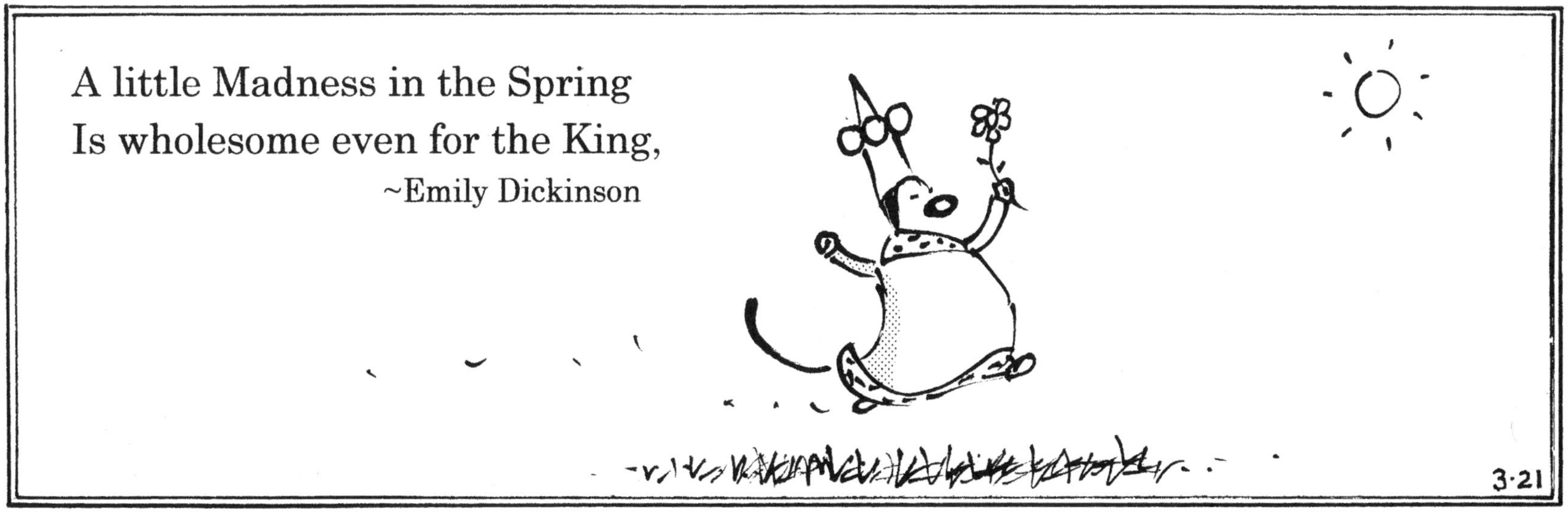
A little Madness in the Spring
Is wholesome even for the King,
~Emily Dickinson
3·21

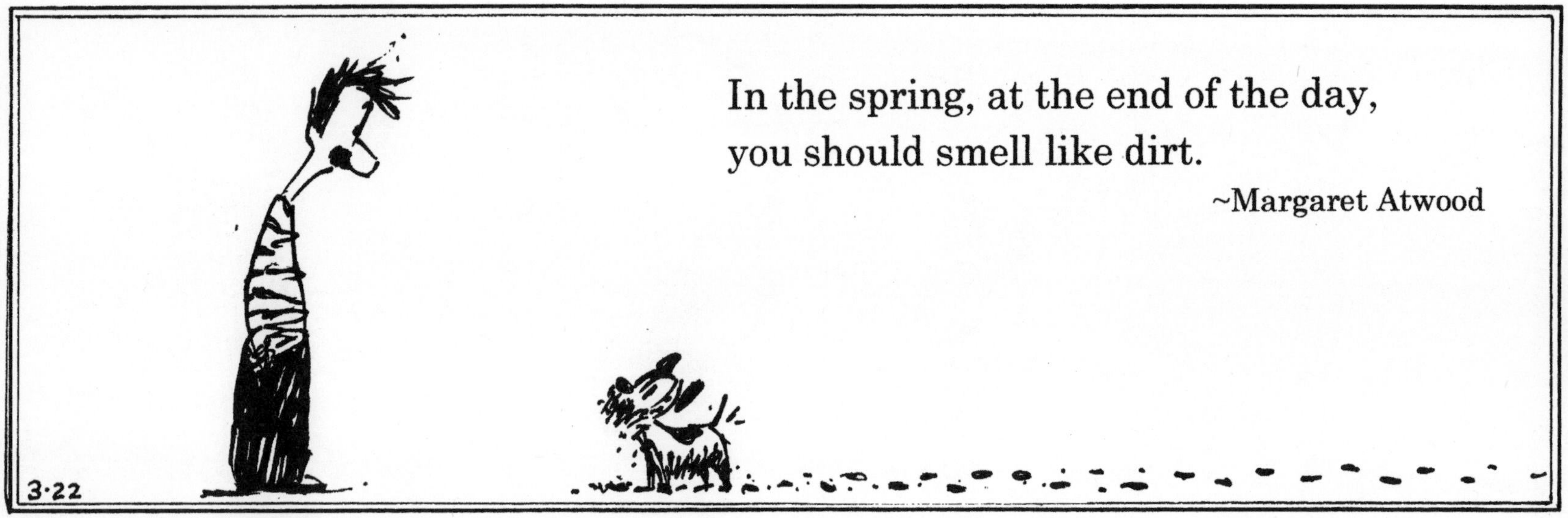
In the spring, at the end of the day,
you should smell like dirt.
~Margaret Atwood
3·22

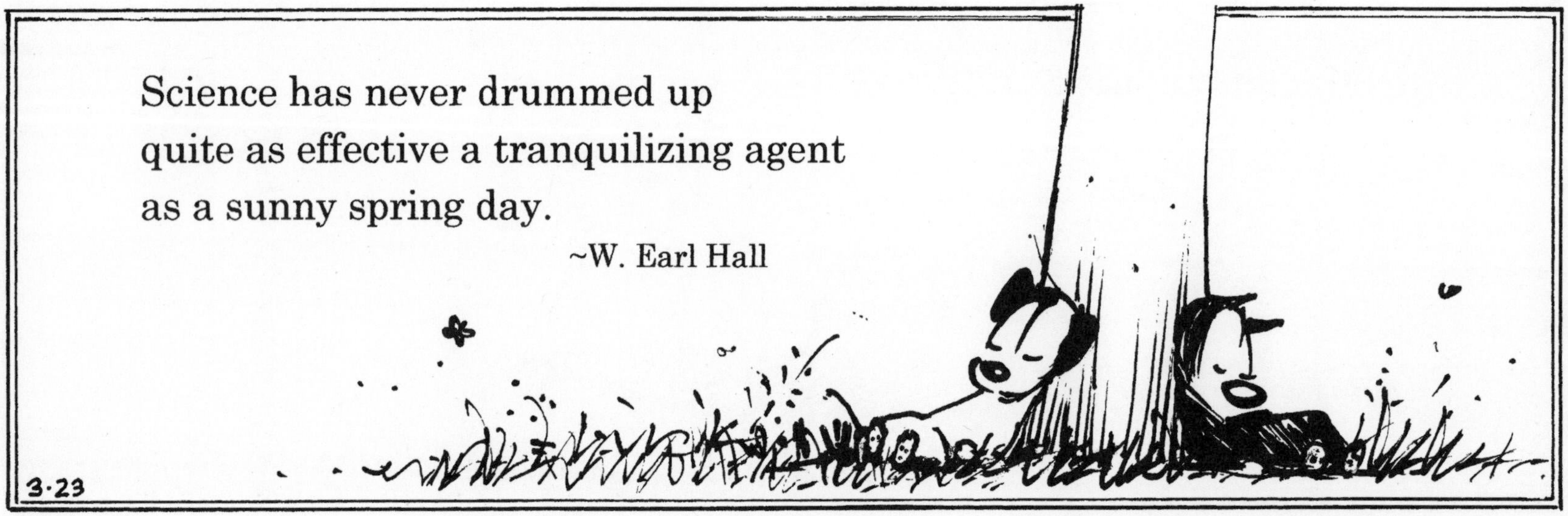
Science has never drummed up
quite as effective a tranquilizing agent
as a sunny spring day.
~W. Earl Hall
3·23

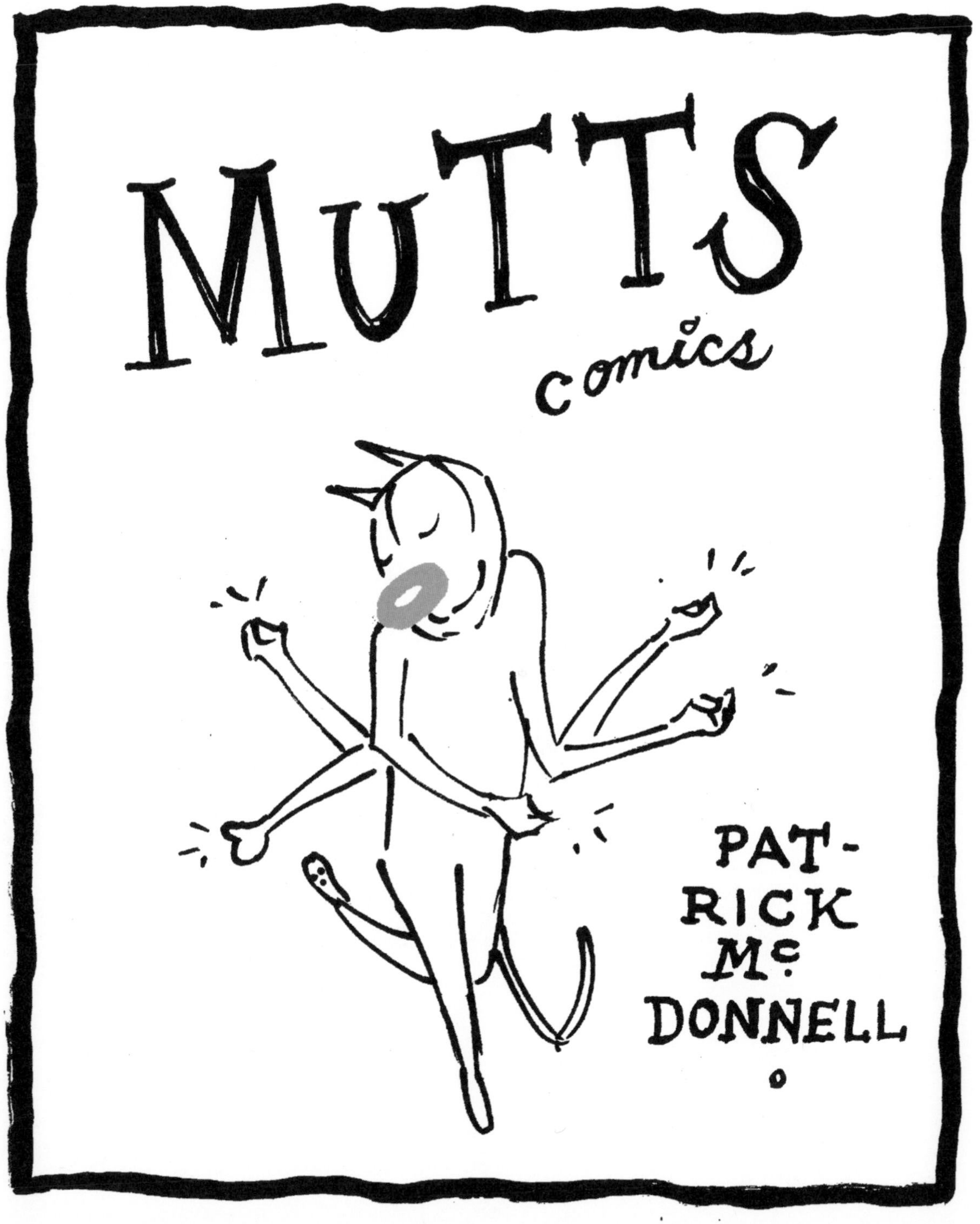
MUTTS
comics
PAT-
RICK
Mc
DONNELL

A DANCE TO SHPRING

A CELEBRATION OF

THE SUN SHINING

THE FLOWERS BLOOMING

THE BIRDS SINGING

THE BEES BUZZING

THE CAT'S SHEDDING !!!

3·18

48

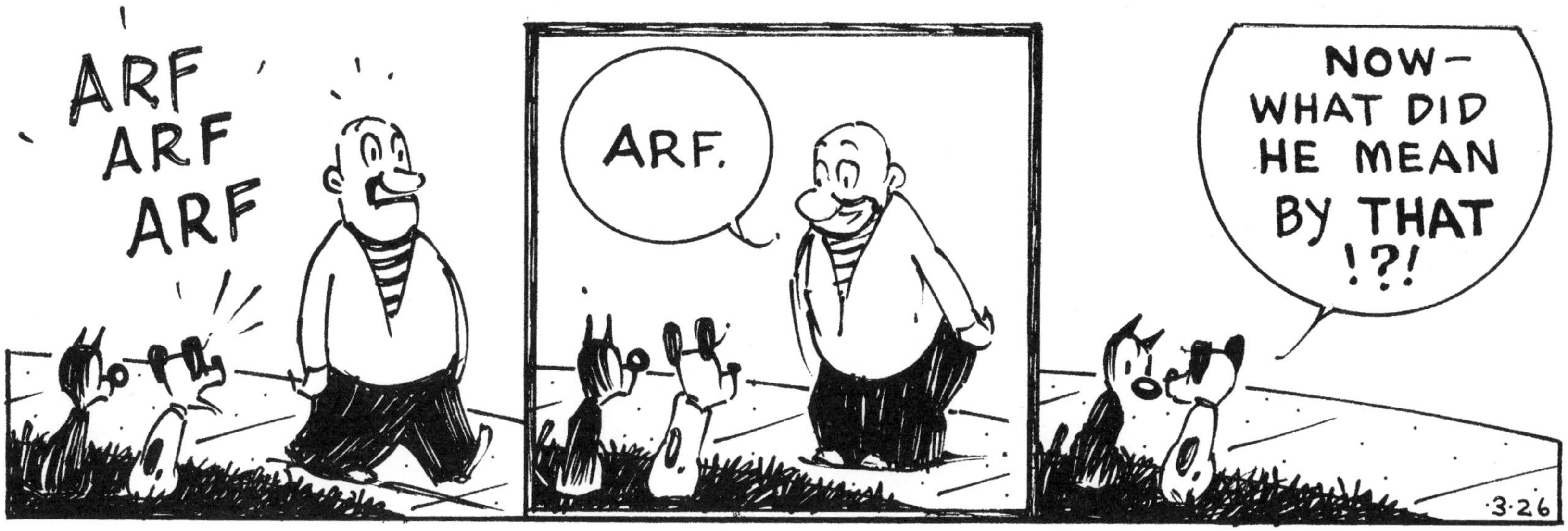
ARF ARF ARF
ARF.
NOW- WHAT DID HE MEAN BY THAT !?!
3·26

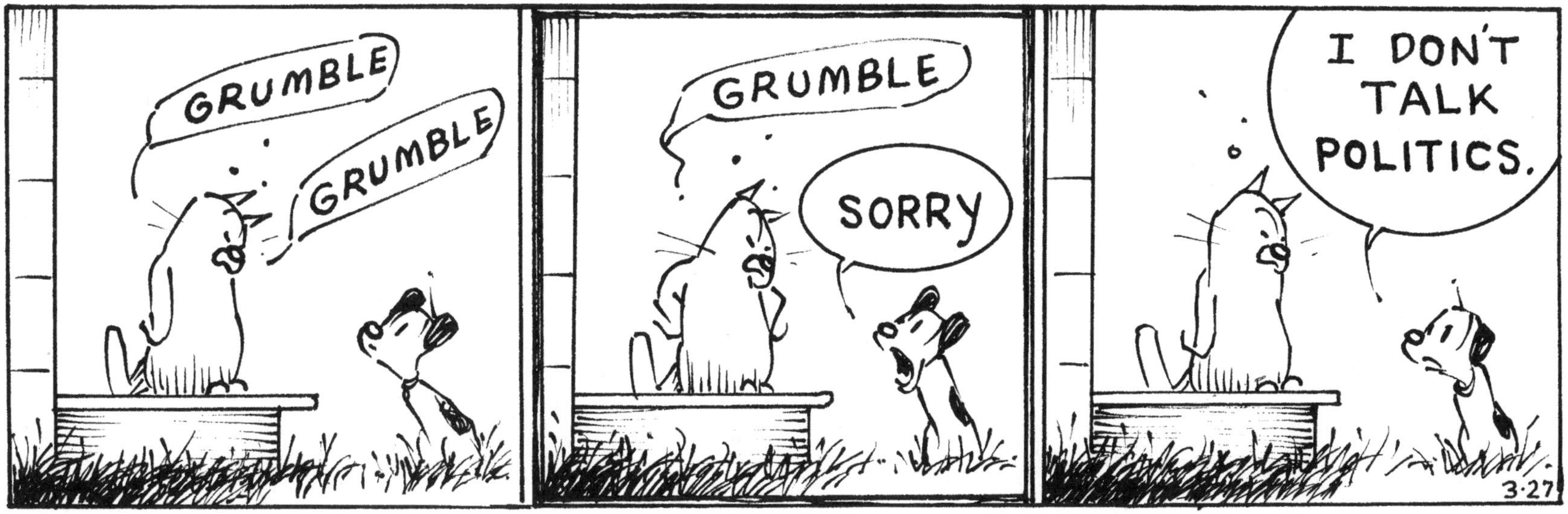
GRUMBLE
GRUMBLE
GRUMBLE
SORRY
I DON'T TALK POLITICS.
3·27

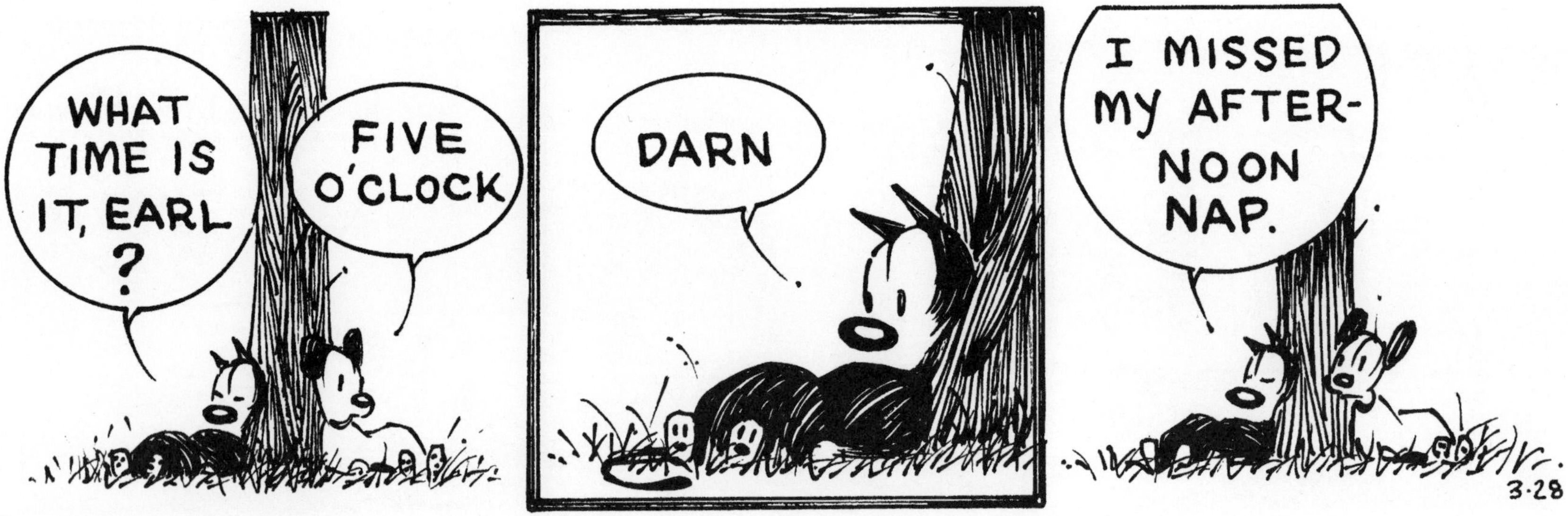
WHAT TIME IS IT, EARL ?
FIVE O'CLOCK
DARN
I MISSED MY AFTER-NOON NAP.
3-28

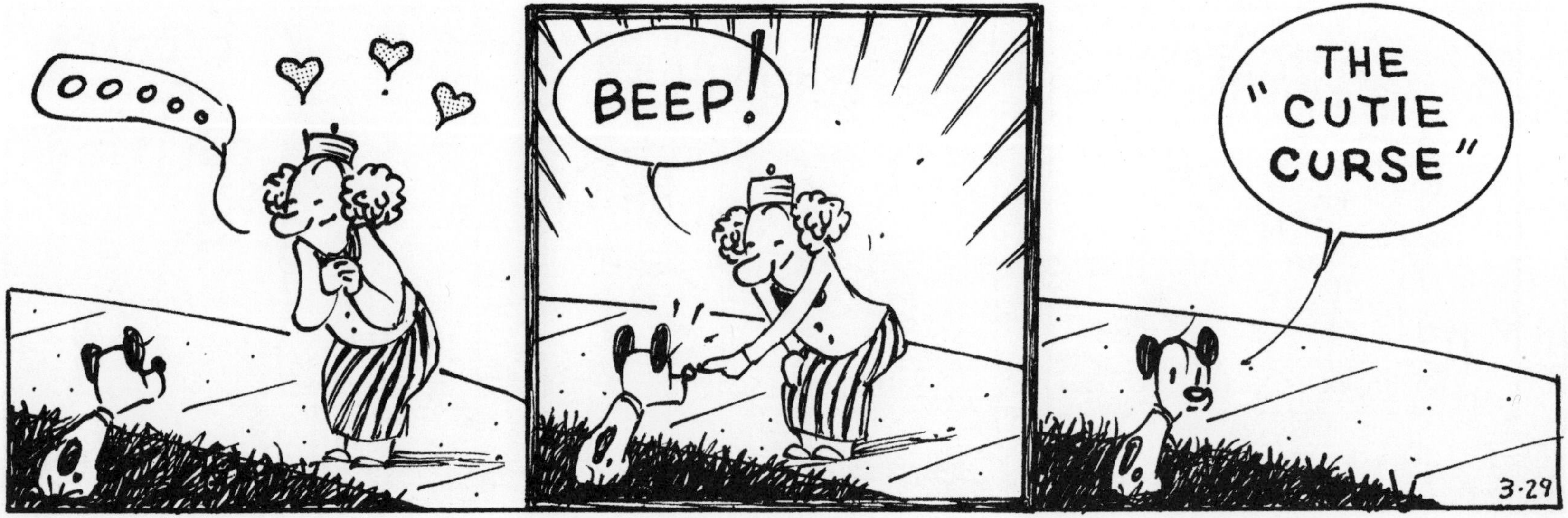
OOOOOO
BEEP!
THE "CUTIE CURSE"
3-29

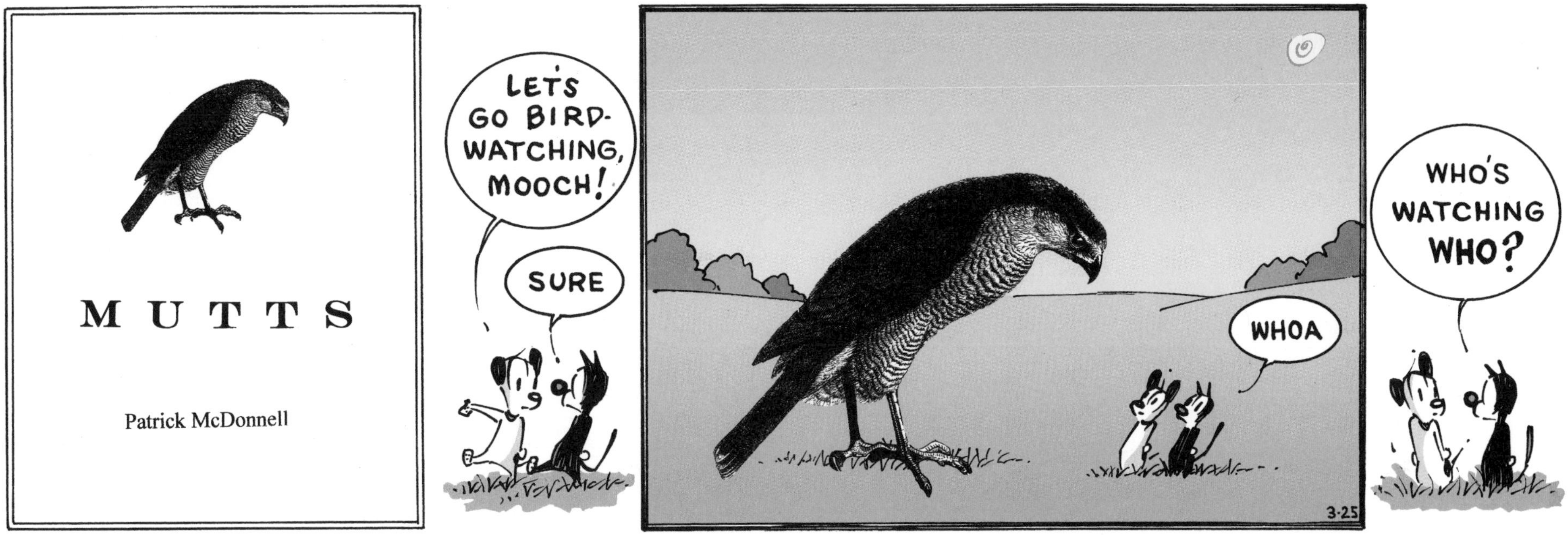
MUTTS
Patrick McDonnell
LET'S GO BIRD-WATCHING, MOOCH!
SURE
WHOA
3·25
WHO'S WATCHING WHO?

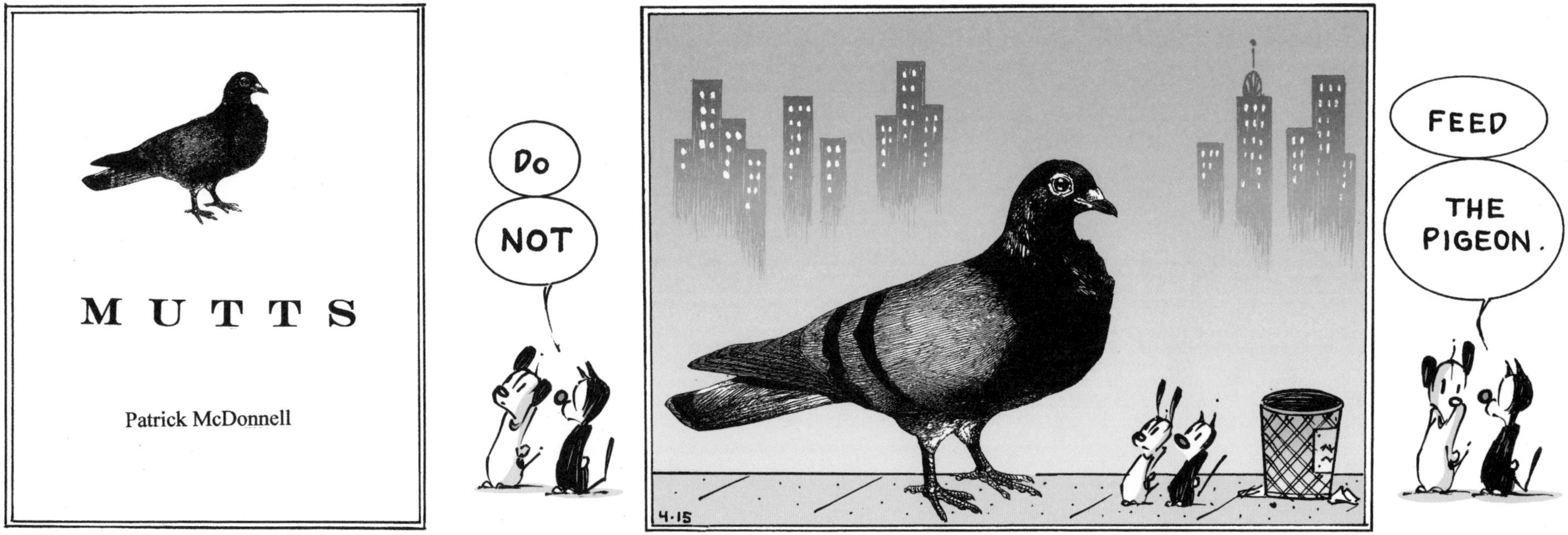
MUTTS
Patrick McDonnell
DO
NOT
FEED
THE PIGEON.
4·15

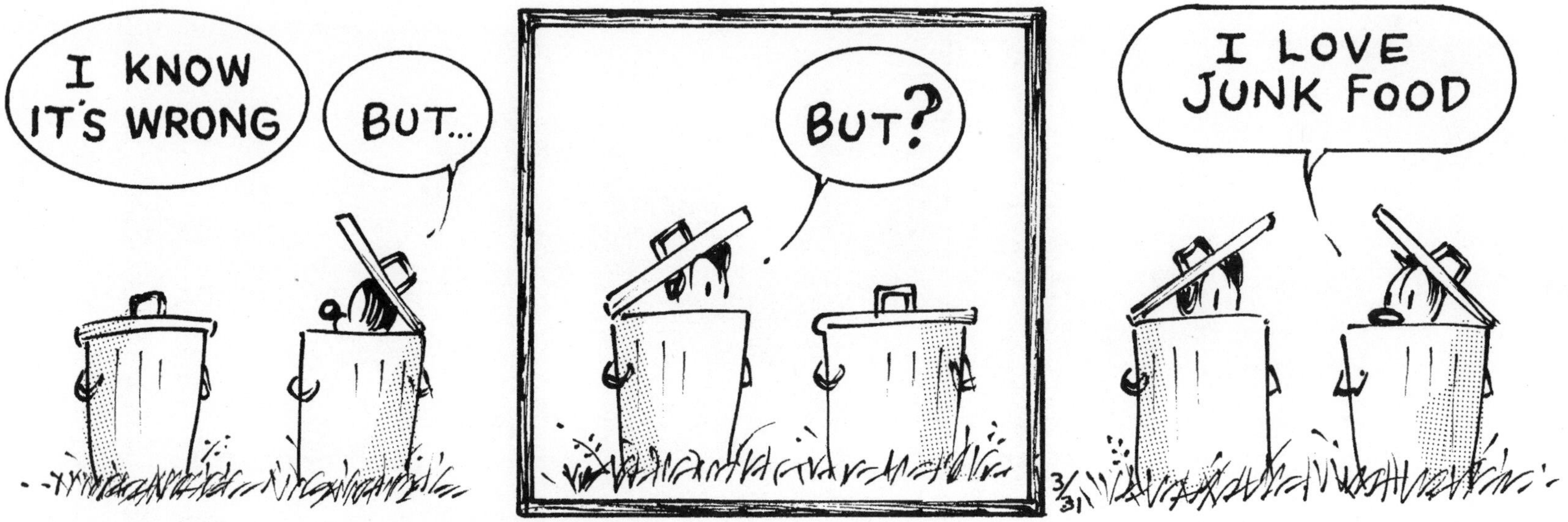
I KNOW IT'S WRONG
BUT...
BUT?
I LOVE JUNK FOOD
3/31

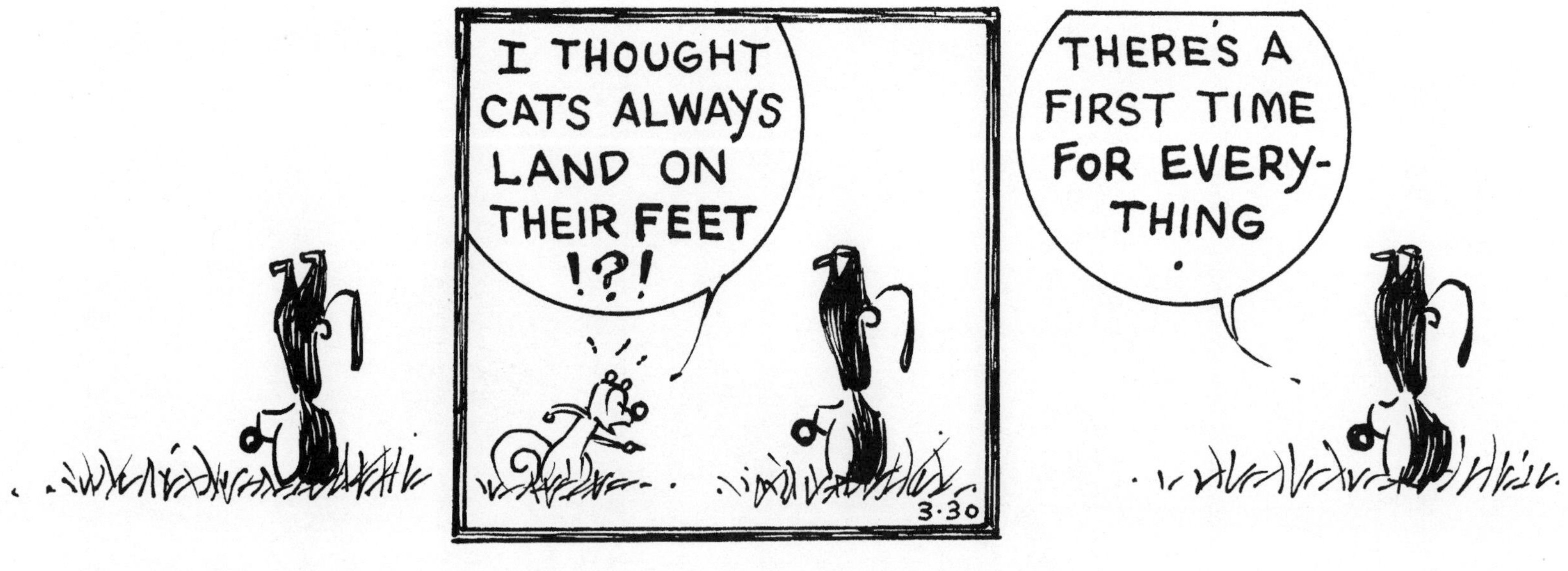
I THOUGHT CATS ALWAYS LAND ON THEIR FEET !?!
3·30
THERE'S A FIRST TIME FOR EVERY-THING.

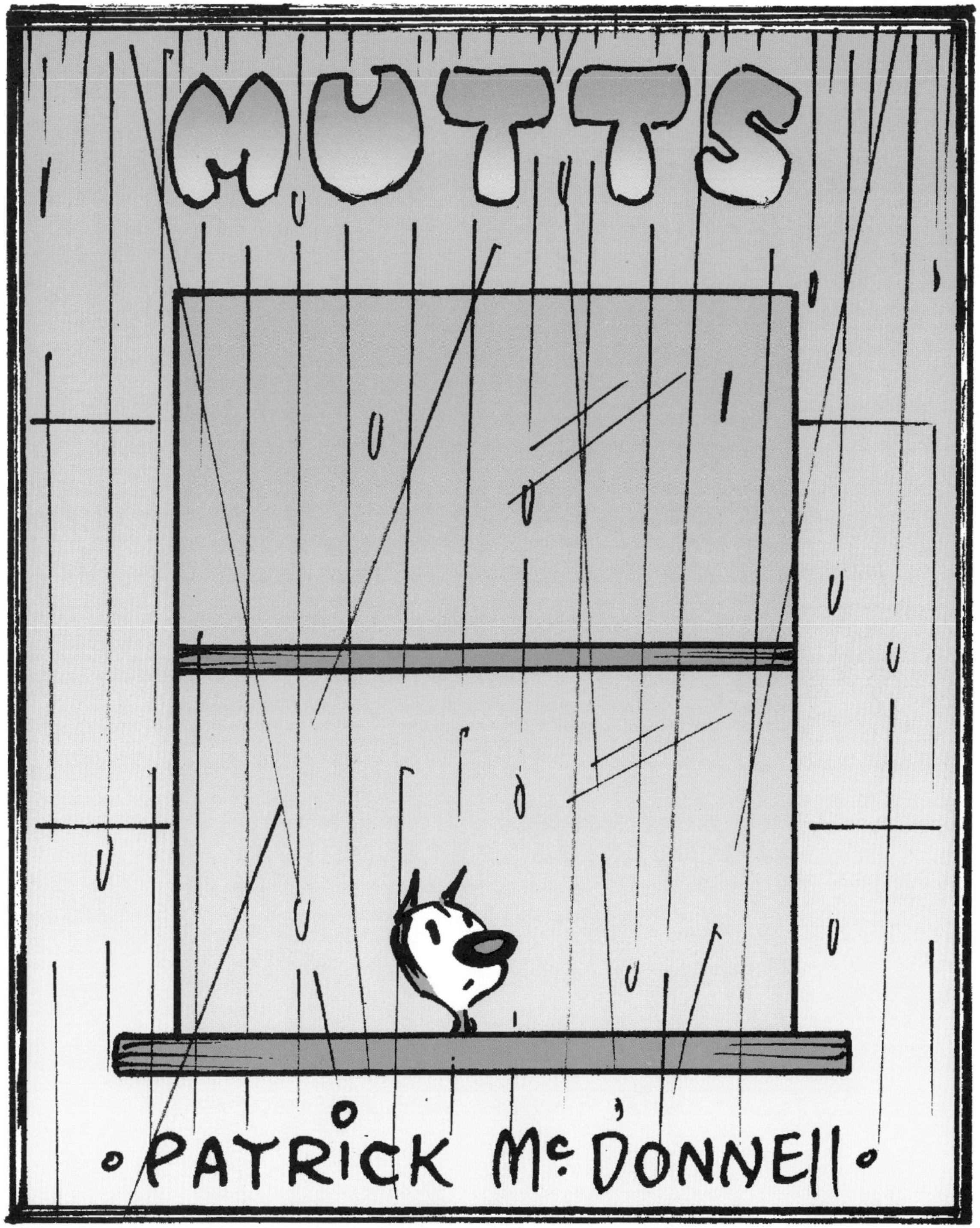
MUTTS
PATRICK McDONNELL

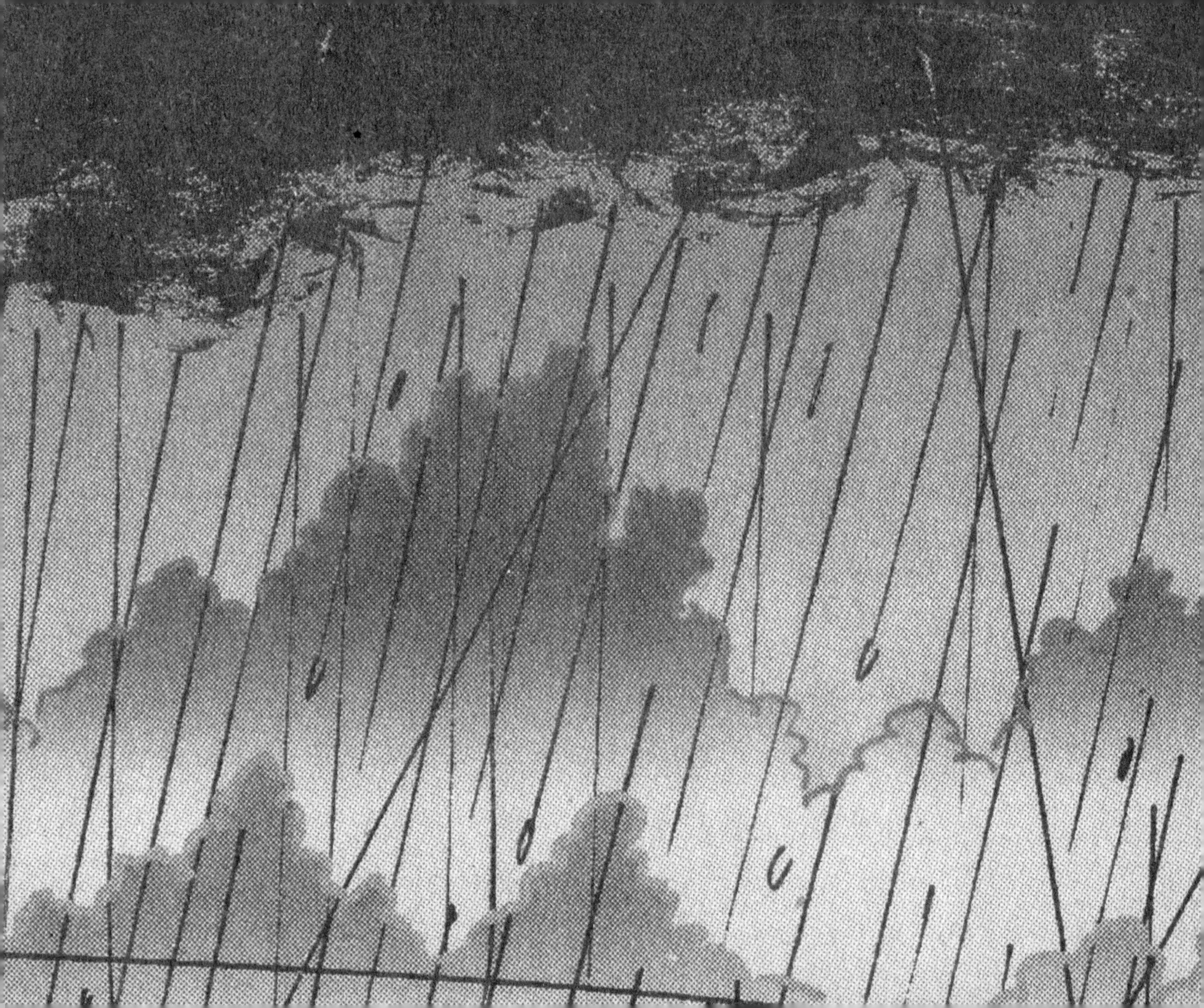

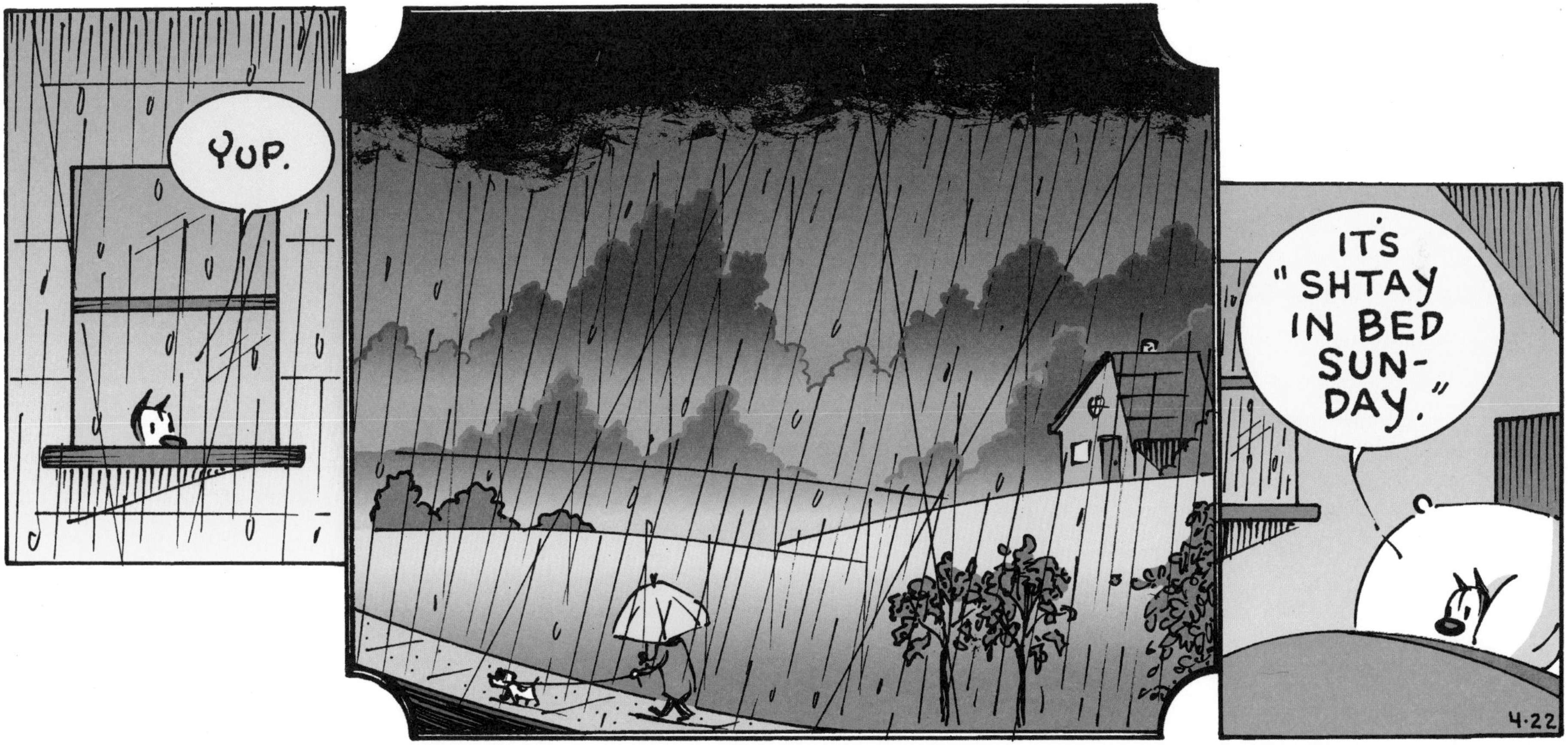
YUP.
IT'S "SHTAY IN BED SUN-DAY."
4-22

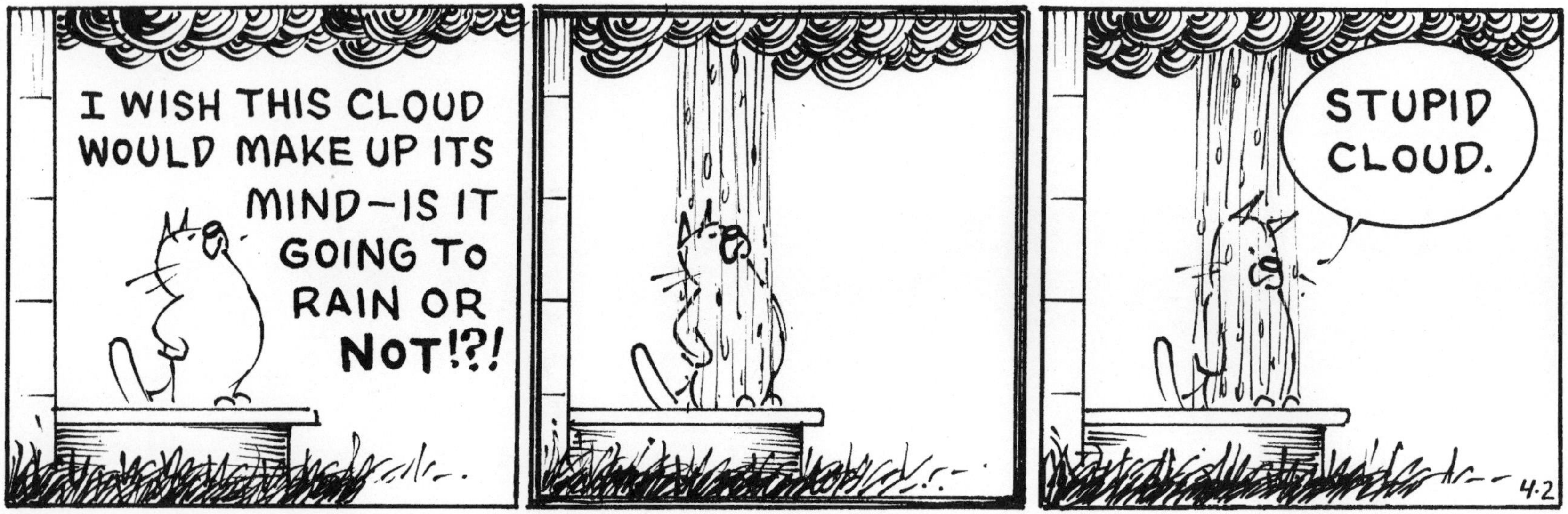
I WISH THIS CLOUD WOULD MAKE UP ITS MIND—IS IT GOING TO RAIN OR NOT!?!
STUPID CLOUD.
4·2

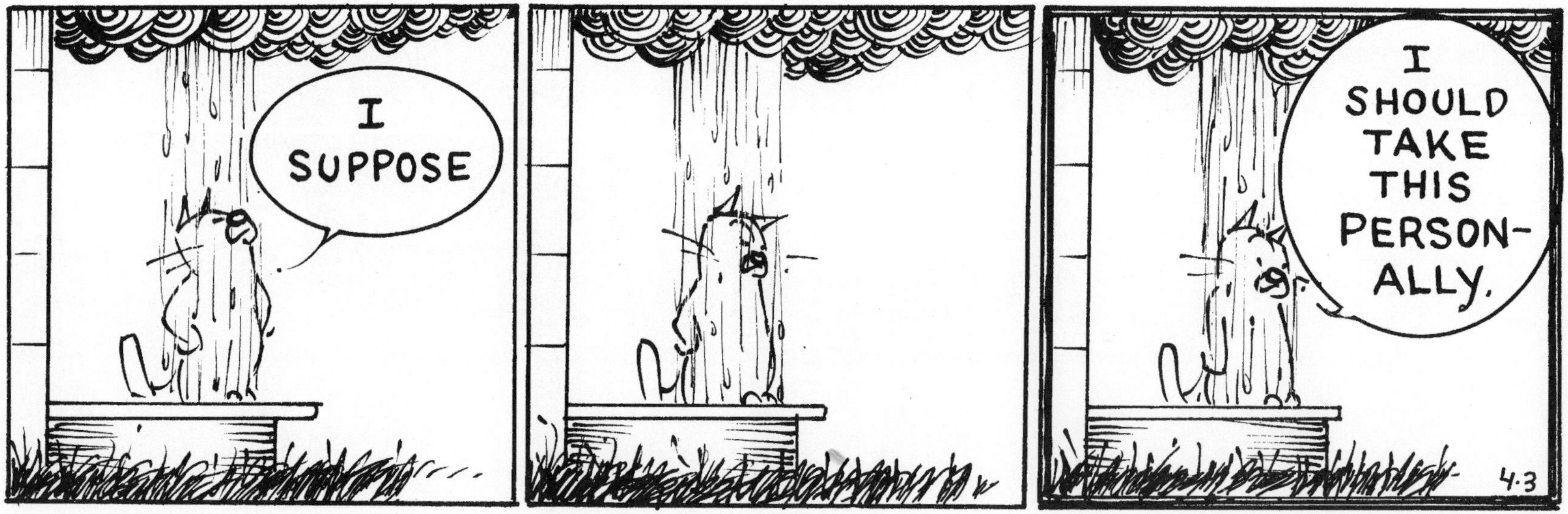
I SUPPOSE
I SHOULD TAKE THIS PERSON-ALLY.
4·3

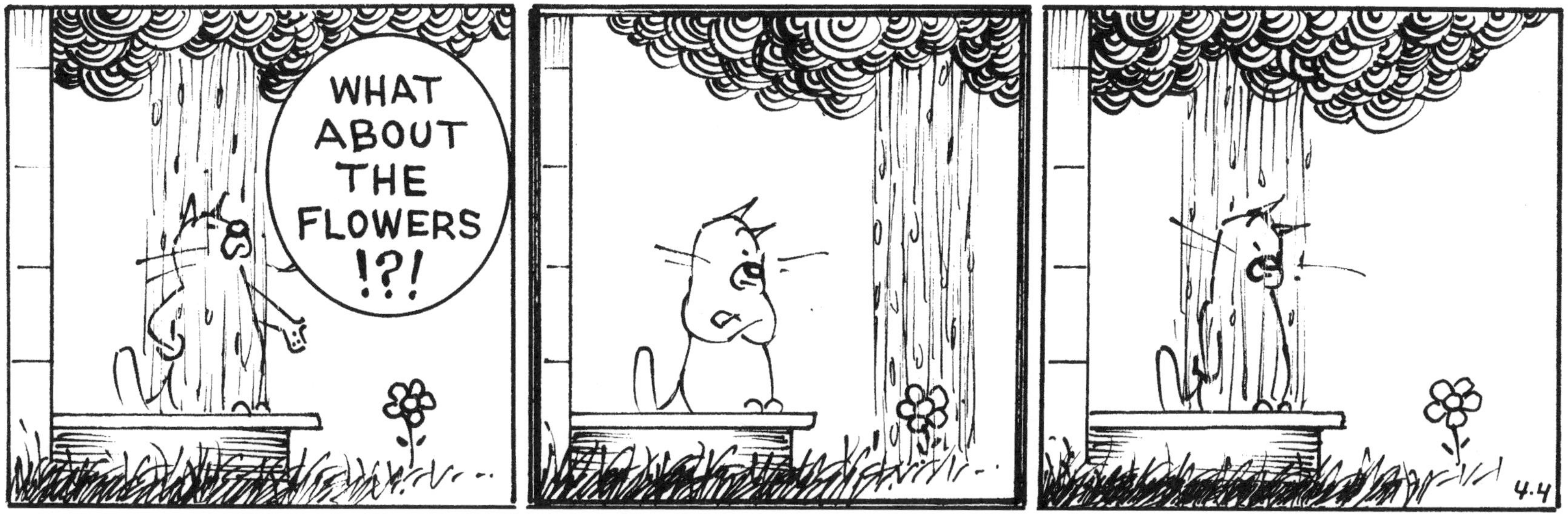
WHAT ABOUT THE FLOWERS !?!

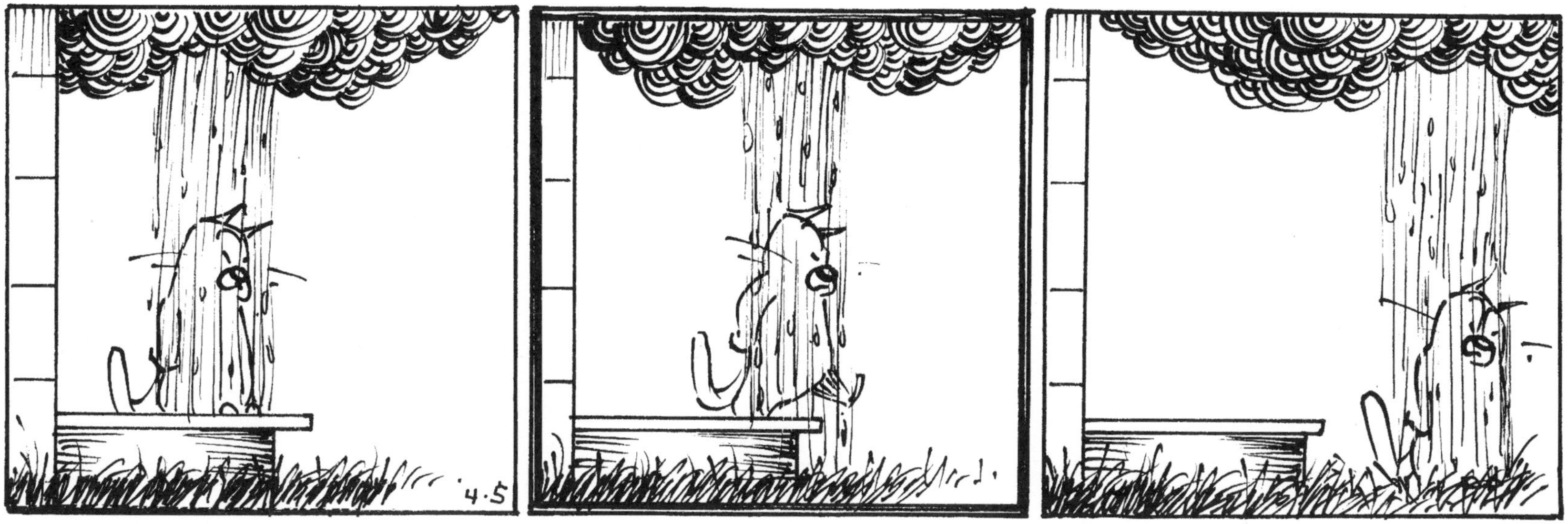

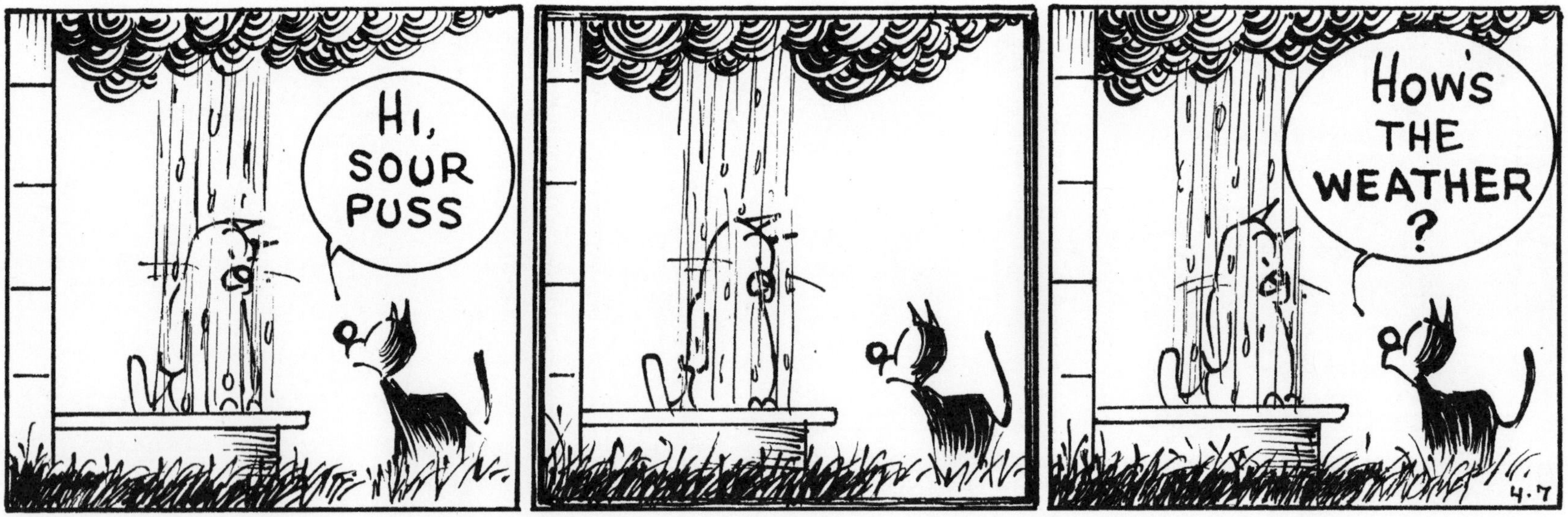
HI, SOUR PUSS
HOW'S THE WEATHER ?
4.7

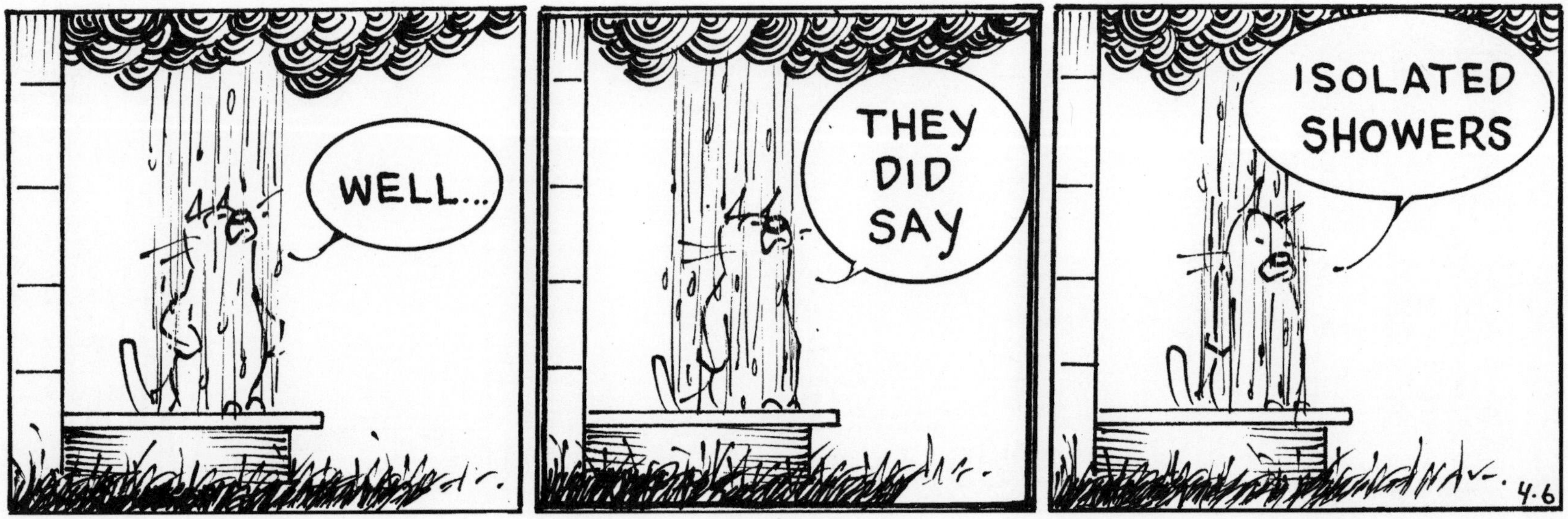
WELL...
THEY DID SAY
ISOLATED SHOWERS
4.6

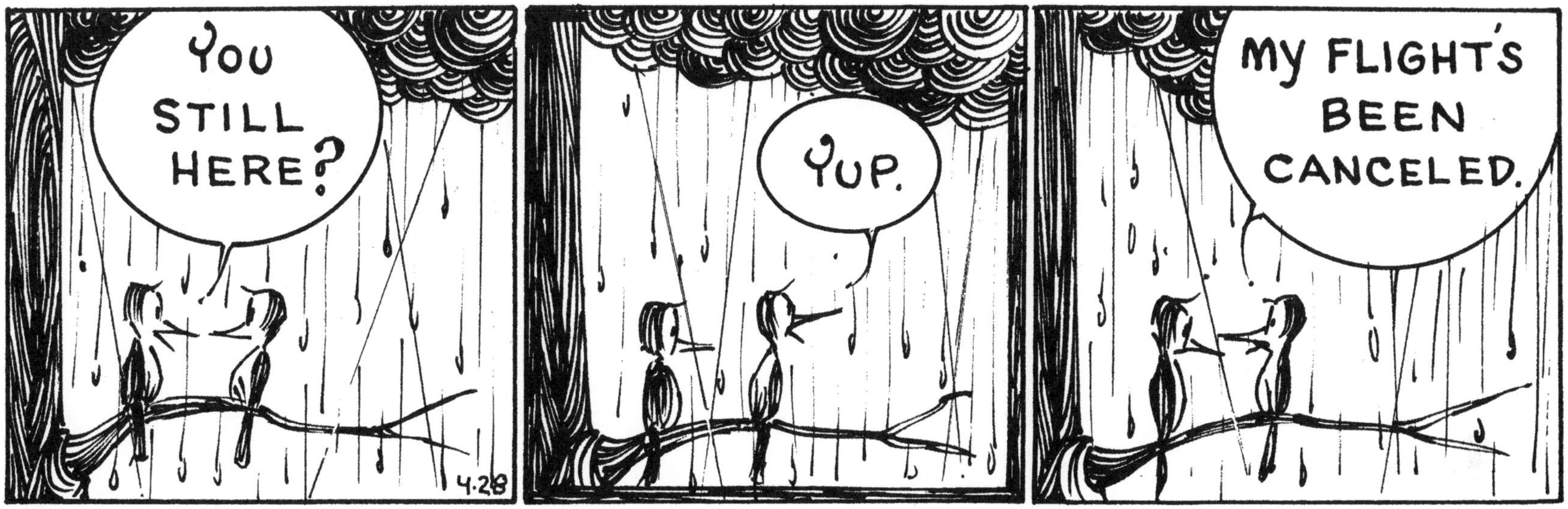
YOU STILL HERE?
YUP.
MY FLIGHT'S BEEN CANCELED.
4·28

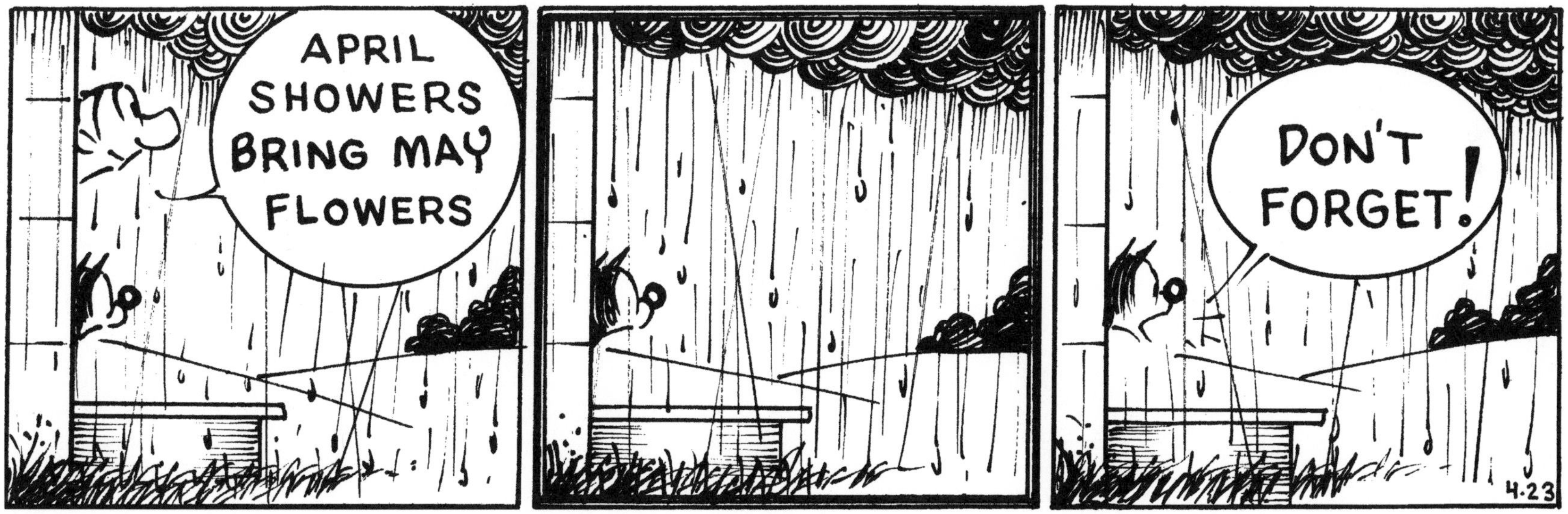
APRIL SHOWERS BRING MAY FLOWERS
DON'T FORGET!
4·23

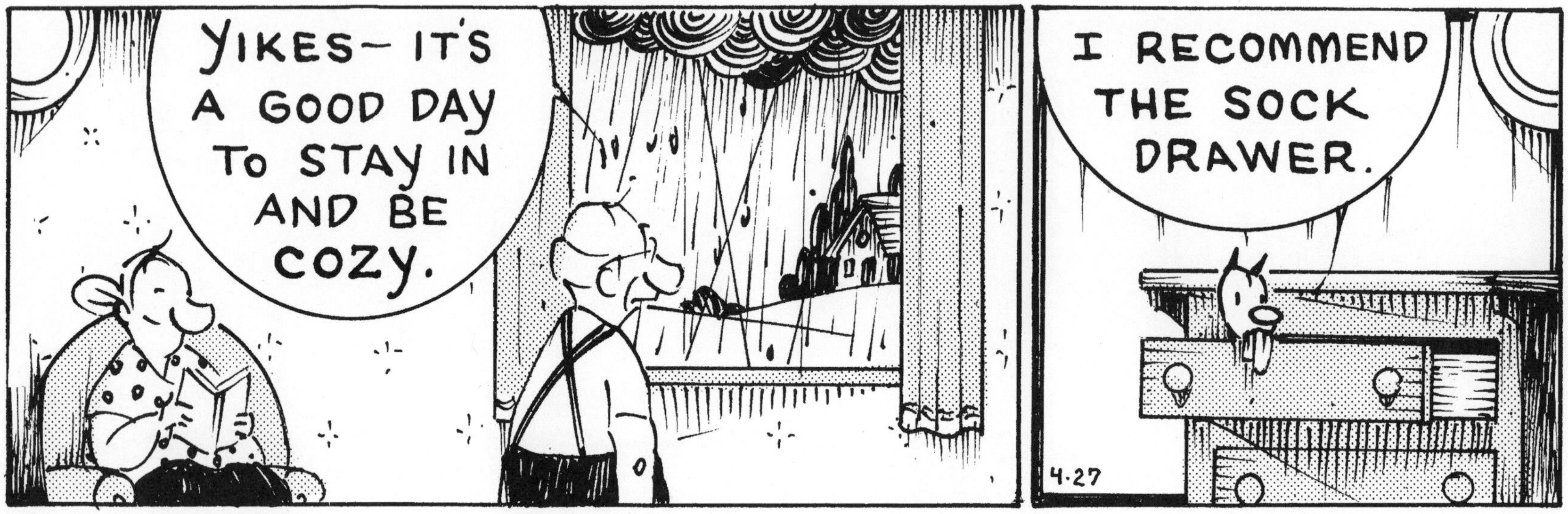
YIKES– IT'S A GOOD DAY TO STAY IN AND BE COZY.
I RECOMMEND THE SOCK DRAWER.
4.27

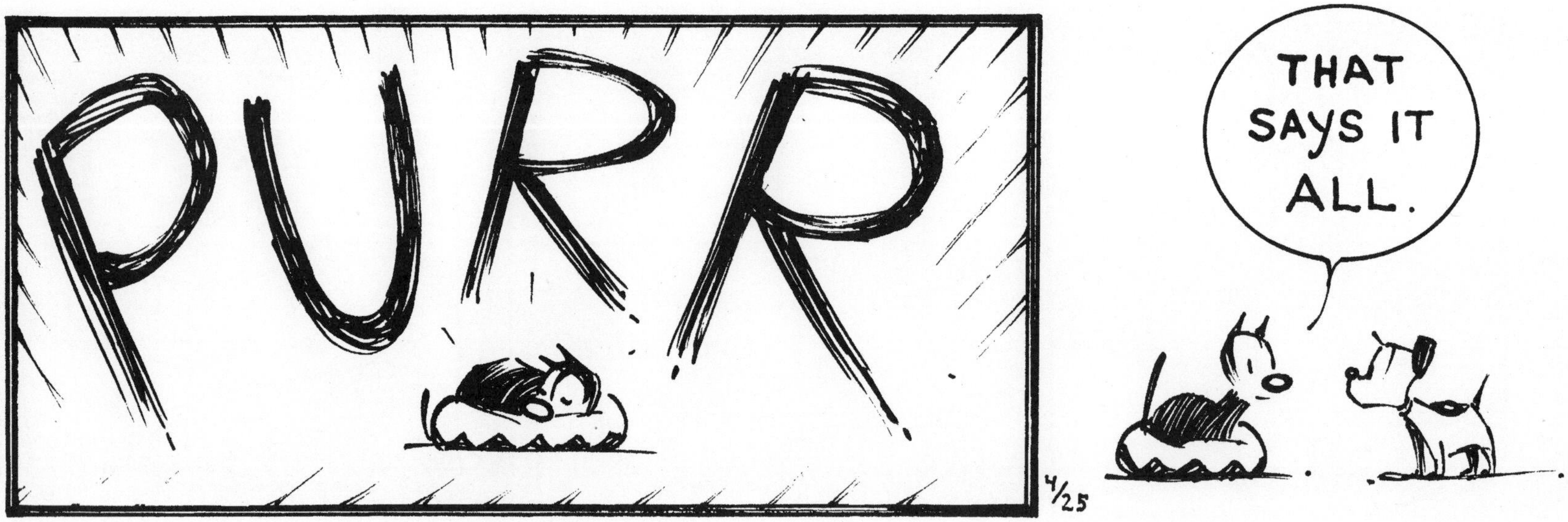
PURR
THAT SAYS IT ALL.
4/25

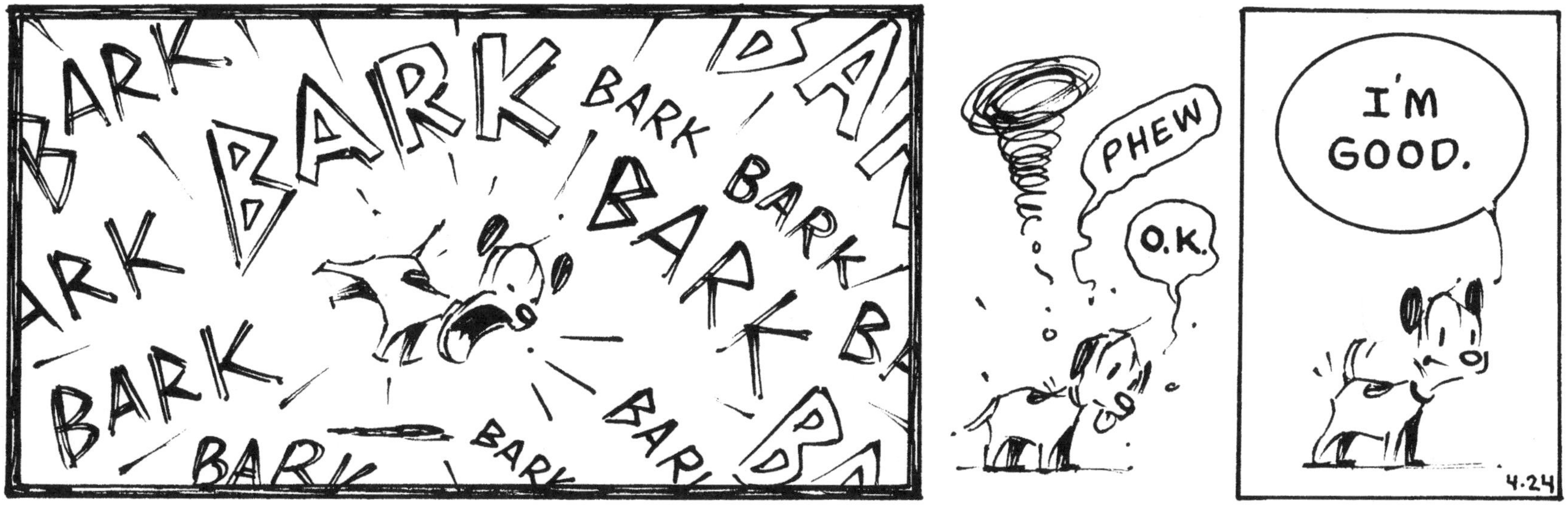
BARK
BARK
BARK
BARK
BARK
PHEW
O.K.
I'M GOOD.
4·24

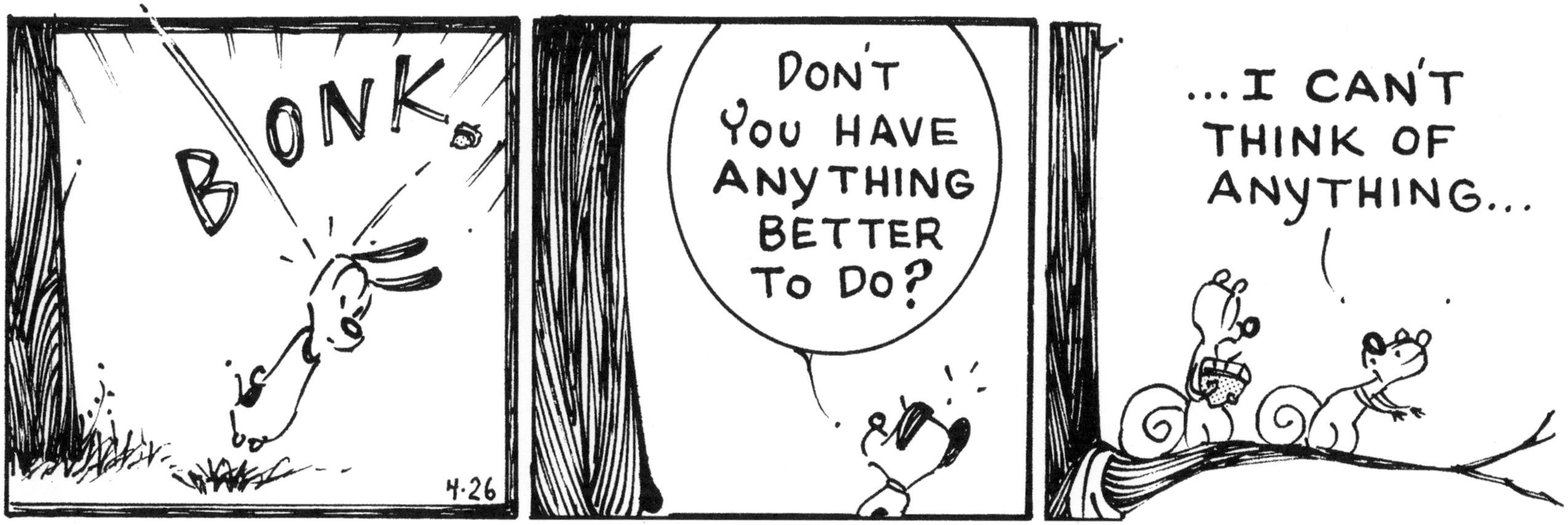
BONK
4·26
DON'T YOU HAVE ANYTHING BETTER TO DO?
...I CAN'T THINK OF ANYTHING...

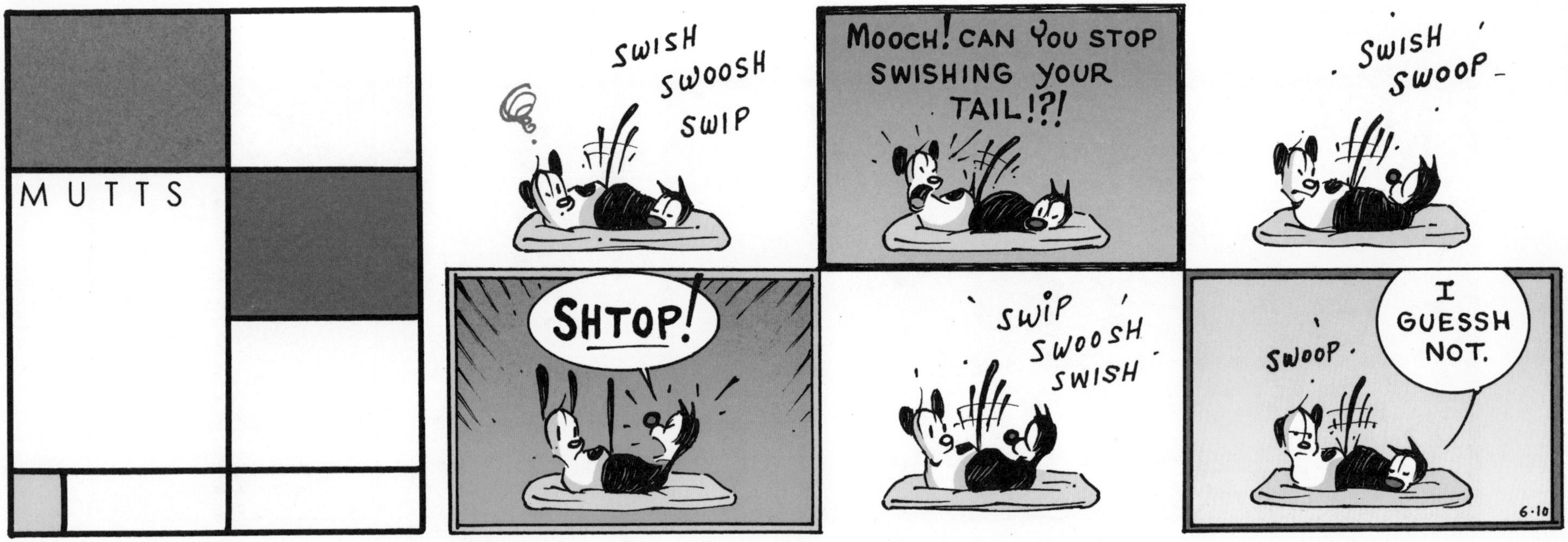
MUTTS
SWISH
SWOOSH
SWIP
MOOCH! CAN YOU STOP SWISHING YOUR TAIL!?!
SWISH
SWOOP
SHTOP!
SWIP
SWOOSH
SWISH
SWOOP
I GUESSH NOT.
6·10

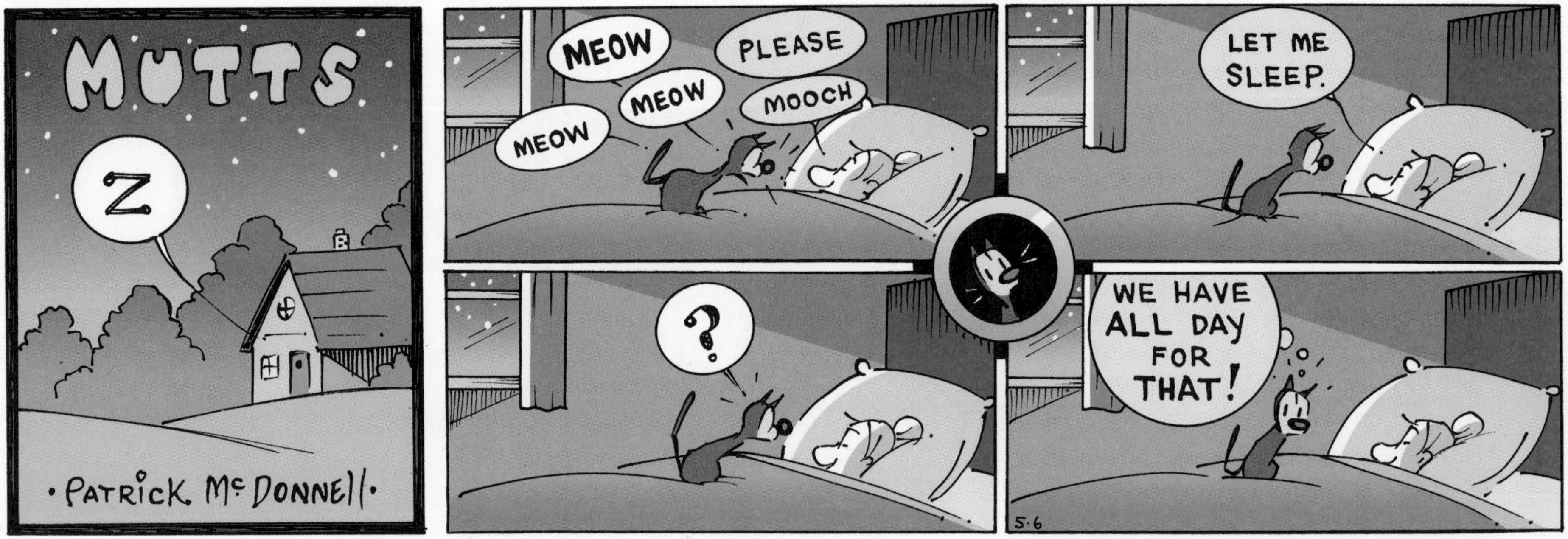
MUTTS
Z
·PATRICK McDONNELL·
MEOW
MEOW
MEOW
PLEASE
MOOCH
LET ME SLEEP.
?
WE HAVE ALL DAY FOR THAT!
5·6

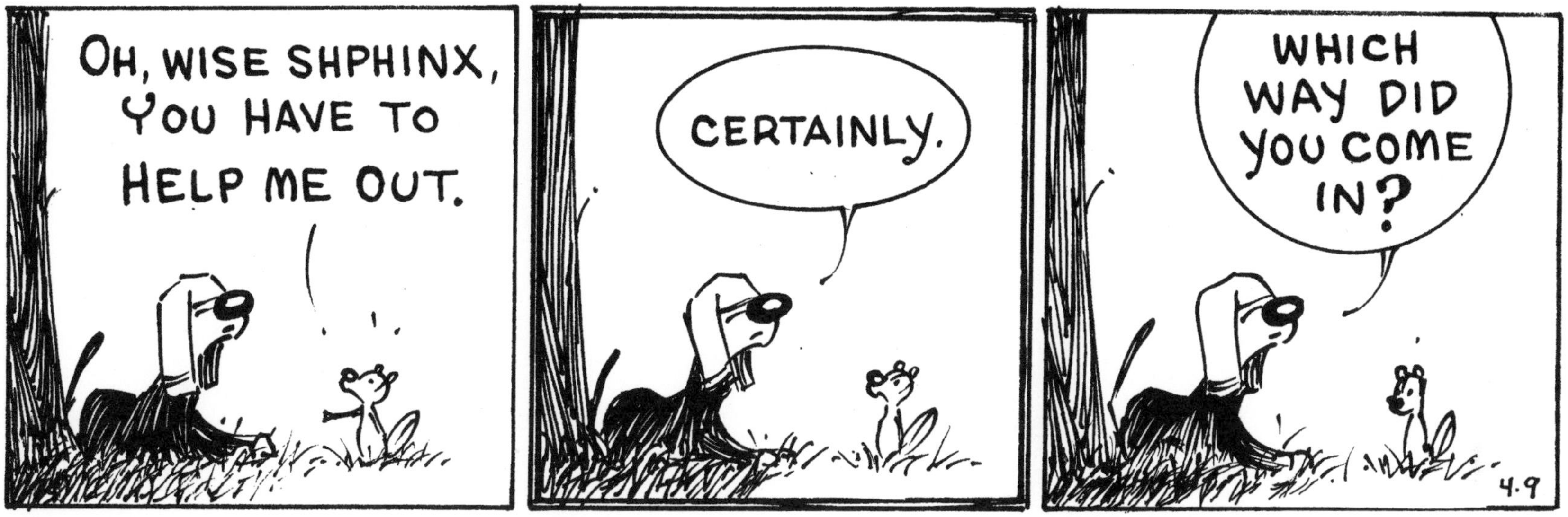
OH, WISE SHPHINX, YOU HAVE TO HELP ME OUT.
CERTAINLY.
WHICH WAY DID YOU COME IN?
4·9

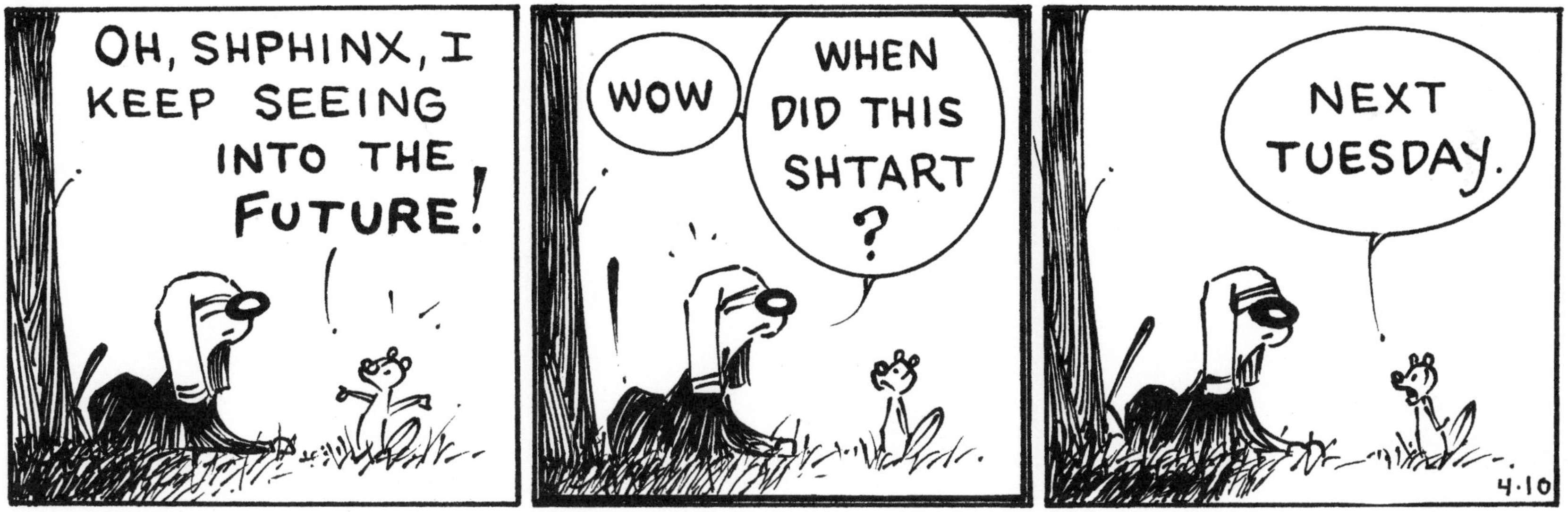
OH, SHPHINX, I KEEP SEEING INTO THE FUTURE!
WOW
WHEN DID THIS SHTART ?
NEXT TUESDAY.
4·10

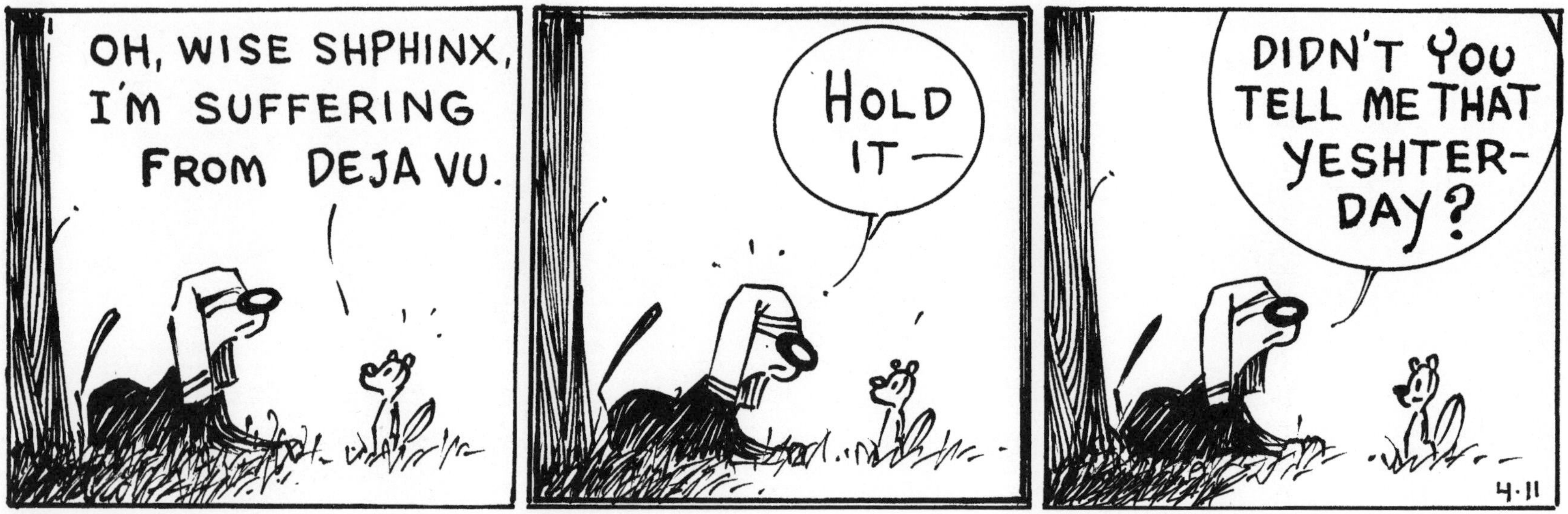
OH, WISE SHPHINX, I'M SUFFERING FROM DEJA VU.
HOLD IT—
DIDN'T YOU TELL ME THAT YESHTER-DAY?
4·11

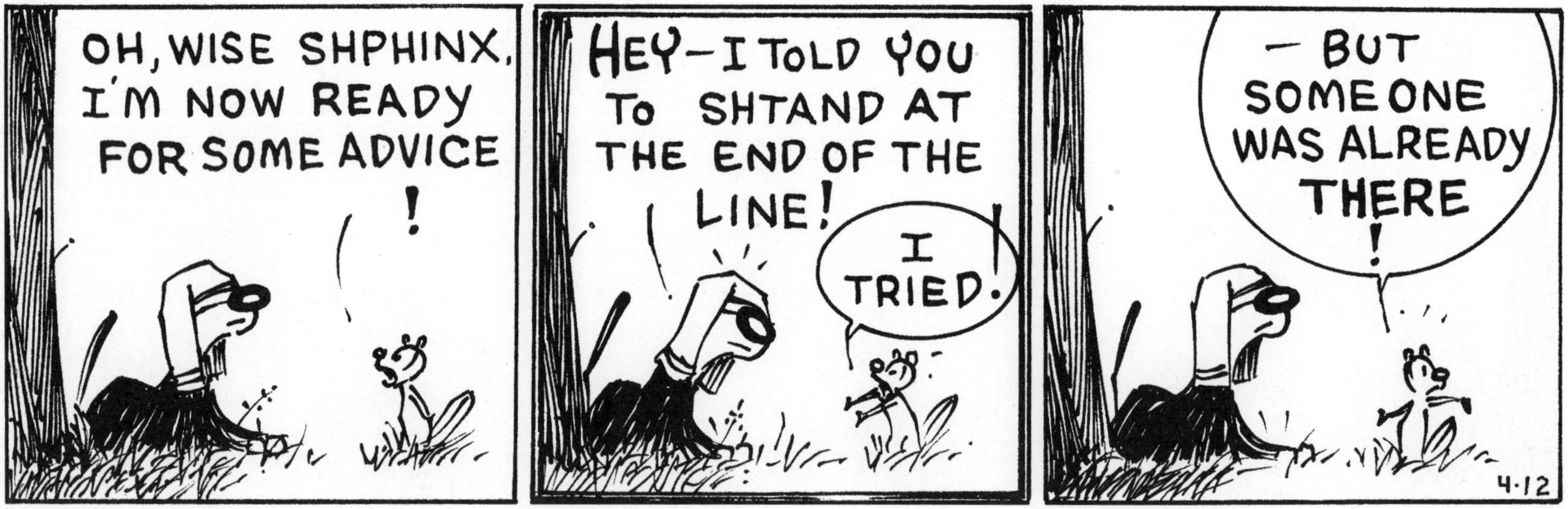
OH, WISE SHPHINX, I'M NOW READY FOR SOME ADVICE!
HEY—I TOLD YOU TO SHTAND AT THE END OF THE LINE!
I TRIED.
—BUT SOMEONE WAS ALREADY THERE!
4·12

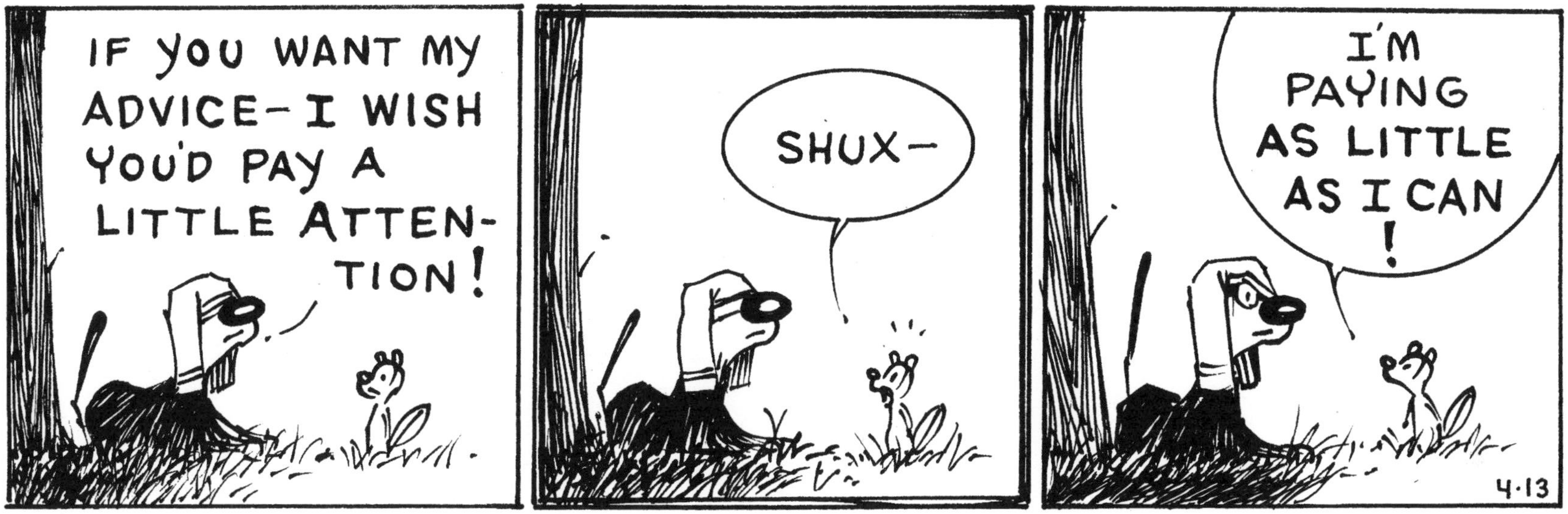
IF YOU WANT MY ADVICE– I WISH YOU'D PAY A LITTLE ATTENTION!
SHUX–
I'M PAYING AS LITTLE AS I CAN!
4·13

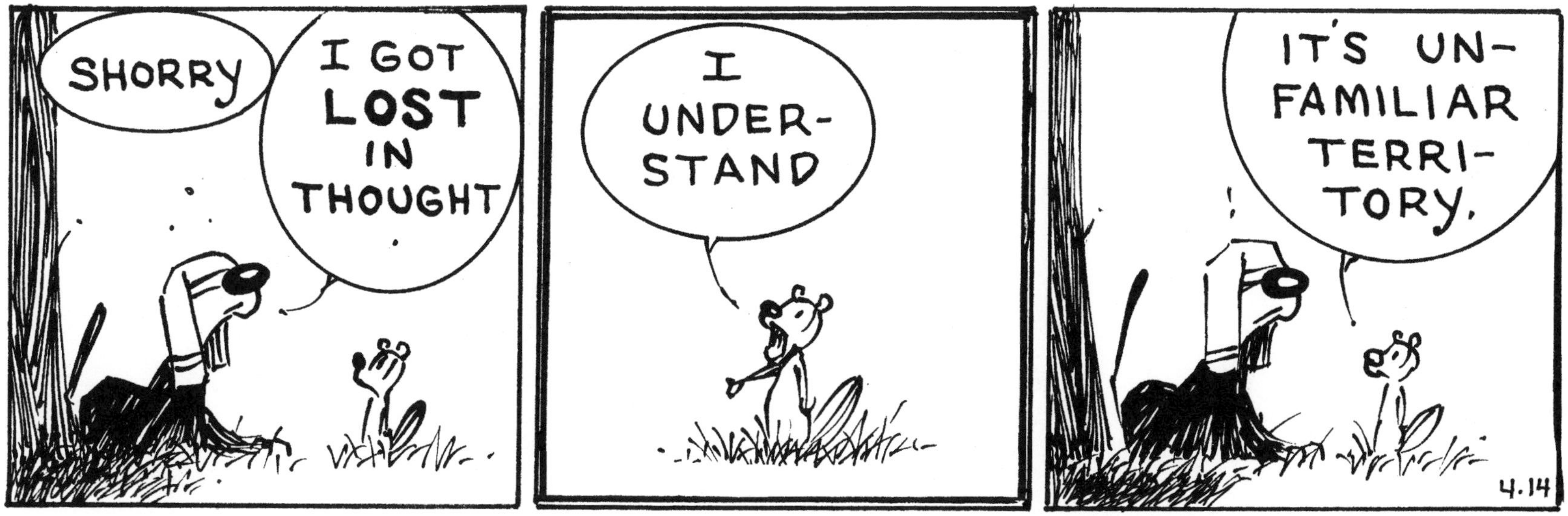
SHORRY
I GOT **LOST** IN THOUGHT
I UNDERSTAND
IT'S UNFAMILIAR TERRITORY.
4·14

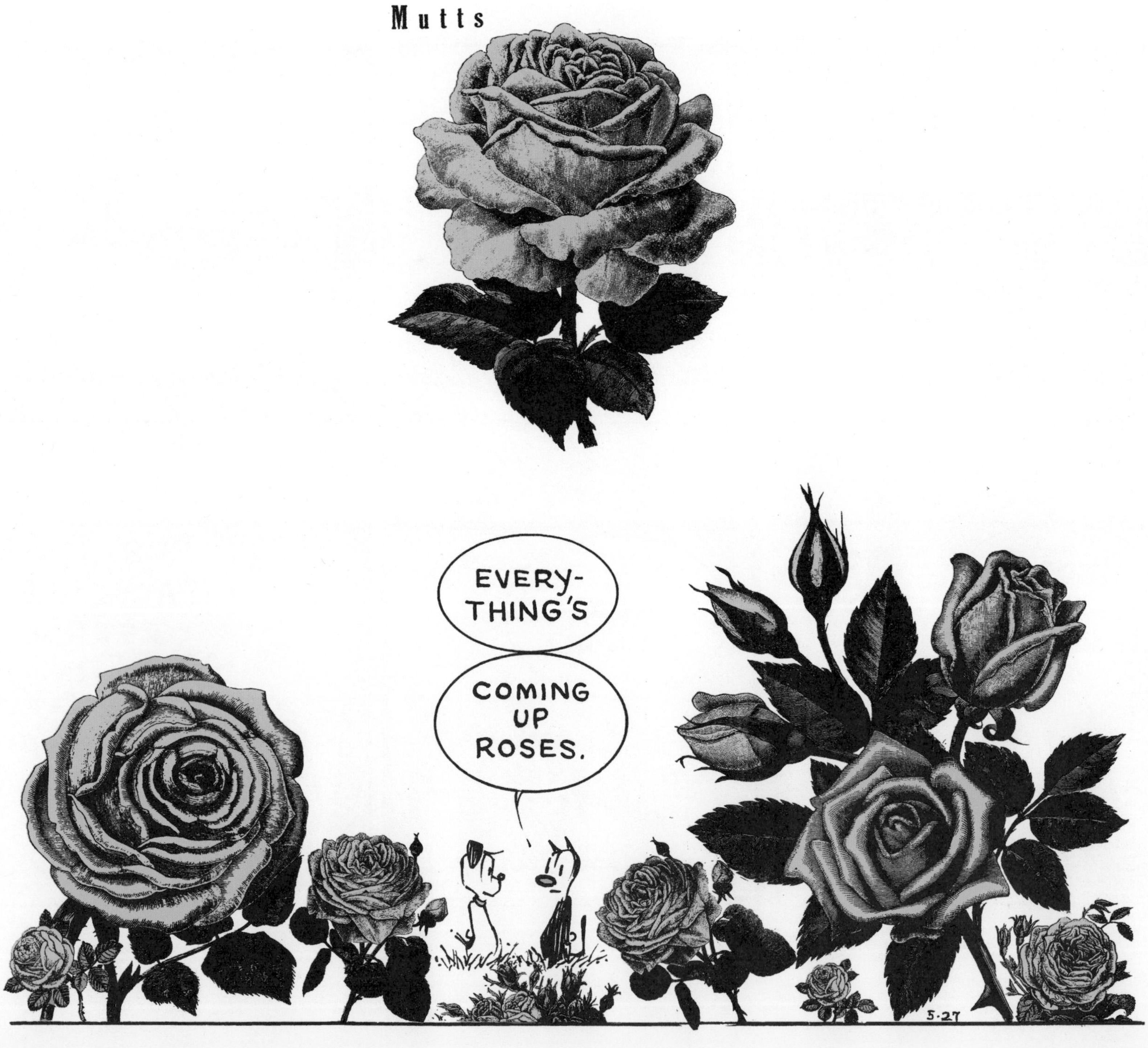
Mutts
EVERY-
THING'S
COMING
UP
ROSES.
5-27

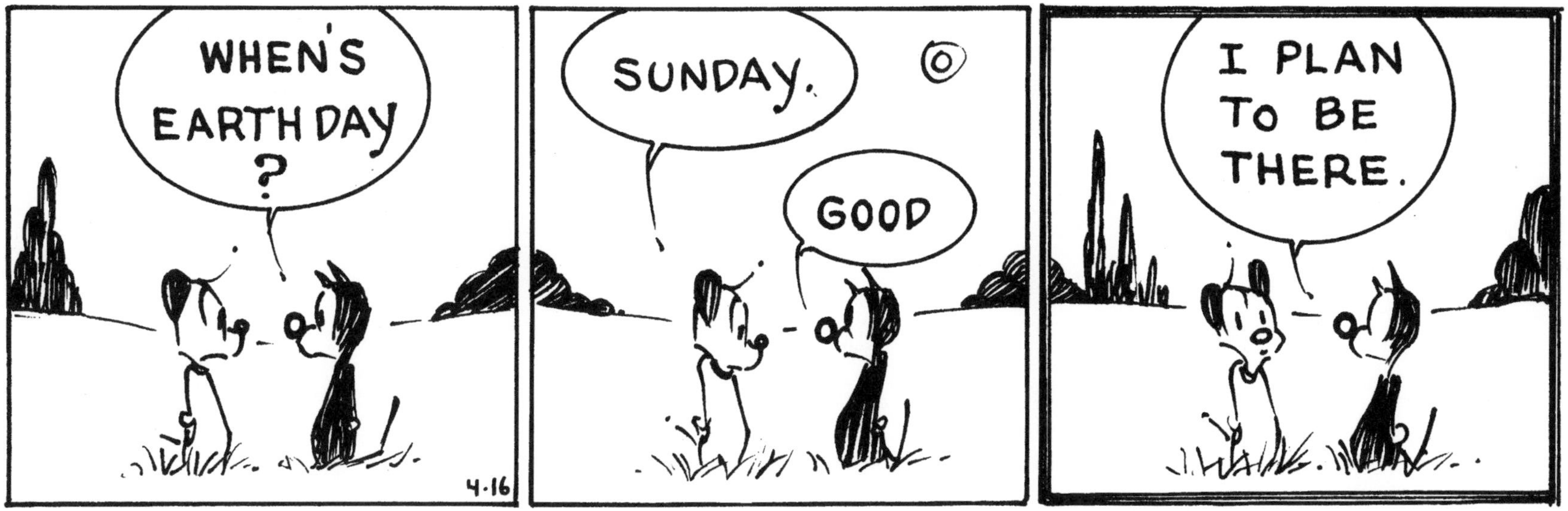
WHEN'S EARTH DAY ?
SUNDAY.
GOOD
I PLAN TO BE THERE.
4·16

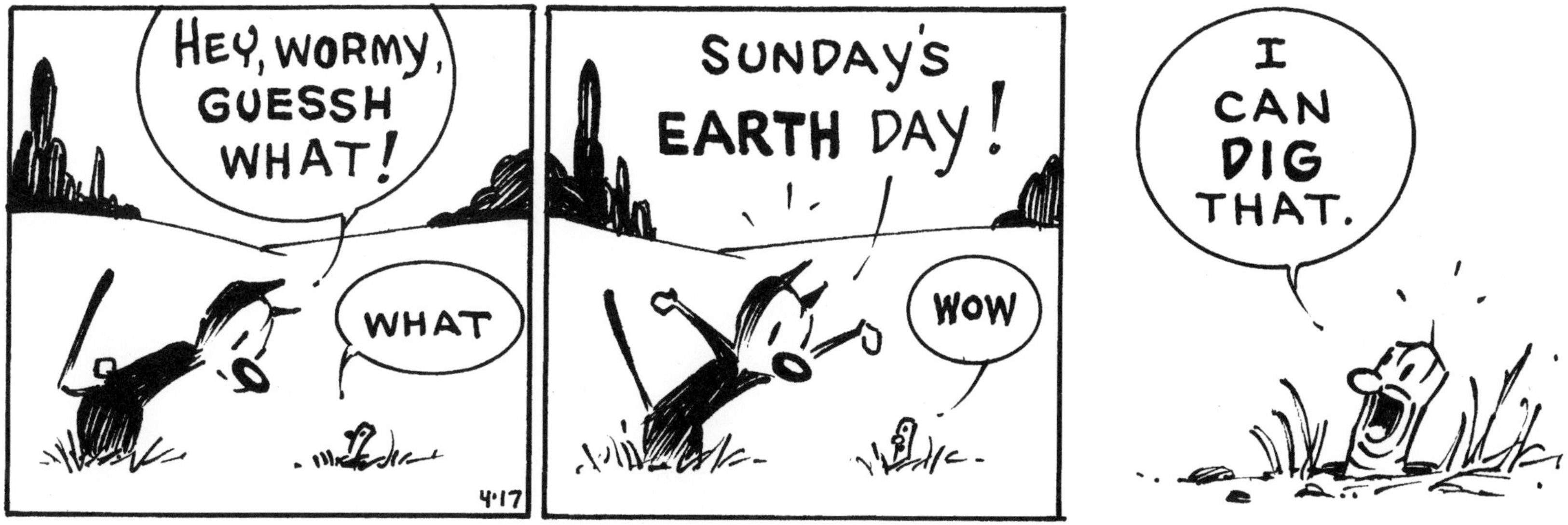
HEY, WORMY, GUESSH WHAT!
WHAT
SUNDAY'S EARTH DAY!
WOW
I CAN DIG THAT.
4·17

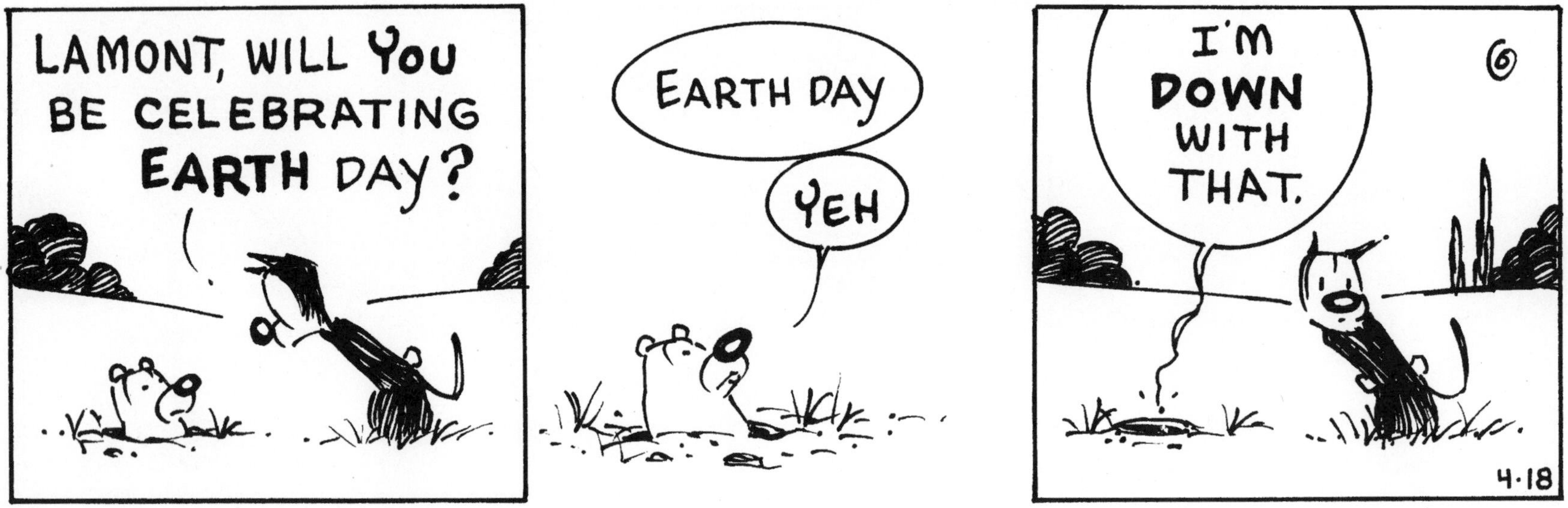
LAMONT, WILL YOU BE CELEBRATING EARTH DAY?
EARTH DAY
YEH
I'M DOWN WITH THAT.
4·18

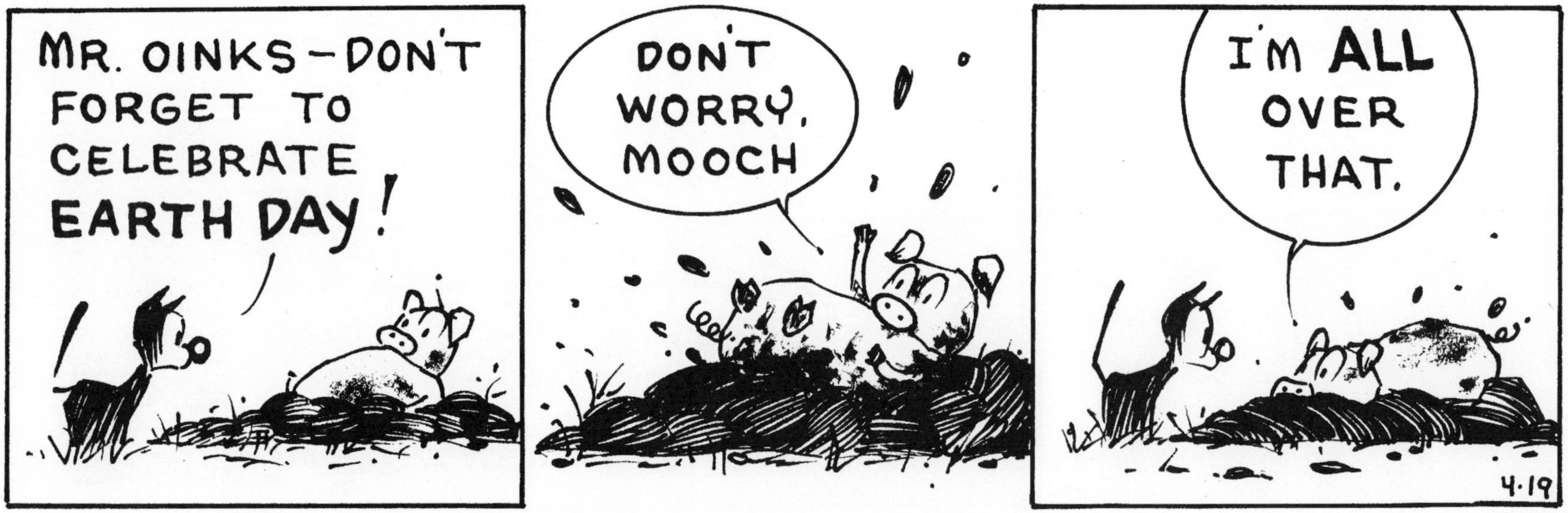
MR. OINKS—DON'T FORGET TO CELEBRATE EARTH DAY!
DON'T WORRY, MOOCH
I'M ALL OVER THAT.
4·19

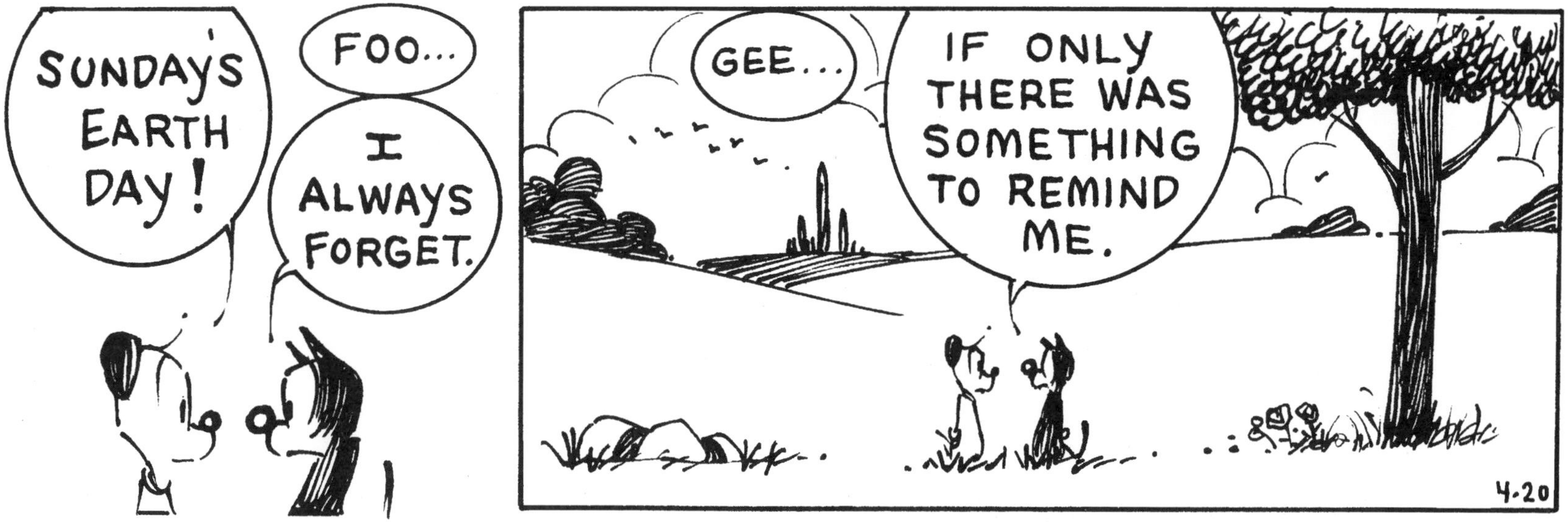
SUNDAY'S EARTH DAY!
FOO...
I ALWAYS FORGET.
GEE...
IF ONLY THERE WAS SOMETHING TO REMIND ME.
4·20

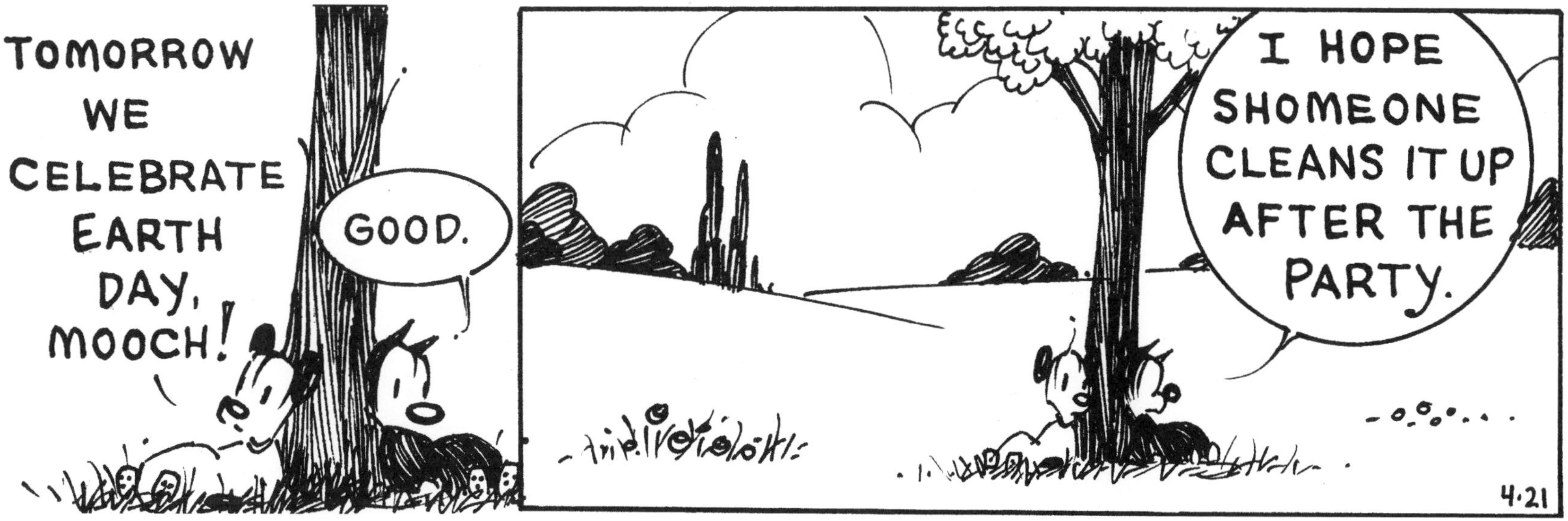
TOMORROW WE CELEBRATE EARTH DAY, MOOCH!
GOOD.
I HOPE SHOMEONE CLEANS IT UP AFTER THE PARTY.
4·21

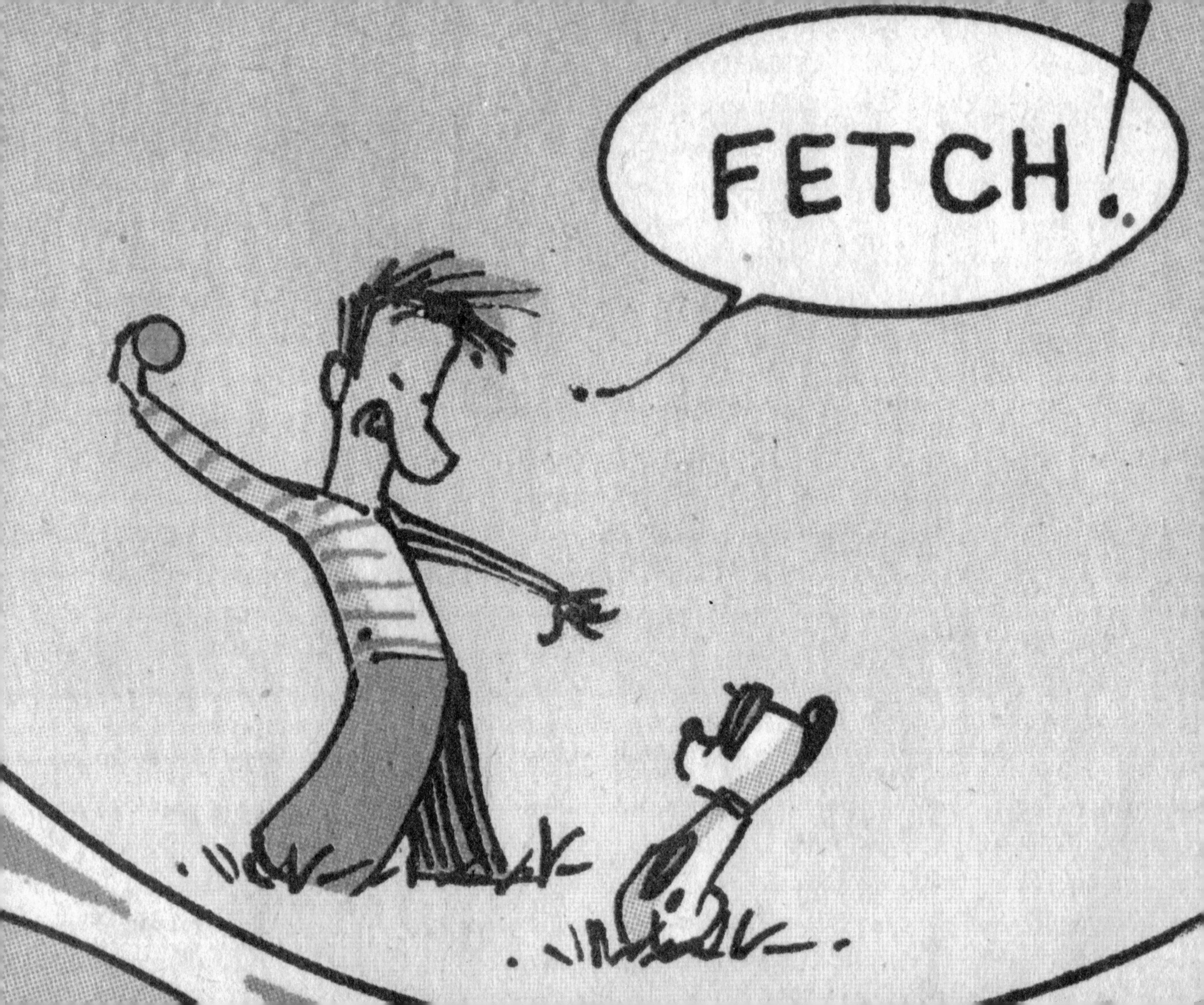
FETCH!

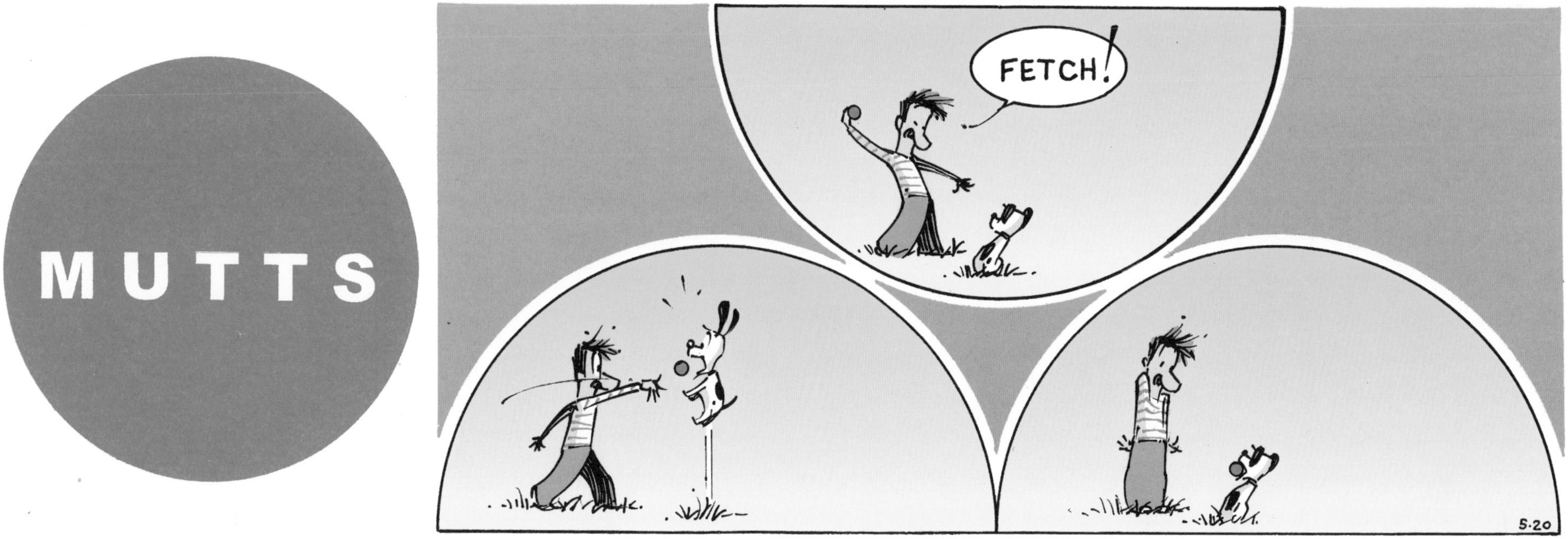
MUTTS
FETCH!
5·20

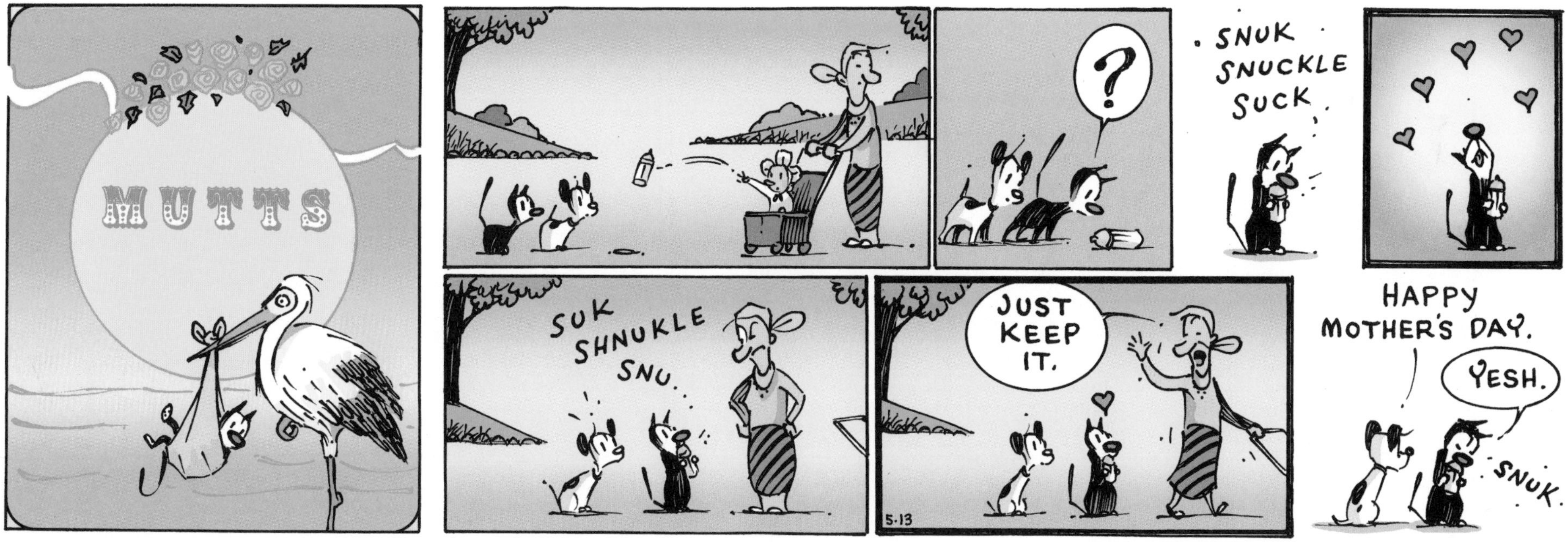
MUTTS
?
SNUK SNUCKLE SUCK
SUK SHNUKLE SNU
JUST KEEP IT.
5·13
HAPPY MOTHER'S DAY.
YESH.
SNUK.

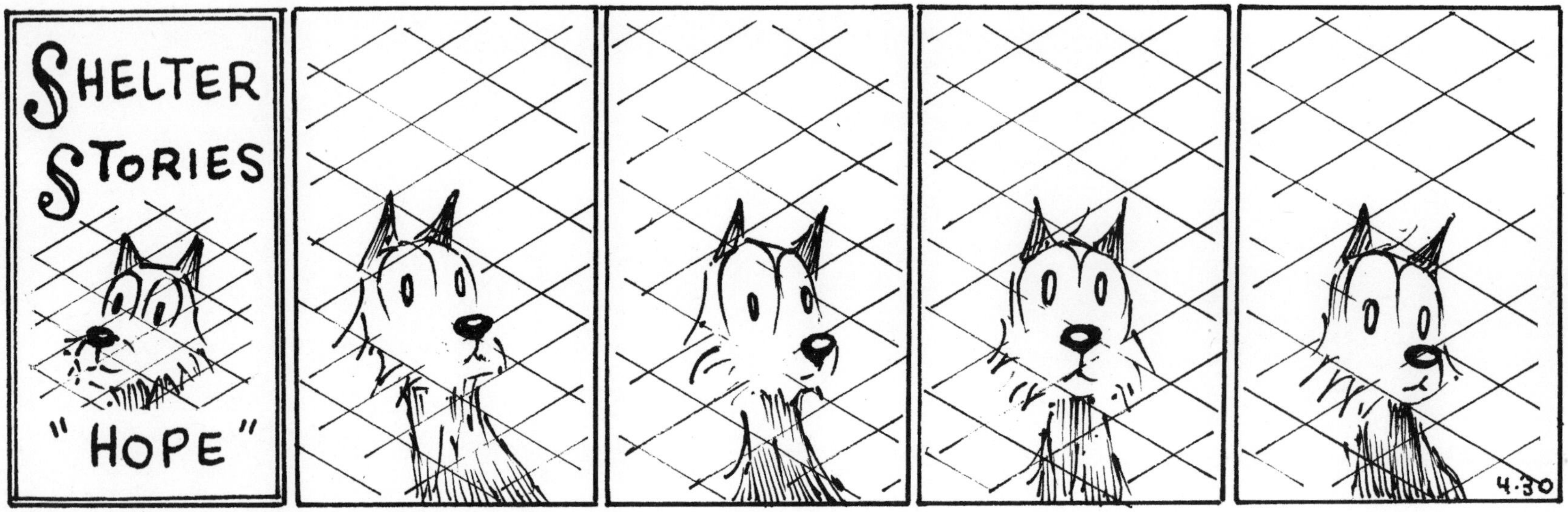
SHELTER STORIES
"HOPE"
4.30

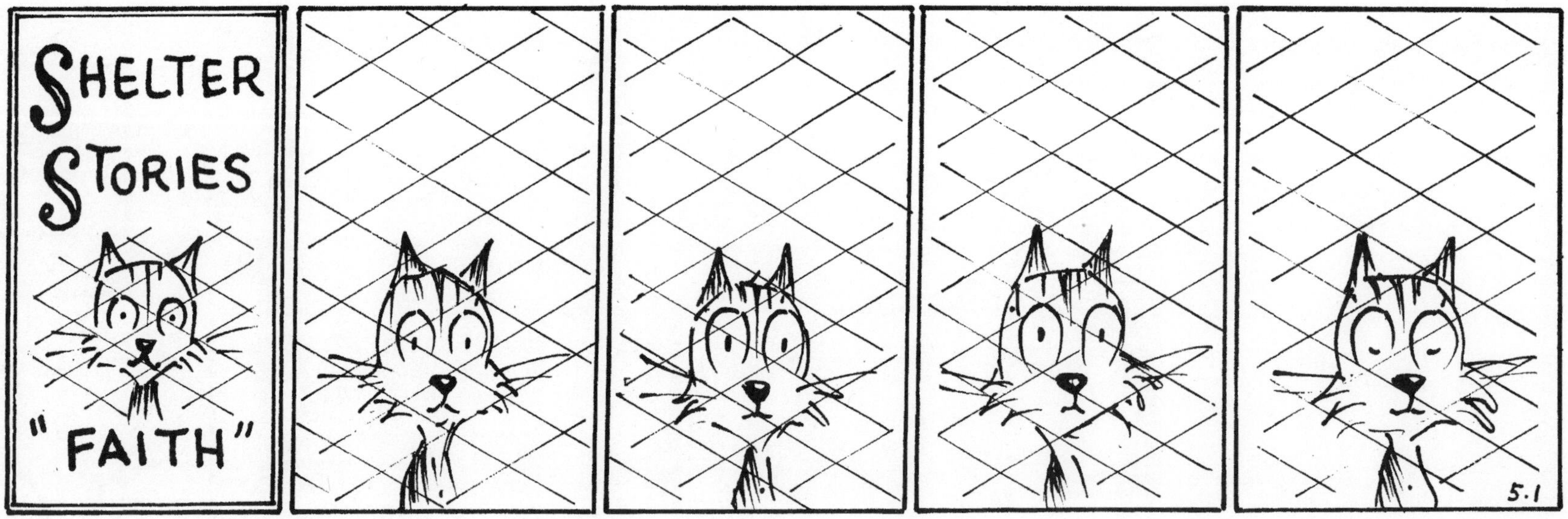
SHELTER STORIES
"FAITH"
5.1

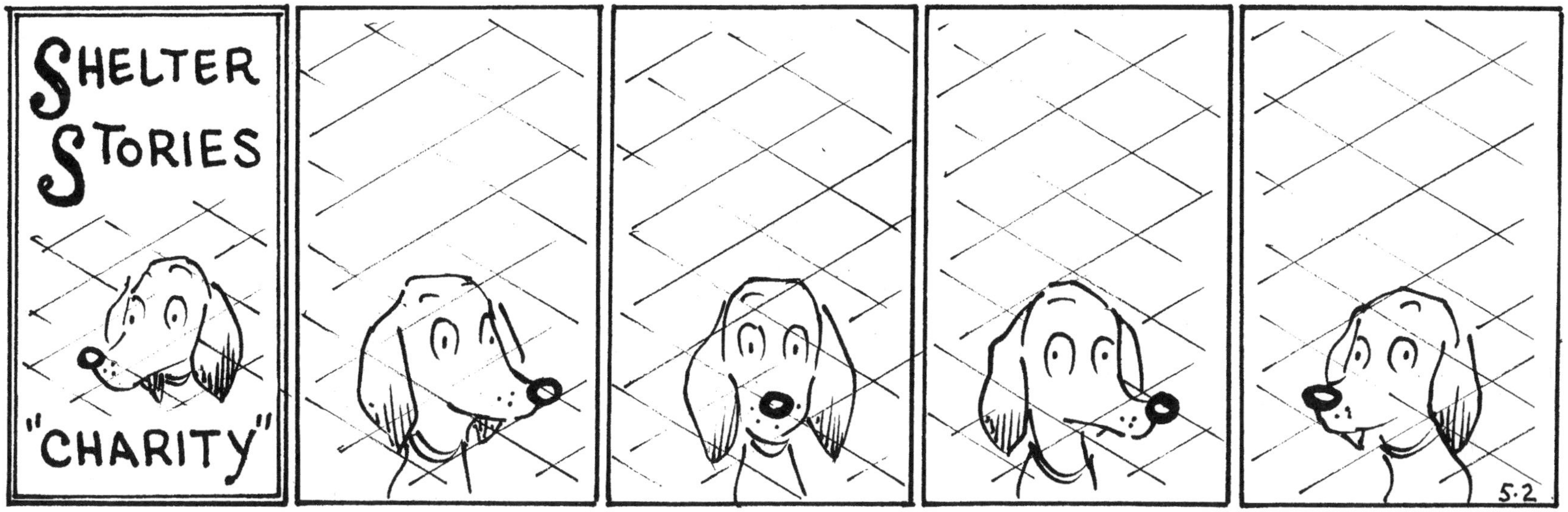
SHELTER STORIES
"CHARITY"
5.2

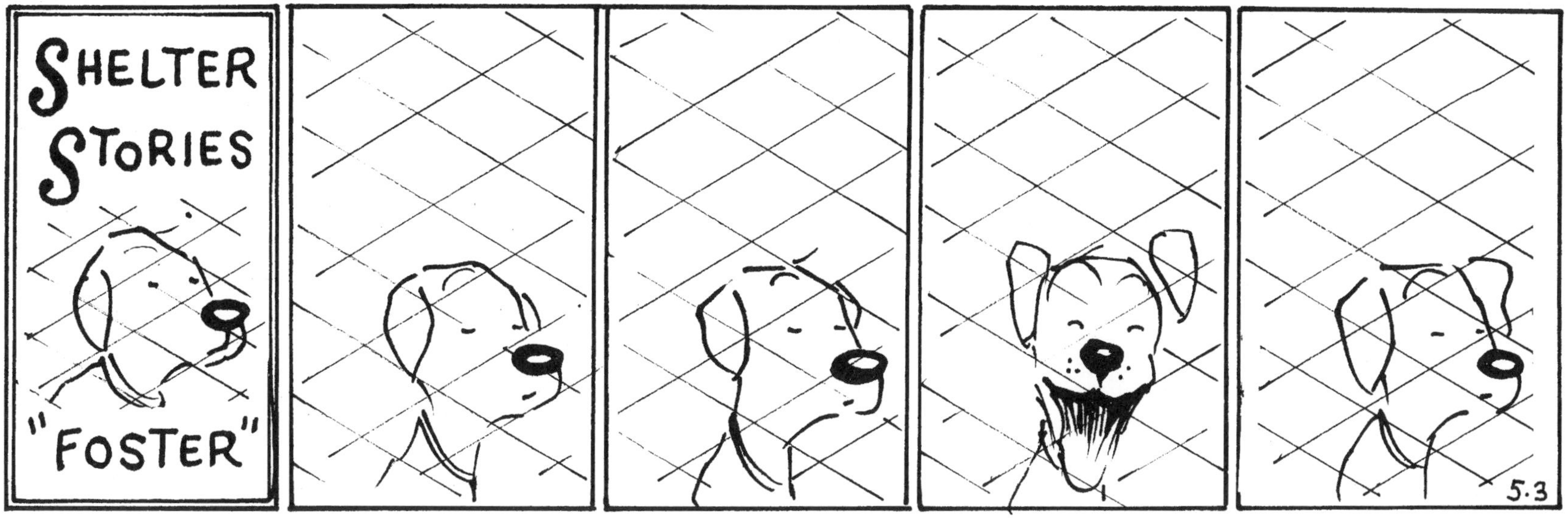
SHELTER STORIES
"FOSTER"
5.3

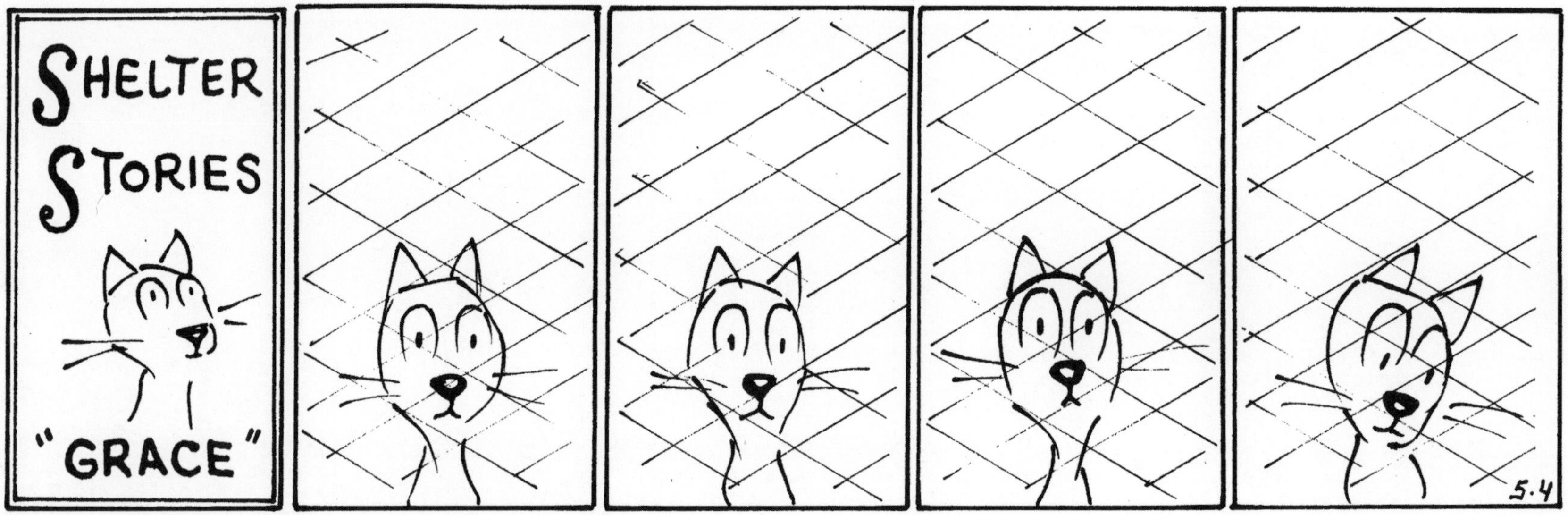
SHELTER STORIES
"GRACE"
5·4

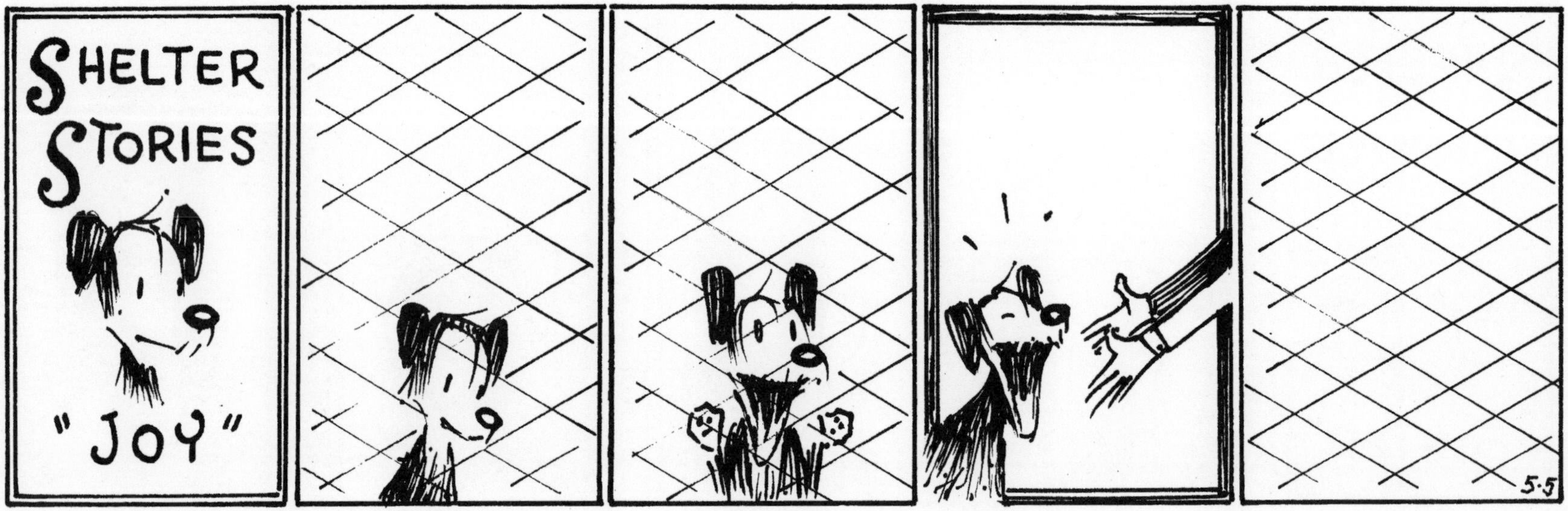
SHELTER STORIES
"JOY"
5·5

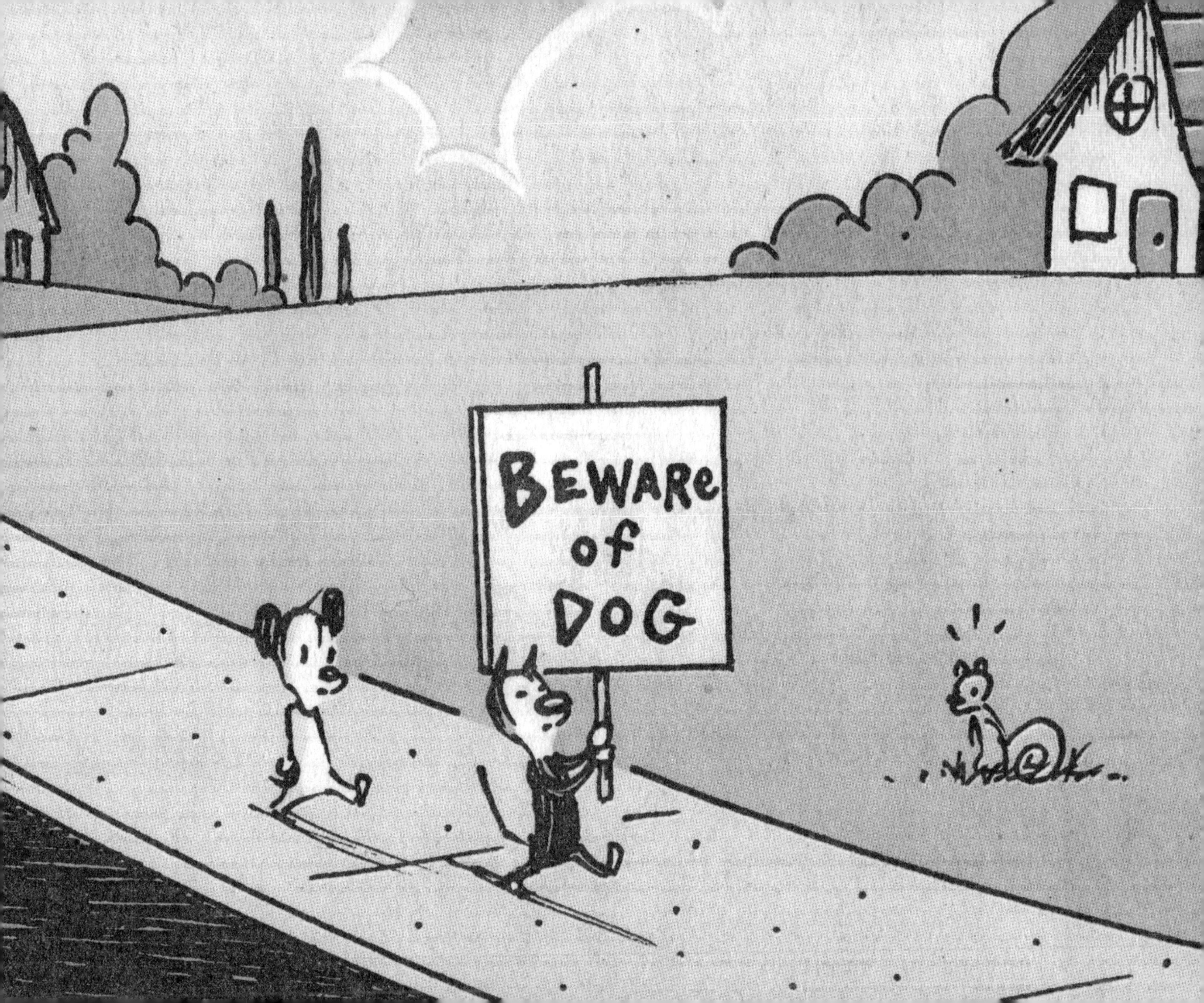
BEWARE
of
DOG

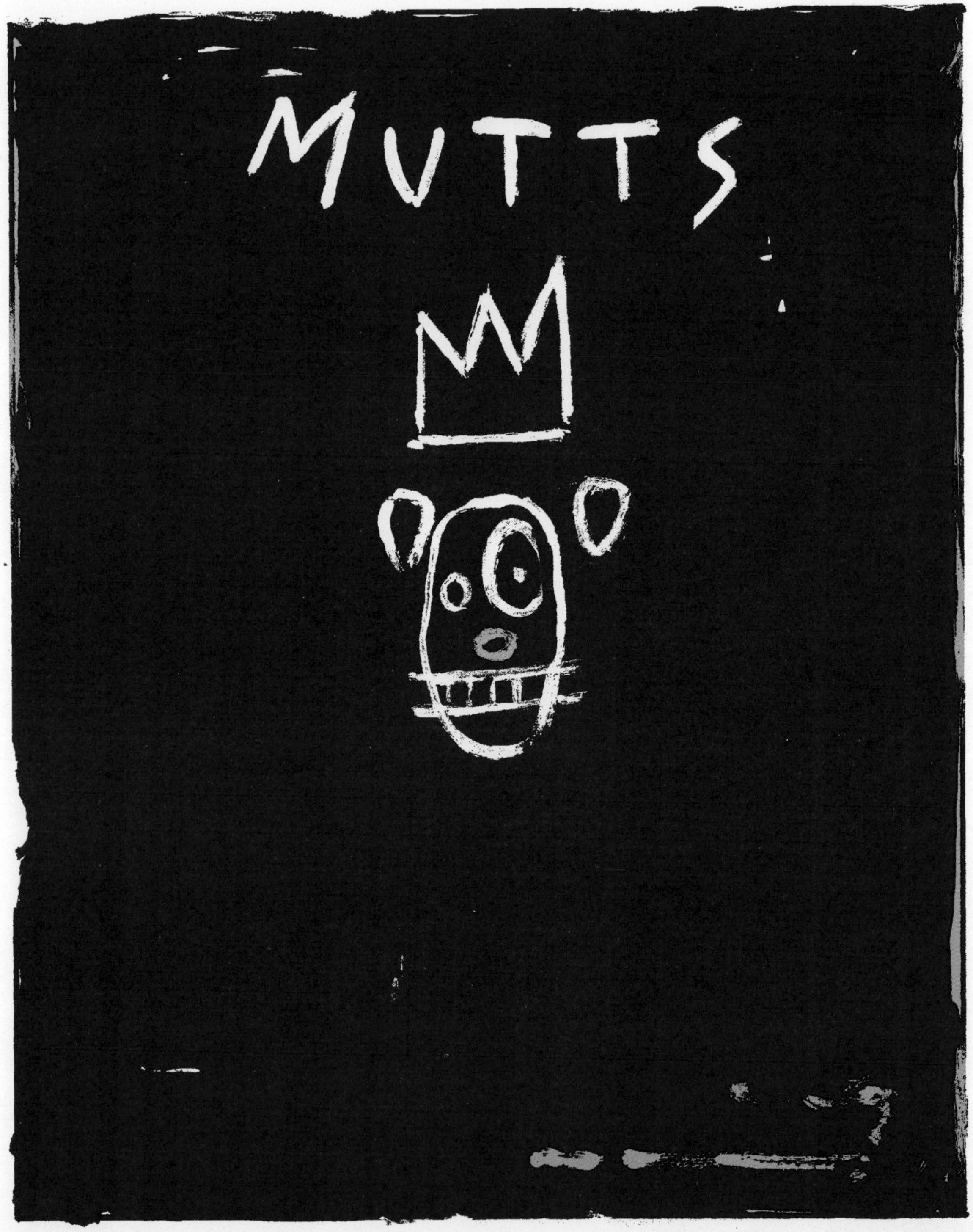
MUTTS

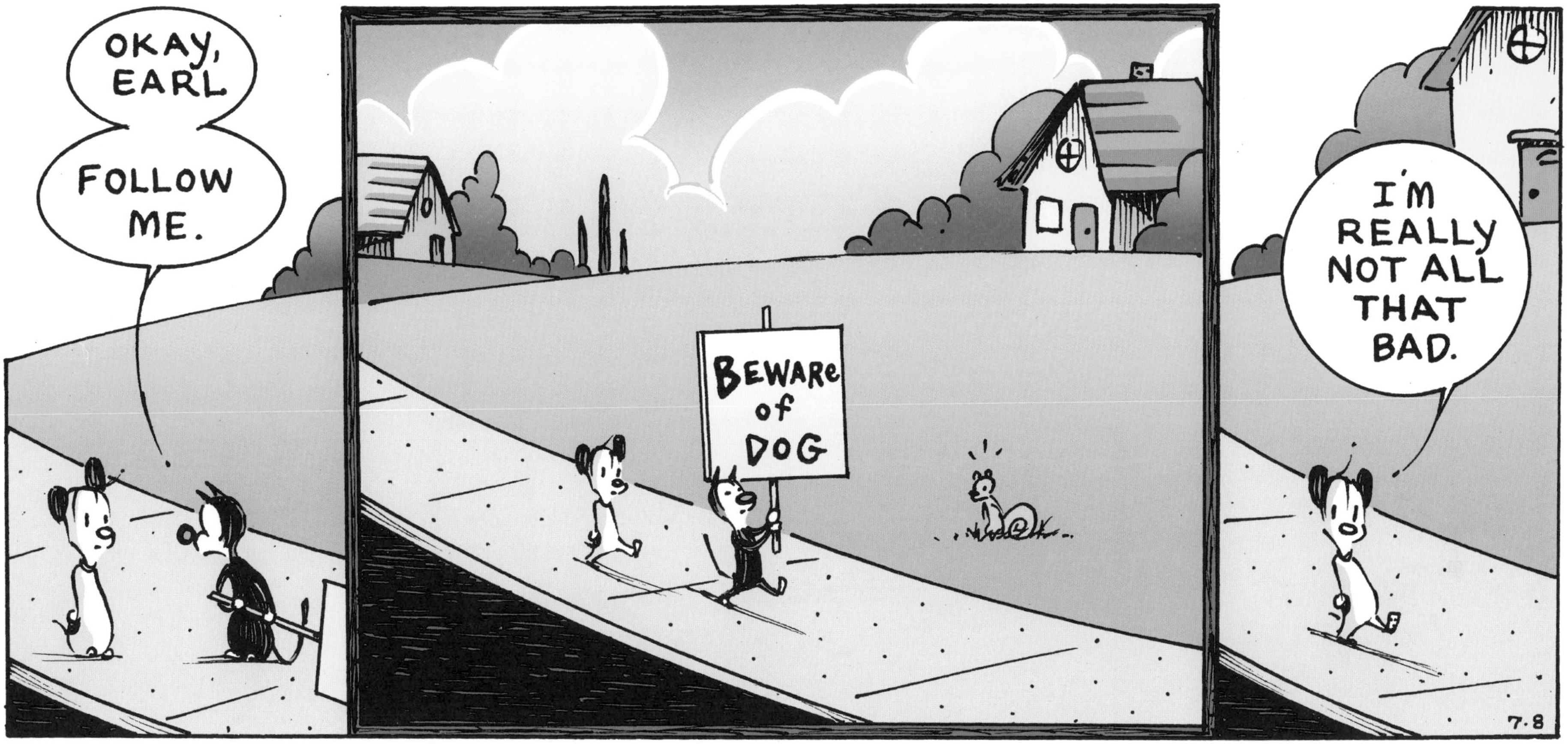
OKAY, EARL
FOLLOW ME.
BEWARE of DOG
I'M REALLY NOT ALL THAT BAD.
7·8

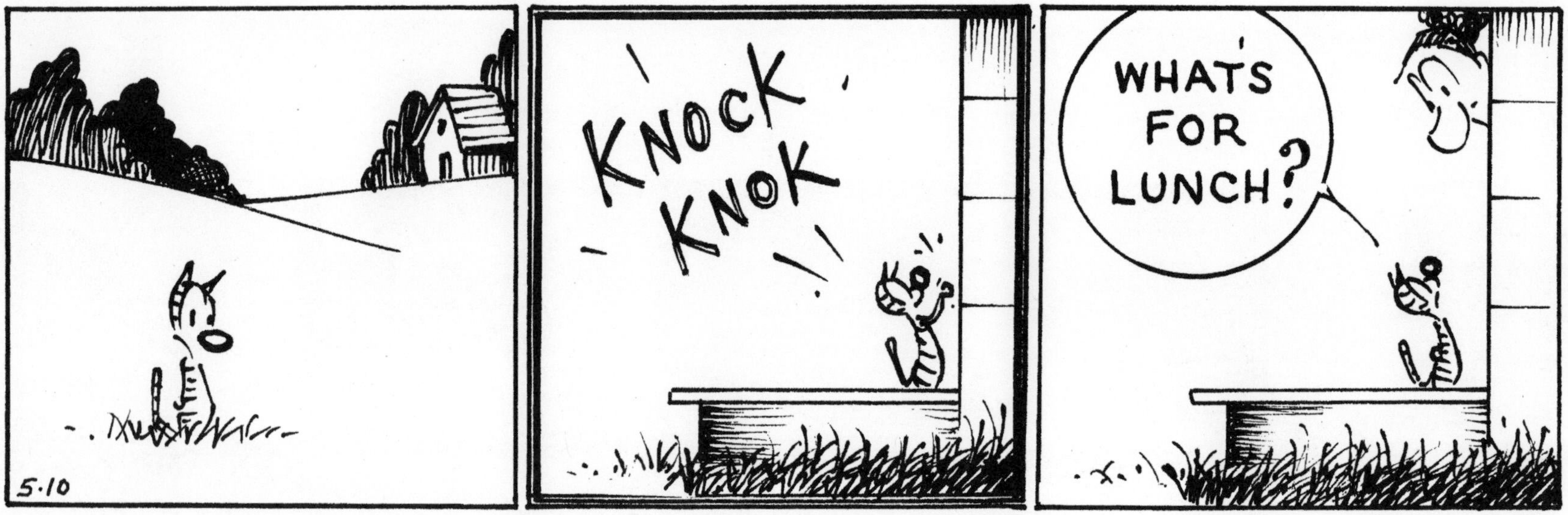
5·10
KNOCK KNOK
WHAT'S FOR LUNCH?

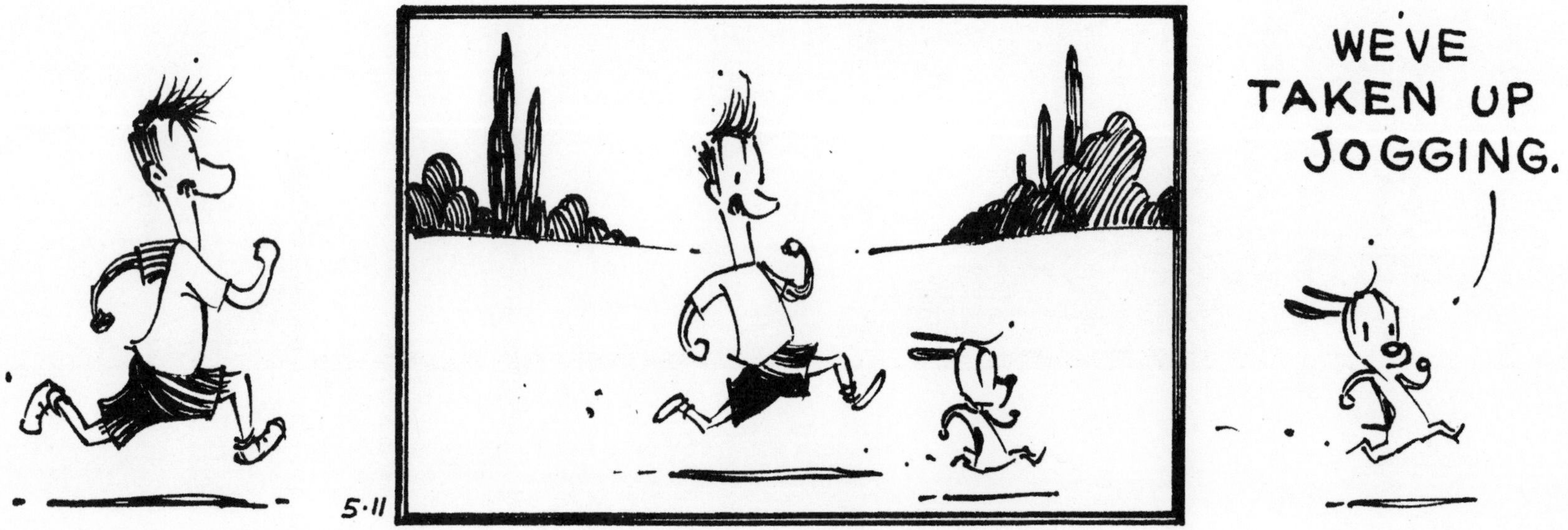
5·11
WE'VE TAKEN UP JOGGING.

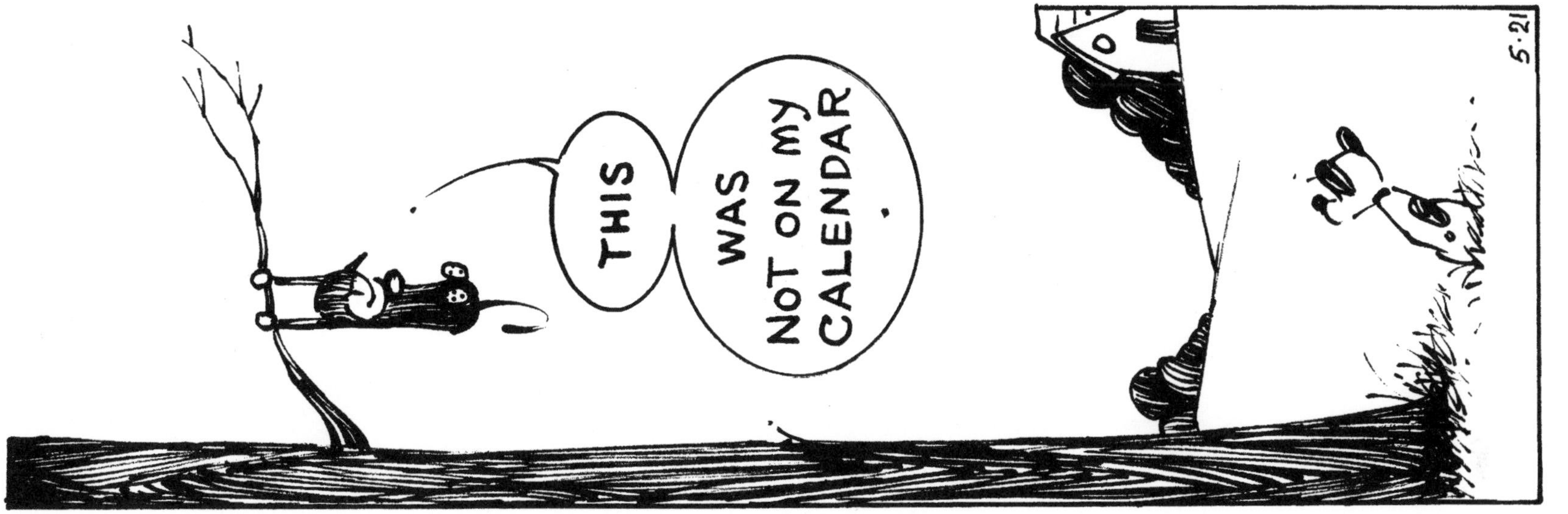
THIS
WAS NOT ON MY CALENDAR.
5·21

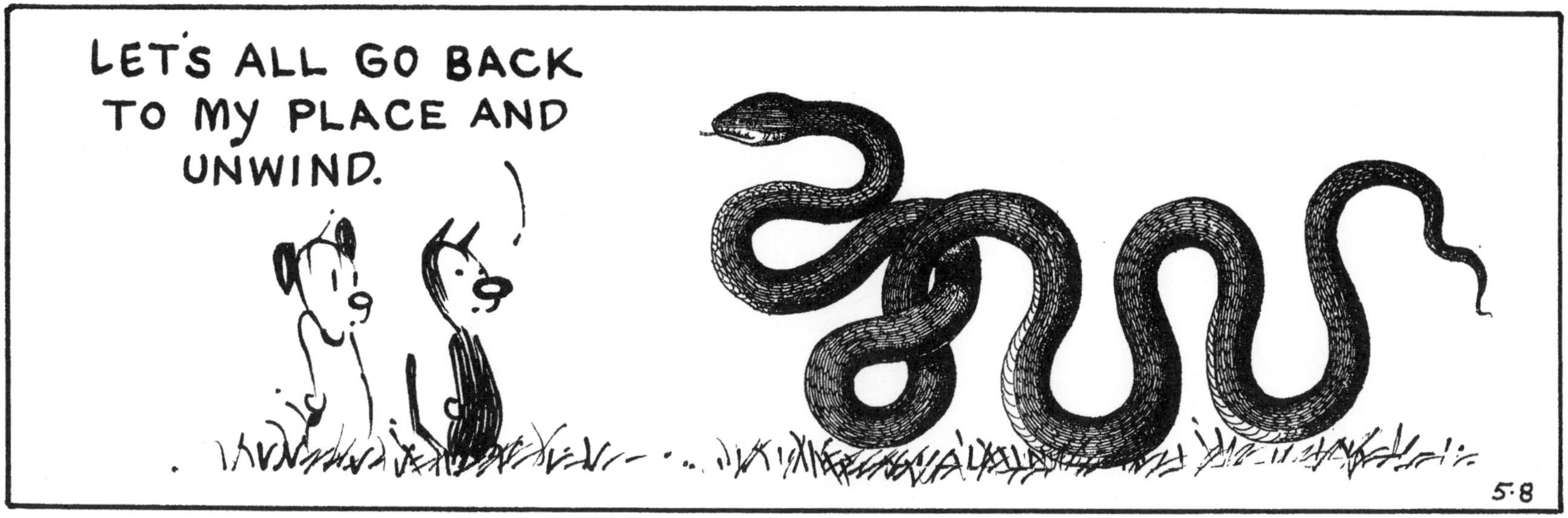
LET'S ALL GO BACK TO MY PLACE AND UNWIND.
5·8

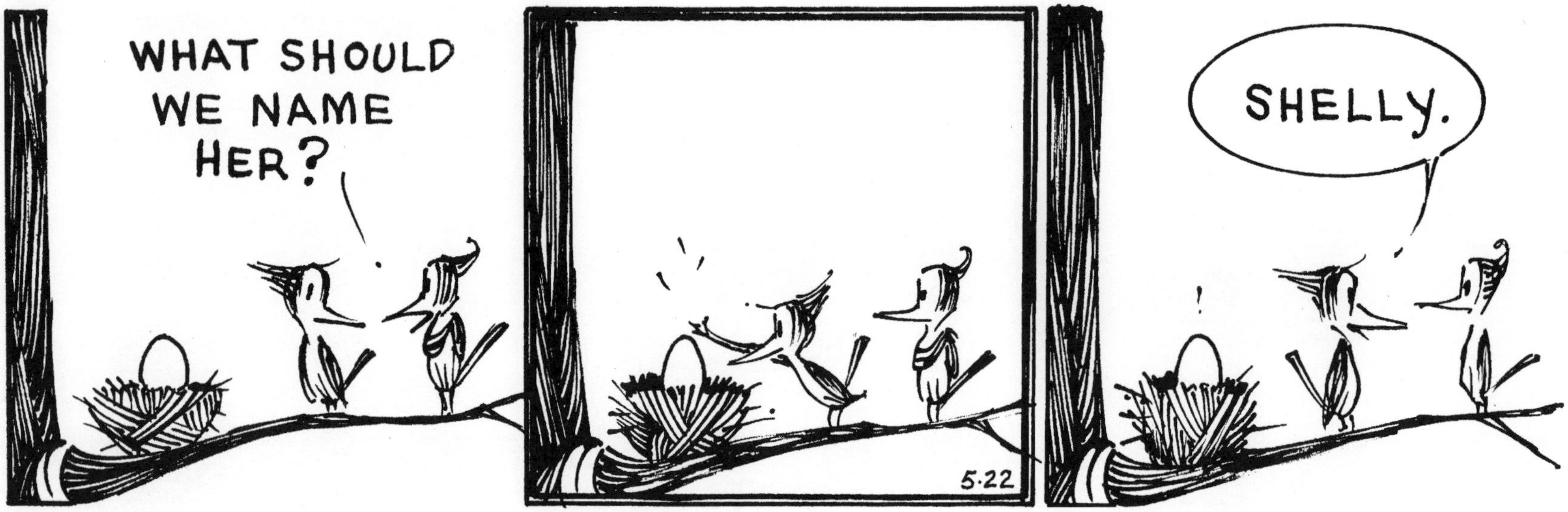
WHAT SHOULD WE NAME HER?
5·22
SHELLY.

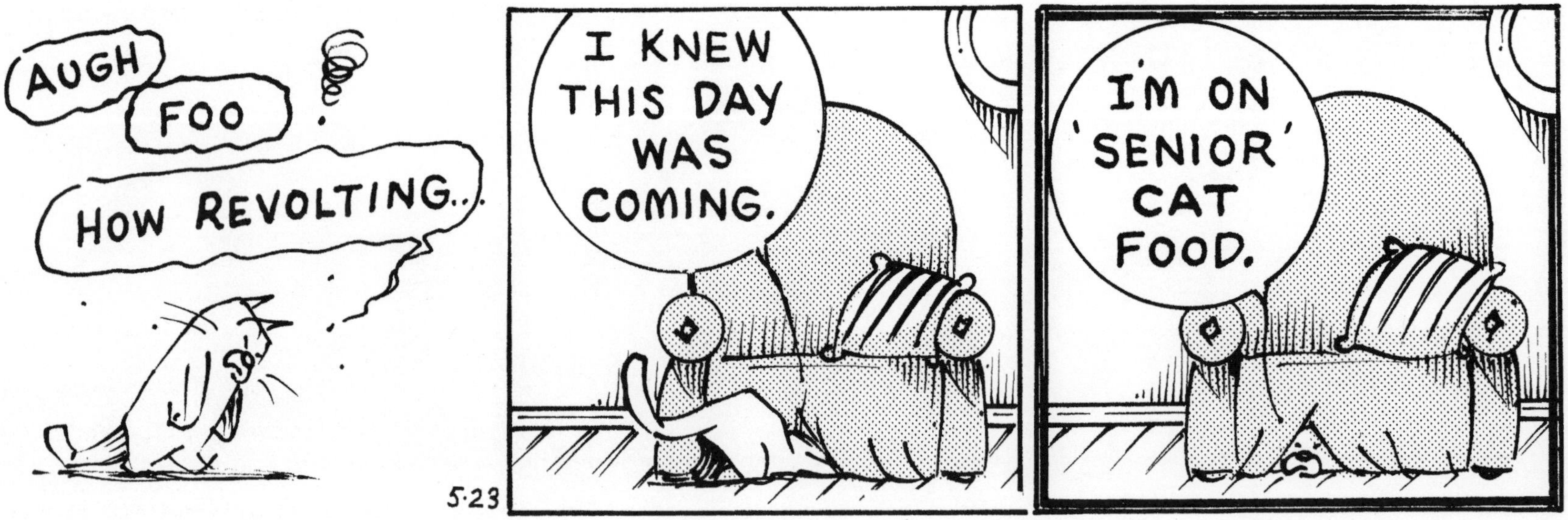
AUGH
FOO
HOW REVOLTING..
5·23
I KNEW THIS DAY WAS COMING.
I'M ON 'SENIOR' CAT FOOD.

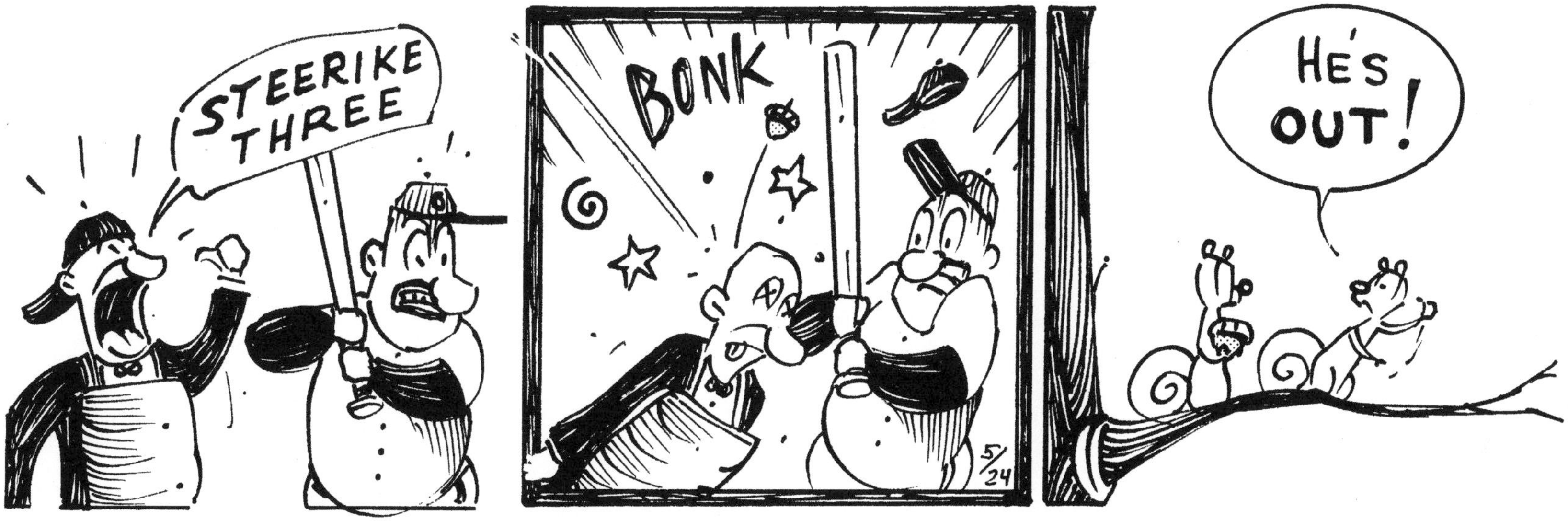
STEERIKE THREE
BONK
5/24
HE'S OUT!

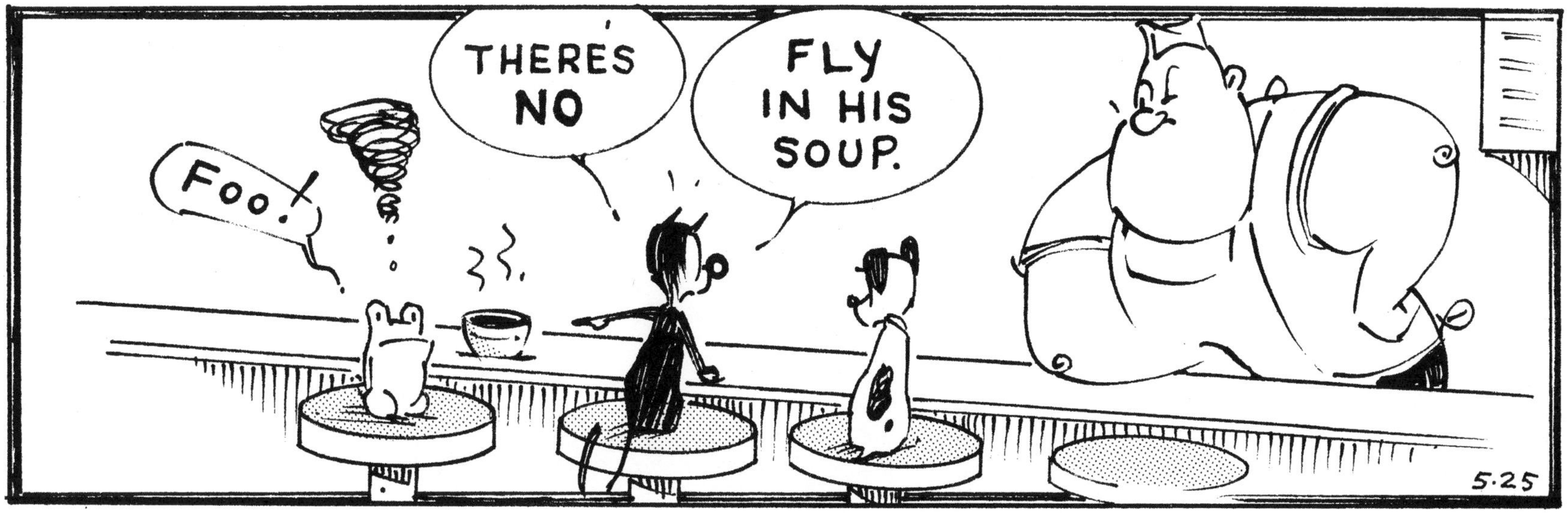
FOO!
THERES NO
FLY IN HIS SOUP.
5.25

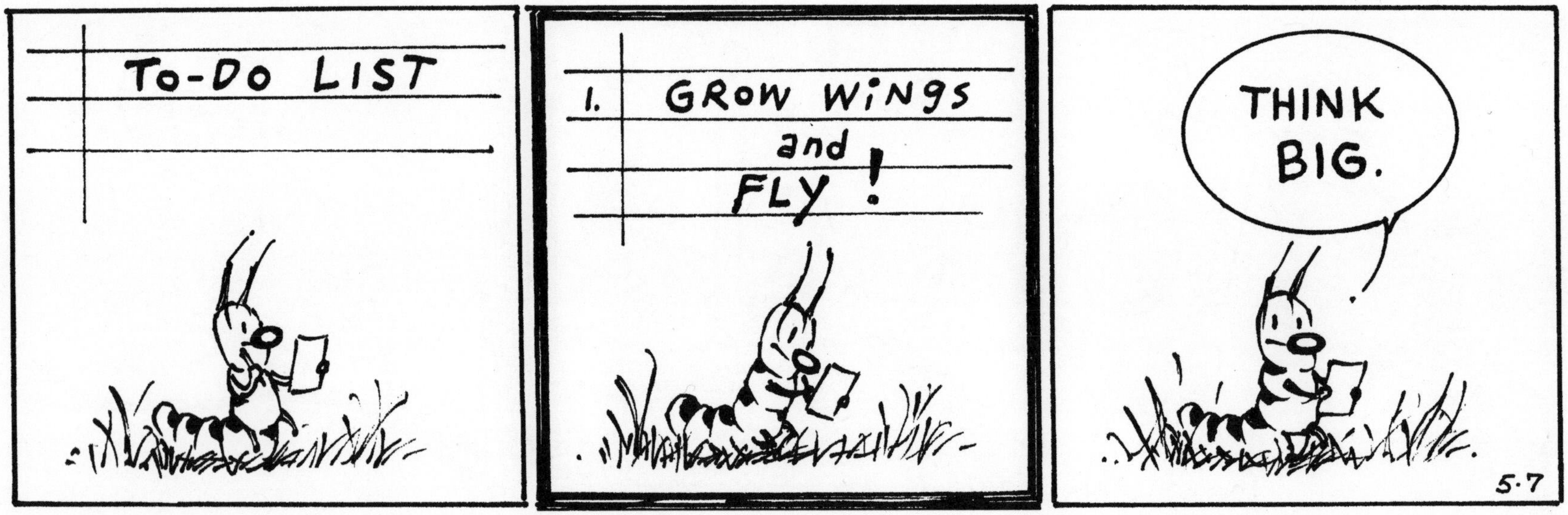

TO-DO LIST
1. GROW WINGS and FLY!
THINK BIG.
5·7

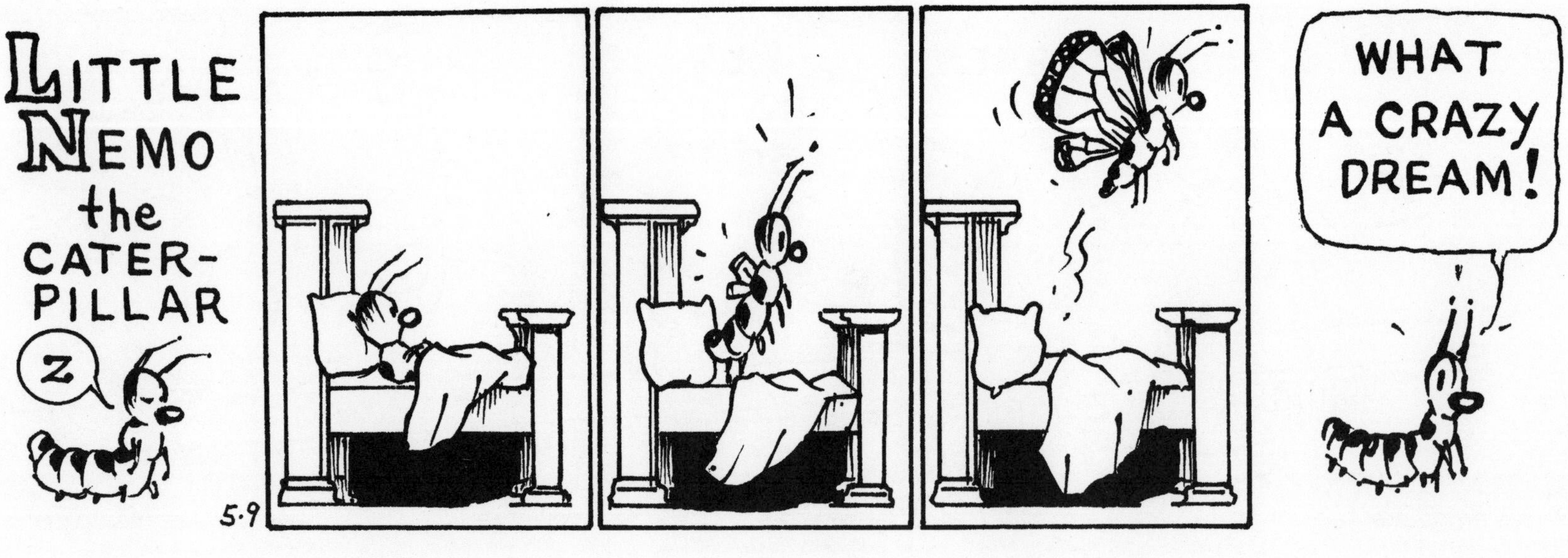

LITTLE NEMO the CATER-PILLAR
Z
5·9
WHAT A CRAZY DREAM!

5·12
THINGS HAPPEN.

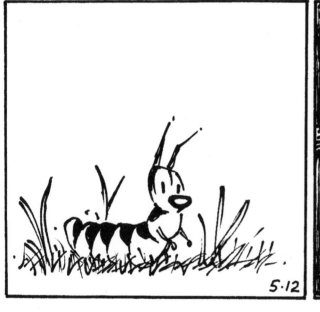

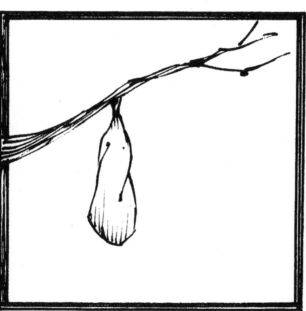

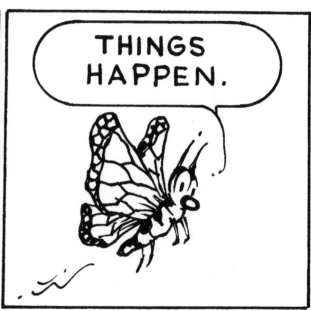

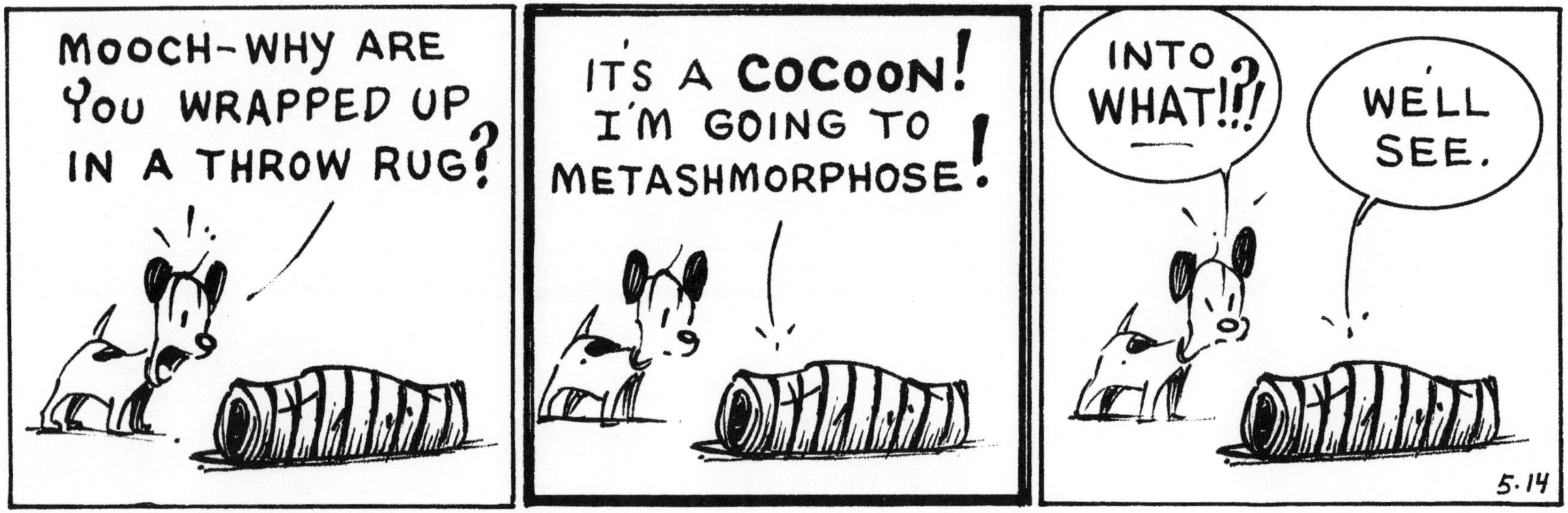
MOOCH-WHY ARE YOU WRAPPED UP IN A THROW RUG?
IT'S A COCOON! I'M GOING TO METASHMORPHOSE!
INTO WHAT!?!
WE'LL SEE.
5.14

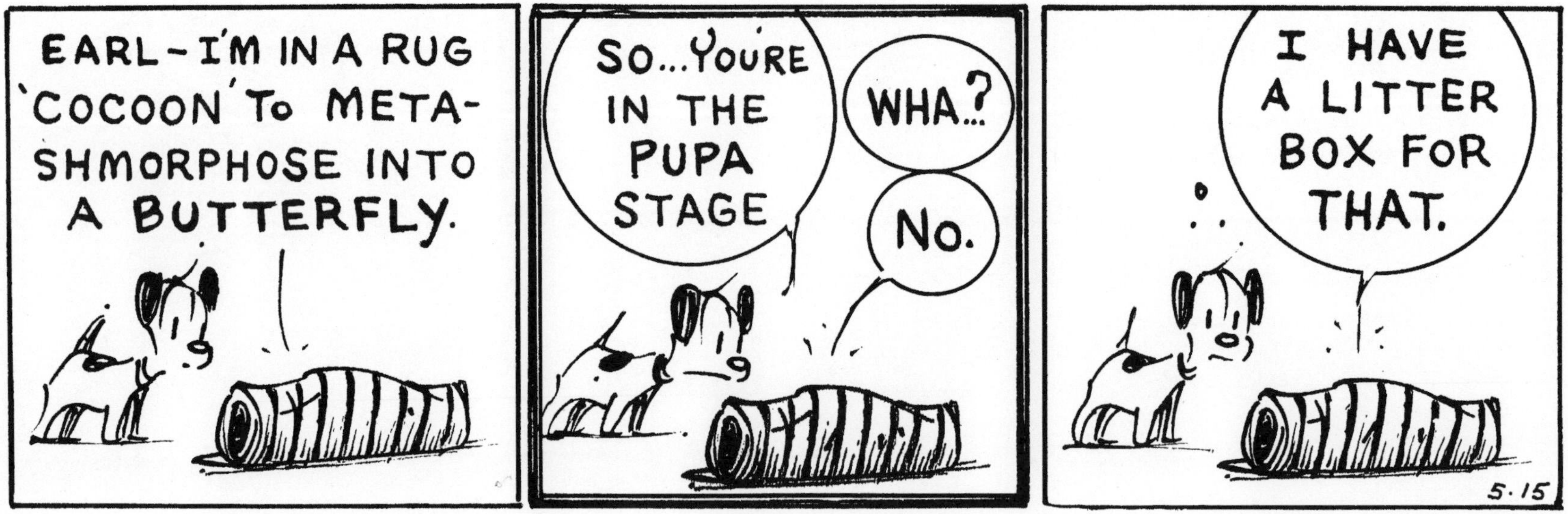
EARL-I'M IN A RUG 'COCOON' TO META-SHMORPHOSE INTO A BUTTERFLY.
SO...YOU'RE IN THE PUPA STAGE
WHA..?
NO.
I HAVE A LITTER BOX FOR THAT.
5.15

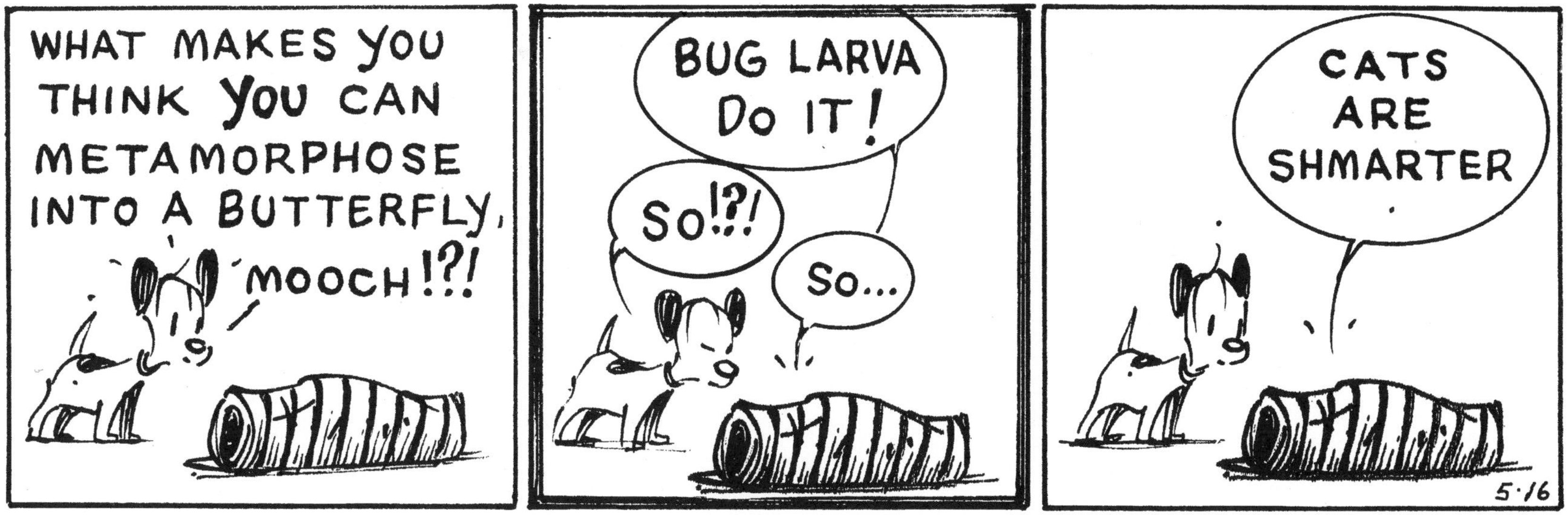
WHAT MAKES YOU THINK YOU CAN METAMORPHOSE INTO A BUTTERFLY, MOOCH!?!
BUG LARVA DO IT!
SO!?!
SO...
CATS ARE SHMARTER
5·16

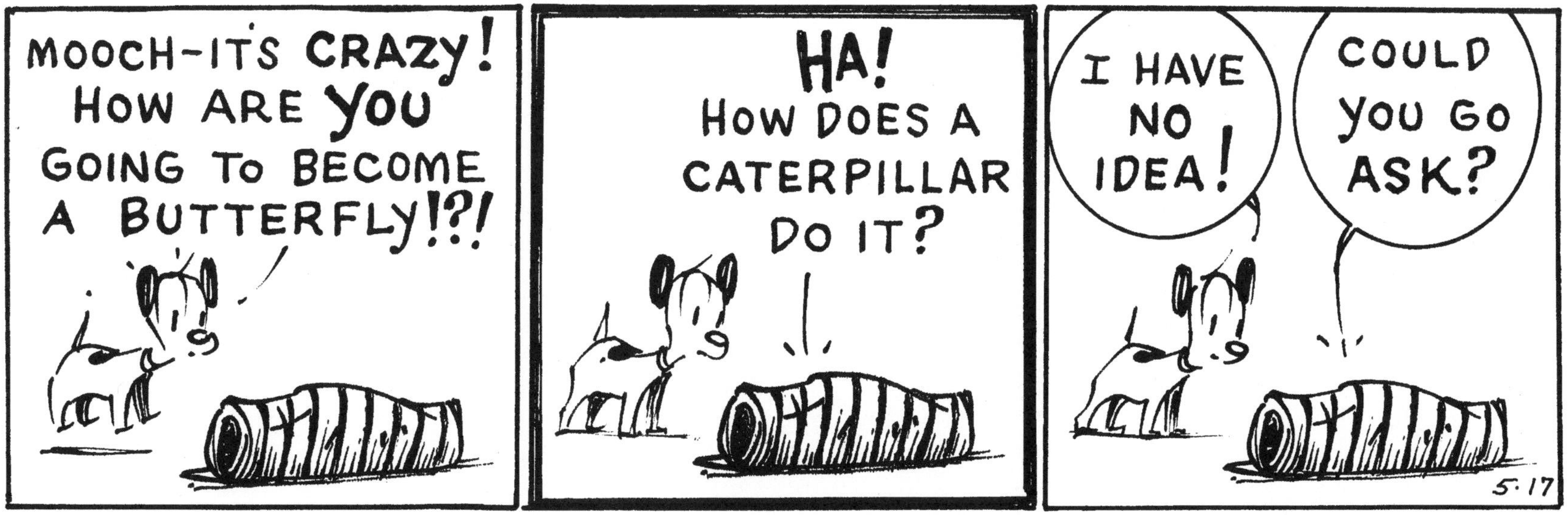
MOOCH-IT'S CRAZY! HOW ARE YOU GOING TO BECOME A BUTTERFLY!?!
HA! HOW DOES A CATERPILLAR DO IT?
I HAVE NO IDEA!
COULD YOU GO ASK?
5·17

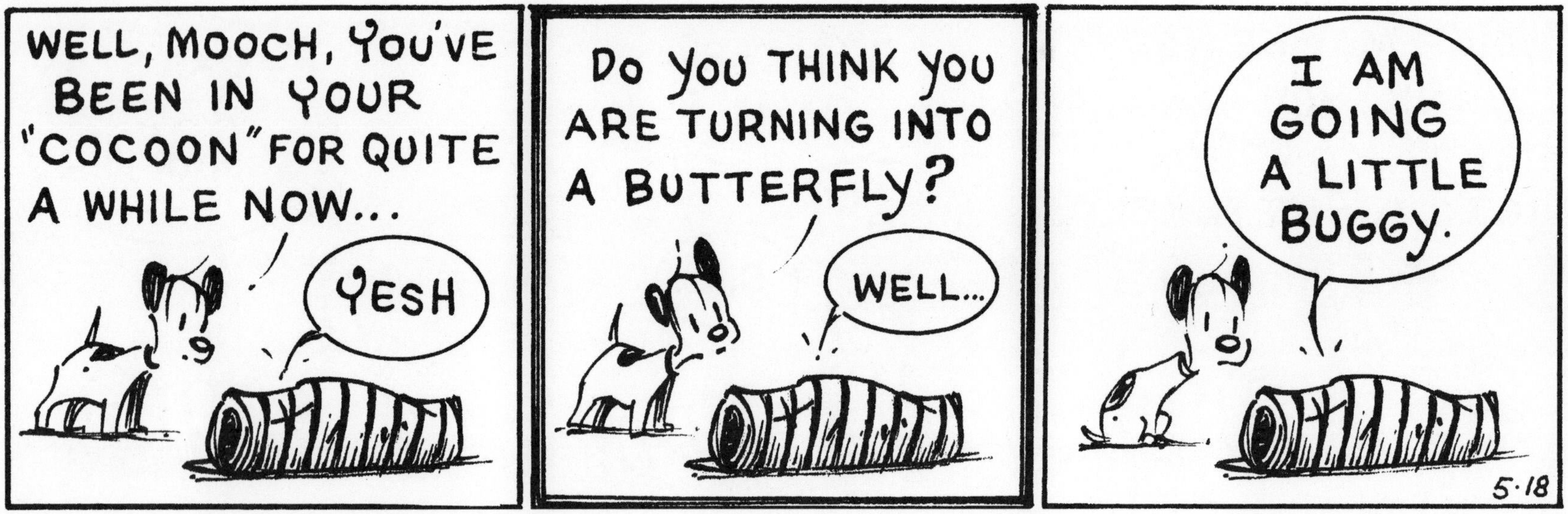
WELL, MOOCH, YOU'VE BEEN IN YOUR "COCOON" FOR QUITE A WHILE NOW...
YESH
DO YOU THINK YOU ARE TURNING INTO A BUTTERFLY?
WELL...
I AM GOING A LITTLE BUGGY.
5·18

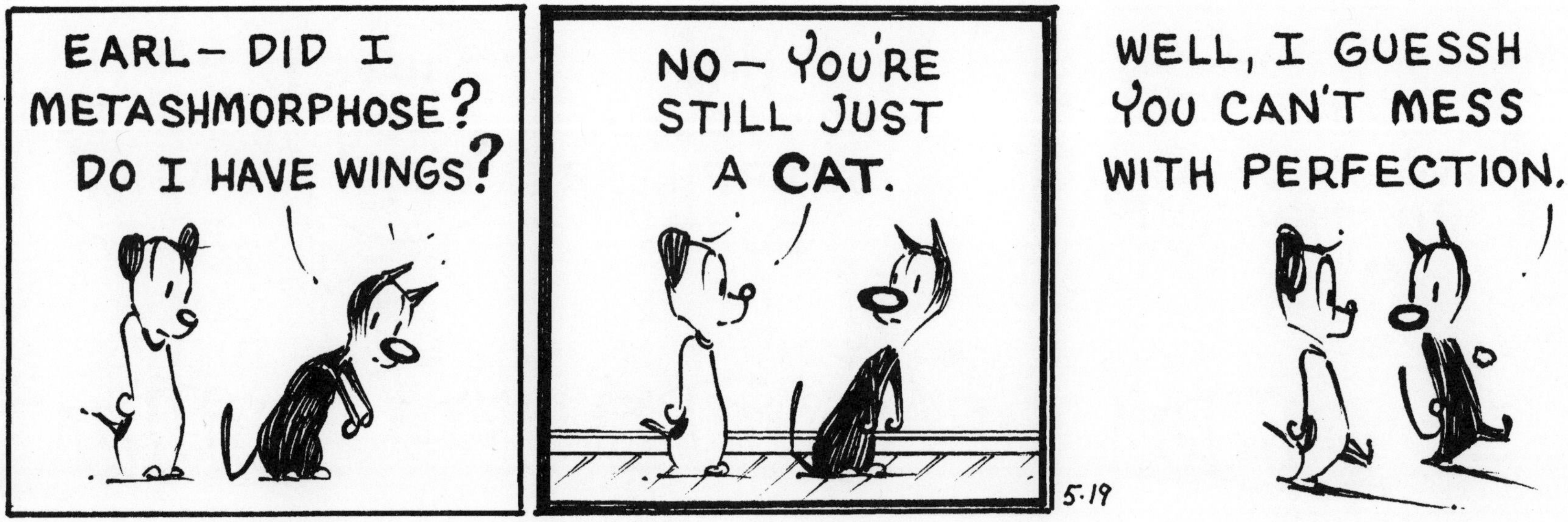
EARL- DID I METASHMORPHOSE? DO I HAVE WINGS?
NO- YOU'RE STILL JUST A CAT.
5·19
WELL, I GUESSH YOU CAN'T MESS WITH PERFECTION.

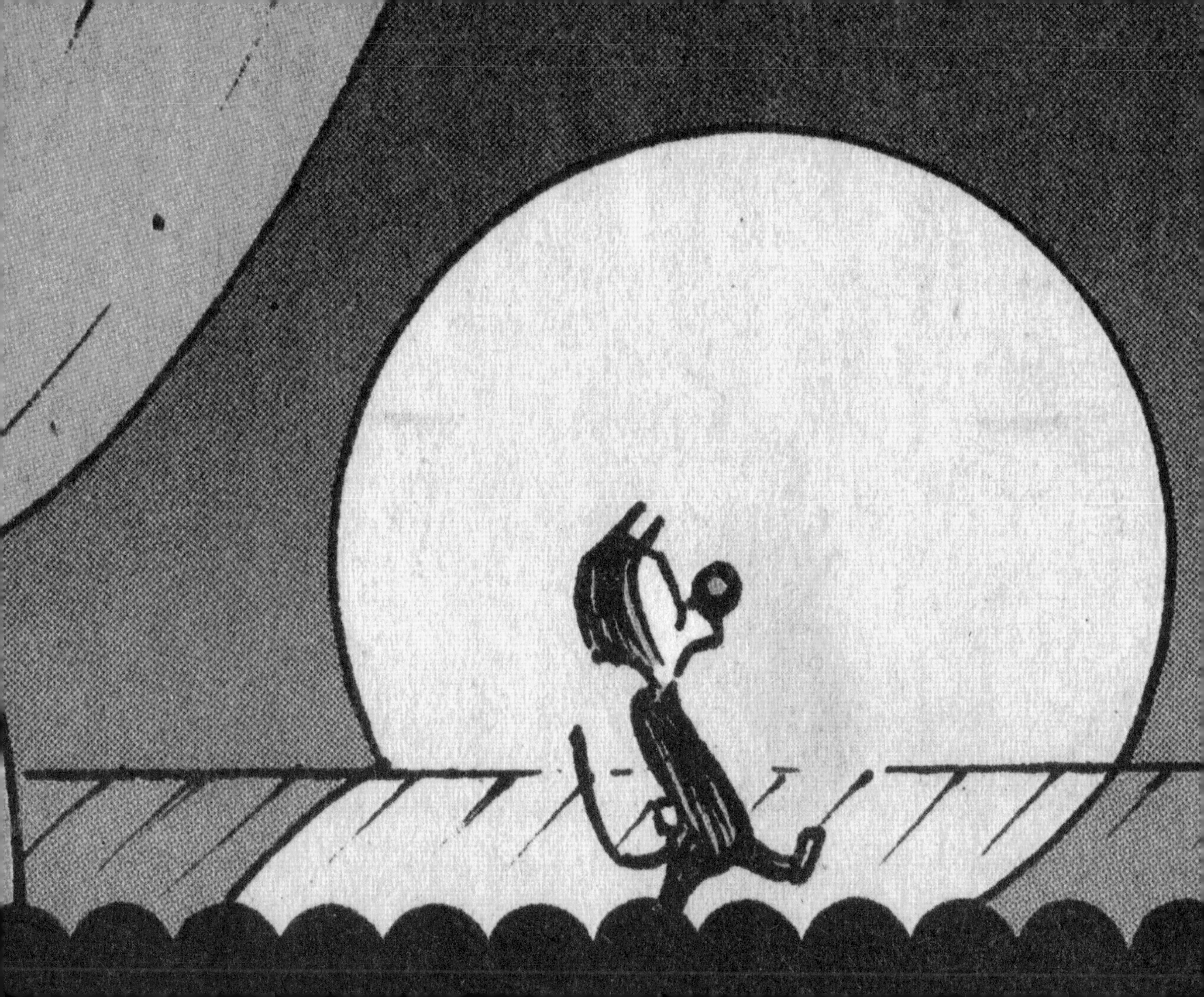

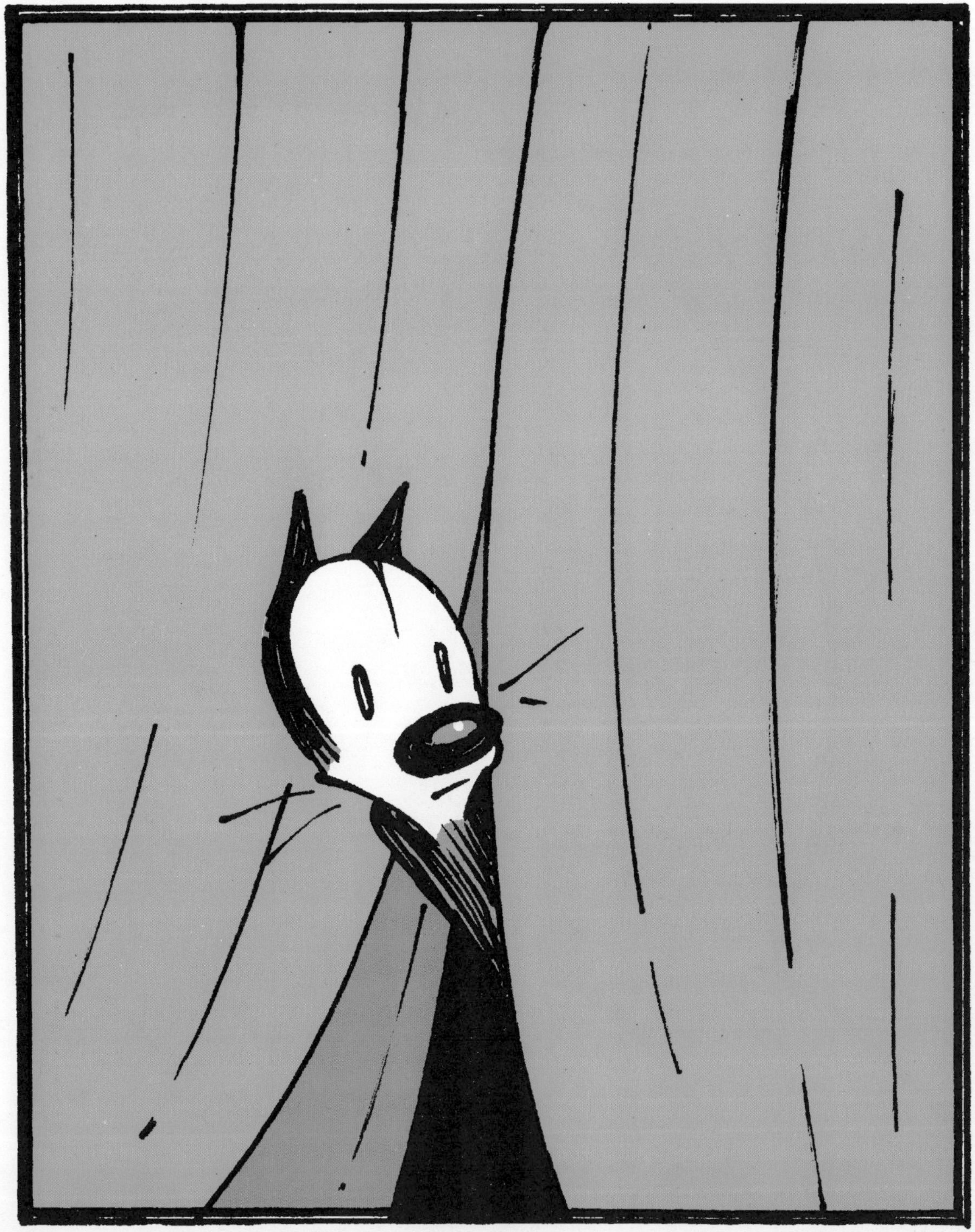

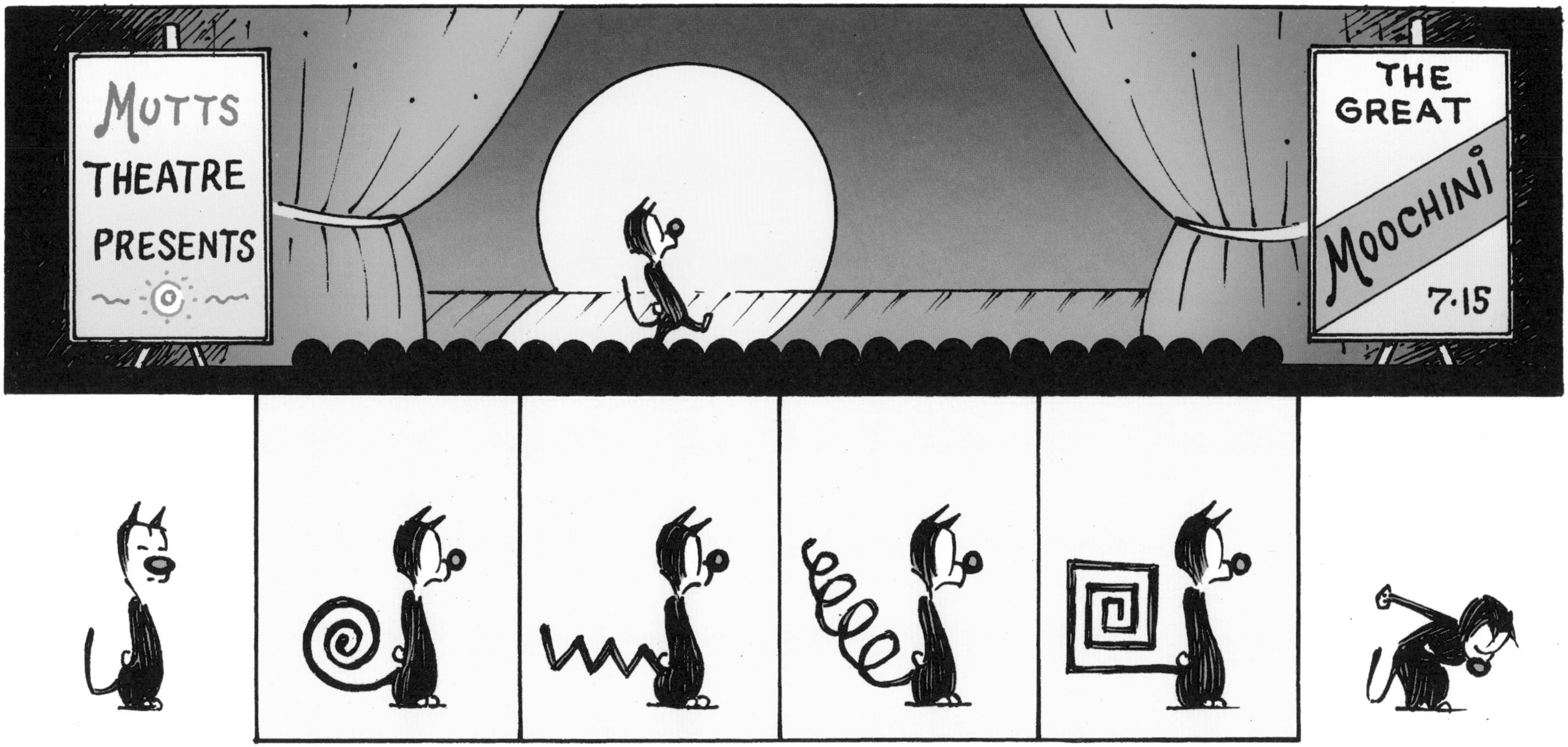
MUTTS
THEATRE
PRESENTS
THE GREAT
MOOCHINI
7·15

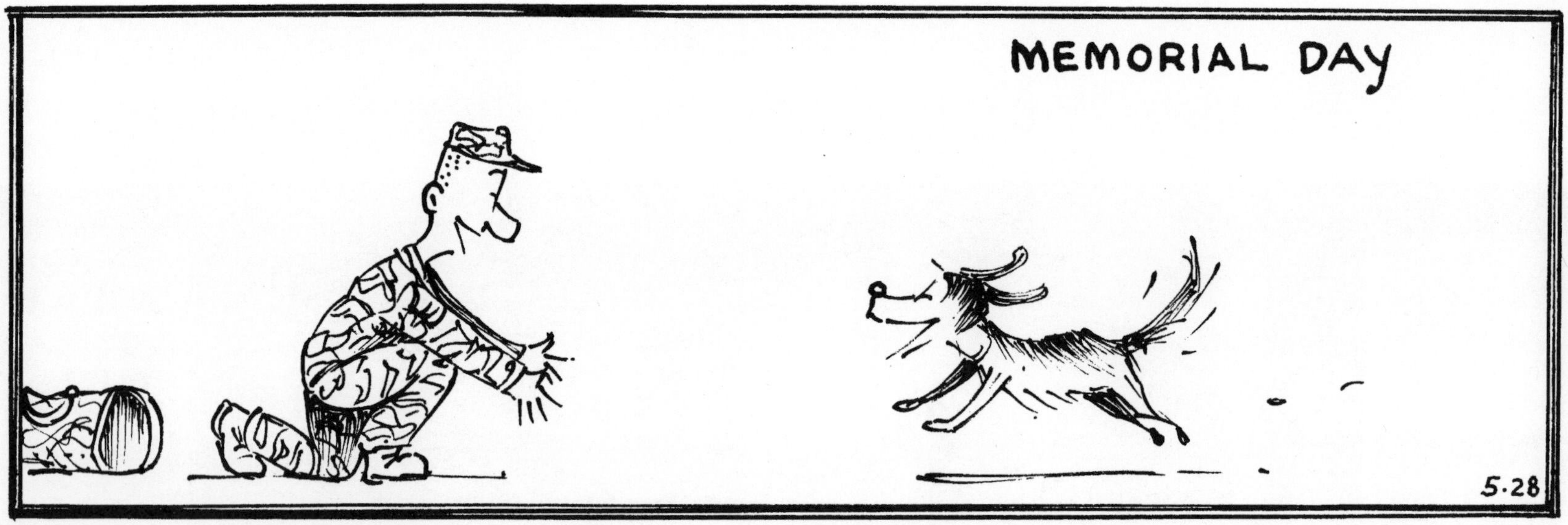
MEMORIAL DAY
5·28

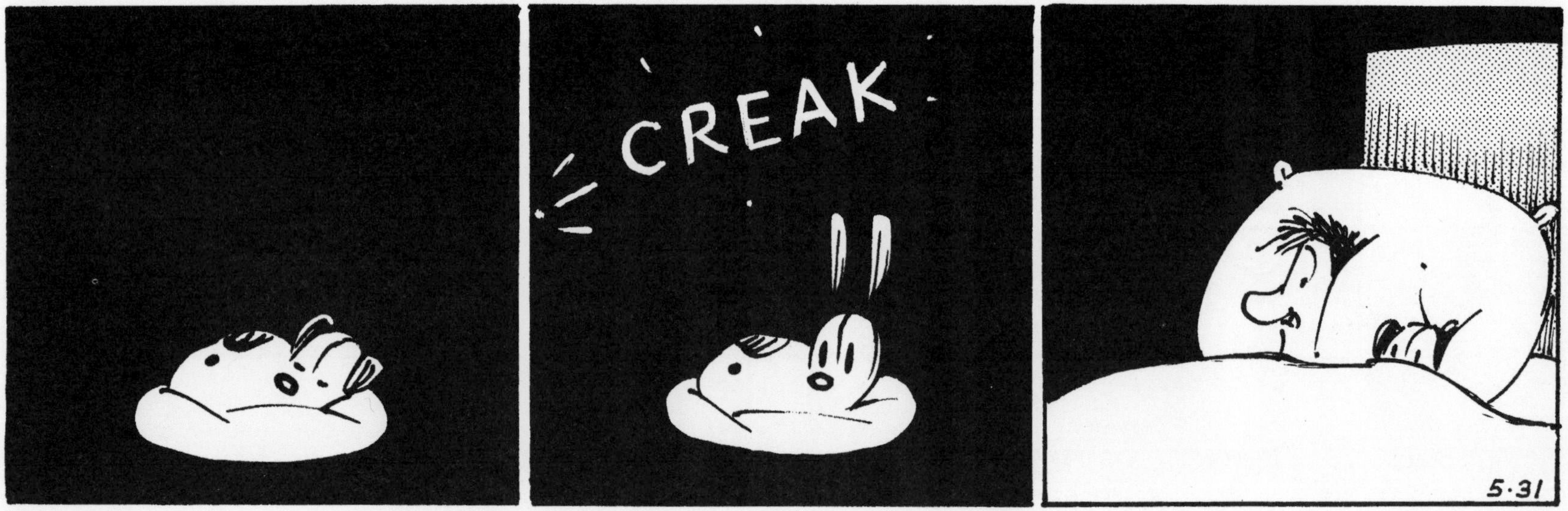
CREAK
5·31

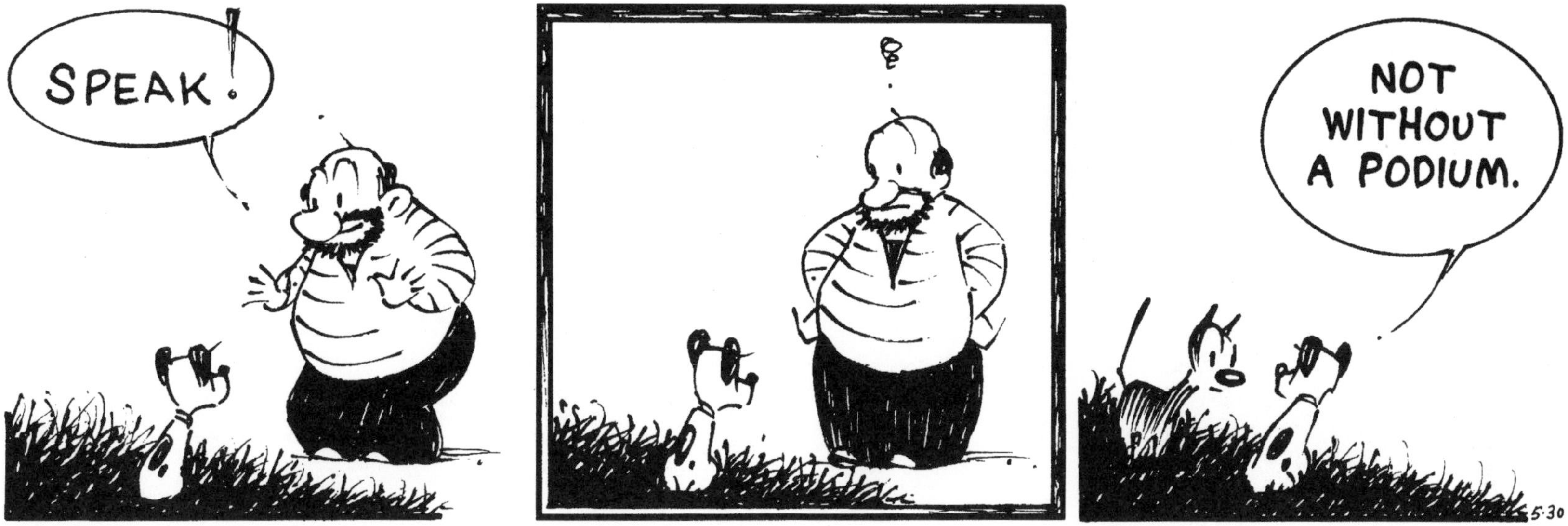
SPEAK!
NOT WITHOUT A PODIUM.
5·30

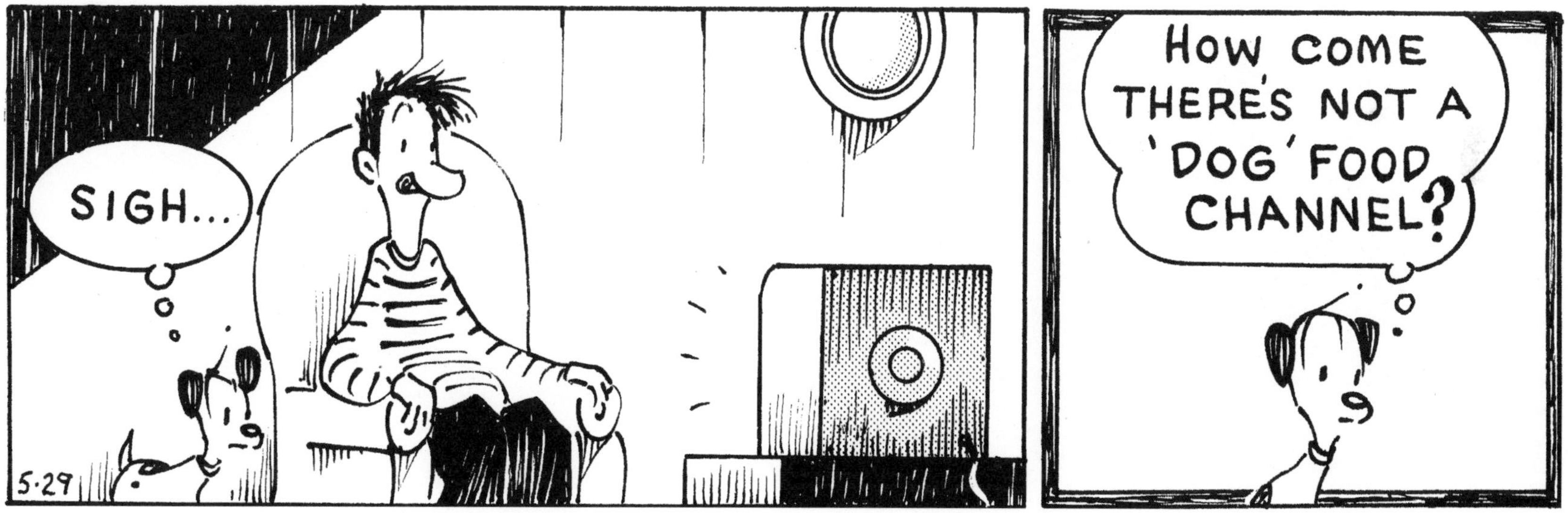
5·29
SIGH...
HOW COME THERE'S NOT A 'DOG' FOOD CHANNEL?

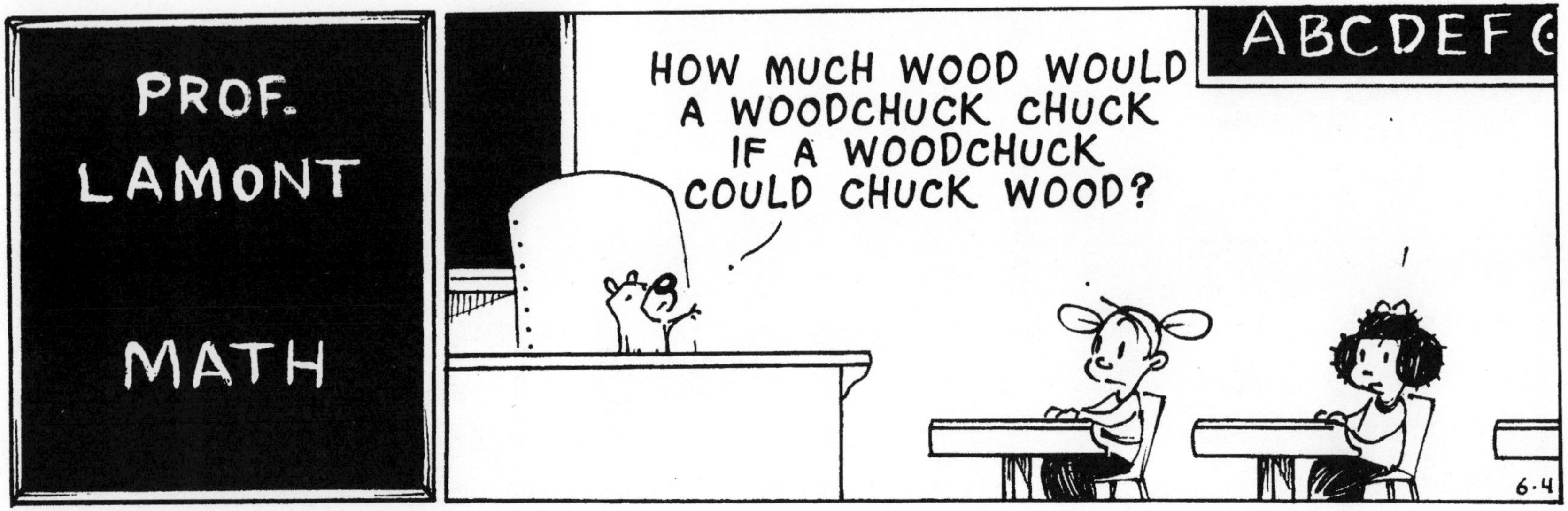
PROF. LAMONT
MATH
HOW MUCH WOOD WOULD A WOODCHUCK CHUCK IF A WOODCHUCK COULD CHUCK WOOD?
ABCDEFG
6·4

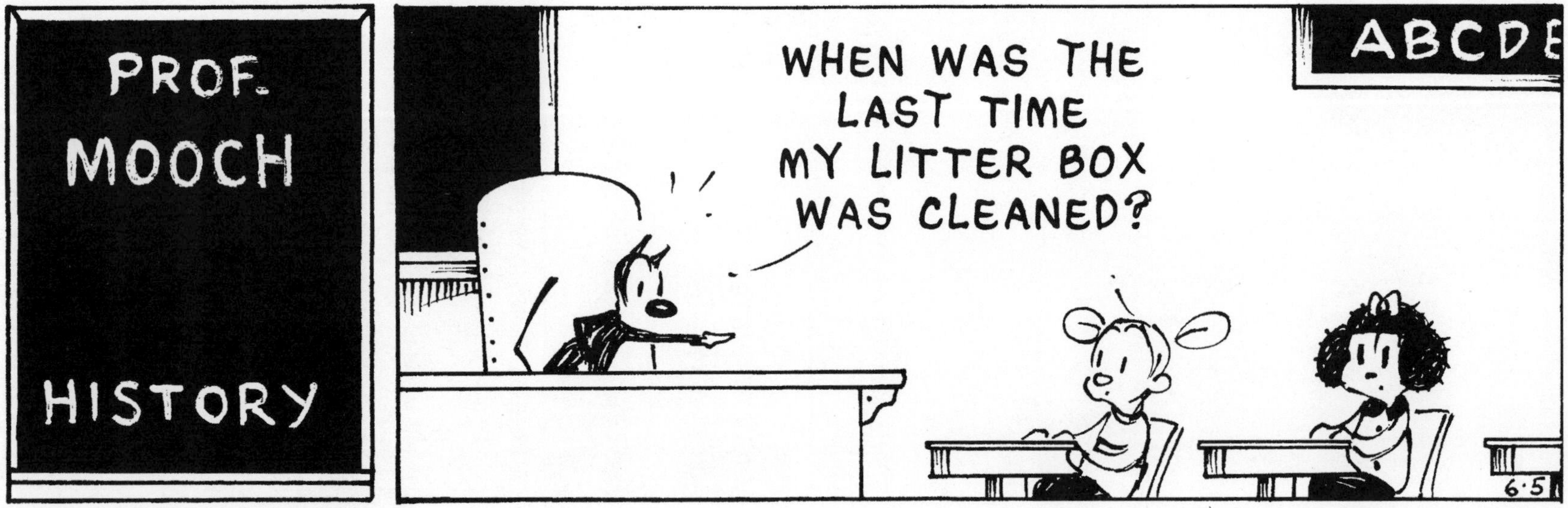
PROF. MOOCH
HISTORY
WHEN WAS THE LAST TIME MY LITTER BOX WAS CLEANED?
ABCDE
6·5

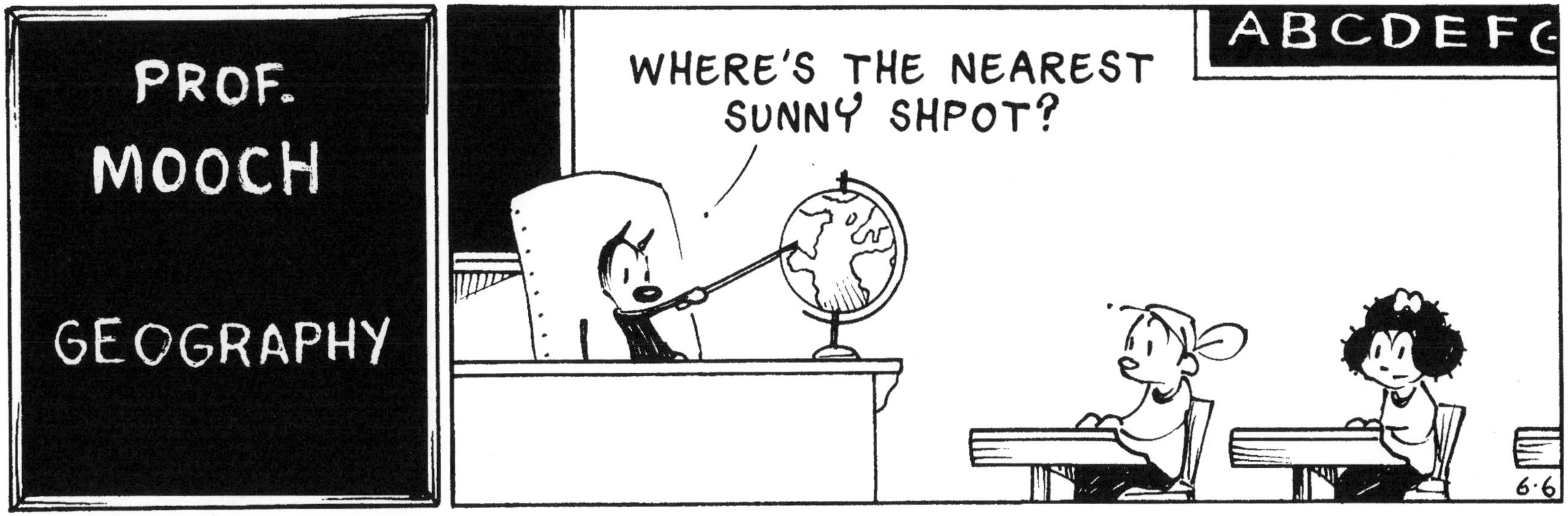
PROF. MOOCH
GEOGRAPHY
ABCDEFG
WHERE'S THE NEAREST SUNNY SHPOT?
6·6

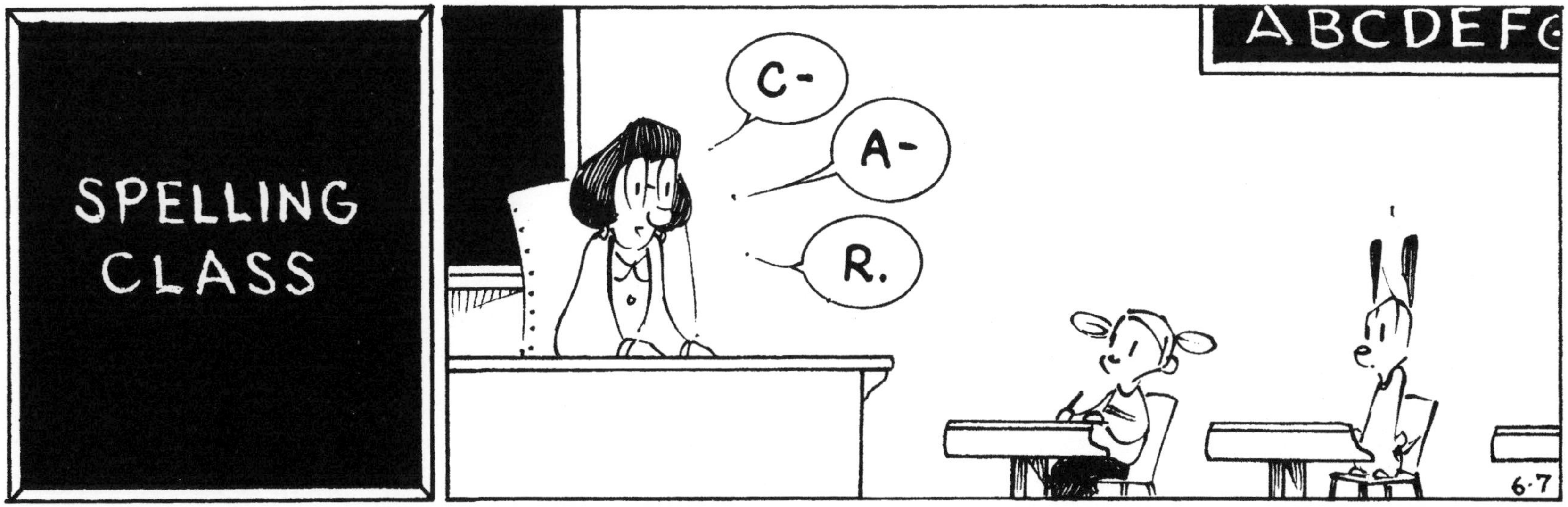
SPELLING CLASS
ABCDEFG
C-
A-
R.
6·7

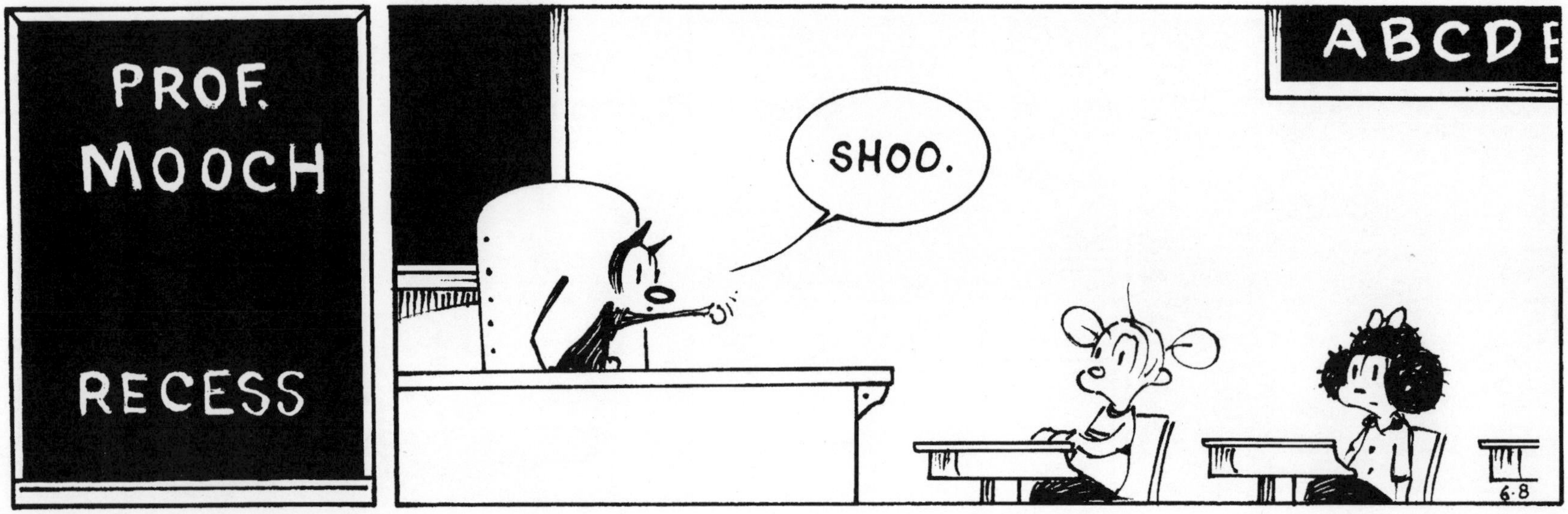
PROF. MOOCH
RECESS
ABCDE
SHOO.
6·8

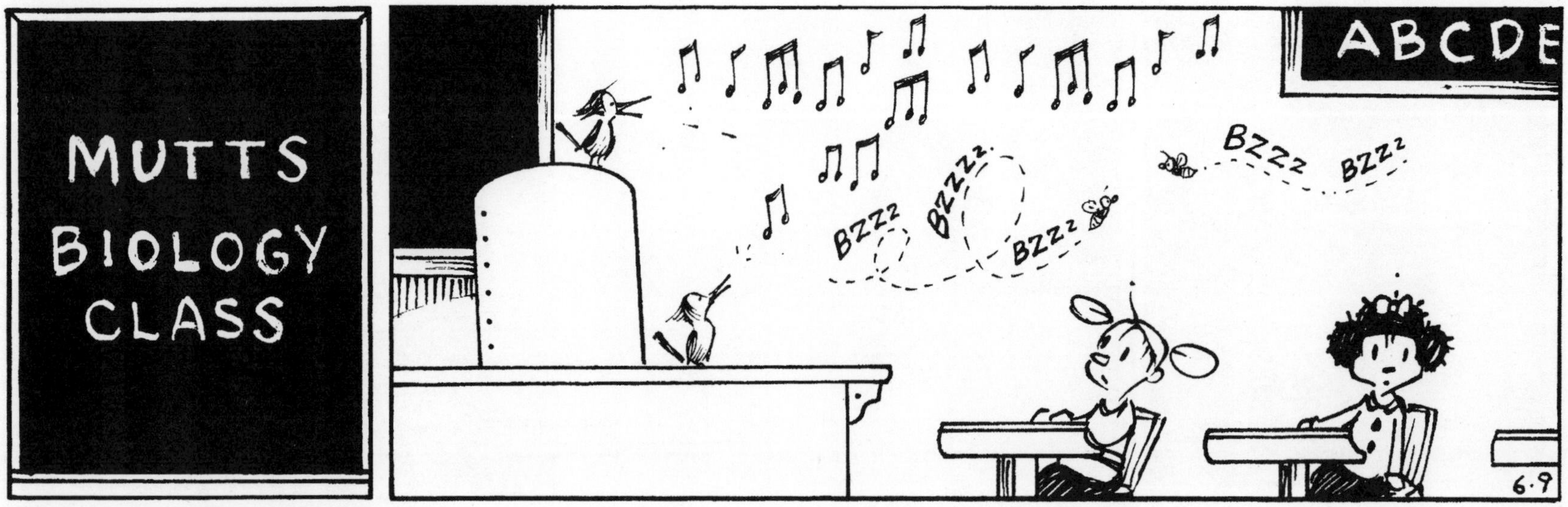
MUTTS BIOLOGY CLASS
ABCDE
BZZZ
BZZZZZ
BZZZ
BZZZ
BZZZ
6·9

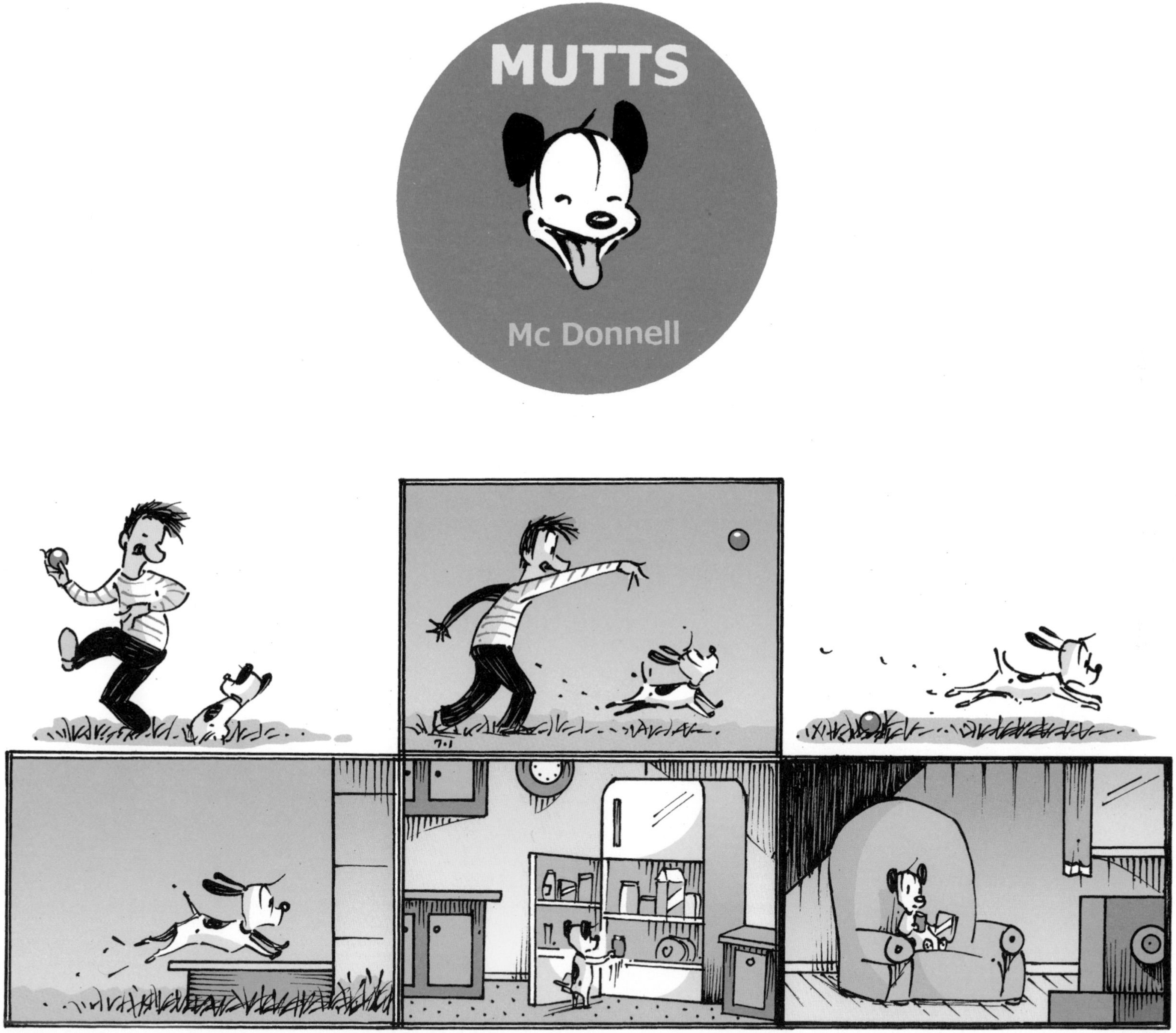
MUTTS
Mc Donnell
7·1

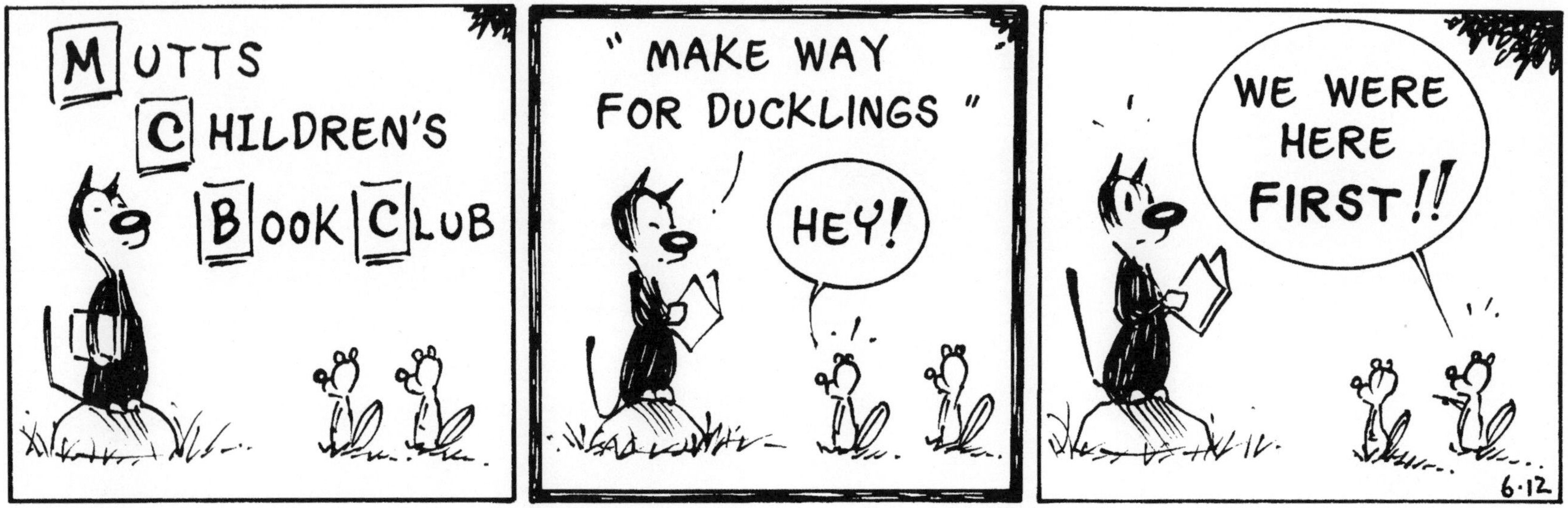
MUTTS CHILDREN'S BOOK CLUB
" MAKE WAY FOR DUCKLINGS "
HEY!
WE WERE HERE FIRST!!
6·12

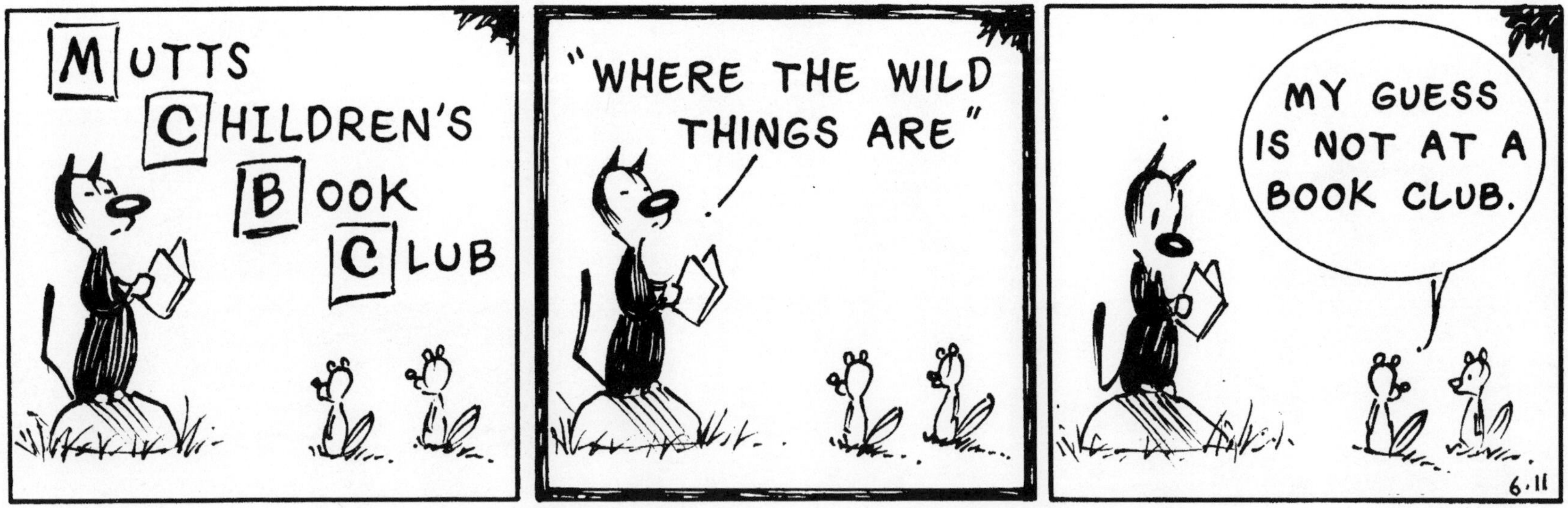
MUTTS CHILDREN'S BOOK CLUB
"WHERE THE WILD THINGS ARE"
MY GUESS IS NOT AT A BOOK CLUB.
6·11

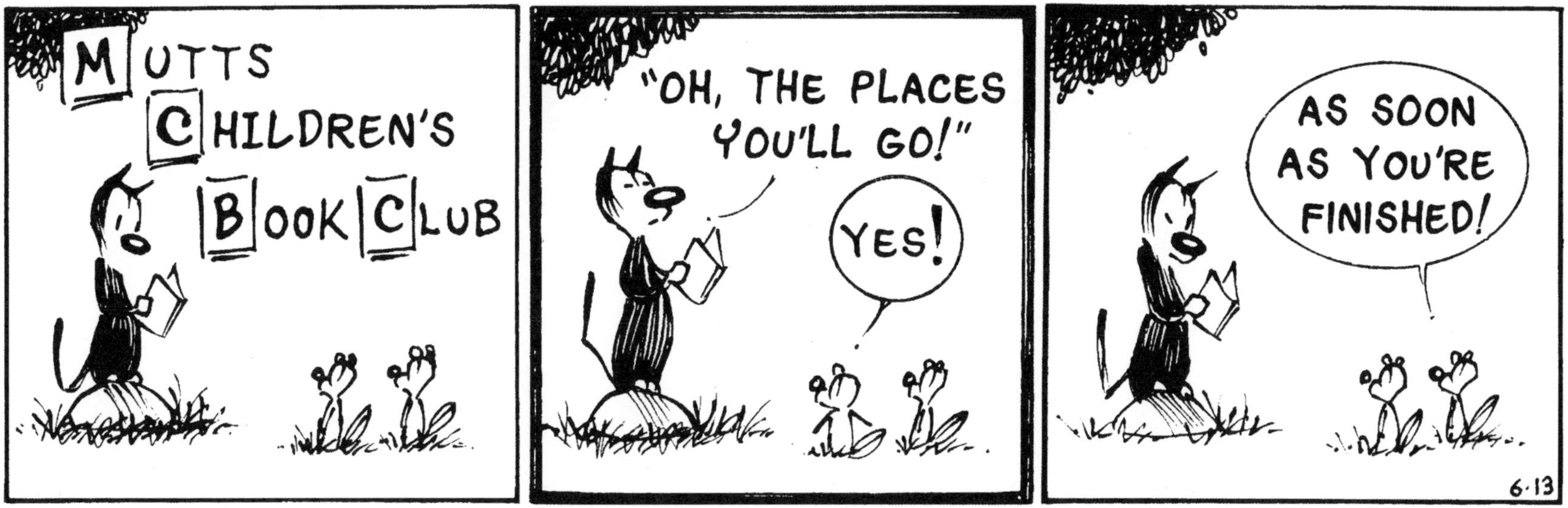
MUTTS CHILDREN'S BOOK CLUB
"OH, THE PLACES YOU'LL GO!"
YES!
AS SOON AS YOU'RE FINISHED!
6·13

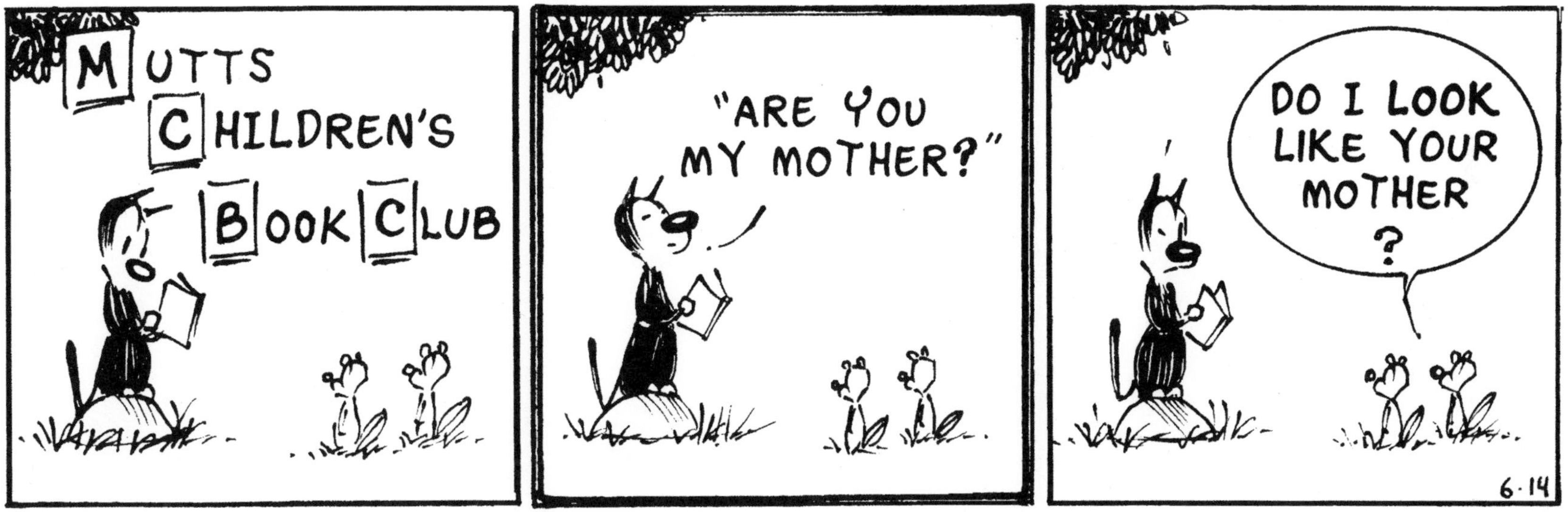
MUTTS CHILDREN'S BOOK CLUB
"ARE YOU MY MOTHER?"
DO I LOOK LIKE YOUR MOTHER ?
6·14

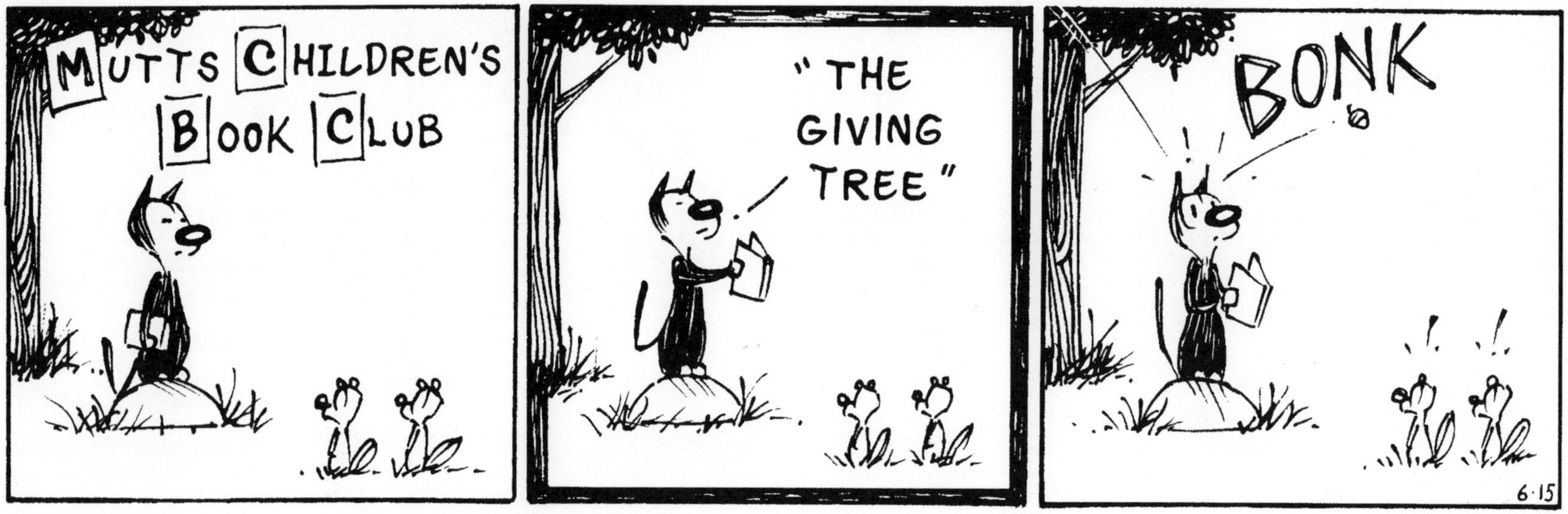
MUTTS CHILDREN'S BOOK CLUB
"THE GIVING TREE"
BONK
6·15

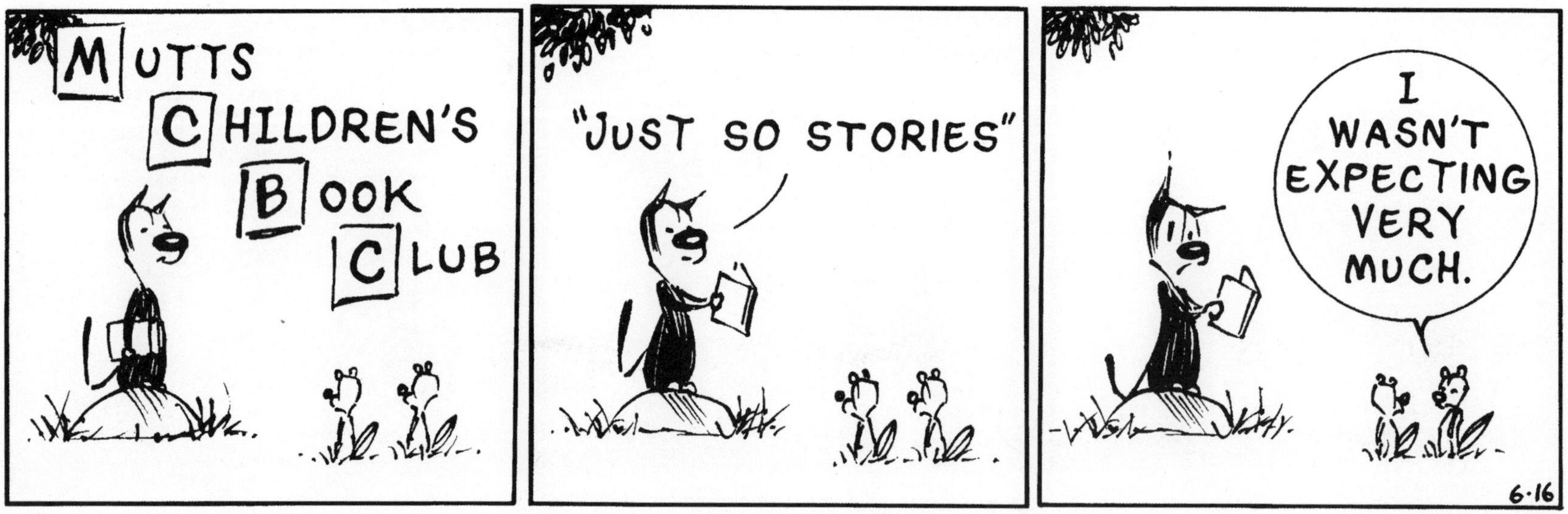
MUTTS CHILDREN'S BOOK CLUB
"JUST SO STORIES"
I WASN'T EXPECTING VERY MUCH.
6·16

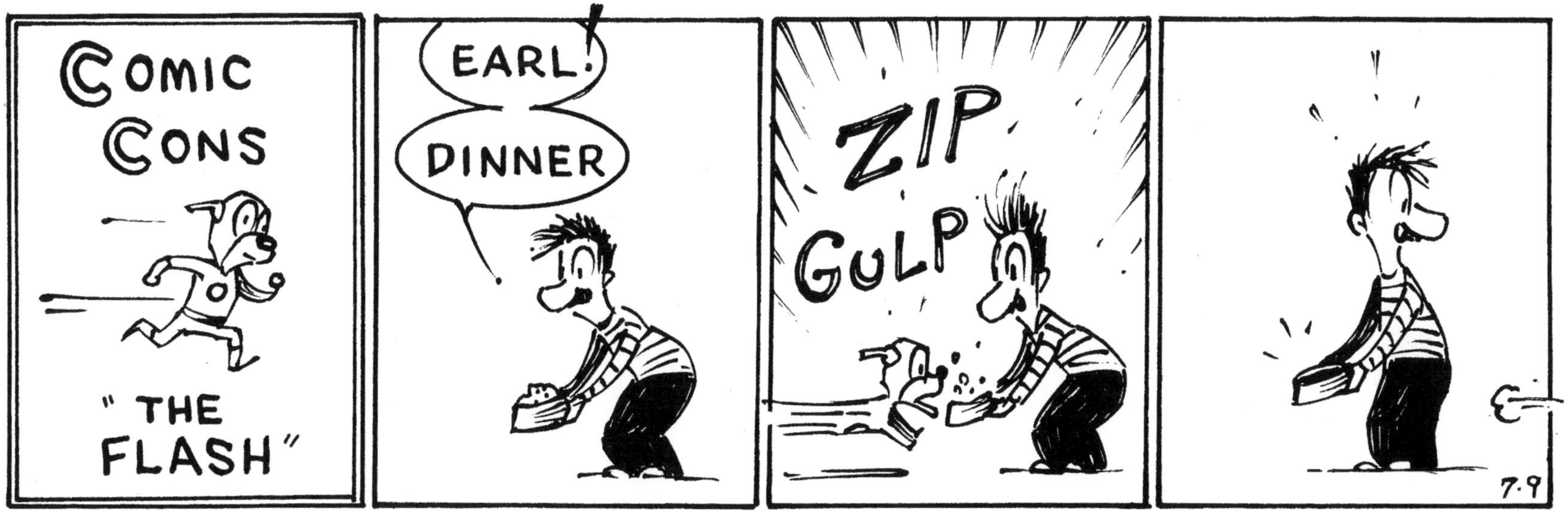
COMIC CONS
" THE FLASH "
EARL!
DINNER
ZIP
GULP
7·9

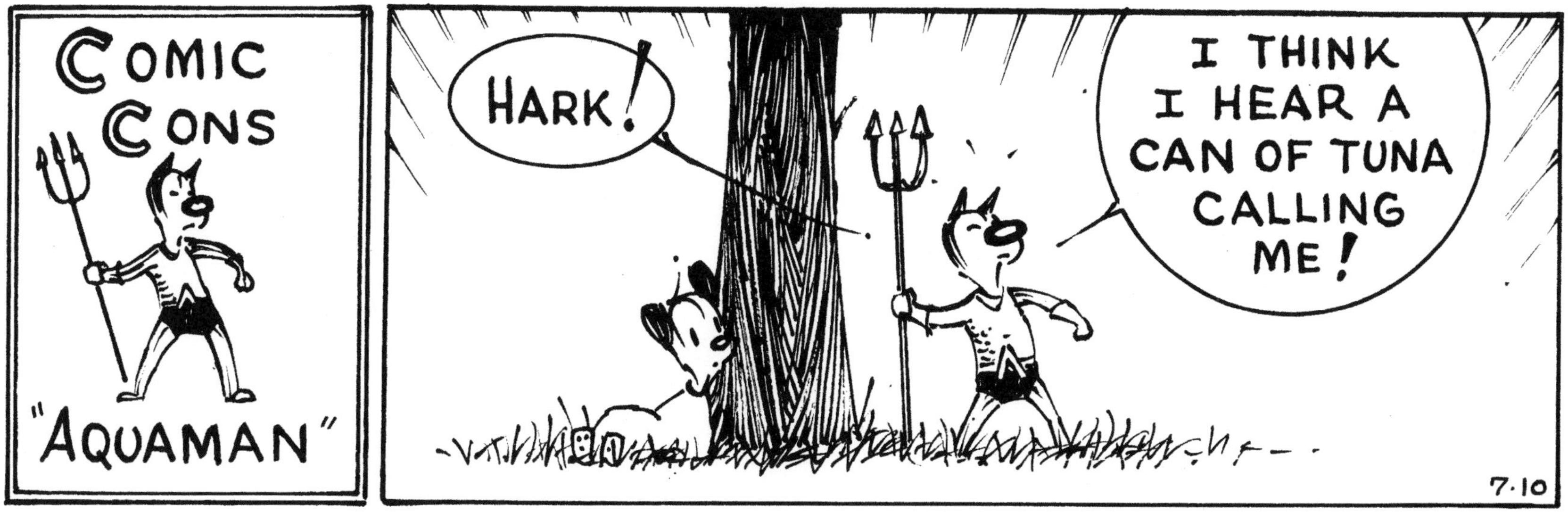
COMIC CONS
"AQUAMAN"
HARK!
I THINK I HEAR A CAN OF TUNA CALLING ME!
7·10

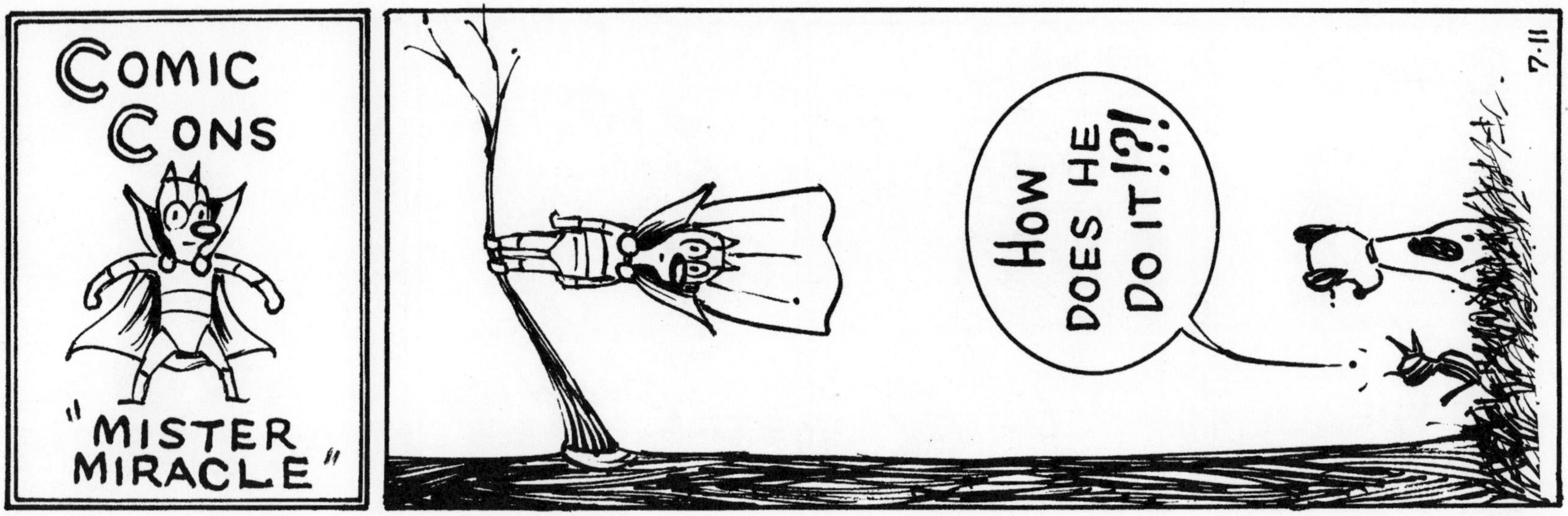
COMIC CONS
"MISTER MIRACLE"
HOW DOES HE DO IT!?!
7·11

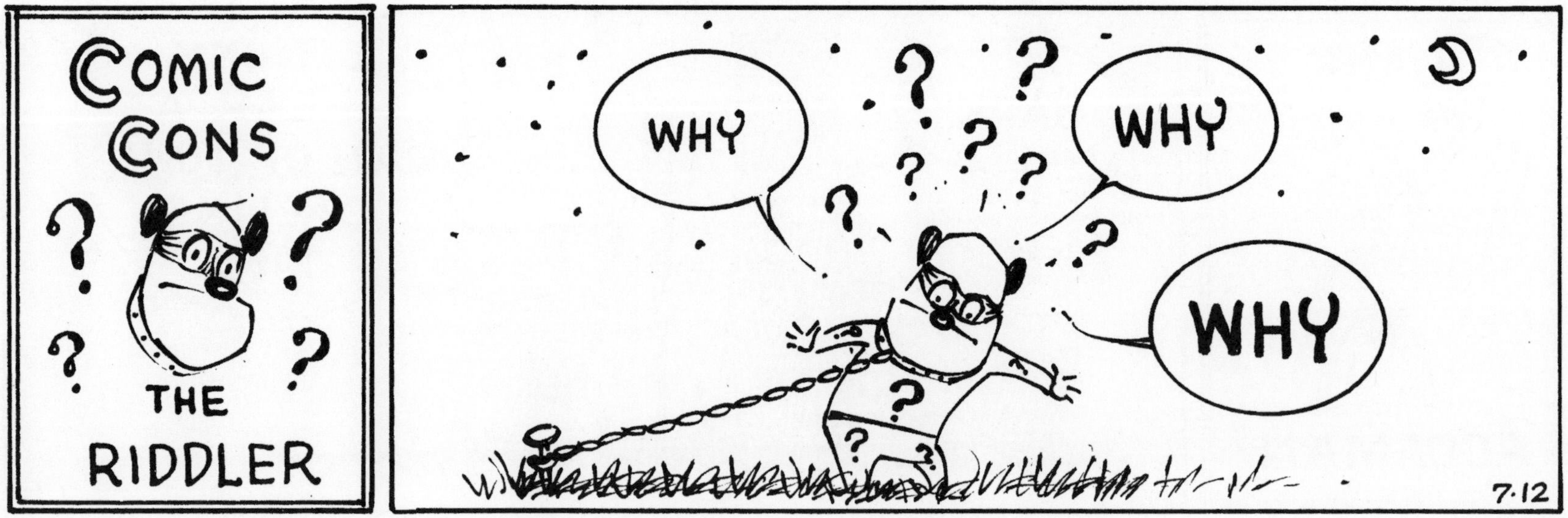
COMIC CONS
THE RIDDLER
WHY
WHY
WHY
7·12

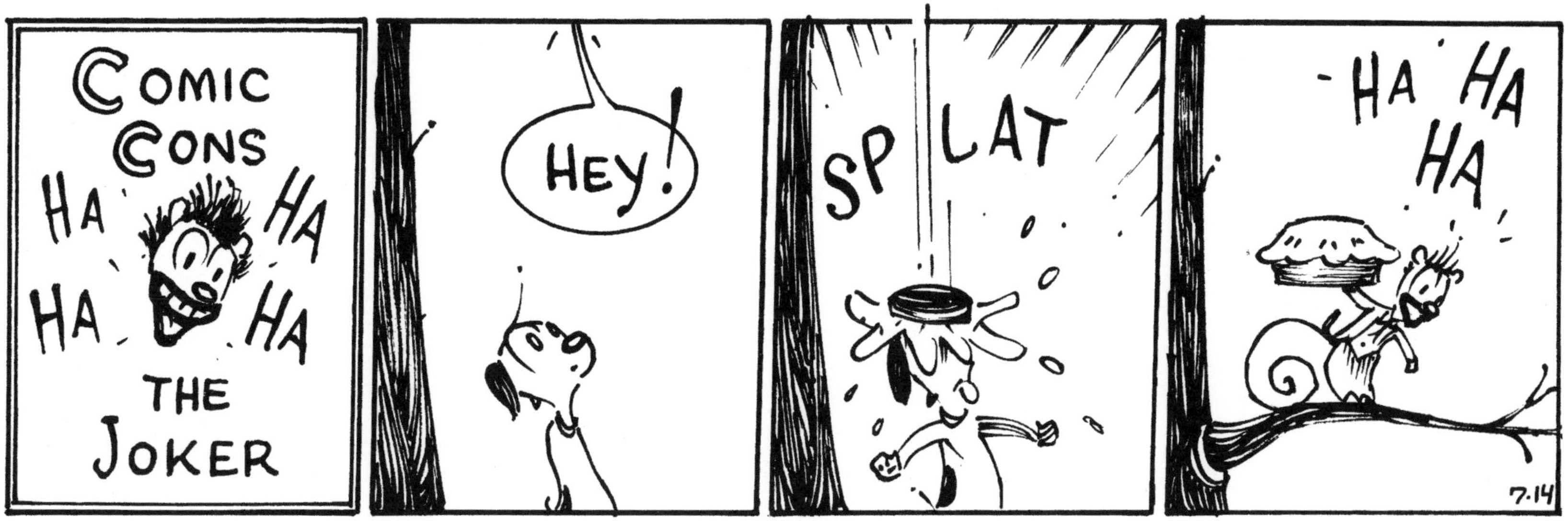
COMIC CONS
HA HA HA HA
THE JOKER
HEY!
SPLAT
HA HA HA
7.14

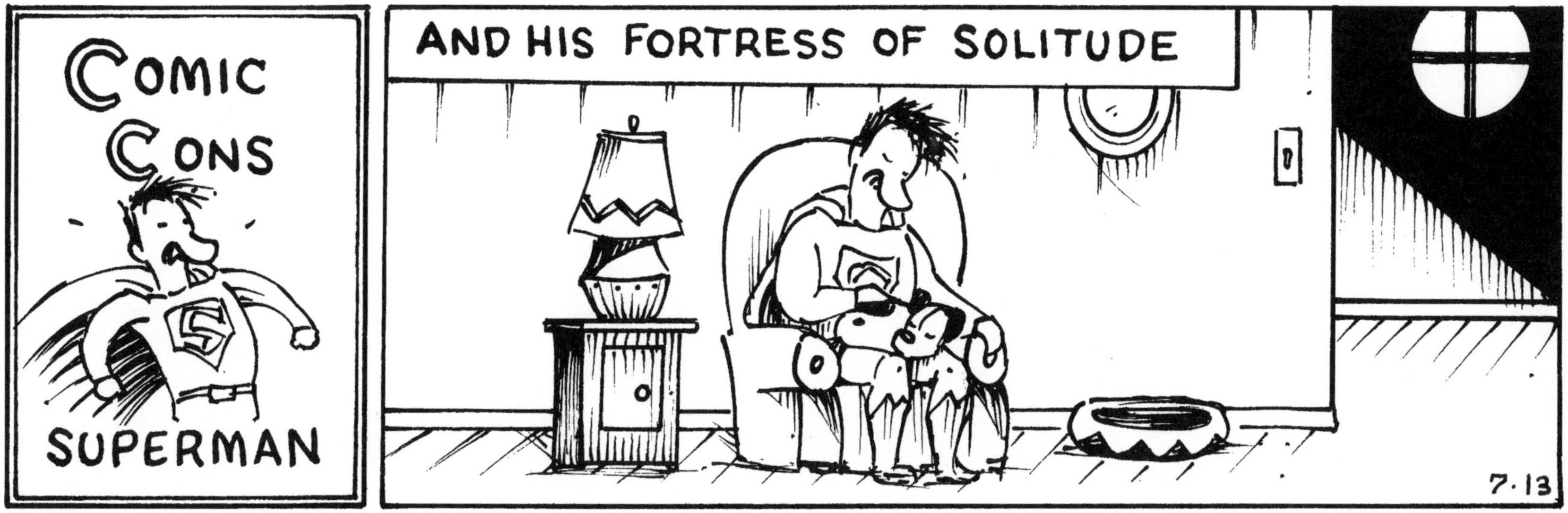
COMIC CONS
SUPERMAN
AND HIS FORTRESS OF SOLITUDE
7.13

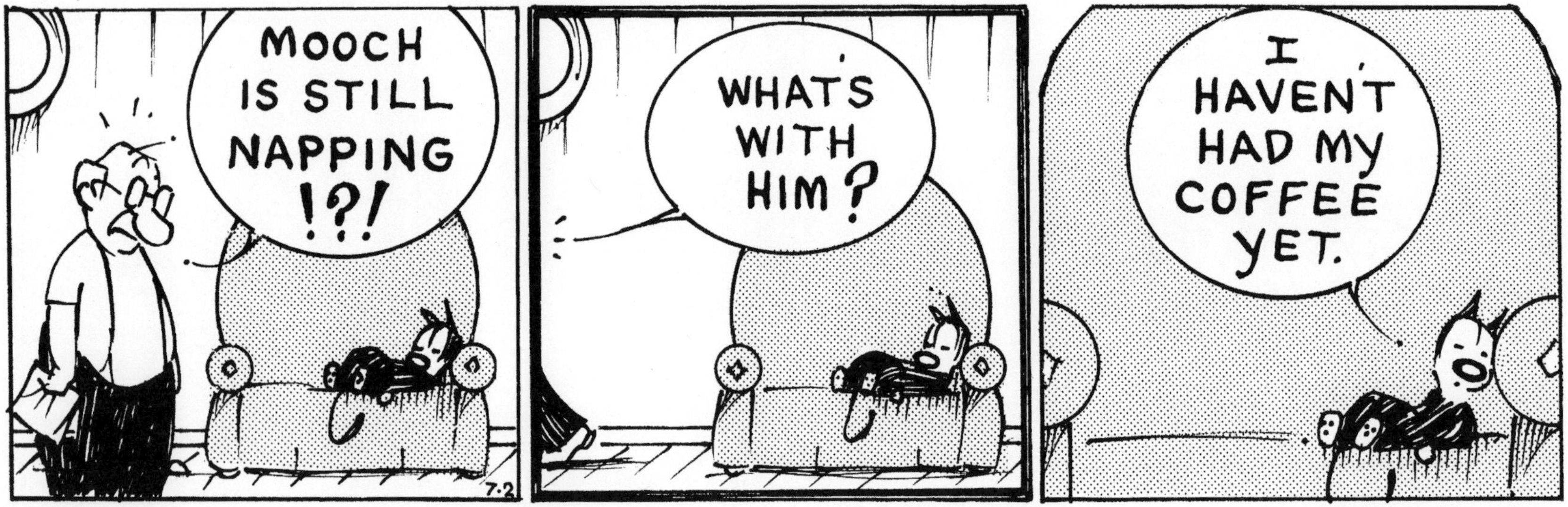
MOOCH IS STILL NAPPING !?!
WHAT'S WITH HIM?
I HAVEN'T HAD MY COFFEE YET.
7·2

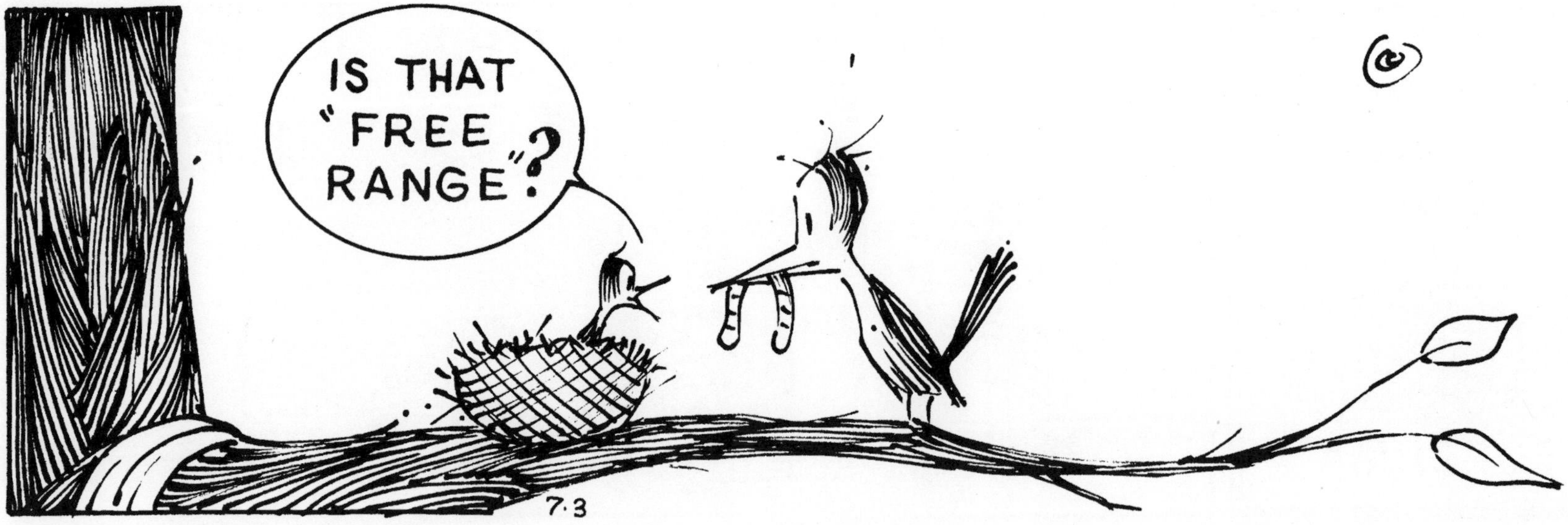
IS THAT "FREE RANGE"?
7·3

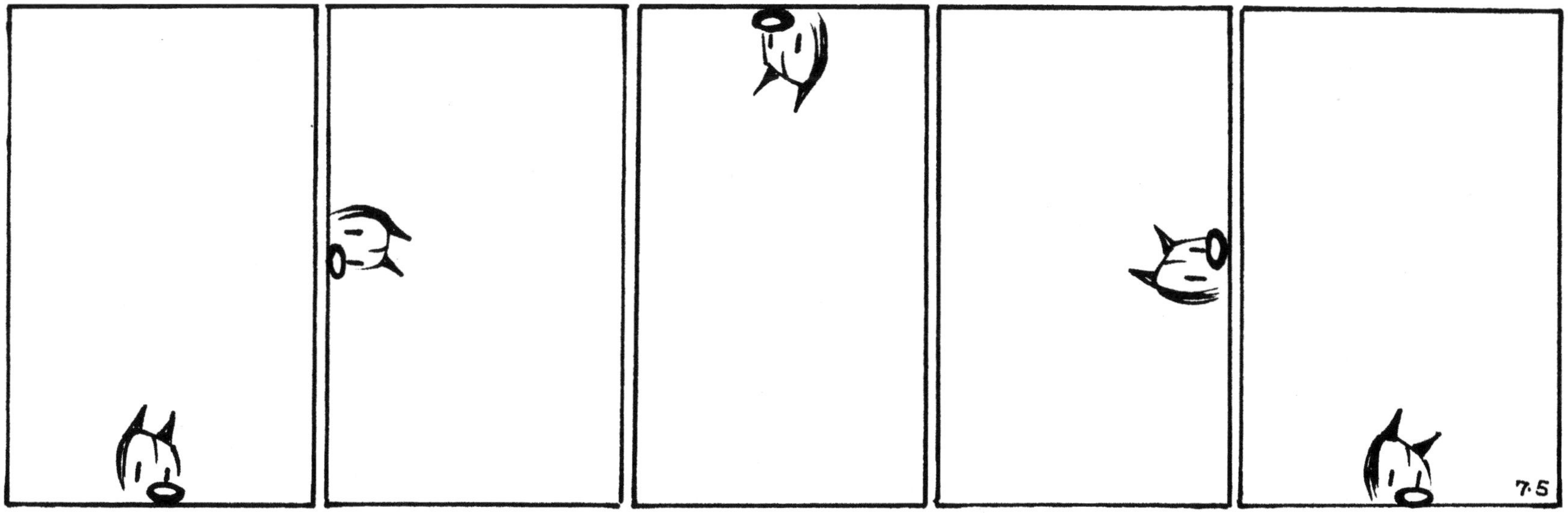
7·5

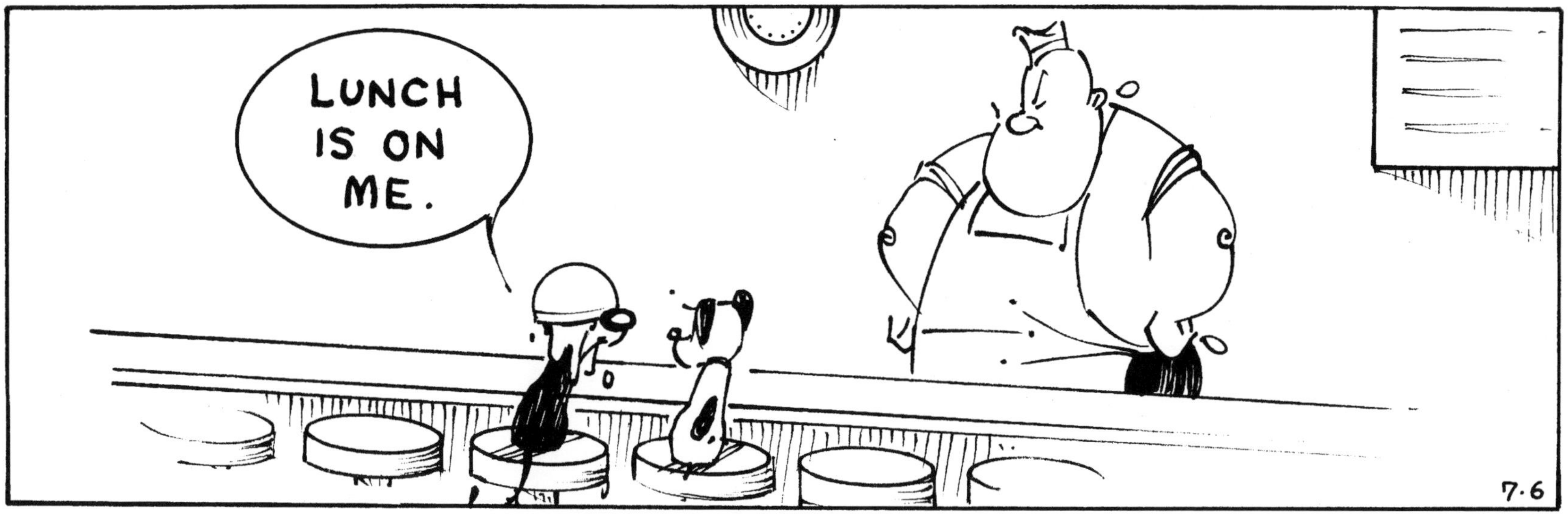
LUNCH IS ON ME.
7·6

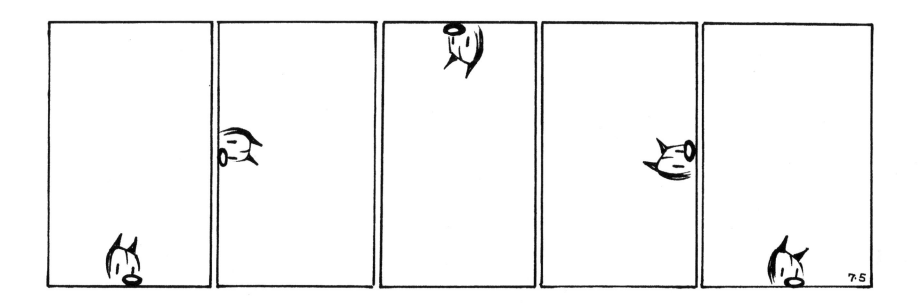

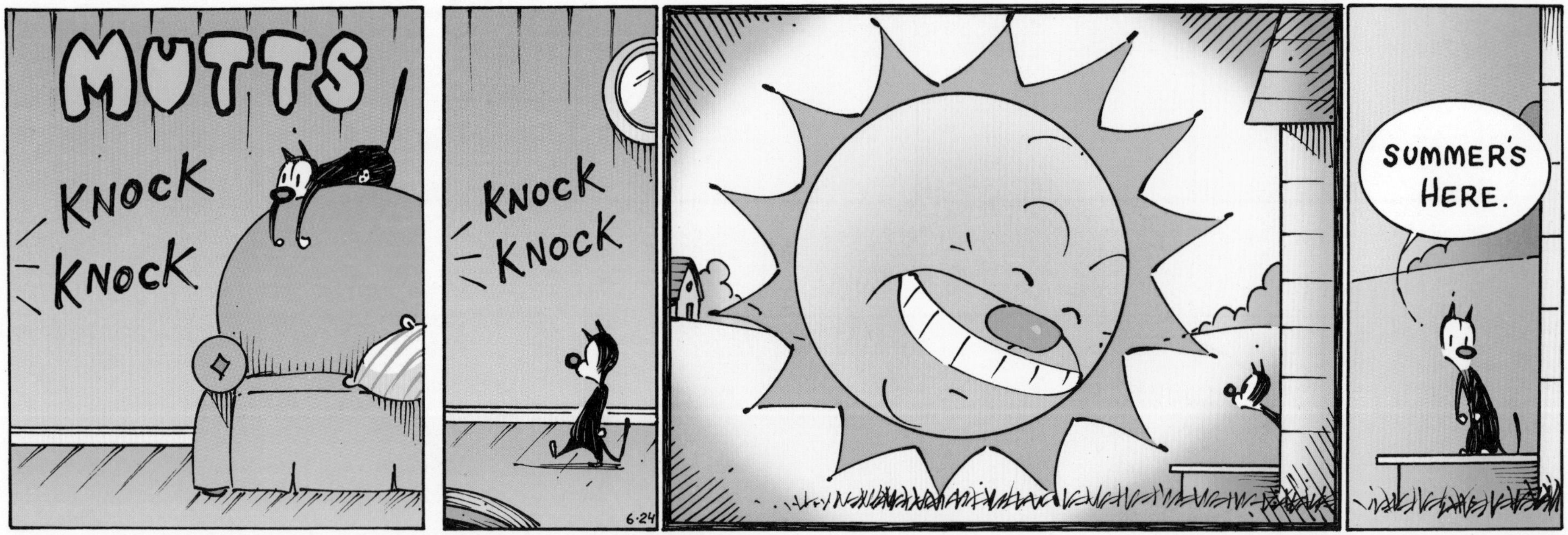
MUTTS
KNOCK
KNOCK
KNOCK
KNOCK
6·24
SUMMER'S HERE.

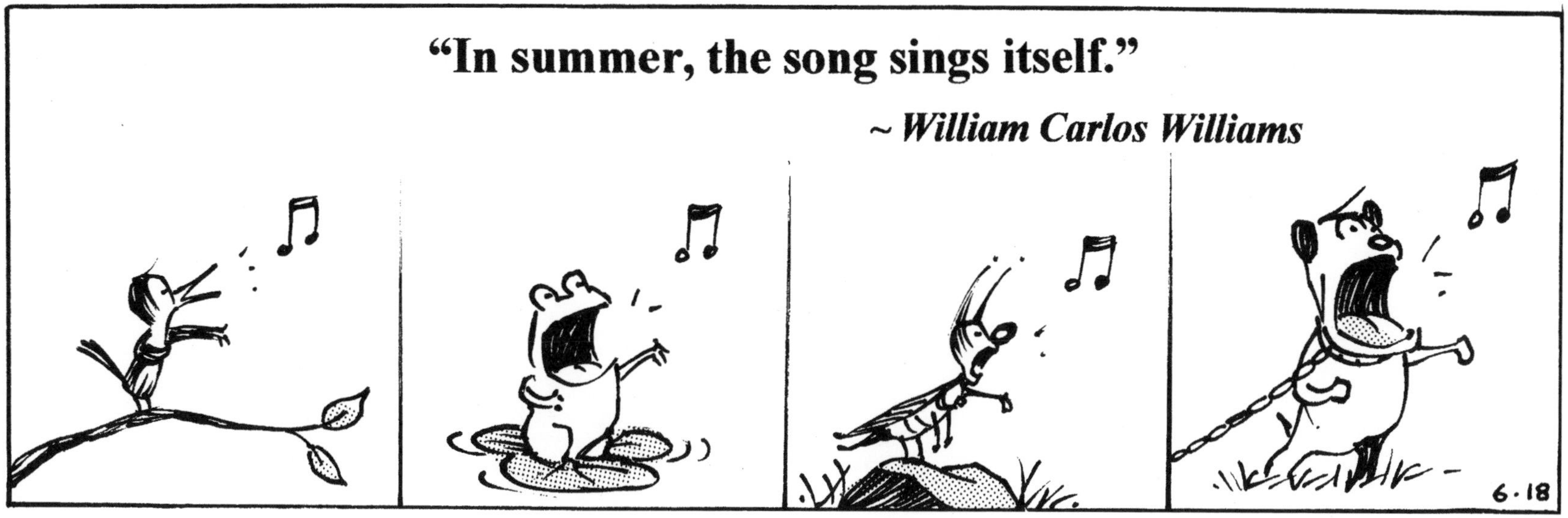
"In summer, the song sings itself."
~ William Carlos Williams
6·18

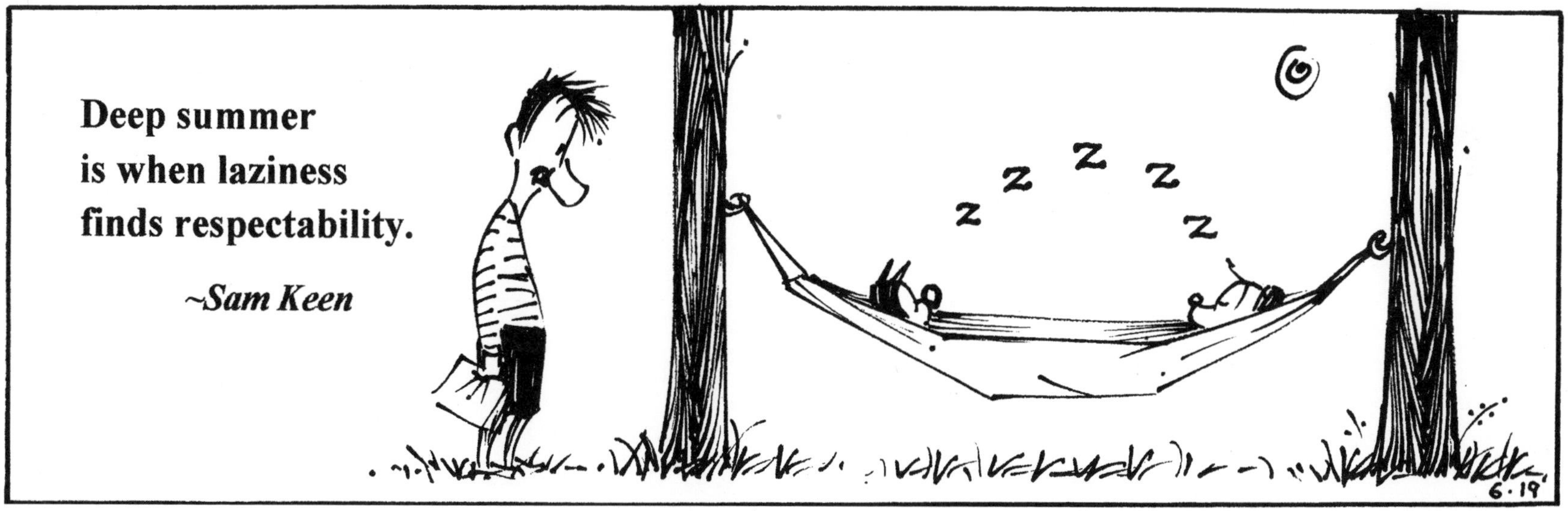
Deep summer
is when laziness
finds respectability.
~Sam Keen
Z Z Z Z Z
6·19

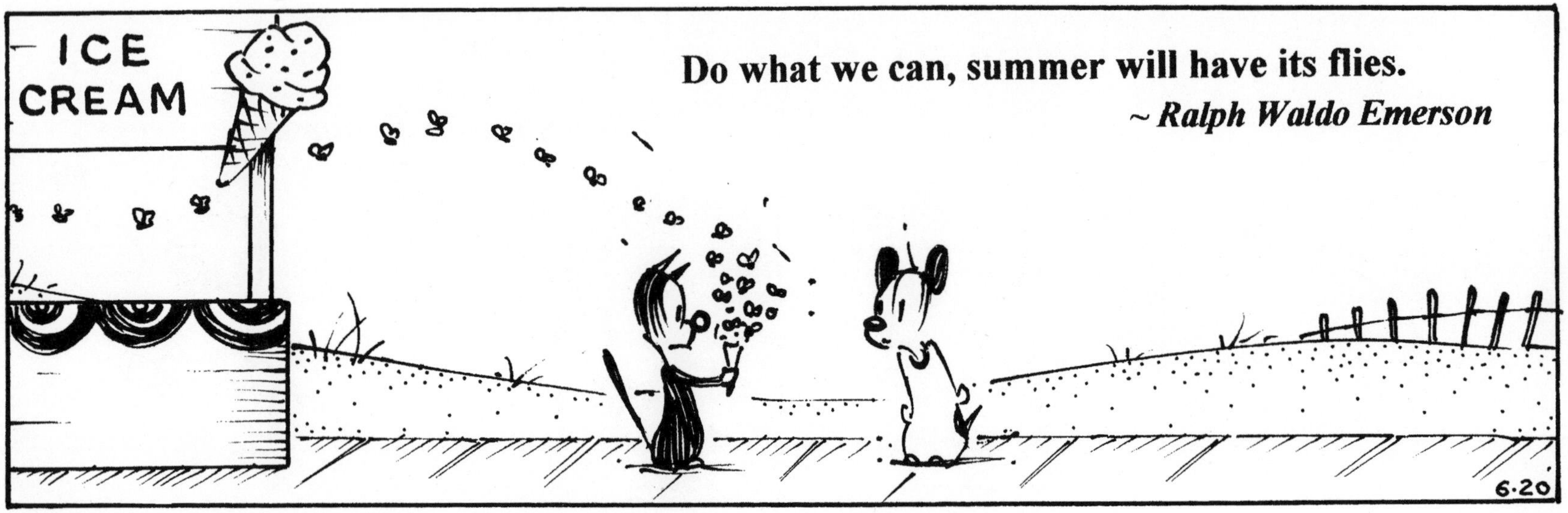

ICE
CREAM
Do what we can, summer will have its flies.
~ Ralph Waldo Emerson
6·20

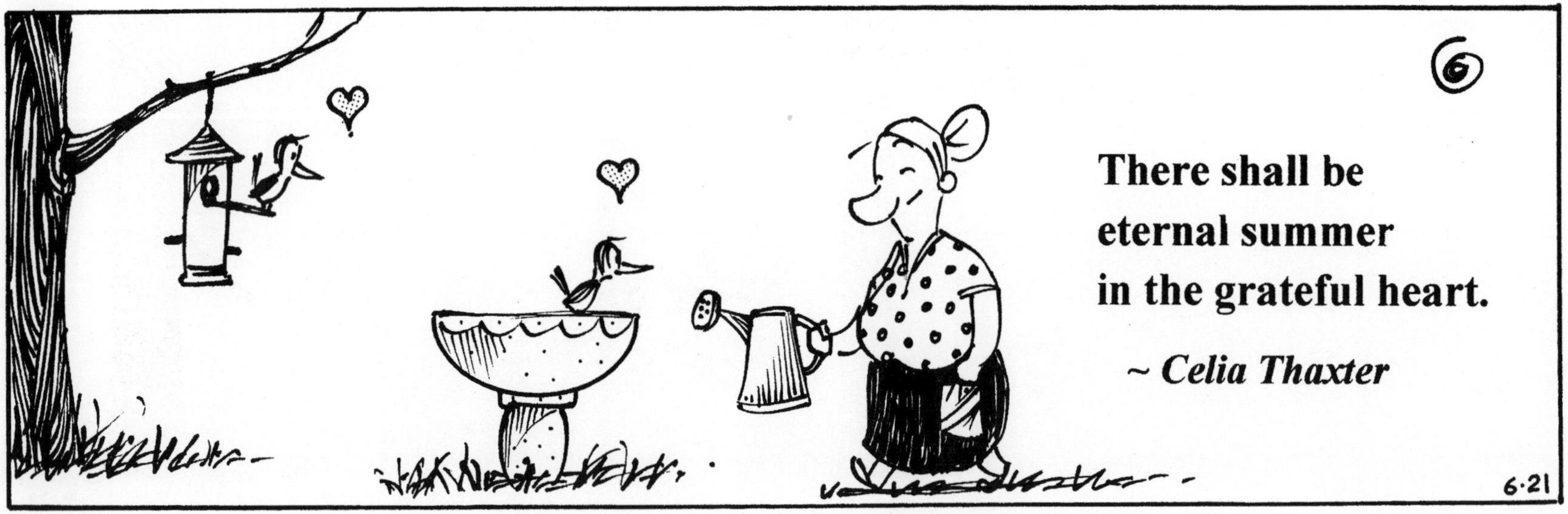

There shall be
eternal summer
in the grateful heart.
~ Celia Thaxter
6·21

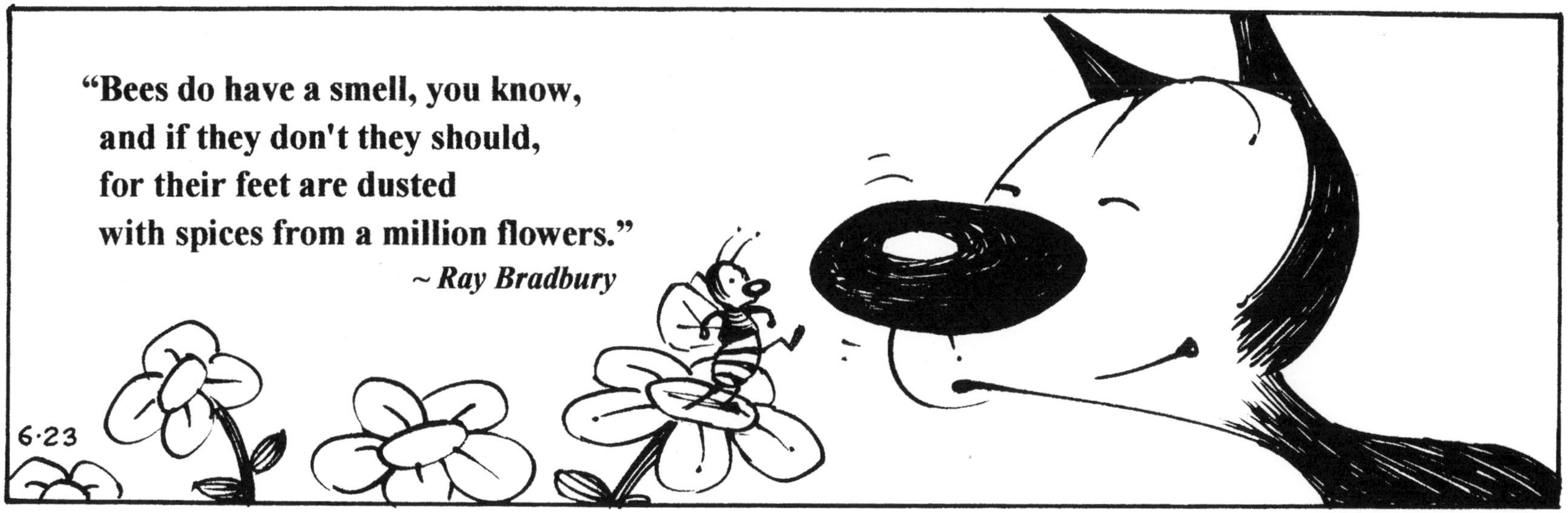
"Bees do have a smell, you know,
and if they don't they should,
for their feet are dusted
with spices from a million flowers."
~ Ray Bradbury
6·23

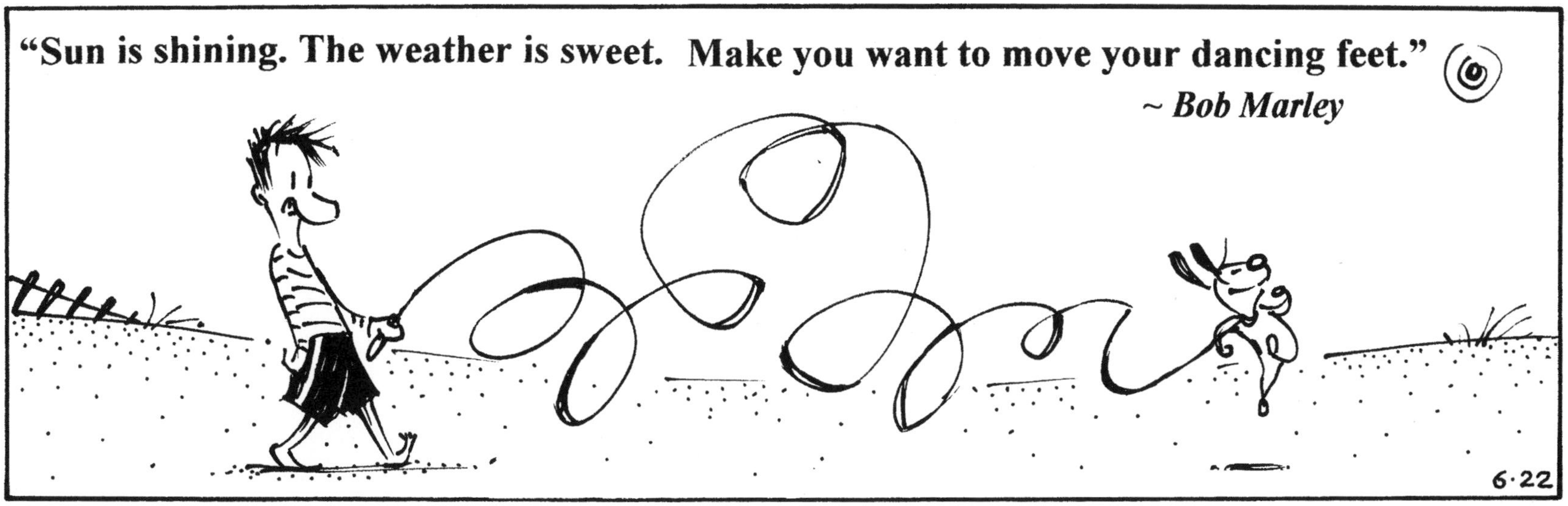
"Sun is shining. The weather is sweet. Make you want to move your dancing feet."
~ Bob Marley
6·22

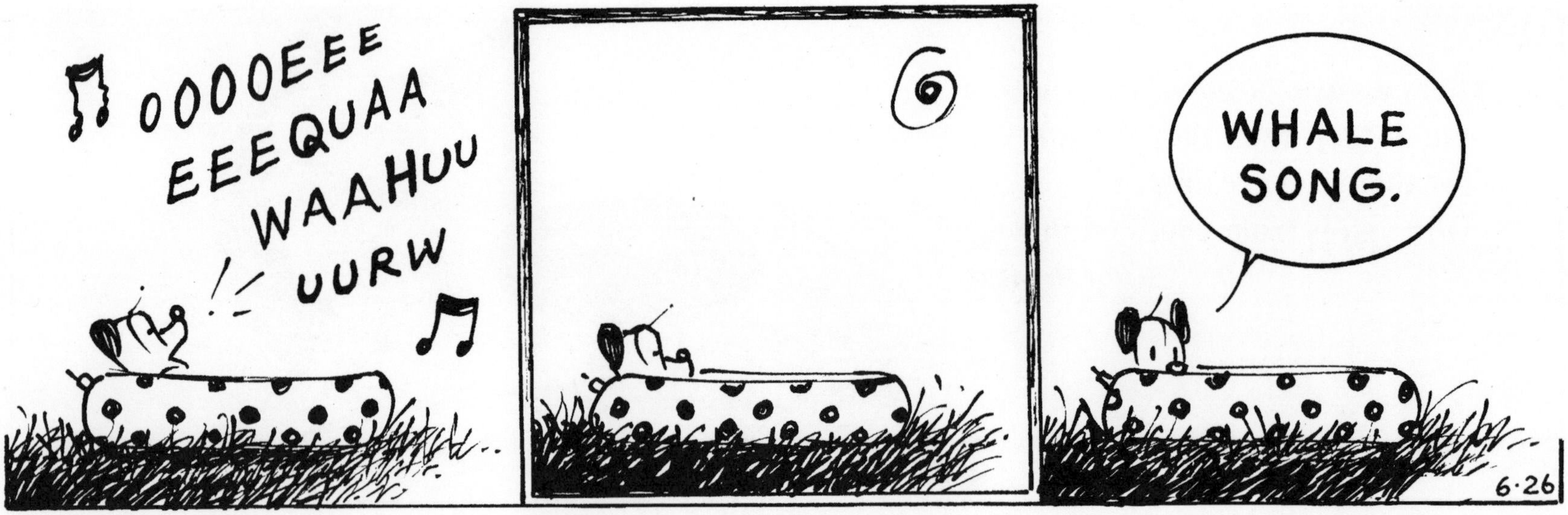
OOOOEEE
EEEQUAA
WAAHUU
UURW
WHALE SONG.
6·26

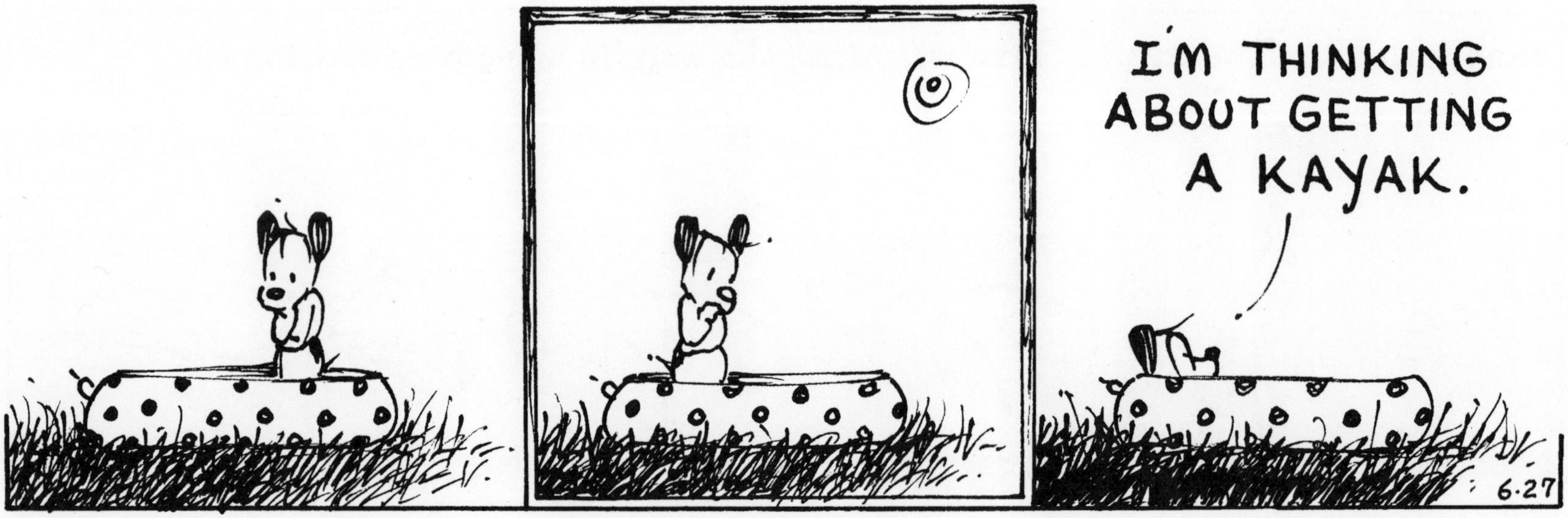
I'M THINKING ABOUT GETTING A KAYAK.
6·27

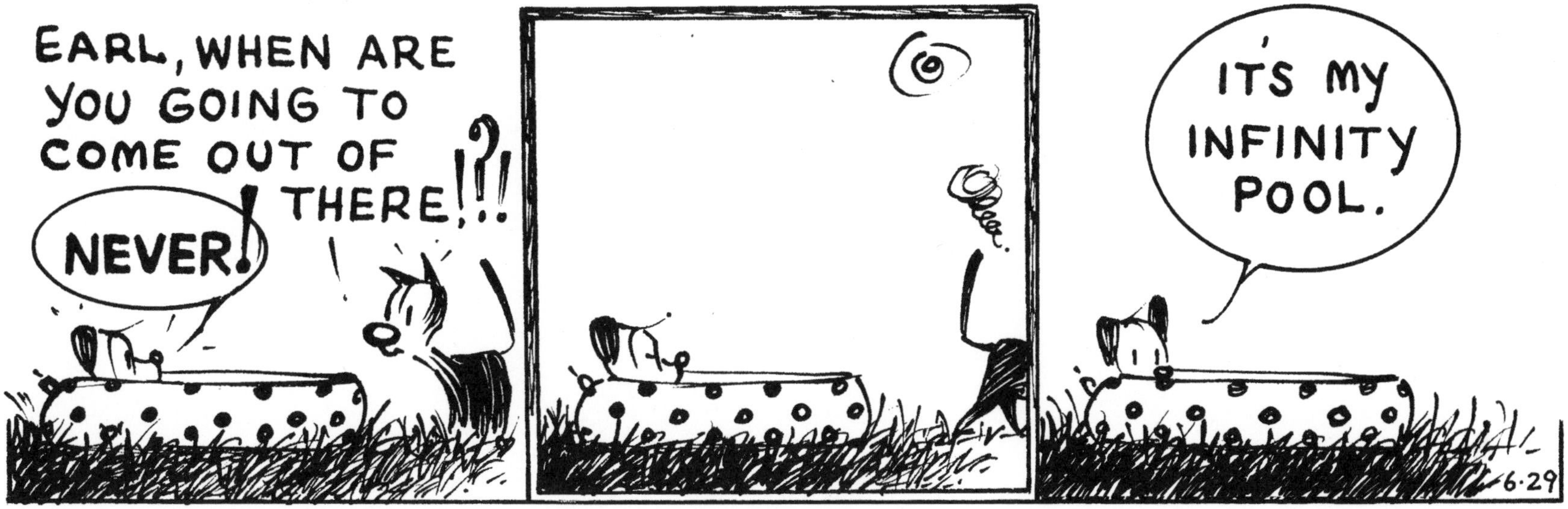
EARL, WHEN ARE YOU GOING TO COME OUT OF THERE!!!
NEVER!
?!
IT'S MY INFINITY POOL.
6·29

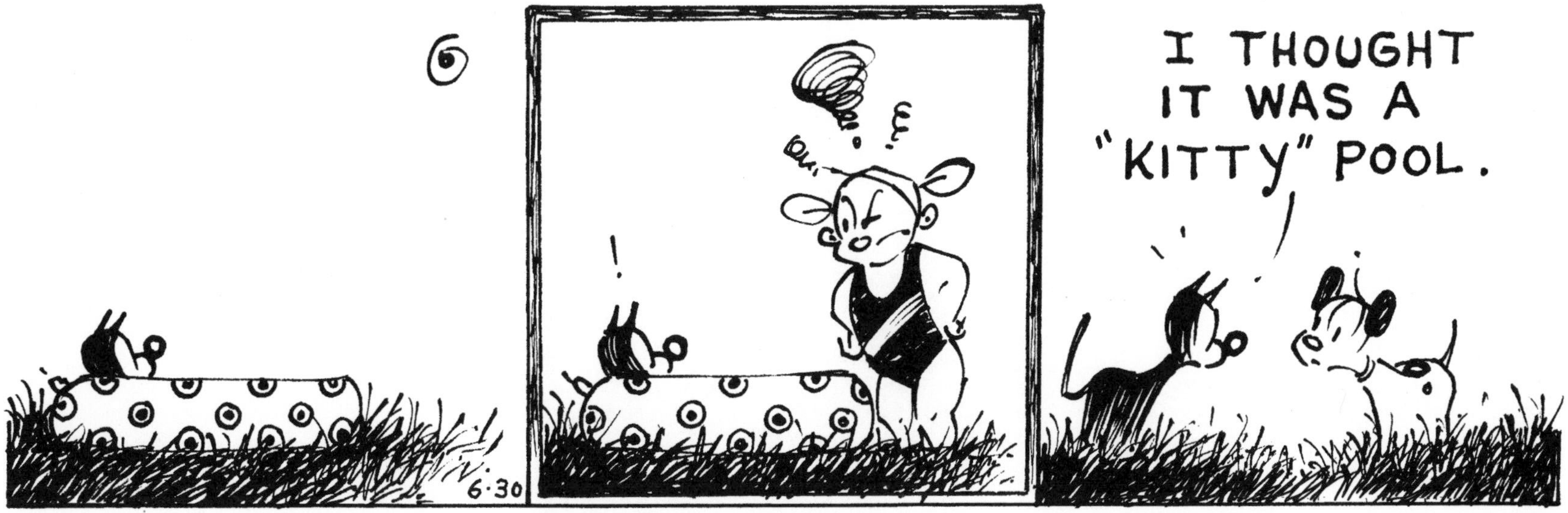
I THOUGHT IT WAS A "KITTY" POOL.
6·30

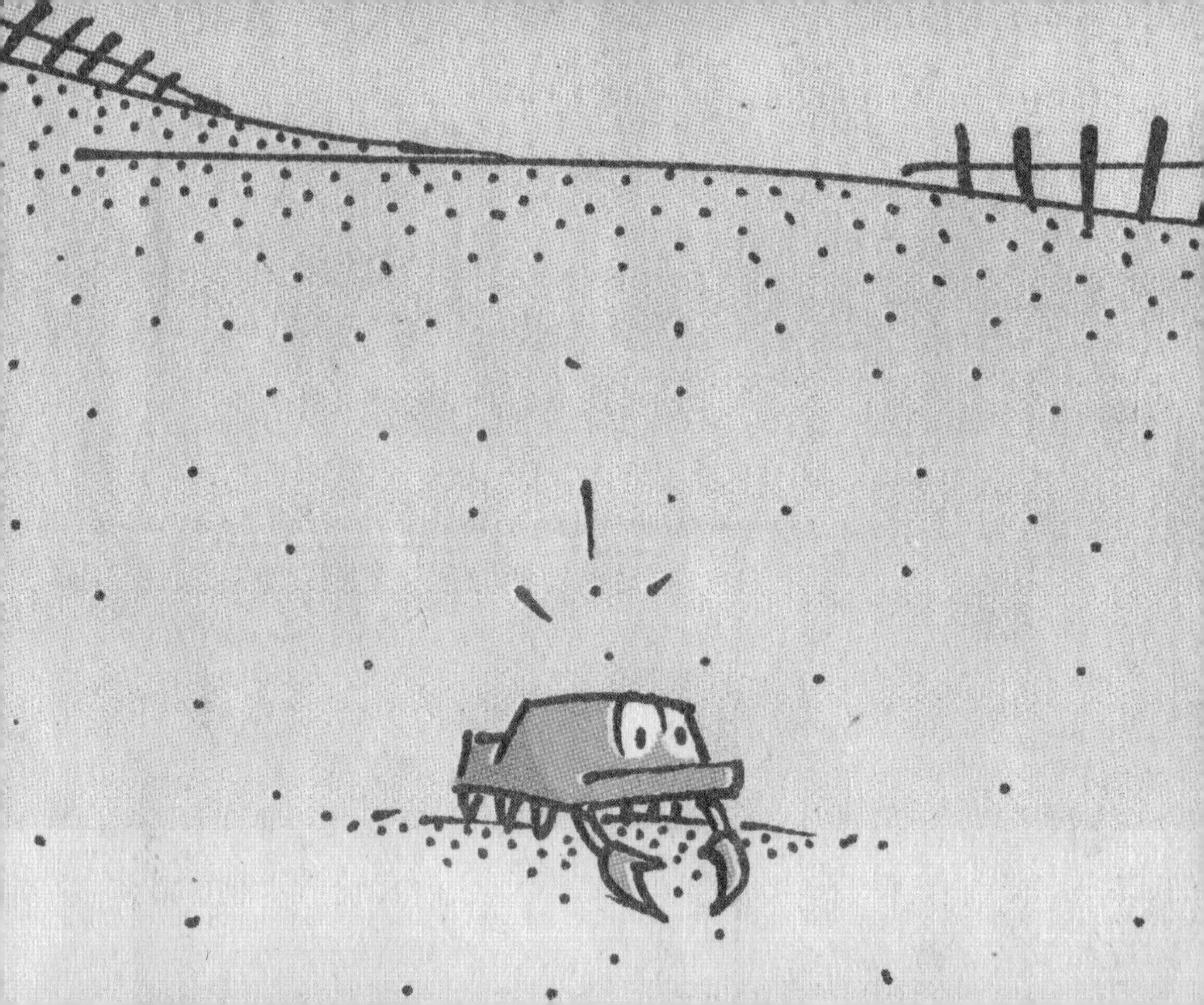

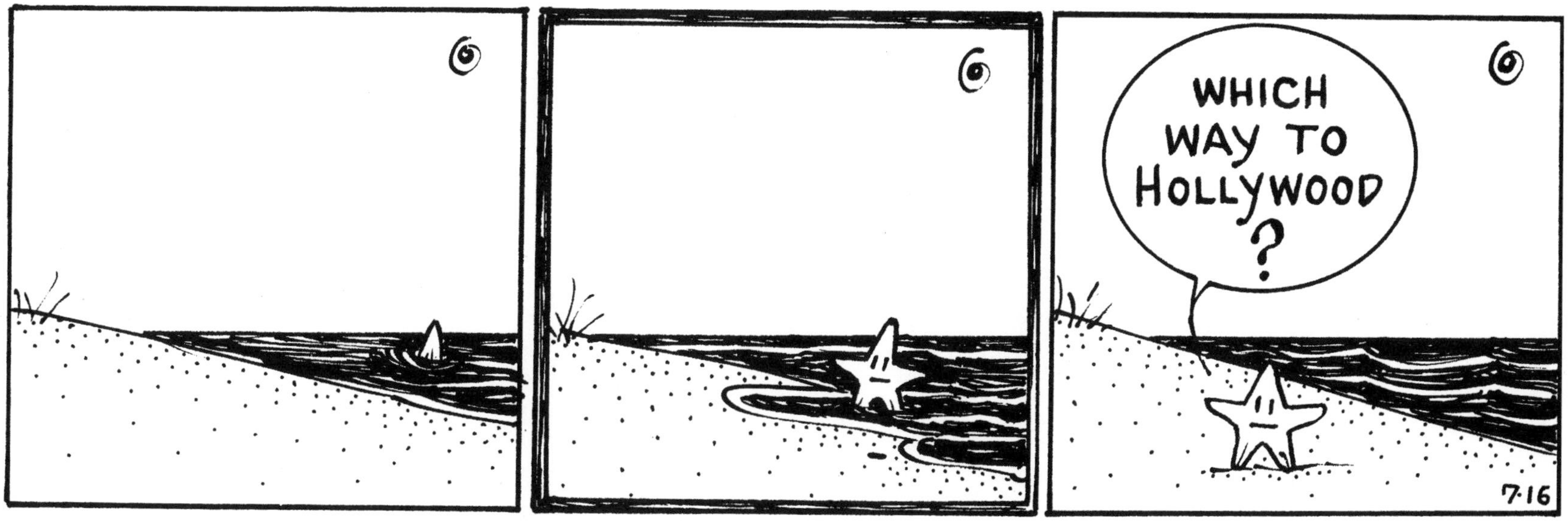
WHICH WAY TO HOLLYWOOD ?
7·16

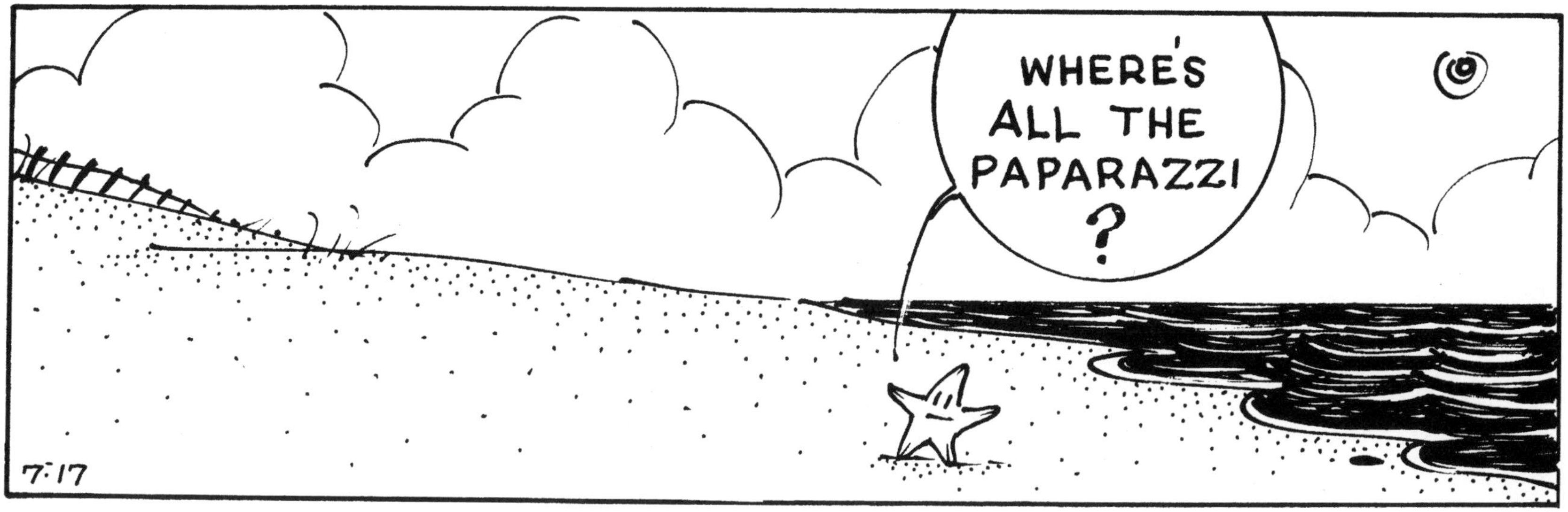
WHERE'S ALL THE PAPARAZZI ?
7·17

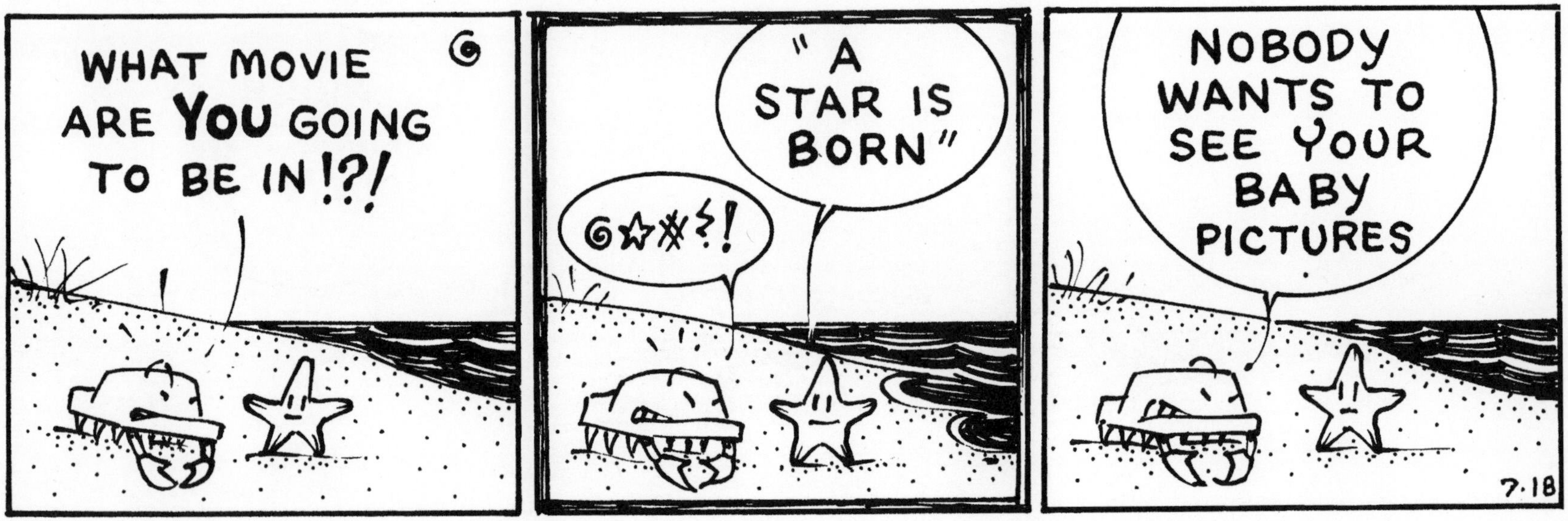
WHAT MOVIE ARE **YOU** GOING TO BE IN!?!
"A STAR IS BORN"
NOBODY WANTS TO SEE YOUR BABY PICTURES
7·18

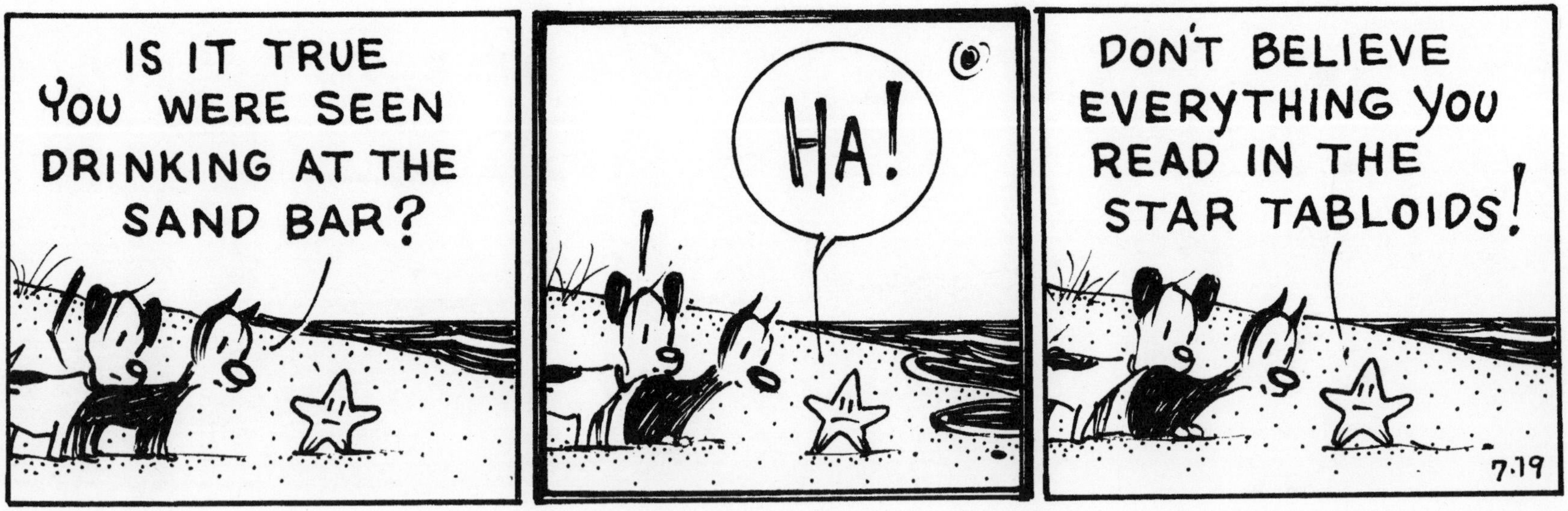
IS IT TRUE YOU WERE SEEN DRINKING AT THE SAND BAR?
HA!
DON'T BELIEVE EVERYTHING YOU READ IN THE STAR TABLOIDS!
7·19

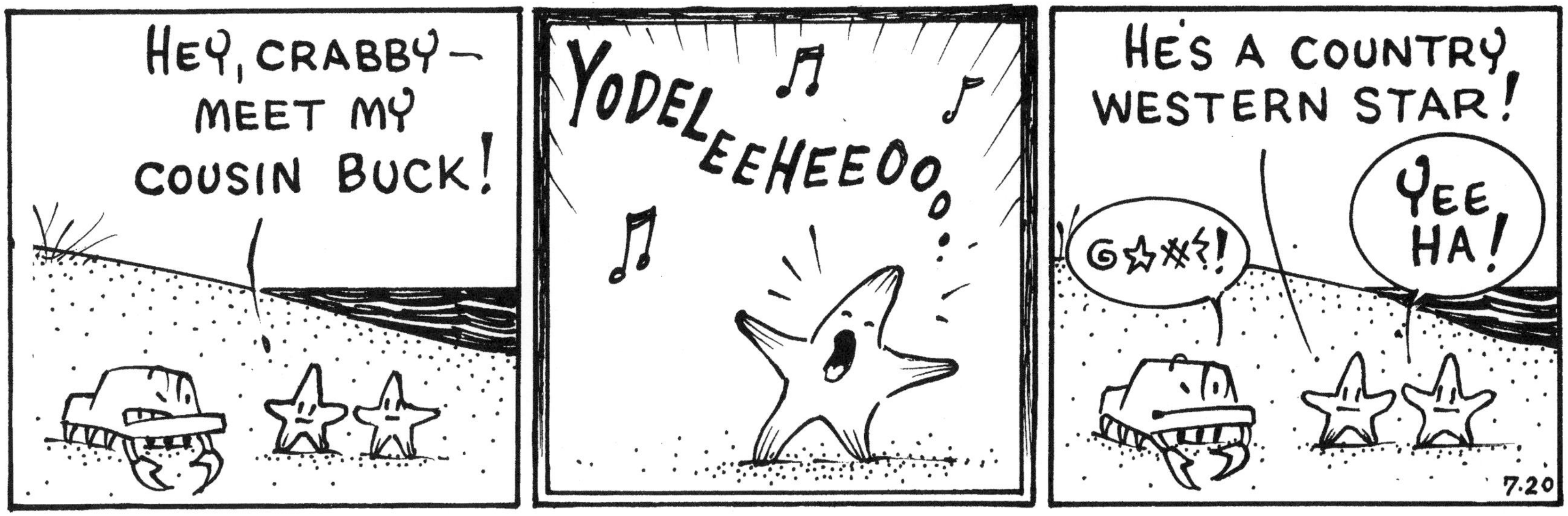
HEY, CRABBY— MEET MY COUSIN BUCK!
YODELEEHEEOOO
HE'S A COUNTRY WESTERN STAR!
YEE HA!
7·20

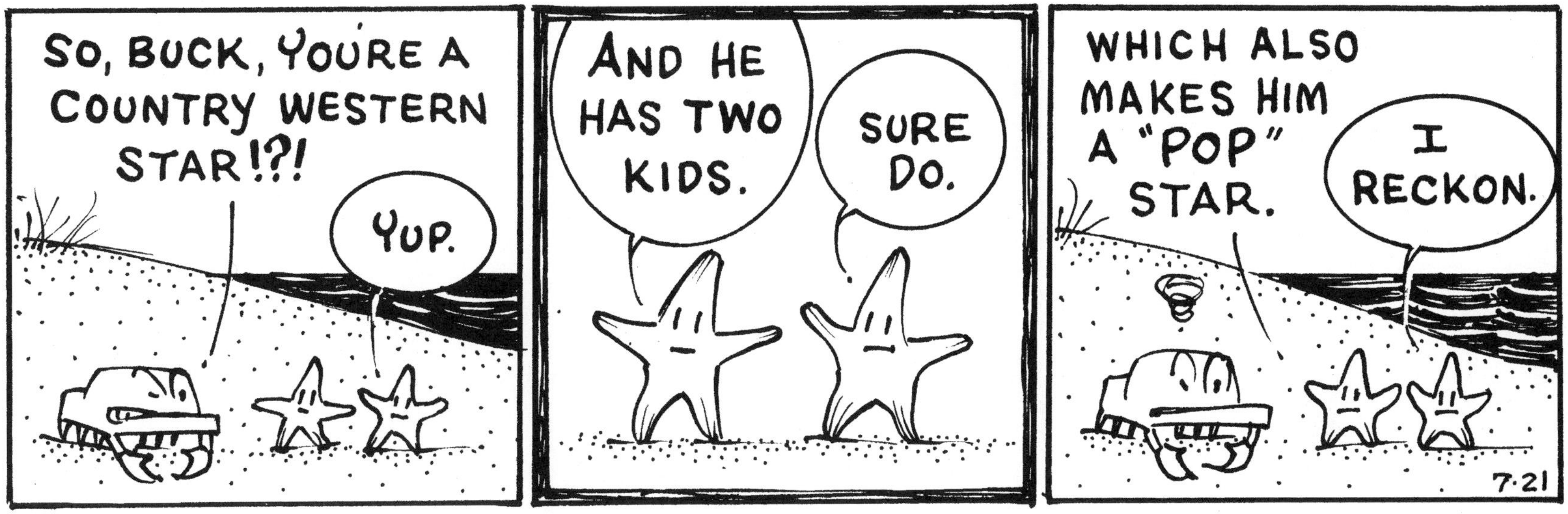
SO, BUCK, YOU'RE A COUNTRY WESTERN STAR!?!
YUP.
AND HE HAS TWO KIDS.
SURE DO.
WHICH ALSO MAKES HIM A "POP" STAR.
I RECKON.
7·21

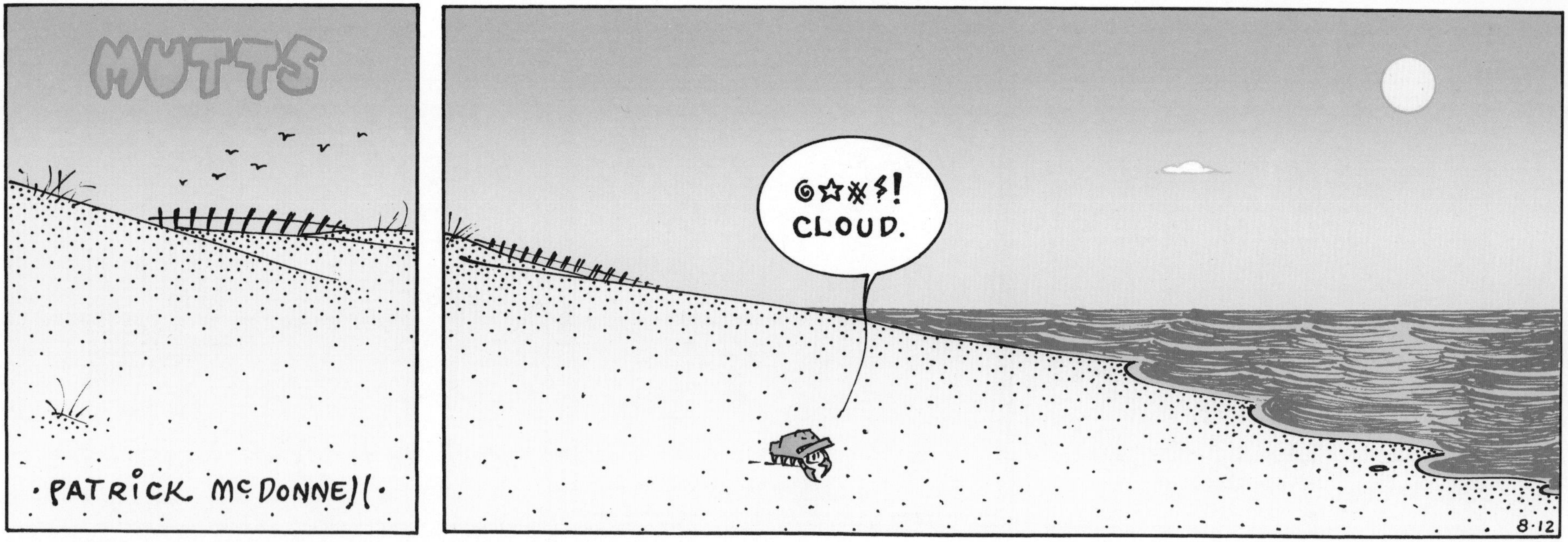
MUTTS
PATRICK McDONNELL
@☆※$! CLOUD.
8·12

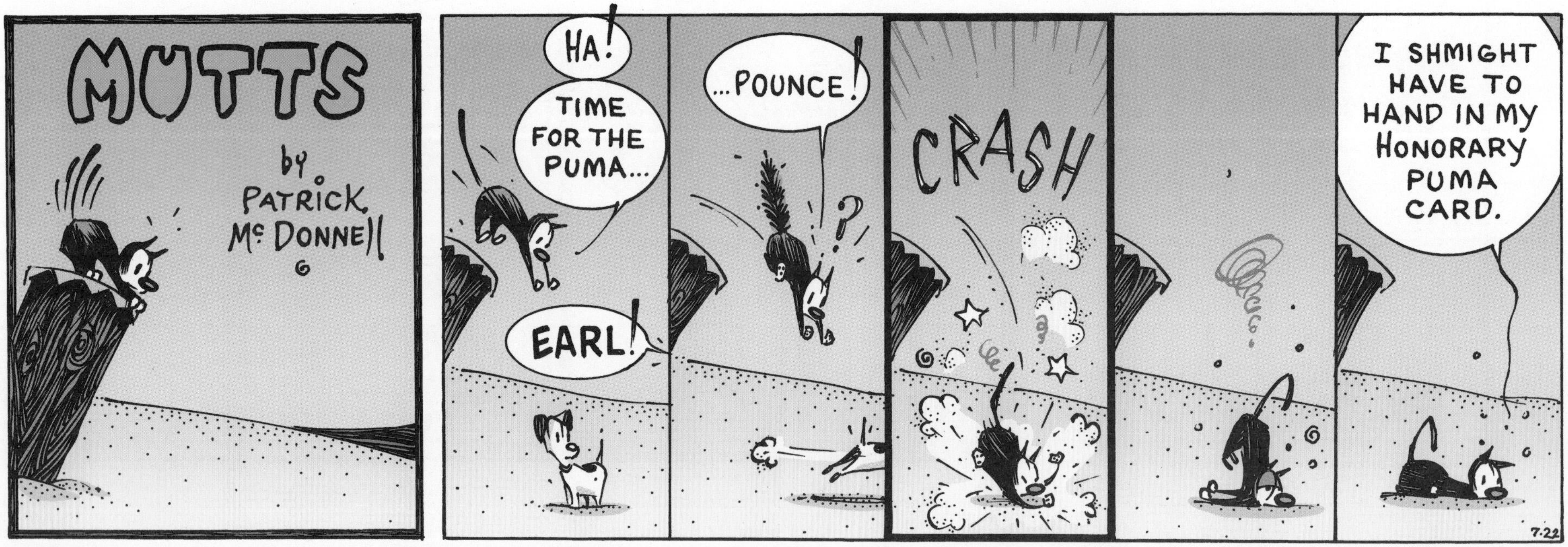
MUTTS
by PATRICK McDONNELL
HA!
TIME FOR THE PUMA...
EARL!
...POUNCE!
CRASH
I SHMIGHT HAVE TO HAND IN MY HONORARY PUMA CARD.
7·22

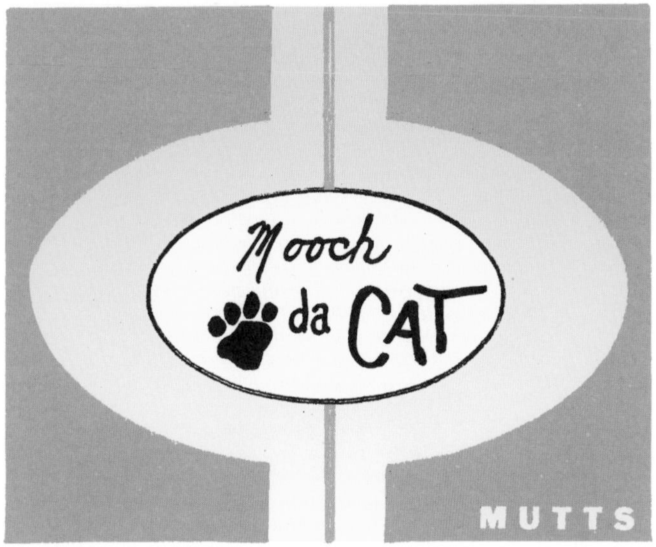
Mooch da CAT
MUTTS

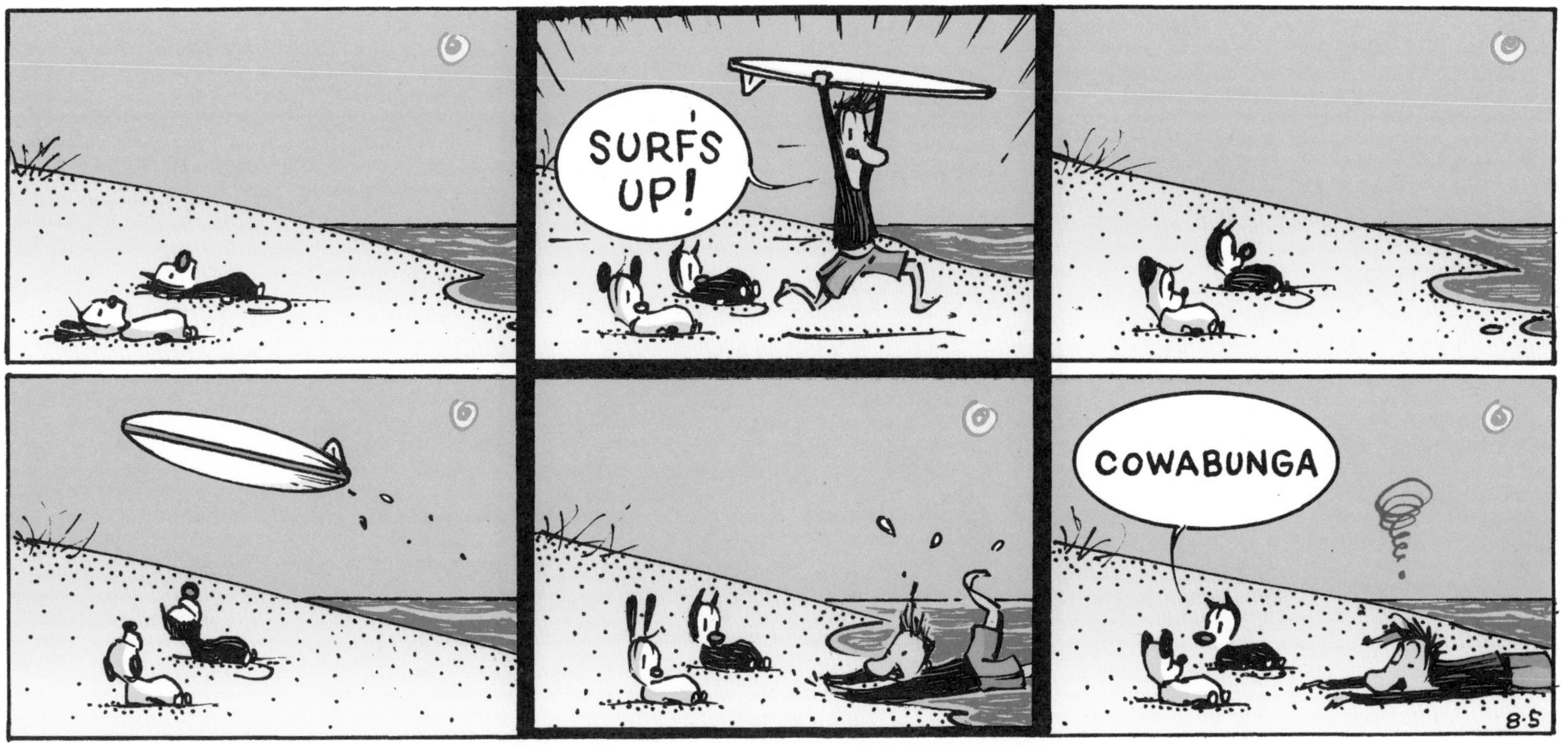
SURF'S UP!
COWABUNGA
8·5

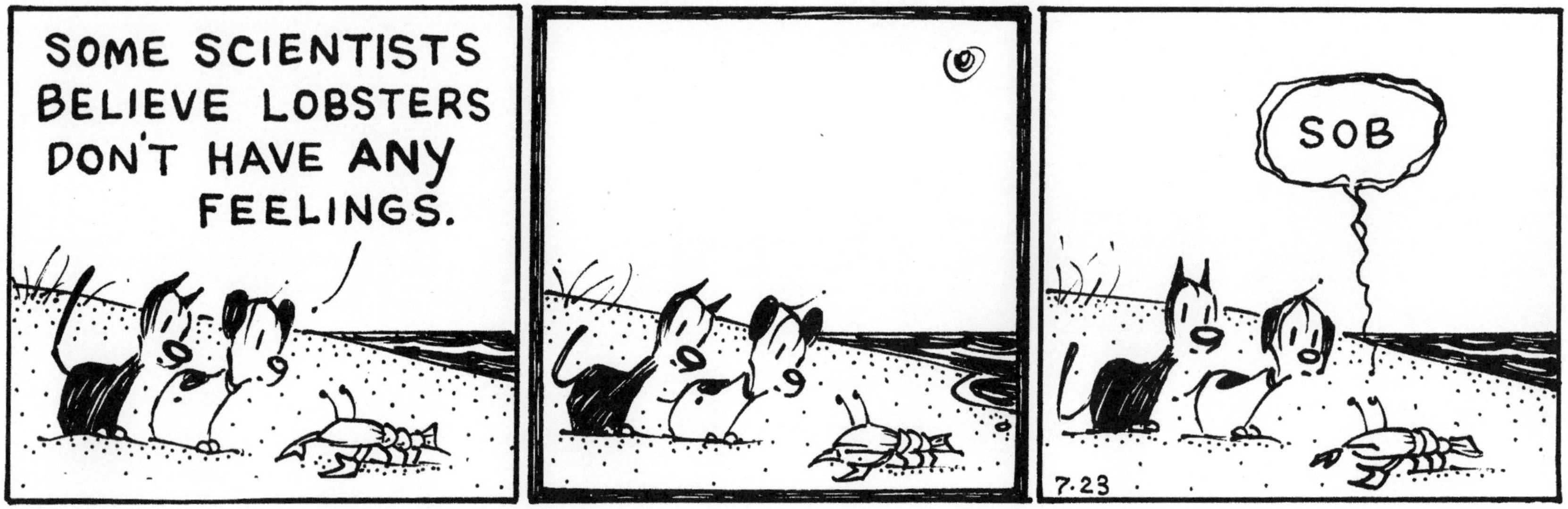
SOME SCIENTISTS BELIEVE LOBSTERS DON'T HAVE ANY FEELINGS.
SOB
7·23

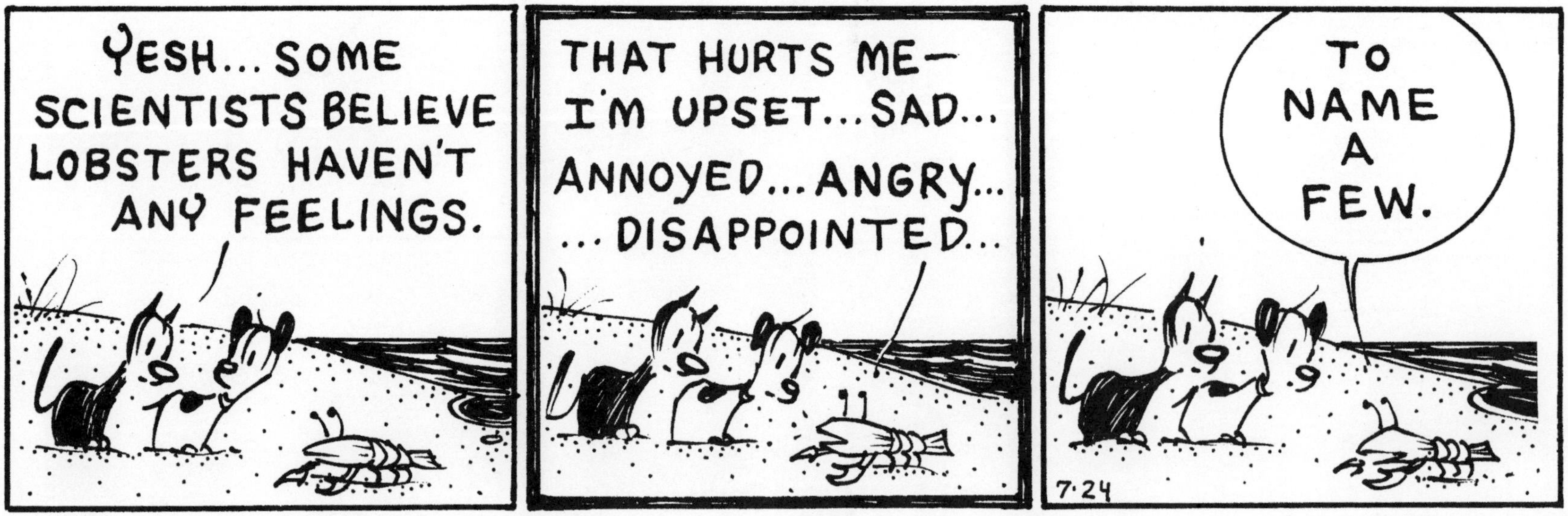
YESH... SOME SCIENTISTS BELIEVE LOBSTERS HAVEN'T ANY FEELINGS.
THAT HURTS ME— I'M UPSET... SAD... ANNOYED... ANGRY... ...DISAPPOINTED...
TO NAME A FEW.
7·24

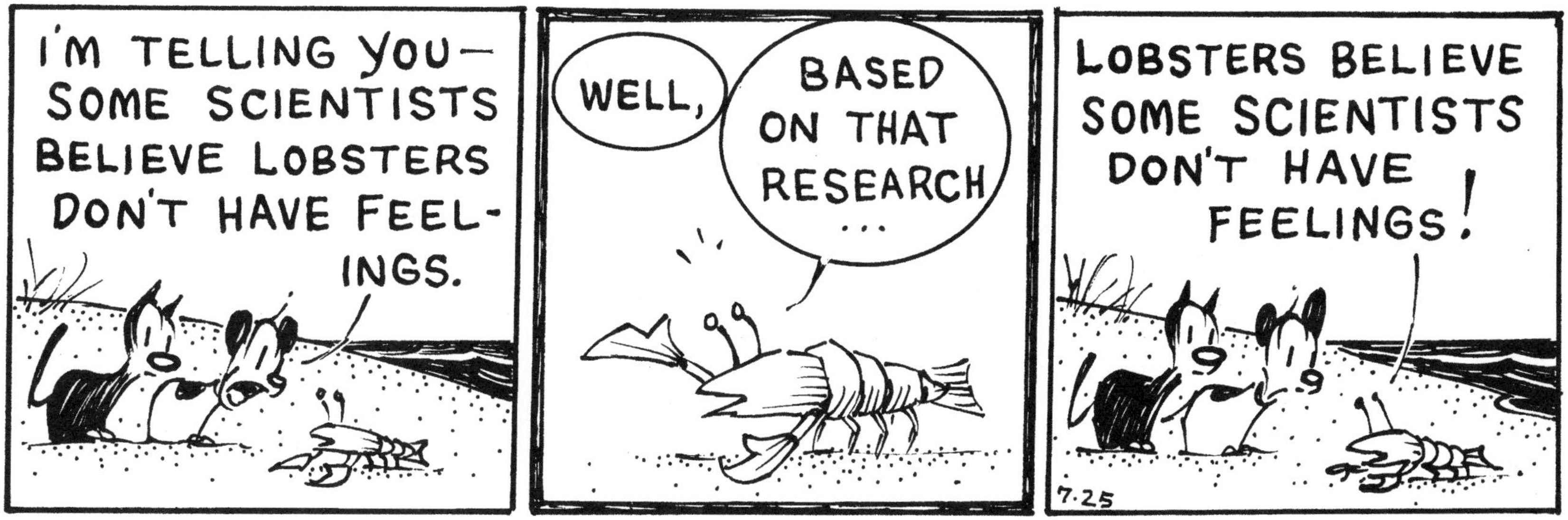
I'M TELLING YOU— SOME SCIENTISTS BELIEVE LOBSTERS DON'T HAVE FEEL- INGS.
WELL,
BASED ON THAT RESEARCH . . .
LOBSTERS BELIEVE SOME SCIENTISTS DON'T HAVE FEELINGS!
7·25

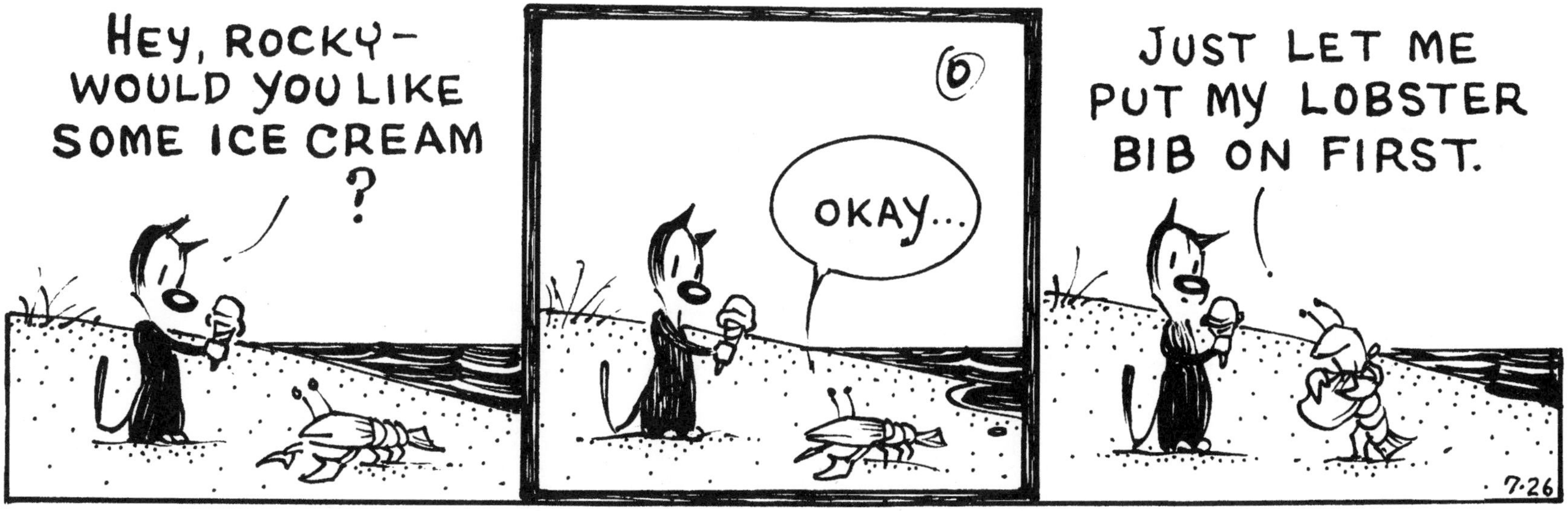
HEY, ROCKY— WOULD YOU LIKE SOME ICE CREAM ?
OKAY...
JUST LET ME PUT MY LOBSTER BIB ON FIRST.
7·26

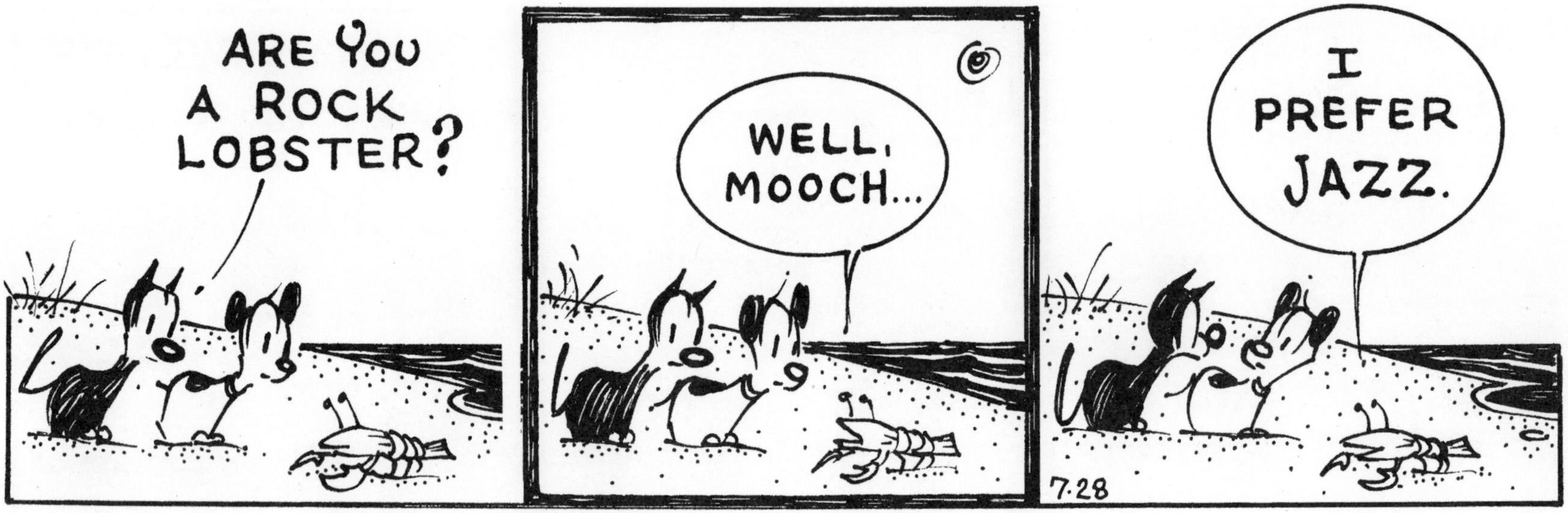
ARE YOU A ROCK LOBSTER?
WELL, MOOCH...
I PREFER JAZZ.
7·28

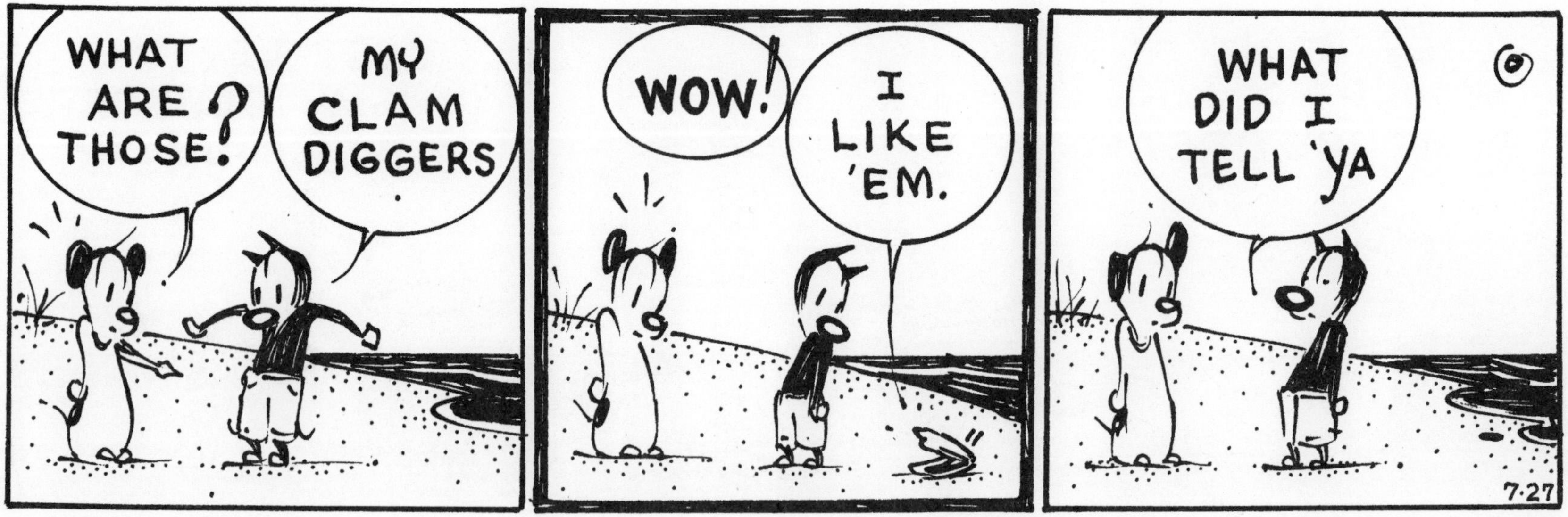
WHAT ARE THOSE?
MY CLAM DIGGERS.
WOW!
I LIKE 'EM.
WHAT DID I TELL 'YA
7·27

MUTTS

Patrick McDonnell

HEY!
THERE'S MELVILLE!
WOW
LOOKS LIKE HE LOST A FEW POUNDS.
7·29

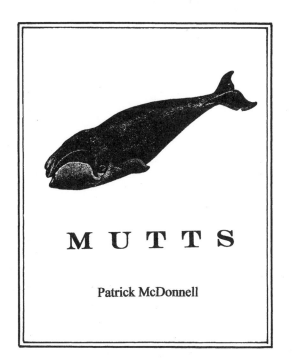

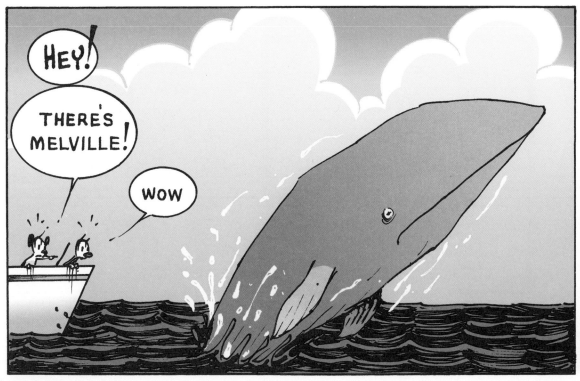

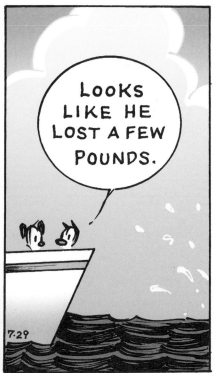

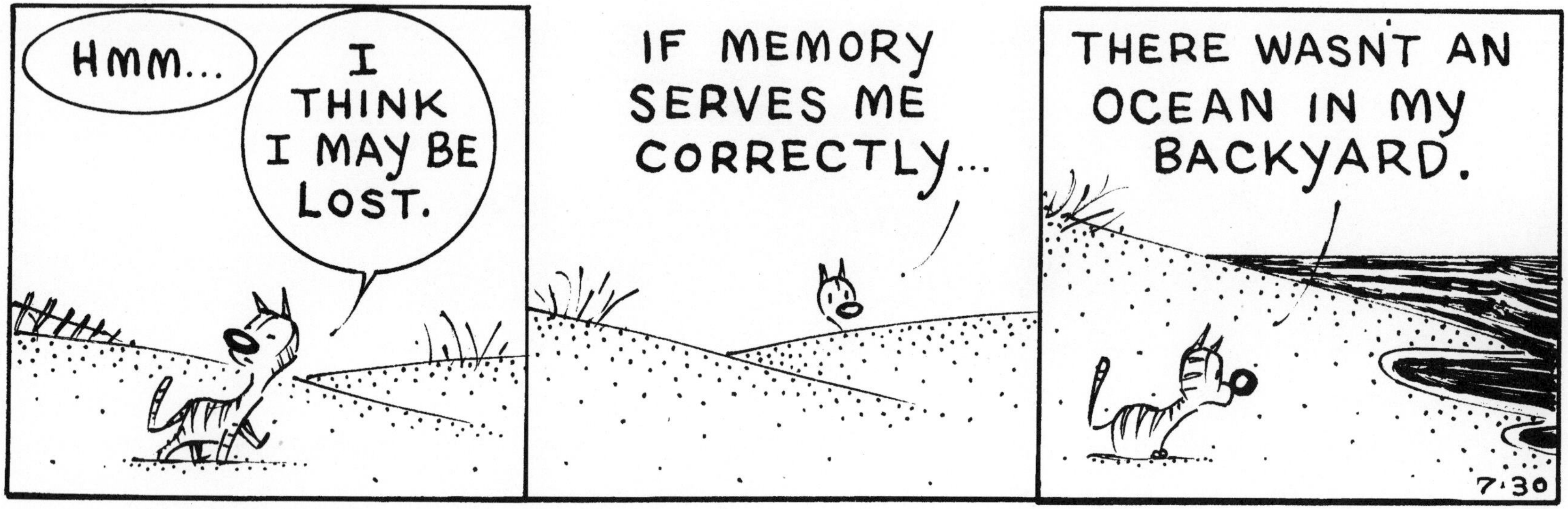
HMM...
I THINK I MAY BE LOST.
IF MEMORY SERVES ME CORRECTLY...
THERE WASN'T AN OCEAN IN MY BACKYARD.
7·30

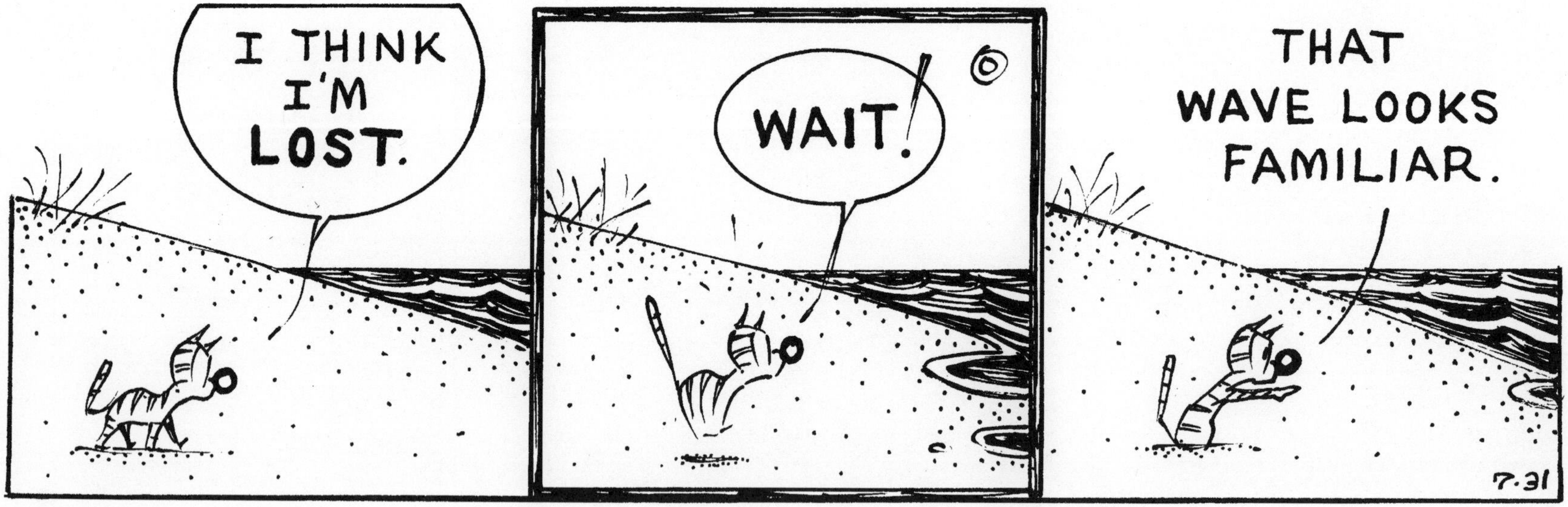
I THINK I'M **LOST**.
WAIT!
©
THAT WAVE LOOKS FAMILIAR.
7·31

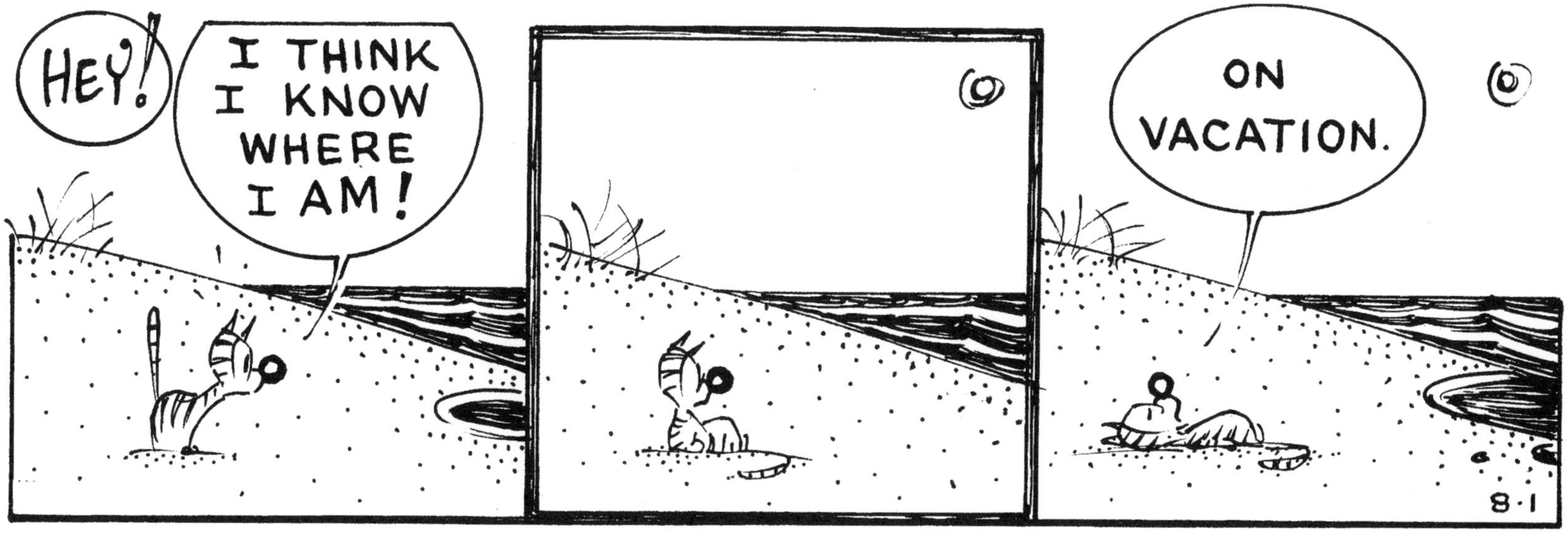
HEY!
I THINK I KNOW WHERE I AM!
ON VACATION.
8·1

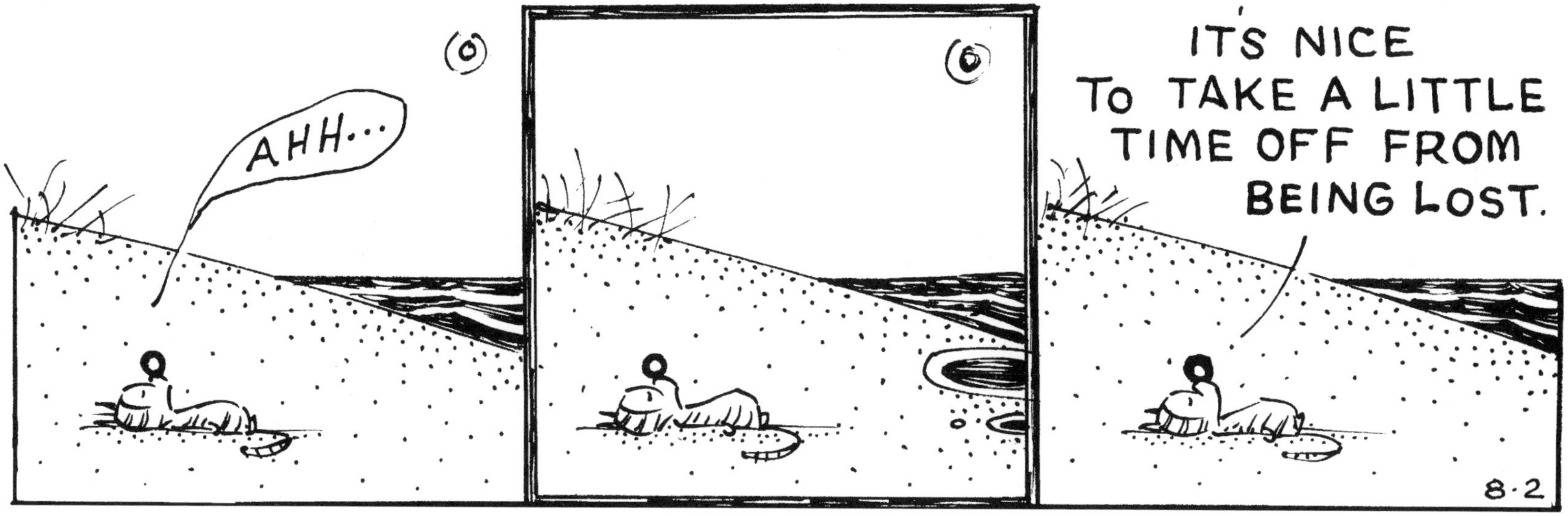
AHH...
IT'S NICE TO TAKE A LITTLE TIME OFF FROM BEING LOST.
8·2

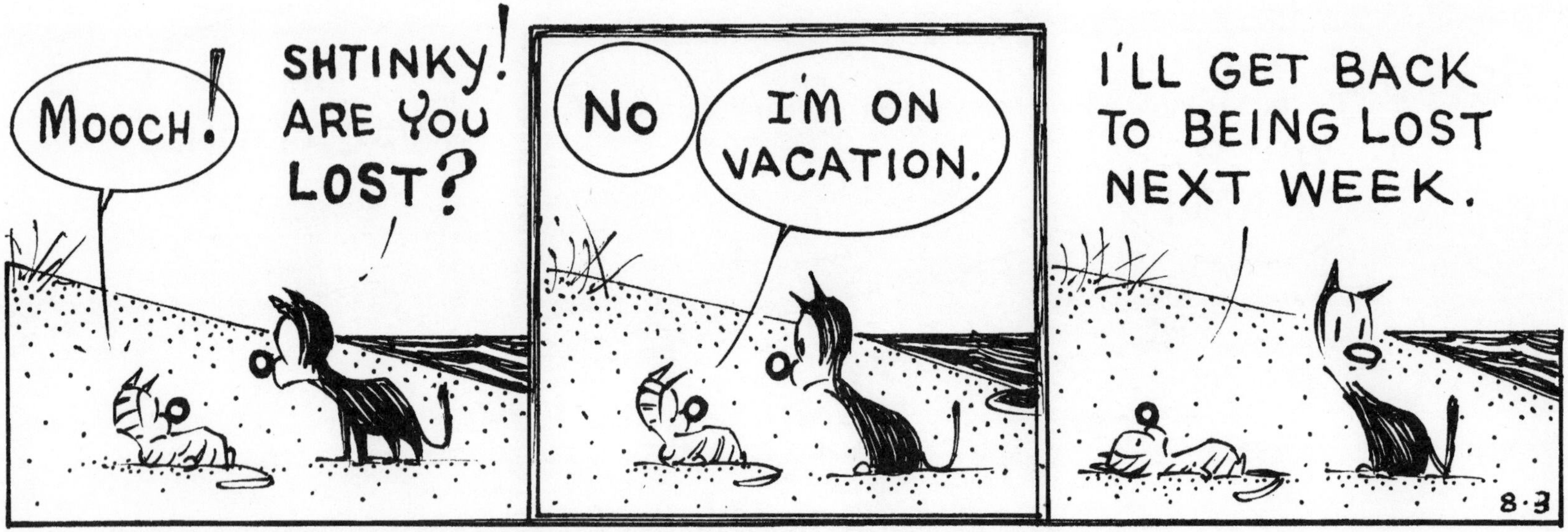
MOOCH!
SHTINKY! ARE YOU LOST?
NO
I'M ON VACATION.
I'LL GET BACK TO BEING LOST NEXT WEEK.
8·3

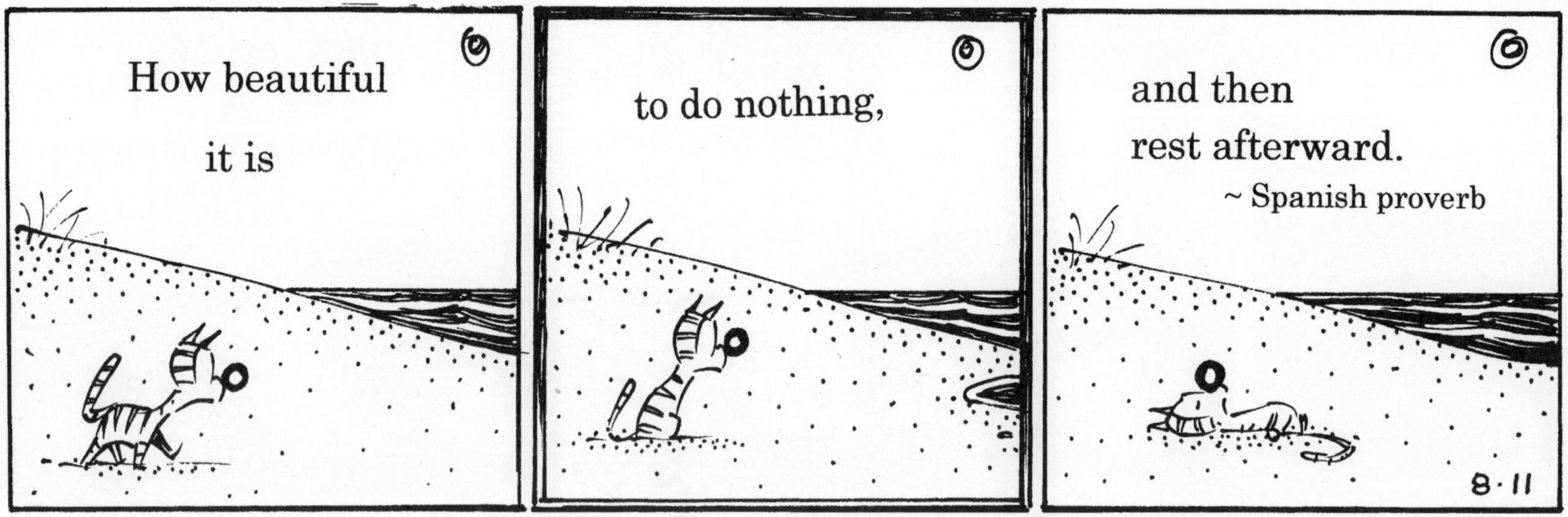
How beautiful
it is
to do nothing,
and then
rest afterward.
~ Spanish proverb
8·11

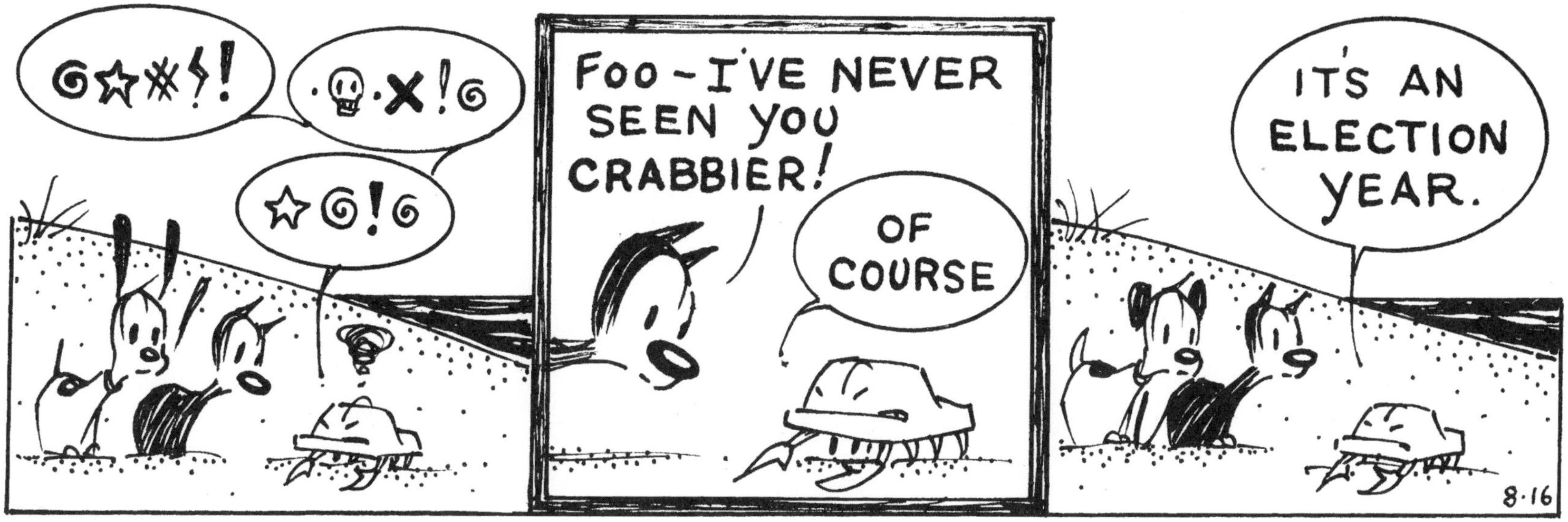
FOO - I'VE NEVER SEEN YOU CRABBIER!
OF COURSE
IT'S AN ELECTION YEAR.
8·16

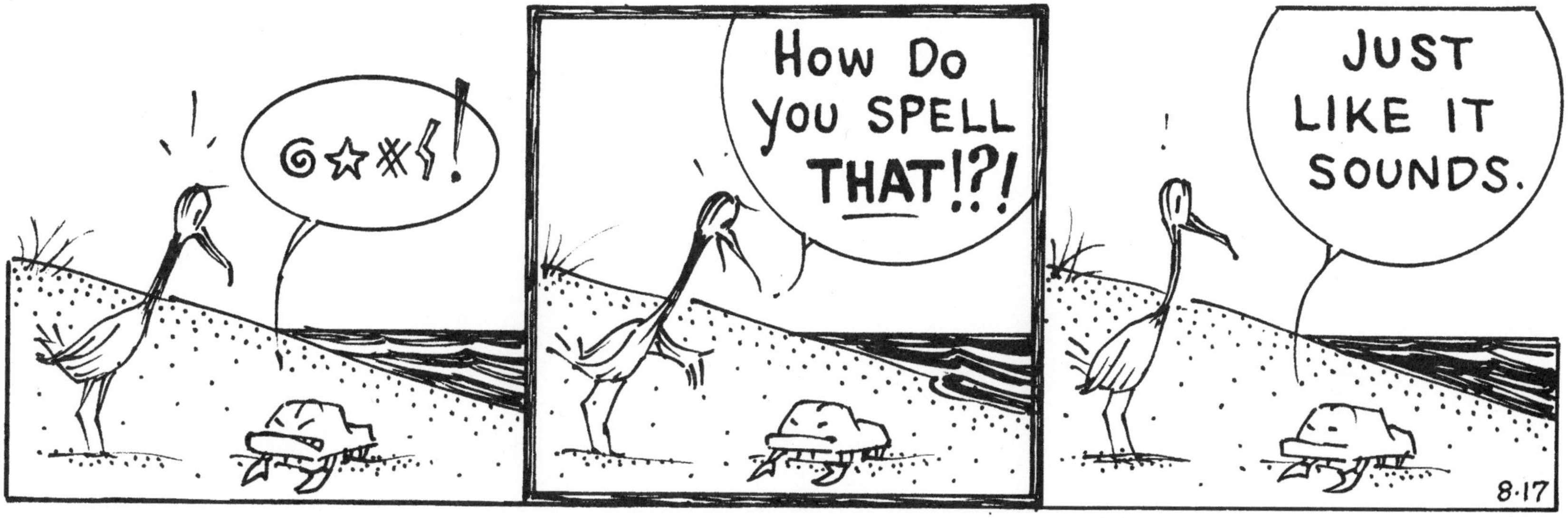
HOW DO YOU SPELL THAT!?!
JUST LIKE IT SOUNDS.
8·17

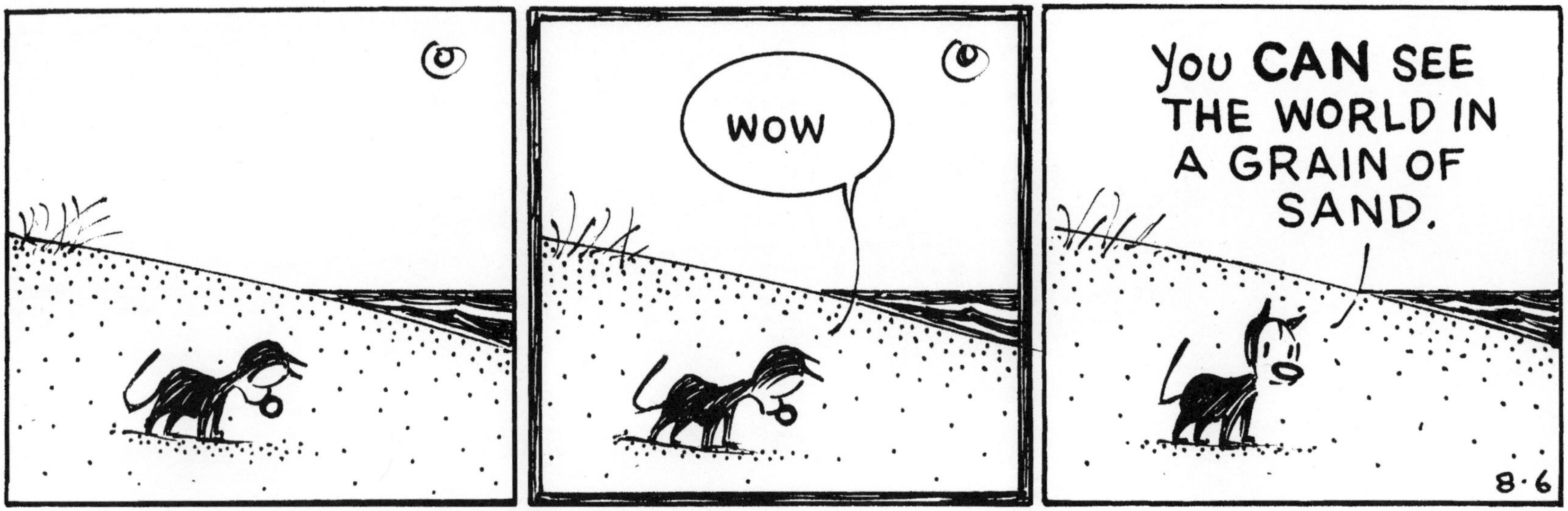
WOW
You CAN SEE THE WORLD IN A GRAIN OF SAND.
8·6

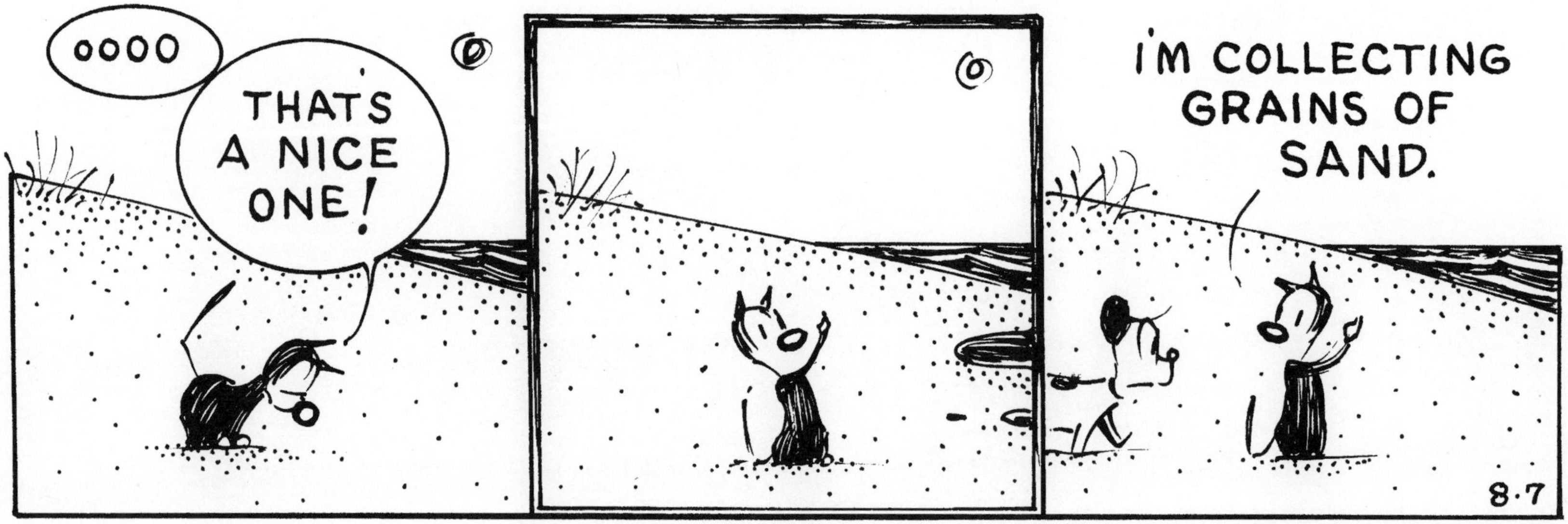
OOOO
THATS A NICE ONE!
I'M COLLECTING GRAINS OF SAND.
8·7

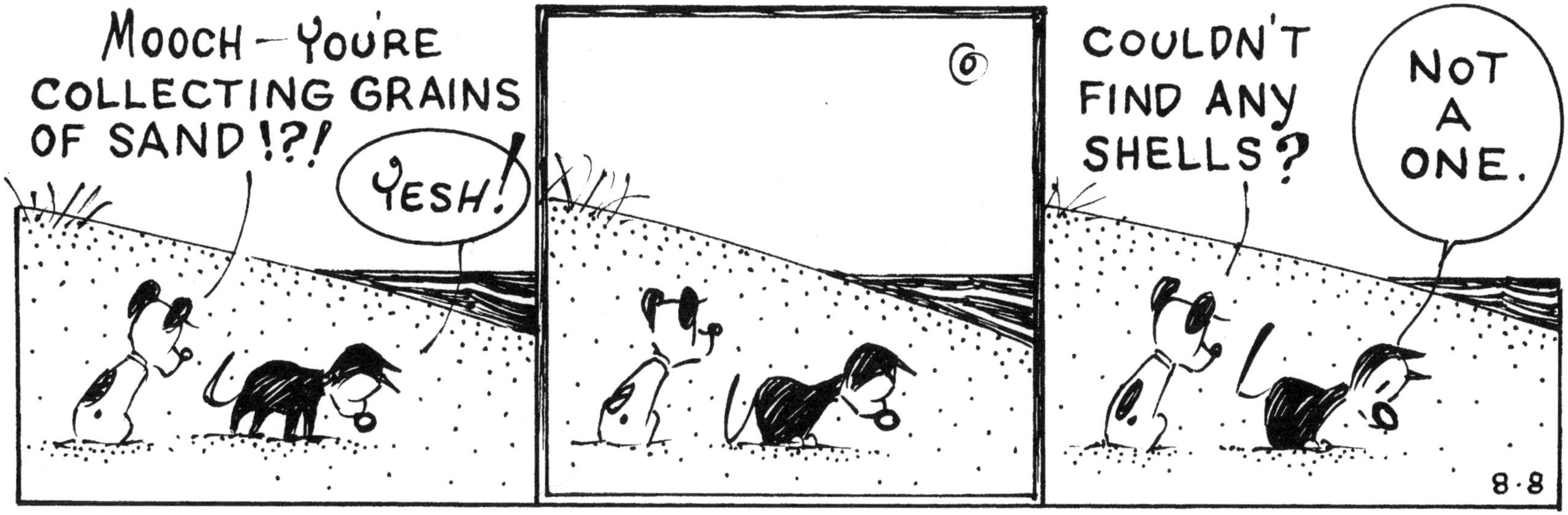
MOOCH—YOU'RE COLLECTING GRAINS OF SAND !?!
YESH!
COULDN'T FIND ANY SHELLS?
NOT A ONE.
8·8

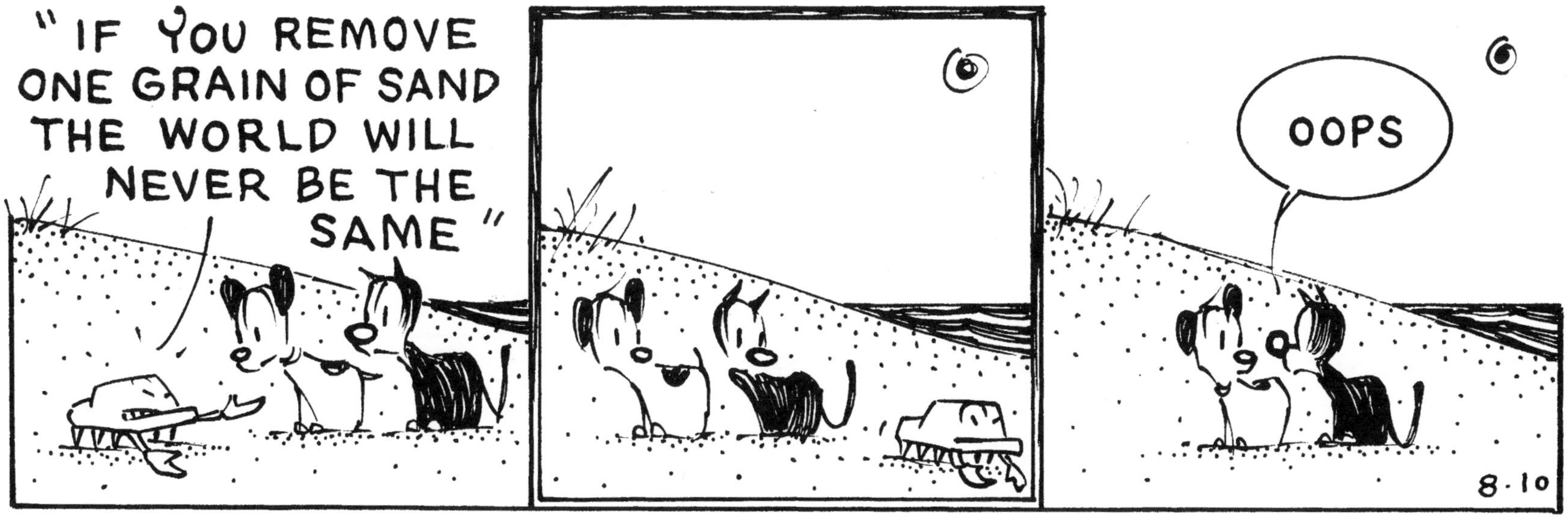
"IF YOU REMOVE ONE GRAIN OF SAND THE WORLD WILL NEVER BE THE SAME"
OOPS
8·10

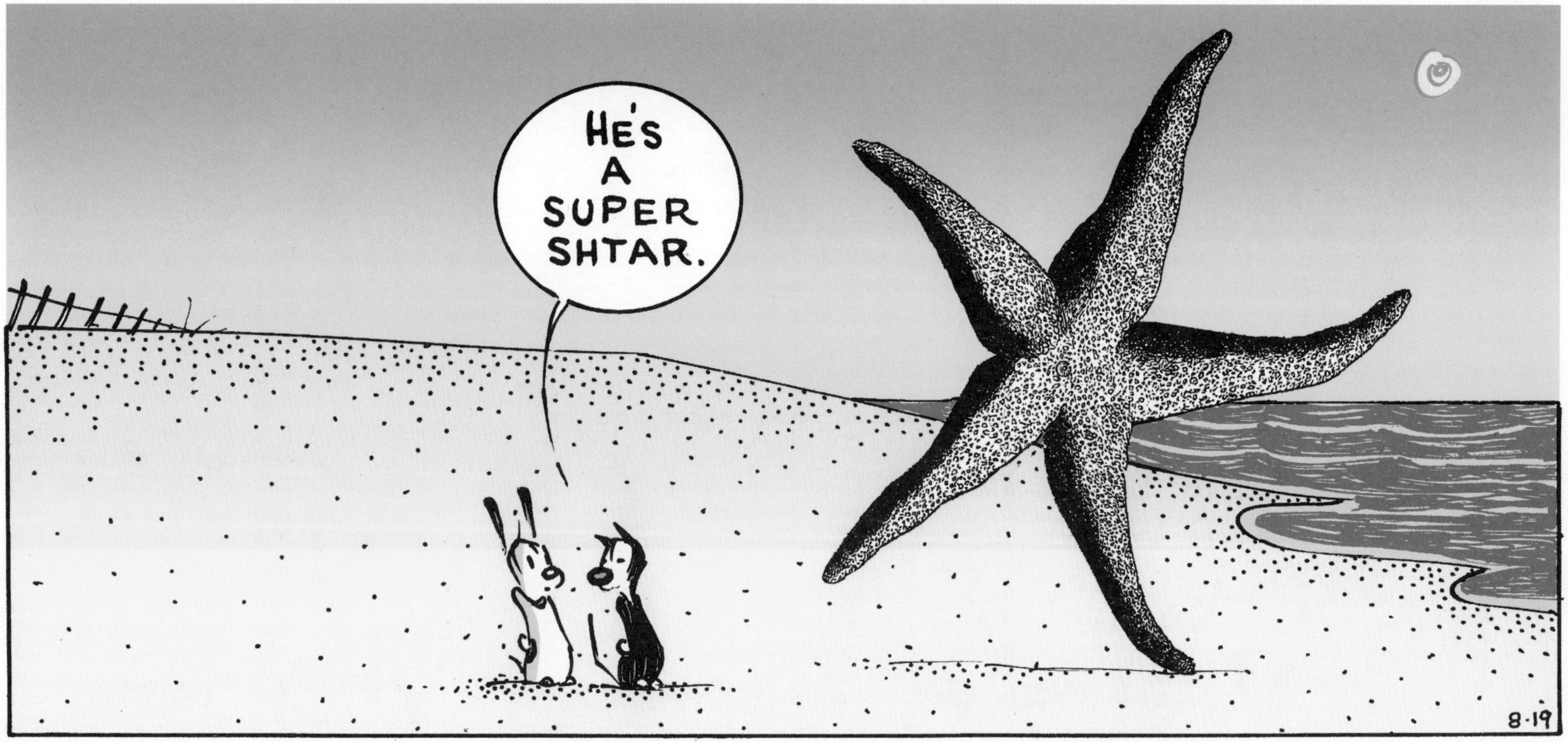
HE'S A SUPER SHTAR.
8·19

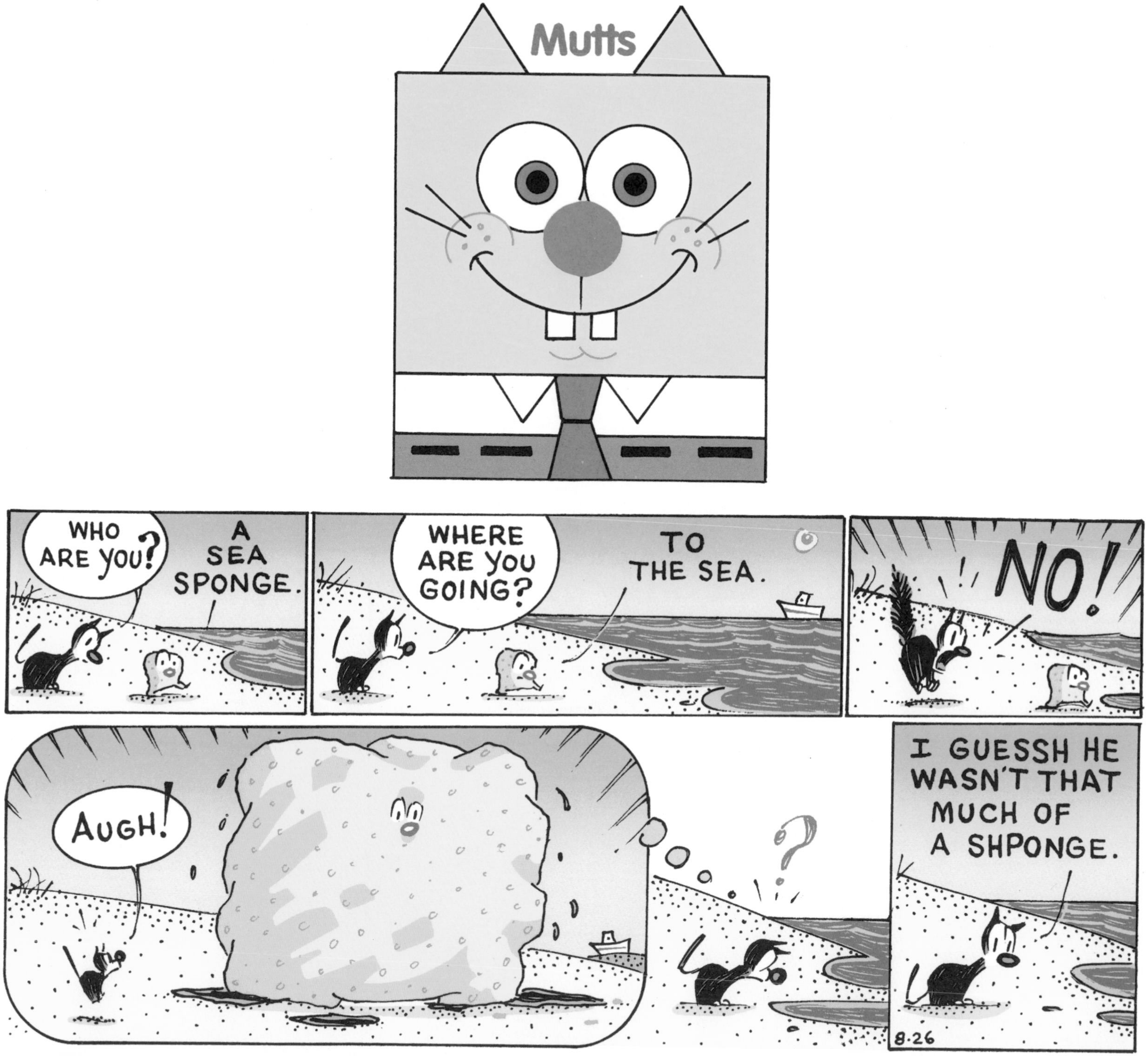
Mutts
WHO ARE YOU?
A SEA SPONGE.
WHERE ARE YOU GOING?
TO THE SEA.
NO!
AUGH!
I GUESSH HE WASN'T THAT MUCH OF A SHPONGE.
8·26

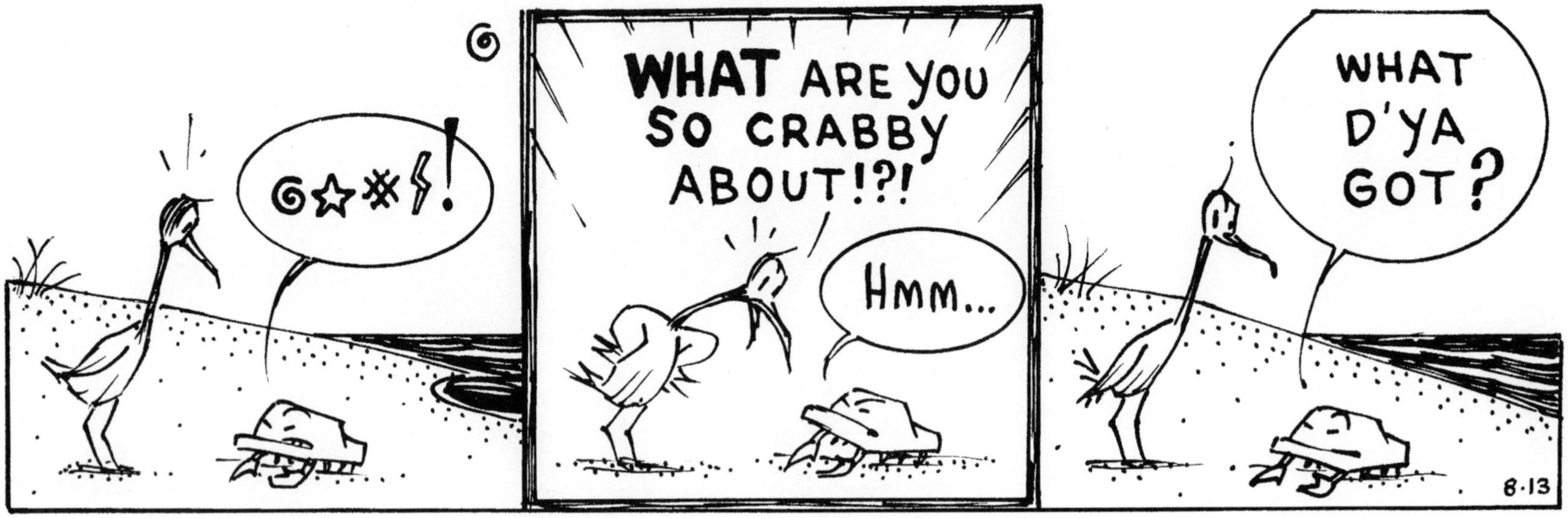
WHAT ARE YOU SO CRABBY ABOUT!?!
HMM...
WHAT D'YA GOT?
8·13

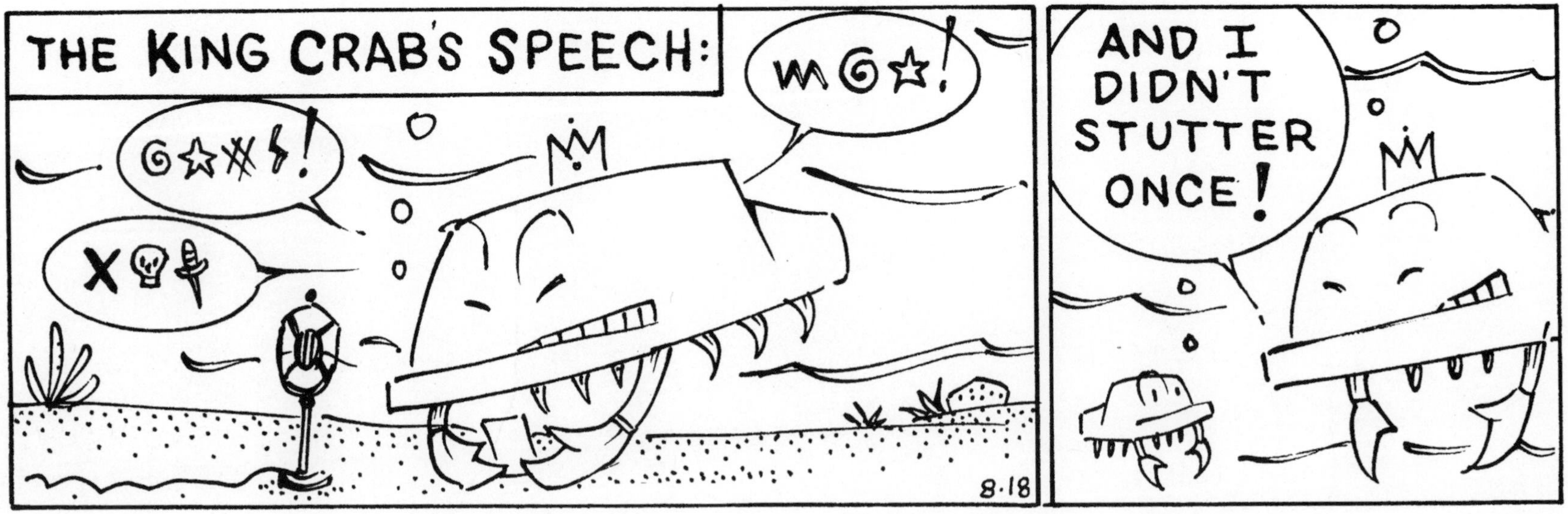
THE KING CRAB'S SPEECH:
AND I DIDN'T STUTTER ONCE!
8·18

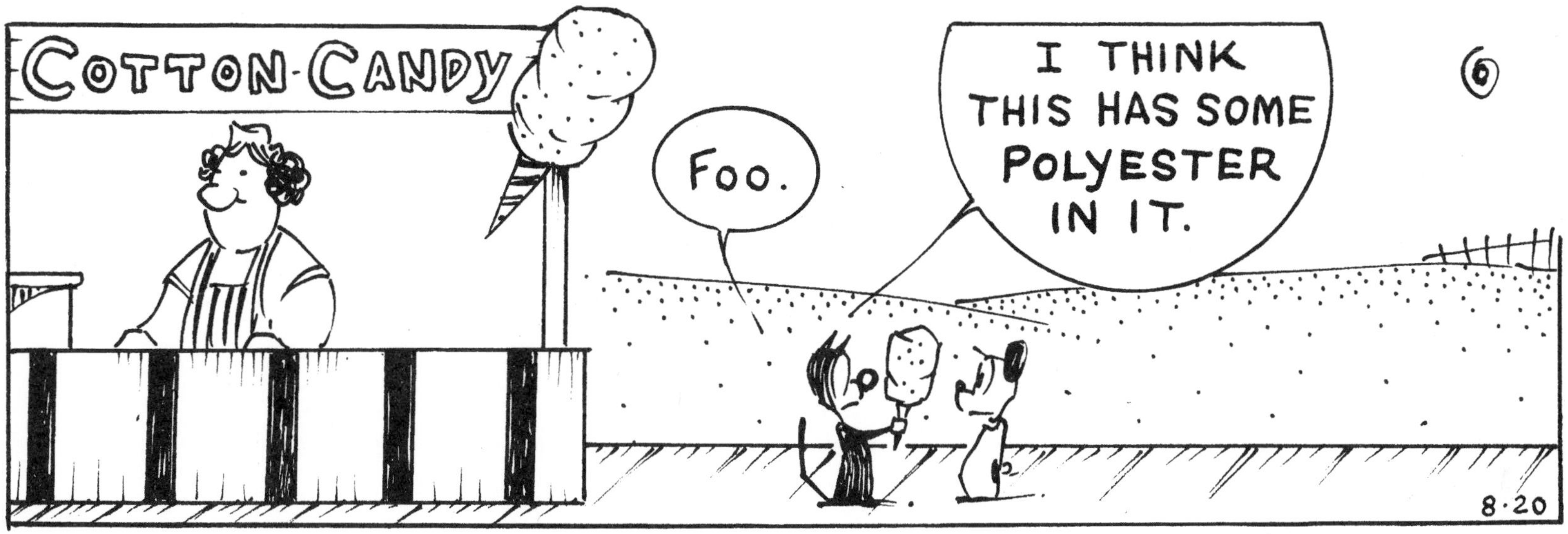
COTTON·CANDY
FOO.
I THINK THIS HAS SOME POLYESTER IN IT.
6
8·20

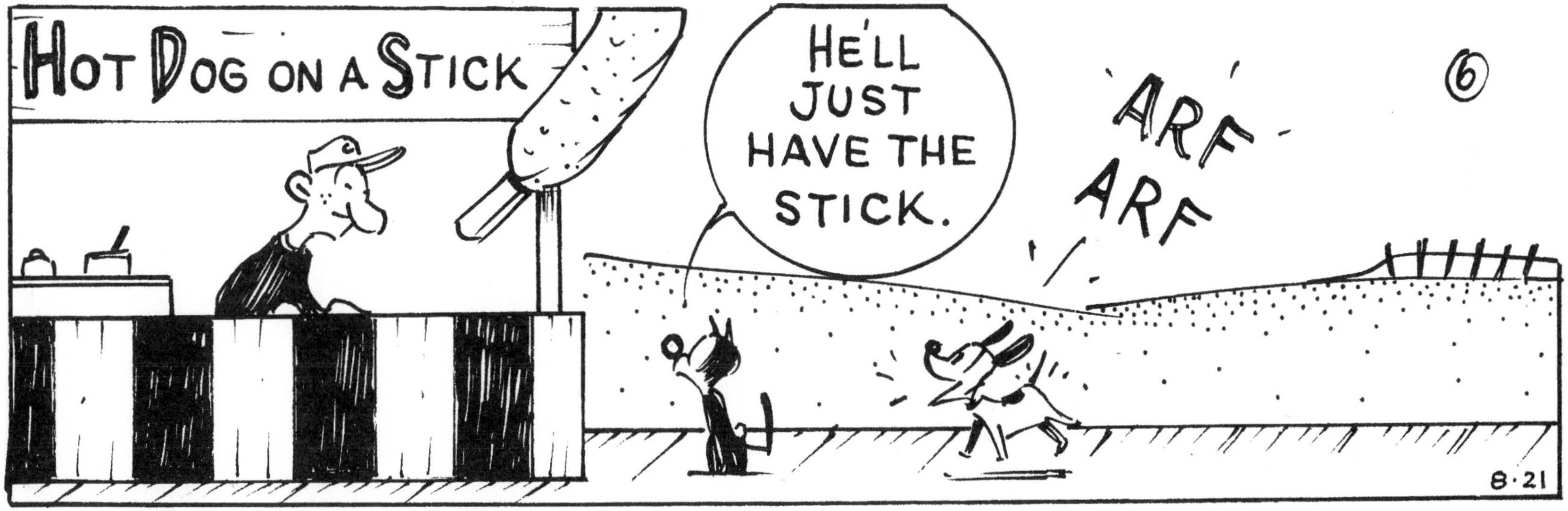
HOT DOG ON A STICK
HE'LL JUST HAVE THE STICK.
ARF ARF
6
8·21

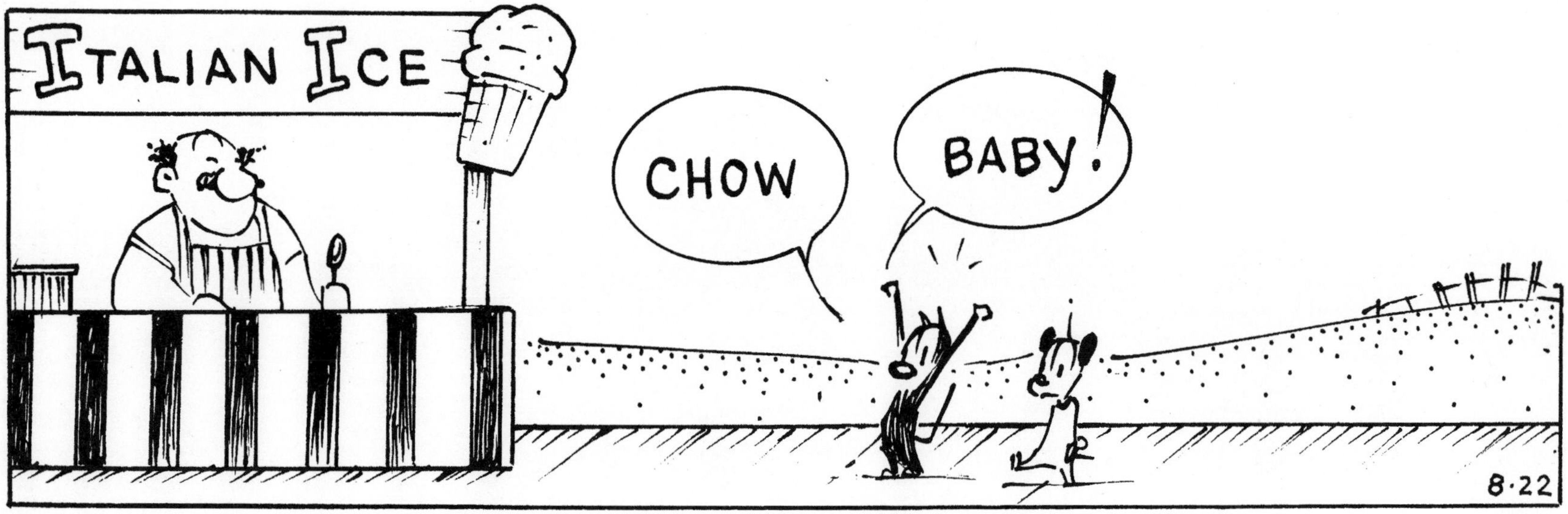
ITALIAN ICE
CHOW
BABY!
8·22

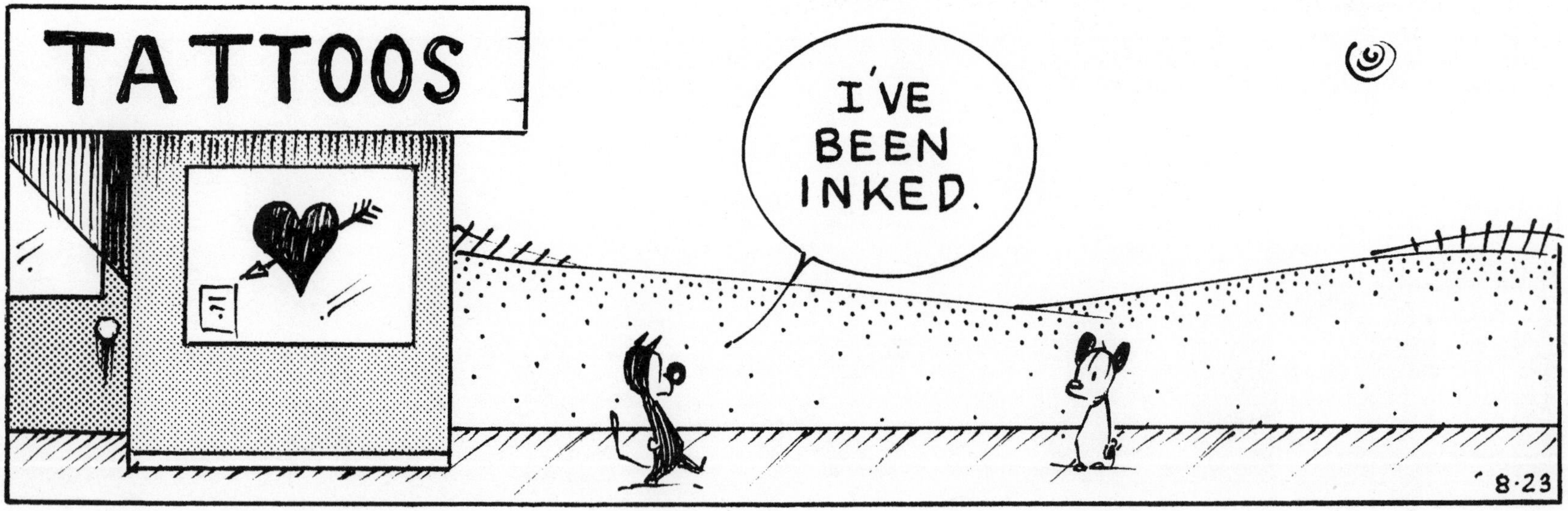
TATTOOS
I'VE BEEN INKED.
8·23

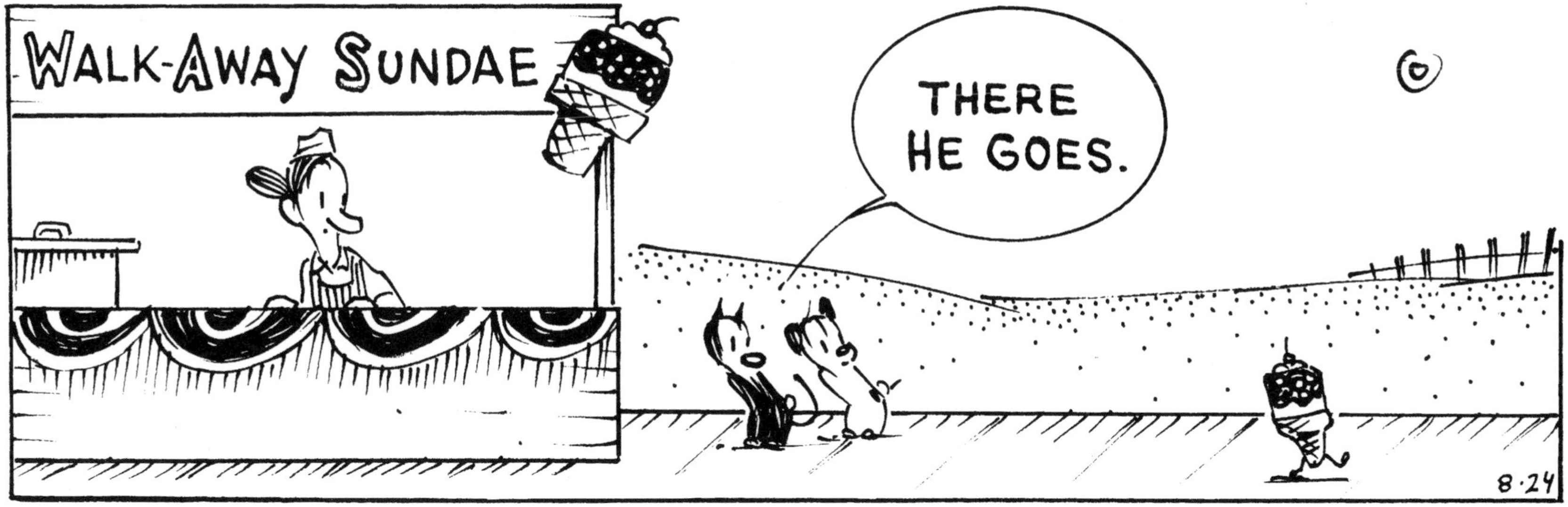
WALK-AWAY SUNDAE
THERE HE GOES.
8·24

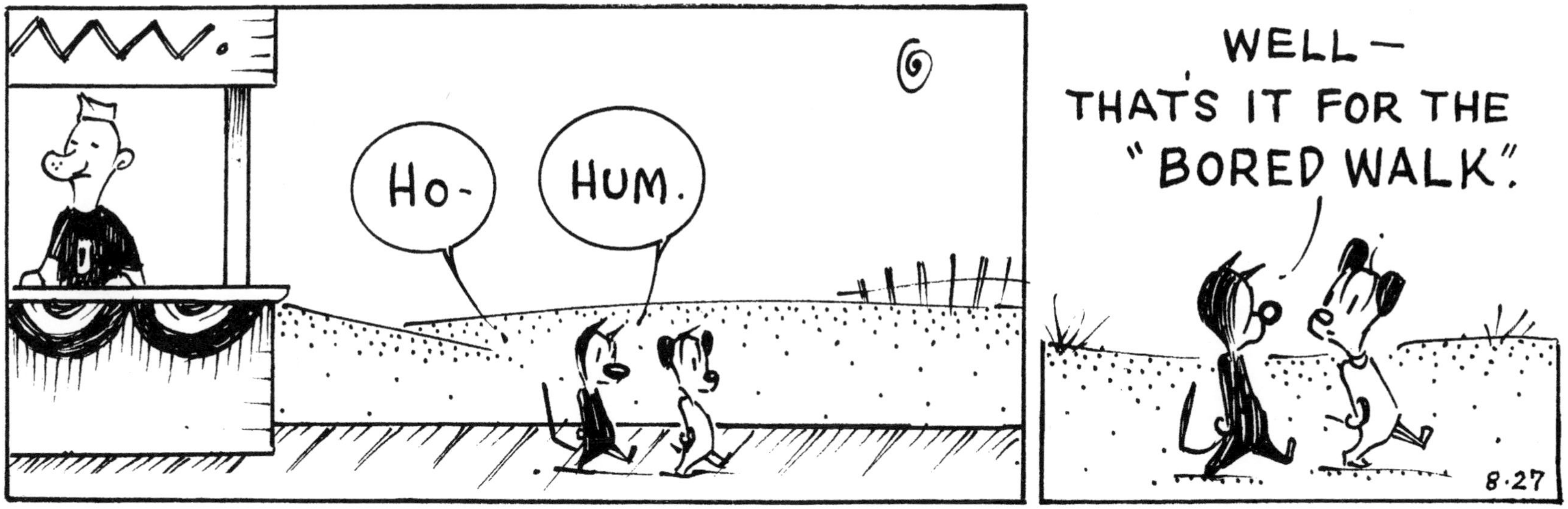
HO-
HUM.
WELL—
THAT'S IT FOR THE
"BORED WALK".
8·27

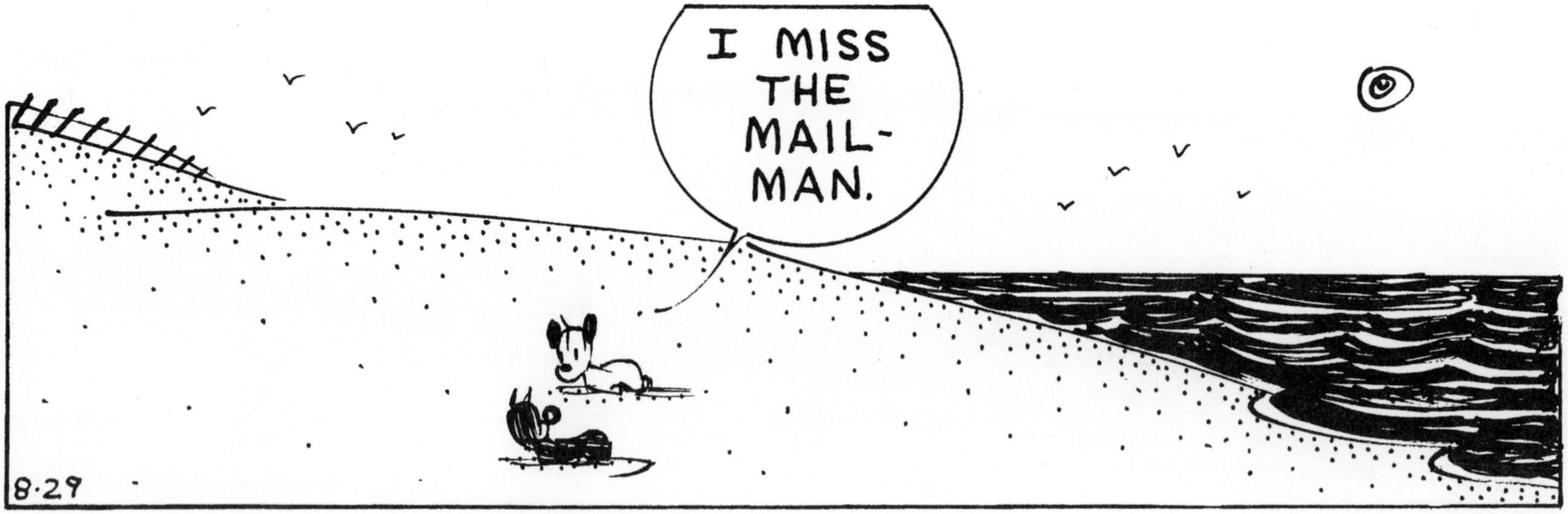
8·29
I MISS THE MAIL-MAN.

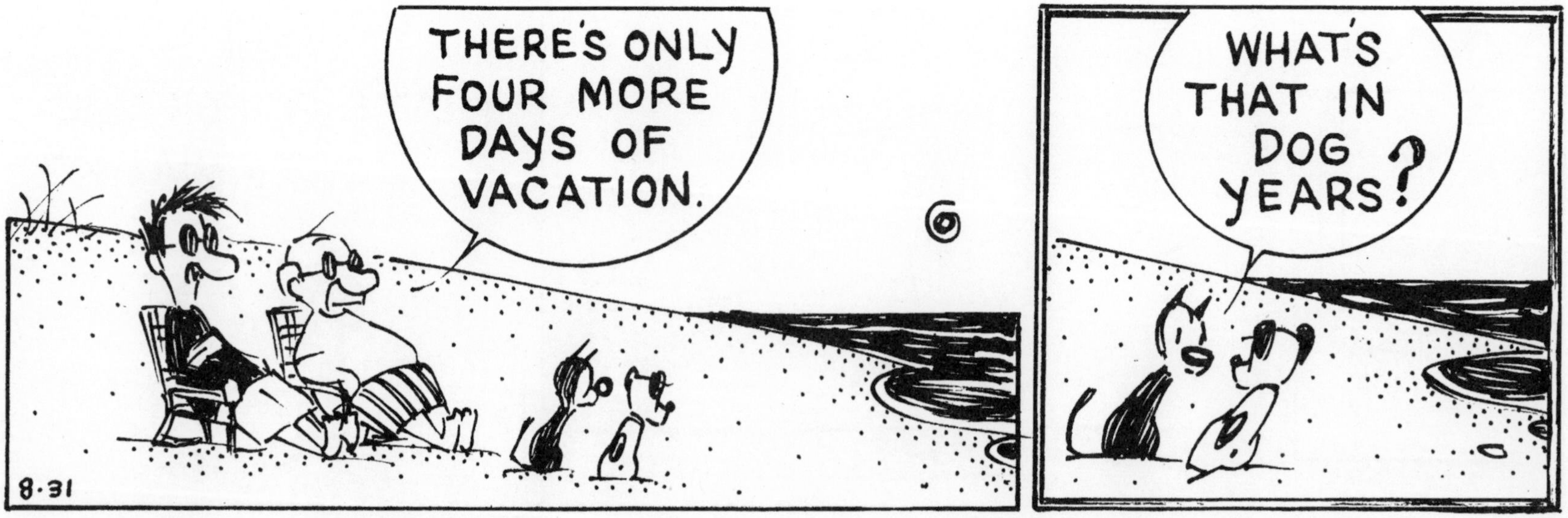
8·31
THERE'S ONLY FOUR MORE DAYS OF VACATION.
WHAT'S THAT IN DOG YEARS?

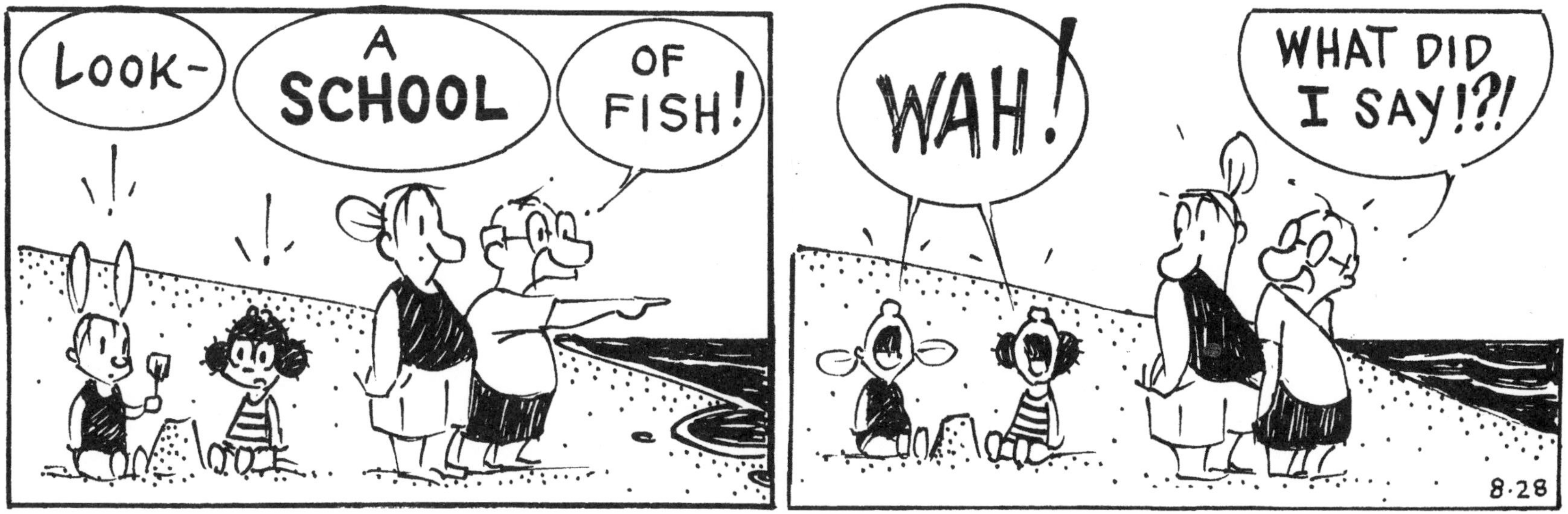
LOOK-
A SCHOOL
OF FISH!
WAH!
WHAT DID I SAY!?!
8·28

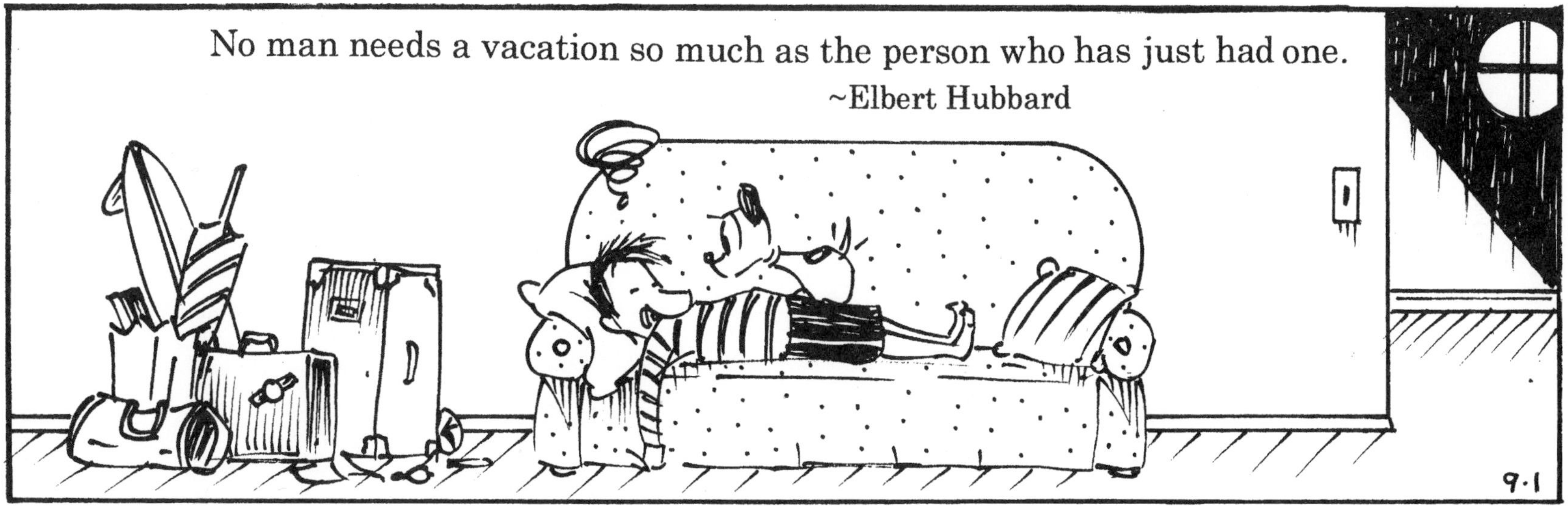
No man needs a vacation so much as the person who has just had one.
~Elbert Hubbard
9·1

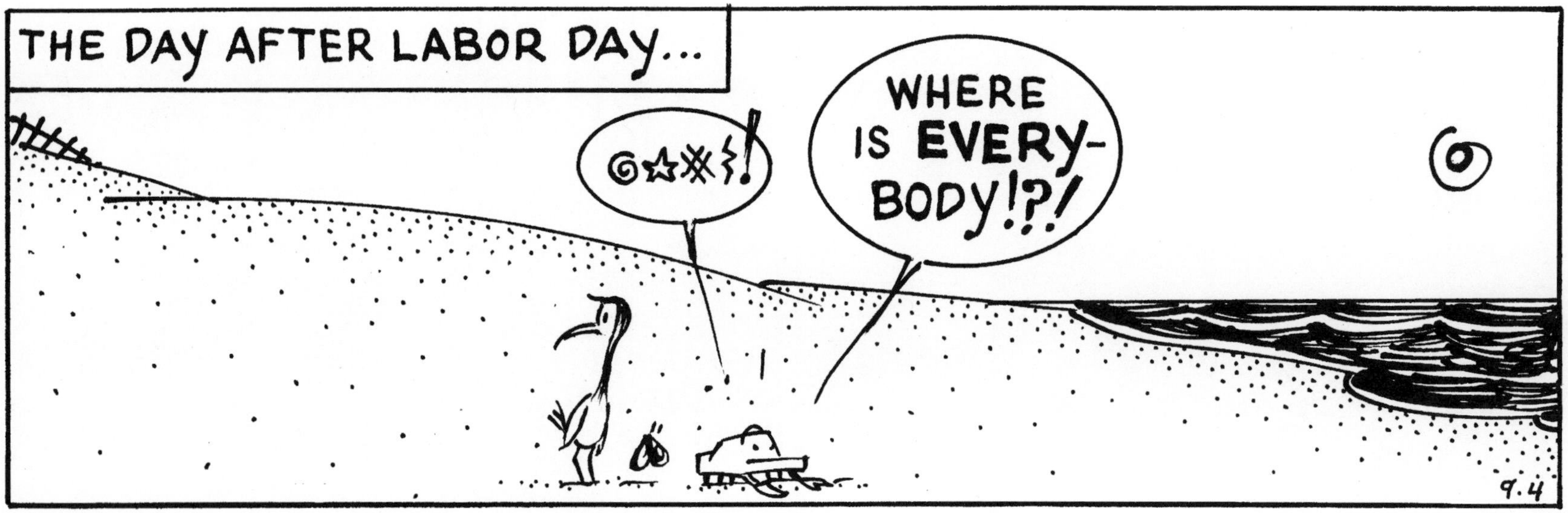
THE DAY AFTER LABOR DAY...
WHERE IS EVERY-BODY!?!
9.4

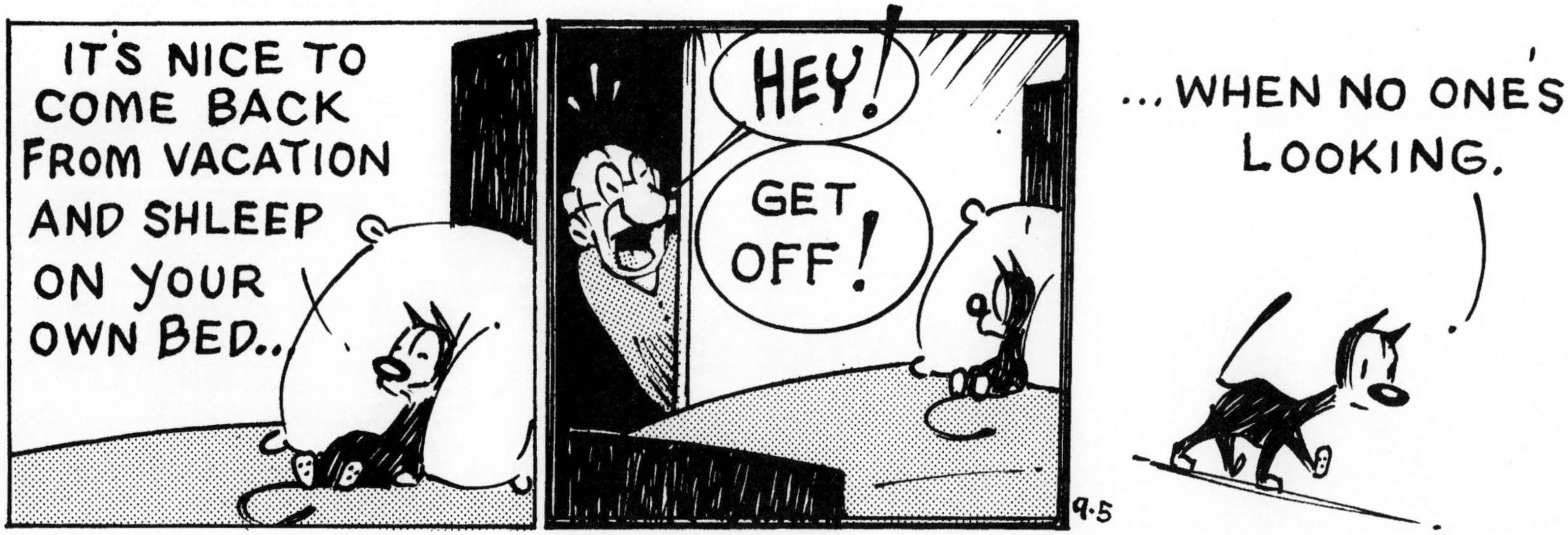
IT'S NICE TO COME BACK FROM VACATION AND SHLEEP ON YOUR OWN BED..
HEY!
GET OFF!
9.5
...WHEN NO ONE'S LOOKING.

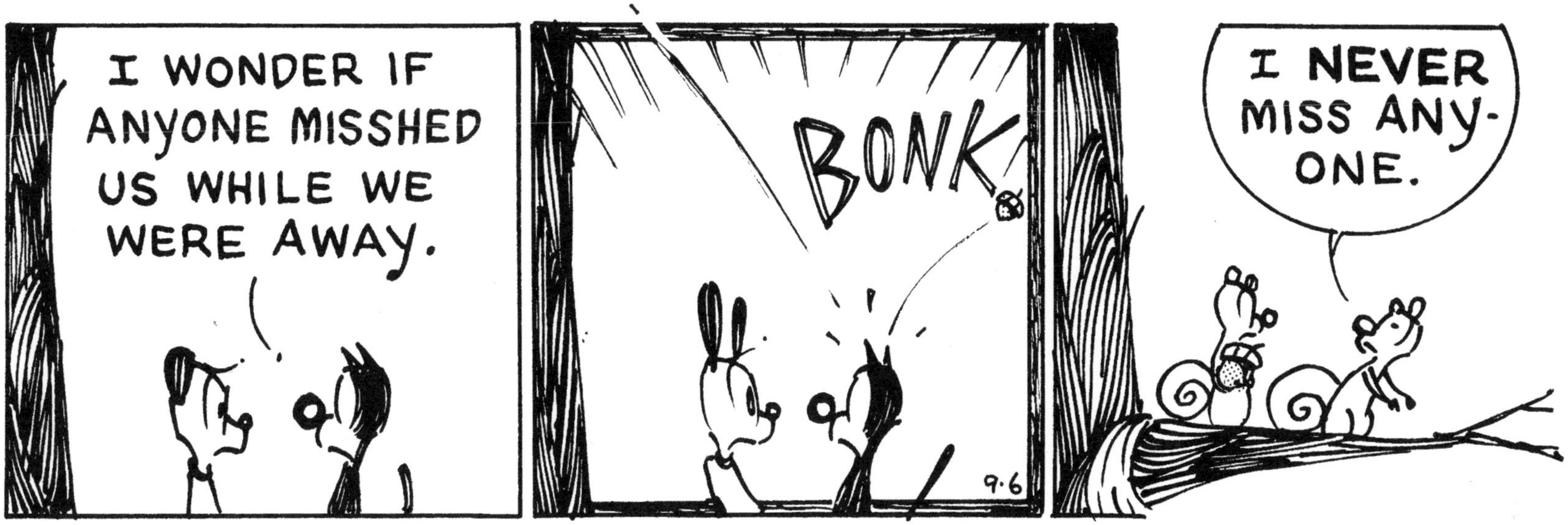
I WONDER IF ANYONE MISSHED US WHILE WE WERE AWAY.
BONK
9.6
I NEVER MISS ANY-ONE.

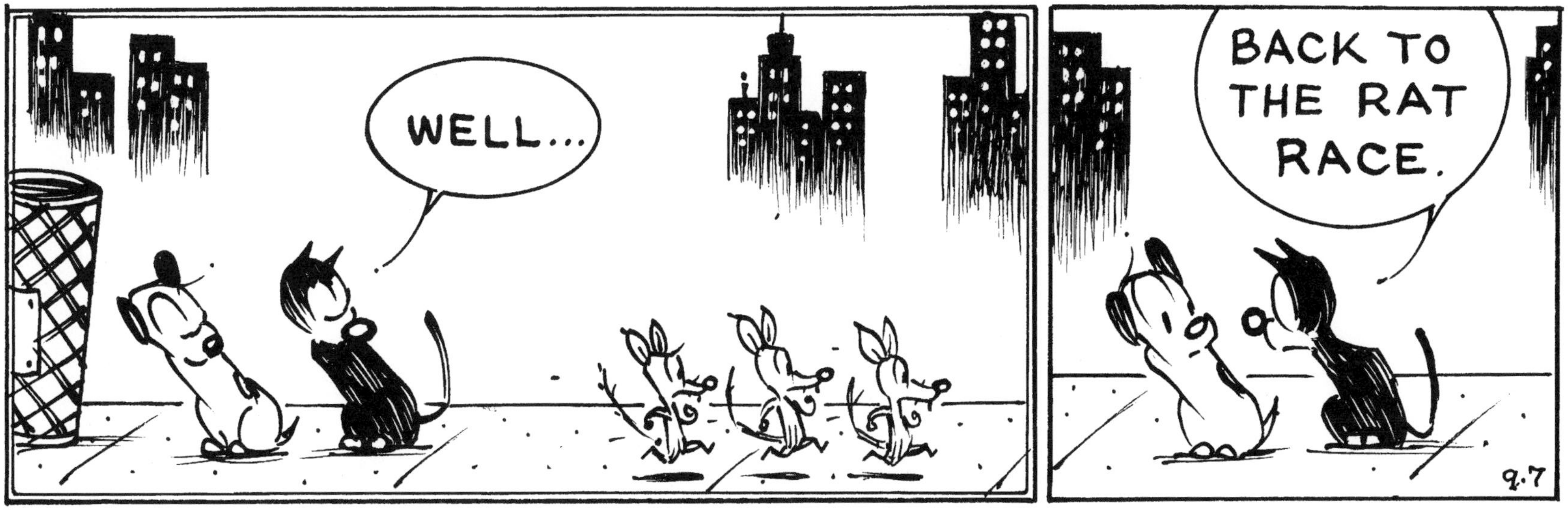
WELL...
BACK TO THE RAT RACE.
9.7

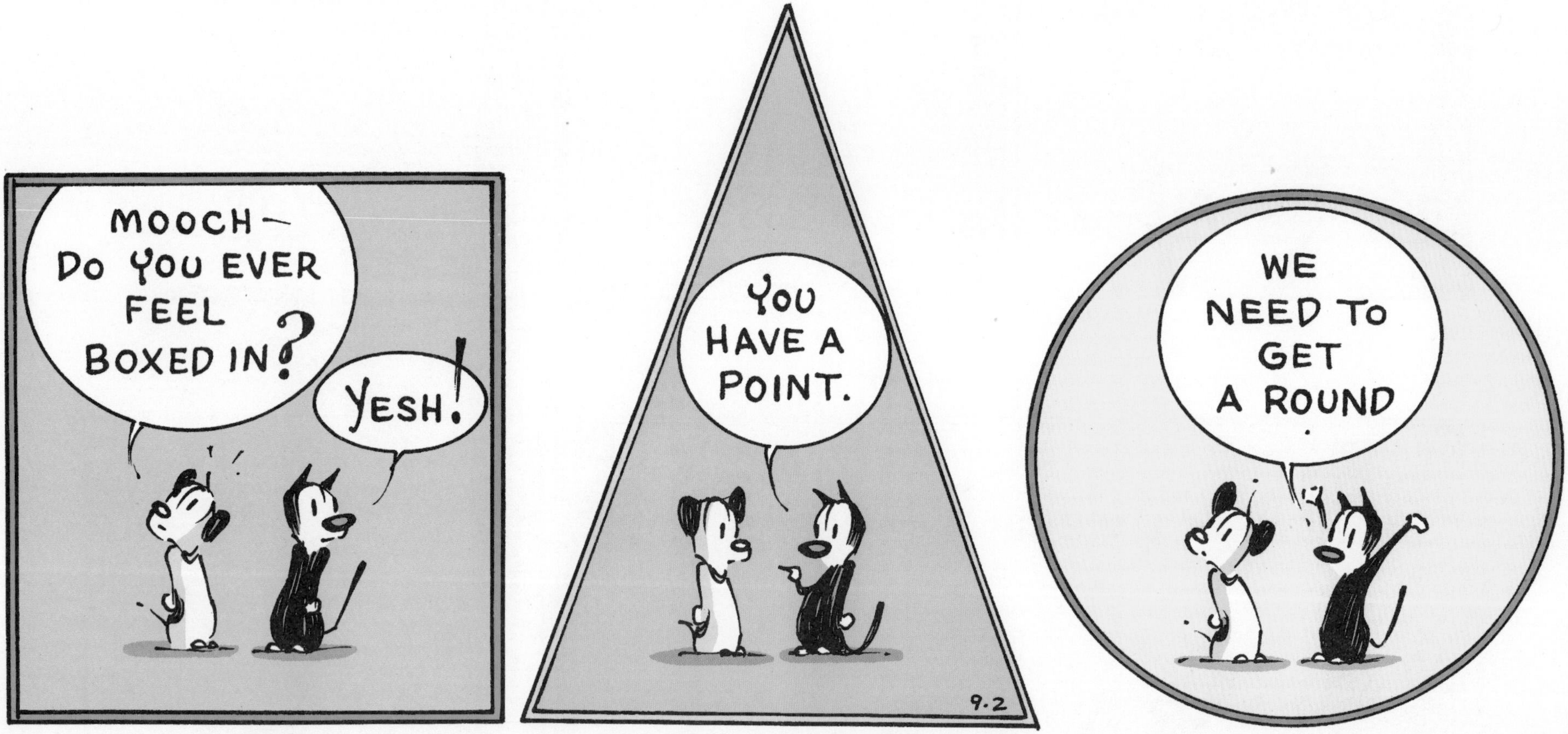
MOOCH— DO YOU EVER FEEL BOXED IN?
YESH!
YOU HAVE A POINT.
9.2
WE NEED TO GET A ROUND.

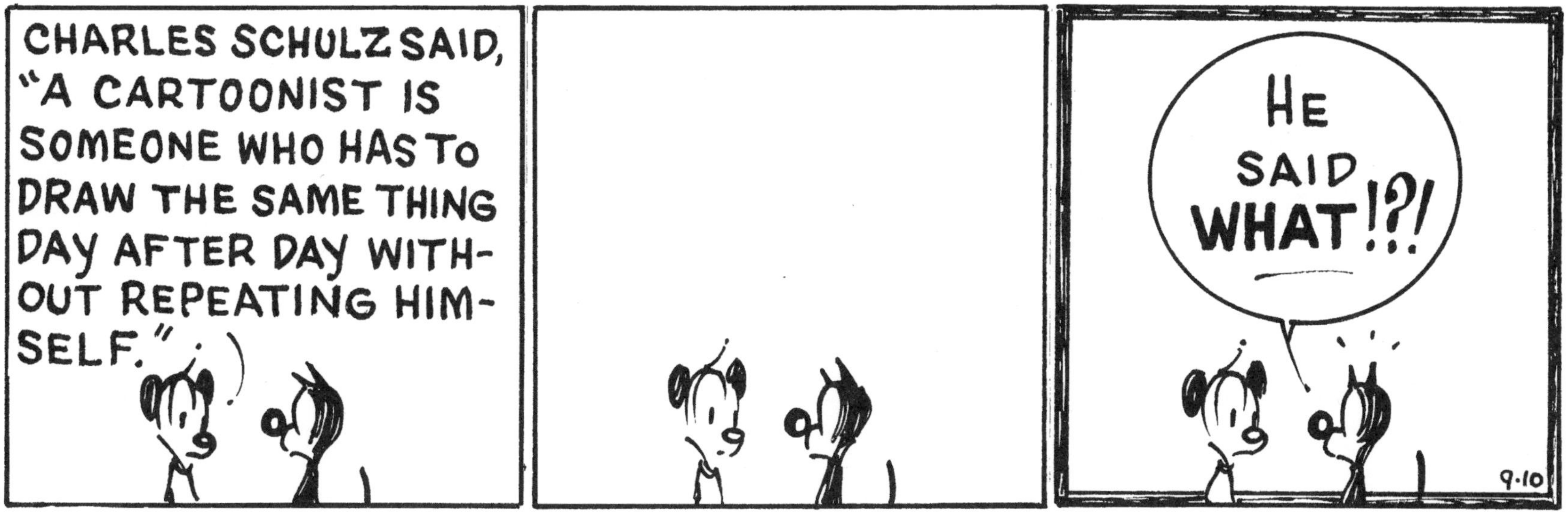
CHARLES SCHULZ SAID, "A CARTOONIST IS SOMEONE WHO HAS TO DRAW THE SAME THING DAY AFTER DAY WITHOUT REPEATING HIMSELF."
HE SAID WHAT!?!
9·10

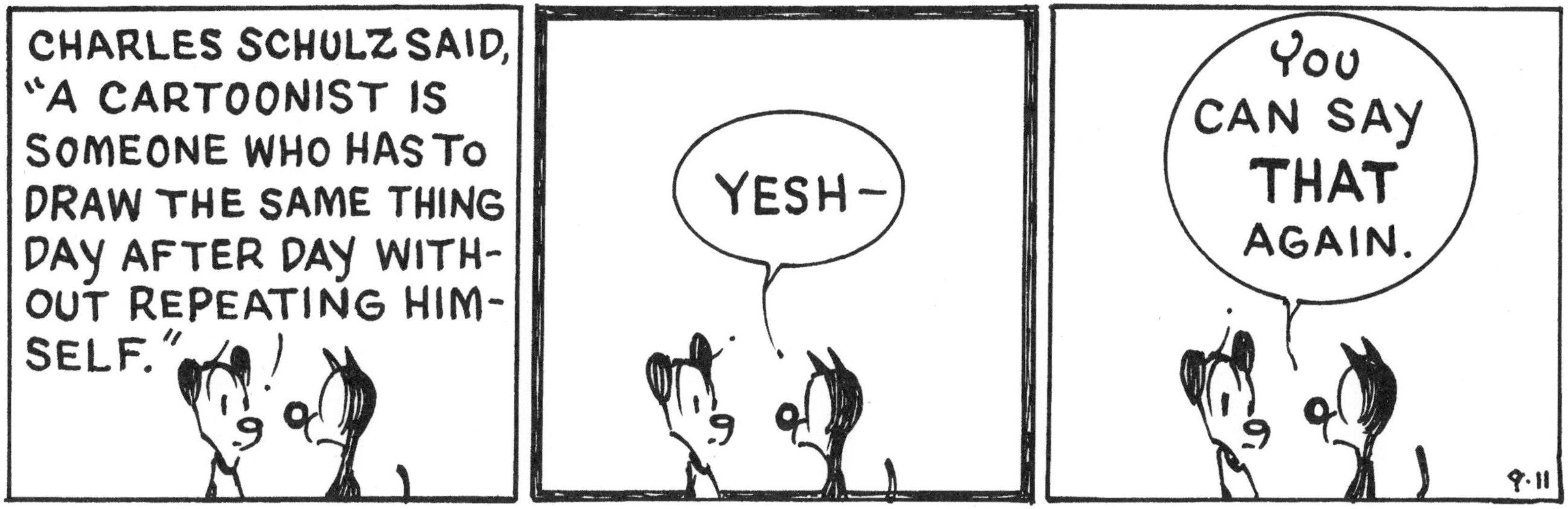
CHARLES SCHULZ SAID, "A CARTOONIST IS SOMEONE WHO HAS TO DRAW THE SAME THING DAY AFTER DAY WITHOUT REPEATING HIMSELF."
YESH–
YOU CAN SAY THAT AGAIN.
9·11

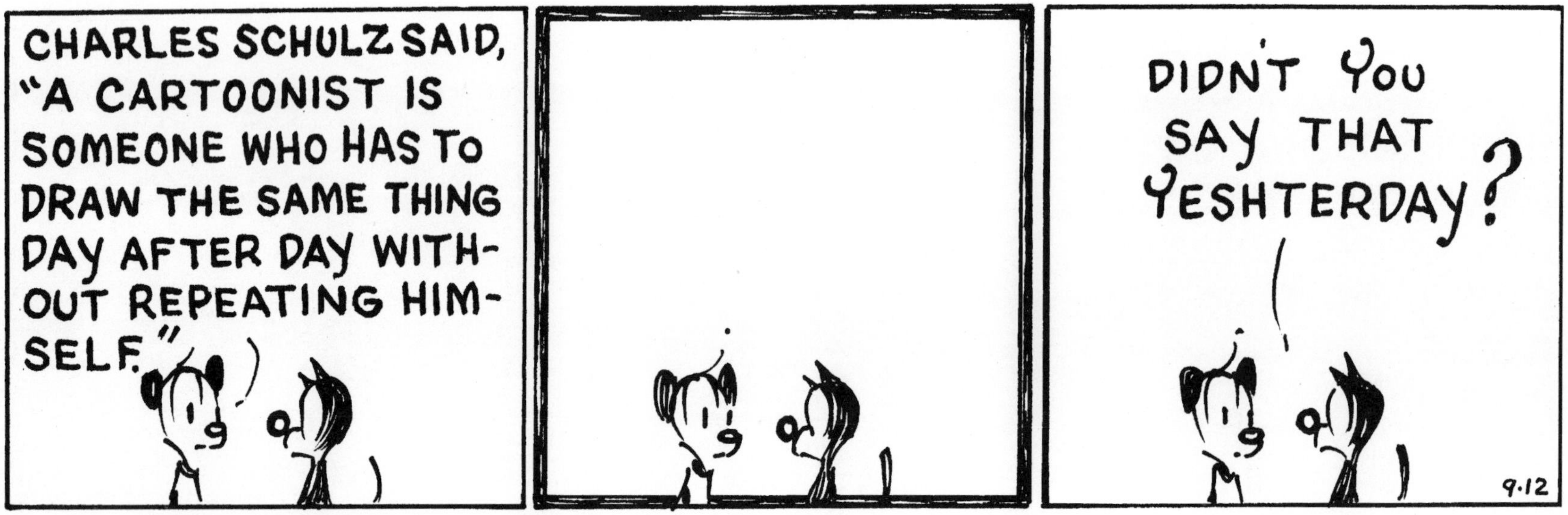
CHARLES SCHULZ SAID, "A CARTOONIST IS SOMEONE WHO HAS TO DRAW THE SAME THING DAY AFTER DAY WITHOUT REPEATING HIMSELF."
DIDN'T YOU SAY THAT YESHTERDAY?
9.12

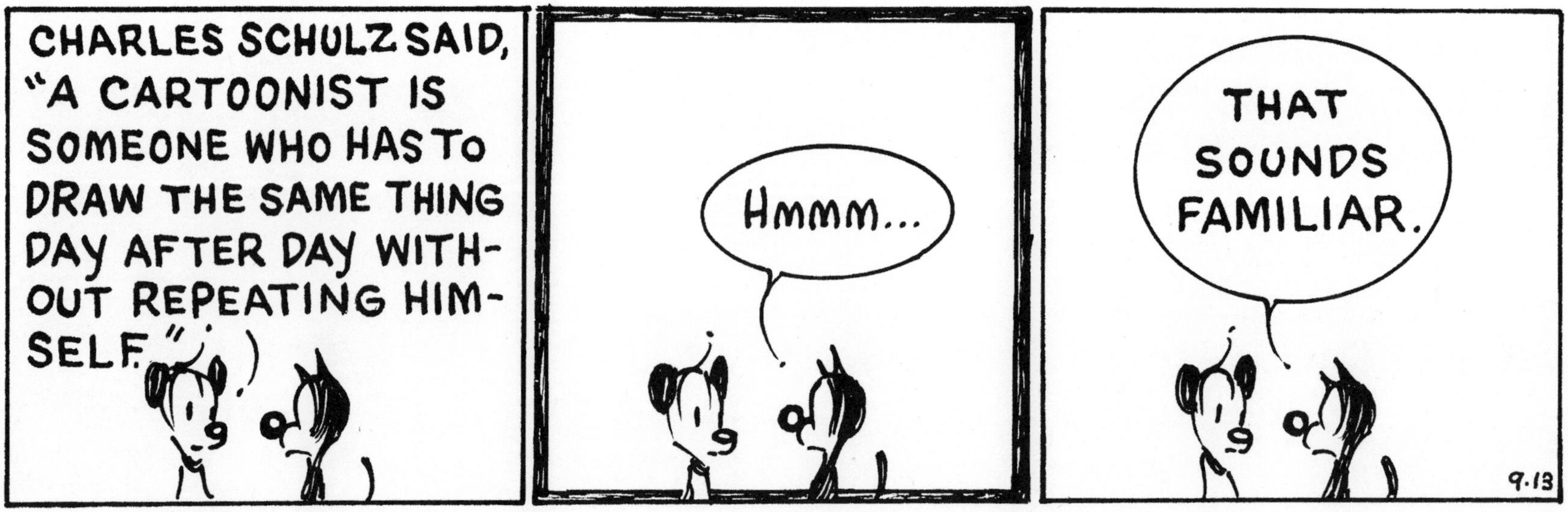
CHARLES SCHULZ SAID, "A CARTOONIST IS SOMEONE WHO HAS TO DRAW THE SAME THING DAY AFTER DAY WITHOUT REPEATING HIMSELF."
Hmmm...
THAT SOUNDS FAMILIAR.
9.13

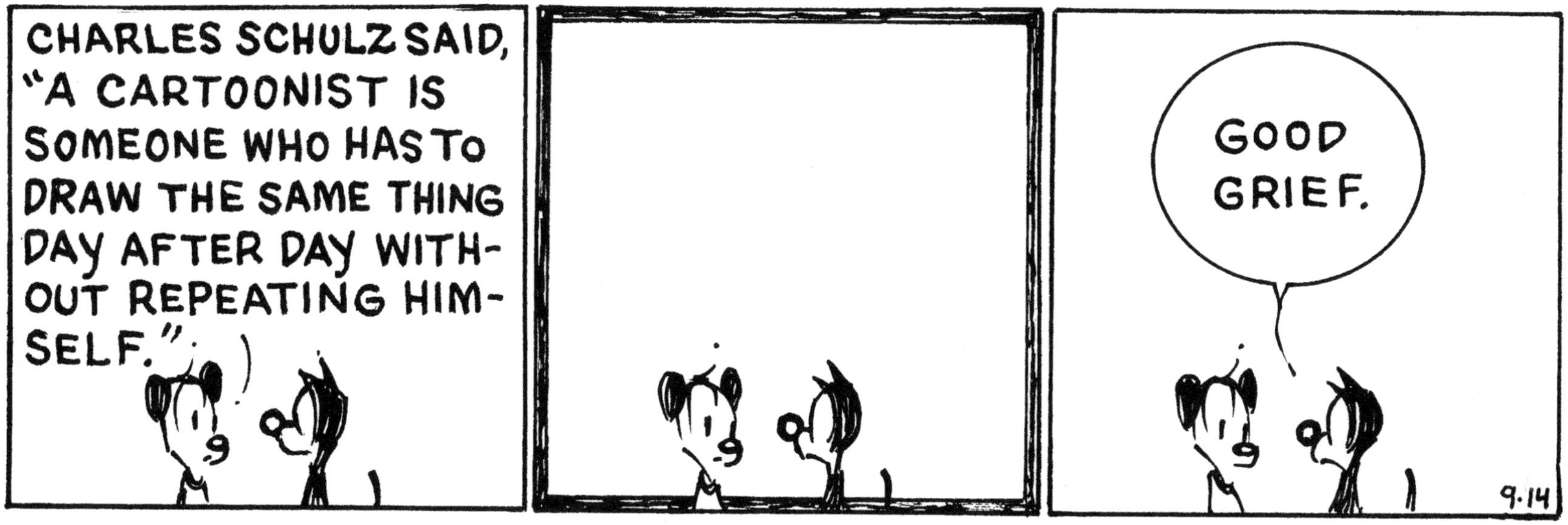
CHARLES SCHULZ SAID, "A CARTOONIST IS SOMEONE WHO HAS TO DRAW THE SAME THING DAY AFTER DAY WITH- OUT REPEATING HIM- SELF."
GOOD GRIEF.
9.14

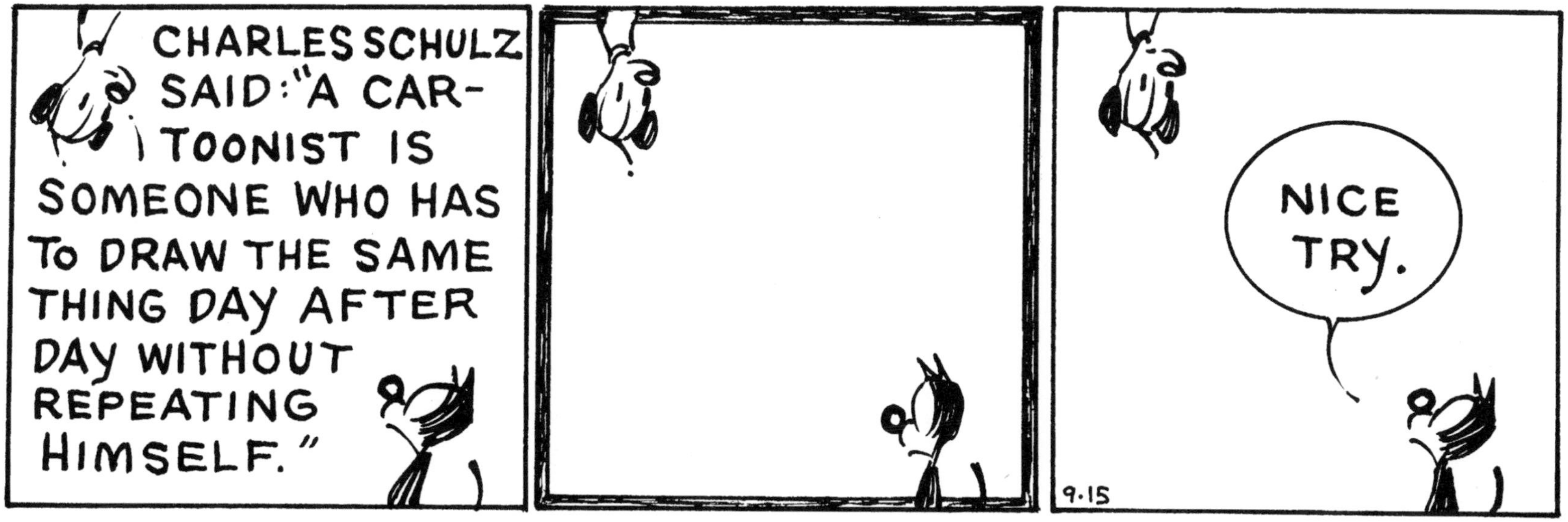
CHARLES SCHULZ SAID: "A CAR- TOONIST IS SOMEONE WHO HAS TO DRAW THE SAME THING DAY AFTER DAY WITHOUT REPEATING HIMSELF."
NICE TRY.
9.15

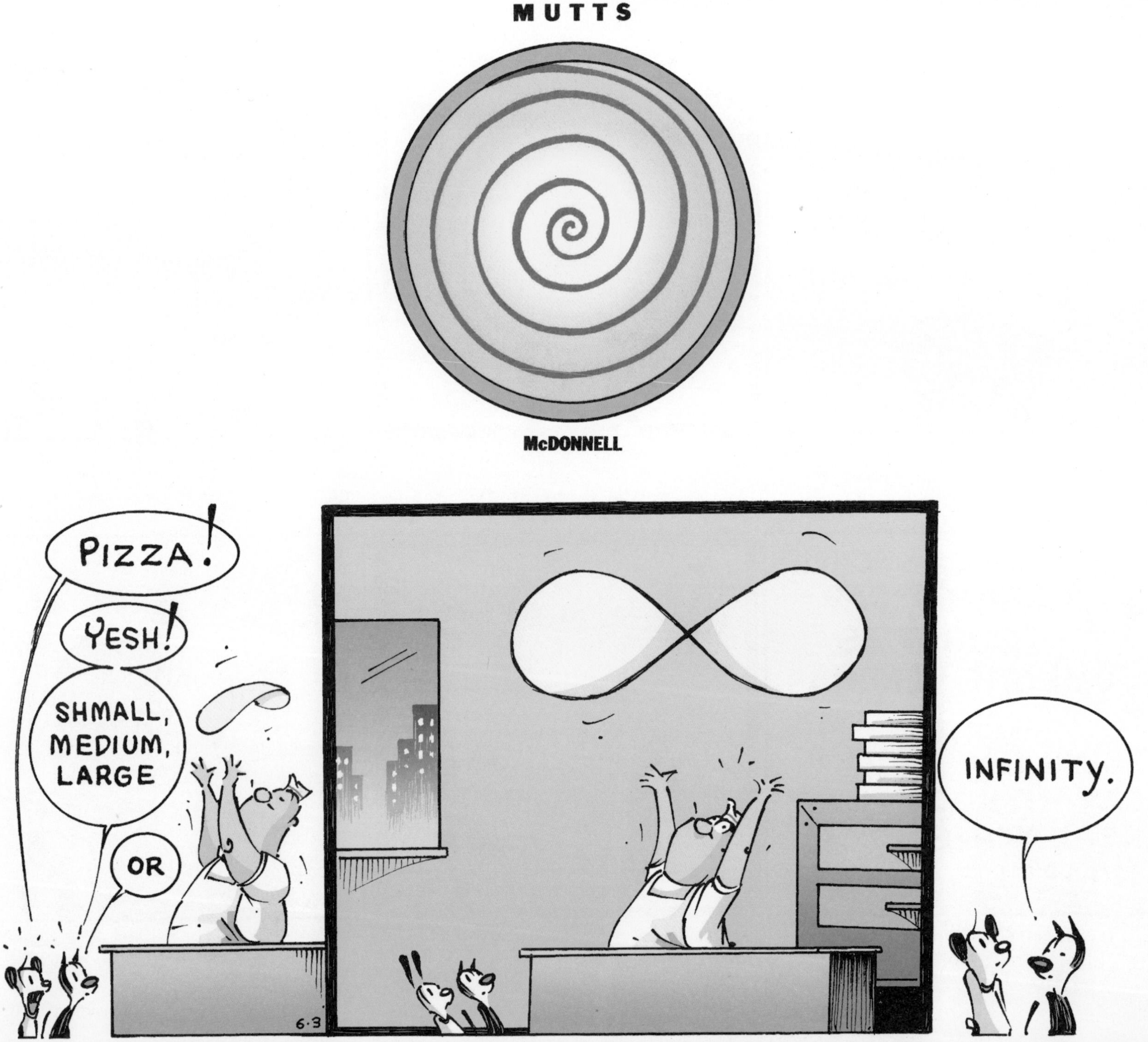
MUTTS
McDONNELL
PIZZA!
YESH!
SHMALL, MEDIUM, LARGE
OR
6·3
INFINITY.

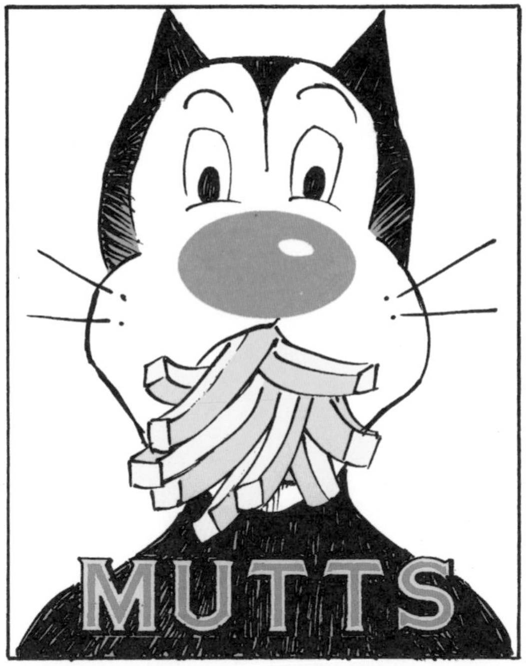
MUTTS

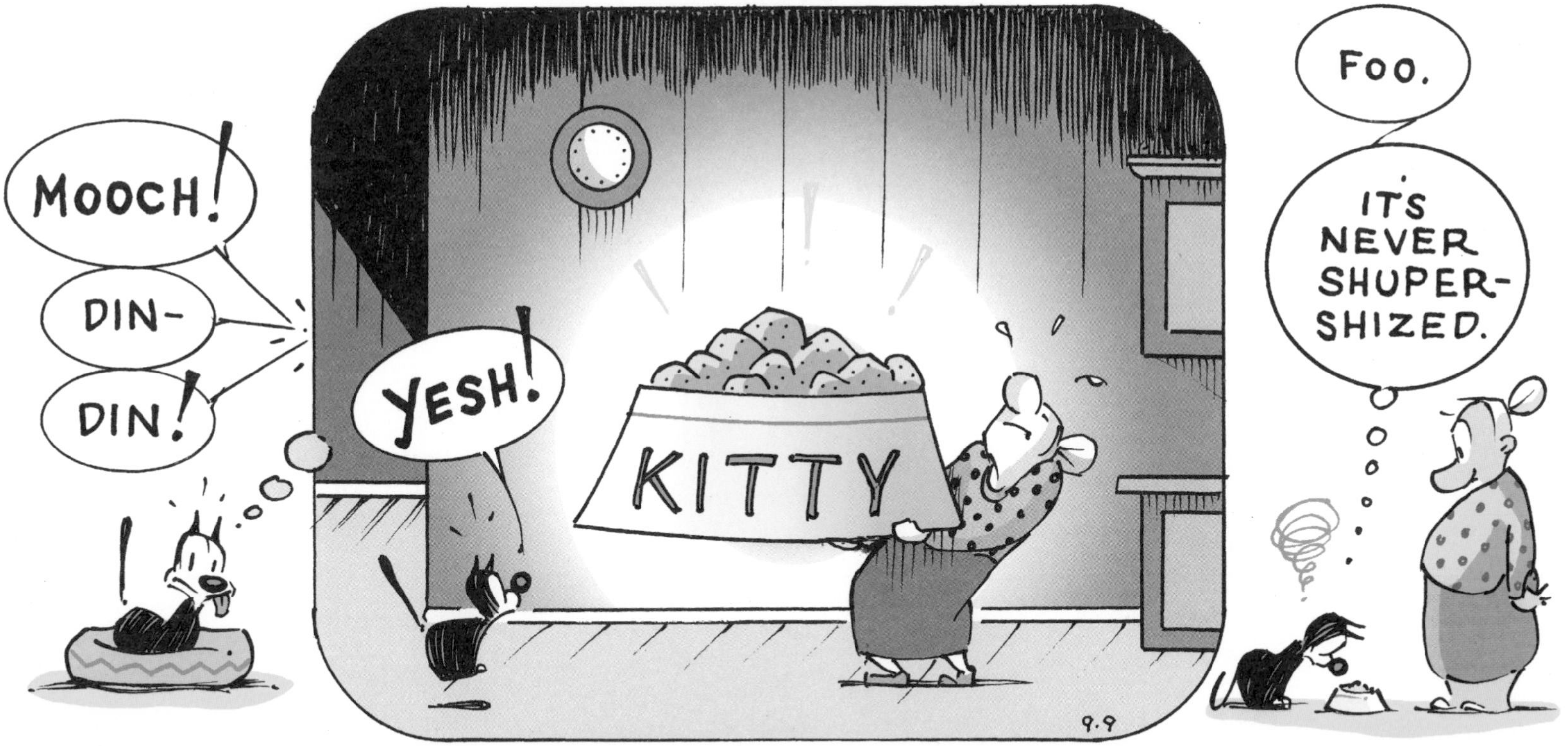
MOOCH!
DIN-
DIN!
YESH!
KITTY
FOO.
IT'S NEVER SHUPER-SHIZED.
9.9

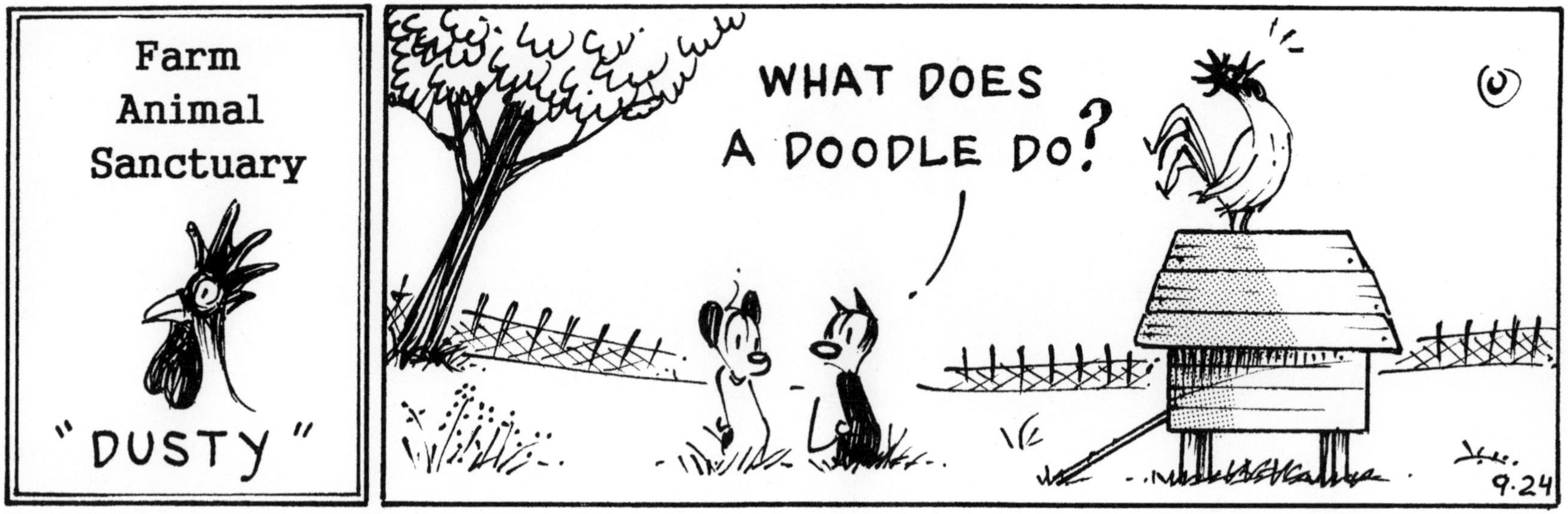
Farm
Animal
Sanctuary
"DUSTY"
WHAT DOES A DOODLE DO?
9·24

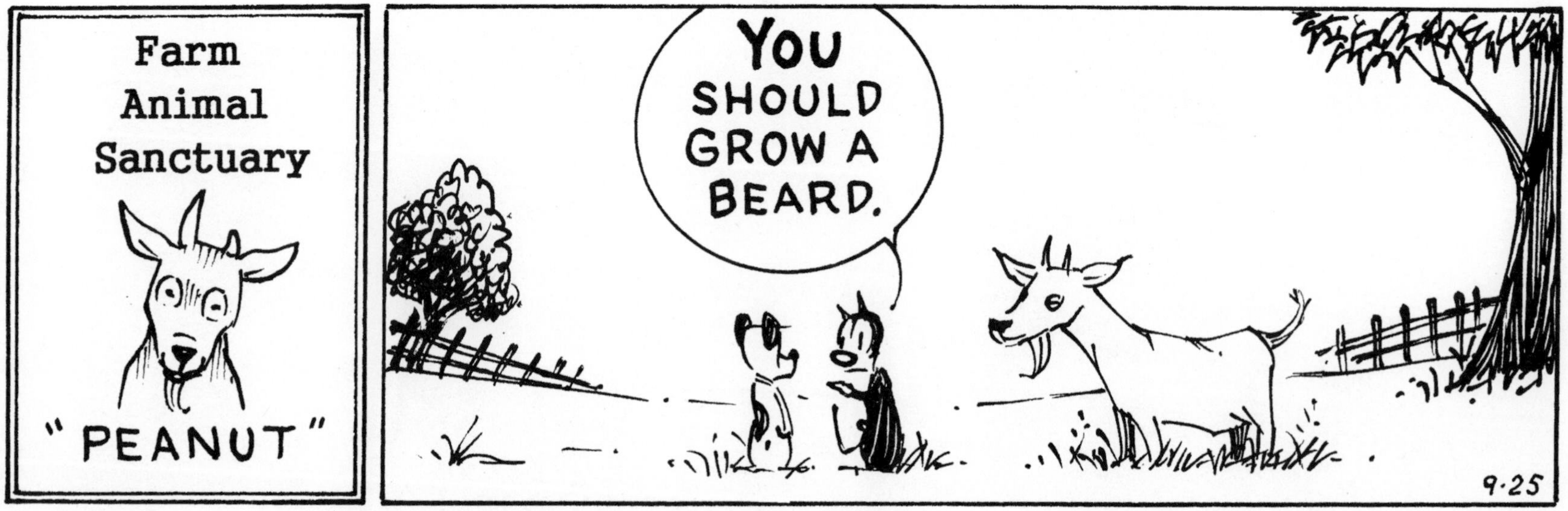
Farm
Animal
Sanctuary
"PEANUT"
YOU SHOULD GROW A BEARD.
9·25

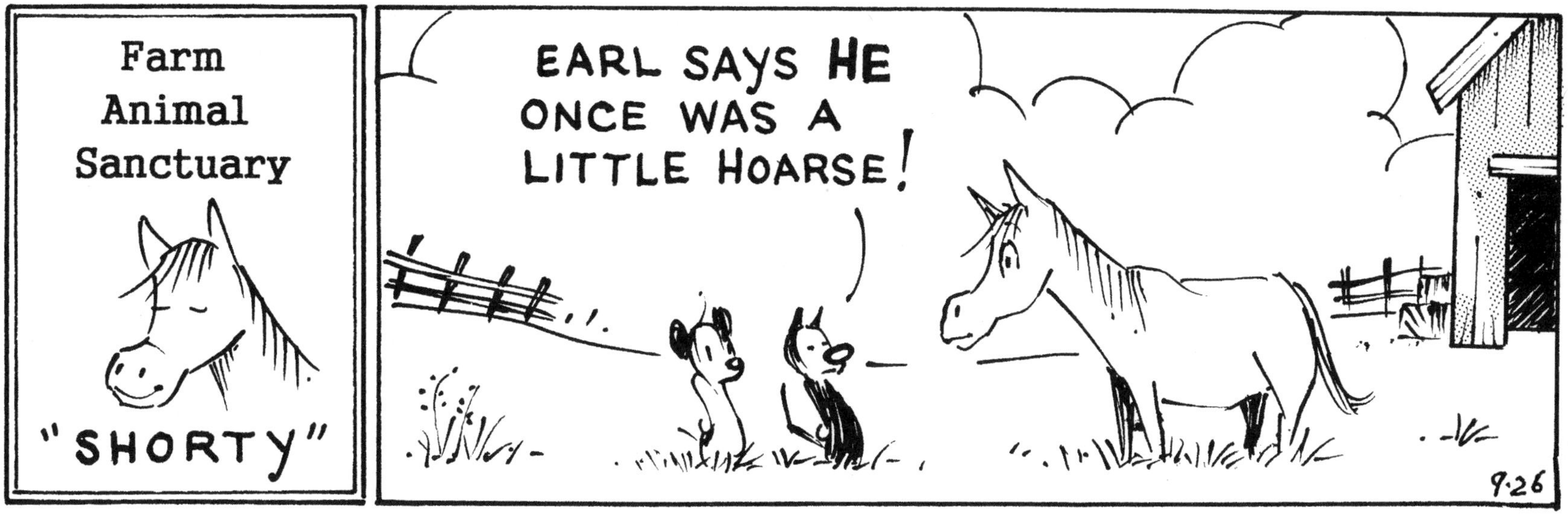
Farm
Animal
Sanctuary
"SHORTY"
EARL SAYS HE ONCE WAS A LITTLE HOARSE!
9·26

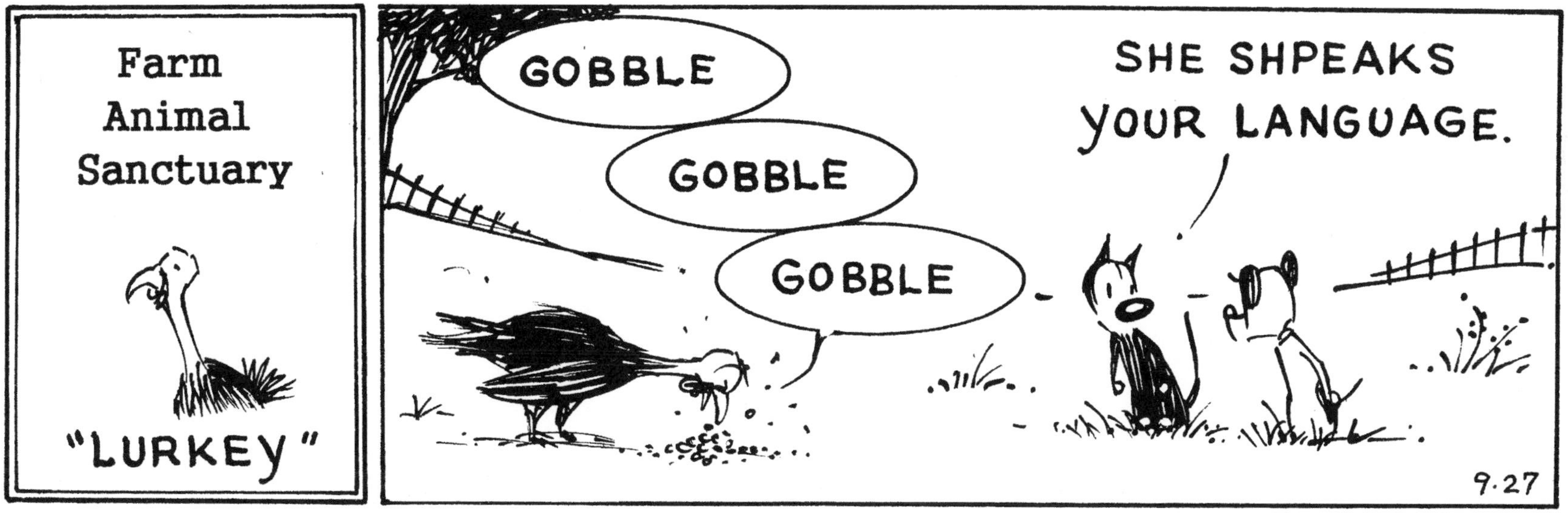
Farm
Animal
Sanctuary
"LURKEY"
GOBBLE
GOBBLE
GOBBLE
SHE SHPEAKS YOUR LANGUAGE.
9·27

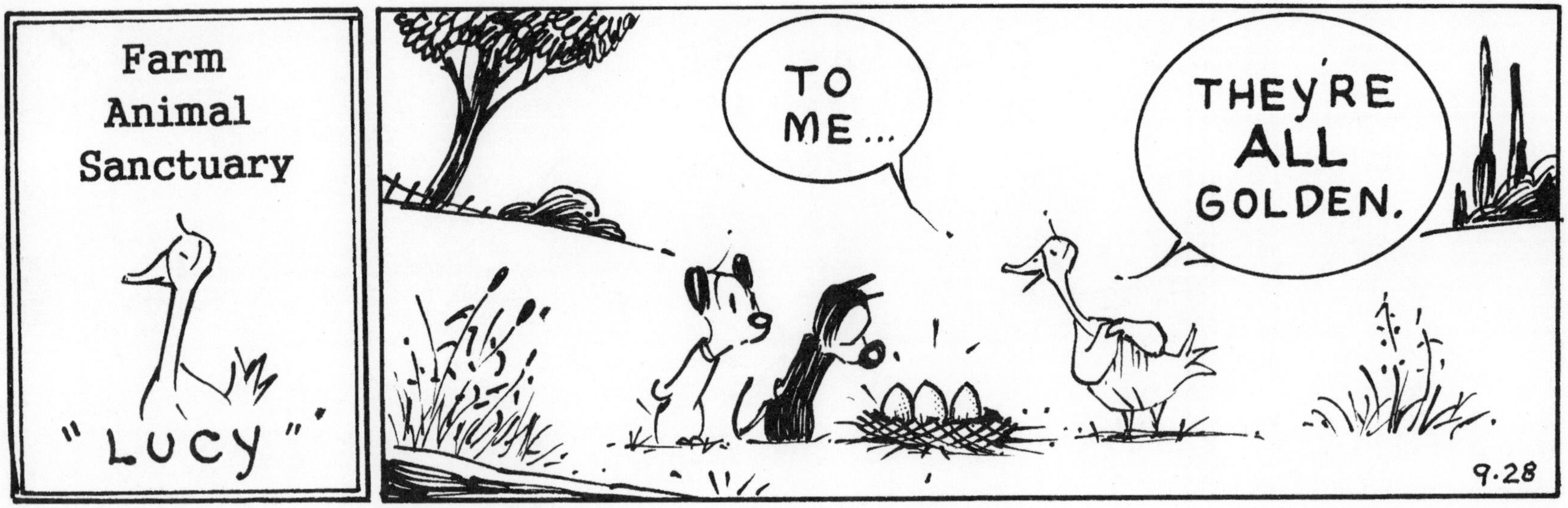
Farm
Animal
Sanctuary
"LUCY"
TO ME...
THEY'RE ALL GOLDEN.
9·28

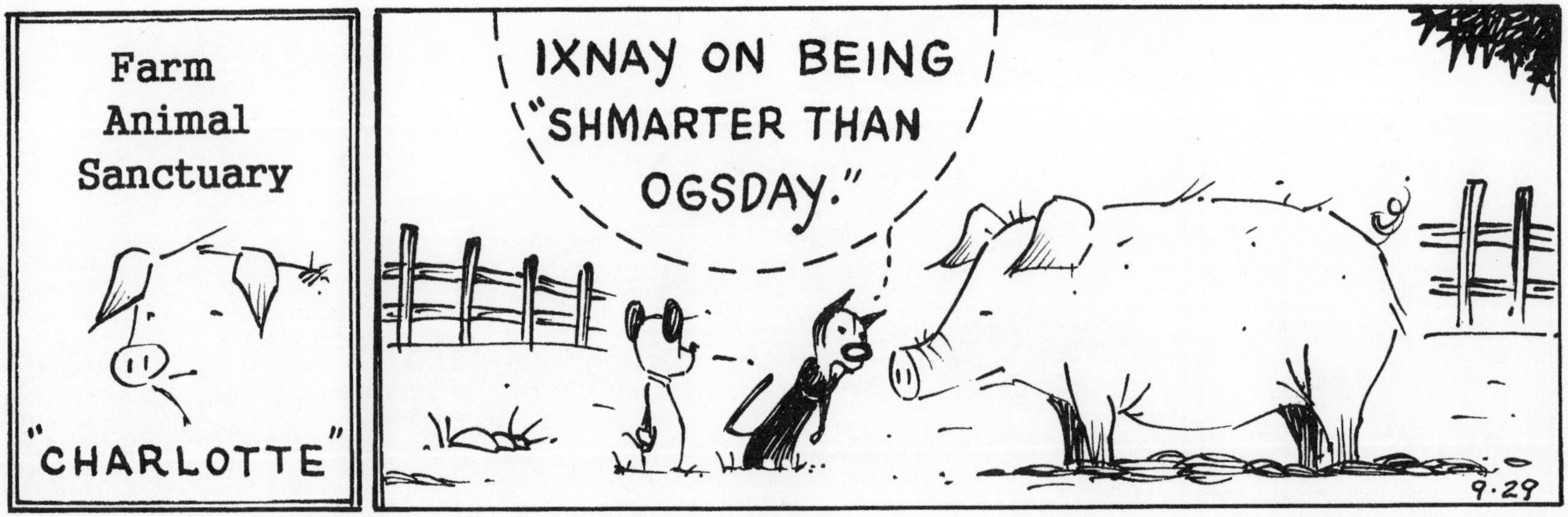
Farm
Animal
Sanctuary
"CHARLOTTE"
IXNAY ON BEING "SHMARTER THAN OGSDAY."
9·29

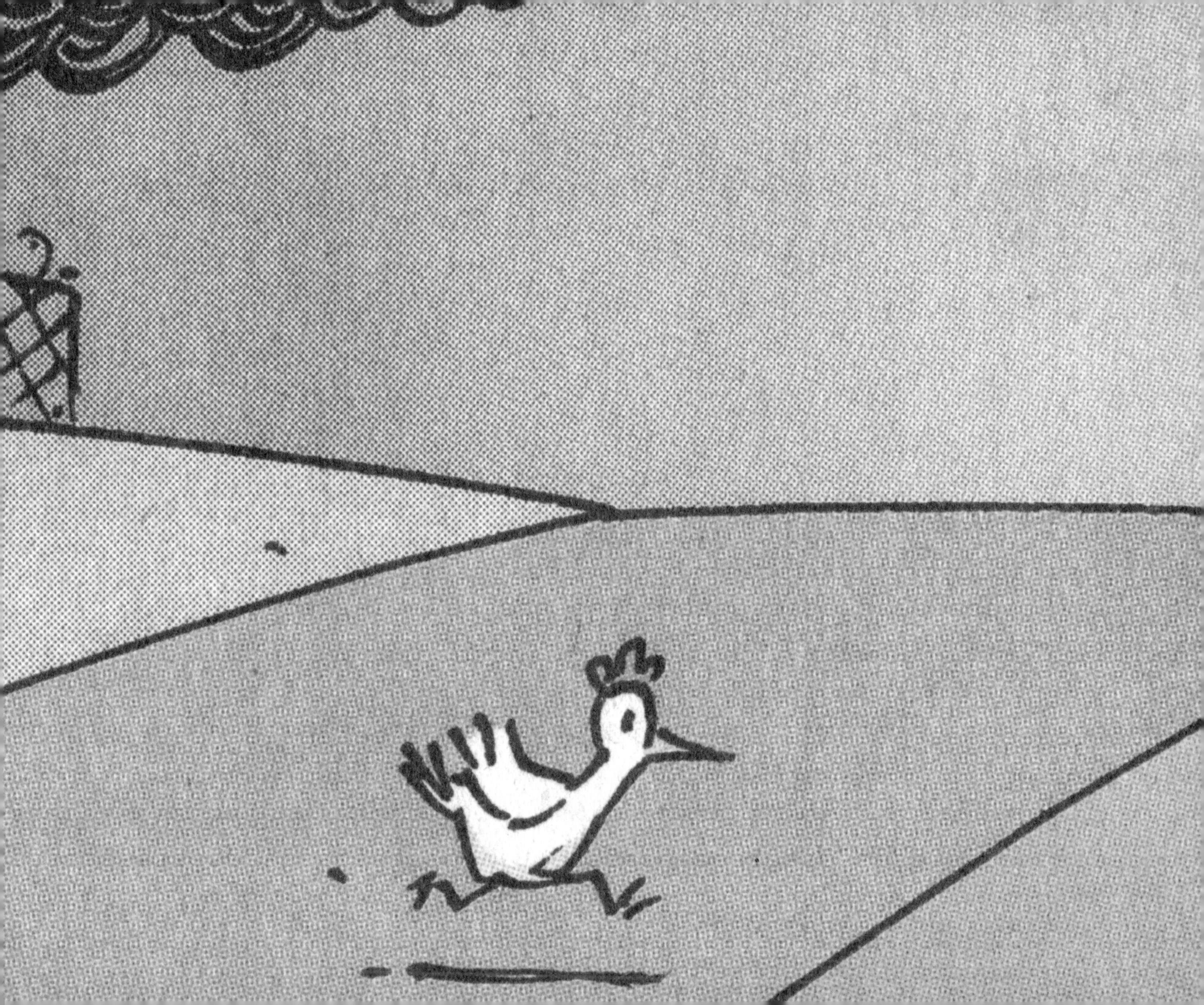

MUTTS
Patrick McDonnell

WHY THE CHICKEN CROSSED THE ROAD:
FACTORY FARM
FARM SANCTUARY
9·30

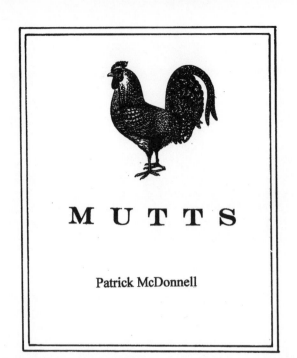

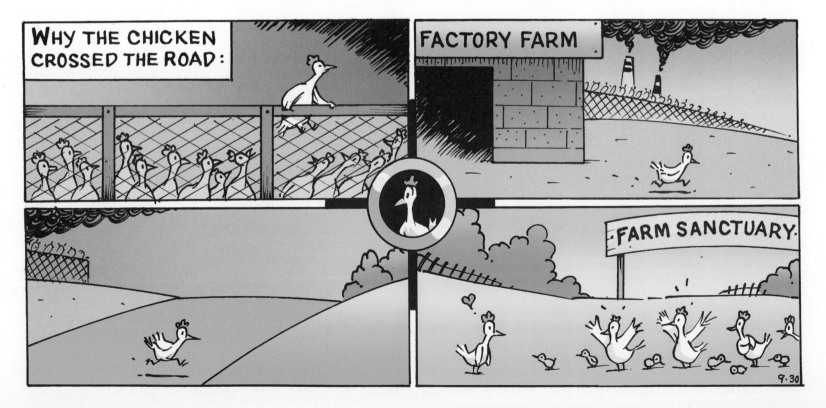

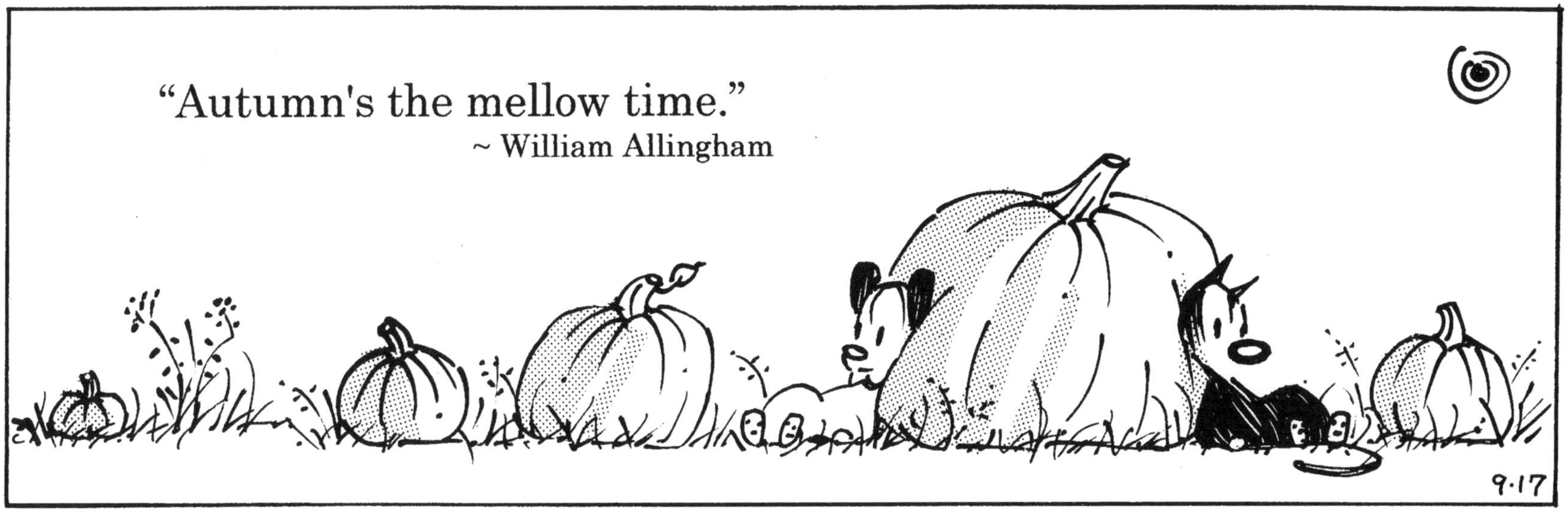
"Autumn's the mellow time."
~ William Allingham
9·17

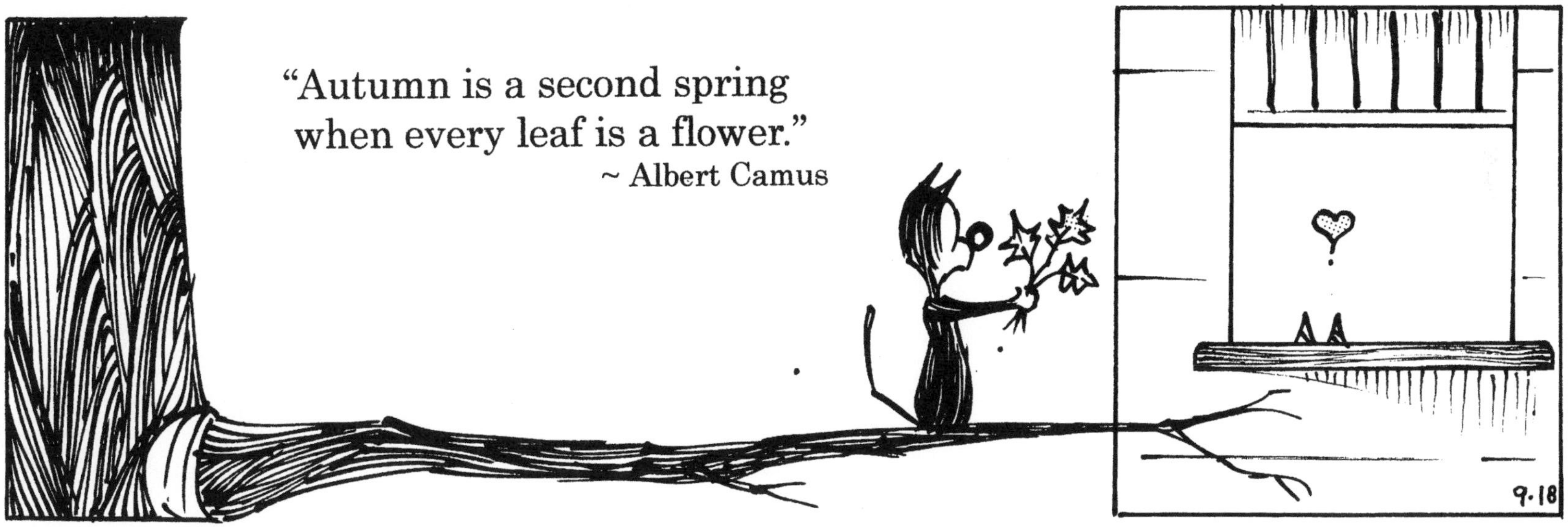
"Autumn is a second spring
when every leaf is a flower."
~ Albert Camus
9·18

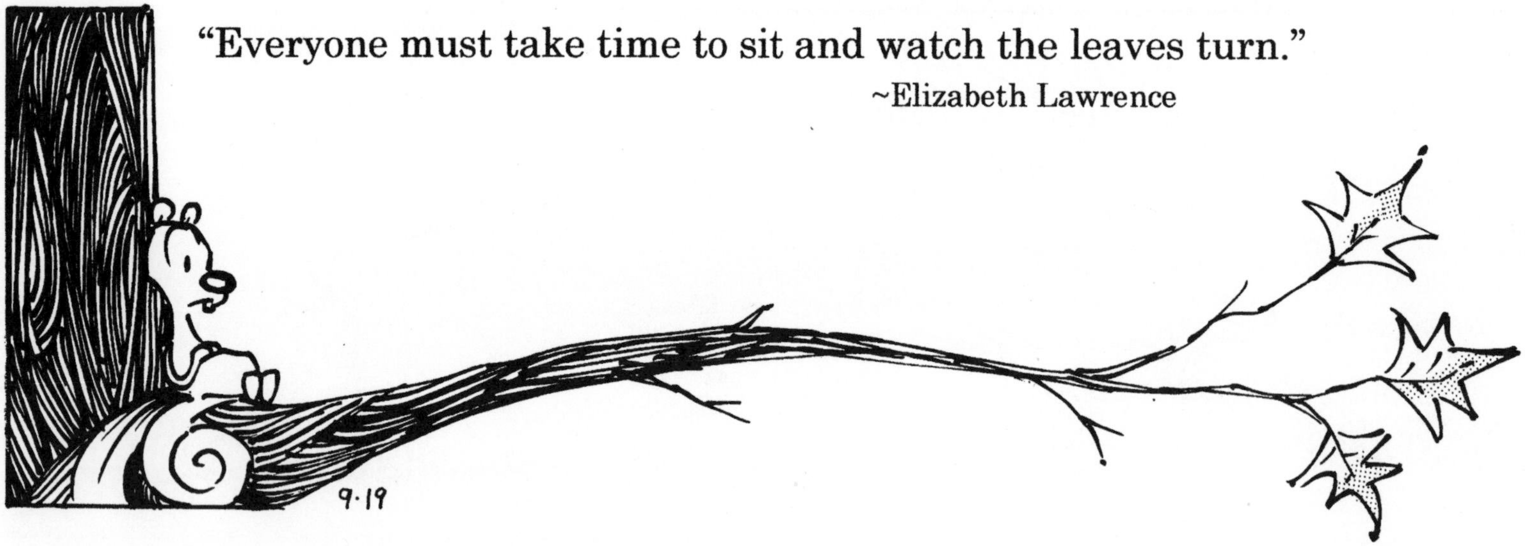
"Everyone must take time to sit and watch the leaves turn."
~Elizabeth Lawrence
9·19

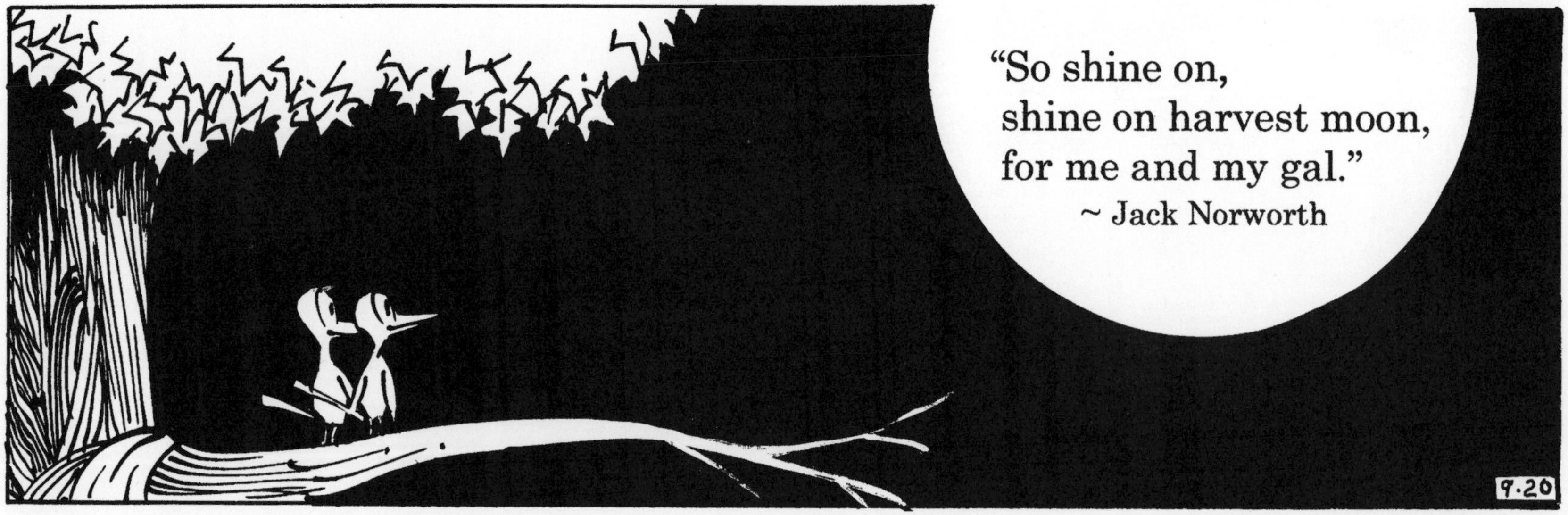
"So shine on,
shine on harvest moon,
for me and my gal."
~ Jack Norworth
9·20

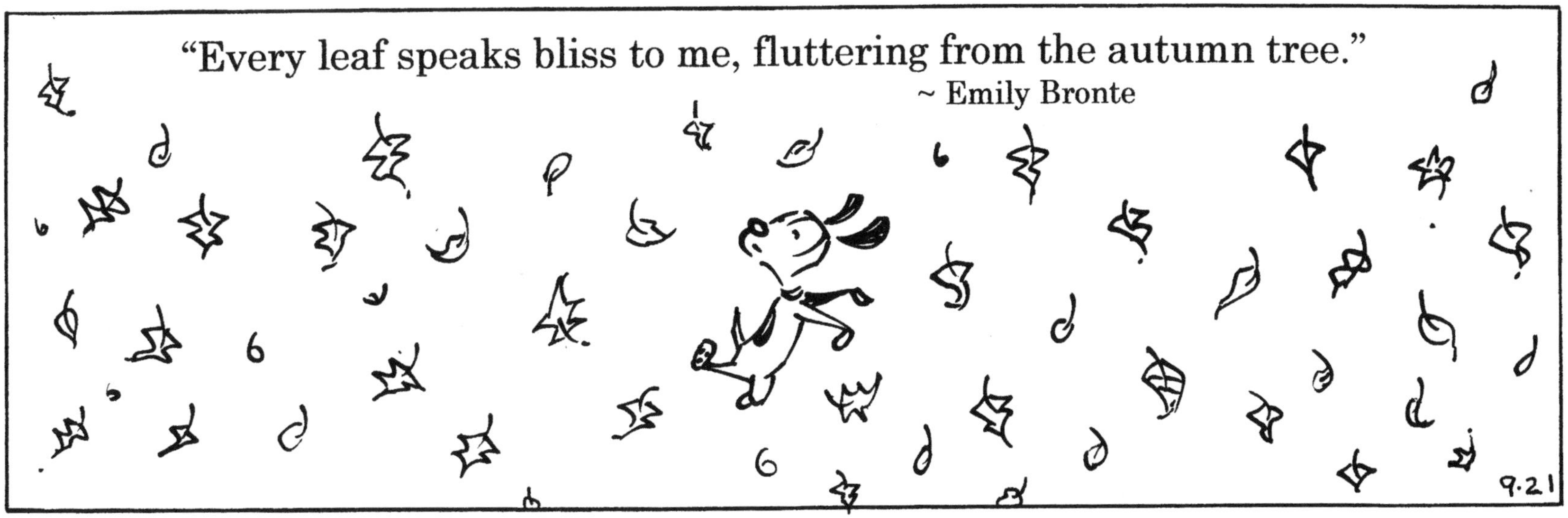
"Every leaf speaks bliss to me, fluttering from the autumn tree."
~ Emily Bronte
9.21

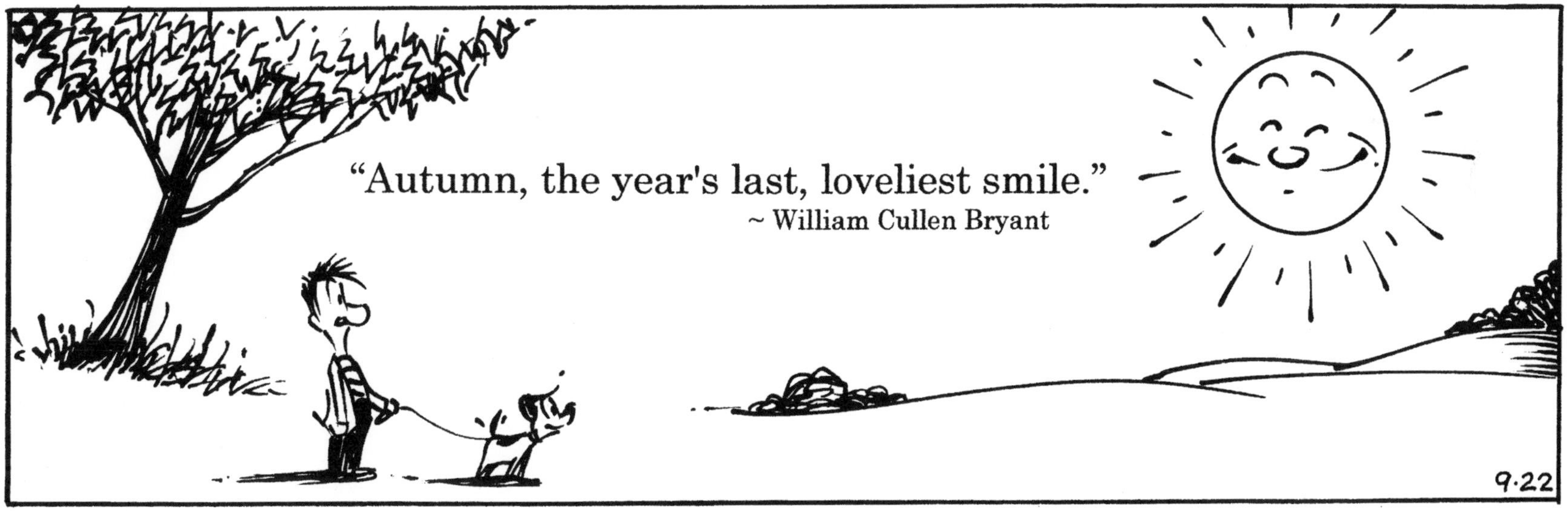
"Autumn, the year's last, loveliest smile."
~ William Cullen Bryant
9.22

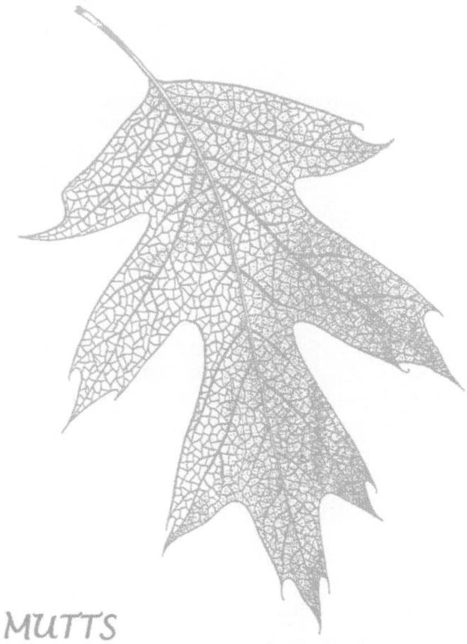

MUTTS

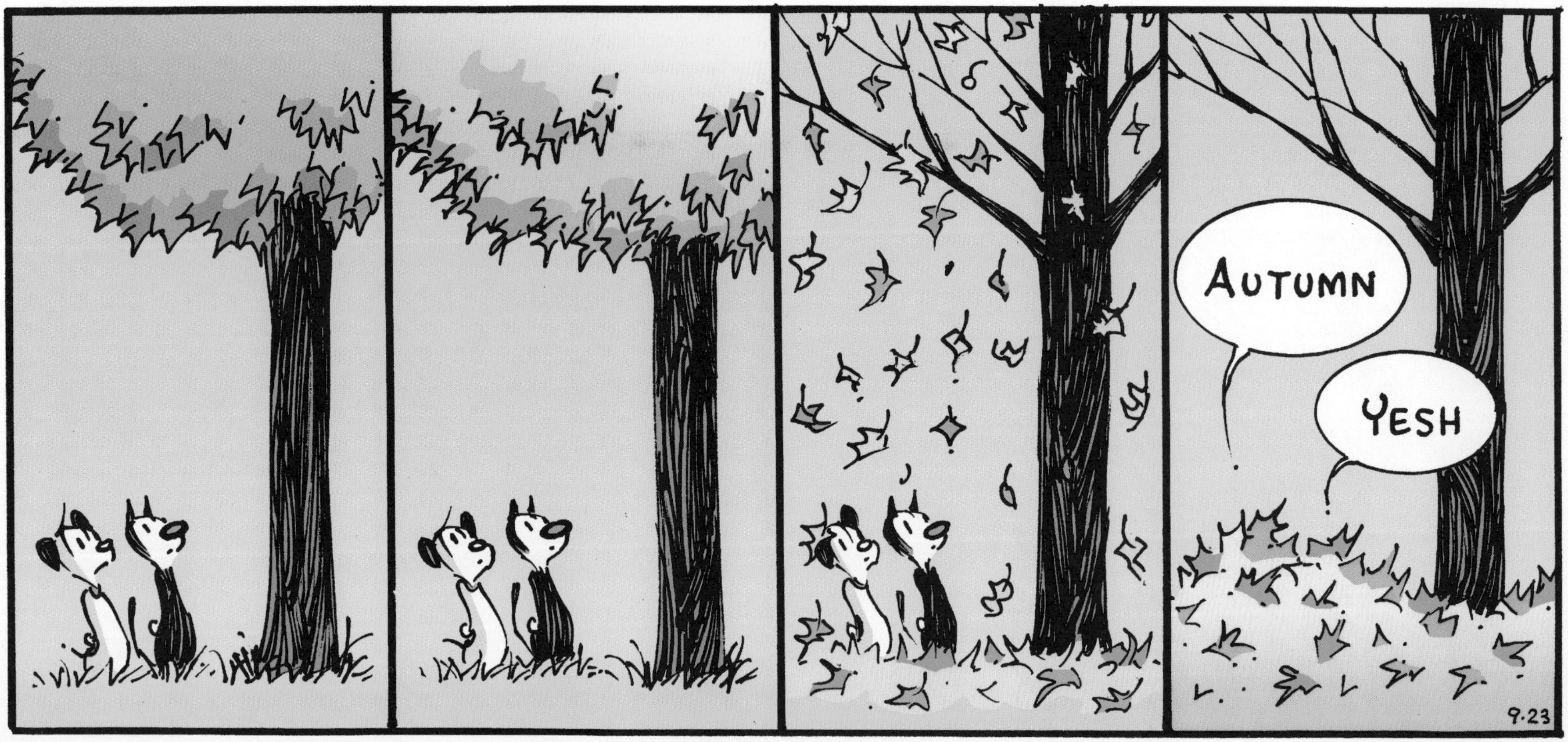
AUTUMN
YESH
9.23

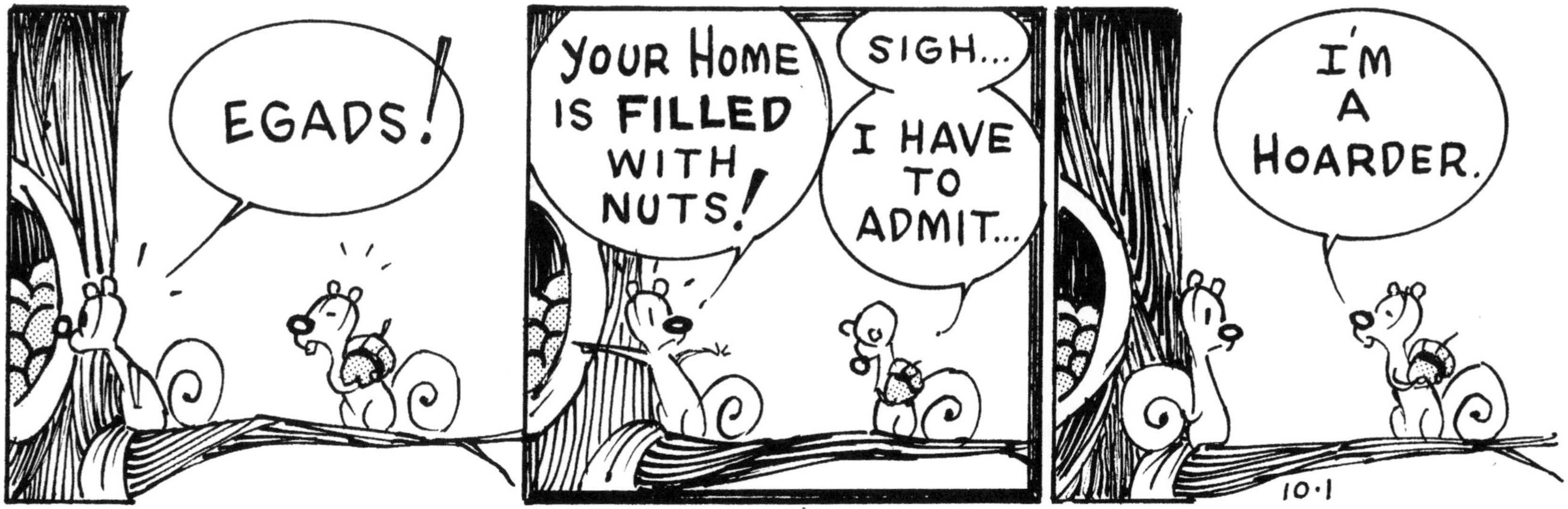
EGADS!
YOUR HOME IS FILLED WITH NUTS!
SIGH...
I HAVE TO ADMIT...
I'M A HOARDER.
10·1

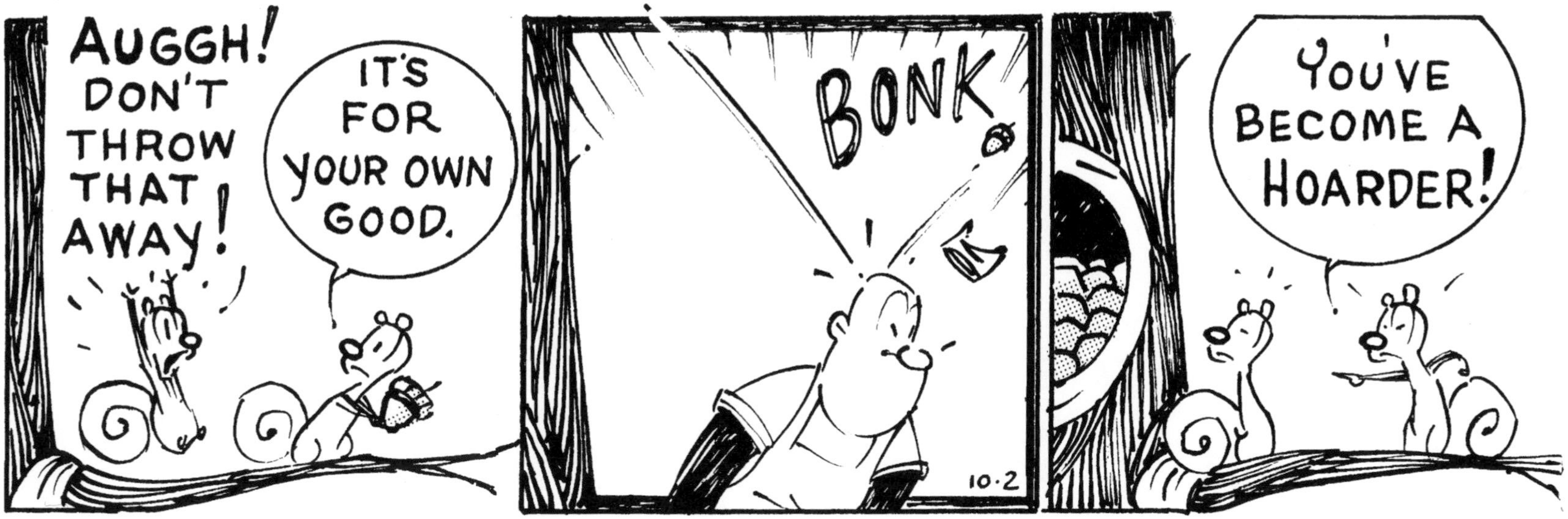
AUGGH! DON'T THROW THAT AWAY!
IT'S FOR YOUR OWN GOOD.
BONK
10·2
YOU'VE BECOME A HOARDER!

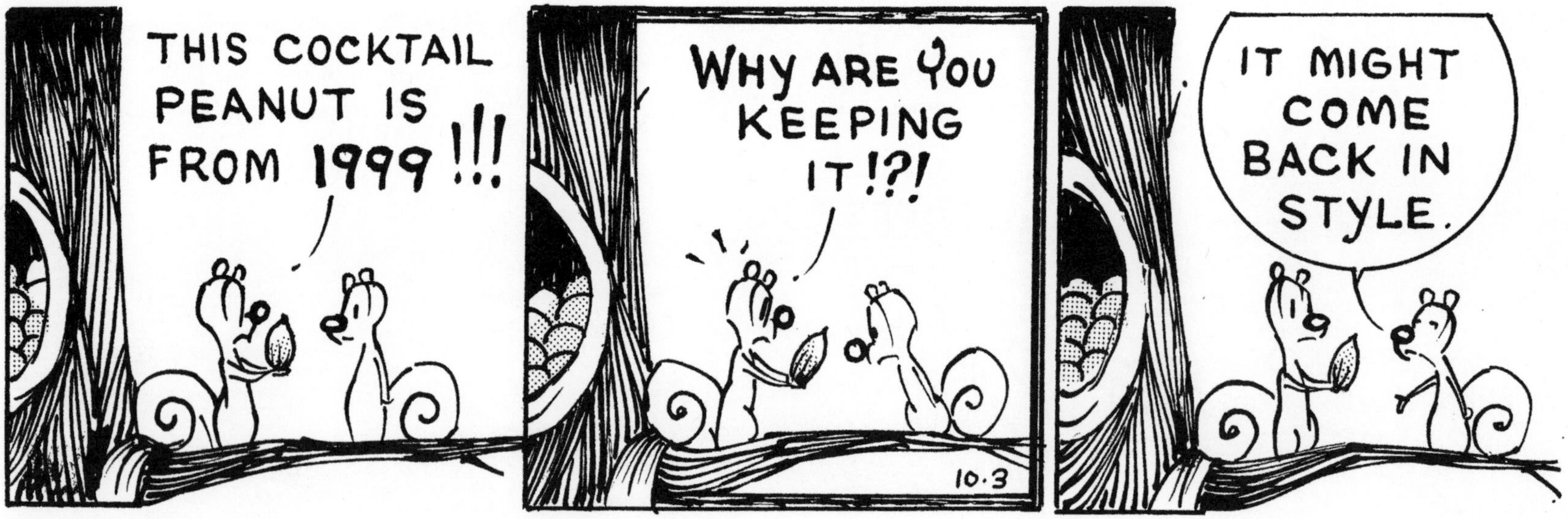
THIS COCKTAIL PEANUT IS FROM 1999!!!
WHY ARE YOU KEEPING IT!?!
10·3
IT MIGHT COME BACK IN STYLE.

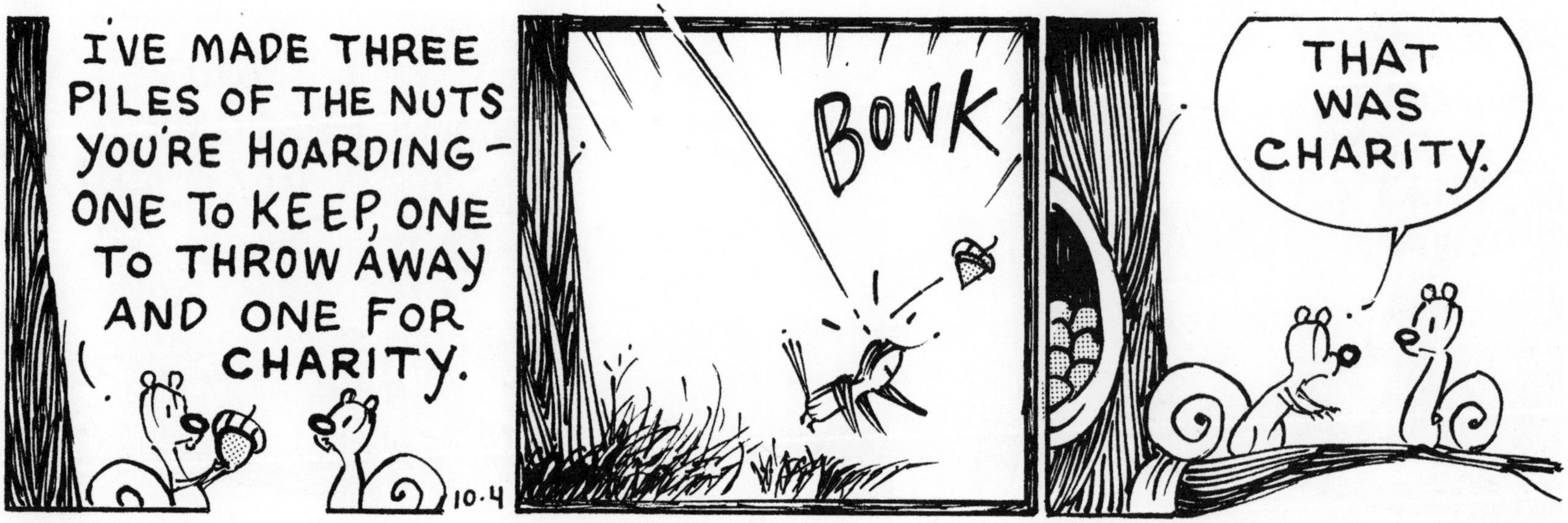
I'VE MADE THREE PILES OF THE NUTS YOU'RE HOARDING - ONE TO KEEP, ONE TO THROW AWAY AND ONE FOR CHARITY.
10·4
BONK
THAT WAS CHARITY.

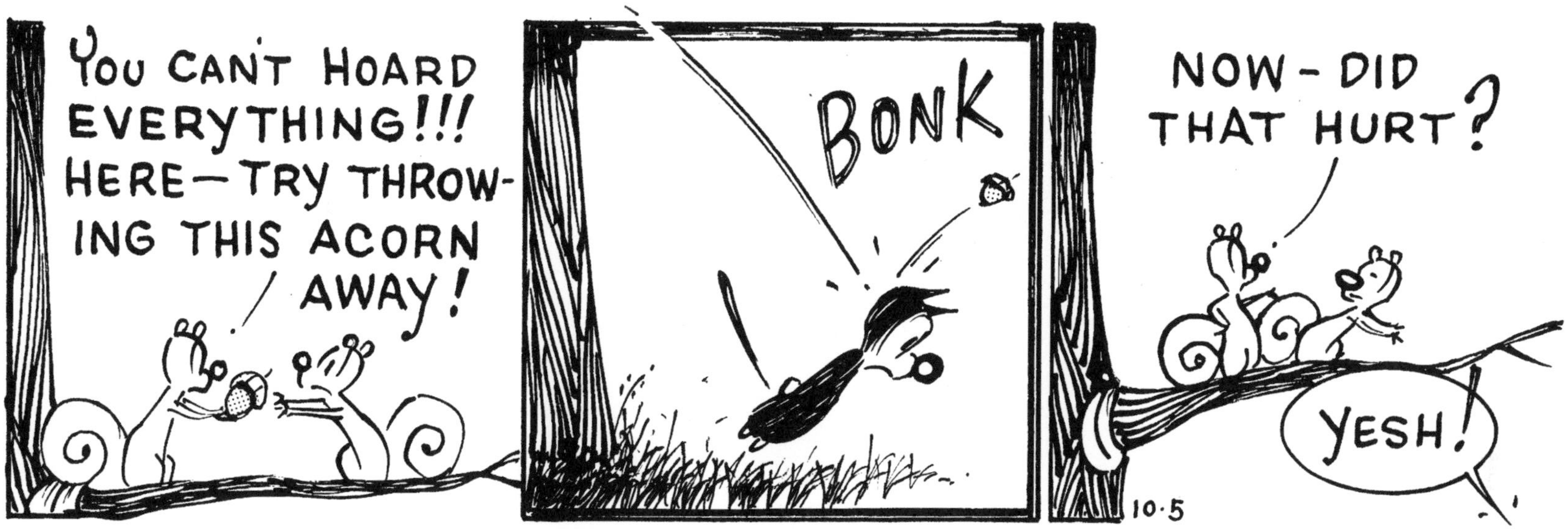
YOU CAN'T HOARD EVERYTHING!!! HERE—TRY THROWING THIS ACORN AWAY!
BONK
NOW-DID THAT HURT?
YESH!
10·5

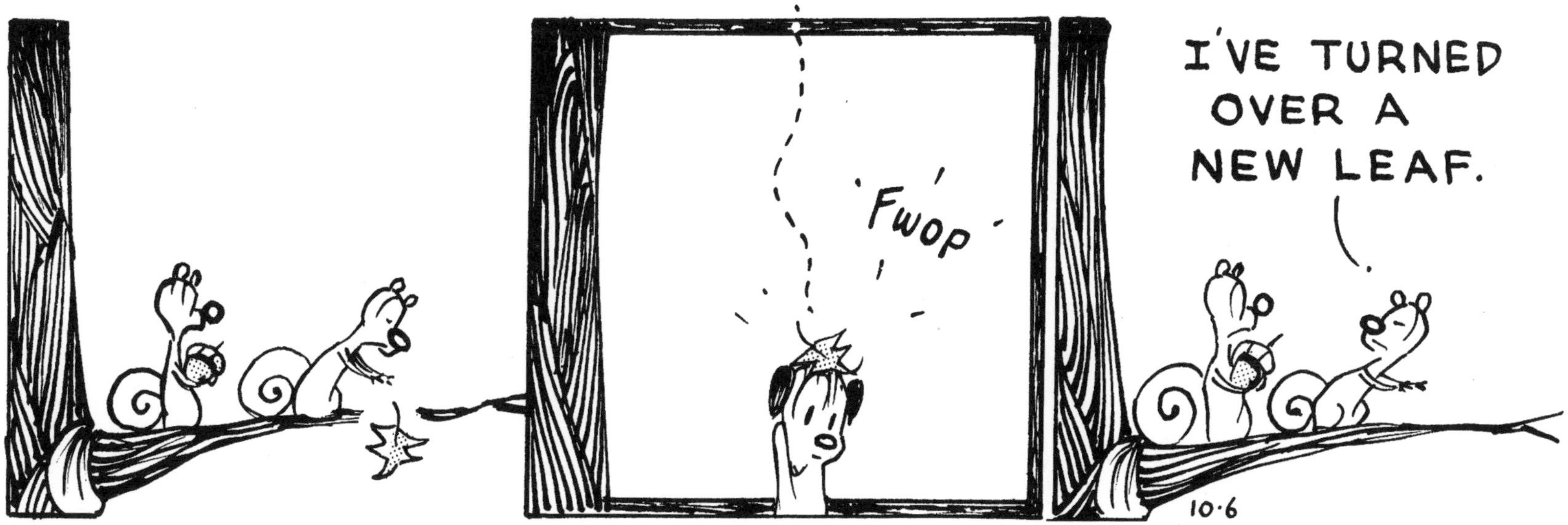
FWOP
I'VE TURNED OVER A NEW LEAF.
10·6

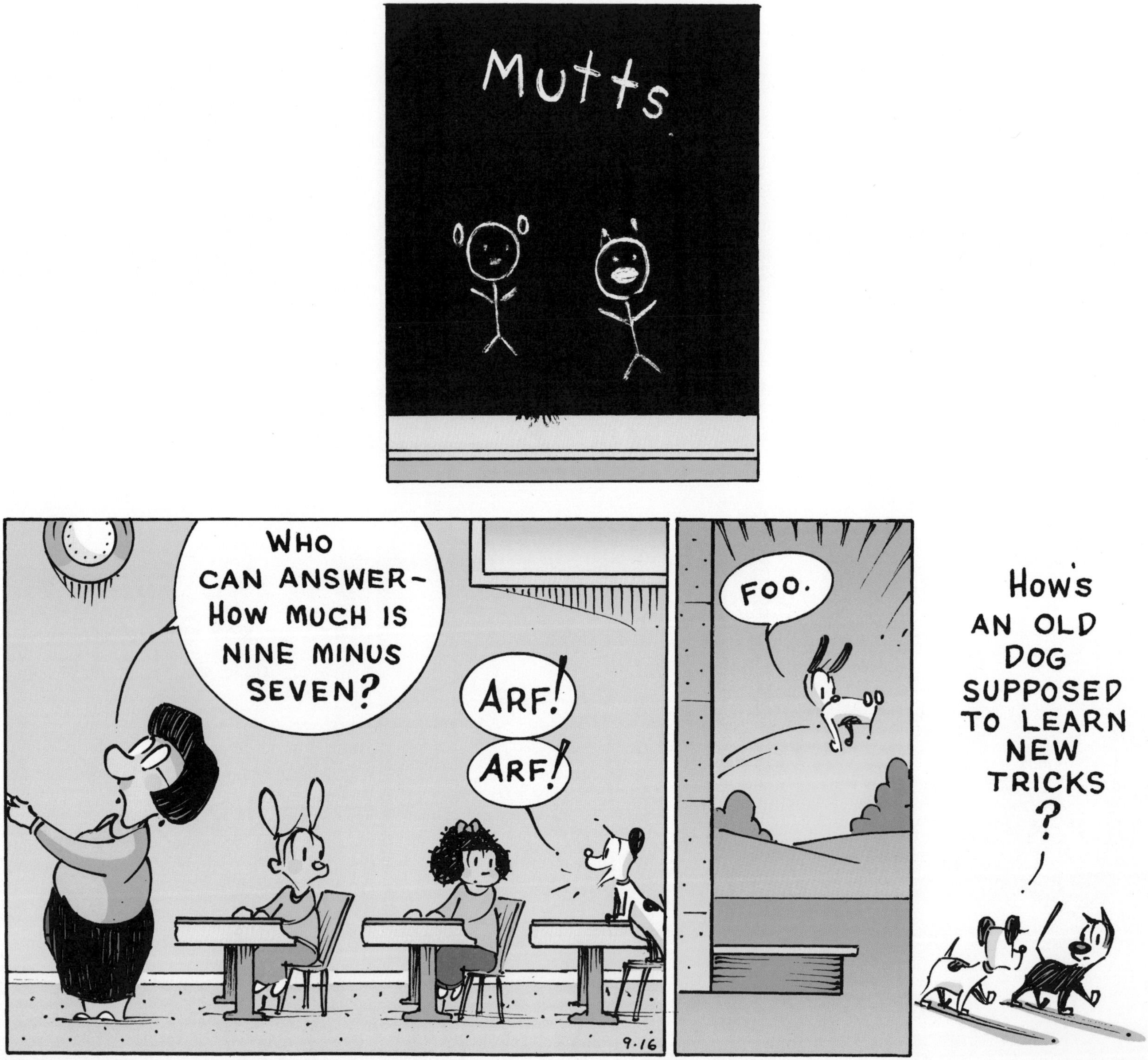
Mutts
WHO CAN ANSWER- HOW MUCH IS NINE MINUS SEVEN?
ARF!
ARF!
9.16
FOO.
HOW'S AN OLD DOG SUPPOSED TO LEARN NEW TRICKS?

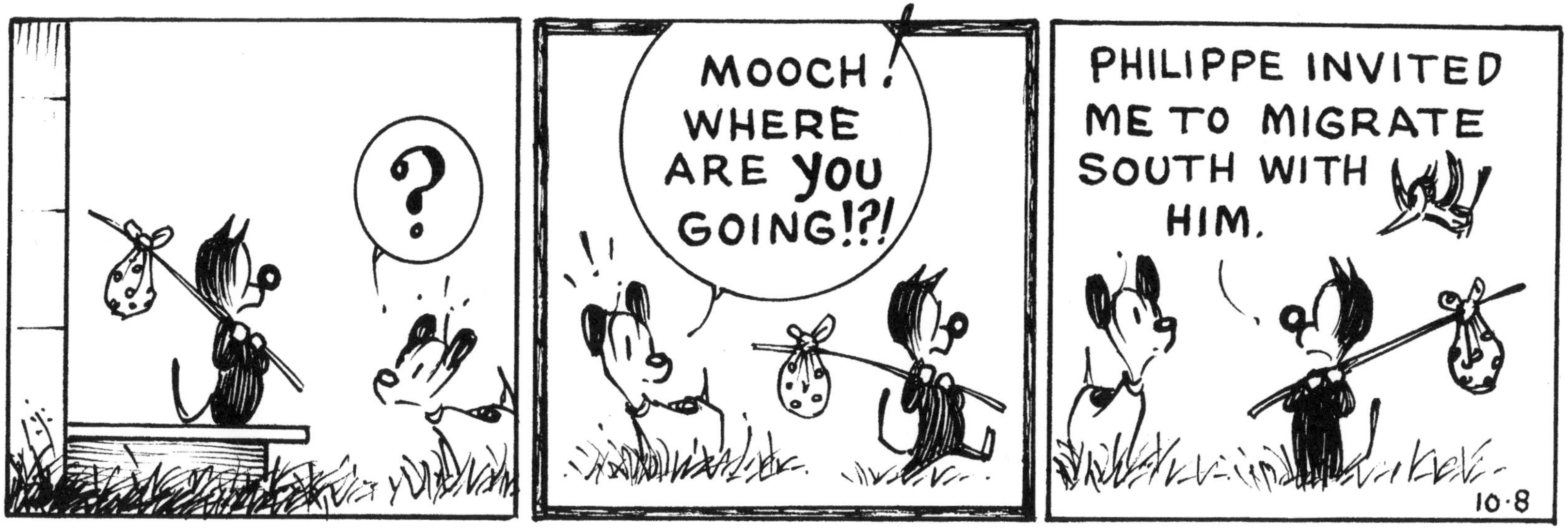
?
MOOCH! WHERE ARE YOU GOING!?!
PHILIPPE INVITED ME TO MIGRATE SOUTH WITH HIM.
10·8

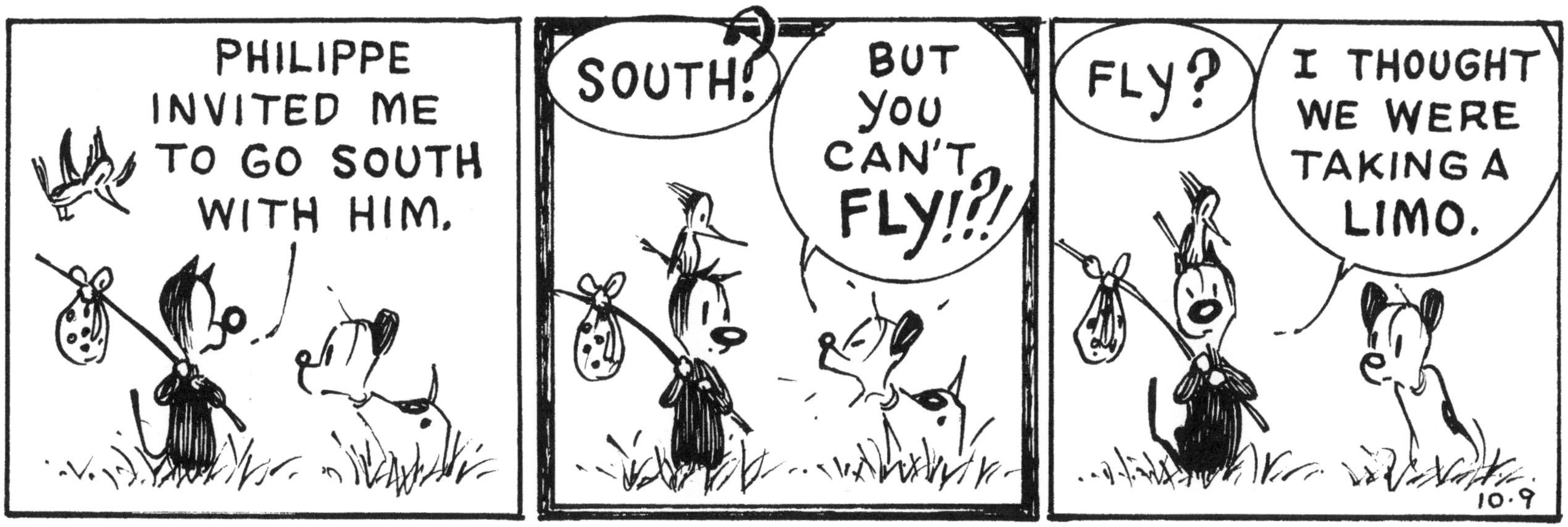
PHILIPPE INVITED ME TO GO SOUTH WITH HIM.
SOUTH?
BUT YOU CAN'T FLY!?!
FLY?
I THOUGHT WE WERE TAKING A LIMO.
10·9

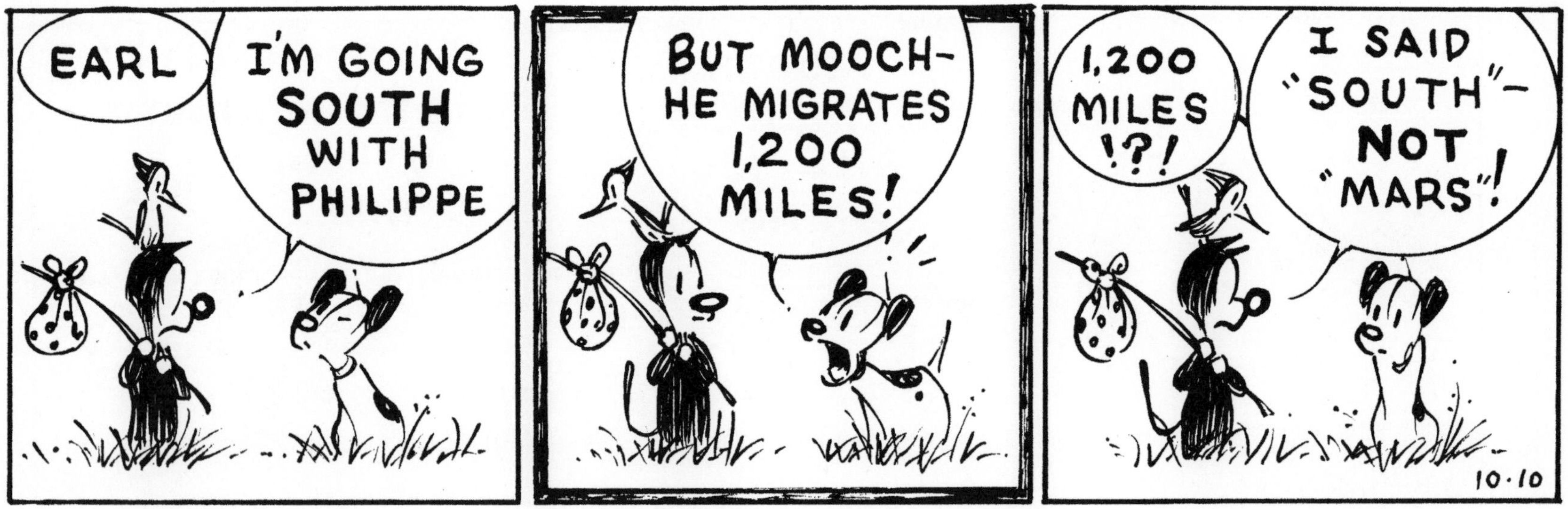
EARL
I'M GOING SOUTH WITH PHILIPPE
BUT MOOCH- HE MIGRATES 1,200 MILES!
1,200 MILES !?!
I SAID "SOUTH"- NOT "MARS"!
10·10

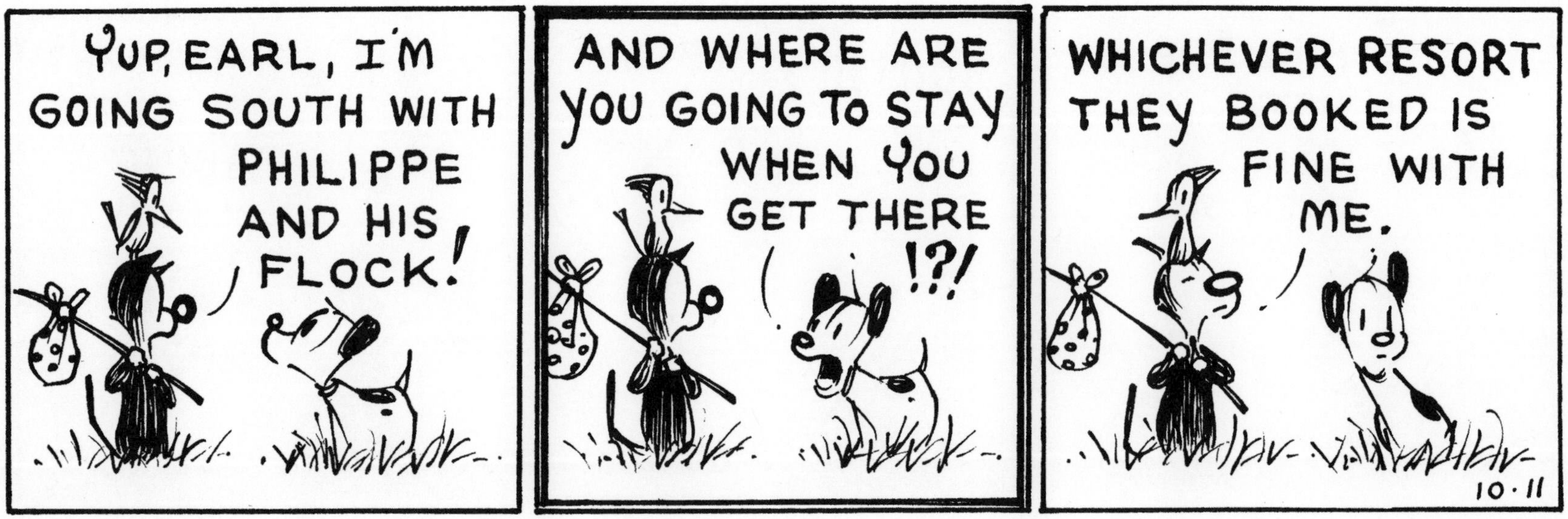
YUP, EARL, I'M GOING SOUTH WITH PHILIPPE AND HIS FLOCK!
AND WHERE ARE YOU GOING TO STAY WHEN YOU GET THERE !?!
WHICHEVER RESORT THEY BOOKED IS FINE WITH ME.
10·11

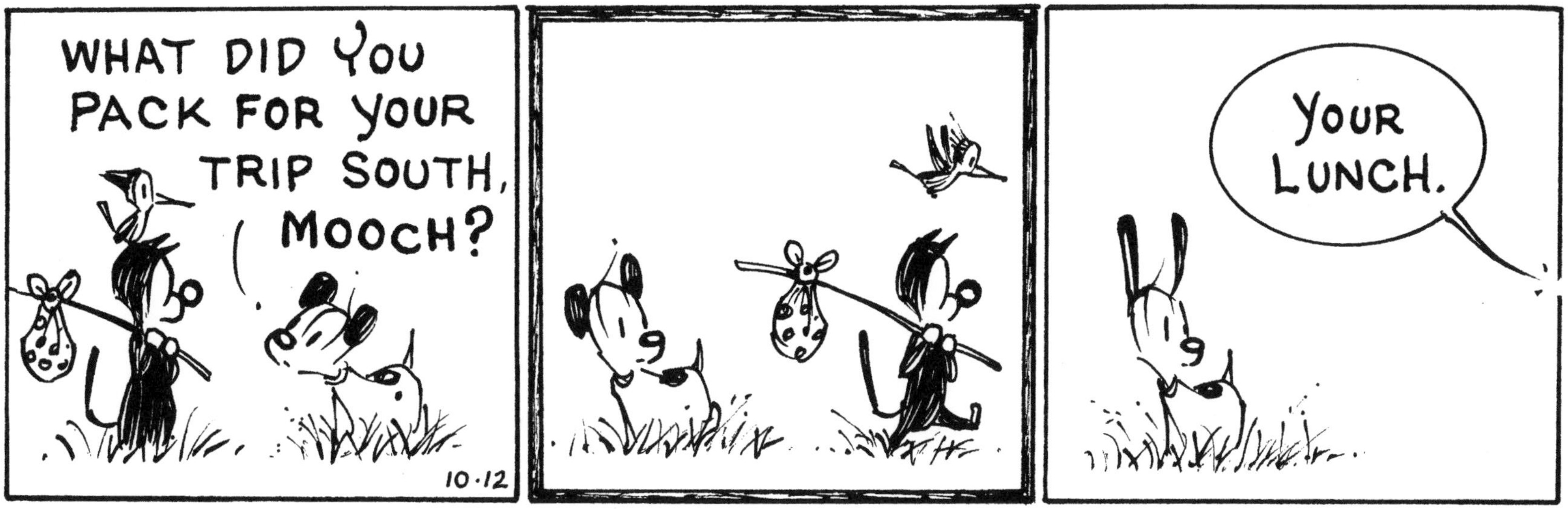
WHAT DID YOU PACK FOR YOUR TRIP SOUTH, MOOCH?
10·12
YOUR LUNCH.

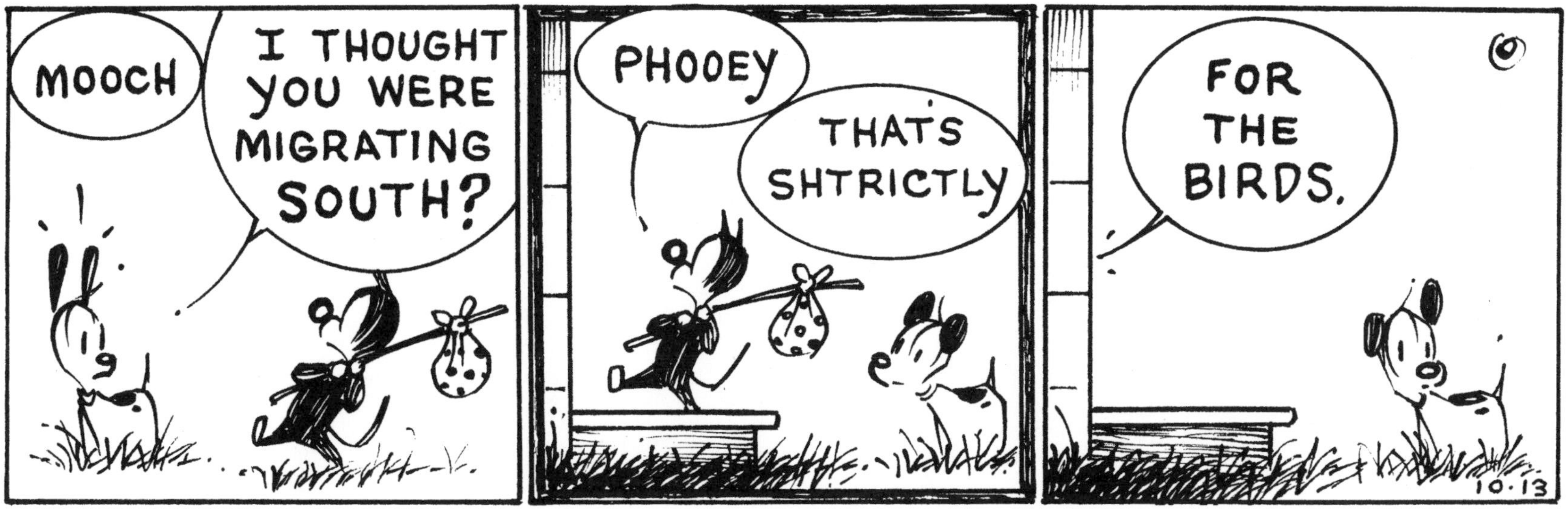
MOOCH
I THOUGHT YOU WERE MIGRATING SOUTH?
PHOOEY
THAT'S SHTRICTLY
FOR THE BIRDS.
10·13

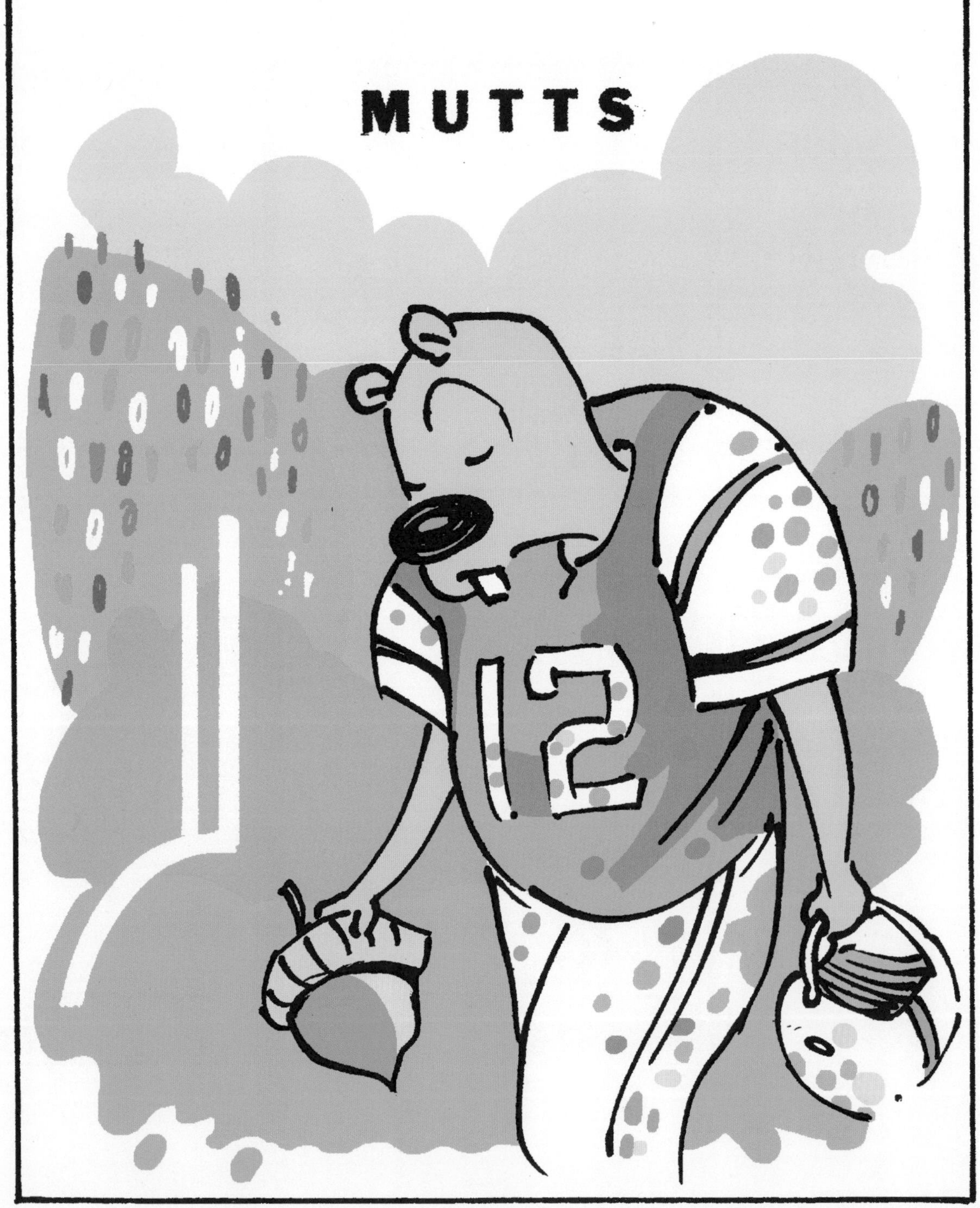
MUTTS
12

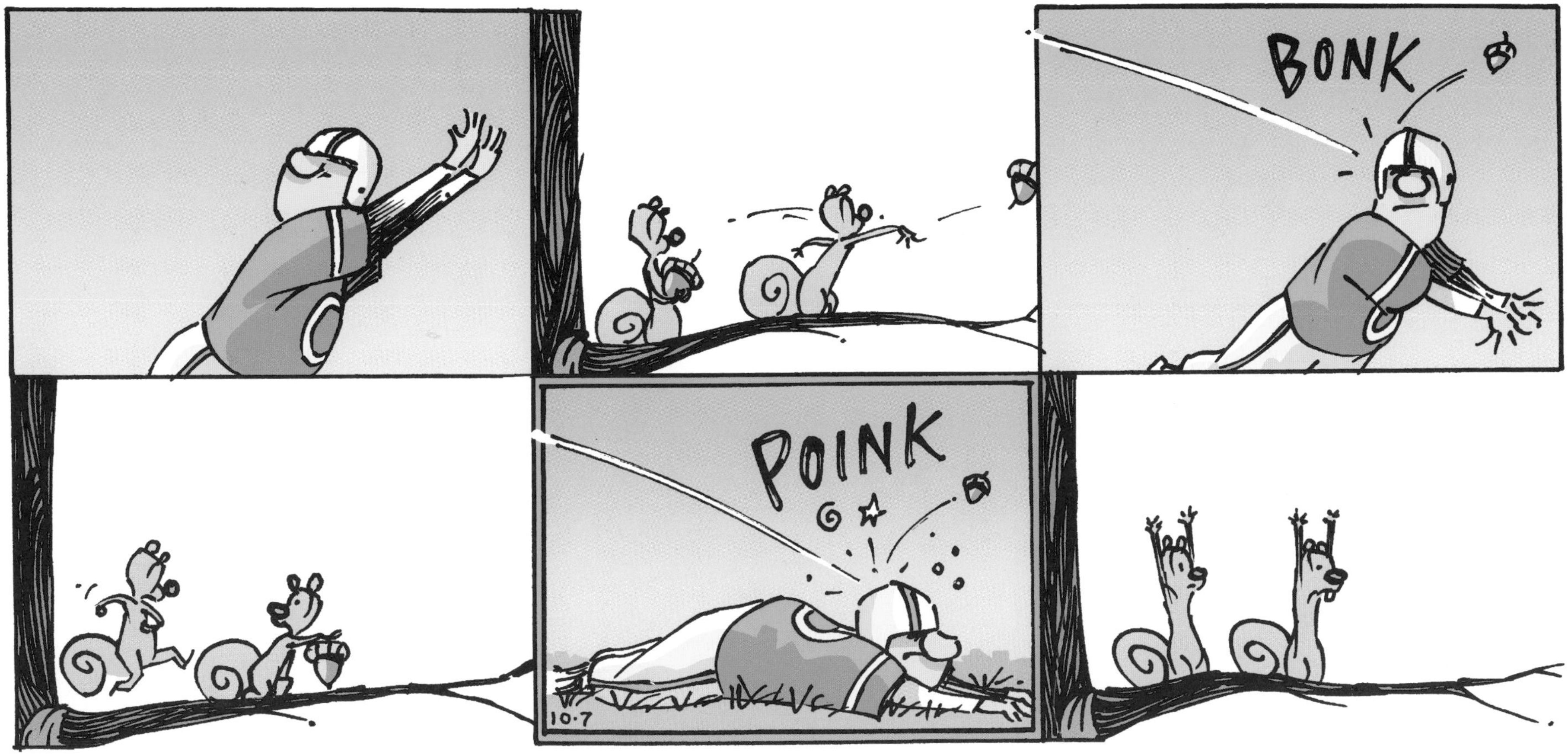
BONK
POINK
10·7

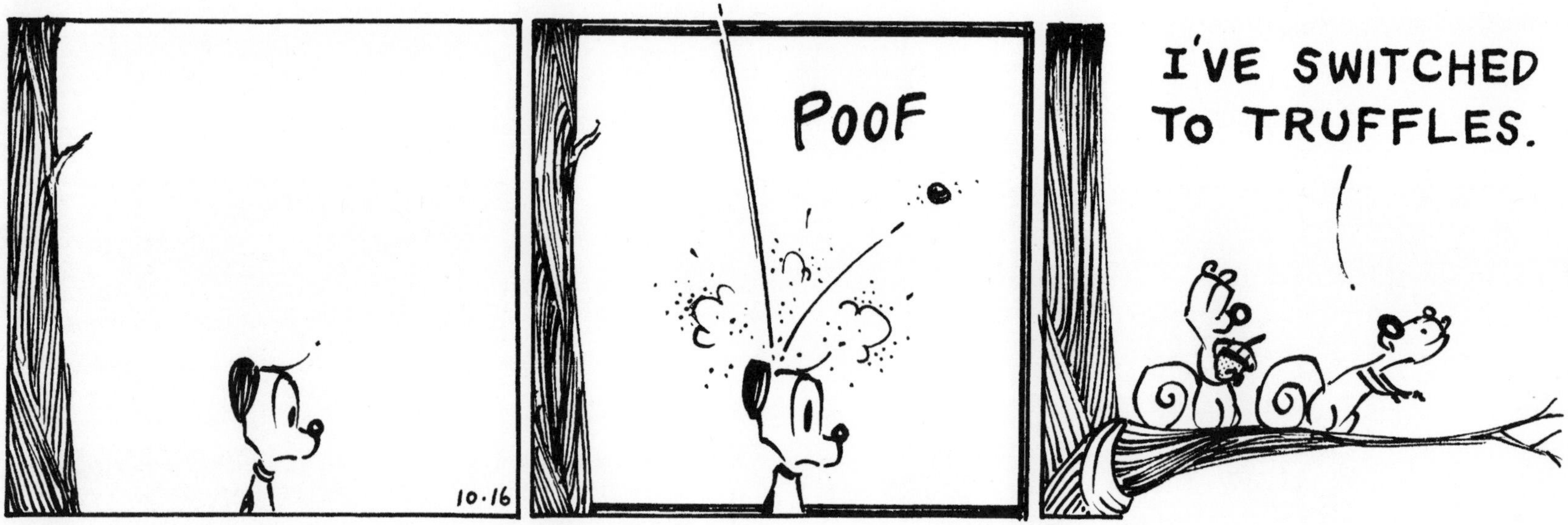
10.16
POOF
I'VE SWITCHED TO TRUFFLES.

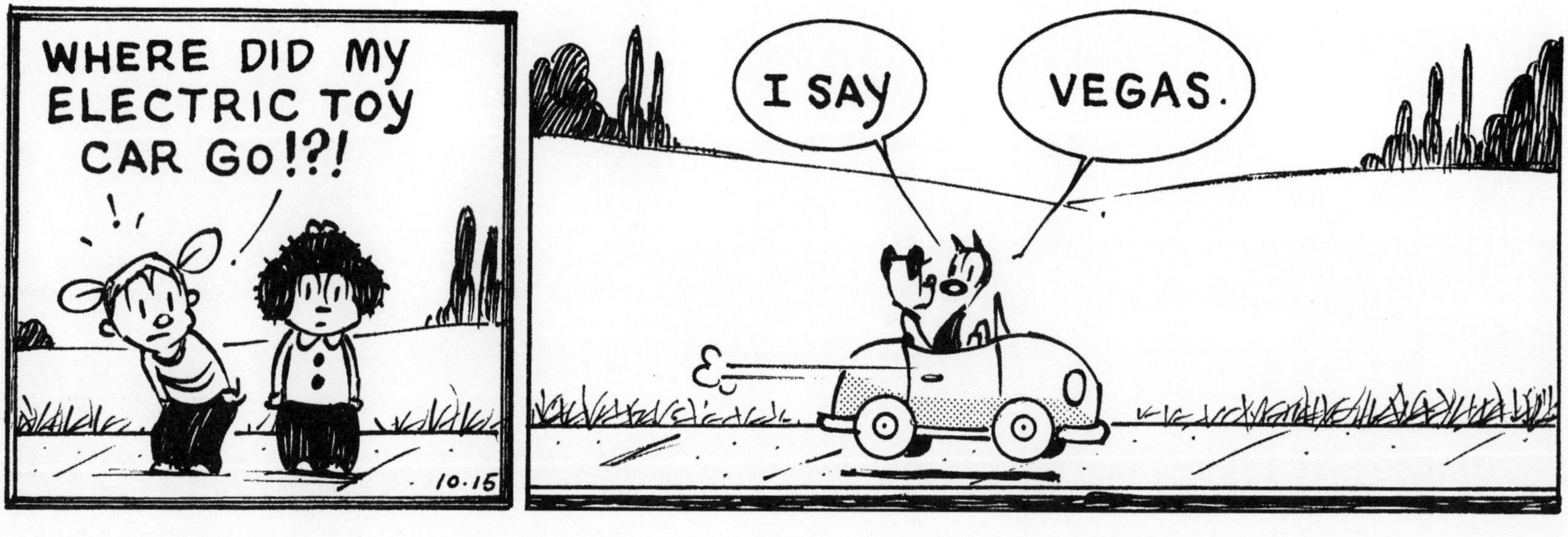
WHERE DID MY ELECTRIC TOY CAR GO!?!
10.15
I SAY
VEGAS.

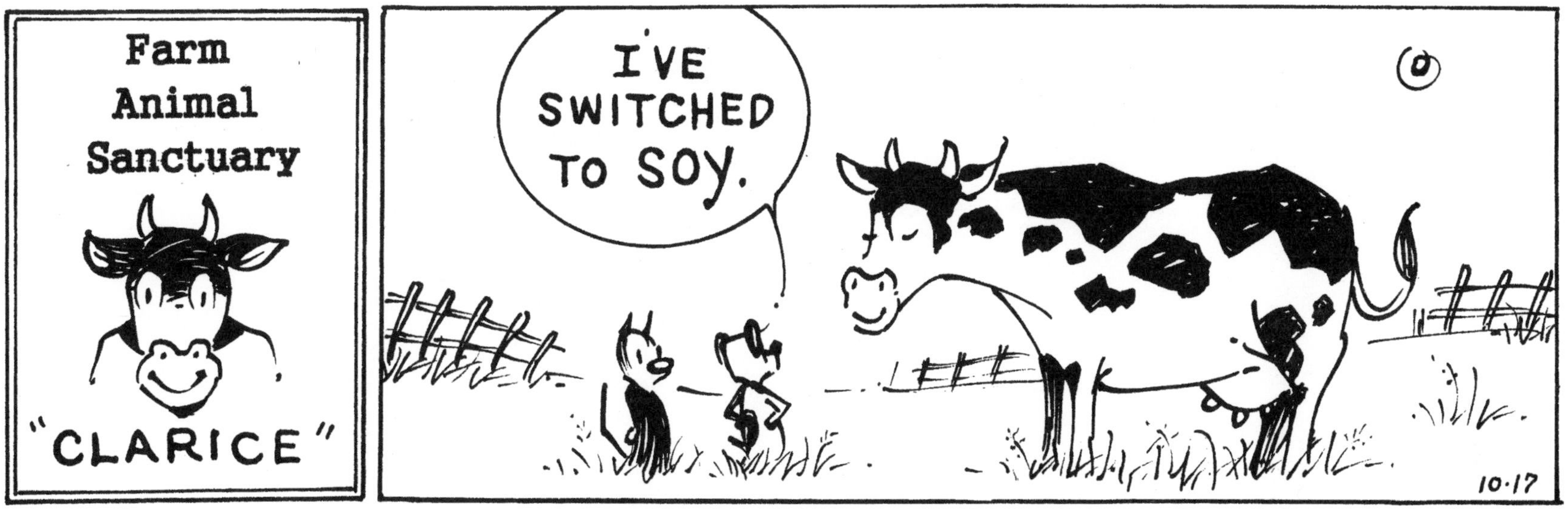
Farm Animal Sanctuary
"CLARICE"
I'VE SWITCHED TO SOY.
10·17

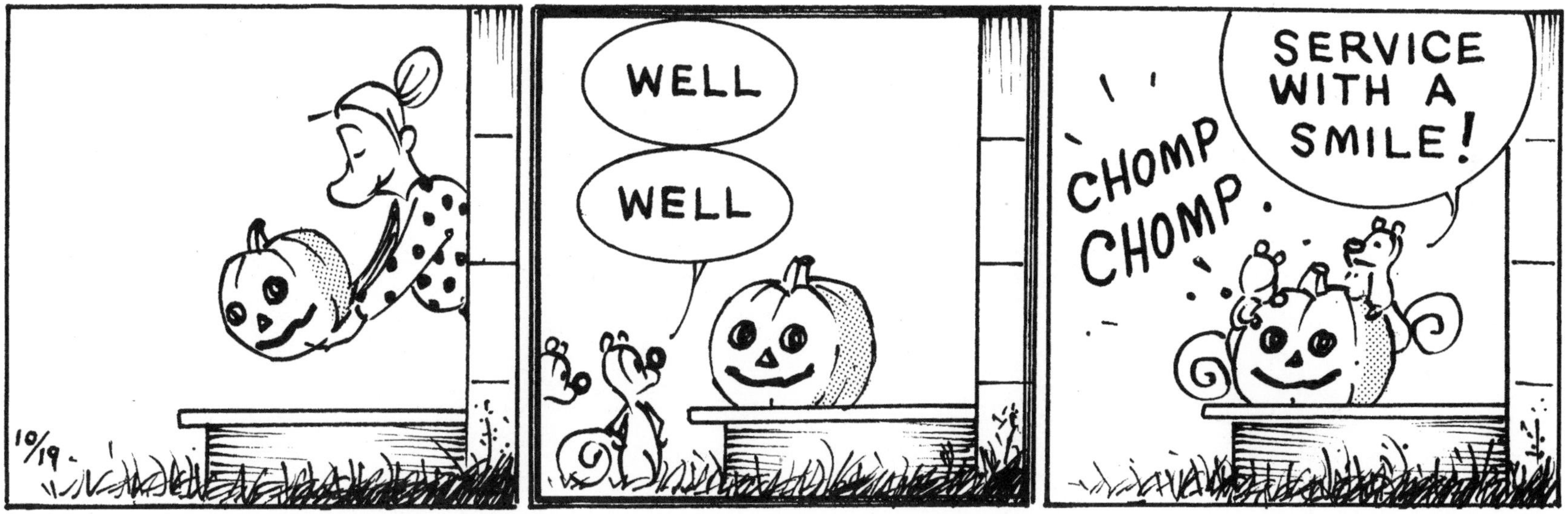
10/19
WELL
WELL
CHOMP CHOMP.
SERVICE WITH A SMILE!

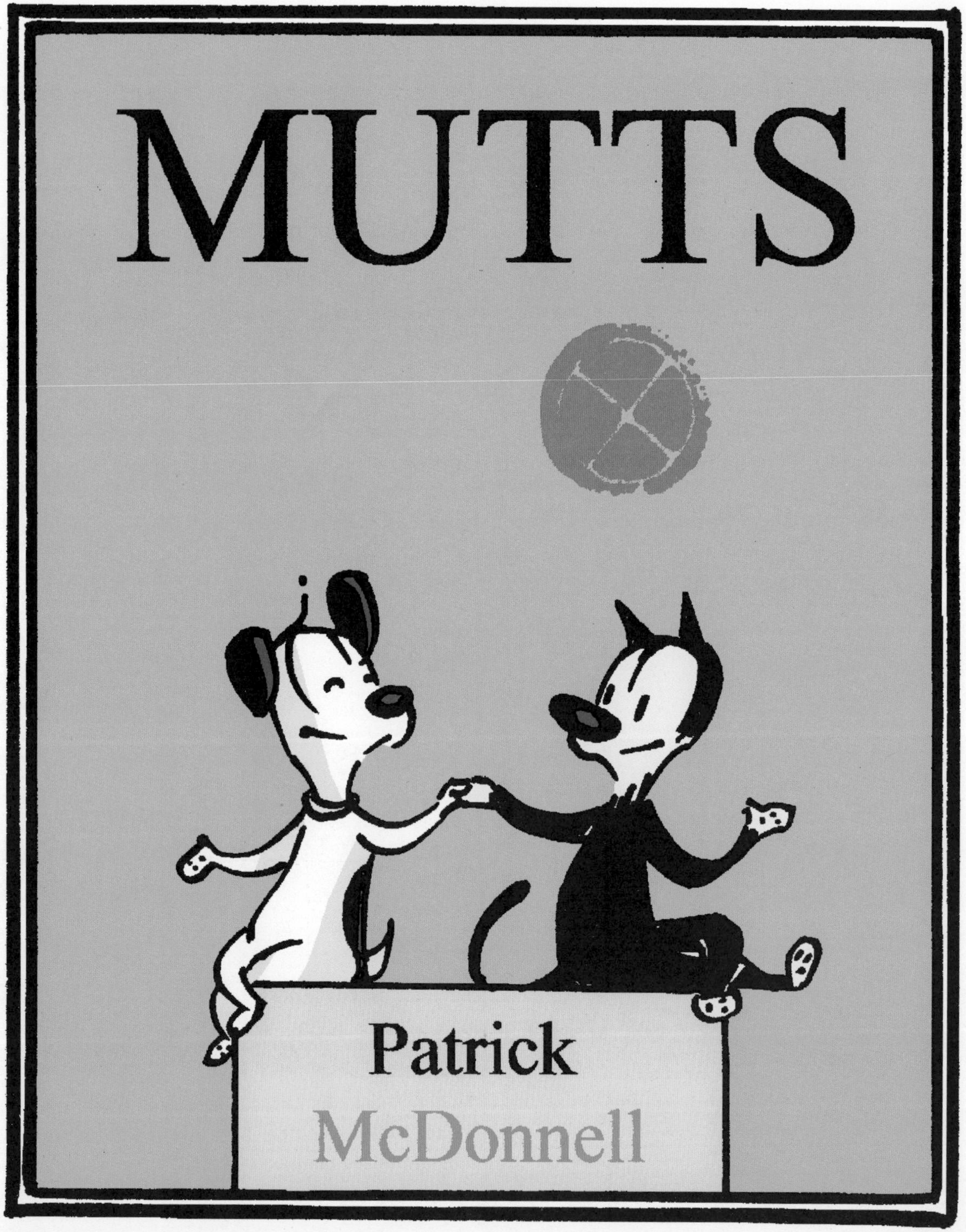
MUTTS
Patrick
McDonnell

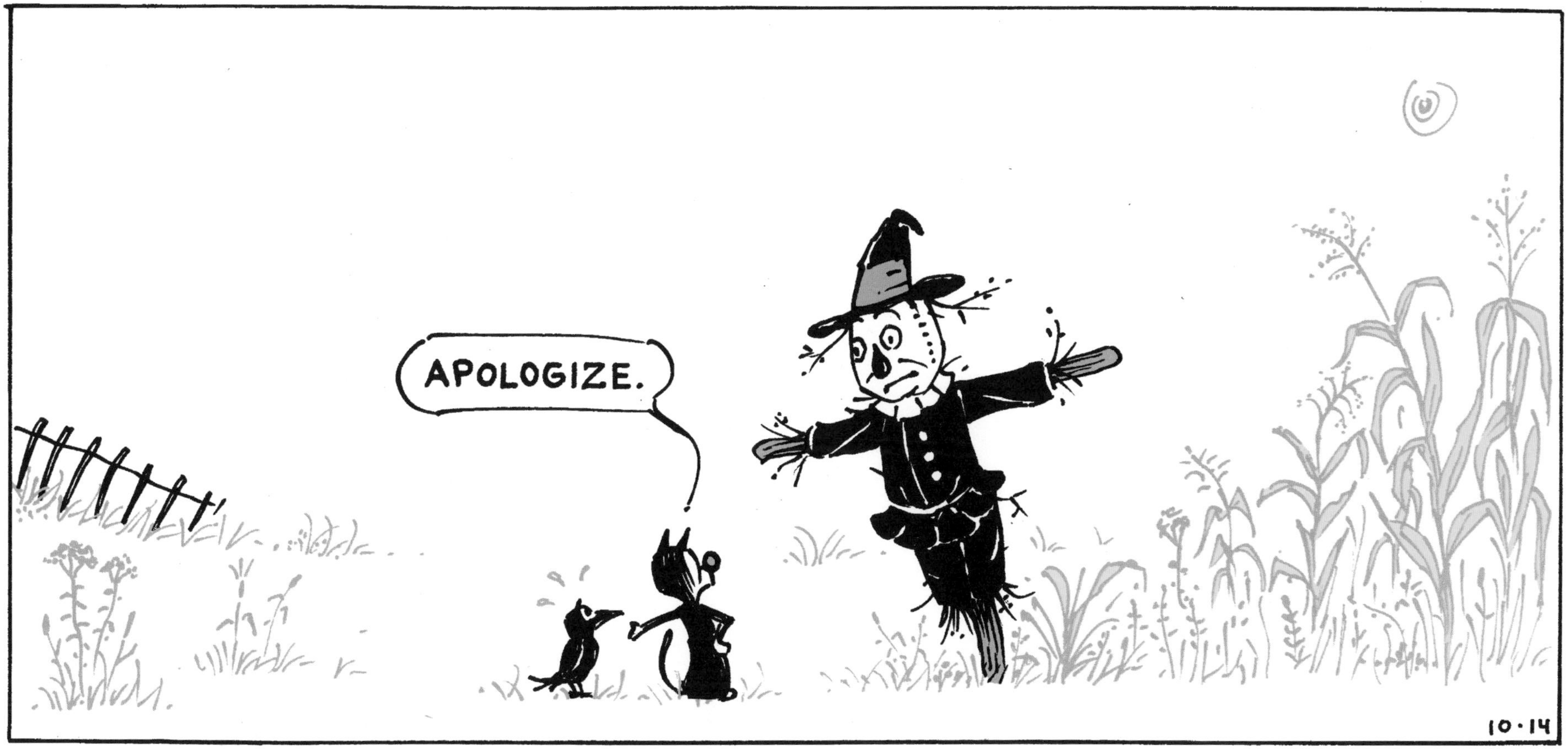
APOLOGIZE.
10 · 14

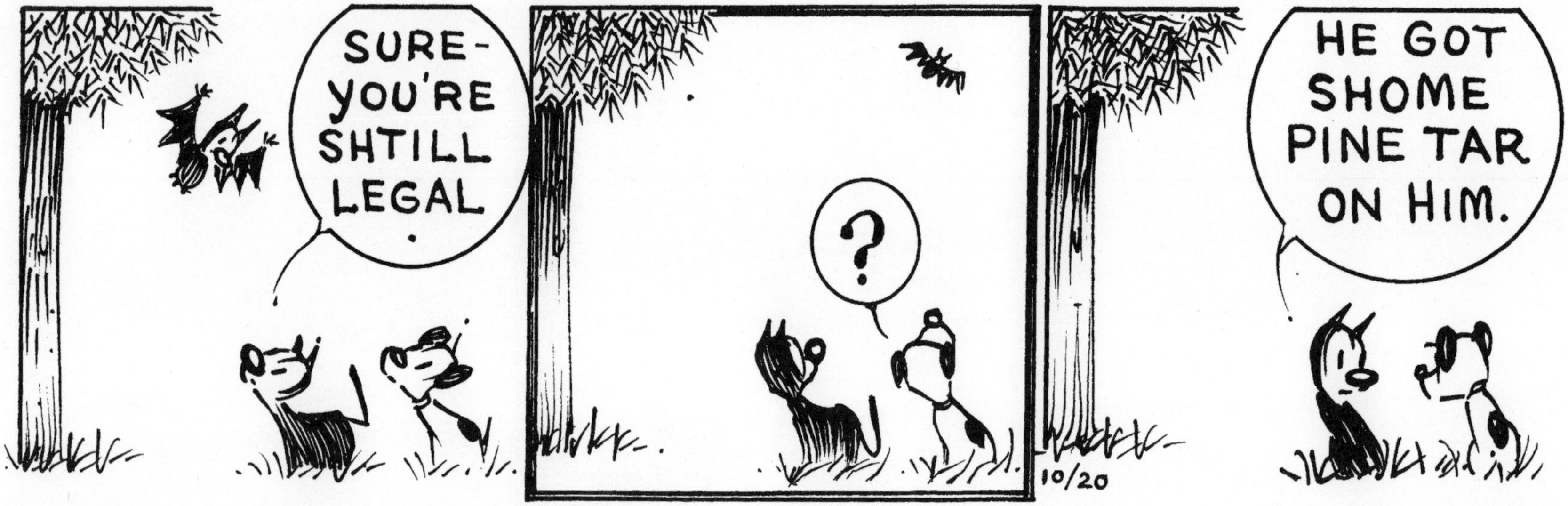
SURE- YOU'RE SHTILL LEGAL.
?
HE GOT SHOME PINE TAR ON HIM.
10/20

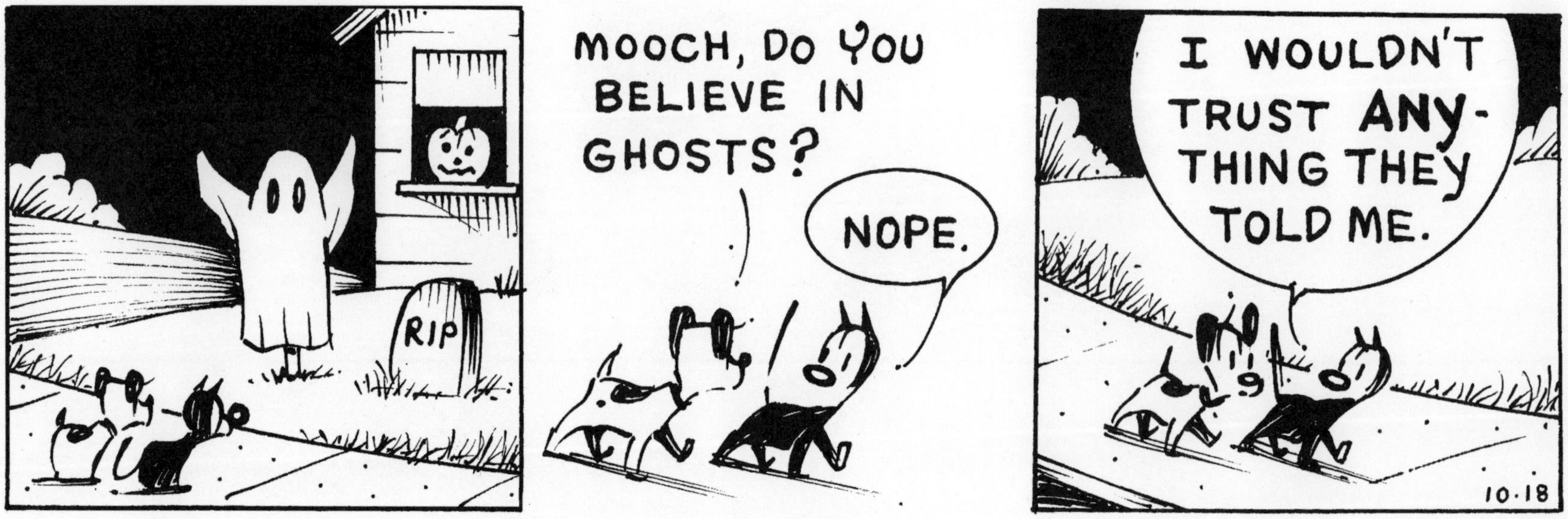
RIP
MOOCH, DO YOU BELIEVE IN GHOSTS?
NOPE.
I WOULDN'T TRUST ANY-THING THEY TOLD ME.
10.18

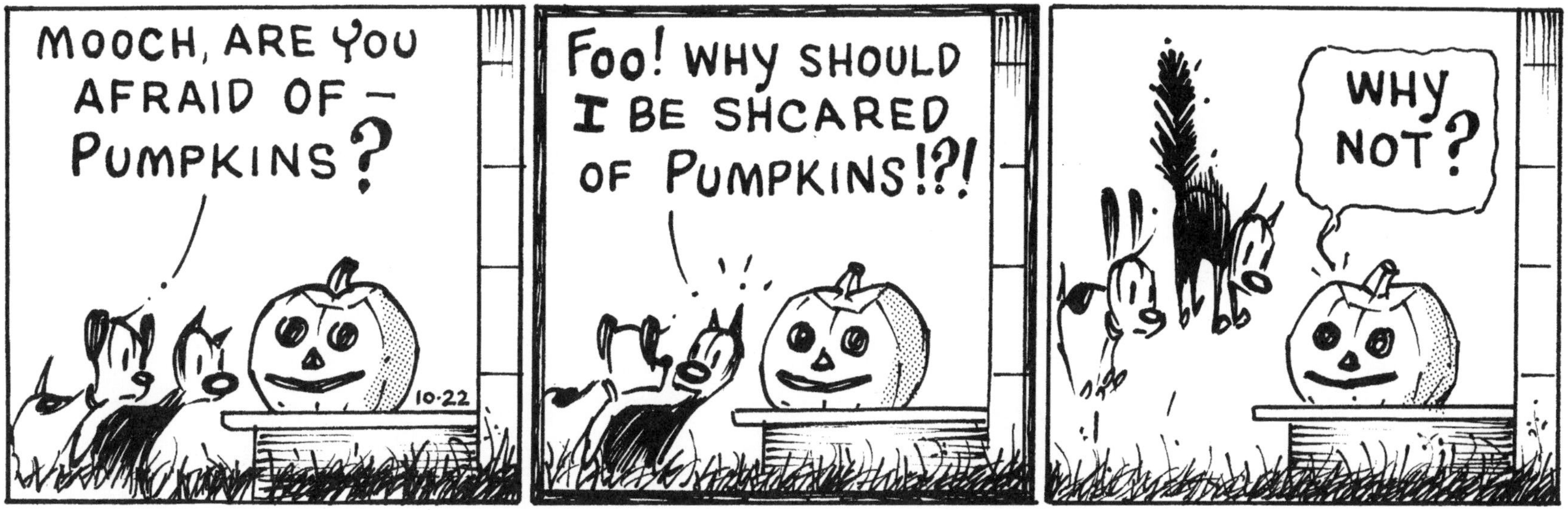
MOOCH, ARE YOU AFRAID OF – PUMPKINS?
10·22
FOO! WHY SHOULD I BE SHCARED OF PUMPKINS!?!
WHY NOT?

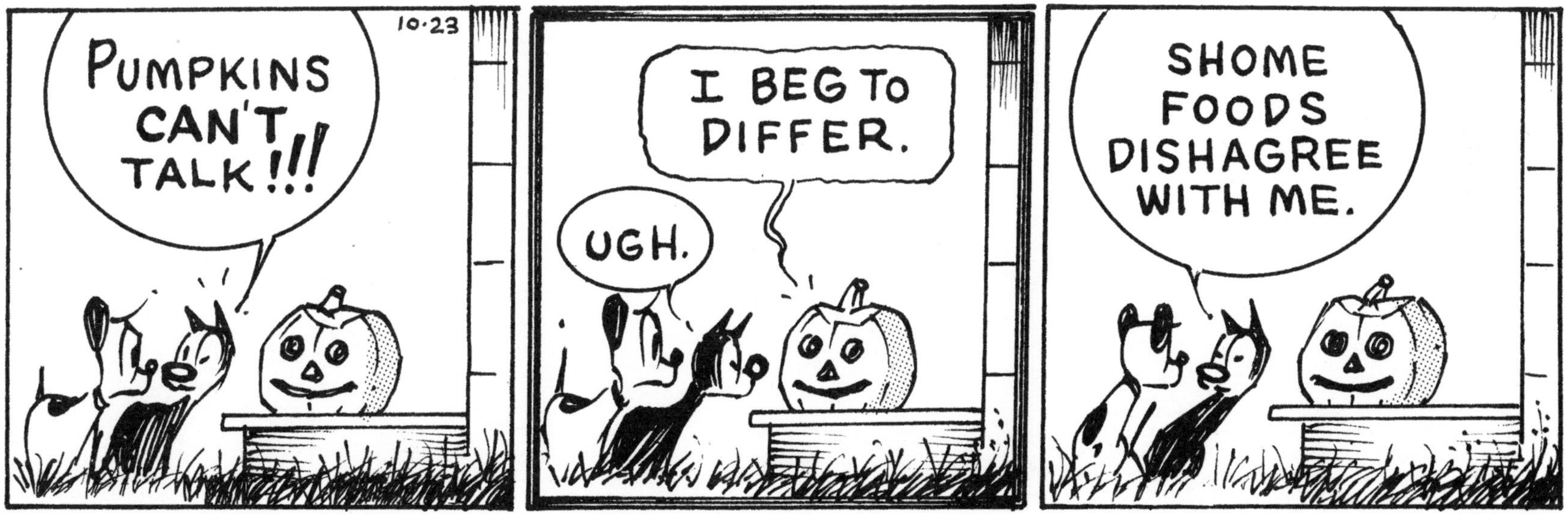
10·23
PUMPKINS CAN'T TALK!!!
UGH.
I BEG TO DIFFER.
SHOME FOODS DISHAGREE WITH ME.

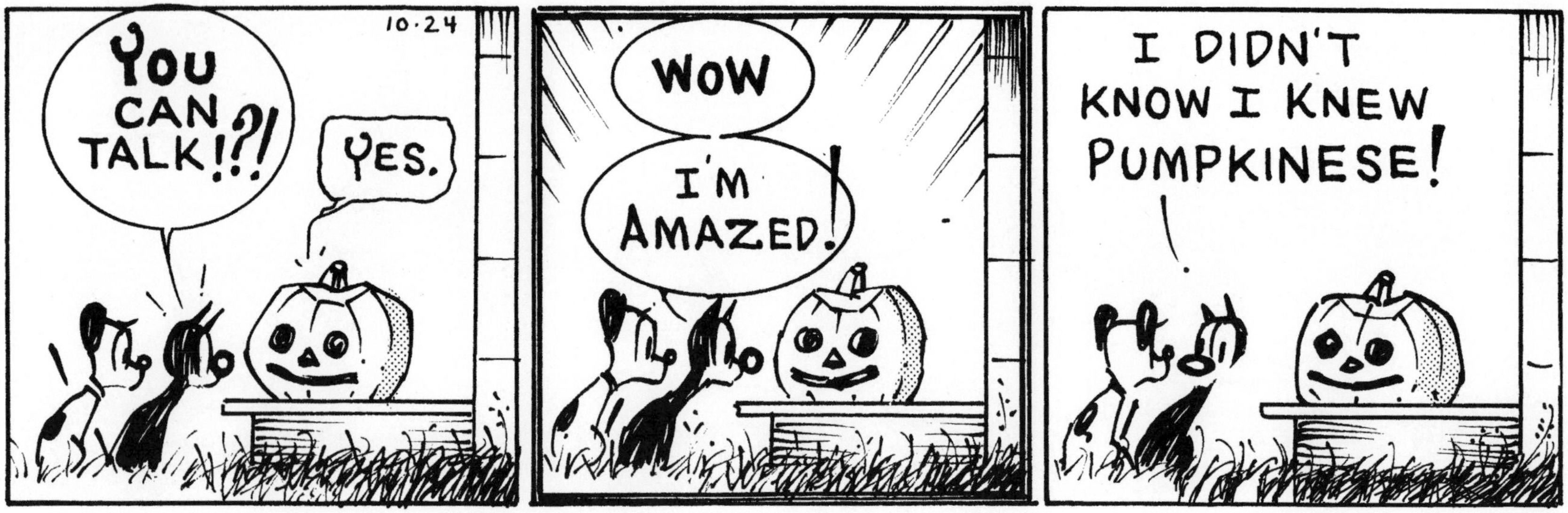
10·24
YOU CAN TALK!?!
YES.
WOW
I'M AMAZED!
I DIDN'T KNOW I KNEW PUMPKINESE!

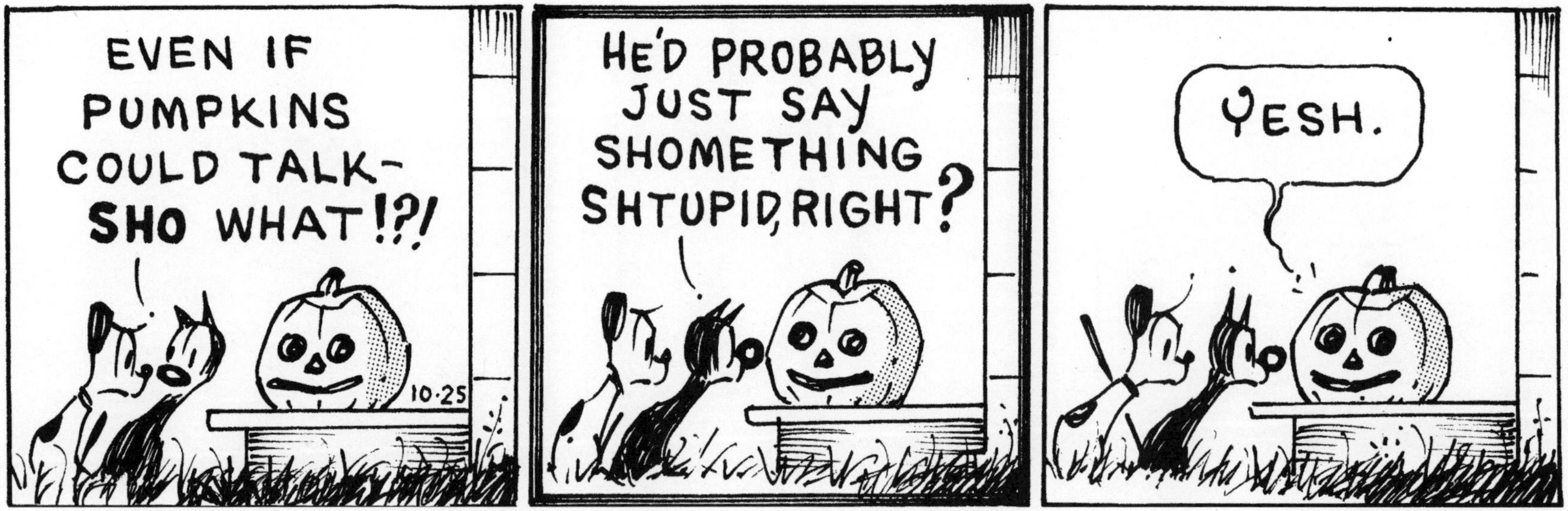
EVEN IF PUMPKINS COULD TALK- SHO WHAT!?!
10·25
HE'D PROBABLY JUST SAY SHOMETHING SHTUPID, RIGHT?
YESH.

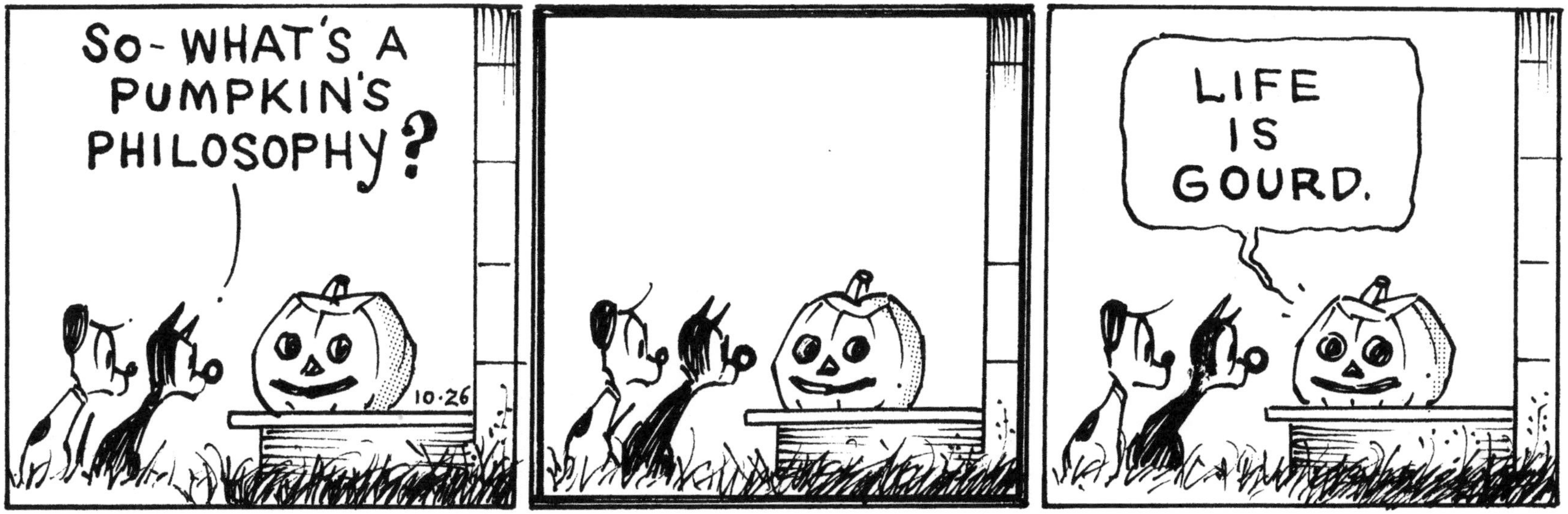
SO- WHAT'S A PUMPKIN'S PHILOSOPHY?
LIFE IS GOURD.
10·26

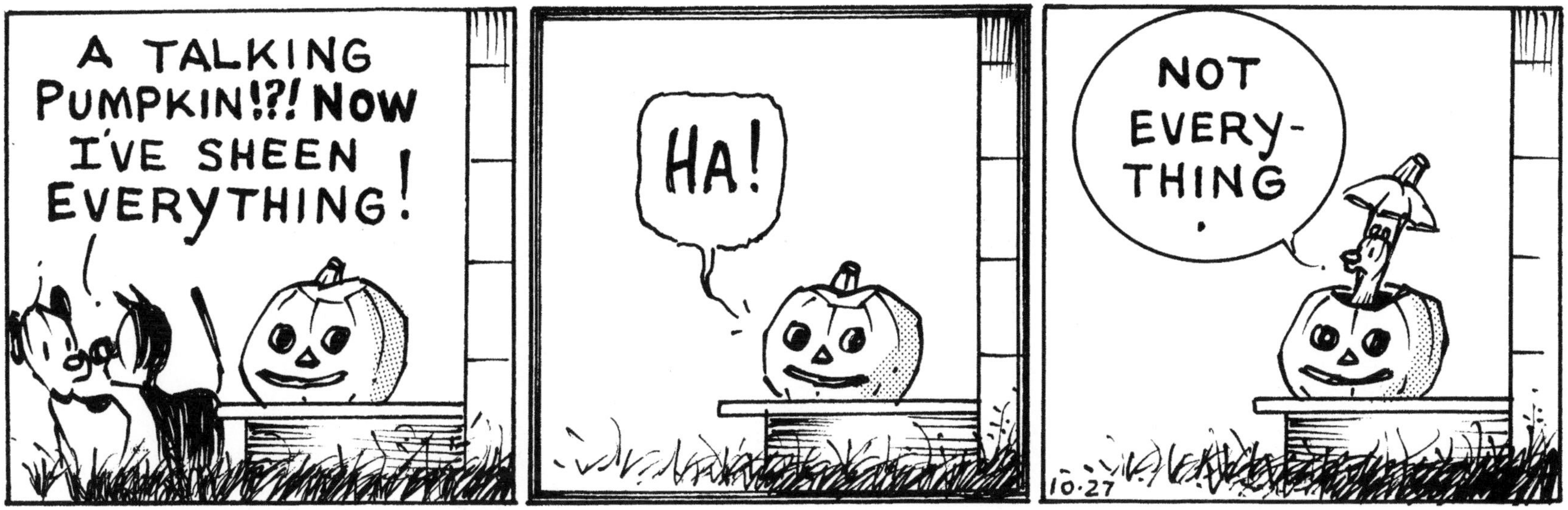
A TALKING PUMPKIN!?! NOW I'VE SHEEN EVERYTHING!
HA!
NOT EVERY-THING.
10·27

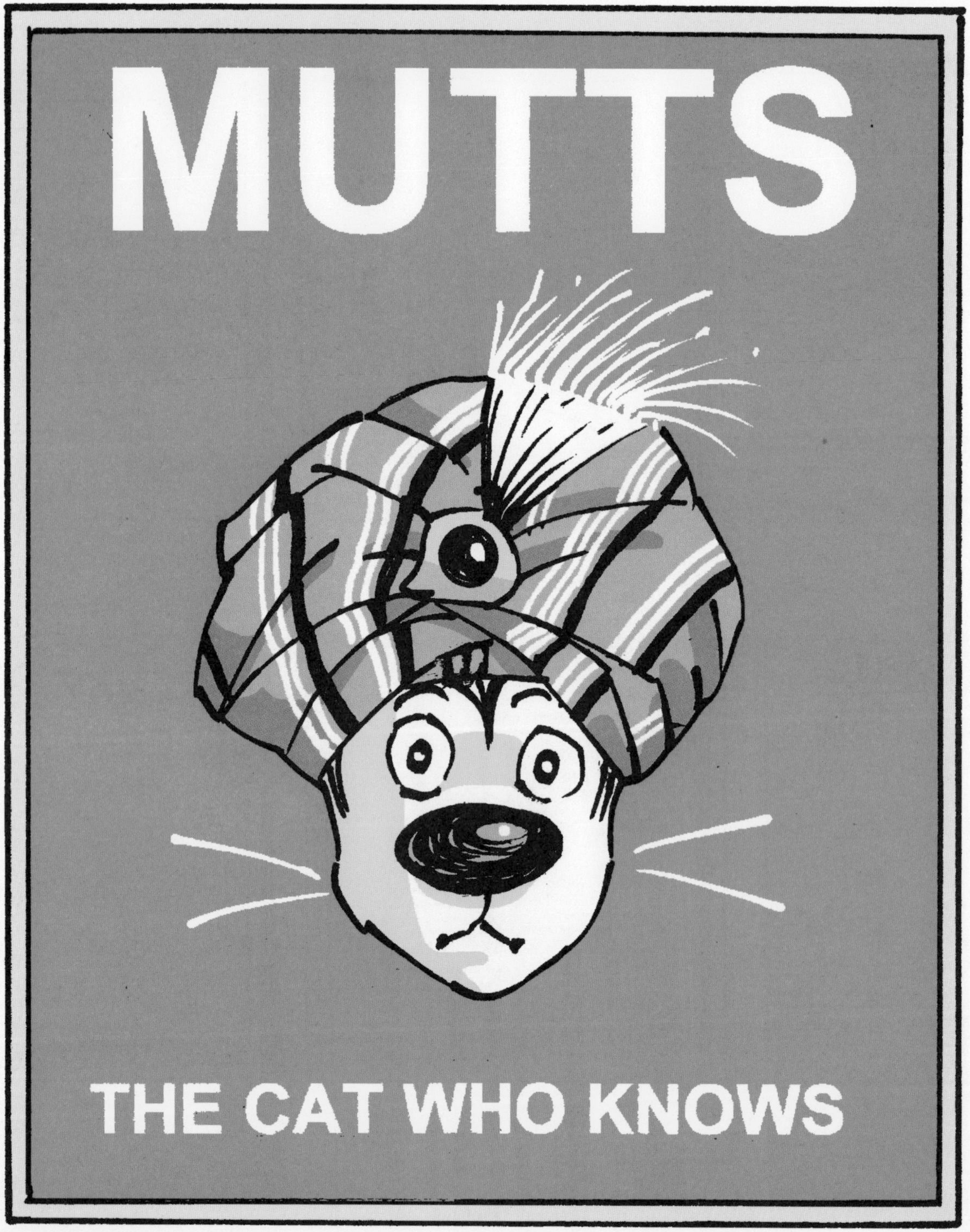
MUTTS
THE CAT WHO KNOWS

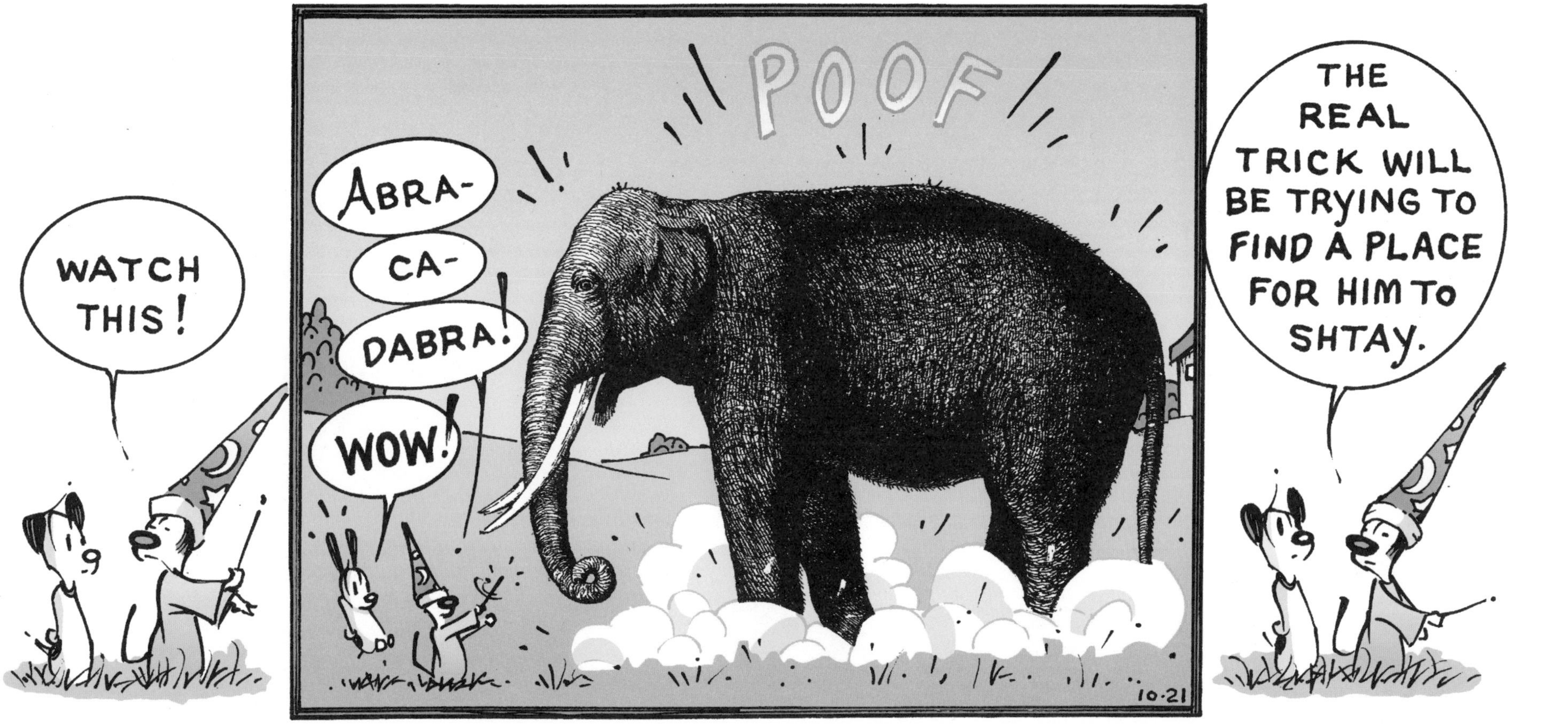
WATCH THIS!
ABRA-
CA-
DABRA!
WOW!
POOF
10·21
THE REAL TRICK WILL BE TRYING TO FIND A PLACE FOR HIM TO SHTAY.

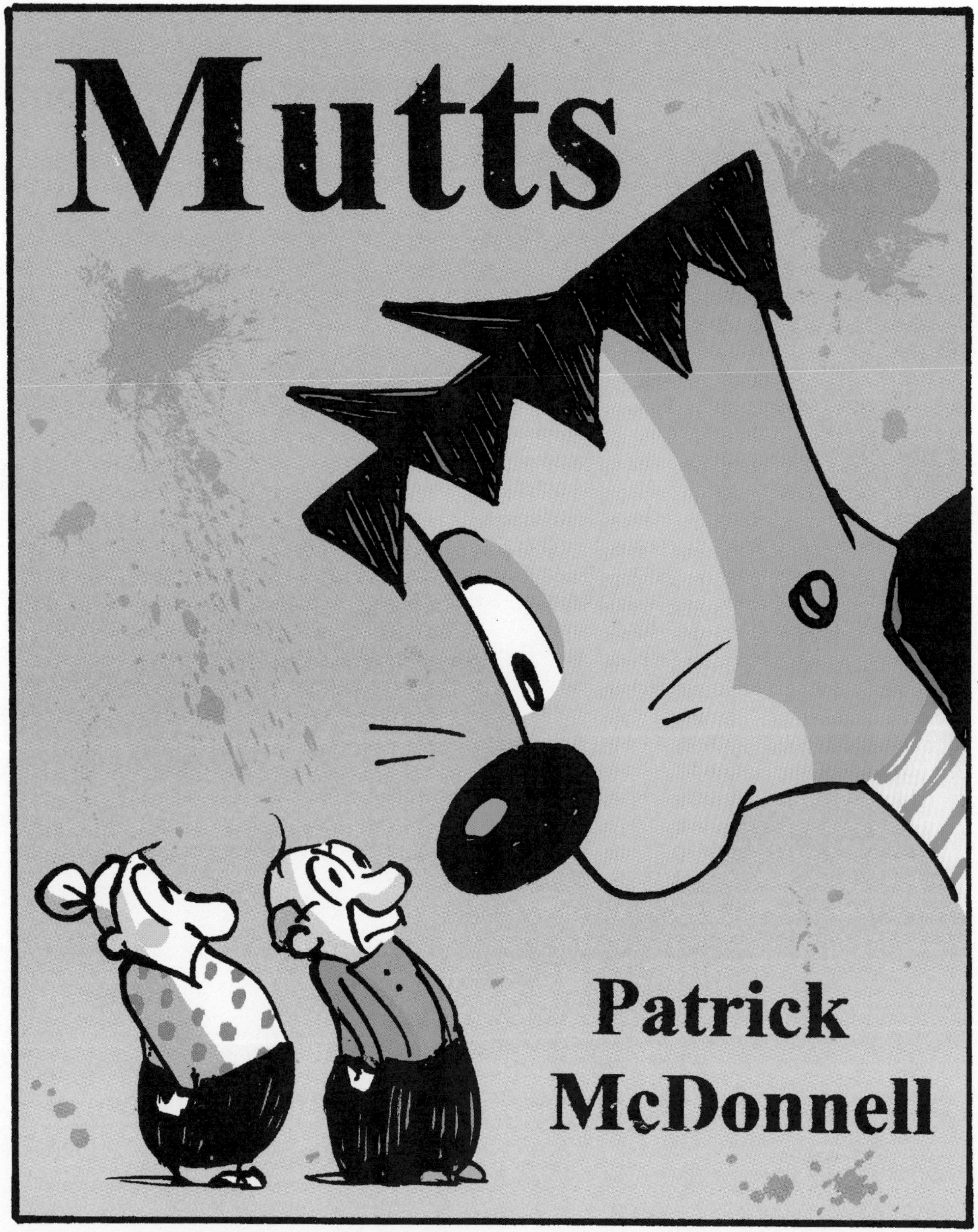
Mutts
Patrick McDonnell

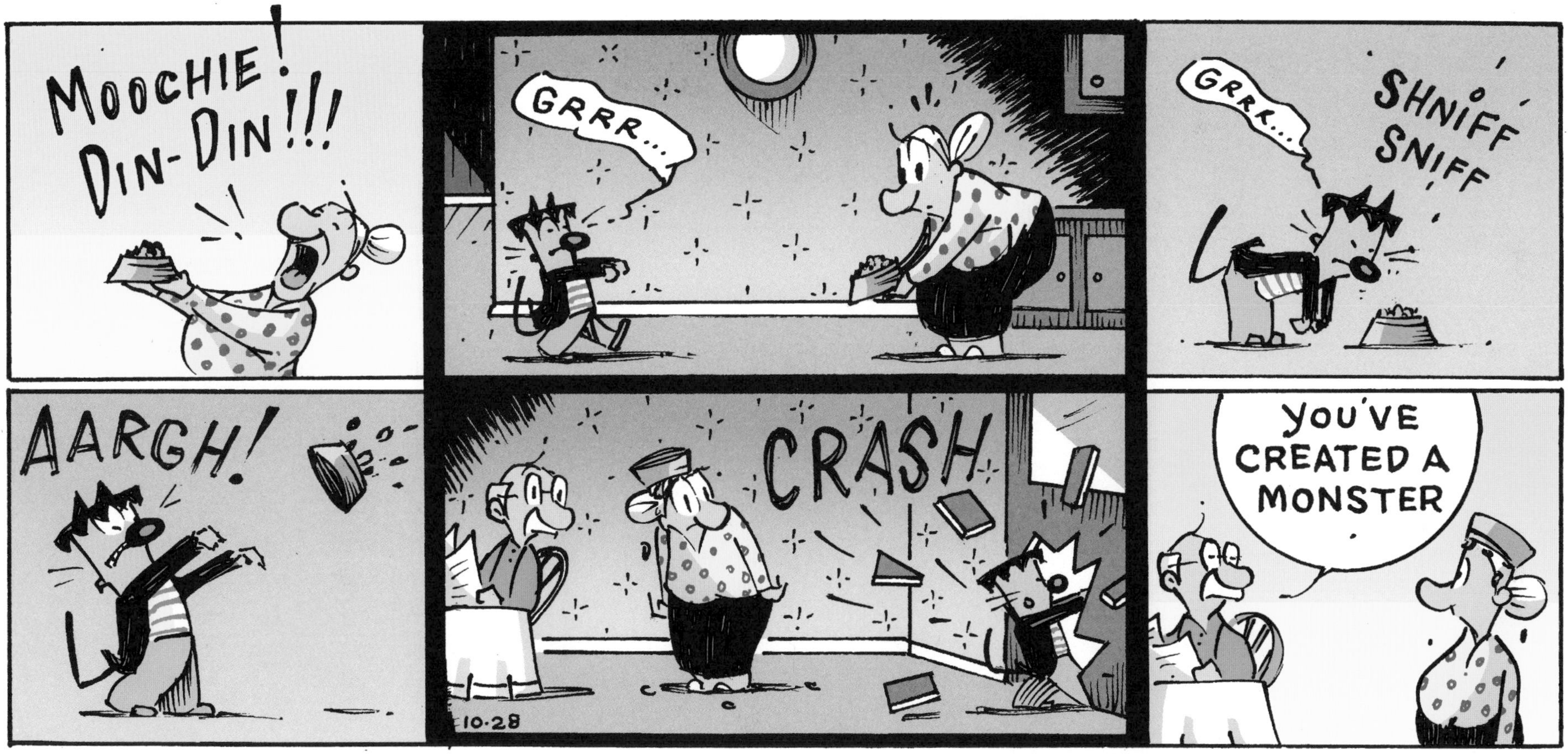
MOOCHIE! DIN-DIN!!!
GRRR...
GRRR...
SHNIFF SNIFF
AARGH!
CRASH
10-28
YOU'VE CREATED A MONSTER

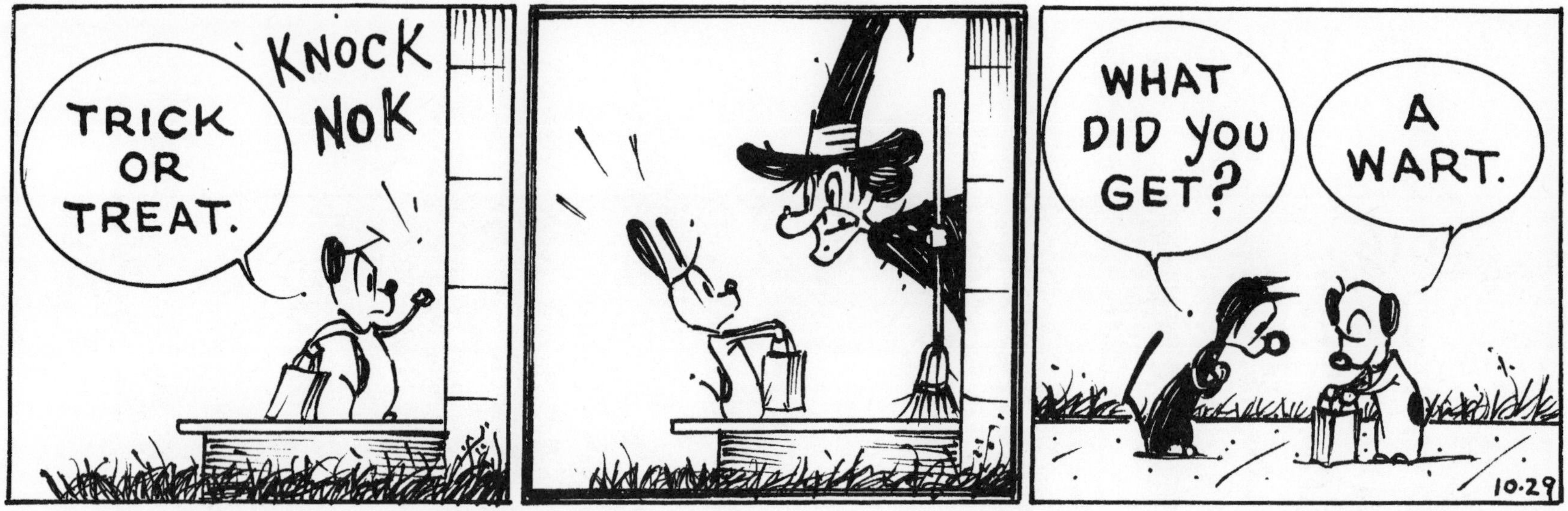
TRICK OR TREAT.
KNOCK NOK
WHAT DID YOU GET?
A WART.
10·29

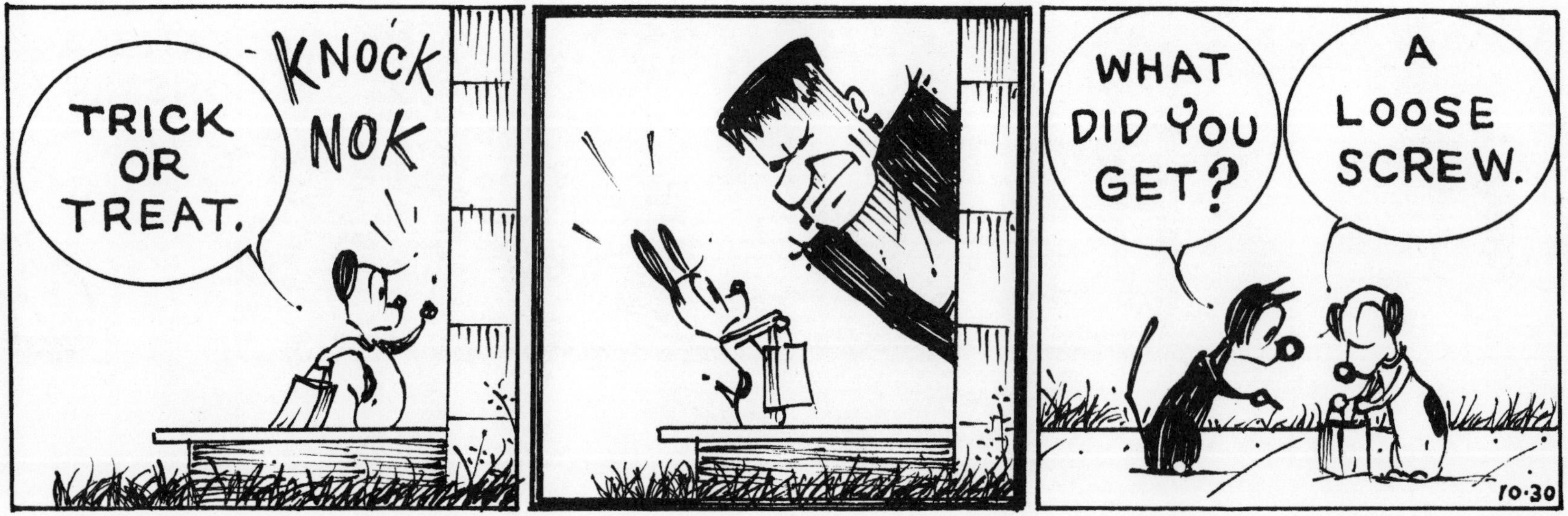
TRICK OR TREAT.
KNOCK NOK
WHAT DID YOU GET?
A LOOSE SCREW.
10·30

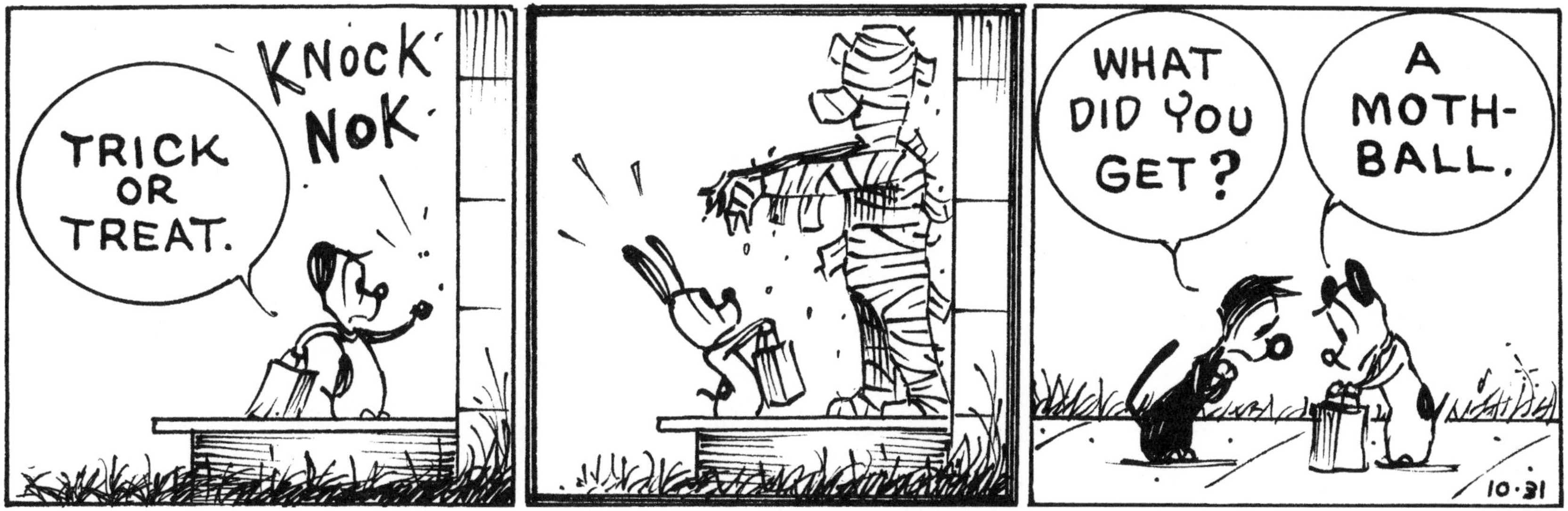
KNOCK NOK
TRICK OR TREAT.
WHAT DID YOU GET?
A MOTH-BALL.
10·31

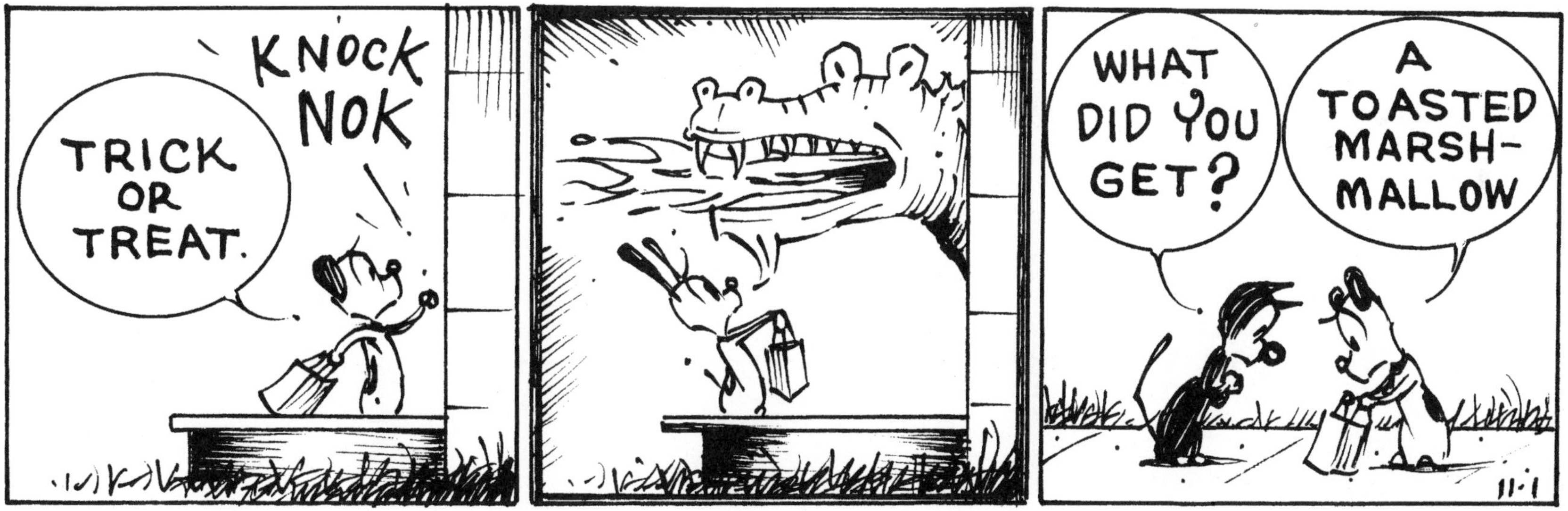
KNOCK NOK
TRICK OR TREAT.
WHAT DID YOU GET?
A TOASTED MARSH-MALLOW
11·1

174

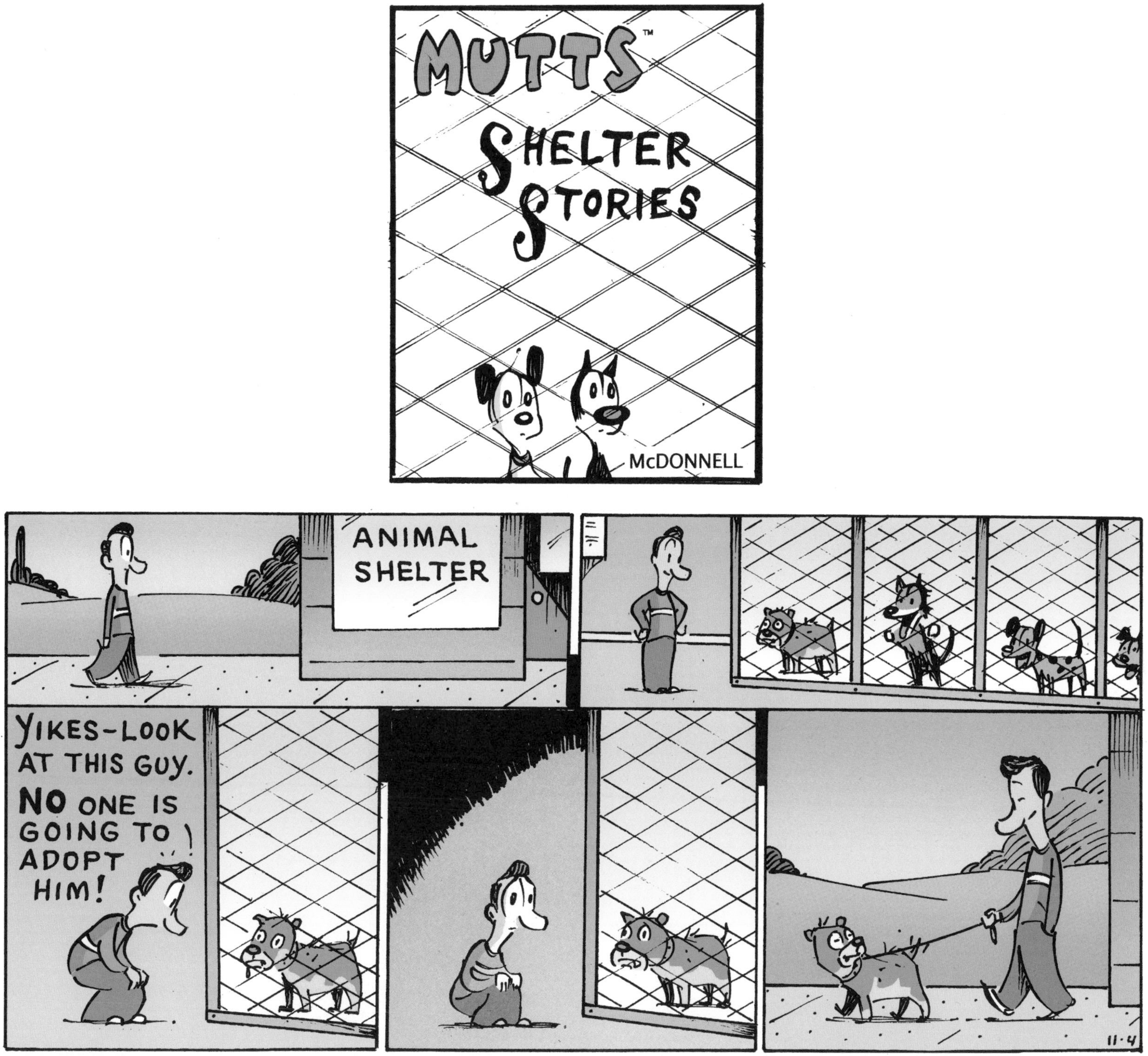
MUTTS™
SHELTER STORIES
McDONNELL
ANIMAL SHELTER
YIKES-LOOK AT THIS GUY. NO ONE IS GOING TO ADOPT HIM!
11·4

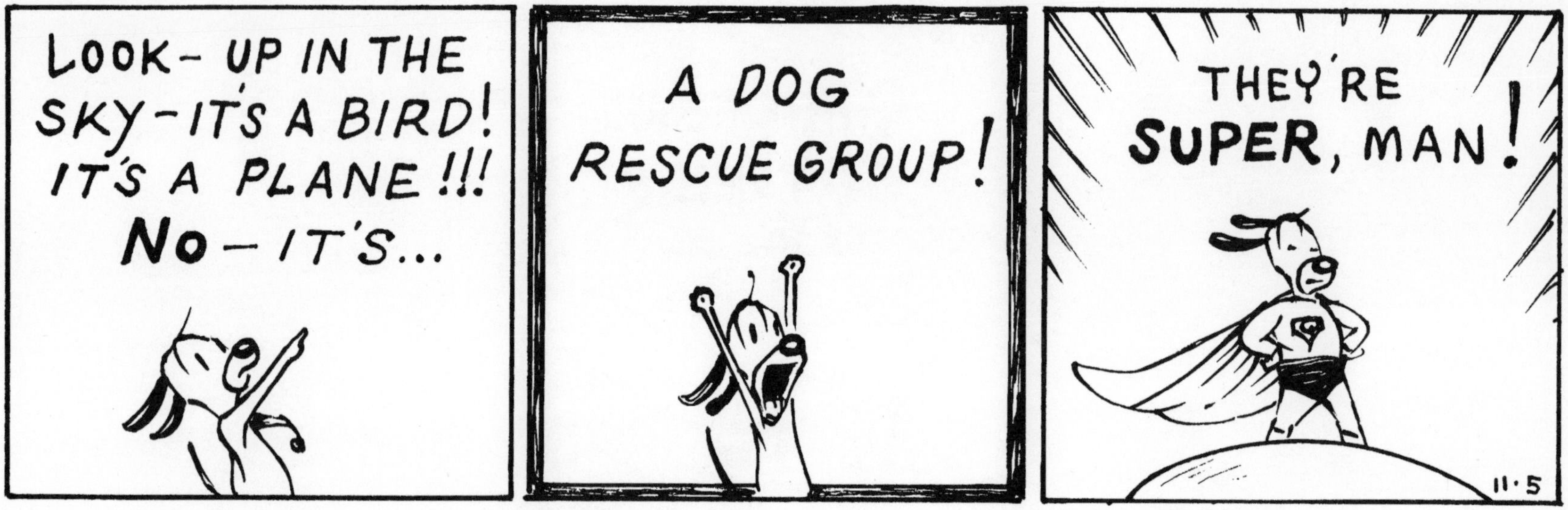
LOOK- UP IN THE SKY-IT'S A BIRD! IT'S A PLANE !!! NO-IT'S...
A DOG RESCUE GROUP!
THEY'RE SUPER, MAN!
11·5

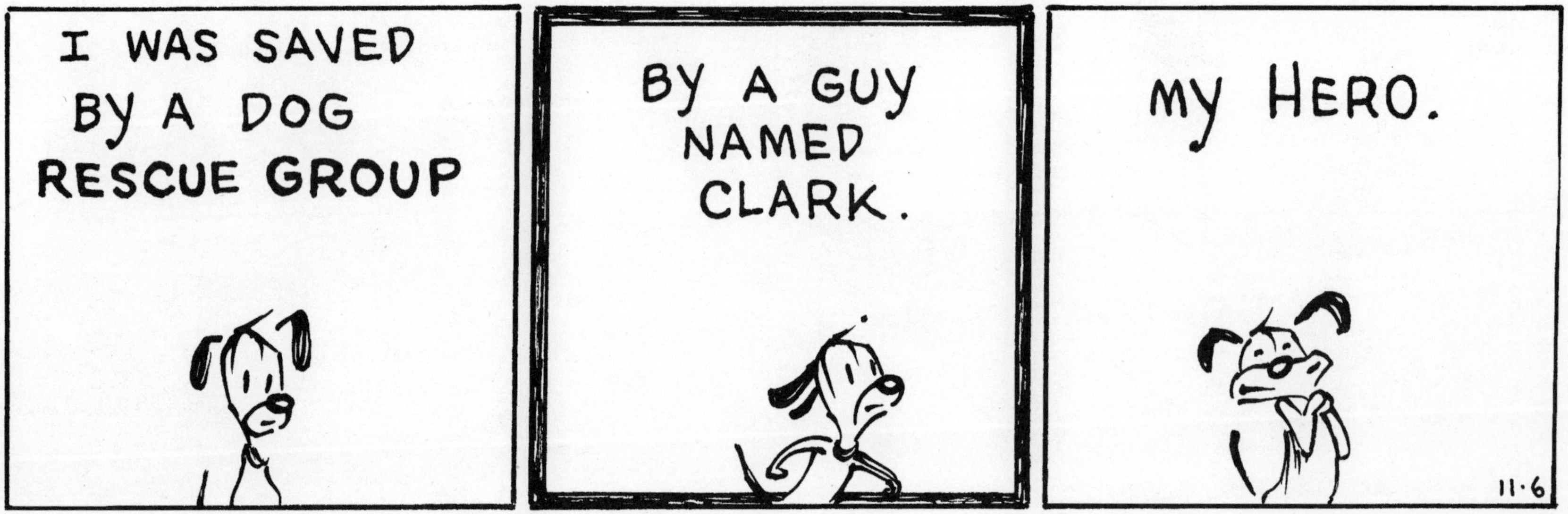
I WAS SAVED BY A DOG RESCUE GROUP
BY A GUY NAMED CLARK.
MY HERO.
11·6

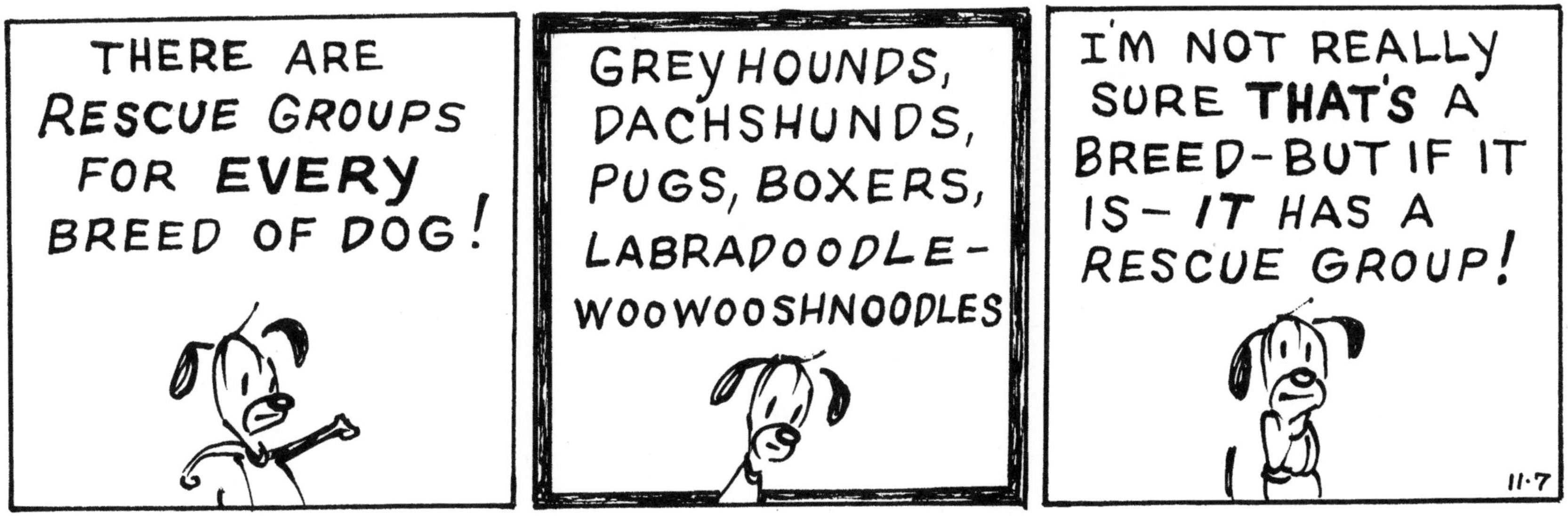
THERE ARE RESCUE GROUPS FOR EVERY BREED OF DOG!
GREYHOUNDS, DACHSHUNDS, PUGS, BOXERS, LABRADOODLE-WOOWOOSHNOODLES
I'M NOT REALLY SURE THAT'S A BREED-BUT IF IT IS- IT HAS A RESCUE GROUP!
11·7

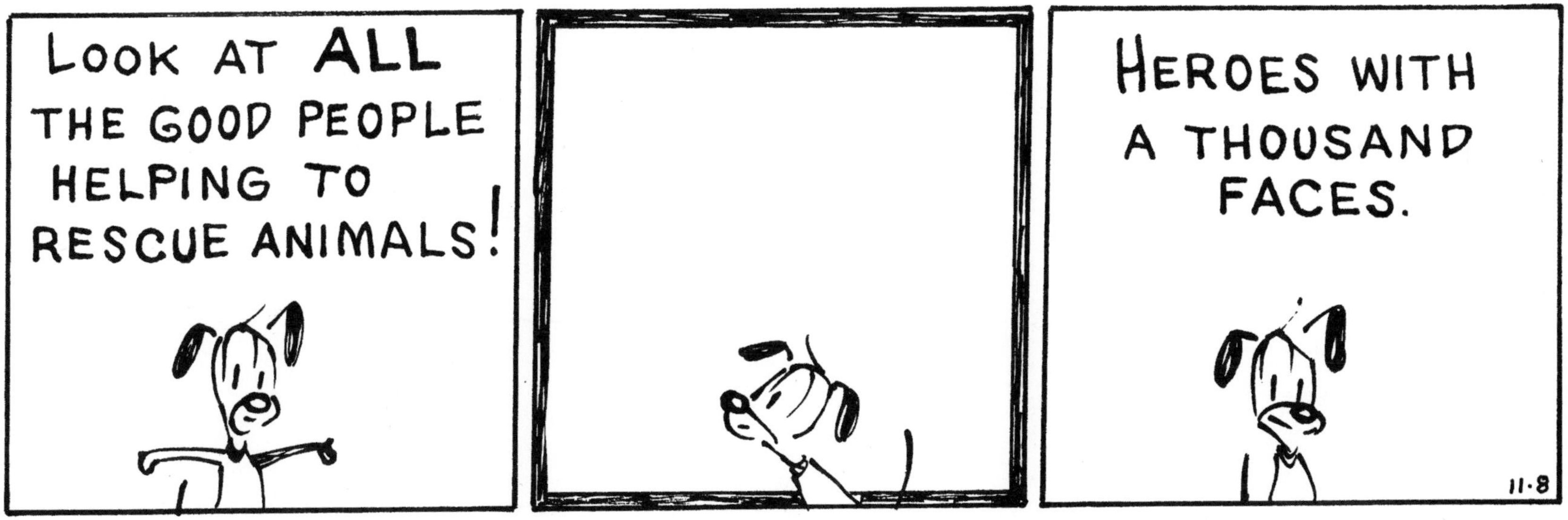
LOOK AT ALL THE GOOD PEOPLE HELPING TO RESCUE ANIMALS!
HEROES WITH A THOUSAND FACES.
11·8

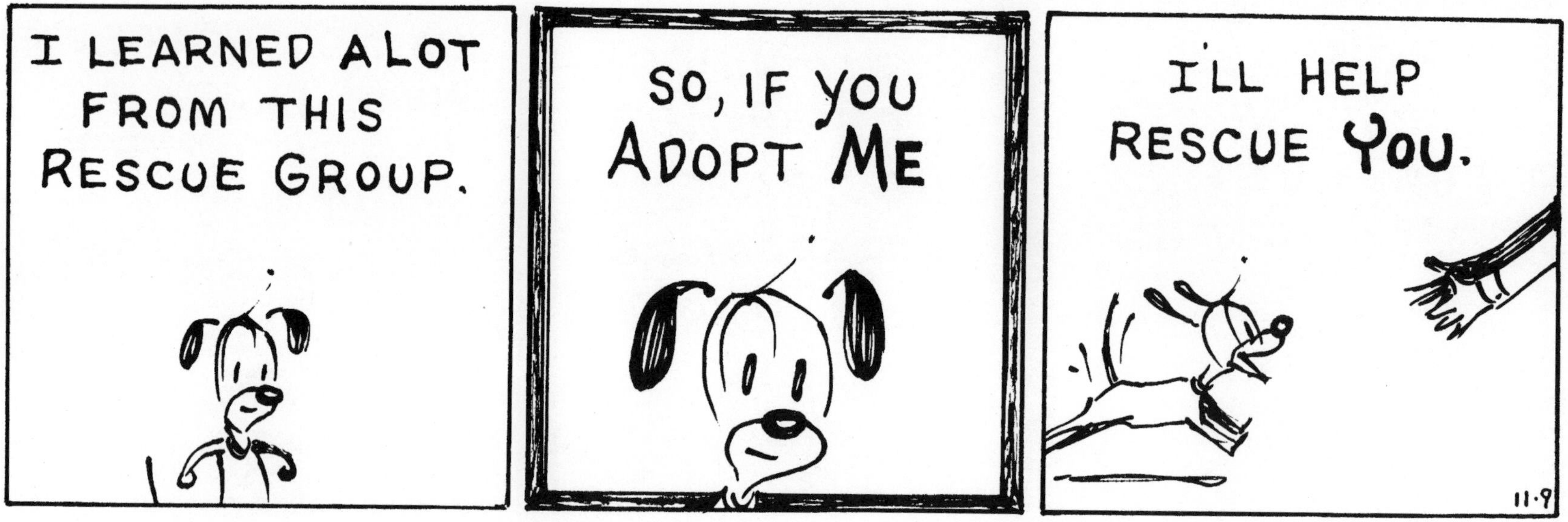
I LEARNED ALOT FROM THIS RESCUE GROUP.
SO, IF YOU ADOPT ME
I'LL HELP RESCUE YOU.
11·9

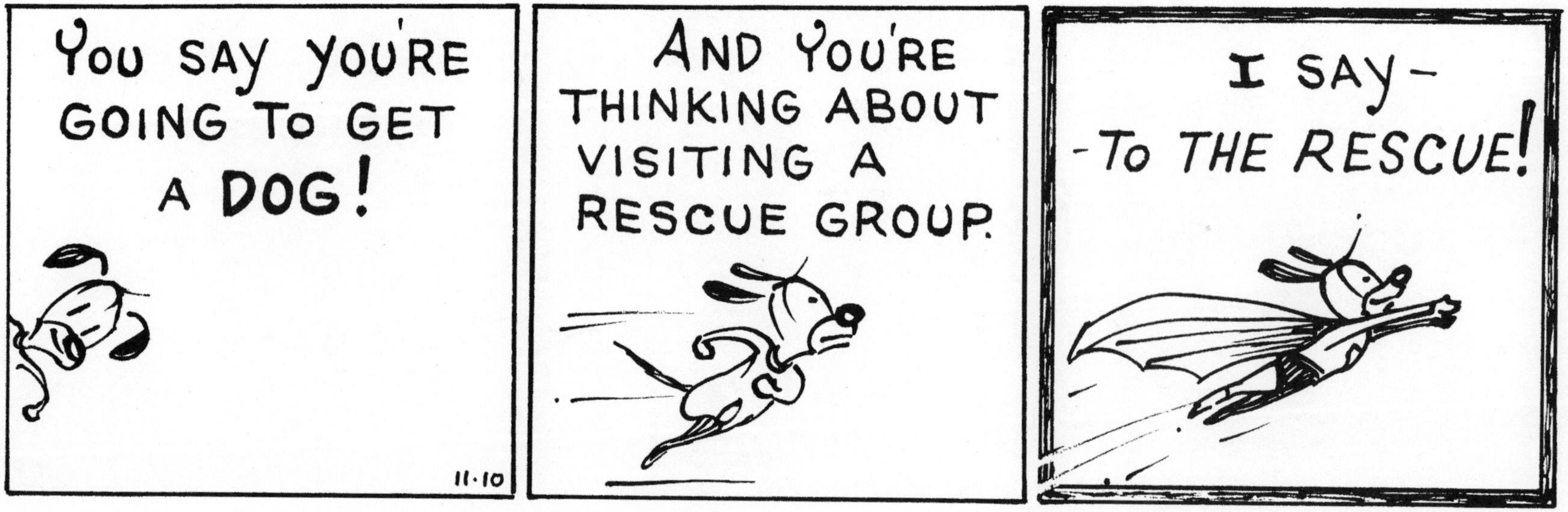
YOU SAY YOU'RE GOING TO GET A DOG!
11·10
AND YOU'RE THINKING ABOUT VISITING A RESCUE GROUP.
I SAY-
-TO THE RESCUE!

**Saving
the world
one kitty
at a time**

12·30

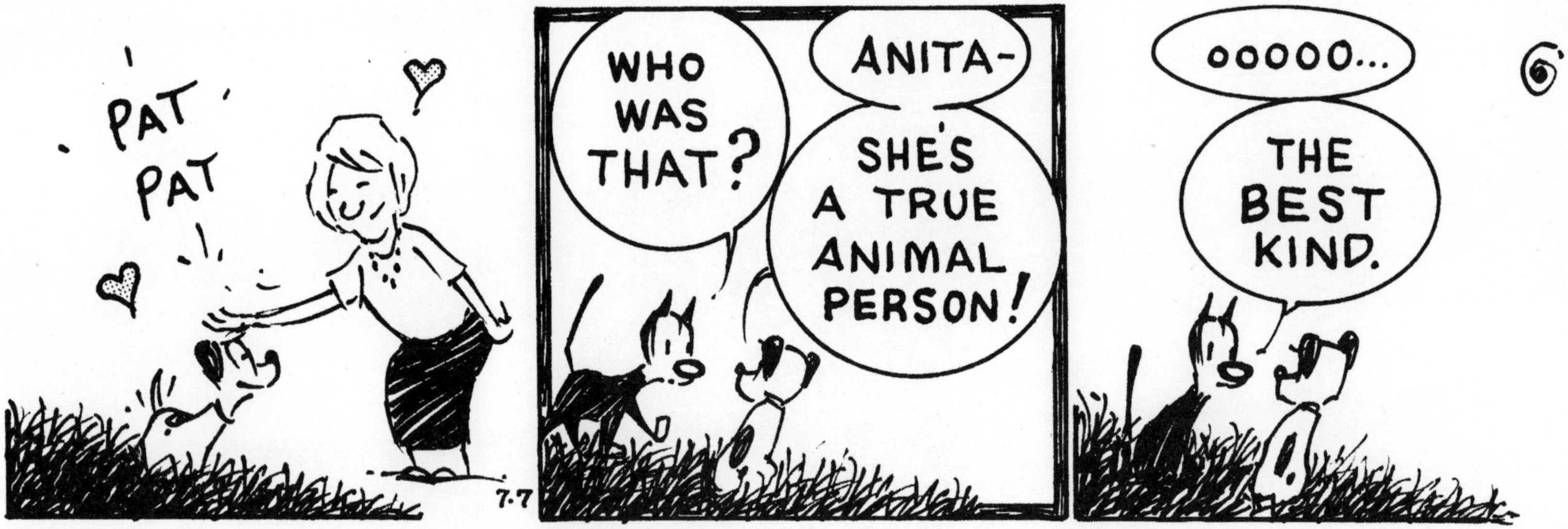
PAT
PAT
WHO WAS THAT?
ANITA-
SHE'S A TRUE ANIMAL PERSON!
OOOOO...
THE BEST KIND.
7·7

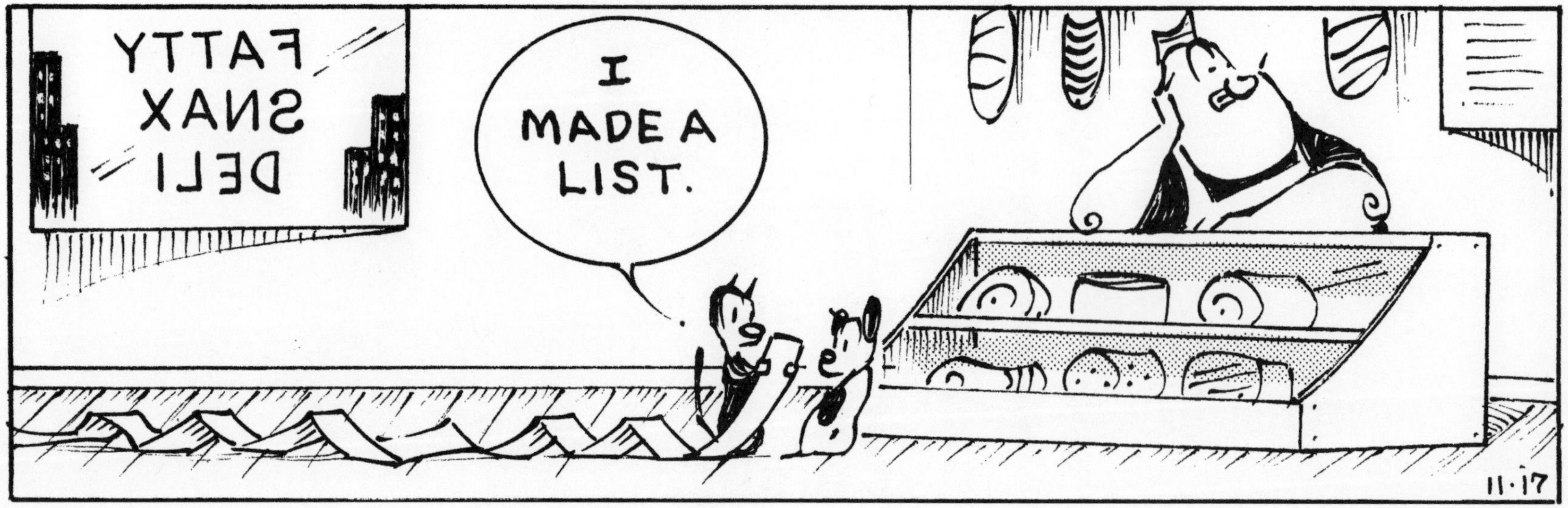
FATTY SNAX DELI
I MADE A LIST.
11·17

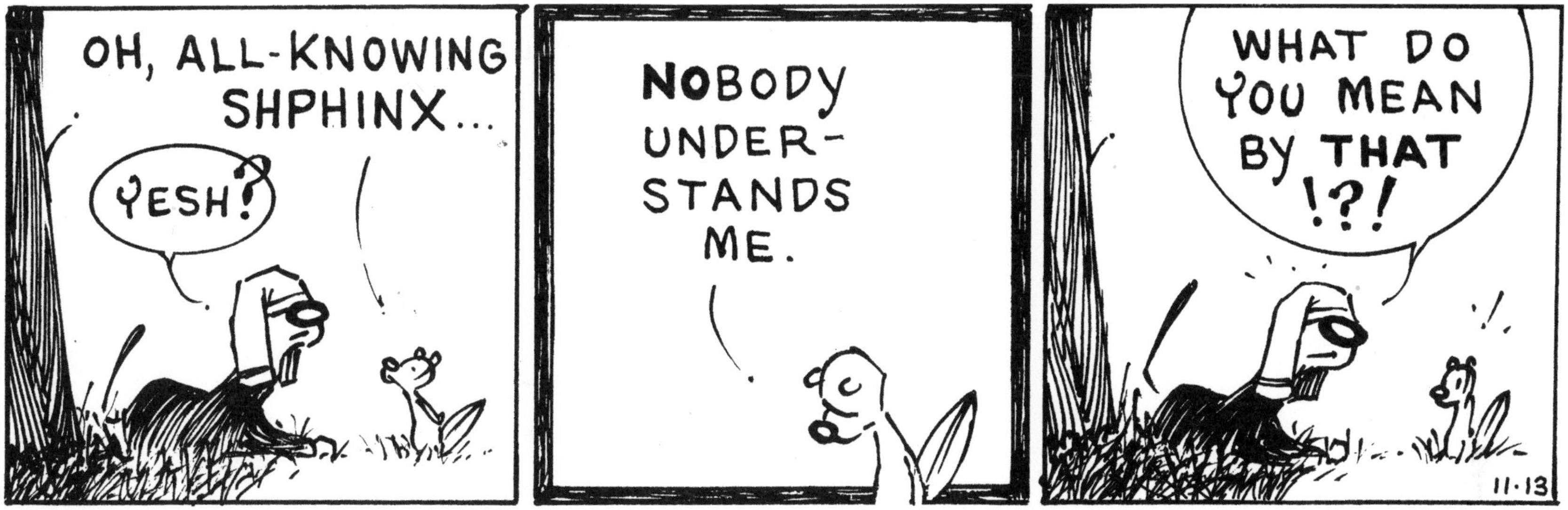
OH, ALL-KNOWING SHPHINX...
YESH?
NOBODY UNDER-STANDS ME.
WHAT DO YOU MEAN BY THAT !?!
11·13

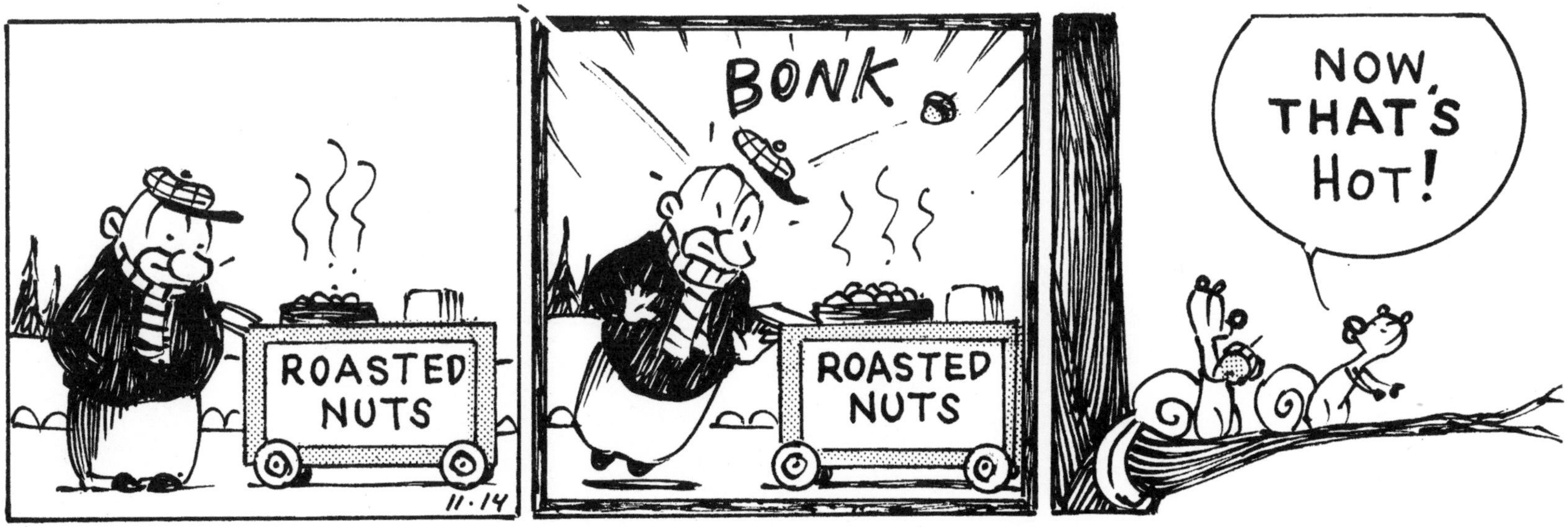
ROASTED NUTS
11·14
BONK
ROASTED NUTS
NOW THAT'S HOT!

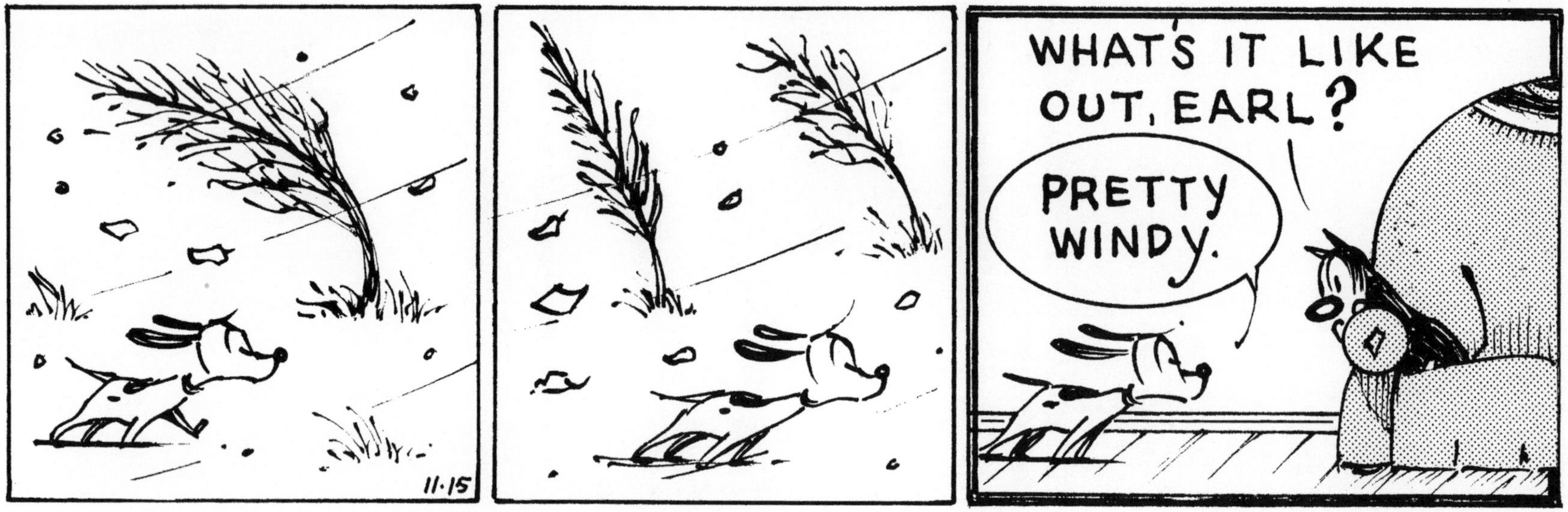
WHAT'S IT LIKE OUT, EARL?
PRETTY WINDY.
11·15

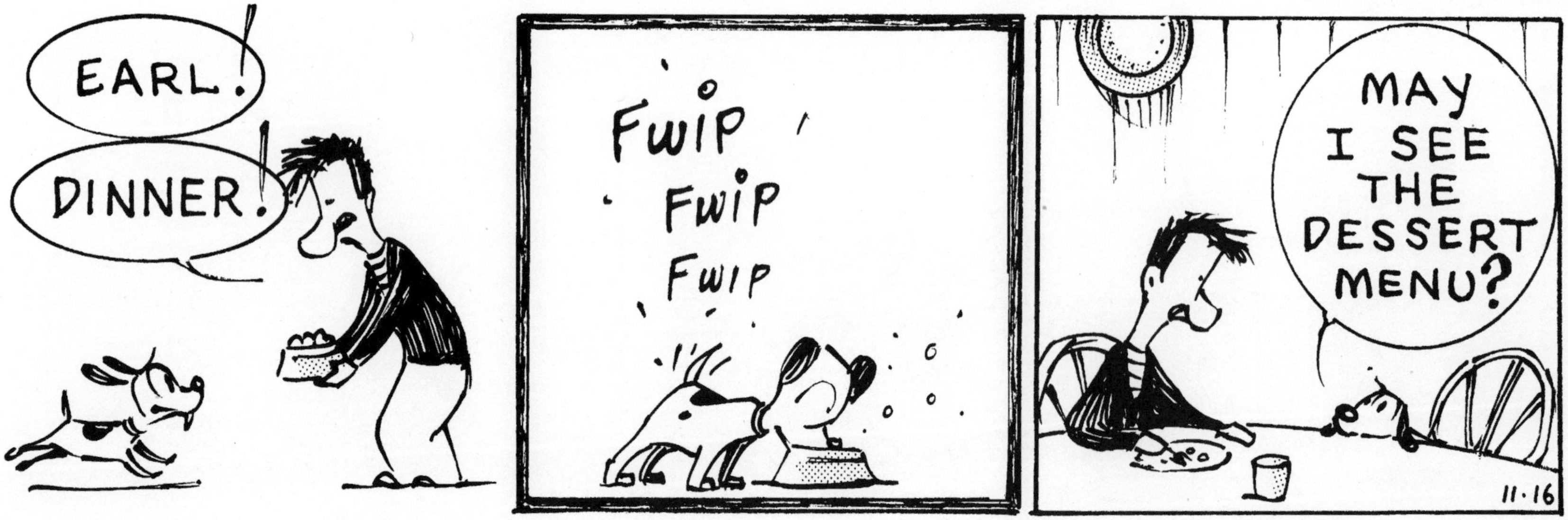
EARL!
DINNER!
FWIP
FWIP
FWIP
MAY I SEE THE DESSERT MENU?
11·16

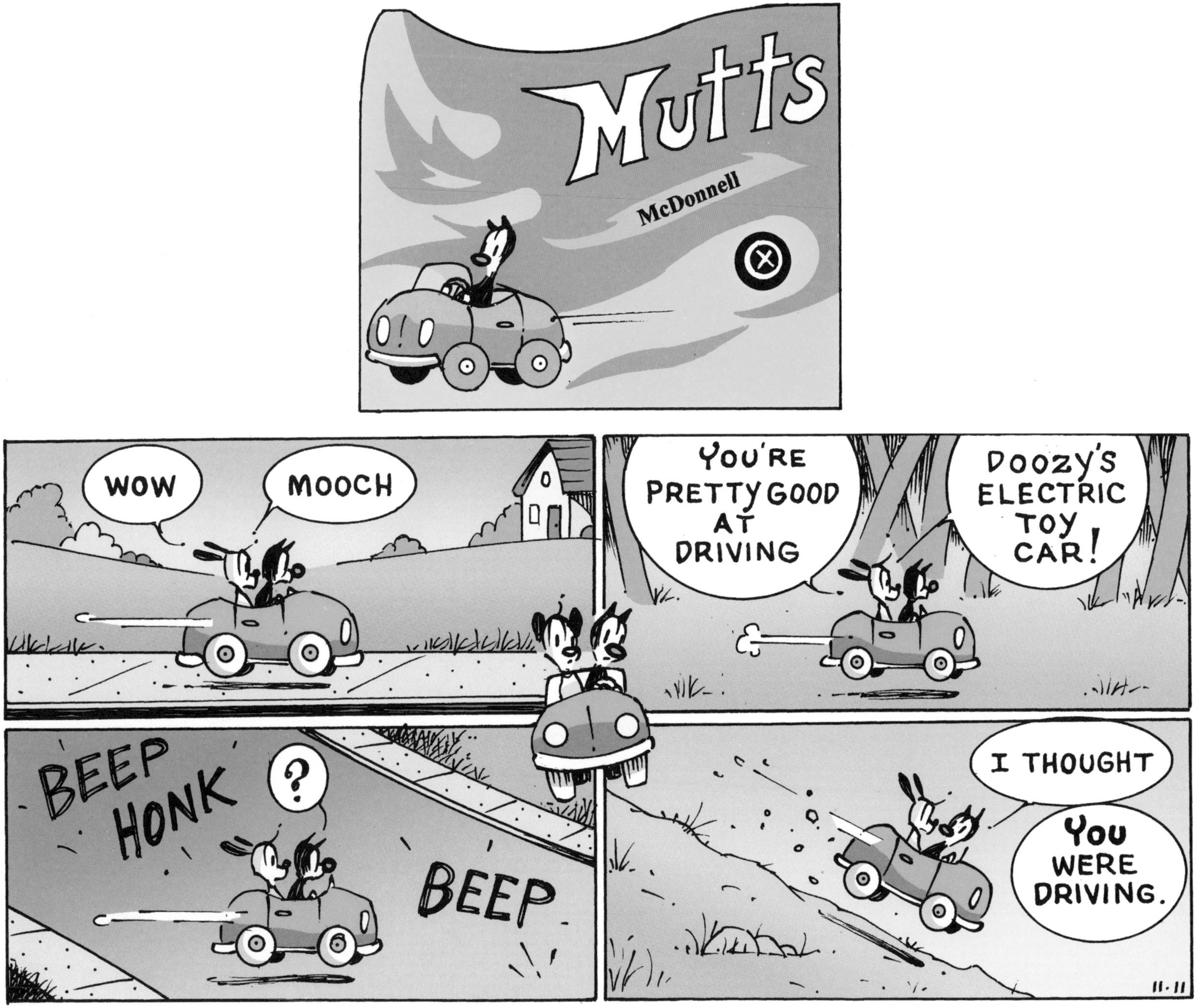
Mutts
McDonnell
WOW
MOOCH
YOU'RE PRETTY GOOD AT DRIVING
DOOZY'S ELECTRIC TOY CAR!
BEEP
HONK
?
BEEP
I THOUGHT
YOU WERE DRIVING.
11.11

MUTTS
by PATRICK McDONNELL
12·2
I DON'T KNOW, EARL...
I FEEL LIKE THEY'RE PUTTING US
IN A VERY
TIGHT
SHPOT.

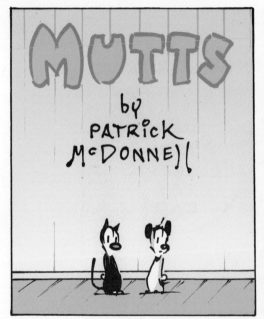

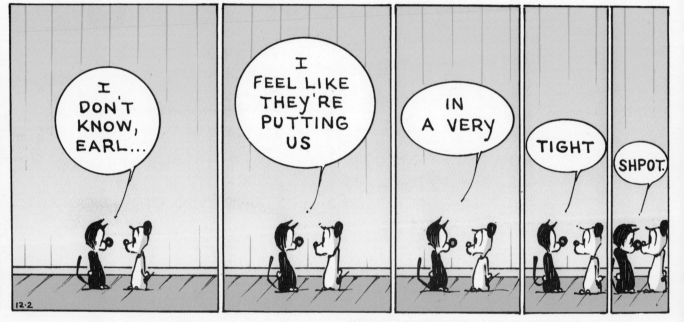

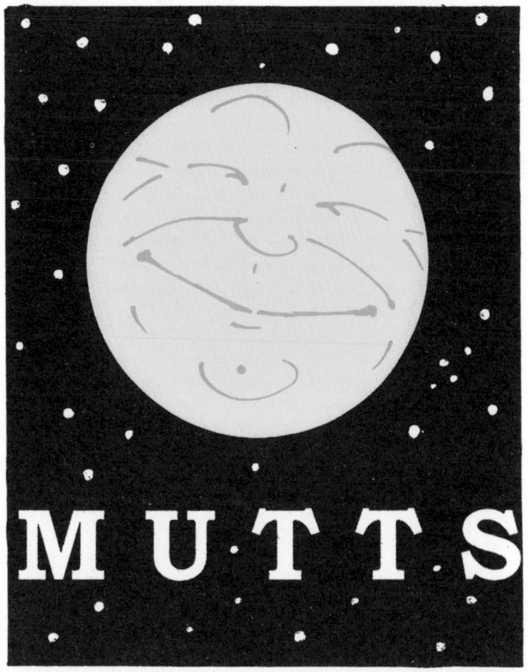
MUTTS

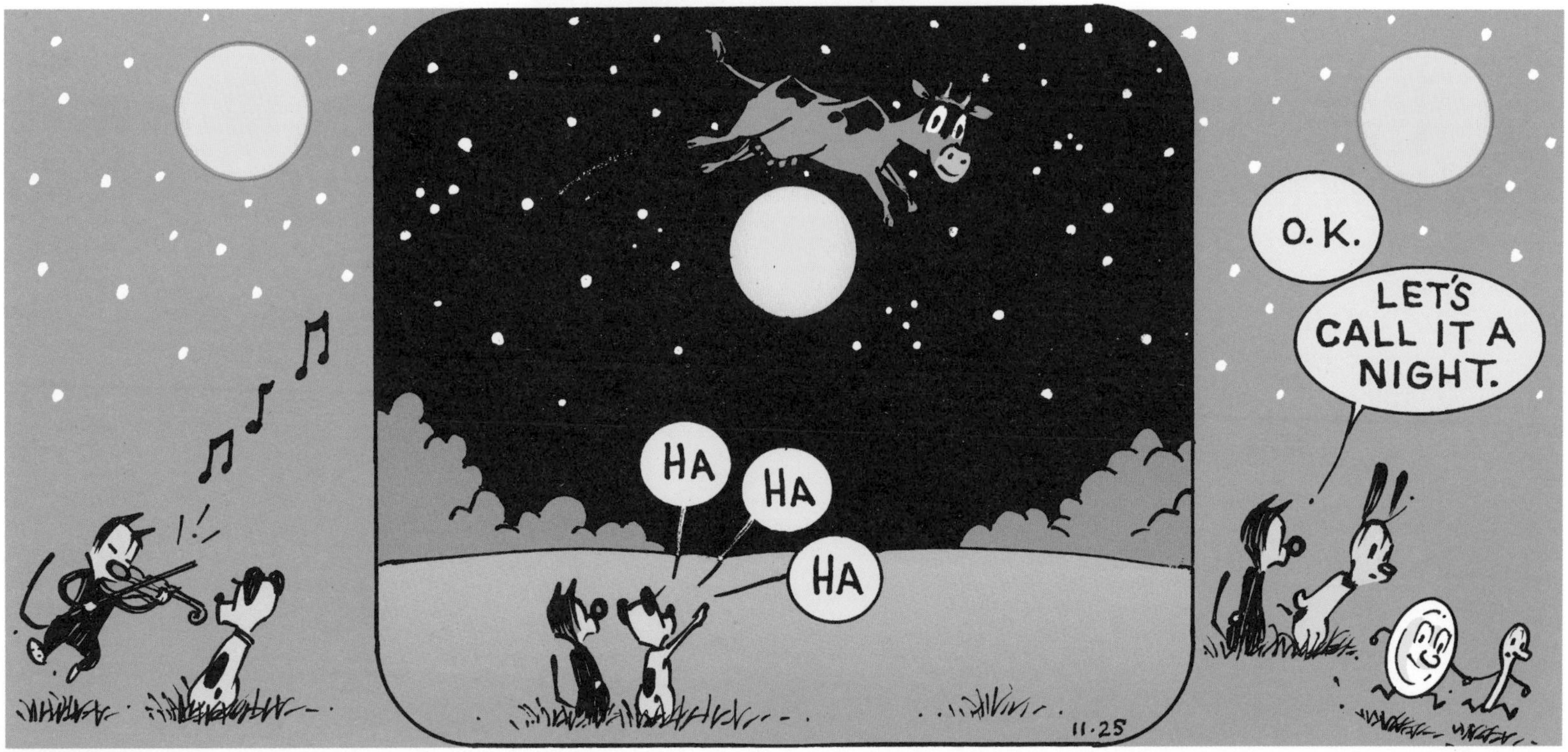
HA
HA
HA
O.K.
LET'S CALL IT A NIGHT.
11·25

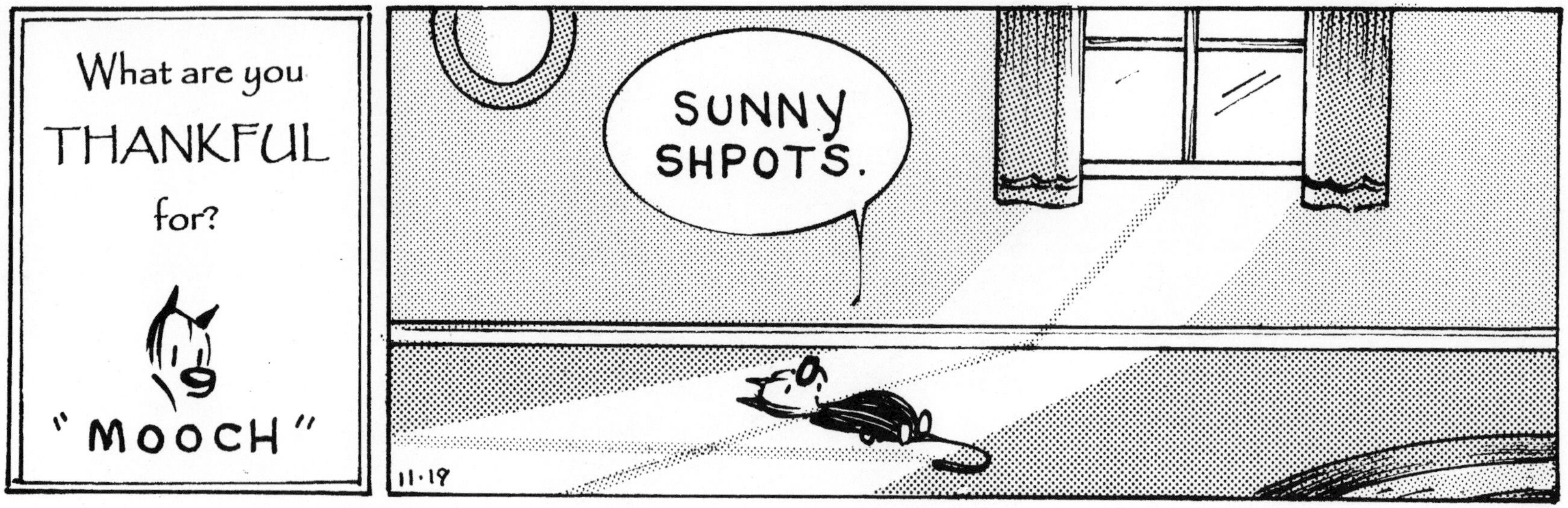
What are you THANKFUL for?
"MOOCH"
SUNNY SHPOTS.
11·19

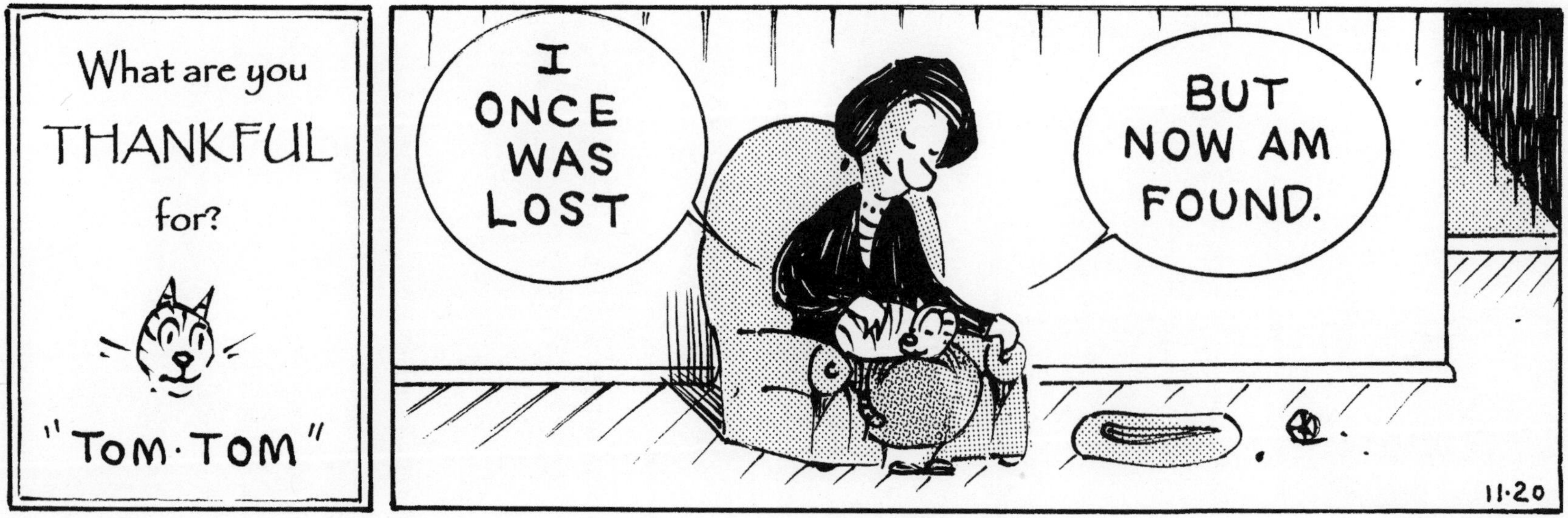
What are you THANKFUL for?
"TOM·TOM"
I ONCE WAS LOST
BUT NOW AM FOUND.
11·20

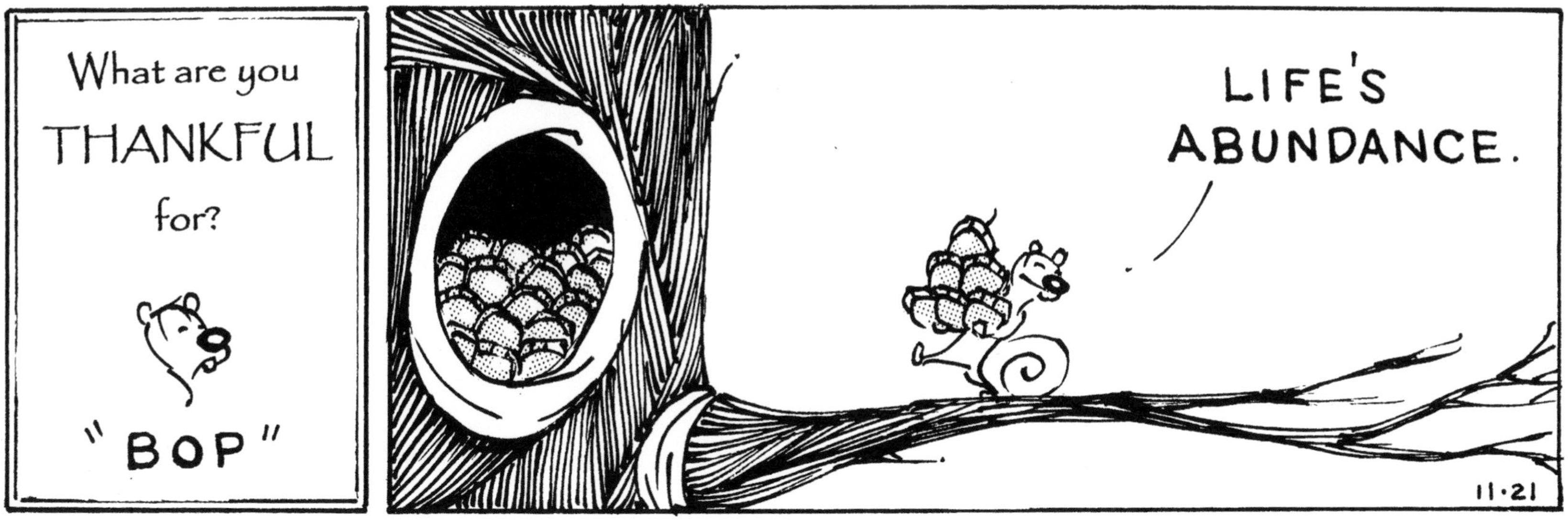
What are you THANKFUL for?
"BOP"
LIFE'S ABUNDANCE.
11·21

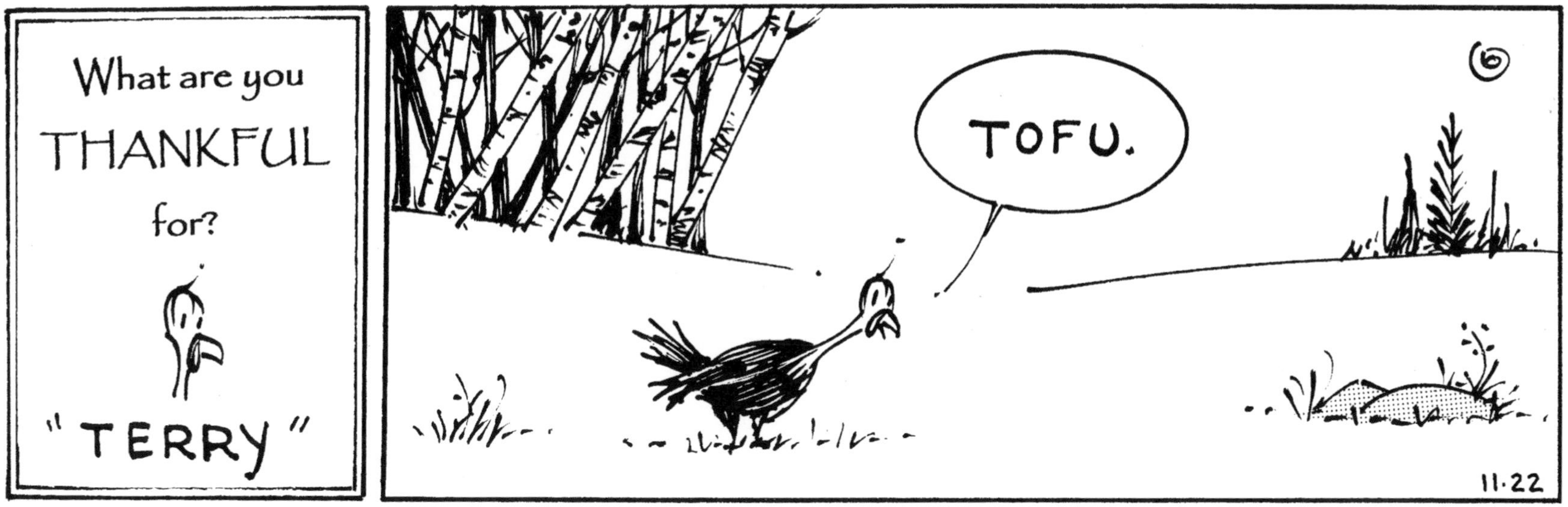
What are you THANKFUL for?
"TERRY"
TOFU.
11·22

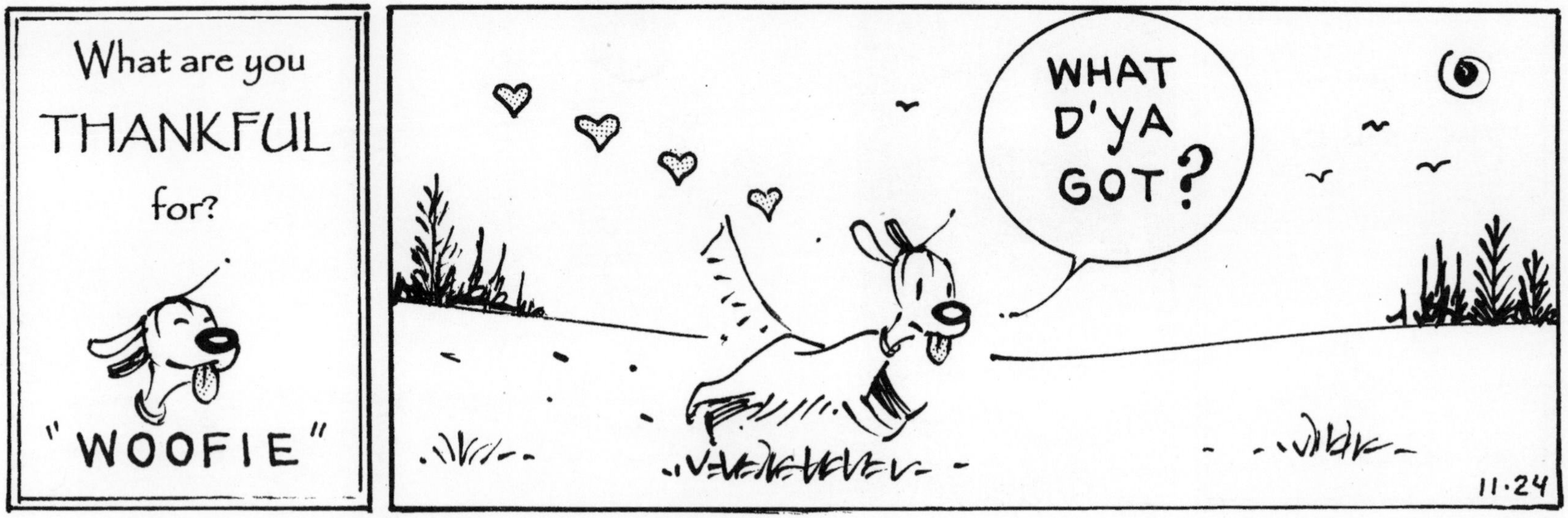
What are you
THANKFUL
for?
"WOOFIE"
WHAT D'YA GOT?
11·24

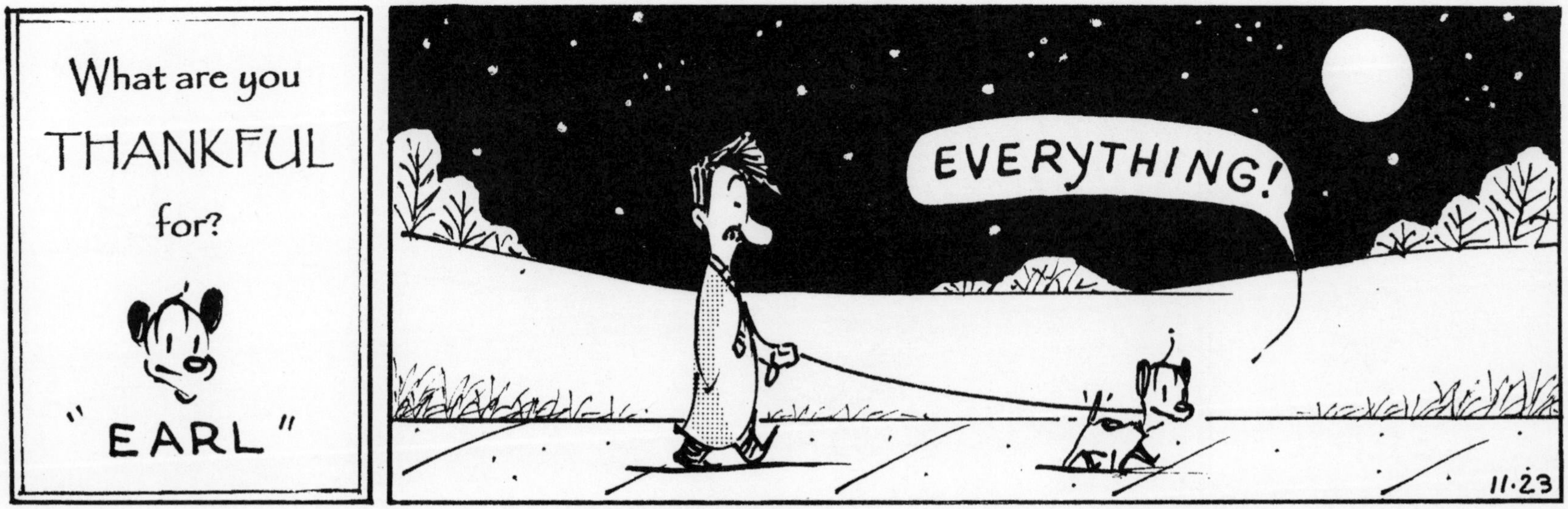
What are you
THANKFUL
for?
"EARL"
EVERYTHING!
11·23

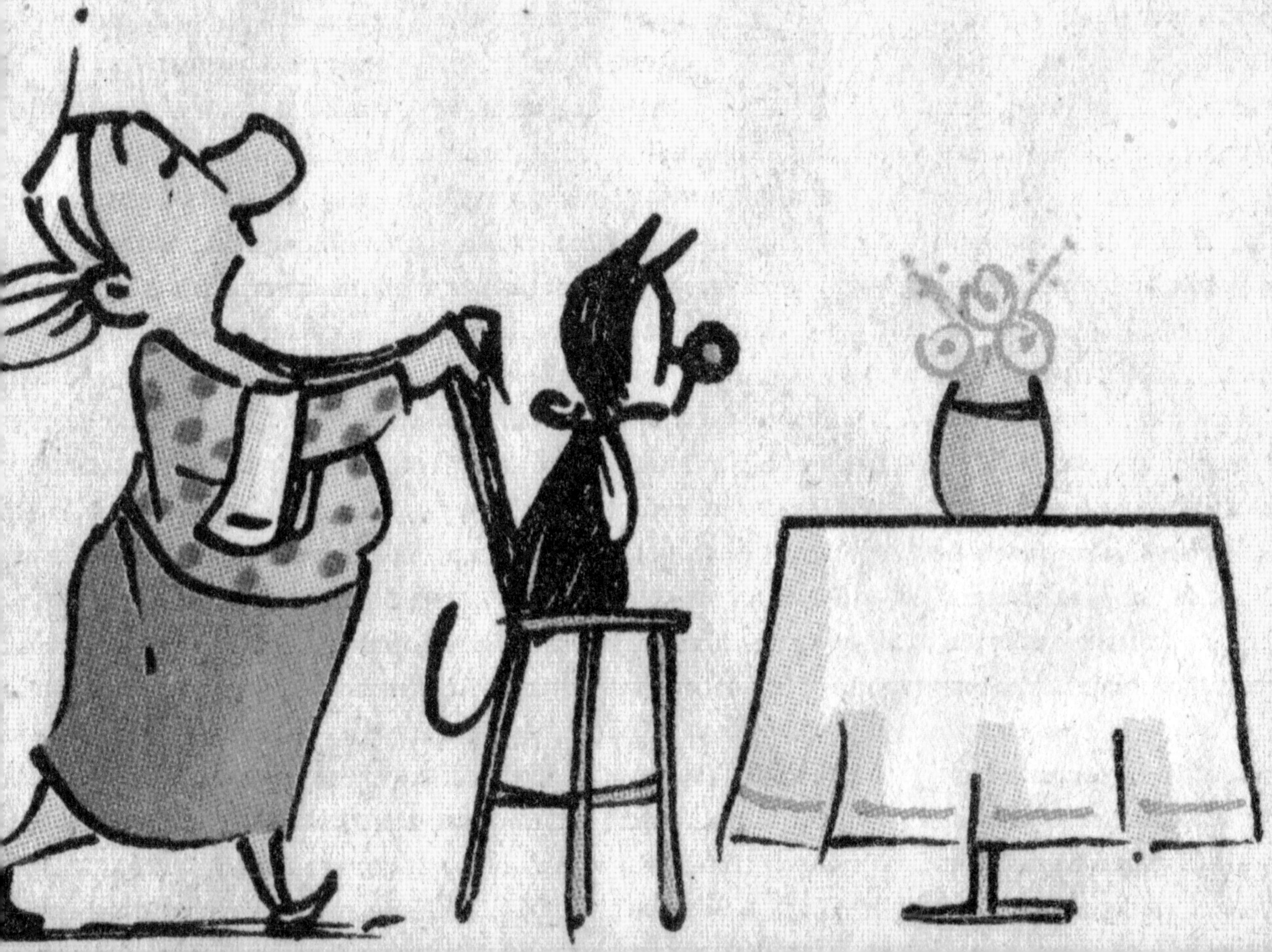

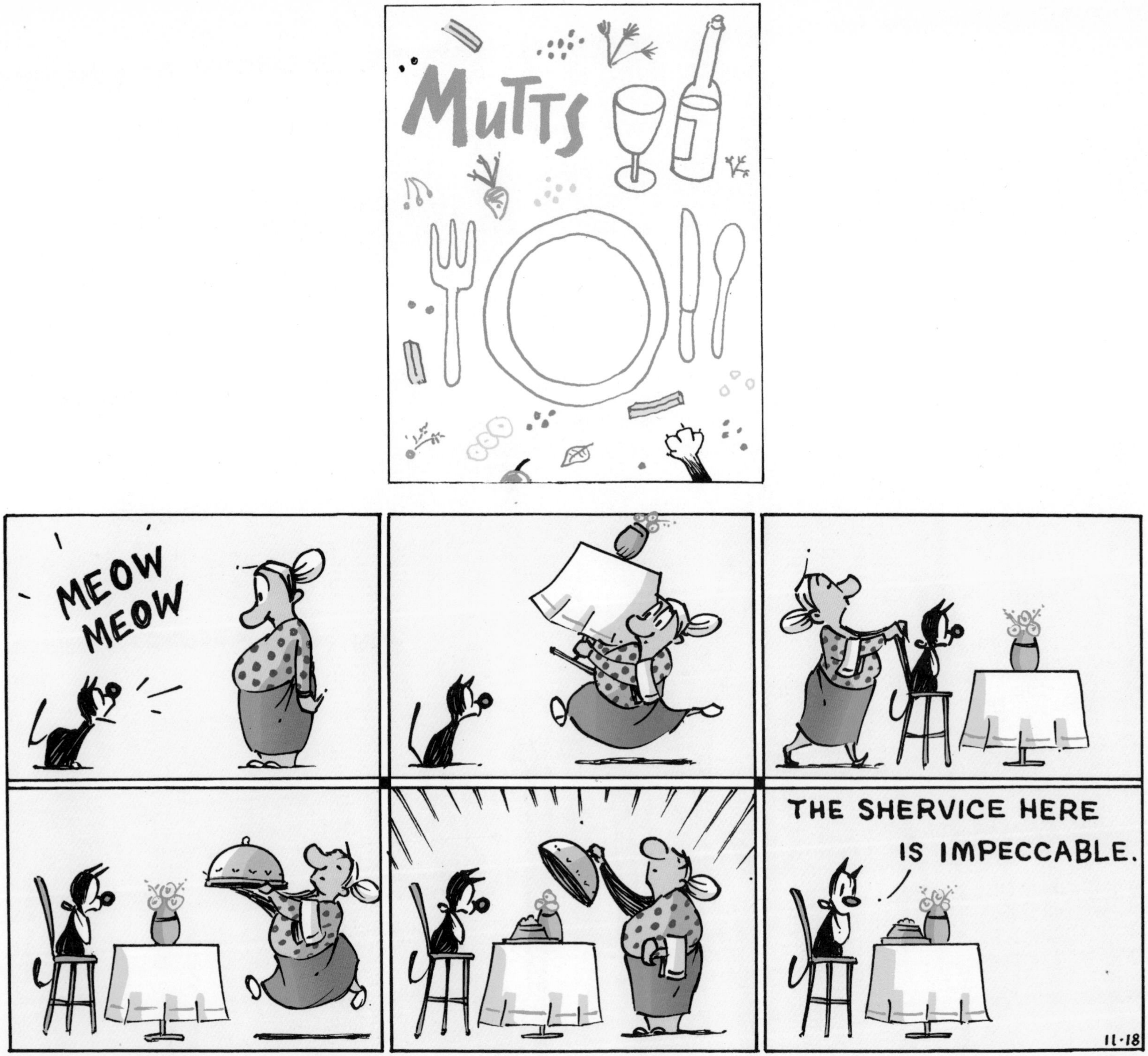
MUTTS
MEOW MEOW
THE SHERVICE HERE IS IMPECCABLE.
11-18

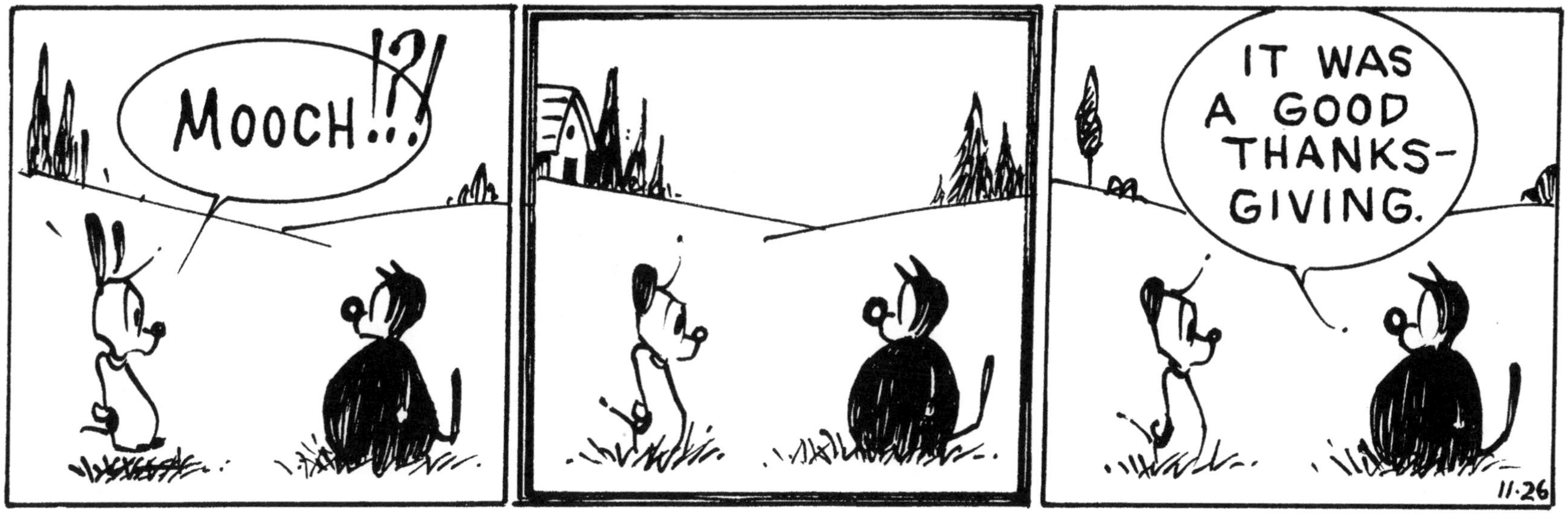
MOOCH!?!
IT WAS A GOOD THANKS-GIVING.
11·26

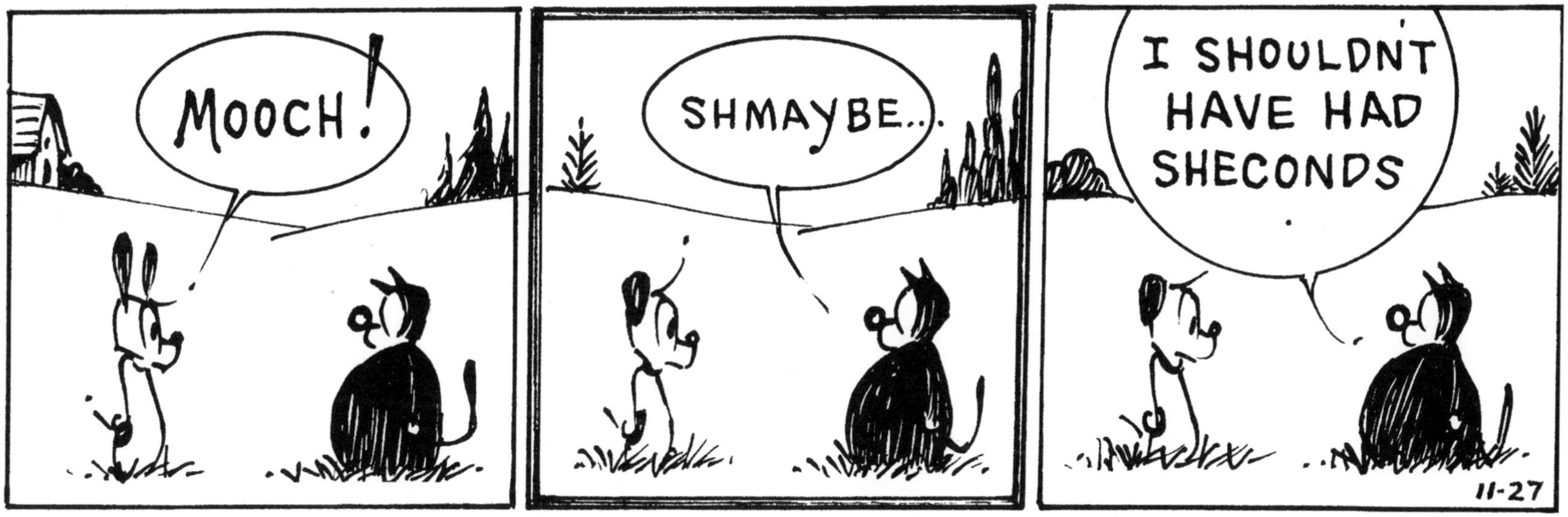
MOOCH!
SHMAYBE...
I SHOULDN'T HAVE HAD SHECONDS
11-27

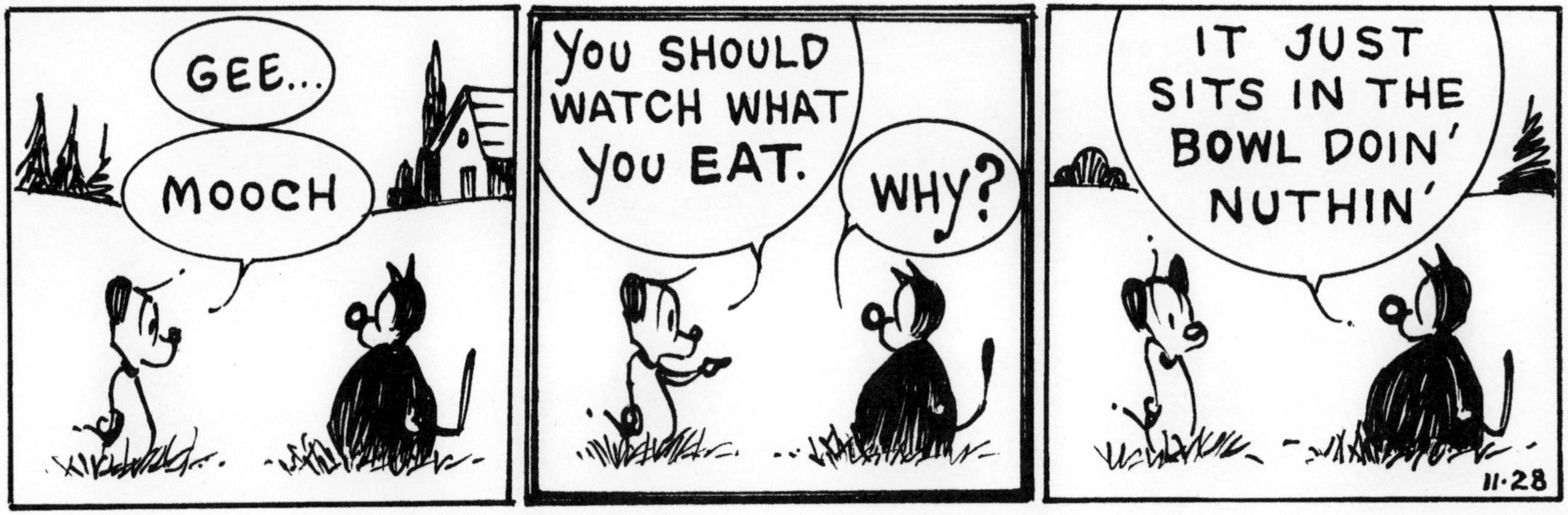
GEE...
MOOCH
YOU SHOULD WATCH WHAT YOU EAT.
WHY?
IT JUST SITS IN THE BOWL DOIN' NUTHIN'
11·28

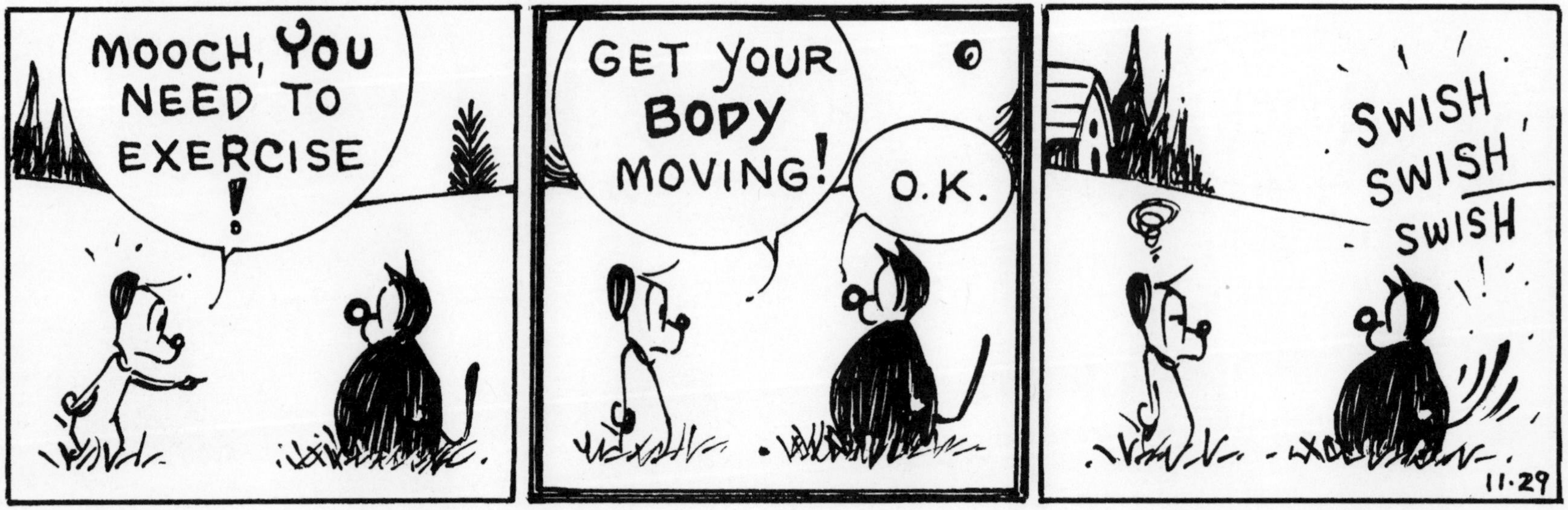
MOOCH, YOU NEED TO EXERCISE!
GET YOUR BODY MOVING!
O.K.
SWISH
SWISH
SWISH
11·29

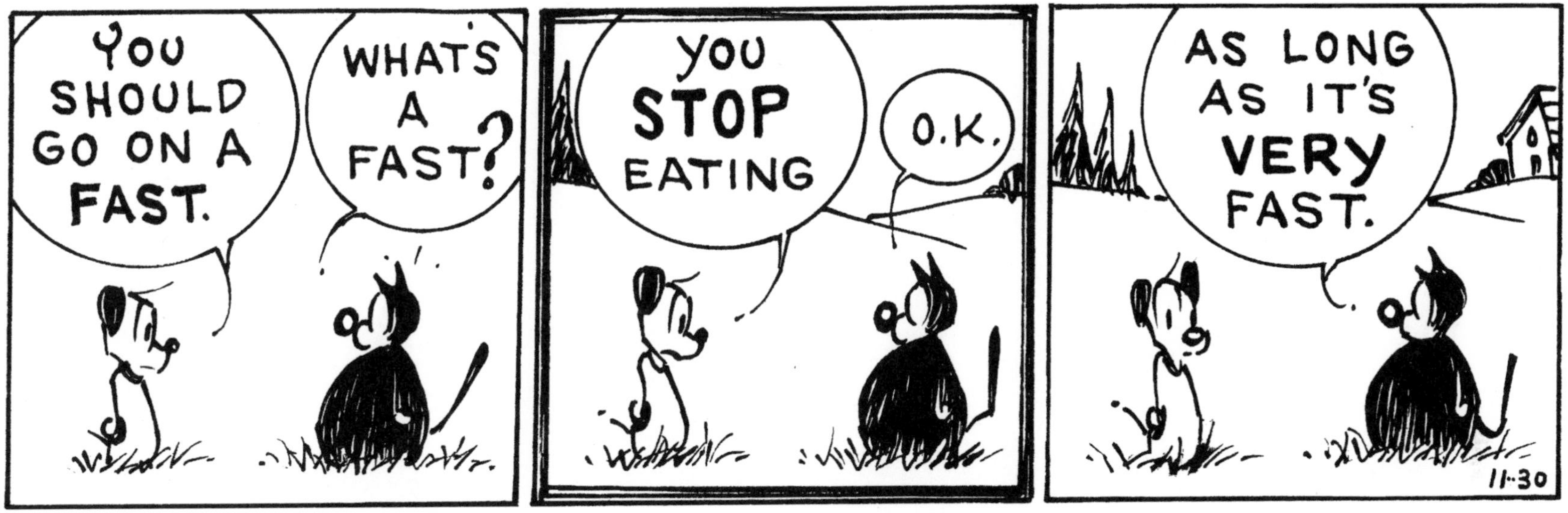
YOU SHOULD GO ON A FAST.
WHAT'S A FAST?
YOU STOP EATING
O.K.
AS LONG AS IT'S VERY FAST.
11-30

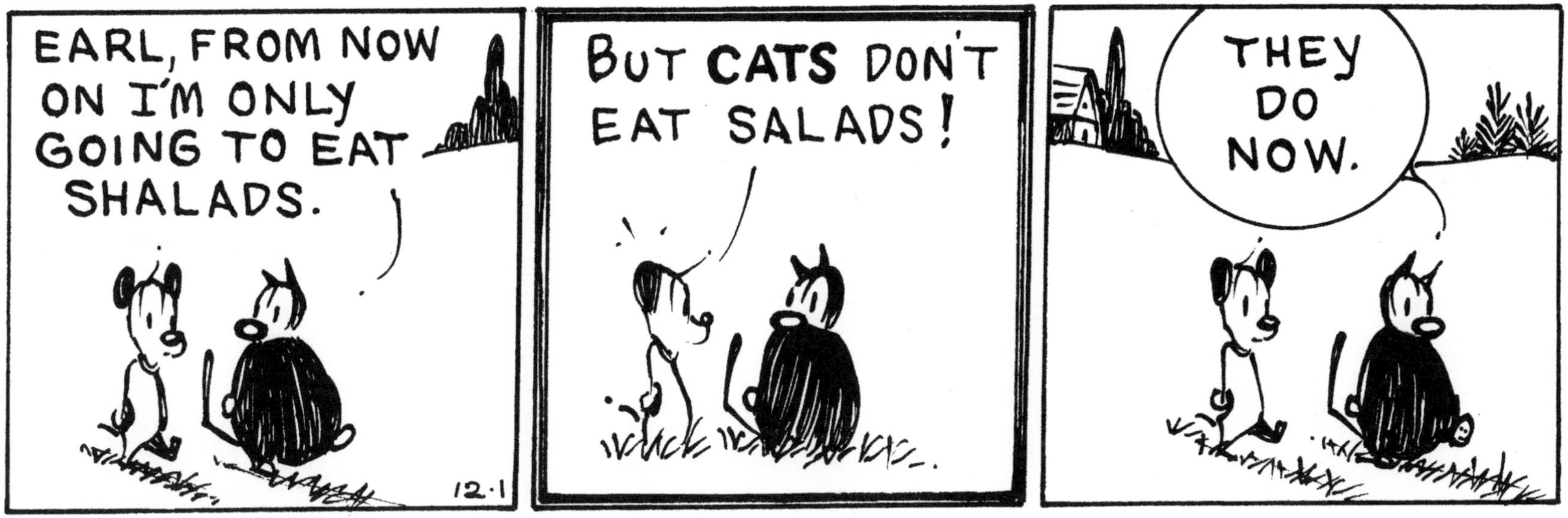
EARL, FROM NOW ON I'M ONLY GOING TO EAT SHALADS.
12-1
BUT CATS DON'T EAT SALADS!
THEY DO NOW.

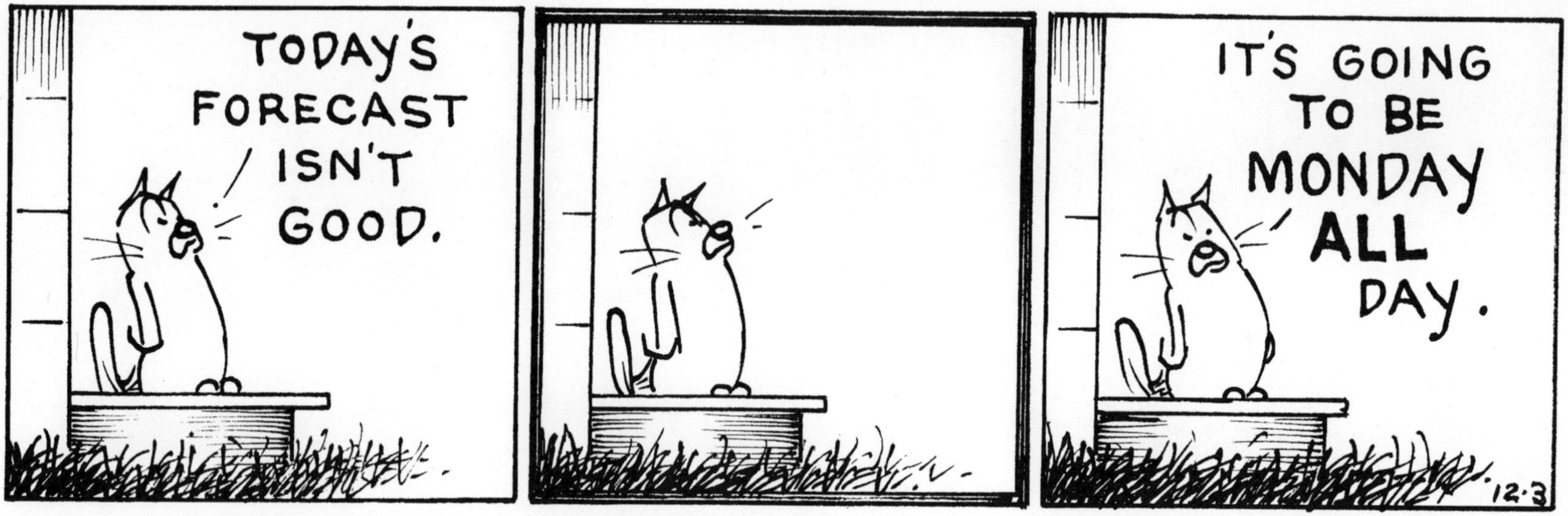
TODAY'S FORECAST ISN'T GOOD.
IT'S GOING TO BE MONDAY ALL DAY.
12·3

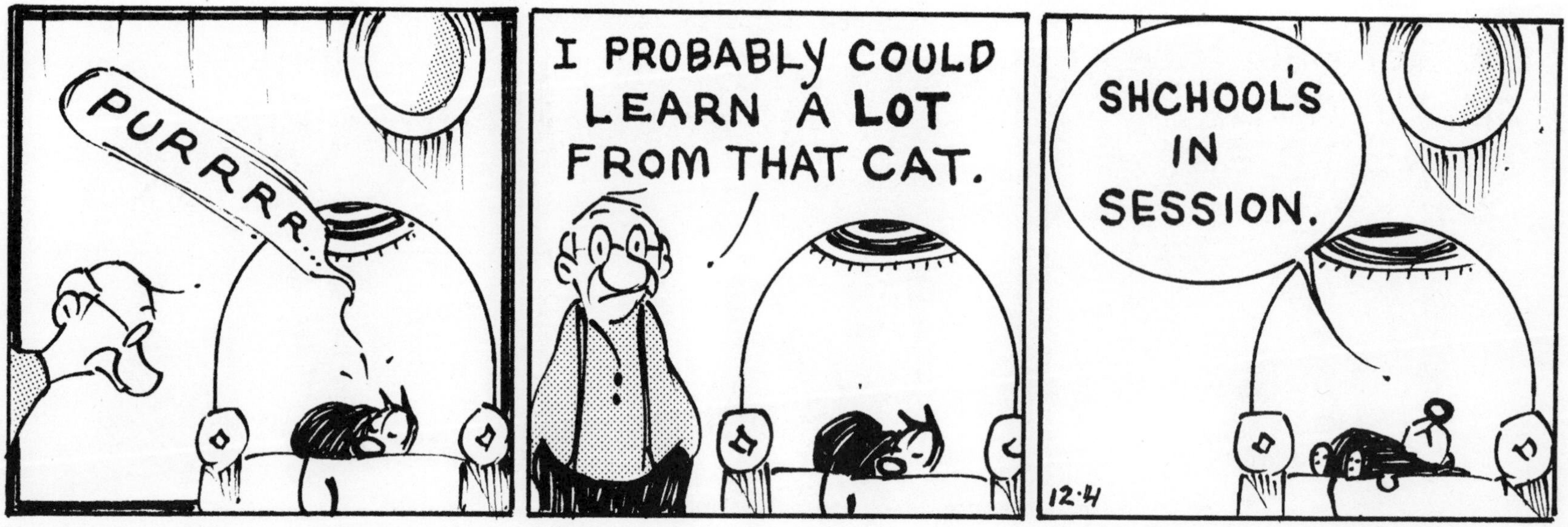
PURRRRR...
I PROBABLY COULD LEARN A LOT FROM THAT CAT.
SHCHOOL'S IN SESSION.
12·4

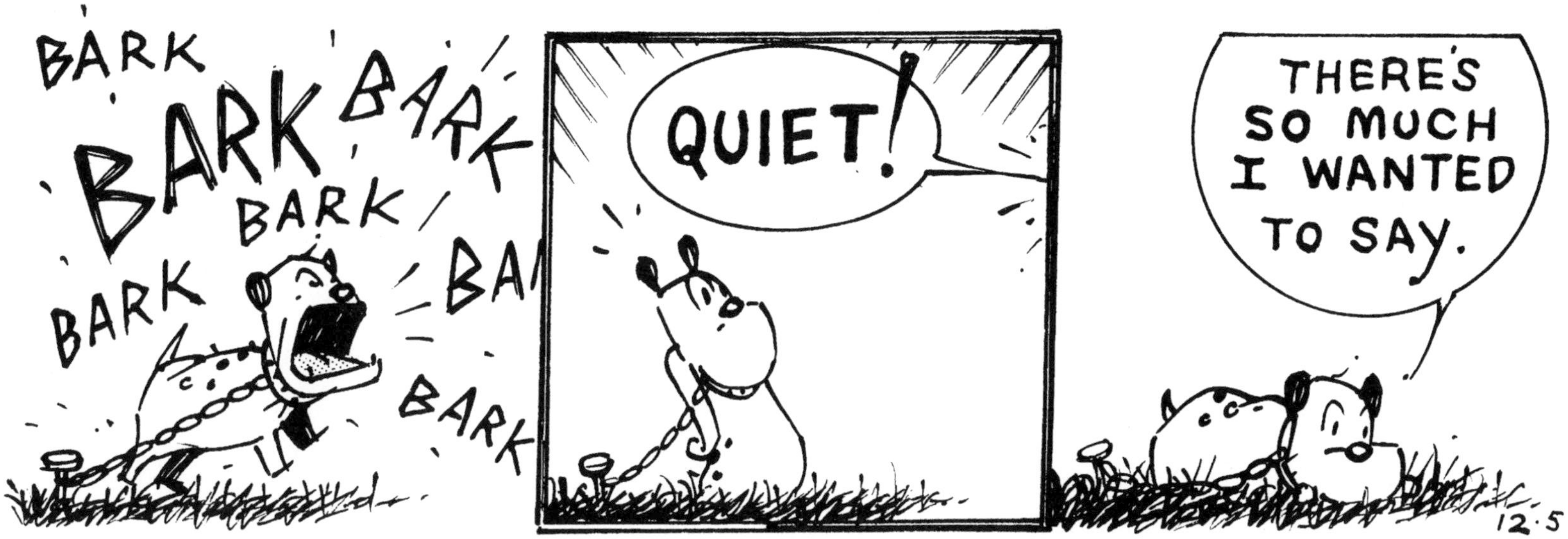
BARK
BARK
BARK
BARK
BARK
BA
BARK
QUIET!
THERE'S SO MUCH I WANTED TO SAY.
12·5

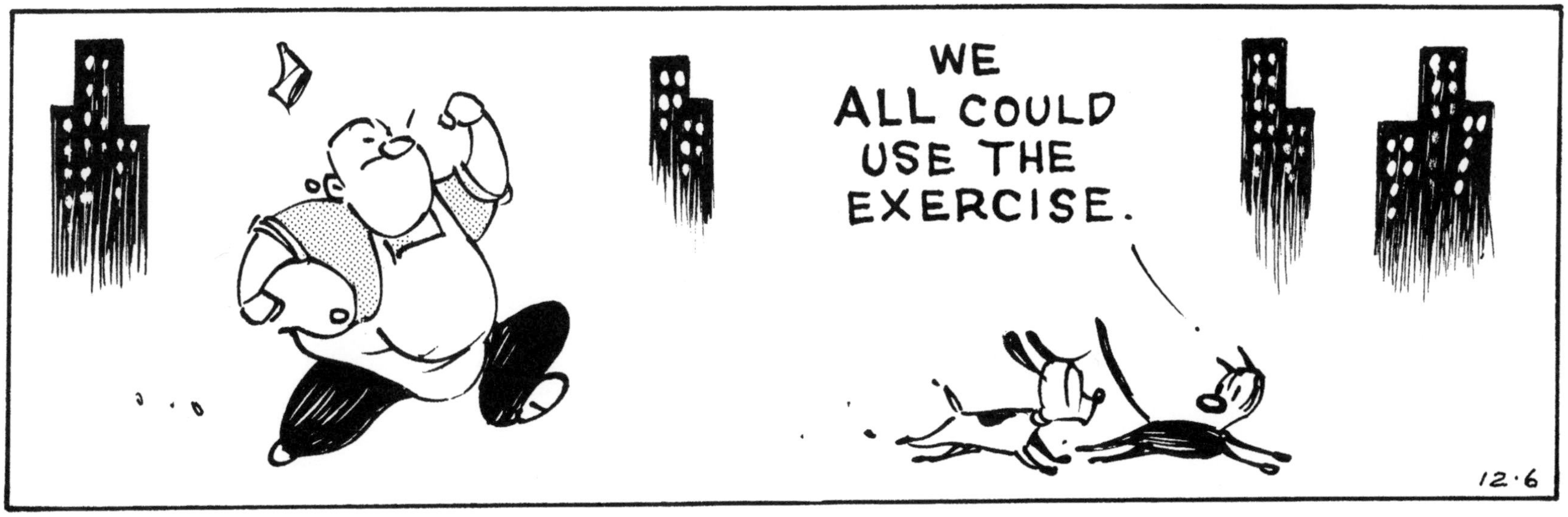
WE ALL COULD USE THE EXERCISE.
12·6

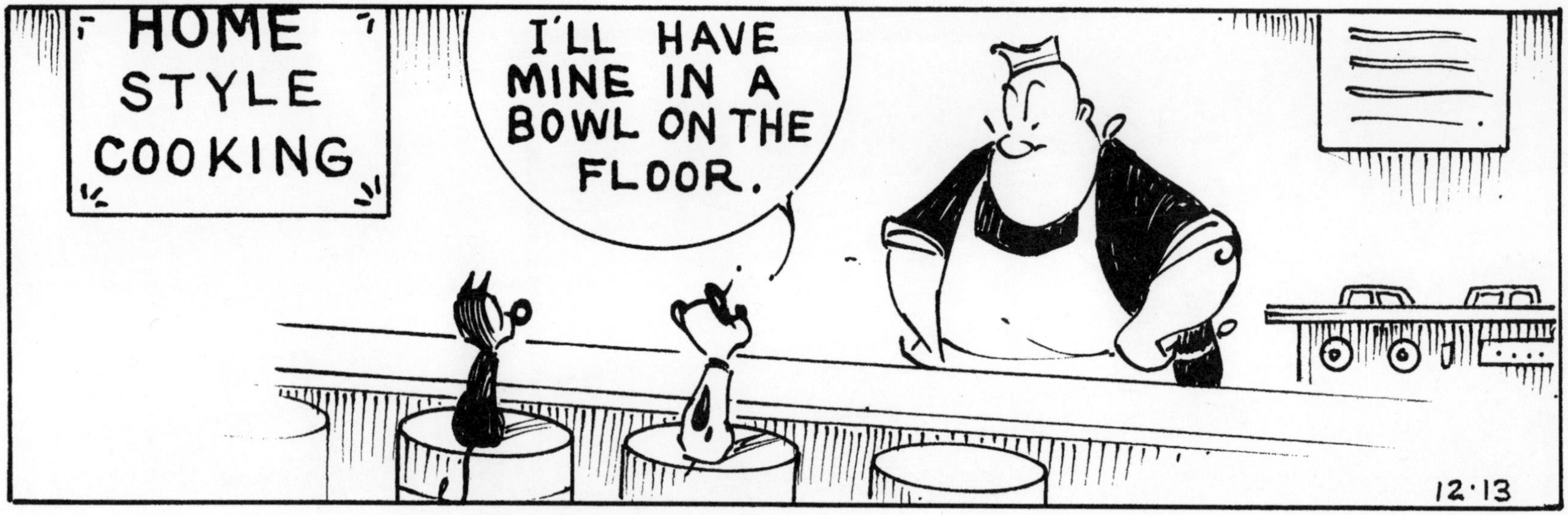
HOME STYLE COOKING
I'LL HAVE MINE IN A BOWL ON THE FLOOR.
12·13

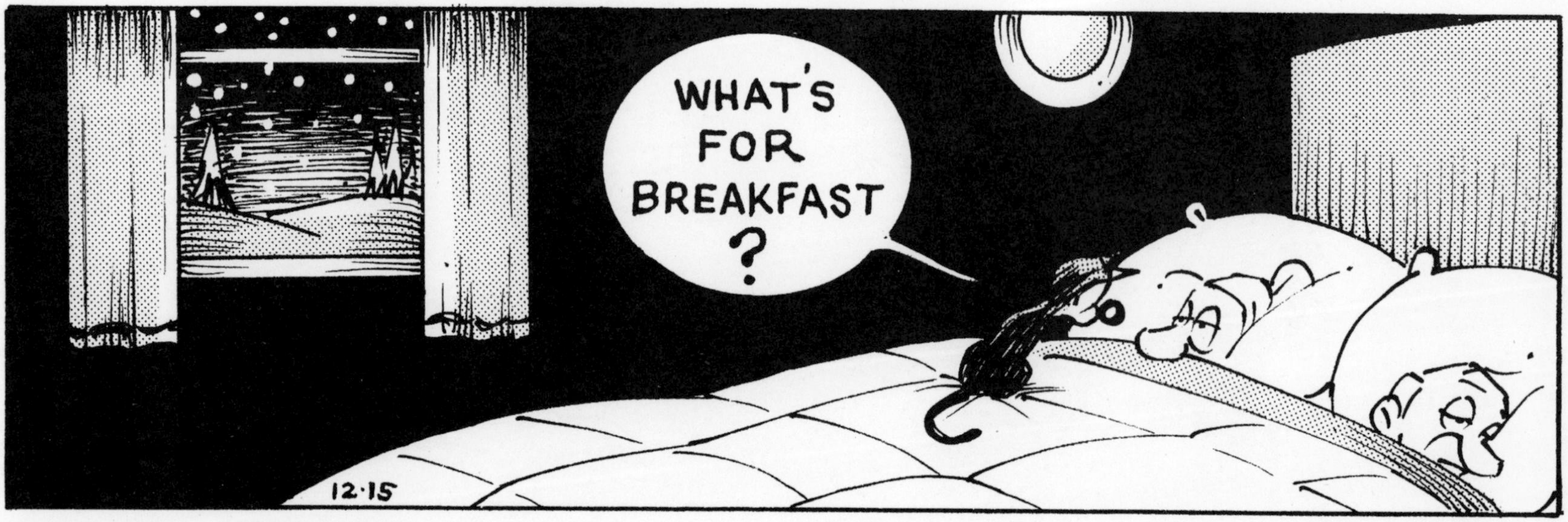
WHAT'S FOR BREAKFAST ?
12·15

LET'S GO FOR A WALK.
HE HAD ME AT "LET'S GO."
12.7

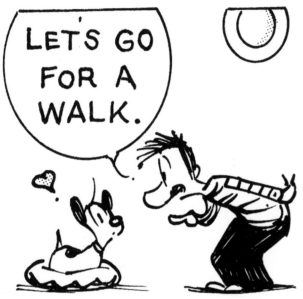

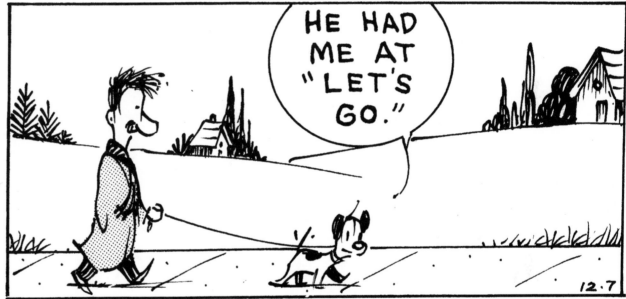

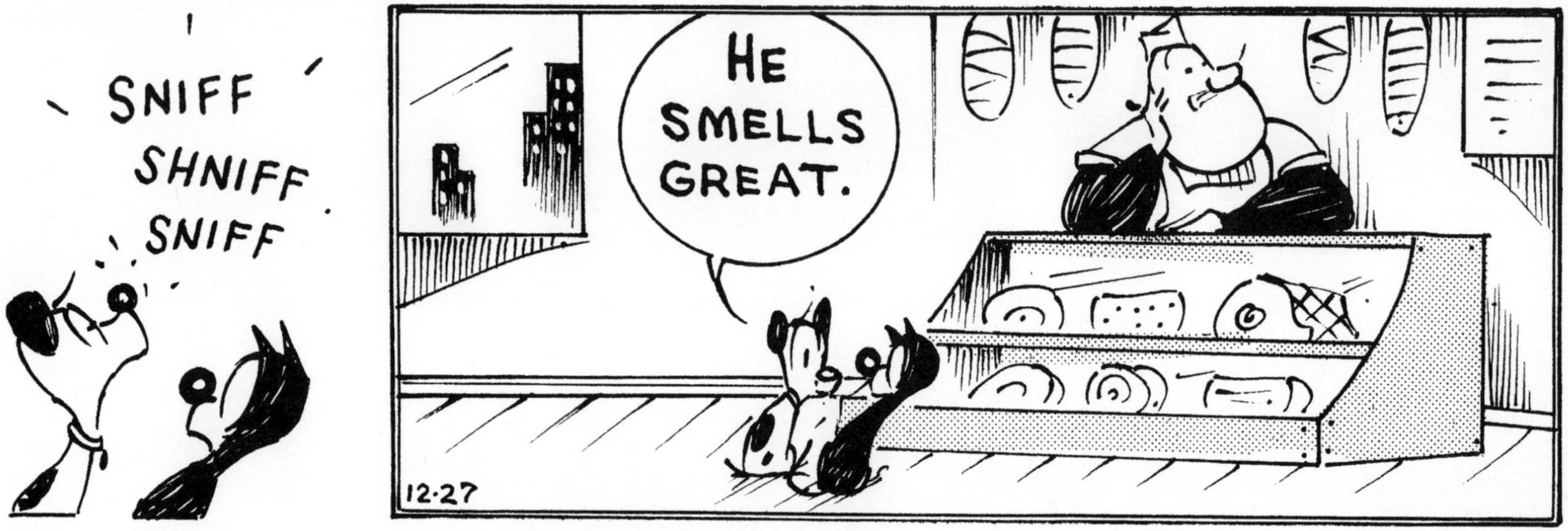
SNIFF
SHNIFF
SNIFF
HE SMELLS GREAT.
12·27

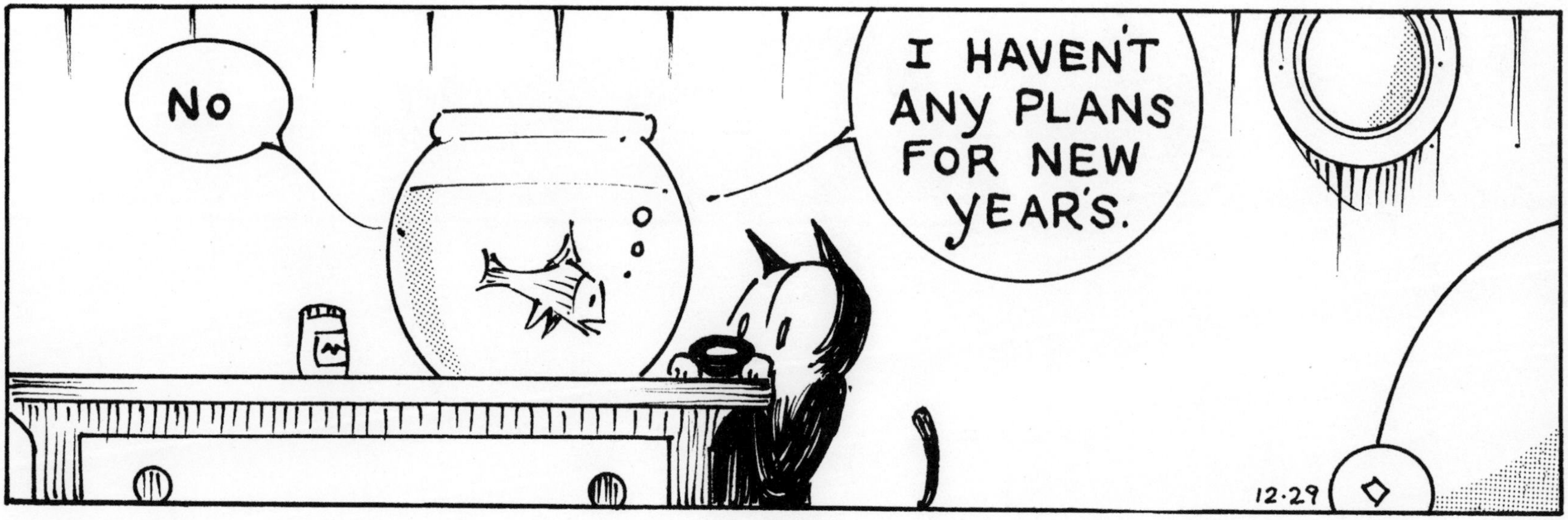
No
I HAVEN'T ANY PLANS FOR NEW YEAR'S.
12·29

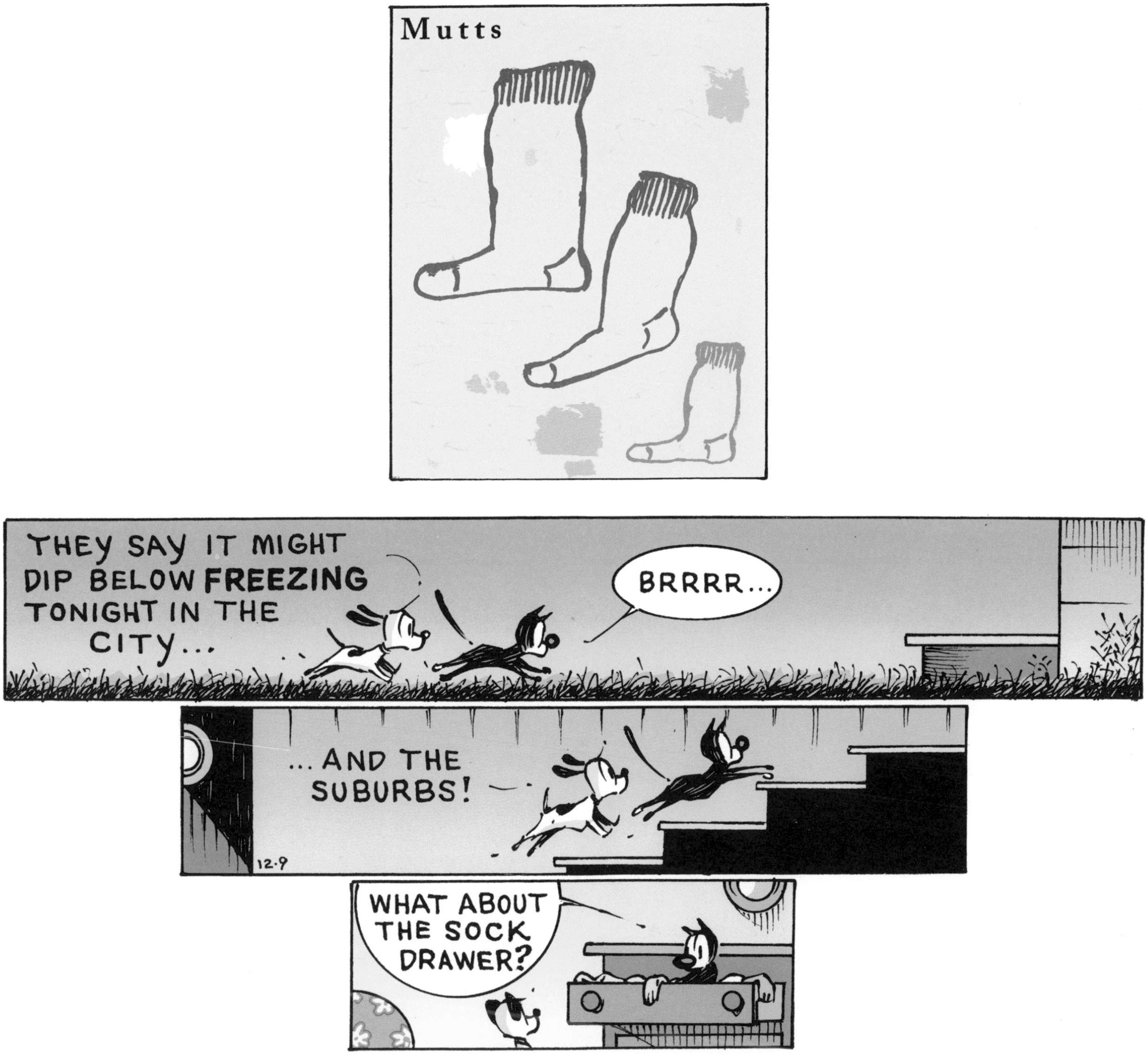
Mutts
THEY SAY IT MIGHT DIP BELOW FREEZING TONIGHT IN THE CITY...
BRRRR...
...AND THE SUBURBS!
12·9
WHAT ABOUT THE SOCK DRAWER?

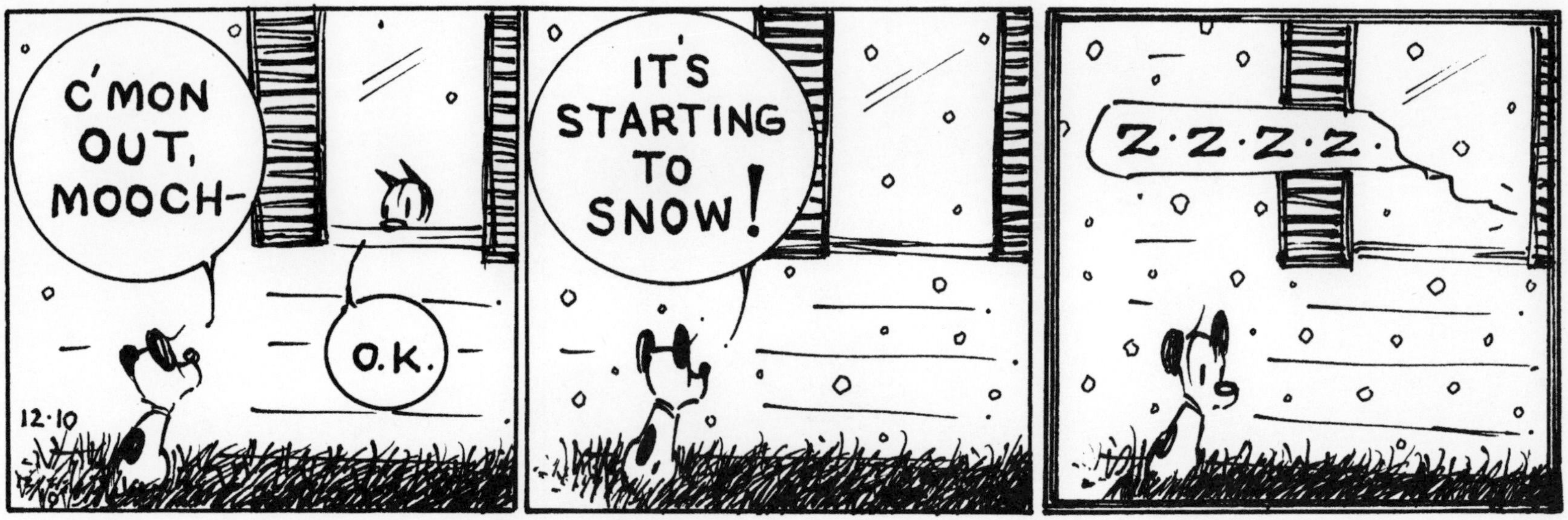
C'MON OUT, MOOCH–
O.K.
12·10
IT'S STARTING TO SNOW!
Z·Z·Z·Z·

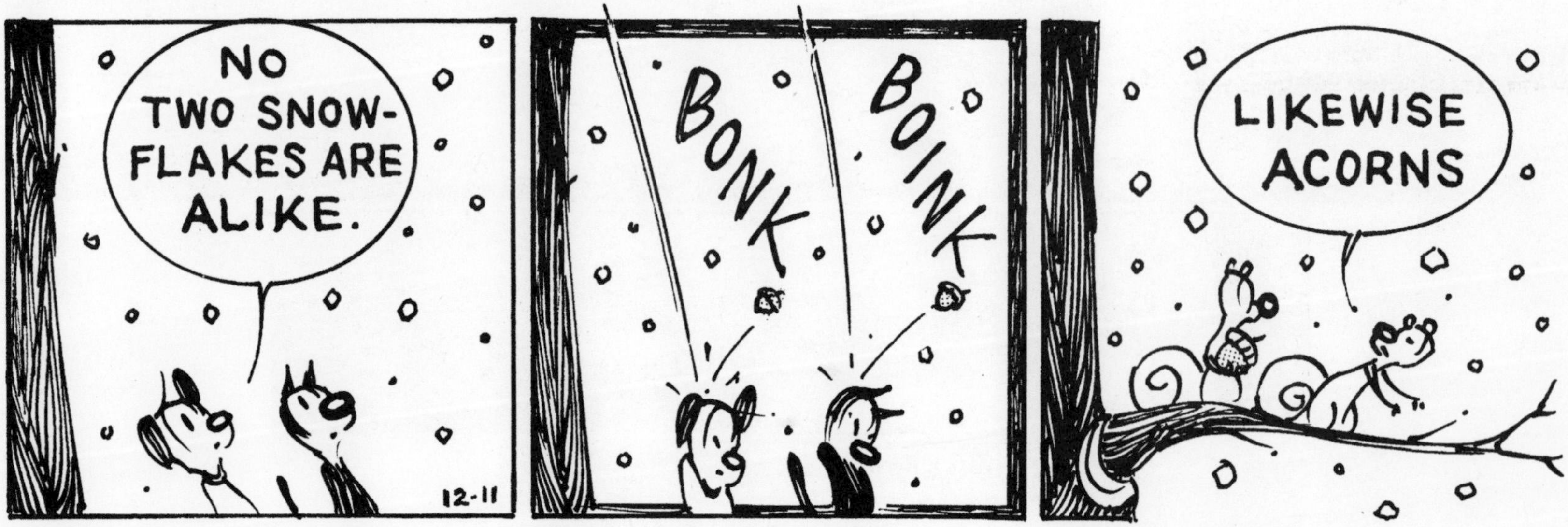
NO TWO SNOW-FLAKES ARE ALIKE.
12-11
BONK
BOINK
LIKEWISE ACORNS

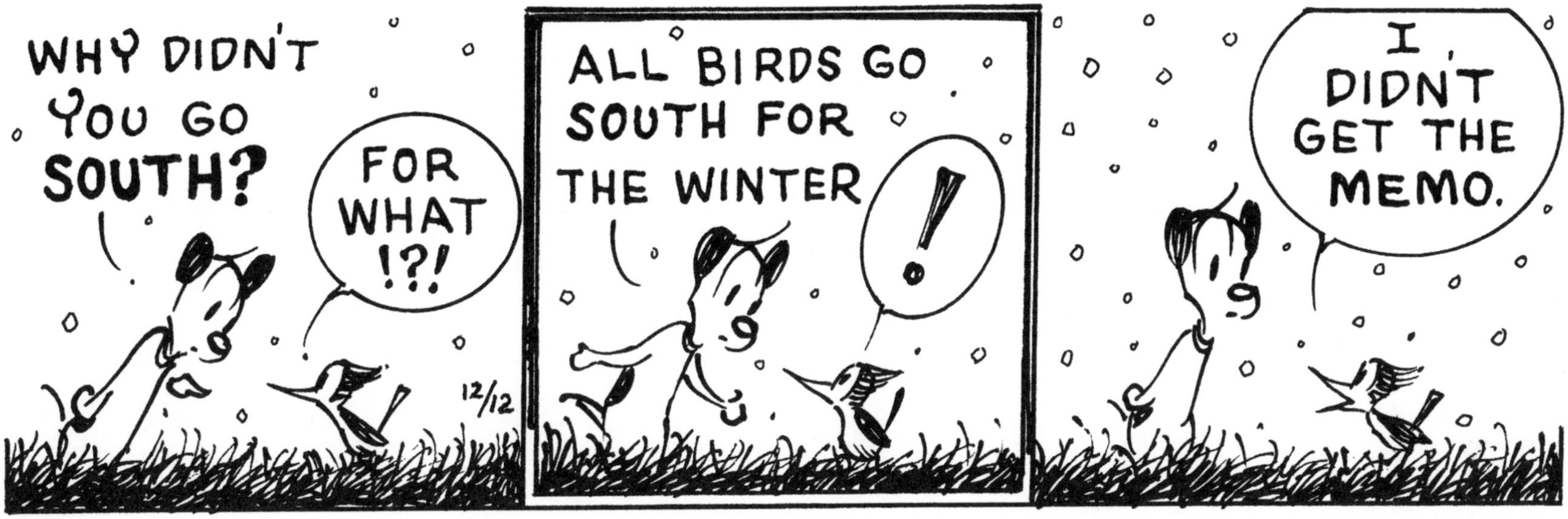
WHY DIDN'T YOU GO SOUTH?
FOR WHAT !?!
12/12
ALL BIRDS GO SOUTH FOR THE WINTER
!
I DIDN'T GET THE MEMO.

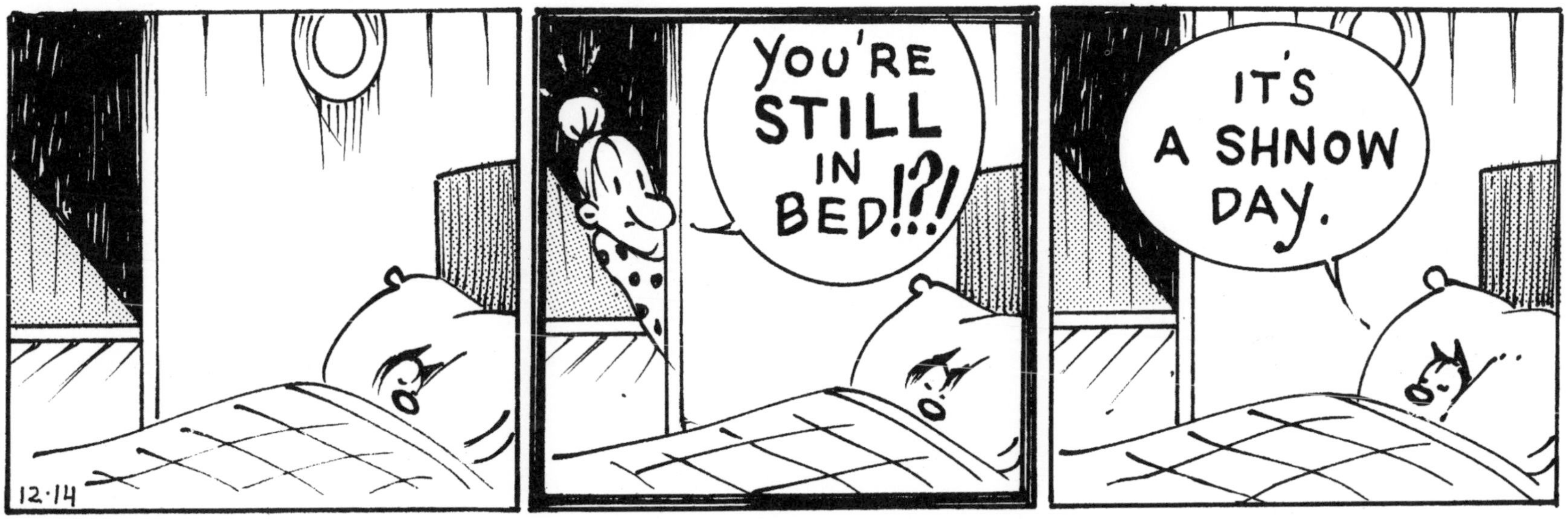
12·14
YOU'RE STILL IN BED!?!
IT'S A SHNOW DAY.

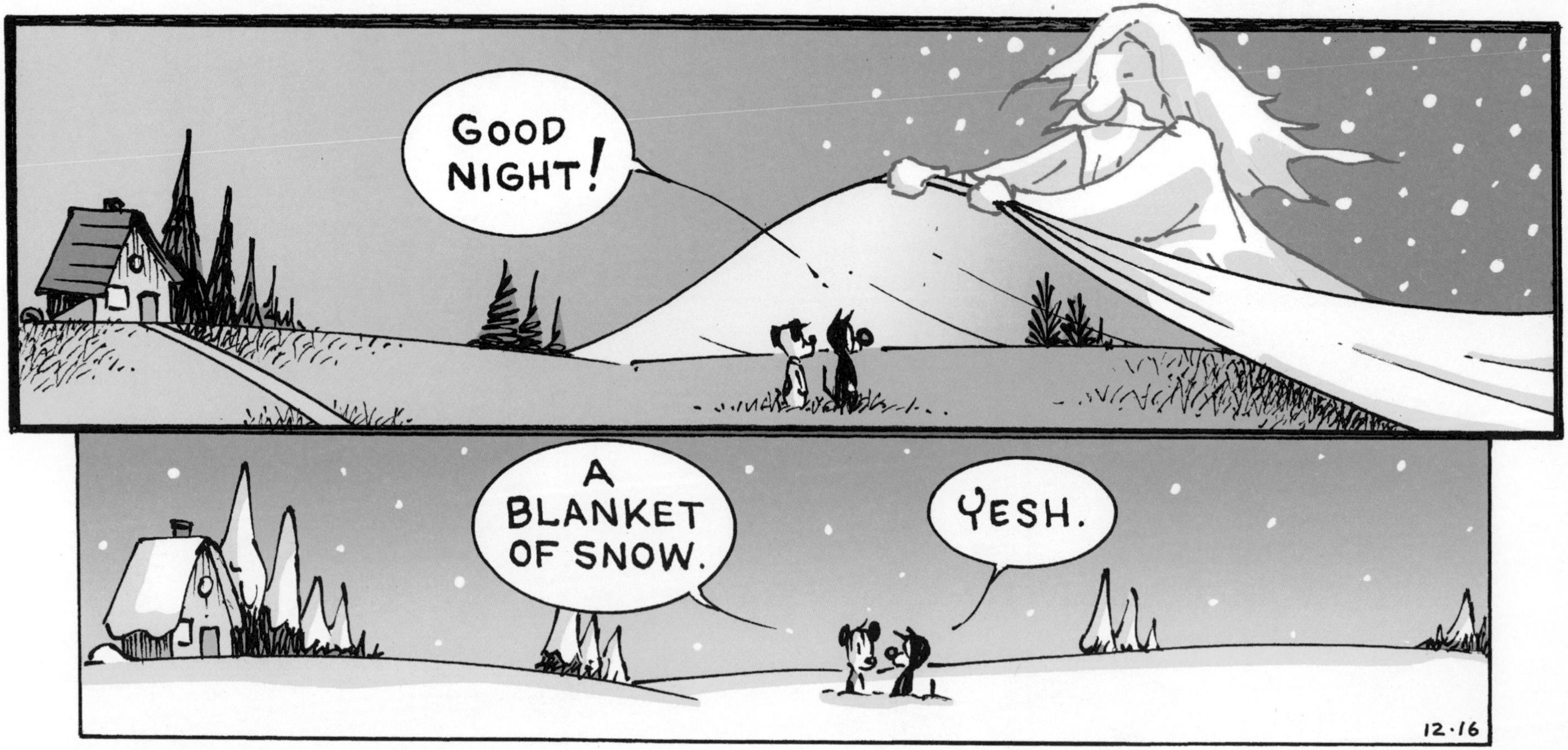
GOOD NIGHT!
A BLANKET OF SNOW.
YESH.
12·16

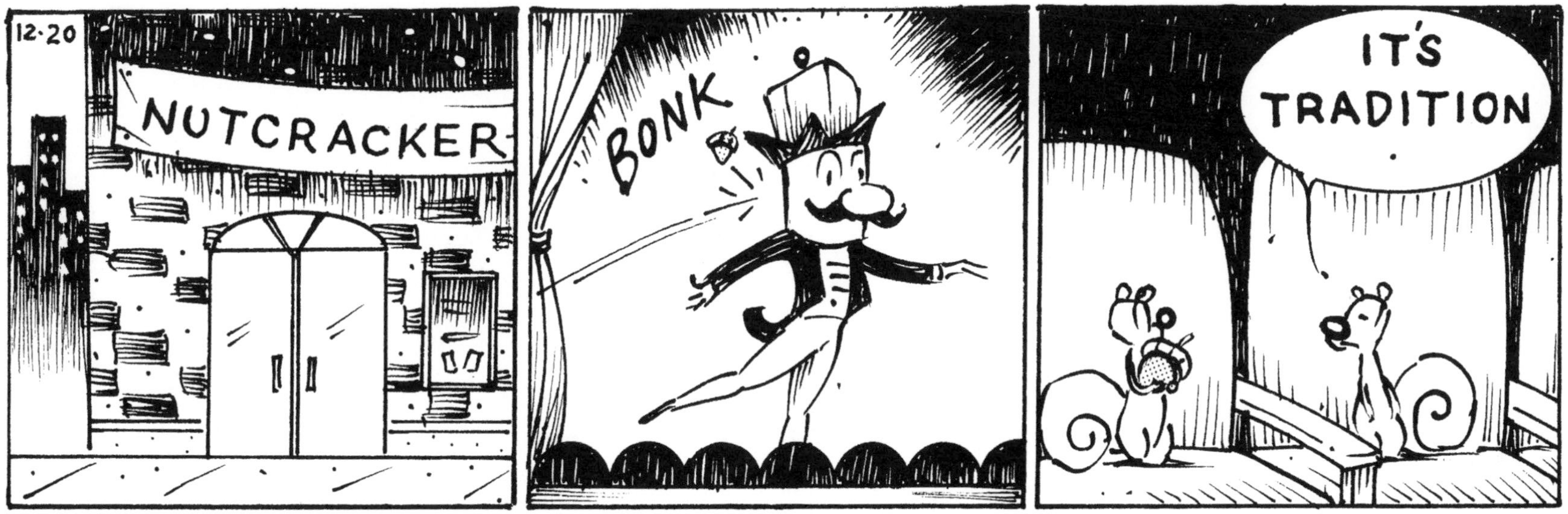
12·20
NUTCRACKER
BONK
IT'S TRADITION

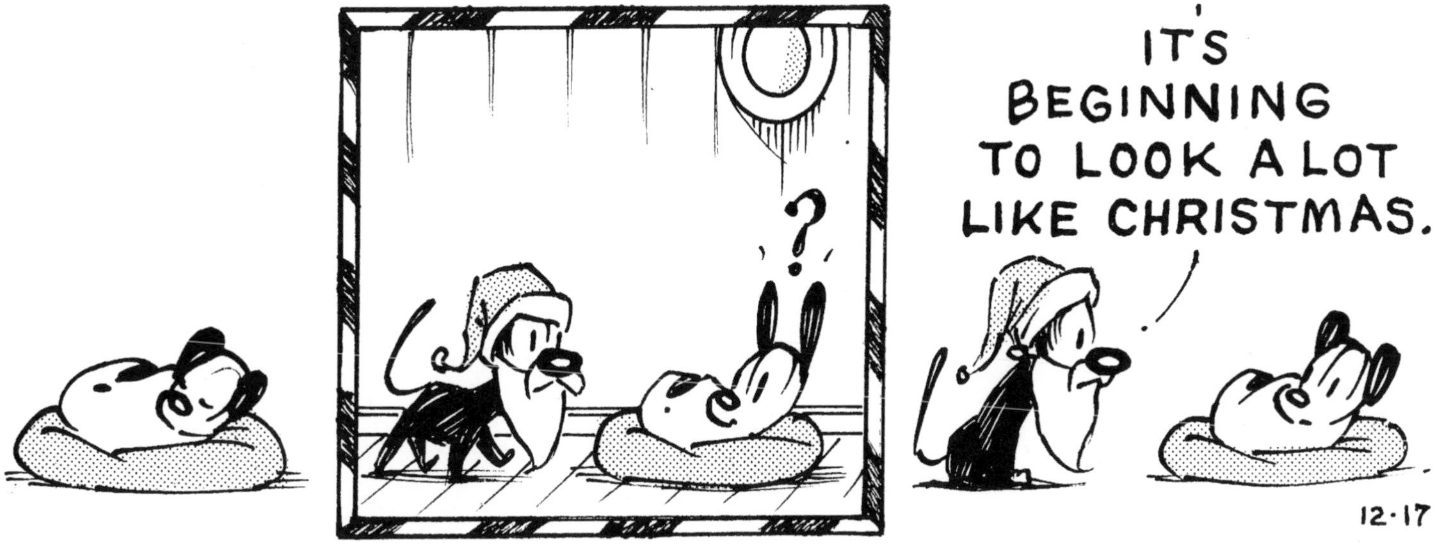
?
IT'S BEGINNING TO LOOK A LOT LIKE CHRISTMAS.
12·17

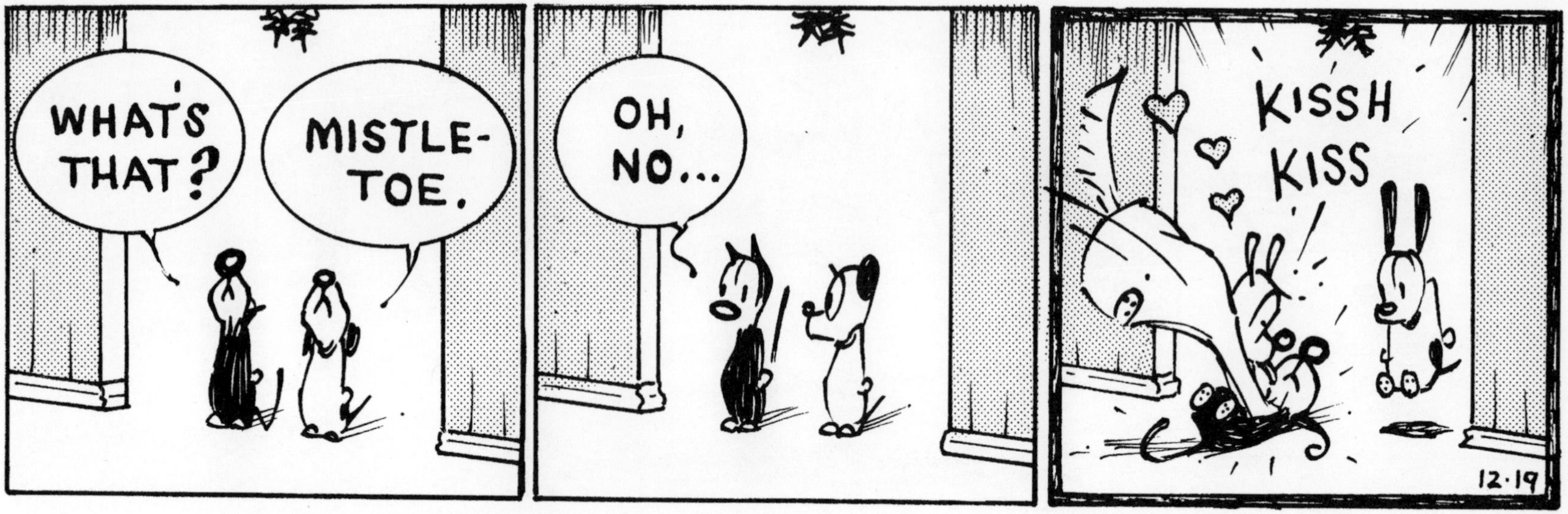
WHAT'S THAT?
MISTLE-TOE.
OH, NO...
KISSH KISS
12·19

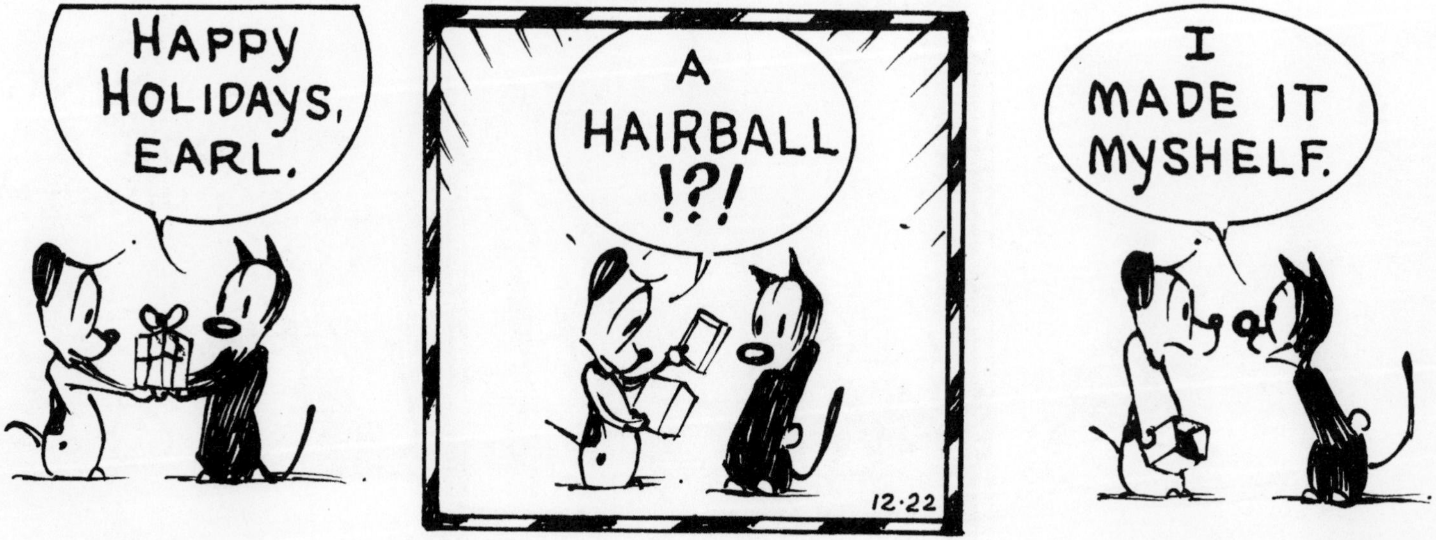
HAPPY HOLIDAYS, EARL.
A HAIRBALL !?!
12·22
I MADE IT MYSHELF.

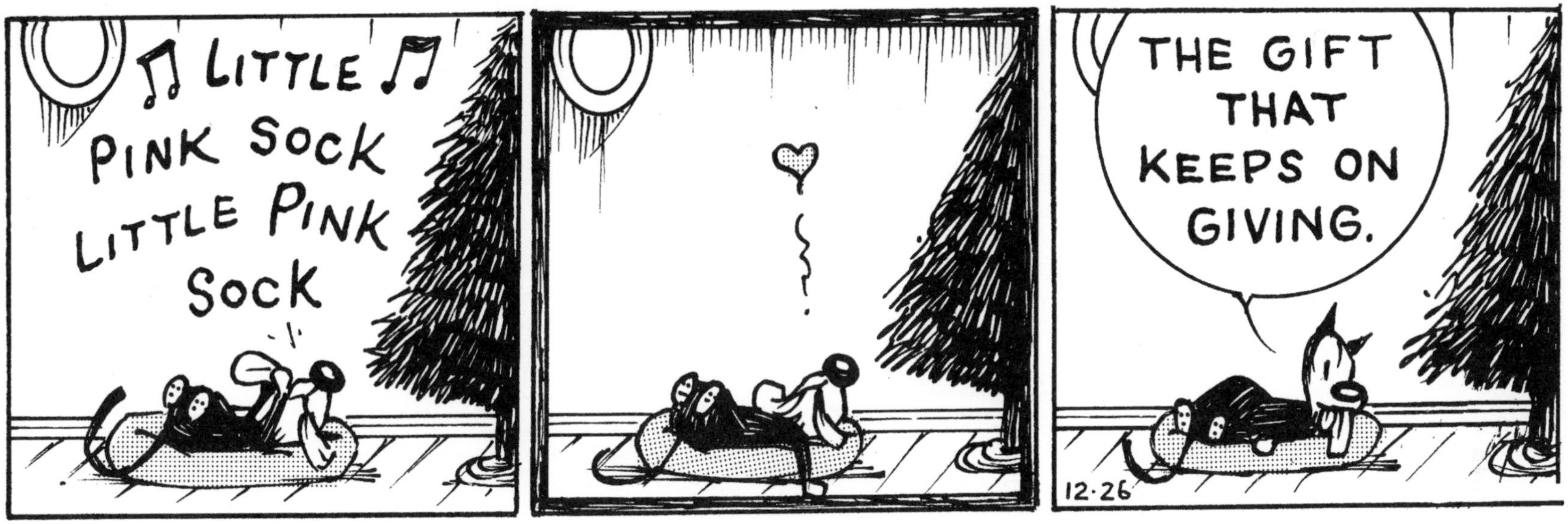
♫ LITTLE ♫ PINK SOCK LITTLE PINK SOCK
THE GIFT THAT KEEPS ON GIVING.
12·26

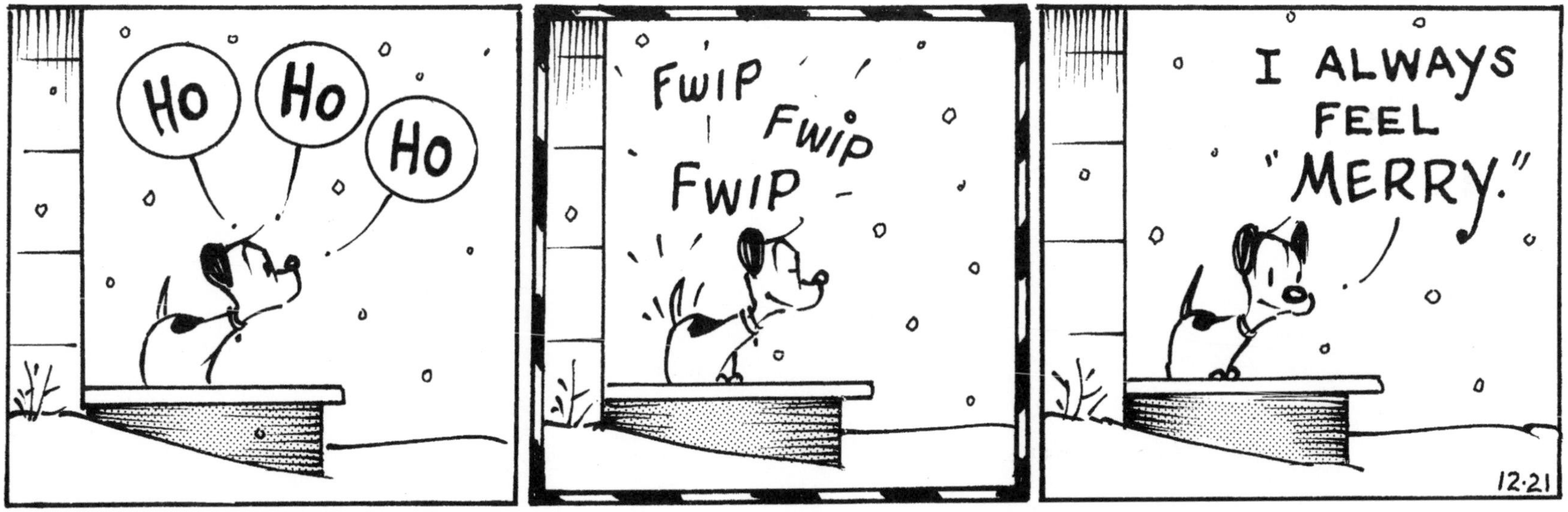
HO
HO
HO
FWIP
FWIP
FWIP
I ALWAYS FEEL "MERRY."
12·21

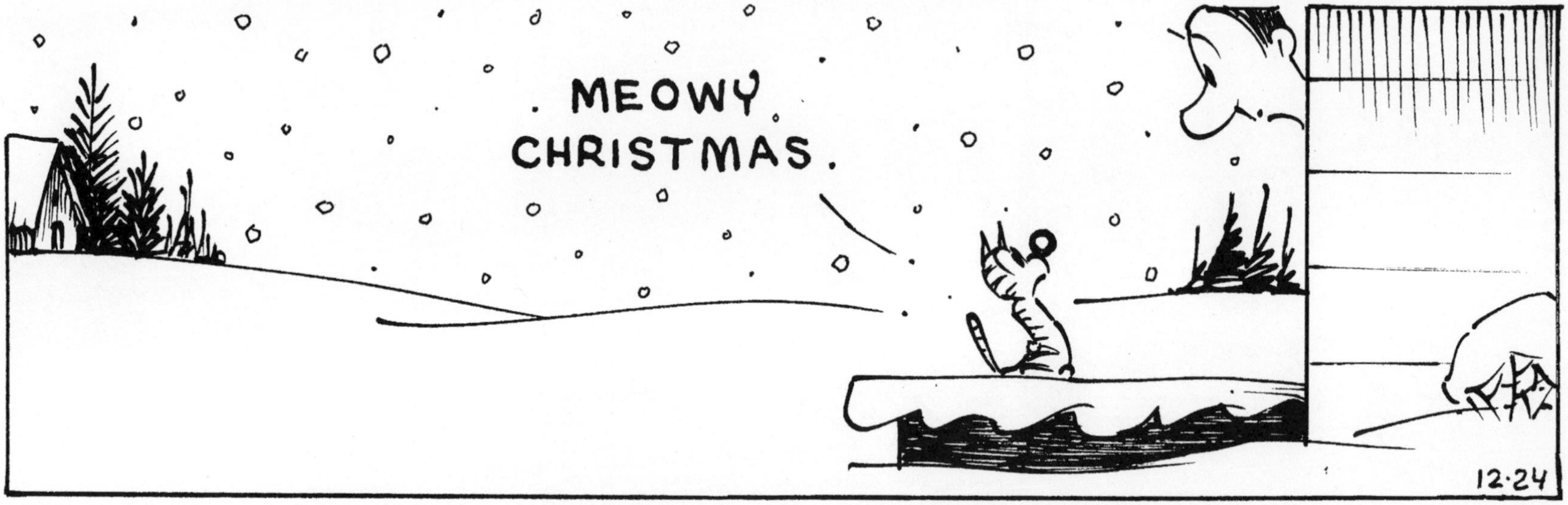
MEOWY CHRISTMAS.
12·24

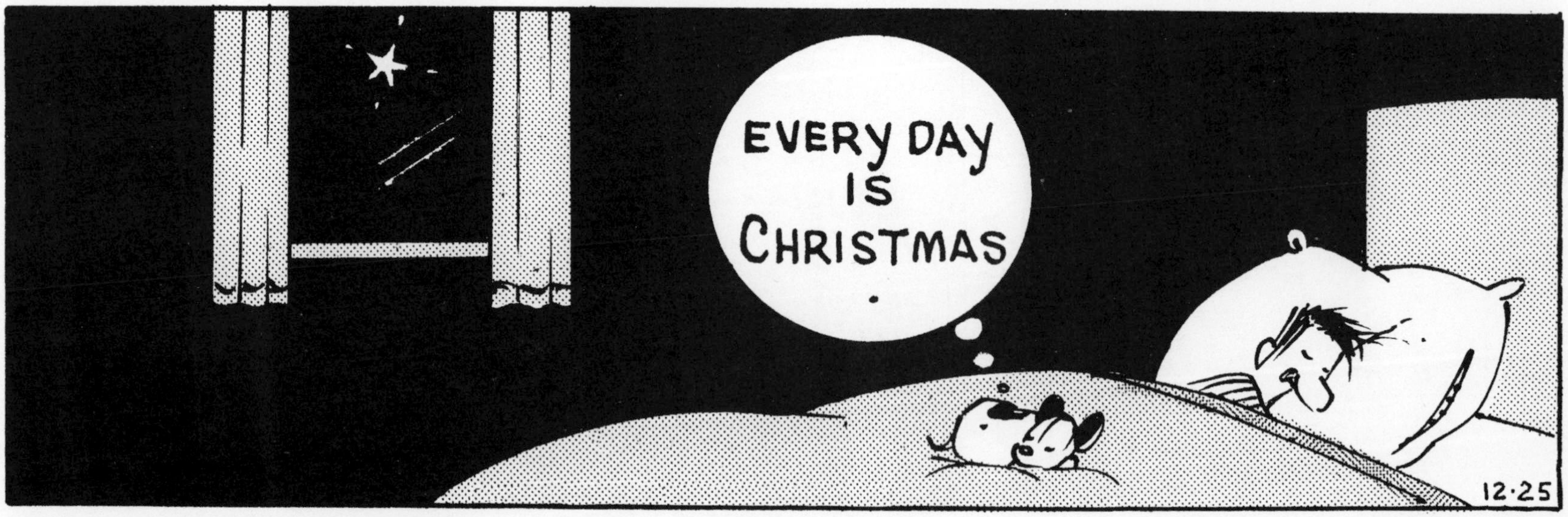
EVERY DAY IS CHRISTMAS.
12·25

MUTTS

PATRICK McDONNELL

ANIMAL SHELTER
HOME FOR THE HOLIDAYS
12·23

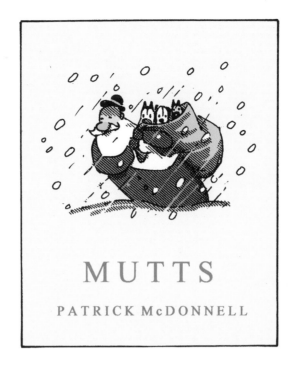

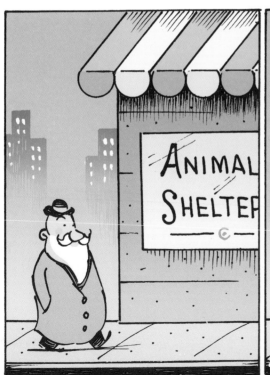

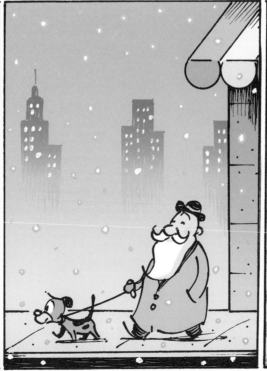

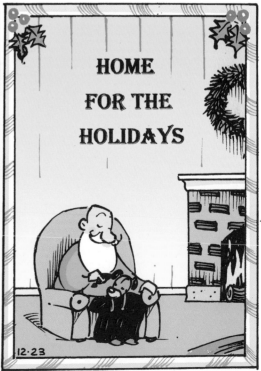

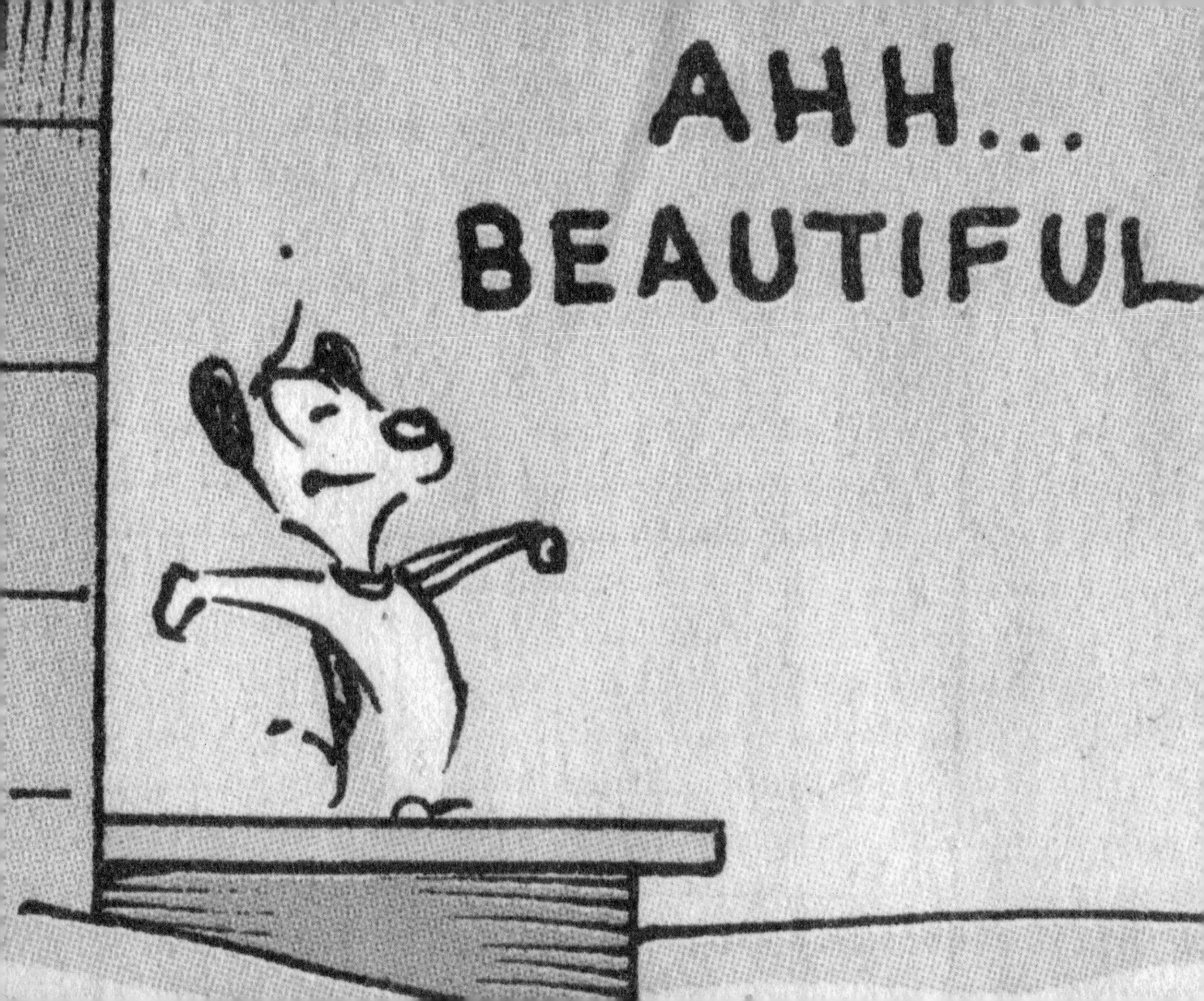
AHH...
BEAUTIFUL